Lecture Notes in Artificial Intelligence   3055

Edited by J. G. Carbonell and J. Siekmann

Subseries of Lecture Notes in Computer Science

T0223701

Springer
Berlin
Heidelberg
New York
Hong Kong
London
Milan
Paris
Tokyo

Henning Christiansen   Mohand-Said Hacid
Troels Andreasen   Henrik Legind Larsen (Eds.)

Flexible
Query Answering
Systems

6th International Conference, FQAS 2004
Lyon, France, June 24-26, 2004
Proceedings

 Springer

Volume Editors

Henning Christiansen
Roskilde University, Computer Science Dept.
P.O. Box 260, 4000 Roskilde, Denmark
E-mail: henning@ruc.dk

Mohand-Said Hacid
Université Lyon 1, LIRIS - UFR d'Informatique
43 boulevard du 11 novembre 1918
69622 Villeurbanne cedex, France
E-mail: mshacid@liris.univ-lyon1.fr

Troels Andreasen
Roskilde University, Department of Computer Science
P.O. Box 260, 4000 Roskilde, Denmark
E-mail: troels@ruc.dk

Henrik Legind Larsen
Aalborg University Esbjerg, Department of Computer Science and Engineering
Niels Bohrs Vej 8, 6700 Esbjerg, Denmark
E-mail: legind@cs.aue.auc.dk

Library of Congress Control Number: 2004106992

CR Subject Classification (1998): I.2, H.3, H.2, H.4, H.5

ISSN 0302-9743
ISBN 3-540-22160-3 Springer-Verlag Berlin Heidelberg New York

Springer-Verlag is a part of Springer Science+Business Media

springeronline.com

© Springer-Verlag Berlin Heidelberg 2004
Printed in Germany

Typesetting: Camera-ready by author, data conversion by Olgun Computergrafik
Printed on acid-free paper   SPIN: 11010753   06/3142   5 4 3 2 1 0

Preface

This volume constitutes the proceedings of the Sixth International Conference on Flexible Query Answering Systems, FQAS 2004, held in Lyon, France, on June 24–26, 2004. FQAS is the premier conference for researchers and practitioners concerned with the vital task of providing easy, flexible, and intuitive access to information for every type of need. This multidisciplinary conference draws on several research areas, including databases, information retrieval, knowledge representation, soft computing, multimedia, and human-computer interaction. With FQAS 2004, the FQAS conference series celebrated its tenth anniversary as it has been held every two years since 1994. The overall theme of the FQAS conferences is innovative query systems aimed at providing easy, flexible, and intuitive access to information. Such systems are intended to facilitate retrieval from information repositories such as databases, libraries, and the Web. These repositories are typically equipped with standard query systems that are often inadequate for users. The focus of FQAS is the development of query systems that are more expressive, informative, cooperative, productive, and intuitive to use.

These proceedings contain contributions from invited speakers and 35 original papers out of more than 100 submissions, relating to the topic of users posing queries and systems producing answers. The papers cover the fields: database management, information retrieval, domain modeling, knowledge representation and ontologies, knowledge discovery and data mining, artificial intelligence, classical and non-classical logics, computational linguistics and natural language processing, multimedia information systems, and human-computer interaction, including reports of interesting applications. We wish to thank the contributors for their excellent papers and the referees, publisher, and sponsors for their effort. Special thanks to Serge Abiteboul, Elisa Bertino, and Yuzuru Tanaka who presented invited talks at the conference. We express our appreciation to the members of the advisory board, and members of the program committee. They made the success of FQAS 2004 possible.

The contributed papers were selected by the following program committee members: Sihem Amer-Yahia, Troels Andreasen, Boualem Benatallah, Djamal Benslimane, Elisa Bertino, Gloria Bordogna, Bernadette Bouchon-Meunier, Torben Brauner, Henrik Bulskov, Sylvie Calabretto, Henning Christiansen, Fabio Crestani, Juan Carlos Cubero, Ernesto Damiani, Rita De Caluwe, Guy De Tre, Hendrik Decker, Robert Demolombe, Marcin Detyniecki, Didier Dubois, Ronald R. Fagin, Rudolf Felix, Elena Ferrari, Jorgen Fischer Nilsson, Norbert Fuhr, Peter Ingwersen, Christian Jacquemin, Janusz Kacprzyk, Etienne Kerre, Rasmus Knappe, Don Kraft, Werasak Kurutach, Mounia Lalmas, Henrik L. Larsen, Christophe Marsala, Maria Jose Martin-Bautista, Saddaki Miyamoto, Amihai Motro, Noureddine Mouaddib, Fred Petry, Olivier Pivert, Olga Pons, Zbigniew Ras, Guillaume Raschia, Brigitte Safar, Michel Scholl, Dietmar Seipel, Andrzej

Skowron, Heiner Stuckenschmidt, Zahir Tari, Hanne Erdman Thomsen, Farouk Toumani, Peter Vojtas, Slawomir T. Wierzchon, Ronald R. Yager, Adnan Yazici, Slawomir Zadrozny, Djamel Zighed,

Additionally, we acknowledge the help in reviewing papers from: Aybar Acar, James Allen, Bernd Amann, Joachim Baumeister, Salima Benbernou, Patrick Bosc, Matilde Celma, Pierre-Antoine Champin, Jérôme Darmont, Martine De Cock, Fabien De Marchi, Susan Dumais, Elod Egyd-Zsigmond, Peter Gursky, Bernd Heumesser, Marbod Hopfner, Mieczyslaw Klopotek, Stanislav Krajci, K.L. Kwok, Monica Landoni, Manish Malhotra, Juan Miguel Medina, Henrik Nottelmann, Jean-Francois Omhover, Jean-Marc Petit, Daniel Rocacher, Khalid Saeed, André Schaefer, Stefan Schlobach, Mihaella Scuturici, Padmini Srinivasan, Anastasios Tombros, Dietrich Van der Weken, Keith van Rijsbergen, Abhinav Vora

March 2004

Henning Christiansen
Mohand-Said Hacid
Troels Andreasen
Henrik Legind Larsen

Table of Contents

Invited Papers

Knowledge Representation

Knowledge Discovery and Data Mining

Domain Modeling, Ontologies and Human Interaction

Computational Linguistics and Natural Language Processing

Web Services

Databases

Information Retrieval

Logic and Artificial Intelligence

Meme Media Architecture for the Reediting and Redistribution of Web Resources

Yuzuru Tanaka and Kimihito Ito

Meme Media Laboratory, Hokkaido University
Sapporo, 060-8628 Japan
{tanaka,itok}@meme.hokudai.ac.jp

Abstract. This paper reviews our R&D studies on meme media technologies and their application to Web resources. Meme media technologies make the Web work as a meme pool, where people can publish their intellectual resources as Web pages, access some Web pages to extract some of their portions as meme media objects through drag-and-drop operations, visually combine these meme media objects together with other meme media objects to compose new intellectual resources, and publish these resources again as Web pages. Such a visual composition through direct manipulation can define not only the layout of components, but also interoperations among these components.

1 Introduction

During the last decade, we have observed the rapid accumulation of intellectual resources on the Web. These intellectual resources include not only multimedia documents, but also application tools running on the client side, and services provided by remote servers. Today, from the Web, you can almost obtain whatever information items, application tools, or services you may think of.

The publication and reuse of intellectual resources using the Web technologies can be characterized by the schematic model in Figure 1 (a). The Web publication uses a compound document representation of intellectual resources. Compound documents denote documents with embedded contents such as multimedia contents, visual application tools, and/or interactive services provided by servers. Such a compound document published on the Web defines a Web page. The model in Figure 1 (a) has no support for us to extract any portion of published Web pages, to combine them together for their local reuse, nor to publish the newly defined composite object as a new Web page. The composition here means not only textual combination but functional federation of embedded tools and services. We need some support to reedit and to redistribute Web contents for their further reuse.

It is widely recognized that a large portion of our paperwork consists of taking some portions of already existing documents, and rearranging their copies in different formats on different forms. Since the reediting is so fundamental in our daily information processing, personal computers introduced the copy-and-paste operation as the most fundamental operation. We need to make this operation applicable not only to multimedia documents but also to documents with embedded tools and services.

H. Christiansen et al. (Eds.): FQAS 2004, LNAI 3055, pp. 1–12, 2004.

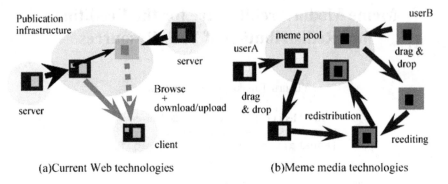

Fig. 1. The publication and reuse of intellectual resources

Figure 1 (b) shows a new model for the worldwide publication, reediting and redistribution of intellectual resources. As in the case of the Web, you can publish a set of your intellectual resources as a compound document into a worldwide publication repository. You can use a browser to view such documents published by other people. In addition to these operations, you can extract any portions of viewed documents as reusable components, combine them together to define a new compound document for your own use, and publish this new compound document into the repository for its reuse by other people. This new model of publishing, reediting and redistributing intellectual resources assumes that all these operations can be performed only through direct manipulation. Meme media technologies proposed by our group [1, 2, 3, 4], when applied to the Web, realize this new model, and make the Web work as a meme pool of intellectual resources. They provide the direct manipulation operations necessary for reediting and redistributing intellectual resources.

Web Service technologies can provide us with similar functions for the interoperation among Web applications [5, 6, 7, 8]. Web Service technologies enable us to interoperate services published over the Web. However, they assume that the API (Application Program Interface) library to access such a service is a priori provided by its server side. You need to write a program to interoperate more than one Web service. Meme media technologies, on the other hand, provide only the client-side direct manipulation operations for users to reedit intellectual resources embedded in Web pages, to define a new combination of them together with their interoperation, and to republish the result as a new Web page. In addition, meme media technologies are applicable not only to the Web, but also to local objects. Meme media can wrap any documents and tools, and make each of them work as interoperable meme media object. You can easily combine Web resources with local tools.

This paper shows how the meme media architecture is applied to the Web to make it work as meme pools. This makes the Web work as a shared repository not only for publishing intellectual resources, but also for their collaborative reediting.

2 Wrapping Web Contents as Meme Media Objects

2.1 Meme Media Architecture IntelligentPad

IntelligentPad is a two-dimensional representation meme media architecture. Its architecture can be roughly summarized as follows for our current purpose. Instead of directly dealing with component objects, IntelligentPad wraps each object with a standard pad wrapper and treats it as a pad. Each pad has both a standard user interface and a standard connection interface. The user interface of every pad has a card like view on the screen and a standard set of operations like 'move', 'resize', 'copy', 'paste', and 'peel'. As a connection interface, every pad provides a list of slots, and a standard set of messages 'set', 'gimme', and 'update'. Each pad defines one of its slots as its primary slot. Most pads allow users to change their primary slot assignments. You may paste a pad on another pad to define a parent-child relationship between these two pads. The former becomes a child of the latter. When you paste a pad on another, you can select one of the slots provided by the parent pad, and connect the primary slot of the child pad to this selected slot. The selected slot is called the connection slot. Using a 'set' message, each child pad can set the value of its primary slot to the connection slot of its parent pad. Using a 'gimme' message, each child pad can read the value of the connection slot of its parent pad, and update its primary slot with this value. Whenever a pad has a state change, it sends an 'update' message to each of its child pads to notify this state change. Whenever a pad receives an 'update' message, it sends a 'gimme' message to its parent pad. By pasting pads on another pad and specifying slot connections, you may easily define both a compound document layout and interoperations among these pads.

2.2 Extraction and Reediting of Web Contents

Web documents are defined in HTML format. An HTML view denotes an arbitrary HTML document portion represented in the HTML document format. The pad wrapper to wrap an arbitrary portion of a Web document specifies an arbitrary HTML view and renders any HTML document. We call this pad wrapper an HTMLviewPad. Its rendering function is implemented by wrapping a legacy Web browser Internet Explorer. The specification of an arbitrary HTML view over a given HTML document requires the capability of editing the internal representation of HTML documents, namely, DOM trees. The DOM tree representation allows you to identify any HTML-document portion, which corresponds to a DOM tree node, with its path expression such as /HTML[0]/BODY[0]/TABLE[0]/TR[1]/TD[1].

The definition of an HTML view consists of a source document specification, and a sequence of view editing operations. A source document specification uses the document URL. Its retrieval is performed by the function 'getHTML' in such a way as

doc = getHTML("http://www.abc.com/index.html", null).

The second parameter will be used to specify a request to the Web server at the retrieval time. Such requests include POST and GET. The retrieved document is kept in

DOM format. The editing of an HTML view is a sequence of DOM tree manipulation operations selected out of the followings:

(1) EXTRACT : Delete all the nodes other than the sub tree with the specified node as its root.
(2) REMOVE : Delete the sub tree with the specified node as its root.
(3) INSERT : Insert a given DOM tree at the specified relative location of the specified node. You may select the relative location out of CHILD, PARENT, BEFORE, and AFTER.

An HTML view is specified as follows:

$$defined\text{-}view = source\text{-}view.DOM\text{-}tree\text{-}operation(node),$$

where source-view may be a Web document or another HTML document, and node is specified by its extended path expression. The following is an example view definition.

```
view1 = doc
        .EXTRACT("/HTML/BODY/TABLE[0]/")
        .EXTRACT("/TABLE[0]/TR[0]/")
        .REMOVE("/TR[0]/TD[1]/");
```

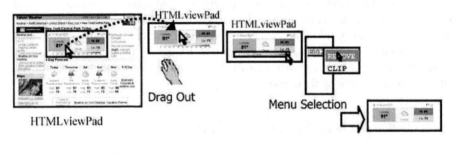

(a) EXTRACT operation   (b) REMOVE operation

Fig. 2. Direct Manipulations for extracting and removing views

2.3 Direct Editing of HTML Views

Instead of specifying a path expression to identify a DOM tree node, we will make the HTMLviewPad to dynamically frame different extractable document portions for different mouse locations so that its user may move the mouse cursor around to see every extractable document portion. When the HTMLviewPad frames what you want to extract, you can drag the mouse to create another HTMLviewPad with this extracted document portion. The new HTMLviewPad renders the extracted DOM tree on itself. Figure 2 (a) shows an example extraction, which internally generates the following edit code.

```
doc = getHTML("http://www.abc.com/index.html", null);
view = doc
       .EXTRACT("/HTML/BODY/TABLE[0]/");
```

The HTMLviewPad provides a pop-up menu of view-edit operations including EXTRACT, REMOVE and INSERT. After you select an arbitrary portion, you may select either EXTRACT or REMOVE. Figure 2 (b) shows an example remove operation, which generates the following code.

```
doc = getHTML("http://www.abc.com/index.html", null);
view = doc
    .EXTRACT(("/HTML/BODY/TABLE[0]/")
    .REMOVE("/TABLE[0]/TR[1]/");
```

The INSERT operation uses two HTMLviewPads showing a source HTML document and a target one. You may first specify INSERT operation from the menu, and specify the insertion location on the target document by directly specifying a document portion and then specifying relative location from a menu including CHILD, PARENT, BEFORE, and AFTER. Then, you may directly select a document portion on the source document, and drag and drop this portion on the target document. Figure 3 shows an example insert operation, which generates the following code, where the target HTMLviewPad uses a different name space to merge the edit code of the dragged-out HTMLviewPad to its own edit code:

```
A::view =A::doc
        .EXTRACT("/HTML/BODY/.../TD[1]/.../TABLE[0]")
        .REMOVE("/TABLE[0]/TR[1]/");
view = doc
    .EXTRACT("/HTML/BODY/.../TD[0]/.../TABLE[0]/")
    .REMOVE("/TABLE[0]/TR[1]/")
    .INSERT("/TABLE[0]", A::view, AFTER);
```

The dropped HTMLviewPad is deleted after the insertion.

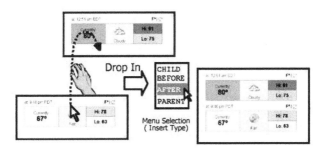

Fig. 3. Direct manipulation for inserting a view in another view

2.4 Automatic Generation of Default Slots

Depending on the type of the node to extract, the HTMLviewPad automatically generates some default slots.

For a general node such as </HTML/.../txt( )>, </HTML/.../attr( )>, or </HTML /.../P/>, the HTMLviewPad automatically defines a default slot, and sets the text in the selected node to this slot. If the text is a numerical string, it converts this string to a numerical value, and sets this value to the slot. Figure 4 shows Yahoo Finance Web page indicating the current Nikkei average stock price in real time. You may extract the Nikkei average index as a pad working as a live copy, and paste it to a DataBufferPad with its connection to #input slot. A DataBufferPad associates each #input slot input with its input time, and outputs this pair in CSV format. You may paste this composite pad on a TablePad with its connection to #data slot. A TablePad adds every #data slot input at the end of the list stored in CSV format. You may paste this TablePad on a GraphPad with its connection to #tabelInput slot. A GraphPad redraws a chart whenever it receives a new #tableInput slot value.

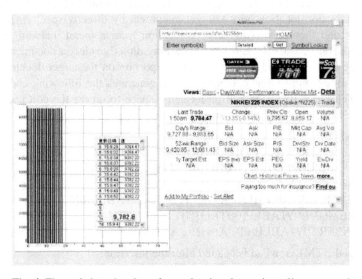

Fig. 4. The real-time drawing of a stock price chart using a live copy pad

For a table node such as </HTML/.../TABLE/>, the HTMLviewPad converts the table value to its CSV (Comma-Separated Value) representation, and automatically generates a new default slot with this value.

For an anchor node such as </HTML/.../A/>, the HTMLviewPad automatically generates the following three default slots:

(1) an output slot with *NameSpace*::#Text as its slot name, and the text in the selected node as its value,
(2) an output slot with *NameSpace*::#refURL as its slot name, and the href attribute of the selected node as its value,
(3) an event listener slot with *NameSpace*::#jumpURL as its slot name, and the URL of the target object as its value.

For example, let us consider a case in which we extract an anchor defined as follows:

```
<A href = ./next.html>
Next Page
</A>
```

The first slot holds "Next Page", while the second slot holds "./next.html" as its value. Whenever the anchor is clicked, the target URL is defined as a concatenation of the current URL and the second slot value, and set to the third slot.

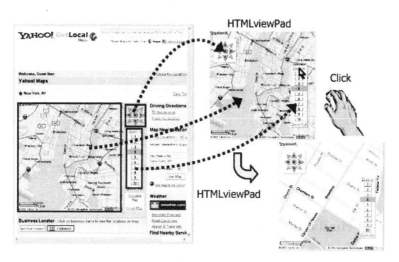

Fig. 5. Composition of a map tool using a map service and its control panels

Figure 5 shows a Yahoo Maps Web page. You may make live copies of its map display portion, its zooming control panel, and its shift control panel, all as pads, and paste the two control panels on the map display with their connections to #Retrieval-Code slot of the map display. Whenever you click some button on either of these control panels, the control panel sets the URL of the requested page, and sends this URL to #RetrievalCode slot of the map display. Such a URL may include a query to the specified server. The map display, then, accesses the requested page with a new map, and extracts the map portion to display.

For a form node such as </HTML/.../FORM/>, the HTMLviewPad automatically generates the following three default slots:

(1) an input and output slot with *NameSpace*::#Input as its name, and the input value as its value,
(2) an event firing slot with *NameSpace*::#FORM_Submit as its name, and a Boolean value as its value,
(3) An event listner slot with *NameSpace*::#FORM_Request as its name, and a server query as its value.

For example, let us consider a case in which we extract a form defined as follows:

```
<FORM action="./search">
<INPUT Type=txt name=keyword >
<INPUT Type=submit value="search">
</FORM>
```

The first slot holds the input keyword. Whenever we submit a form input, TRUE is set to the second slot, and the HTMLviewPad triggers a form-request event. The third slot has the EventListener type. Whenever an event to send a form request occurs, the HTMLviewPad concatenates the server URL and the corresponding query, sets this value to the third slot, and sends this query to the server.

Each HTMLviewPad has the additional following four default slots. The #UpdateInterval slot specifies the time interval for the periodical polling of referenced HTTP servers. A view defined over a Web document refresh its contents by periodically retrieving this Web document in an HTTP server. The #RetrievalCode slot stores the code to retrieve the source document. The #ViewEditingCode slot stores the view definition code. The #MappingCode slot stores the mapping definition code that defines the automatic generation of default slots. Because of the limited space, we have to omit the details of the mapping definition code in this paper. The HTMLviewPad updates itself by accessing the source document, whenever either the #RetrievalCode slot or the #ViewEditingCode slot is accessed with a set message, the interval timer invokes the polling, a user specifies its update, or it becomes active after its loading from a file.

3   Visual Definition of Slots for Extracted Web Resources

Our HTMLviewPad allows users to visually specify any HTML-node to work as a slot. In its node specification mode, an HTMLviewPad frames different extractable document portions of its content document for different mouse locations so that its user may change the mouse location to see every selectable document portion. When the HTMLviewPad frames what you want to work as a slot, you can click the mouse to pop up a dialog box to name this slot. Since each extracted Web component uses an HTMLviewPad to render its contents, it also allows users to specify any of its portions to work as its slot. We call such a slot thus defined an HTML-node slot. The value of an HTML-node slot is the HTML view of the selected portion. The HTMLviewPad converts ill-formed HTML into well-formed HTML to construct its DOM-tree. Therefore, you may connect an HTMLviewPad to an HTML-node slot to view the corresponding HTML view. If the HTML-node slot holds an anchor node, the HTMLviewPad connected to this slot shows the target Web page.

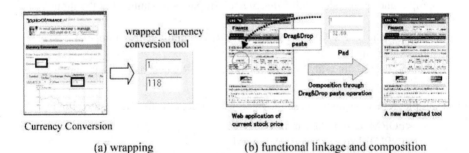

(a) wrapping   (b) functional linkage and composition

Fig. 6. Direct manipulation for wrapping and linking of Web applications

Figure 6 (a) shows an HTMLviewPad showing a Yahoo Web page with an embeded Web application to convert US dollar to Japanese yen based on the current exchange rate. On this pad, you can visually specify the input form for inputting dollar amount and the output text portion showing the equivalent yen amount to work as slots. The HTML-path of the input-form is represented as HTML[0]/BODY[0] /DIV[0]/FORM[0]/INPUT[0]/text[(.*)], while the HTML-path of the selected output text portion is represented as HTML[0]/BODY[0]/TABLE[0]/TR[0]/TD[1]/A[0]/ attr[href].

You may name the corresponding HTML-node slots as #dollarAmount and #yen-Amount respectively. The HTMLviewPad allows you to suspend the rendering of its contents. In this mode, you may use an HTMLviewPad with an HTML view as a blank pad with an arbitrary size. Figure 6 (a) shows, on its right hand side, a currency rate converter pad. You can define this pad from the above mentioned Web page just by defining two slots, resizing the HTMLviewPad, and pasting two text IO pads with their connections to #dollarAmount and #yenAmount slots.

Such a pad wraps a Web application, providing slots for the original's input forms and output text strings. We call such a pad a wrapped Web application. Since a wrapped Web application is such a pad that allows you to change its primary slot assignment, you may specify any one of its slots to work as a primary slot.

Figure 6 (b) shows an HTMLviewPad showing a Lycos' Web page for a real time stock-price browsing service. You can wrap this page defining a slot for the current stock price. Then you can paste the wrapped currency conversion Web application with its #dollarAmount specified as its primary slot on this wrapped Lycos stock-price page. You may connect the conversion pad to the newly defined current stock price slot as shown in this figure. For the input of different company names, you may use the input form of the original Web page. Since this Web application uses the same page layout for different companies, the same path expression correctly identifies the current stock-price information part for every different company.

4   Redistribution and Publication of Meme Media Objects as Web Contents

Whenever you save a wrapped Web document portion extracted from a Web page, the system saves only the pad type, namely 'HTMLviewPad', the values of all the slots, and the path expression, the name, and the value of each user-defined slot. Copies of such a live copy pad share only such meta information with the original. They access the source Web page whenever they need to update themselves. This is an important feature from a copyright point of view, since every update of such a copy requires a server access. The redistribution of a live copy across the Internet needs to send only its save format representation.

For the reediting of extracted Web contents, our framework provides two methods. One of them allows you to insert an HTML view into another HTML view without any functional linkage. The other allows us to paste an HTML view as a pad on another HTML view as a pad with a slot connection between them. The former composition results in a new HTML view, while the latter composition is no longer an HTML view.

In order to publish composed documents and/or tools as HTML documents in the Web, we need to convert non HTML view compositions to HTML views. We call such a conversion a *flattening* operation. While there may be several different methods to flatten composite pads, we chose the use of IFrame (inline frame) representation of composite pads. An HTML view representation of a composite pad can be inserted as a new IFrame element in the HTML view representation of the parent pad. This insertion defines a new HTML view composition.

Script

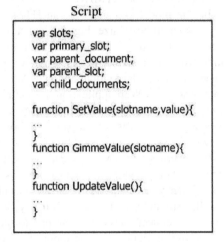

```
var slots;
var primary_slot;
var parent_document;
var parent_slot;
var child_documents;

function SetValue(slotname,value){
  ...
}
function GimmeValue(slotname){
  ...
}
function UpdateValue(){
  ...
}
```

Fig. 7. A JavaScript program to define slots in an HTML view

Non HTML view composition treats HTML views as pads, and combines them through slot connections. A script language, such as JavaScript, enables an HTML view to be connected to another HTML view with a slot connection between them. Using the same visual operation to insert an HTML view in another HTML view, you can visually insert a composite pad as a new HTML element in an arbitrary HTML view. For the HTML representation of an HTML view working as a pad, we use script variables to represent its slots, its primary slot, its parent pad, the parent's slot it is connected, and the list of child pads. As shown in Figure 7, we use JavaScript to define SetValue function to set a new value to a specified slot, GimmeValue function to read out the value of a specified slot, and UpdateValue function to update the primary slot value and to invoke every child pad's UpdateValue function. To update the primary slot value, we define a script program to invoke the parent's GimmeValue function with the connection slot as its parameter, and to set the return value to the own primary slot. Figure 7 shows an HTML view defined with two slots #increment and #number and the three standard functions. This HTML view works as a counter with a number display and a button to increment the number. The HTML view defines these components in HTML.

Figure 8 shows an HTML view composition with three simple HTML views; two works as child pads of the other. The parent HTML view is the counter with two slots,

#increment and #number. One child HTML view works as a button with its primary slot #click, while the other child HTML view works as a number display with its primary slot #value. The composition rewrites the HTML definition of the base pad to embed the HTML definitions of the other two using <IFRAME> tags, and adds a script code using <SCRIPT> tags to define slot connection linkages among them. The composed HTML view works exactly the same as a composite pad combining the pad representations of these three HTML views. Users may use a legacy Web browser to show this composite view and to play with it.

Our framework uses this mechanism to flatten a composite pad that uses only those pads extracted from some Web pages.

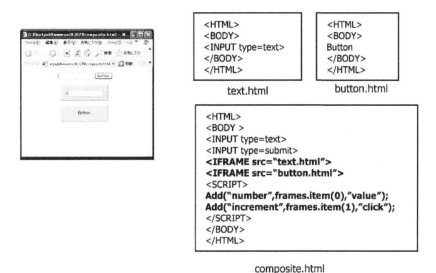

Fig. 8. Use of a JavaScript program for an HTML-view composition

5   Conclusion

Meme media architectures work as the enabling technologies for interdisciplinary and international availability, distribution and exchange of intellectual assets including information, knowledge, ideas, pieces of work, and tools in reeditable and redistributable organic forms. When applied to the Web, they make the Web work as a shared repository not only for publishing intellectual resources, but also for their collaborative reediting and reorganization. Meme media technologies allow us to reedit multimedia documents with embedded tools and services, and to combine their functions through copy-and-paste manipulations of these documents. Meme media over the Web will make the Web work as a meme pool, and significantly accelerate the evolution of memes in our societies.

References

1. Tanaka, Y. and Imataki, T.: IntelligentPad: A Hypermedia System allowing Functional Composition of Active Media Objects through Direct Manipulations. Proc. of IFIP'89 (1989) 541-546
2. Tanaka, Y.: Meme media and a world-wide meme pool. Proc. ACM Multimedia 96 (1996) 175-186
3. Ito, K. and Tanaka, Y.: A Visual Environment for Web Application Composition, In Proc of 14th ACM Conference on Hypertext and Hypermedia, 184-193 (2003)
4. Tanaka, Y.: Meme Media ad Meme Market Architectures –Knowledge Media for Editing, Distributing, and Managing Intellectual Resources–. IEEE Press & Wiley-Interscience, NJ (2003)
5. Stal, M.: Web Services: Beyond Component-based Computing, Communications of the ACM, Vol.45 10 (2002) 71-76
6. Pierce,M., Fox, G., Youn, C., Mock, S., Mueller, K., Balsoy, O.: Interoperable Web Services for Computational Portals, Proceedings of the 2002 ACM/IEEE conference on Supercomputing (2002) 1-12
7. Agrawal, R., Bayardo, R.J., Gruhl, D., Papadimitriou, S.: Vinci: A Service-oriented Architecture for Rapid Development of Web Applications, Proceedings of the tenth international conference on World Wide Web (2001) 355-365
8. Anzböck, R., Dustdar, S., Gall, H.: Web-based Tools, Systems and Environments: Software Configuration, Distribution, and Deployment of Web-Services, Proceedings of the 14th international conference on Software engineering and knowledge engineering (2002) 649-656

A Flexible Access Control Model
for Web Services

Elisa Bertino[1] and Anna C. Squicciarini[2]

[1] Computer Science Department and CERIAS
Purdue University, West LaFayette, IN
bertino@cerias.purdue.edu
[2] Universitá degli Studi di Milano
squiccia@dico.unimi.it

A Web service [8] is a Web-based application that can be published, located and invoked across the Web. Compared to centralized systems and client-server environments, a Web service environment is much more dynamic and security for such an environment poses unique challenges. However, while Web services are rapidly becoming a fundamental paradigm for the development of complex Web applications, several security issues still need to be addressed. Some proposals for securing Web services have been presented [1, 2, 4] over the last two years. In particular, the SAML [1] and XACML [6] standards provide a sound basis for the development of the secure infrastructure for Web services. SAML, acronimous of Security assertion markup language, is an XML based framework for exchanging security information, developed by the OASIS XML-Based Security Services Technical Committee, whereas XACML is a specification that is used in conjunction with SAML, and it provides a means for standardizing access control decision for XML documents. However, none of these technologies provide a general and formal model for access control of web services. Indeed, among the various open issues concerning security, an important issue is represented by the development of suitable access control models, able to restrict access to Web services to authorized users. At first glance, it may seem that such an issue may be solved by relying on security technologies commonly adopted for Web sites. Indeed, there is a number of embedded software applications whose purpose is to control access to web service applications. But such an approach is not adequate when dealing with loosely coupled applications as the Web service technology asks, and can just be considered as a temporary solution until more appropriate techniques be devised.

An alternative approach might be the adoption of existing access control models for Web services application. However, Web services are very different with respect to objects typically protected in conventional systems, like files or documents, since they consist of software modules, to be executed, upon service requests, according to a set of associated input parameters. Further, when Web services are published and located across Web, access requests may come from users belonging to different domains not known to the parties providing the services. Based on such considerations, we have devised an ad-hoc access control model for Web services, for use within the SOAP [5] standard, characterized by

H. Christiansen et al. (Eds.): FQAS 2004, LNAI 3055, pp. 13–16, 2004.
© Springer-Verlag Berlin Heidelberg 2004

capabilities for negotiating service parameters. The goal of our model, referred to as *Ws-Aba*, is to express, validate and enforce access control policies without assuming pre-established trust in the users of the web services, while at the same time being in line with recent developments on identity management [7]. Access conditions in Ws-Aba are thus expressed in terms of *identity attributes*[1] (attributes, for short) of the requesters. Moreover, in order to support a fine tuning of access control, access conditions also take into account the parameters characterizing web services. It is thus possible to specify that a user is authorized to use a given web service but only for some specific values of the service parameters. Furthermore our model supports the concept of *access negotiation*. Although the notion of negotiation has been extensively used in secure communication protocols to establish trust among entities, this notion is only now emerging in the area of access control policies. Web service negotiation deals with the possibility for users whose associated attributes have been validated by the server to dynamically change their access requests in order to obtain authorizations. The negotiation option makes Ws-Aba an adaptive system able to ask subjects to refine their requests and so to gain resource accesses by updating web services parameters in order to fully comply with access control policies.

In the next section we briefly overview the model we have developed and show a sketch of the a system architecture implementing the model.

1   Overview of the Model

Informally, the way Ws-Aba works can be summarized as follows. Access control policies are specified by constraining service parameters, and attributes that subjects should possess in order to obtain a service. An example of Web service application might be, for instance, a service providing flight tickets information to generic customers, according to a set of specific parameters, like discount or fare, which actually define the type of service invoked, by users presenting qualifying properties, like the age or the possession of membership cards.

A service request in Ws-Aba is specified by assigning values to a set of parameters describing the service itself, and disclosing the credentials corresponding the requested attributes. Service requests are matched against corresponding access control policies, in order to establish whether access can be granted, or must be rejected or have to be negotiated and executed in a different form. More precisely, an access request that can be accepted, either totally or partially, is said to be *compliant*. A compliant access request for a certain policy defined for the same service is a request presenting attributes that satisfy the list of attribute conditions specified in the policy, according to the attributes sent together with the access request. Note that the concept of compliance does not deal with the parameters used to specify access request. Parameter evaluation is used to establish whether a full or partial authorization may be granted. A full acceptance is granted if the parameters appearing in the access request are

---

[1] By Identity attributes we refer to properties that can be associated with users, like name, birth-date, credit cards.

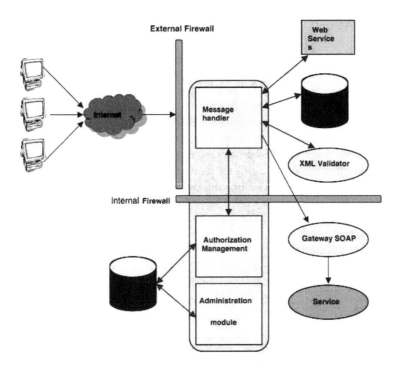

Fig. 1. Ws-Aba system architecture

all and only the parameters specified in the associated policy, and their value is compatible with the values admitted by the policy. Partial acceptance, by contrast, may occur when the access request is compliant with the policy, but it cannot be fully accepted due to the lack or wrong specification of one or more of its parameters. In such case the missing parameters may be negotiated. A request negotiation, indeed, may involve elimination or modification of some of the service parameters that the current invoker is not allowed to specify.

The actual negotiation process consists of an access request counterproposal (single or multiple, depending on the specific implementation of the server) sent by the server specifying the set of legal parameter values that may be accepted, and corresponding reply by the requesting user with an updated and possibly fully compliant access request.

Ws-Aba also provides a system architecture implementing the model (see Figure 1). The main functionality of the system deals with three different aspects: *access request management, authorization management* and *system administration*, concerning the administration of the WS-Aba system itself (for instance, access policies definition and management). An implementation of the sketched system is currently in progress, on a platform based on Java and a CORBA server. Such protoype system will allow us to develop a systematic benchmark to asses the system performance under a variety of conditions.

2   Future Work

In designing Ws-Aba we have identified a number of open issues that we believe relevant for future research on Web Services access control model. Such issues deal with strategies for parameter negotiations, delegation, cached policies and certificates and policy protection. The work we have done so far mainly focuses on the negotiation issue, however delegation is also partially supported by carrying certificates of delegated entities in the SOAP header of access requests. For what concerns the issue of cached policies and policy protection we have already developed a number of techniques and strategies for protection of sensitive policies and caching in trust negotiation contexts [3]. We will explore the possibility of integrating such approaches in the Ws-Aba system.

Currently, we are extending our model by introducing the possibility of specifying policies that apply to group of services and authorization derivation rules, allowing authorizations on a service to be automatically derived from authorizations specified on other services.

References

1. Advancing SAML, an XML-based security standard for exchanging authnetication and authorization information.
   http://www.oasis-open.org/ committees/security.
2. B. Atkinson et al. Web services security (ws-security), April 2002.
   http://msdn.microsoft.com/ws/2002/04/Security
3. E. Bertino, E. Ferrari, A. Squicciarini, Trust-$\mathcal{X}$: A Peer to Peer Framework for Trust Negotiations. *To appear in IEEE Transactions on Knowledge and Data Engineering.*
4. E. Damiani, S. Di Capitani di Vimercati, Towards securing XML Web services. *Proceedings of the 2002 ACM workshop on XML security* November 2002, Fairfax, VA.
5. D. Box et. al. Simple Object Access Protocol (SOAP) 1.1, Technical Report W3C, 2000.
6. Defining XACML, an XML specification for expressing policies for information access over the internet http://www.oasis-open.ord /committes/xacml
7. Liberty Alliance Project http://www.projectliberty.org/
8. World Wide Web Consortium. Web Service http://www.w3.org/2002/ws/
9. World Wide Web Consortium XML Signature Syntax and Processing 2001 W3C Candidate Reccomendation
   http://www.w3.org/TR/2001/CR-xmldisigcore-20010419

Active XML and Active Query Answers[*]

Serge Abiteboul[**], Omar Benjelloun, and Tova Milo[***]

INRIA-Futurs and[†] LRI

Abstract. XML and Web services are revolutioning the automatic management of distributed information, somewhat in the same way that
HTML, Web browser and search engines modified human access to world
wide information. We argue in this paper that the combination of XML
and Web services allows for a novel query answering paradigm, where
the exchanged information mixes materialized and intensional, active,
information.
We illustrate the flexibility of this approach by presenting Active XML
that is based on embedding Web service calls in XML data. We discuss
advantages of an approach of query answering based on intensional and
active data.

1 Introduction

Alice: What is the meaning of "intensional"?
Mom: Look it up in the dictionary

There is typically more in answering a query than just listing plain facts. Indeed,
as shown by the dialogue between Alice and her mom, a smart answer may
teach you more than what you have asked. If Alice looks up "intensional" in the
dictionary, she will not only learn the meaning of this particular word, but will
also learn how one may find, in general, the meaning of words, and she will be
able to reuse this knowledge later.

We refer to a response that gives the means to obtain an answer without answering explicitly, as an *active answer*. Many other examples and motivations for
the use of such active answers are presented further. We will argue that Active
XML (AXML in short), a new paradigm that combines XML and Web services,
provides a simple and unified platform for such active answers, thereby introducing a new dimension to flexible query answering in the distributed context
of the Web.

The field of distributed data management has centered for many years around
the relational model. More recently, the Web has made the world wide (or in-
tranet) publication of data much simpler, by relying on HTML as a standard

---

[*] The research was partly funded by EC Project DBGlobe (IST 2001-32645), the
RNTL Project e.dot and the French ACI MDP2P.
[**] Also Xyleme SA.
[***] On leave from Tel Aviv University.
[†] Gemo Team, PCRI Saclay, a joint lab between CNRS, Ecole Polytechnique, INRIA
and Université Paris-Sud.

language, universally understood by Web browsers, on plain-text search engines
and on query forms. However, because HTML is more of a presentation language for documents than a data model, and because of limitations of the core
HTTP protocol, the management of distributed information remained cumbersome. The situation is today dramatically improving with the introduction of
XML and Web services. The Extensible Markup Language, XML [18], is a self-
describing, semi-structured data model that is becoming the standard format
for data exchange over the Web. Web services [21] provide an infrastructure
for distributed computing at large, independently of any platform, system or
programming language. Together, they provide the appropriate framework for
distributed management of information.

Active XML (AXML, for short), is a declarative framework that harnesses
these emerging standards for the integration and management of distributed
Web data. An AXML document is an XML document where some of the data
is given explicitly, while some portions are given only intensionally by means
of embedded calls to Web services. By calling the services, one can obtain up-
to-date information. In particular, AXML provides control of the activation of
service calls both from the client side (pull) or from the server side (push).
AXML encourages an approach to query answering based on *active answers*,
that is, answers that are AXML documents.

Choosing which parts of a query answer should be given explicitly and which
should be given in an active/intensional manner may be motivated and influenced by various parameters. These include logical considerations, such as knowledge enrichment or context awareness, and physical considerations like performance or capabilities. We will give an overview of these various aspects, and
describe some possible solutions for guiding this crucial choice.

It should be noted that the idea of mixing data and code is not new. Functions
embedded in data were already present in relational systems [14] as stored procedures. Also, method calls form a key component of object-oriented databases [7].
In the Web context, scripting languages such as PHP or JSP have made popular the integration of (query) processing inside HTML or XML documents.
Embedding calls to Web services in XML documents is just one step further,
but is indeed a very important one. The novelty here is that since both XML
and Web services are becoming standards, AXML documents can be universally
understood, and therefore can be *exchanged*. We focus here on the new flexibly
brought to query answering by this paradigm of exchanging AXML documents.

The rest of this paper is organized as follows. We first briefly recall some
key aspects of XML, Web services (Section 2) and Active XML (Section 3).
The following two sections informally discuss motivations for the use of active
data in query answers, both logical (Section 4) and physical (Section 5). The
last section concludes by mentioning some supporting techniques around AXML
that are important for query processing.

2 XML and Web Services

XML is a new data exchange format promoted by the W3C [20] and widely adopted by industry. An XML document can be viewed as a labeled ordered tree, as seen on the example of[1] Figure 1. XML is becoming a lingua franca, or more precisely an agreed upon syntax, that most pieces of software can understand or will shortly do. Unlike HTML, XML does not provide any information about the document presentation. This is typically provided externally using a CSS or XSL stylesheet.

XML documents may be typed using a language called XML Schema [19]. A schema mainly enforces structural relationships between labels of elements in the document tree. For instance, it may request a *movie* element to consist of a *title*, zero or more *author*s and *reviews*. The typing proposed by XML Schema is very flexible, in the sense that it can describe, for instance, an HTML webpage, as well as a relational database instance, thus marrying the document world with the structured or semistructured world of databases. The presence of structure in XML documents enables the use of queries beyond keyword search, using query languages such as XPath or XQuery.

Web Services are a major step in the evolution of the Web. Web servers, that originally provide HTML pages for human consumption, become gateways to available services. Although most of the hype around Web services comes from e-commerce, one of their main current uses is for the management of distributed information. If XML provides the data model, Web services provide the adequate abstraction level to describe the various actors in data management such as databases, wrappers or mediators and to manage the communications between them.

Web services in fact consist of an array of emerging standards. To find the desired service, one can query the yellow-pages: a UDDI [17] directory (Universal Discovery Description and Integration). Then, to understand how to interact with it, one relies on WSDL [22] (Web Service Definition Language), something like Corba's IDL. One can then access the service using SOAP [16], an XML-based lightweight protocol for the exchange of information. Of course, life is more complicated, so one often has to sequence operations (see Web Services Choreography [23]) and consider issues such as confidentiality, transactions, etc.

XML and Web services are nothing really new from a technical viewpoint. However, their use as a large scale infrastructure for data sharing and communication provides a new, trendy environment to utilize some old ideas in a new context. For instance, tree automata techniques regained interest as they best model essential manipulations on XML, like typing and querying.

This new distributed, setting for data and computation also raises many new challenges for computer science research in general, and query answering

---

[1] We will see in the next section that this XML document is also an Active XML document.

```
<directory>
  <movies>
    <director>Hitchcock</director>
    <sc service="movies@allocine.com" >Hitchcock</sc>
    <movie> <title>Vertigo</title>
      <actor>J. Stewart</actor> <actor>K. Novak</actor>
      <reviews> <sc service="reviews@cine.com" >Vertigo</sc></reviews>
    </movie>
    <movie> <title>Psycho</title>
      <actor>N. Bates</actor>
      <reviews> <sc service="reviews@cine.com" >Psycho</sc></reviews>
    </movie>
  </movies>
</directory>
```

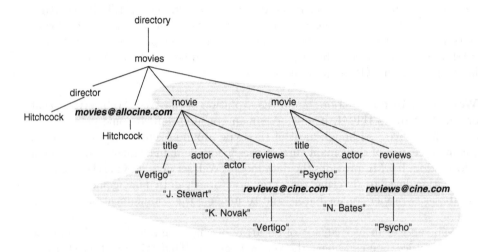

Fig. 1. An Active XML document and its tree representation

in particular. For instance, data sources ought to be discovered and their informations integrated dynamically, and this may involve data restructuring and semantic mediation. Classical notions such as data consistency and query complexity must be redefined to accommodate the huge size of the Web and its fast speed of change.

3   Active XML

To illustrate the power of combining XML and Web services, we briefly describe Active XML, a framework based on the idea of embedding calls to Web services in XML documents. This section is based on works done in the context of the Active XML project [6].

In Active XML (AXML for short), parts of the data are given explicitly, while other parts consist of calls to Web services that generate more data. AXML is based on a P2P architecture, where each AXML peer acts as a client, by activating Web service calls embedded in its documents, and also acts as a server, by providing Web services that correspond to queries or updates over its repository of documents. The activation of calls can be finely controlled to happen periodically, or in reaction to some particular (in the style of database triggers), or in a "lazy" way, whenever it may contribute data to the answer of a query.

AXML is an XML dialect, as illustrated by the document in Figure 1. (Note that the syntax is simplified in the example for presentation purposes.) The `sc` elements are used to denote embedded service calls. Here, reviews are obtained from `cine.com`, and information about more Hitchcock movies may be obtained from `allocine.com`. The data obtained from the call to `allocine.com` corresponds to the shaded part of the tree. In case the relashionship between data and the service call is maintained, we say that data is *guarded* by the call.

The data obtained by a call to a Web service may be viewed as intensional (it is originally not present). It may also be viewed as dynamic, since the same service call possibly returns different, data when called at different times. When a service call is activated, the data it returns is inserted in the document that contains it. Therefore, documents evolve in time as a consequence of call activations. Of particular importance is thus the decision to activate a particular service call. In some cases, this activation is decided by the peer hosting the document. For instance, a peer may decide to call a service only when the data it provides is requested by a user; the same peer may choose to refresh the data returned by another call on a periodic basis, say weekly. In other cases, the service provider may decide to send updates to the client, for instance because the latter registered to a subscription-based, continuous service.

A key aspect of this approach is that AXML peers exchange AXML documents, i.e., documents with embedded service calls. Let us highlight an essential difference between the exchange of regular XML data and that of AXML data. In frameworks such as Sun's JSP or PHP, dynamic data is supported by programming constructs embedded inside documents. Upon request, all the code is evaluated and replaced by its result to obtain a regular, fully materialized HTML or XML document. But since Active XML documents embed calls to Web services, and the latter provide a standardized interface, one does not need to materialize all the service calls before sending some data. Instead, a more flexible data exchange paradigm is possible, where the sender sends an XML document with embedded service calls (namely, an AXML document) and gives the receiver the freedom to materialize the data if and when needed. In the following sections, we will investigate both logical and physical motivations for exchanging AXML documents, in particular as answers to queries, and discuss the benefits obtained from doing so.

4   Logical Motivations for Active Answers

In this section, we present the main *logical* motivations for returning active answers to queries, namely reasons motivated by the desire to provide more functionality. *Physical* motivations will be considered in the next section.

We consider three classes of logical motivations.

Reusability of Answers

A first family of motivations is about enabling the client to reuse autonomously some of the information in the query answer without having to ask the query again, by giving her more knowledge about its origin or means to get it.

Dynamicity. Perhaps the main motivation for returning active answers is to capture the fact that parts of the answer may change over time. For instance, suppose someone asks for the description of a ski resort, say Megève. A portion of the answer may describe the snow condition, an information that is typically volatile. If this answer is inspected tomorrow or in a month, we would like the information to still be up-to-date, without having to ask the initial query again. So we may want to make the snow condition part active, that is, to guard it with a Web service call to provide real-time snow conditions.

Knowledge. In the dialogue between Alice and her mom, the mother answers intensionally. By looking in a dictionary, Alice will learn something beyond the meaning of the word "intensional": She may learn how to obtain the meaning *of any word*. In general, by obtaining the information via a service call, the client becomes more independent knowledge-wise and may be able to *generalize* the use of the service, by reusing it over time, or calling it with different parameters, e.g. other ski resorts in the snow conditions example, or other words in the case of Alice.

Partial Answers

A second family of motivations has to do with providing the client with a partial representation of query answers, instead of the full computed result of the query.

Summarization. If the client of the query is a human user, then the full answer may simply be too large and unreadable for her. The natural way to summarize it is to "intensionalize" some of it. We are here at the border between man machine interfaces and query answer. Active data may be viewed as an environment to provide several views of a query answer, as well as means to navigate between them, by zooming in and out. This can easily be accomplished using AXML, with the service calls acting as navigational links.

Incompleteness. Another important reason is that we may want the answer to be incomplete. For instance, the answer may be very large and we may be satisfied with just some of it, e.g., we ask the query "XML" to Google and there are 22 300 000 answers. The server decides not to send them all but provide, say the first 10, and a link to obtain more. This may be viewed as a very simplistic form of active data but the situation does not have to be so simple. Consider a search engine that is aggregating three different data sources. It receives a query and one of the sources is down. Then the search engine may want to answer in AXML with the concrete data it knows of, and with a call to the last source with the meaning that more data may be obtained from there when the source will come back up.

Partial computations. Active data may also be used to represent computations that still need to be carried out to obtain the full answer. An example of this comes from the management of security and encryption. A secret phone number may be sent encrypted. So, the answer has to be decrypted to be understood, so the answer is active. As another example, some news systems provide as results lists of news headlines, each of them with a summary and the means to buy the article (say using a Web service). With an active data approach, this may be viewed as part of the answer, to be obtained by the data receiver via some additional computation (calling the service and paying the required fee).

Enriching Answers

A last family of motivations consists in enriching the query answer with active parts that provide the client with extra functionality that better fits her needs.

Metadata. Consider, as an example of a "raw" query answer, the result of a scientific experiment. This is very static information. By activating it, we can add some meta-information to it. For instance, the document may be in AXML with some service calls to obtain details on the data provenance and others to access existing annotations that were made on this experiment or to attach some new annotation. The metadata could also allow obtaining different versions of the same document and access related information. The active part may be in charge of maintaining (possibly implicitly) the metadata and, in particular, the provenance information.

Context awareness and personalization. A piece of information, be it extensional or intensional, may depend on some context. For instance, if a user obtained a list of restaurants, the content of the list may depend on predefined preferences, like the user's taste for certain kinds or food, or on religious restrictions. Also, the explicit presence of some details in this list may be guided by the device used by the user, possibly to accommodate limitations of her screen, or by the way the information will be used. For instance, all data should be extensional if the information is to be used off-line.

Enriching data. This is the process of adding value to an answer by applying some external tools. The enrichment may occur at the level of the entire query result or at a different granularity, e.g., an XML element. Typical enrichment may include links with the user context, extracting related concepts from an ontology, transforming from one type (XML schema) to another, or translating the answer to a preferred language.

In all these various scenarios, an active answer may be viewed as an agent in charge of managing the answer and providing it to the user.

5   Physical Motivation for Active Answers

In the previous section, we considered motivations for using active answers to provide more functionality. We next briefly illustrate how the notion of active answer may be useful for guiding the evaluation of queries, when information and query processing are distributed.

The presence of intensional information in data that is transfered between systems on the Web is rather standard. For instance, in PHP or JSP pages, the code that is inserted inside HTML or XML documents is a form of intensional information. But typically, all this intensional data is materialized *before* being sent, and only "plain" data is exchanged. This does not have to be the case in a Web service setting. The decision whether to invoke service calls before or after the data transfer may be influenced by physical considerations such as the current system load or the cost of communication. For instance, if the server is overloaded or if communication is expensive, the server may prefer to send smaller files and delegate as much materialization of the data as possible to the client. Otherwise, it may decide to materialize as much data as possible before transmission, in order to reduce the processing on the client's side.

Note however that although Web services may in principle be called remotely from anywhere on the Internet, it may be the case that the particular client of the intensional document cannot perform them, e.g., a newspaper reader's browser may not be able to handle the intensional parts of a document, or the user may not have access to a particular service, e.g., by lack of access rights. In such cases, it is compulsory to materialize the corresponding information before sending the document.

More generally, it is interesting to note that there are analogs to most of the aspects that played a role at the logical level. We next illustrate some of them.

To see one aspect that typically plays an important role on the performance and quality of Web servers, consider *Dynamicity*. Suppose some Web server S publishes a book catalog and that a comparative shopping site S' downloads the pages of the catalog regularly. The cache of S' will contain these pages, but information such as book prices that change rapidly will often be stale. The Web server S may decide to make catalog pages active. Then a reload of a page that is now controlled by a Web service may just result in sending the "delta" between the old and the new page (e.g., just a change of prices). This results in savings in communication. Furthermore, in an Active XML framework, S' is able to subscribe to price changes and to be notified of such changes without having to reload pages regularly. As a consequence, the cache of S' will have a more accurate copy of the catalog.

As another example, consider *Knowledge*. Knowledge may be exchanged in the form of intensional information, for instance to facilitate tasks such as routing. Suppose some peer A requests some data from peer B and B in fact finds the data in some peer C. Then the data from C to A would transit via B. However, if B answers A intensionally, then A may obtain the data directly from C, which possibly results in saving in communication.

6 Supporting Techniques

We have briefly discussed XML and Web services and the advantages of answering queries with active data. We presented AXML, that enables such answering style. To conclude this paper, we mention three important issues in this setting, and recent works performed in these directions.

To call or not to call. Suppose someone asks a query about the "Vertigo" movie. We may choose to call `cine.com` to obtain the reviews or not before sending the data. As we saw, this decision may be guided by considerations such as performance, cost, access rights, security, etc. Now, if we choose to activate the service call, it may return a document with embedded service calls and we have to decide whether to activate those or not, and so on, recursively. We introduce in [11] a technique to decide whether some calls should be activated or not based on typing. First, a negotiation between the peers determines the schema of data to exchange. Then, some complex automata manipulation are used to cast the query answer to the type that has been agreed upon. The general problem has deep connections with alternating automata, i.e., automata alternating universal and existential states [13].

The choice of a schema for data exchange between peers in general, or for query answers in particular is itself an interesting reasoning problem. We need some formal model to describe preferences of the peers as well as their knowledge of the context that will guide this selection.

Lazy service calls and query composition. As mentioned earlier, it is possible in AXML to specify that a call is activated only when the data it returns may be needed, e.g., to answer a query. Suppose that a user has received some active document and wants to extract some information from it, by evaluating a query. A difficulty is then to decide whether the activation of a particular call is needed or not to answer that query. For instance, if someone asks for information about the actors of "The 39 steps" of Hitchcock, we need to call `allocine.com` to get more movies by this director. Furthermore, if this service is sophisticated enough, we may be able to ask only for information about that particular movie (i.e., to "push" the selection to the source). Algorithms for guiding the invocation of relevant calls, and pushing queries to them are presented in [1]. Some surprising connections between this problem and optimization techniques for deductive database and logic programming are exhibited in [5].

Cost model. We describe in [3] a framework for the management of distribution and replication in the context of AXML. We introduce a cost model for query evaluation and show how it applies to user queries and service calls. In particular, we describe an algorithm that, for a given peer, chooses data and services that the peer should replicate in order to improve the efficiency of maintaining and querying its dynamic data. This is a first step towards controlling the use of intensional answers in a distributed setting.

Efficient query processing of structured and centralized data was made feasible by relational databases and its sound logical foundation [14, 4]. Deep connections with descriptive complexity have been exhibited [9, 4]. For the management of answers with active components, we are now at a stage where a field is building and a formal foundation is still in its infancy. The development of this foundation is a main challenge for the researchers in the field.

References

1. S. Abiteboul, O. Benjelloun, B. Cautis, I. Manolescu, T. Milo, N. Preda: Lazy Query Evaluation for Active XML, Sigmod 2004.
2. S. Abiteboul, P. Buneman, and D. Suciu, Data on the Web, Morgan Kaufmann Publishers, 2000.
3. S. Abiteboul, A. Bonifati, G. Cobena, I. Manolescu, T. Milo, Active XML Documents with Distribution and Replication, ACM SIGMOD, 2003.
4. S. Abiteboul, R. Hull and V. Vianu, Foundations of databases, Addison-Wesley, 1995.
5. S. Abiteboul and T. Milo, Web Services meet Datalog, 2003, submitted.
6. The AXML project, INRIA,
   http://www-rocq.inria.fr/verso/Gemo/Projects/axml.
7. The Object Database Standard: ODMG-93, editor R. G. G. Cattell, Morgan Kaufmann, San Mateo, California, 1994.
8. Tata, Tree Automata Techniques and Applications, H. Comon, M. Dauchet, R. Gilleron, F. Jacquemard, D. Lugiez, S. Tison and M. Tommasi, www.grappa.univ-lille3.fr/tata/
9. N. Immerman, Descriptive Complexity, Springer 1998.
10. M. Lenzerini, Data Integration, A Theoretical Perspective, ACM PODS 2002, Madison, Winsconsin, USA, 2002.
11. T. Milo, S. Abiteboul, B. Amann, O. Benjelloun, F. Dang Ngoc, Exchanging Intensional XML Data, ACM SIGMOD, 2003.
12. M.T. Ozsu, and P. Valduriez, Principles of Distributed Database Systems, Prentice-Hall, 1999.
13. A. Muscholl, T. Schwentick, and L. Segoufin, Active Context-Free Games, Symposium on Theoretical Aspects of Computer Science, 2004.
14. J.D. Ullman, Principles of Database and Knowledge Base Systems, Volume I, II, Computer Science Press, 1988.

15. F. M. Cuenca-Acuna, C. Peery, R. P. Martin, T. D. Nguyen, Using Gossiping to Build Content Addressable Peer-to-Peer Information Sharing Communities, Department of Computer Science, Rutgers University, 2002.
16. The SOAP Specification, version 1.2, http://www.w3.org/TR/soap12/
17. Universal Description, Discovery and Integration of Web Services (UDDI), http://www.uddi.org/
18. The Extensible Markup Language (XML), http://www.w3.org/XML/
19. XML Typing Language (XML Schema), http://www.w3.org/XML/Schema
20. The World Wide Web Consortium (W3C), http://www.w3.org/
21. The W3C Web Services Activity, http://www.w3.org/2002/ws/
22. The Web Services Description Language (WSDL), http://www.w3.org/TR/wsdl/
23. W3C, Web Services Choreography, http://www.w3.org/2002/ws/chor/

Towards Flexible Querying of XML Imprecise Data in a Dataware House Opened on the Web

Patrice Buche[1], Juliette Dibie-Barthélemy[1],
Ollivier Haemmerlé[1,2], and Mounir Houhou[1]

[1] UMR BIA INA P-G/INRA
16, rue Claude Bernard, F-75231 Paris Cedex 05
[2] LRI (UMR CNRS 8623 - Université Paris-Sud) / INRIA (Futurs)
Bâtiment 490, F-91405 Orsay Cedex, France
{Patrice.Buche,Juliette.Dibie,Ollivier.Haemmerle}@inapg.inra.fr

Abstract. This paper describes a new subsystem of the Sym'Previus knowledge base. This knowledge base contains information useful to help experts in the field of predictive microbiology. Information has several specific properties: it is incomplete, imprecise and heterogeneous. In the pre-existing Sym'Previus knowledge base, stable data are stored in a relational database and data which do not fit the relational structure are stored in a conceptual graph knowledge base. The MIEL language permits to scan simultaneously both bases in a transparent way for the user, using fuzzy queries. The new subsystem described in the paper contains information found on the Web to complete the knowledge base. This information is stored in XML format. Firstly, we extend the XML model of the knowledge base to represent imprecise data as possibility distributions. Secondly, we present the mapping process used to translate a MIEL query into an XML query to scan the XML knowledge base.

1 Introduction

Our team is involved in a national project, called Sym'Previus, which aims at building a tool to help experts in the field of predictive microbiology. This tool is composed of two subsystems: (1) a knowledge base which gathers knowledge about the behaviour of pathogenic germs in food products, (2) a simulation tool. This paper is dedicated to the knowledge base subsystem. The information stored in this knowledge base is characterized by several specific properties: it is incomplete, imprecise and weakly-structured. This information is incomplete by nature because it is not possible to store information about all existing food products and all existing germs. It is imprecise because of the complexity of the underlying biological processes. It is weakly-structured because the information comes from heterogeneous sources (bibliographical literature, industrial partners, ...) and from knowledge about predictive microbiology, which is still a field of research, and as such is then evolving rapidly. To take those properties into account, we have made choices in the design of the Sym'Previus knowledge base and its querying system, called MIEL (see [7,8]). The more stable information

H. Christiansen et al. (Eds.): FQAS 2004, LNAI 3055, pp. 28–40, 2004.
© Springer-Verlag Berlin Heidelberg 2004

(in terms of structure) is stored in a relational database. The information which does not fit the relational structure is stored in a more flexible representation model: the conceptual graph model. The imprecise information stored in the Sym'Previus knowledge base is represented by possibility distributions in both bases.

The MIEL querying system has several properties: (1) it scans both bases simultaneously in a transparent way (the final user does not know that the knowledge is stored in two different formats); (2) by using MIEL, the final user queries the bases through views which hide the complexity of bases schemas; (3) MIEL executes a fuzzy query: predefined selection attributes are available in the views and the final user has only to specify his/her preferences expressed as fuzzy sets; (4) answers are returned ordered according to their relevance to the selection criteria. In the framework of another national project, called E.dot, our aim is to complete the Sym'Previus knowledge base with information, semi-automatically found on the Web. Information retrieved from the Web in different formats (html, pdf, excel, ...) is stored in XML format in an additional local knowledge base especially adapted to store XML documents: the Xyleme Zone server (see [16]).

Our paper may be related to three types of works. In a first category of study, the fuzzy set framework has been shown to be a sound scientific choice to model flexibles queries (see [5]). It is a natural way of representing the notion of preference using a gradual scale. In a second category of works, the fuzzy set framework has also been proposed to represent imprecise values by means of possibility distributions (see [18]). Several authors have developed this approach in the context of databases (see [3, 6, 10]). In a third category of paper, flexible query languages have been proposed to scan XML data (see [4, 9, 11, 13]). Some flexibility is provided by using similarity relationships [13], partial structural match techniques [2, 9, 11, 12], and flexible constraints to determine significance degrees of indexed terms in the data [4].

Our paper is a very first step to adapt the MIEL system in order to be able to query an XML knowledge base. As we already did for the relational database and the conceptual graph knowledge base, we make the assumption that XML data fit predefined XML schemas. The aims of this paper are: (1) to propose a way of representing imprecise information expressed as possibility distribution in an XML knowledge base, (2) to extend MIEL to be able to scan the additional XML knowledge base. We recall briefly in section 2: firstly, the fuzzy set framework we have used to represent preferences in the queries and imprecise data and secondly, the MIEL language. In section 3 we propose an extension of the XML model to represent imprecise information. In section 4 we present the translation process of a MIEL query to scan the XML knowledge base.

2   Background

2.1   Fuzzy Set Theory

We use, in this article, the representation of fuzzy sets proposed in [17, 18].

Definition 1 A **fuzzy set** f on a definition domain $Dom(f)$ is defined by a membership function μ_f from $Dom(f)$ to $[0,1]$ that associates the degree to which x belongs to f with each element x of $Dom(f)$.

Definition 2 For any fuzzy set f defined on a definition domain $Dom(f)$ with μ_f its membership function, we note $\mathbf{support}(f) = \{x \in Dom(f)|\mu(x) > 0\}$ and $\mathbf{kernel}(f) = \{x \in Dom(f)|\mu(x) = 1\}$.

The fuzzy set formalism can be used in two different ways: (1) in the knowledge base, in order to represent imprecise data expressed in terms of possibility distributions or (2) in the queries, in order to represent fuzzy selection criteria which express the preferences of the final user. In order to answer queries in a knowledge base involving fuzzy sets, we must be able to compare fuzzy sets. We studied several comparison degrees in [14]. We present here the "possibility degree" which is classically used to evaluate the compatibility between a fuzzy selection criterion and an imprecise datum. A fuzzy set can be defined on a continuous or discrete definition domain.

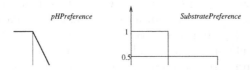

Fig. 1. The fuzzy set pHPreference noted [4,5,6,7] is a continuous fuzzy set and the fuzzy set SubstratePreference noted (1/Fresh cheese + 0.5/Soft cheese) is a discrete one.

Definition 3 Let f and g be two fuzzy sets defined on the same definition domain Dom, representing respectively a selection criterion and an imprecise datum, and μ_f and μ_g being their respective membership functions. The **possibility degree of matching** between f and g is $\Pi(f,g) = sup_{x \in Dom}(min(\mu_f(x), \mu_g(x)))$.

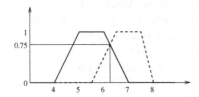

Fig. 2. The possibility degree of matching between the two fuzzy sets is 0.75.

Remark 1 *The evaluation of the possibility degree between a fuzzy selection criterion and a crisp datum is a particular case of definition 3.*

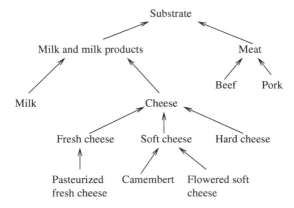

Fig. 3. A part of the ontology composed of the attribute Substrate and its hierarchized symbolic definition domain.

2.2   The MIEL Query Language

In the MIEL system, the interrogation of a knowledge base is made through the MIEL query language. This interrogation relies on a set of pre-written queries, called views, which are given to help the final user to express his/her queries and an ontology which contains the vocabulary used to express the queries. We introduce the MIEL query language by presenting successively the ontology, the views, the queries and the answers to a query.

The ontology. The ontology of a knowledge base in the MIEL system is composed of the set of attributes which can be queried by the final user and their corresponding definition domain. As a matter of fact, each attribute is defined on a definition domain which can be of three kinds: (1) numeric, it is then completely ordered (for example the real numbers), (2) "flat" symbolic, it is then composed of unordered constants (for example a set of authors) or (3) hierarchized symbolic, it is then partially ordered by the "kind-of" relation.

The views. Final users are not experts and cannot write queries from scratch. The views are the way given to the final user to query the knowledge base, without having to know the complexity of the schema of the base. In the MIEL system, a view is composed of a visible part which is the set of "queryable" attributes and a hidden part which is the description of the structure of the view (the way the attributes are linked together in the knowledge base).

The queries. A query is an instanciation of a given view by the final user, by specifying, among the set of queryable attributes of the view, which are the selection attributes and the projection attributes of the query.

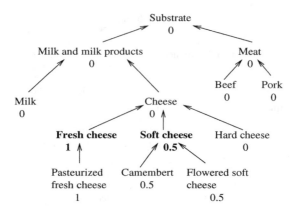

Fig. 4. Fuzzy set in extension corresponding to the fuzzy set SubstratePreference.

Definition 4 A **query** Q asked on a view V defined on n attributes $\{a_1, \ldots, a_n\}$ is defined by $Q = \{V, a_1, \ldots, a_l, <a_{l+1}, v_{l+1}>, \ldots, <a_m, v_m>\}$, $1 \leq l \leq m \leq n$, where $a_1, \ldots, a_l$ represent the list of the projection attributes and $a_{l+1}, \ldots, a_m$ represent the conjonction of the selection attributes with their respective values $v_{l+1}, \ldots, v_m$. The crisp or fuzzy values v_i, $i \in [l+1, m]$, must belong to the definition domain of the attributes a_i.

We are interested in the fuzzy value of a selection attribute which has a hierarchized symbolic definition domain. In that case, the fuzzy set used to represent the fuzzy value can be defined on a subset of the hierarchized symbolic definition domain of the selection attribute. Such a fuzzy set is called a **fuzzy set in intention** since it is considered to define degrees implicitly on the whole definition domain of the selection attribute. In order to take those implicit degrees into account, a **fuzzy set in extension** is associated with every fuzzy set in intention (see [14, 15] for more details).

Example 1 *Let us consider the fuzzy value (1/Fresh cheese + 0.5/Soft cheese) (see figure 1) assigned by the final user to the selection criterion Substrate. It can be interpreted as "the final user wants fresh cheese as a substrate and he/she also accepts soft cheese but with a lower interest". Since the selection criterion Substrate has a hierarchized symbolic definition domain (see figure 3), we can consider that the final user who is interested in fresh cheese is also interested in all the kinds of fresh cheese such as pasteurized fresh cheese. The fuzzy set in extension given in figure 4 takes the "kind-of" relation into account by propagating the degree associated with a value to all the specializations of that value.*

When a fuzzy set is used to represent a selection criterion defined on a hierarchized symbolic definition domain, the fuzzy set in extension is computed and used to search for satisfying answers in the knowledge base. Note that this mechanism of transformation of a fuzzy set in intention into a fuzzy set in extension can also be used when the fuzzy set is used to represent a fuzzy datum.

The answers. An answer to a query Q must (1) satisfy all the selection criteria of Q in the meaning of definition 5 given below and (2) associate a constant value with each projection attribute of Q.

Definition 5 Let $<a, v>$ be a selection criterion and a value v' of the attribute a stored in the knowledge base. The selection criterion $<a, v>$ is satisfied iff $\Pi(v, v') > 0$ in the meaning of definition 3.

As the selection criteria of a query are conjonctive, we use the *min* operator to compute the adequation degree associated with the answer.

Definition 6 An **answer** A to a query $Q= \{V, a_1, \ldots, a_l, <a_{l+1}, v_{l+1}>, \ldots, <a_m, v_m>\}$, is a set of tuples, each of the form $\{v_1, \ldots, v_l, ad\}$, where $v_1, \ldots, v_l$ correspond to the crisp or fuzzy values associated with each projection attribute $a_1, \ldots, a_l$ of Q, where all the selection criteria $a_{l+1}, \ldots, a_m$ of Q are satisfied with the respective possibility degree $\Pi_{l+1}, \ldots, \Pi_m$ and where ad is the adequation degree of the answer A to the query Q defined as follows: $ad=min_{i=l+1}^{m}(\Pi_i)$.

3   The Sym'Previus XML Knowledge Base

In order to store the information retrieved from the Web in different formats (html, pdf, xml, excel, ...), we propose to add a third knowledge base in the Sym'Previus knowledge base, represented with the XML format. We propose to use the tree-based model as the one proposed in the Xyleme Project [1, 16] in order to represent the XML knowledge base with a clear formalization. One of the specificities of the data stored in the Sym'Previus knowledge base is their imprecision. We propose an extension of the tree-based model in order to represent such fuzzy data. First, we briefly give the definitions of the tree-based model used to represent the XML knowledge base. Second, we describe how to represent fuzzy values in the XML knowledge base. Third, we present the Sym'Previus XML knowledge base.

3.1   Preliminaries Notions: The Tree-Based Model

In the tree-based model, an XML knowledge base is a set of data trees, each of them representing an XML document.

Definition 7 A **data tree** is a triple (t, l, v) where t is a finite tree, l a labelling function that assigns a label to each node in t and v a partial value function that assigns a value to nodes of t. The pair (t, l) is called a **labelled tree**.

The schema of a data tree is defined by a **type tree** which is a labelled tree such that no node has two children labelled the same. A data tree (t, l, v) is said to be an **instance** of a type tree (t_T, l_T) if there exists a strict type homomorphism from (t, l) to (t_T, l_T) as defined below.

Definition 8 Let (t, l) and (t', l') be two labelled trees. The mapping h from nodes of t into nodes of t' is a **strict structural homomorphism** if and only if (1) h preserves the root of t: $\text{root}(t') = h(\text{root}(t))$ and (2) h preserves the structure of t: whenever node m is a child of node n, $h(m)$ is a child of $h(n)$. The mapping h is a **strict type homomorphism** if and only if h is a strict structural homomorphism which preserves the labels of t: for each node n of t, $l(n)=l'(h(n))$.

The **schema** of an XML knowledge base is defined by the set of type trees which are associated with the data trees that it contains.

3.2   The Representation of Fuzzy Values in the Tree-Based Model

We propose to use the fuzzy set formalism in order to represent imprecise data expressed in terms of possibility distributions. In the tree-based model, a fuzzy set is represented by a data tree. We give the definition of a continuous fuzzy set and then of a discrete one.

Definition 9 Let f be a continuous fuzzy set. f is represented by a data tree which is composed of a root labelled *CFS* and composed of four leaves labelled *minSup*, *minKer*, *maxKer*, *maxSup* of respective values $\min(\text{support}(f))$, $\min(\text{kernel}(f))$, $\max(\text{kernel}(f))$ and $\max(\text{support}(f))$.

Fig. 5. Data tree representing the continuous fuzzy set pHPreference of figure 1.

Definition 10 Let f be a discrete fuzzy set. f is represented by a data tree which is composed of a root labelled *DFS* and such that for each element x of $\text{Dom}(f)$, there exists a node labelled *ValF* that has two children labelled *Item* and *MD* (for Membership Degree) of respective values x and $\mu(x)$.

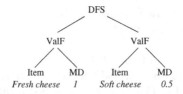

Fig. 6. Data tree representing the discrete fuzzy set SubstratePreference of figure 1.

3.3   The Sym'Previus XML Knowledge Base

The Sym'Previus XML knowledge base is a set of data trees, which are instance of type trees, and allow one to represent fuzzy values. According to definition 7, a data tree is a triple (t, l, v) where (t, l) is a labelled tree and v is a partial value function that assigns a value to nodes of t. In a fuzzy data tree, the nodes to which a value can be assigned by the function v are of two types. Firstly, they can be nodes having a (continuous or discrete) fuzzy value, that is to say nodes having only one child labelled CFS or DFS according to definitions 9 and 10. Secondly, they can be leaves that are not descendants of nodes labelled CFS or DFS (those leaves have then a crisp value). These two types of nodes are called respectively **fuzzy and crisp leaves**.

Definition 11 A **fuzzy data tree** is a triple (t, l, v) where (t, l) is a labelled tree and v is a partial value function that assigns a value to crisp and fuzzy leaves of t. The value assigned to a crisp leaf is an atomic value and the one assigned to a fuzzy leaf is a data tree with a root labelled CFS or DFS respectively conform to definitions 9 and 10.

Example 2 *The fuzzy data tree $\mathcal{D}$ of figure 7 talks about experimental data retrieved from the bibliographical source Partner1_03. It concerns the behaviour of Bacillus Cereus in a substrate which may be Fresh Cheese (but it may be also camembert) whose pH value is between 6 and 6.8. This experience studies the influence of conservation temperature on the level of contamination of the substrate by Bacillus Cereus. Two temperature have been tested (8 and 25 celsius degrees). At 8° C, the initial contamination was 1950 CFU/g. After 3 days, it was 1000 CFU/g...*

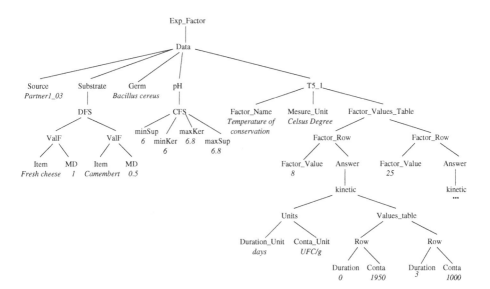

Fig. 7. Fuzzy data tree $\mathcal{D}$ representing one experimental result belonging to the bibliographical source Partner1_03.

Remark 2 Assigning a value to a continuous (resp. discrete) fuzzy leaf means assigning a value to each of its leaves labelled *minSup*, *minKer*, *maxKer* and *maxSup* (resp. to each of its leaves labelled *Item* and *MD*).

Example 3 *The data tree* $\mathcal{D}=(t_\mathcal{D}, l_\mathcal{D}, v_\mathcal{D})$ *of figure 7 is an instance of the type tree* $\mathcal{T}=(t_\mathcal{T}, l_\mathcal{T})$ *of figure 8: there exists a strict type homomorphism from* $(t_\mathcal{D}, l_\mathcal{D})$ *to* $\mathcal{T}$ *(see definition 8). Note that the mapping between the nodes of* $t_\mathcal{D}$ *and the nodes of* $t_\mathcal{T}$ *only concerns a subset of the nodes of* $t_\mathcal{T}$.

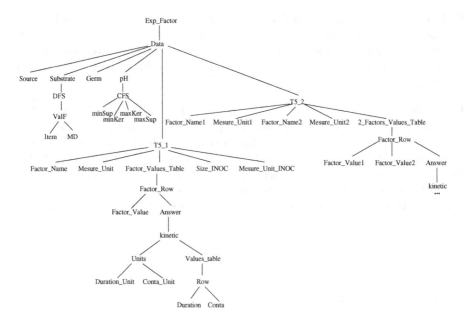

Fig. 8. Type tree $\mathcal{T}$ representing one experimental result belonging to a bibliographical source.

4   The Interrogation of the XML Knowledge Base in the MIEL System

In order to ensure a uniform interrogation of Sym'Previus knowledge base, we propose to query the XML knowledge base, represented in the tree-based model, by means of the MIEL query language. In order to ensure a mapping between the MIEL query language and the XML subsystem of the MIEL system, we define successively the ontology, the views, the queries and the answers in this subsystem.

4.1   The Ontology

In the XML knowledge base, the ontology defined in section 2.2 is represented as a set of trees stored in a XML document. Each tree materializes the definition domain and the partially ordered "kind-of" relation associated with a queriable leaf of the XML knowledge base (queriable leaf Substrate by example shown in figure 3).

4.2   The Views

The XML subsystem relies on a set of views, which allow one to query the XML knowledge base.

Definition 12 A **view conform to a type tree** (t_T, l_T) is a triple $V=(t_V, l_V, w_V)$ where (t_V, l_V) is an instance of (t_T, l_T) and w_V is a partial function that assigns the value ql to crisp and fuzzy leaves of t_V, indicating that such leaves are queryable ones.

4.3   The Queries

A query is an instanciation of a given view by the final user, by specifying, in the set of queryable leaves of the view, which are the selection leaves and which are the projection leaves of the query.

Definition 13 A **query** conform to a type tree (t_T, l_T) is a 6-tuple $Q=(t_Q, l_Q, w_Q, p_Q, s_Q, ws_Q)$ where:

- (t_Q, l_Q, w_Q) is a view conform to (t_T, l_T);
- p_Q is a partial function that assigns the value pl to queryable leaves of the view, allowing one to identify the **projection leaves** of the query;
- s_Q is a partial function that assigns the value sl to queryable leaves of the view, allowing one to identify the **selection leaves** of the query, also called selection criteria;
- ws_Q is a partial value function that assigns a value to the selection leaves of the query, such that the value assigned to a crisp leaf is an atomic value and the one assigned to a fuzzy leaf is a data tree with a root labelled CFS or DFS respectively conform to definitions 9 and 10.

The value of a selection criterion given by the final user can be crisp as well as fuzzy. In the second case, the fuzzy set formalism is used to represent a fuzzy selection criterion which expresses the preferences of the final user.

Example 4 *The following query Q (see figure 9) expresses that the final user wants to obtain the germ, the factor name and the substrate from the view Exp_Factor. Moreover, the fuzzy value assigned by the final user to the selection criterion Substrate can be interpreted as "he wants fresh cheese as a substrate, but he also accepts soft cheese but with a lower interest".*

Remark 3 *When a fuzzy set is used to represent a fuzzy selection criterion defined on a hierarchized symbolic definition domain, the fuzzy set in extension is computed and used to search for satisfying answers in the knowledge base as seen in subsection 2.2.*

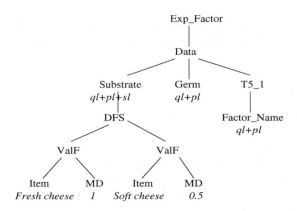

Fig. 9. Query Q in the view Exp_Factor which contains the results of the effect of one factor in biological experiments.

4.4   The Answers

An answer to a query Q must (1) satisfy all the selection criteria of Q in the meaning of definition 5 and (2) associate a constant value with each projection leaf of Q. The search of the answers to a query in an XML knowledge base is made through the valuation of the query on the data trees of the knowledge base as defined below.

Definition 14 Let $Q=(t_Q, l_Q, w_Q, p_Q, s_Q, ws_Q)$ be a query conform to a type tree $T=(t_T, l_T)$ and $D=(t_D, l_D, v_D)$ be a data tree instance of the type tree T. A **valuation** of Q with respect to D is a mapping σ_D from the tree t_Q of Q into the tree t_D of D such that (1) σ_D is a strict type homomorphism from (t_Q, l_Q) into (t_D, l_D) and (2) σ_D satisfies each selection criterion n_s^i, $i \in [1,m]$, of Q with the possibility degree $\Pi(ws_Q(n_s^i), v_D(\sigma_D(n_s^i)))$. The adequation degree of the data tree D to the query Q through the valuation σ_D is $ad_D = min_{i \in [1,m]}(\Pi(ws_Q(n_s^i), v_D(\sigma_D(n_s^i))))$.

We can now give the definition of an answer to a query in an XML knowledge base. An answer is a set of tuples, each tuple corresponding to a set of values given to each projection leaf of the query.

Definition 15 An **answer** to a query $Q=(t_Q, l_Q, w_Q, p_Q, s_Q, ws_Q)$ composed of m projection leaves noted $n_p^1, \ldots, n_p^m$ in an XML knowledge base $\mathcal{KB}$ is a set of tuples, each tuple being defined as follows: $\{ \cup_{i=1}^m v_D(\sigma_D(n_p^i)) \cup ad_D \mid D$ is a data tree of $\mathcal{KB}$ and σ_D is a valuation of Q with respect to $D\}$.

Example 5 The answer to the query Q of figure 9 in the XML knowledge base of figure 7 is: {(1/Fresh cheese, 0.5/Camembert), Bacillus cereus, Temperature of conservation, ad=1.0}.

5   Conclusion

In this article, we have defined the basic framework of a new subsystem in the MIEL system, the XML subsystem, in order to store the information retrieved from the Web in the field of predictive microbiology. The XML subsystem is composed of an XML knowledge base which had to take into account the specificities of the knowledge stored in the Sym'Previus knowledge base and had to be able to be queried by means of the MIEL query language, this in order to ensure its integration in the MIEL system. We have chosen to use the tree-based model in order to represent the XML knowledge base. We have proposed an extension of the tree-based model proposed in the Xyleme project (see [16]) in order to represent imprecise data expressed as possibility distribution in the XML knowledge base. We have also adapted the tree-based model in order to allow one to query the XML knowledge base by means of the MIEL query language. Consequently, we have proposed an XML querying language adding flexibility on the searched values in the leaves (selection criteria expressing preferences, preferences in extension for selection criteria defined on symbolic definition domains, fuzzy pattern matching to compare selection criteria to data). At the moment, the XML querying subsystem has been implemented in Java. We have used XML Schema to define the schemas (called type trees in this article) of the XML documents of the knowledge base, the schemas of the ontology and the schemas of the views. We have used XQuery to query the knowledge base and to obtain the answers. The knowledge base can be queried by a final user through an Internet browser.

As mentioned in the introduction, we make in this article the assumption that XML data fit XML schemas which are used in the querying process. We have evaluated this first version of our new XML subsystem by creating manually XML documents checking this hypothesis. Our next step will be to study ways to relax this assumption by introducing, for example, flexibility on the tree query structure or similarity relationships on tree labels. The design of this next version will be guided by the properties of the pertinent XML documents which are retrieved semi-automatically from the Web.

References

1. V. Aguiléra, S. Cluet, P. Vetri, D. Vodislav, and F. Wattez, *Querying the xml documents on the web*, Proceedings of the ACMSIGIR Workshop on XML and I.R. (Athens), July 2000.
2. S. Amer-Yahia, SungRan Cho, and Divesh Srivastava, *Tree pattern relaxation*, Proceedings of the 8th International Conference on Extending Database Technology (EDBT 2002), 2002.
3. G. Bordogna and G. Pasi, *A fuzzy object oriented data model managing vague and uncertain information*, International Journal of Intelligent Systems **14** (1999), no. 6, SCI 3495.
4. Gloria Bordogna and Gabriella Pasi, *Flexible querying of web documents*, Proceedings of the ACM Symposium Applied Computing (Madrid, Spain), 2002, pp. 675–680.

5. P. Bosc, L. Lietard, and O. Pivert, *Soft querying, a new feature for database management system*, Proceedings DEXA'94 (Database and EXpert system Application), Lecture Notes in Computer Science #856, Springer-Verlag, 1994, pp. 631–640.

6. Patrick Bosc, L. Lietard, and Olivier Pivert, *Fuzziness in Database Management Systems*, ch. Fuzzy theory techniques and applications in data-base management systems, pp. 666–671, Academic Press, 1999.

7. P. Buche and O. Haemmerlé, *Towards category-based fuzzy querying of both structured and semi-structured imprecise data*, Proceedings of the Fourth International Conference on Flexible Query Answering Systems (FQAS'2000) (Warsaw, Poland), Springer-Verlag, October 2000, pp. 362–375.

8. P. Buche, O. Haemmerlé, and R. Thomopoulos, *Integration of heterogeneous, imprecise and incomplete data: an application to the microbiological risk assessment*, Proceedings of the 14th International Symposium on Methodologies for Intelligent Systems, ISMIS'2003 (Maebashi, Japan), Lecture Notes in AI #2871, Springer, October 2003, pp. 98–107.

9. P. Ciaccia and W. Penzo, *Adding flexibility to structure similarity queries on xml data*, Proceedings of the Fifth International Conference on Flexible Query Answering Systems (FQAS'2002) (Copenhagen, Denmark), Lecture Notes in AI #2522, Springer, 2002, pp. 124–139.

10. H. Prade, *Lipski's approach to incomplete information data bases restated and generalized in the setting of Zadeh's possibility theory*, Information Systems **9** (1984), no. 1, 27–42.

11. T. Schlieder, *Similarity search in xml data using cost-based query transformations*, Proceedings of the Fourth International Workshop on the Web and Databases (WebDB 2001), 2001.

12. Torsten Schlieder, *Schema-driven evaluation of approximate tree-pattern queries*, Proceedings of the 8th International Conference on Extending Database Technology (EDBT 2002), 2002.

13. A. Theobald and G. Weikum, *Adding relevance to xml*, Proceedings of the Third International Workshop on the Web and Databases (WebDB 2000), 2000, pp. 35–40.

14. R. Thomopoulos, P. Buche, and O. Haemmerlé, *Different kinds of comparison between fuzzy conceptual graphs*, Proceedings of the 11th International Conference on Conceptual Structures, ICCS'2003, Lecture Notes in Artificial Intelligence 2746 (Dresden, Germany), Springer, July 2003, pp. 54–68.

15. Rallou Thomopoulos, P. Buche, and O. Haemmerlé, *Sous-ensembles flous définis sur une ontologie*, Revue des Nouvelles Technologies de l'Information E-2, Vol 1, EGC'2004, pp 147–158.

16. Lucie Xyleme, *A dynamic warehouse for xml data of the web*, IEEE Data Engineering Bulletin (2001).

17. L. Zadeh, *Fuzzy sets*, Information and control **8** (1965), 338–353.

18. Lofti Zadeh, *Fuzzy sets as a basis for a theory of possibility*, Fuzzy Sets and Systems **1** (1978), 3–28.

Fuzzy Closeness Relation as a Basis
for Weakening Fuzzy Relational Queries

Patrick Bosc, Allel HadjAli, and Olivier Pivert

IRISA/ENSSAT
6, rue de Kerampont - BP 447
22305 Lannion Cedex, France
{bosc,hadjali,pivert}@enssat.fr

Abstract. Query weakening is the modification of the conditions involved in a query in order to obtain a less restrictive variant and then a non empty set of answers. The aim of the paper is to propose an approach for dealing with this problem in the case of fuzzy queries against relational databases. The approach rests on a transformation mechanism that consists in applying a tolerance relation on fuzzy predicates contained in the query. A particular tolerance relation, which can be conveniently modeled in terms of a parameterized fuzzy closeness relation, is discussed. The modified fuzzy predicate is obtained by a simple arithmetic operation on fuzzy numbers. The transformation must guarantee that the weakened query is not semantically speaking too far from the initial one, and its limits are handled in a non-empirical rigorous way without requiring any additional information from the user.

1 Introduction

One of the main benefits of fuzzy query processing systems [3] with respect to traditional ones is to contribute to avoid empty sets of answers when the queries are too restrictive. The use of a finer discrimination scale, [0, 1] instead of {0, 1}, increases the chances that an element satisfies the filter. Nevertheless, it may still happen that none of the elements satisfies the criterion formulated by the user. In such a case, two kinds of solutions can be thought of: i) giving the user information explaining why there is no answer ; ii) weakening the query, i.e., making it more tolerant in order to obtain a non empty answer. As stressed by Motro [8], in the case where no satisfactory data (with respect to the criterion) are present in the database, a solution consists in retrieving the data which are as close as possible to the initial query. Note that in this study, the notion of an empty answer corresponds to the situation where none of the items of the database satisfies the fuzzy query with a degree higher than 0.

Weakening a failing fuzzy query consists in modifying the constraints contained in the query in order to obtain a less restrictive variant. To the best of our knowledge, this problem has not received much attention in the literature [1, 2]. Let Q be a fuzzy query of the form P_1 and P_2 and ... and P_k (where P_i is a fuzzy predicate), and assume that the set of answers to Q is empty. A simple way to weaken the query Q, in order to obtain a non empty set of answers, is to apply a basic uniform transformation to each predicate P_i. To be effective, this transformation must increase the cardinality of the support of P_i. In [1], to extend the support of a fuzzy term, the authors apply a particu-

H. Christiansen et al. (Eds.): FQAS 2004, LNAI 3055, pp. 41–53, 2004.
© Springer-Verlag Berlin Heidelberg 2004

lar linguistic modifier to this term such that: i) no membership degree of any element of the domain of P_i decreases and ii) some degrees which were initially zero become positive. For instance, the simple query "find the employees who are *young*" can be transformed into "find the employees who are *more-or-less young*" where the modifier is expressed by *more-or-less*.

In this paper, we propose an alternative method to transform a fuzzy predicate P_i into an enlarged one, with the objective to keep it semantically close to the initial one, and where the notion of proximity plays a central role. Let us note that the proximity used here originally stems from qualitative reasoning about orders of magnitude and has been applied to define a fuzzy set of values that are close to some real-valued x. Obviously, the set of values *close to 10* and the set of values *close to 5000*, for instance, are not built in a similar way, especially from the point of view of the width of their supports. More generally, a proximity relation is intended for defining a set of predicates that are close to a given predicate P semantically speaking. This is why this notion appears appropriate in the perspective of relaxing queries. Nevertheless, the way to address the problem using this notion of proximity can be viewed as an original philosophy in query weakening, since known approaches proceed differently and are based on other concepts.

The proposed approach for fuzzy query weakening is based on a tolerance mechanism that consists in applying a tolerance relation to each fuzzy term involved in the query. The obtained terms are more permissive and then the associated query is less restrictive. Let us mention that the notion of a tolerance relation has already been used by Dubois and Prade in the context of fuzzy pattern matching [5]. A particular tolerance relation, which is of interest in the context of query weakening, is discussed in this paper. This relation can be conveniently modeled by a fuzzy relative closeness relation parameterized by a tolerance indicator. Based on this fuzzy relation, the proposed approach satisfies the properties required for any weakening process, as we will see later. Section 2 introduces the background on fuzzy query weakening based on linguistic modifiers, on the one hand, and the fuzzy modeling of the closeness relation, on the other hand. In section 3, we show how fuzzy closeness can be used for performing fuzzy predicate weakening, and we examine the main benefits of this approach. Section 4 describes a fuzzy closeness-based weakening strategy for multi-predicates queries. An illustrative example is also provided in this section. To conclude, the main interesting points of the approach are briefly recalled and some future working directions are outlined.

2 Background

2.1 Symmetric Fuzzy Weakening

Let us first consider a query that involves only one fuzzy predicate. It has been pointed out in [1] that the only way to weaken such a query is to apply a linguistic modifier to the fuzzy term. For instance, the query "find the employees who are *young*" can be transformed into "find the employees who are *more-or-less young*". If we want *more-or-less*(P) to be a weakening of P, the linguistic modifier "*more-or-less*" must satisfy the two following properties: i) it does not decrease the membership degree for any element of the domain, i.e. $\forall\, x \in$ domain(A), $\mu_{\text{more-or-less(P)}}(x) \geq \mu_P(x)$ where A denotes the attribute concerned by P; ii) it extends the support of the fuzzy term, i.e. $\{x \,|\, \mu_P(x) > 0\} \subset \{x \,|\, \mu_{\text{more-or-less(P)}}(x) > 0\}$.

A family of linguistic modifiers, denoted by m, that satisfies both of these properties, is the one proposed by Bouchon-Meunier in [4]. Let f be a fuzzy term whose membership function is defined by five parameters (A, B, a, b, ε) such that f(x) = ε if $x \leq A - a$ or $x \geq B + b$, f(x) = 1 if $A \leq x \leq B$, and f(x) = f'(x) if $A - a \leq x \leq a$, f(x) = f''(x) if $B \leq x \leq B + b$, for two functions f' and f'' respectively non decreasing for $x \leq A$ and non increasing for $x \geq B$, with f'(A) = f''(B) = 1 and f'(A − a) = f''(B + b) = ε. The term f is associated with a function φ such that φ(x) = 1 if $A \leq x \leq B$, φ(x) = f'(x) if $x \leq A$ and φ(x) = f''(x) if $x \geq B$. The behavior of the family of modifiers m is defined as follows (where U is the universe of discourse):

$$\forall\, x \in U,\ g(x) = m(f(x)) = \min\,(1,\ \max(0,\ \alpha\varphi(x) + \beta)), \tag{1}$$

for two real parameters α and β. In terms of a parameterized trapezoidal membership function, g can be represented by five parameters (A', B', a', b', ε').

One modifier of this family, called *v-rather*, is of particular interest for the purpose of query weakening. It corresponds to the values $\alpha = v \in [1/2, 1[$ and $\beta = 1 - v$, such that $\forall\, x \in U,\ g(x) = \max(0,\ v\varphi(x) + 1 - v)$ corresponding to the parameters (A, B, a', b', ε) with a' = a/v and b' = b/v (see figure 1). Let us write a' = a + θ·a and b' = b + θ·b, with $\theta = (1 - v)/v \in\,]0, 1]$. Then, we can easily see that the resulting weakening effects in the left and right sides are obtained using the same parameter θ. This is why the approach is said to be *symmetric*. As we can also see, this modifier enables to preserve the specificity of the attribute, which means that f and g have the same set of significant values (i.e., $\{x \,|\, \mu_f(x) = 1\} = \{x \,|\, \mu_g(x) = 1\}$), but the set of values where f is zero strictly contains the one where g is zero (since a' > a and b' > b). Then, this modifier satisfies the above two properties, required for query weakening.

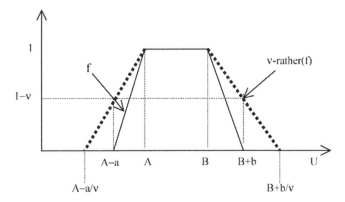

Fig. 1. Behavior of the modifier v-rather

Let us now explain how this modifier can be used in order to weaken a query involving one predicate P. If the set of answers is empty, the query Q is transformed into Q_1 = rather (P) and the process can be repeated n times until the answer to the question Q_n = rather(rather(.....rather (P).....)) is not empty. In practice, the difficulty when applying this weakening mechanism, concerns its semantic limits. Namely, what is the maximum number of weakening steps that is acceptable according to the user, i.e., such that the final modified query Q_n is not too far, semantically speaking, from the original one. To deal with this problem, a solution is proposed in [1] which consists in asking the user to specify, along with his query, a fuzzy set F_p of forbidden values in the related domain. Then, an element x would get a satisfaction degree equal to $\min(\mu_{Qi}(x), 1 - \mu_{FP}(x))$ with respect to the modified query resulting from i weakening steps. The weakening process will stop when the answer is non empty or when the complement of the support of Q_i is included in the core of F_p. In our opinion, this solution is not very practical since the user is asked to provide a fuzzy set F_p for which he may be sometimes unable to come up with an estimate.

In the general case of a query involving several fuzzy predicates linked by connectors, two options can be envisaged for the weakening procedure (see [1]): i) a global query modification which consists in applying the modifier to all the terms in the query; ii) a local query modification which affects only some terms (or sub-queries). The fuzzy set framework also provides another approach to weaken a complex fuzzy query. The method is based on the replacement of one or more connectors by less restrictive variants along the scale with disjunction as the least and conjunction as the most restrictive connector. For instance, if Q is a conjunctive query of the form P_1 *and* P_2 *and* ... *and* P_k (where P_i is a fuzzy predicate), the idea is to replace one or several *and* operators by a less strict one. For more details on this method, see [2].

2.2   Fuzzy Relative Closeness

A fuzzy set-based approach for handling relative orders of magnitude stated in terms of closeness and negligibility relations has been proposed in [7]. At the semantic level, these relations are represented by means of fuzzy relations controlled by tolerance parameters. The idea of relative closeness expresses the approximate equality between two real numbers x and y and can be captured by the following definition [7].

Definition 1. The closeness relation (Cl) is a reflexive and symmetric fuzzy relation such that:

$$\mu_{Cl}(x, y) = \mu_M(x/y),\qquad(2)$$

where the characteristic function μ_M is that of a fuzzy number "*close to* 1", such that $\mu_M(1) = 1$ since x is close to x, and $\mu_M(t) = 0$ if $t \leq 0$ assuming that two numbers which are close should have the same sign[1]. M is called a *tolerance parameter*.

---

[1] This is natural in a ratio-based view since the division by 0 is undefined. It does not lead to serious limitations in the expressiveness of qualitative relative orders of magnitude. Indeed, the statement that a variable is close to 0 (with an undefined sign) is an absolute statement; moreover, difference-based relations would enable us to express that x and y are close without having the same sign necessarily, but would have other limitations [7], and especially they correspond to a different viewpoint than that considered in this study.

Since closeness is naturally symmetric, i.e. $\mu_{Cl}(x, y) = \mu_{Cl}(y, x)$, M should satisfy $\mu_M(t) = \mu_M(1/t)$. So, the support of the fuzzy number M (denoted by S(M)) is of the form $[1-\varepsilon, 1/(1-\varepsilon)]$ with $\varepsilon \in [0, 1[$. Strict equality is recovered for $M = 1$ defined as $\mu_1(x/y) = 1$ if $x = y$ and $\mu_1(x/y) = 0$ otherwise. In this relative point of view, we evaluate the extent to which the ratio x/y is close to 1. The closer x and y are, the closer to 1 x/y must be.

The negligibility relation can be defined from closeness as follows.

Definition 2. Negligibility (Ne) is a fuzzy relation defined from the closeness relation Cl based on a fuzzy number M via the following : x is *negligible* with respect to y if and only if (x + y) is *close to* y. Then

$$\mu_{Ne}(x, y) = \mu_{Cl}(x + y, y)$$

$$= \mu_M((x + y) / y) = \mu_M(1 + x/y). \tag{3}$$

In the following, $(x, y) \in$ Cl[M] (resp. Ne[M]) expresses that the more or less possible pairs of values for x and y are restricted by the fuzzy set Cl[M] (resp. Ne[M]).

It has been demonstrated in [7] that the fuzzy number M which parameterizes closeness and negligibility should be chosen such that its support S(M) lies in the *validity interval* $\mathbb{V} = [(\sqrt{5} - 1)/2, (\sqrt{5} + 1)/2]$ ($\cong [0.61, 1.61]$) in order to ensure that the closeness relation be more restrictive than the relation "not negligible". In other terms, each level cut of M is of the form $[1 - \varepsilon, 1/(1 - \varepsilon)]$, with $\varepsilon \in [0, (3 - \sqrt{5})/2]$ ($\cong [0, 0.38]$). This means that if the support of a tolerance parameter associated with a closeness relation Cl is not included in $\mathbb{V}$, then the relation Cl is not in agreement with the intuitive semantics underlying this notion. The same applies for the negligibility relation Ne. It is worth noticing that the *validity interval* $\mathbb{V}$ plays a key role in the weakening process. As it will be shown later, it constitutes the basis for defining a stopping criterion of an iterative weakening process.

3   Fuzzy Closeness-Based Approach for Predicate Weakening

3.1   Principle of the Approach

Starting with the idea that allowing for a possible weakening of a query is connected with the intuitive idea of introducing some tolerance into it, one way to perform query weakening is to apply a tolerance relation to the fuzzy terms involved in the query. A particular tolerance relation which is of interest in the context of query weakening is considered. This relation can be conveniently modeled by the proposed parameterized closeness relation due to the fact that it expresses a proximity relation and satisfies the properties of reflexivity (i.e. $\forall u \in U, \mu_{Cl[M]}(u, u) = 1$) and symmetry (i.e. $\forall u \in U, \forall u' \in U, \mu_{Cl[M]}(u, u') = \mu_{Cl[M]}(u', u)$).

Let us consider a query which only involves one fuzzy predicate P, and a closeness relation parameterized by a tolerance indicator M, Cl[M]. Now, to weaken this query we replace the predicate P by an enlarged fuzzy predicate P' defined as follows:

$$\forall\, u \in U,\ \mu_{P'}(u) = \sup_{u' \in U} \min\, (\mu_P\, (u'),\, \mu_{Cl[M]}\, (u,\, u')). \tag{4}$$

From (4), it is easy to see that P' gathers the elements of P and the elements outside P which are somewhat close to an element in P.

Proposition 1. P' = P $\otimes$ M where $\otimes$ is the product operation extended to fuzzy numbers.

Indeed,

$$\forall\, u \in U,\quad \mu_{P'}(u) = \sup_{u' \in U} \min\, (\mu_P\, (u'),\, \mu_{Cl[M]}\, (u,\, u'))$$
$$\mu_{P'}(u) = \sup_{u' \in U} \min\, (\mu_P\, (u'),\, \mu_M\, (u/u')),\ \text{since}\ \mu_{Cl[M]}\, (u,\, u') = \mu_M\, (u/u')$$
$$\mu_{P'}(u) = \mu_{P \otimes M}\, (u),\ \text{observing that } u' \cdot (u/u') = u.$$

Then, P' = P $\otimes$ M. For more details about the arithmetic operations on fuzzy numbers, see [6].

The two desirable properties required for any weakening process are satisfied by the predicate P'. Namely, we have: i) $\forall\, u$, $\mu_{P'}(u) \geq \mu_P(u)$; ii) $S(P) \subset S(P')$. In terms of parameterized membership functions, if P = (A, B, a, b) and M = (1, 1, ε, $\varepsilon/(1 - \varepsilon)$), with $\varepsilon \in [0, (3 - \sqrt{5})/2]$, then, P' = (A, B, a + A$\cdot\varepsilon$, b + B$\cdot\varepsilon/(1 - \varepsilon)$) by applying the above proposition. Taking a' = a + A$\cdot\varepsilon$ and b' = b + B$\cdot\varepsilon/(1 - \varepsilon)$, the membership function of P' is illustrated in figure 2.

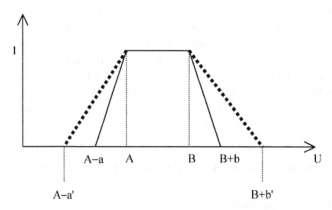

Fig. 2. Behavior of the fuzzy closeness-based weakening

In practice, if Q is a query containing one predicate P (i.e., Q = P) and if the set of answers to Q is empty, then Q is weakened by transforming it into $Q_1 = P \otimes M$. This transformation is repeated n times until the answer to the question $Q_n = P \otimes M^n$ is not empty. Now, in order to ensure that the query Q_n is semantically close to the original one, the support of $M^{n\,2}$ should be included in the interval of validity $\mathbb{V}$. In effect, the

---

[2] In order to preserve the symmetry of the initial fuzzy number M, we use a global approximation to compute the product M $\otimes$ M. Namely, if M = (1, 1, ε, $\varepsilon/(1 - \varepsilon)$) with S(M) = [1 - ε, $1/(1 - \varepsilon)$] then, M^2 = M $\otimes$ M = (1, 1, 2ε - ε^2, (2ε - ε^2)/(1 - ε)^2) with S(M^2) = [(1 - ε)^2, 1/(1 - ε)^2].

relation $Cl[M^n]$ is no longer a closeness relation semantically speaking when $S(M^n)$ does not lie in $\mathbb{V}$, despite its appearance at the syntactic level. Then, the above procedure will stop either when the answer is non empty or when $S(M^n) \not\subset \mathbb{V}$.

This weakening process can be formalized by algorithm 1. The choice of ε will be discussed in section 4.

Now as stressed in subsection 2.1, the modifier-based weakening approach makes use of an external criterion for stopping the weakening process (namely, the fuzzy set F_p); here such a criterion is a direct by-product of the fuzzy semantics of a closeness relation. Moreover, it is worth noticing that the values of the bounds of the core of the predicate P (i.e., the parameters A and B) are taken into account when computing the left spread a' and the right spread b' of the predicate P' (which are expressed by a + A·ε and b + B·ε/(1 − ε) respectively). This means that significant values of P are used in the weakening process which implies that the non empty answers might be obtained rather quickly. In the modifier-based weakening approach, these spreads are independent of the bounds of the core of P. This may constitute an actual disadvantage since the approach fails when the query only involves a precise (non fuzzy) predicate. For instance, let Q be the query "find the cars whose price is *between 5500 and 7500*" where the predicate P, *between_5500_and_7500*, is represented by the following trapezoidal membership function P = (5500, 7500, 0, 0). The linguistic modifier-based approach does not allow for a weakening of this query since ν-*rather*(P) = P. Now, applying the tolerance-based weakening (with ε = 0.01 as a tolerance value), Q can be weakened replacing P by the enlarged predicate P' = (5500, 7500, 55, 83.33).

```
let Q = P
let ε be a tolerance value          (* ε ∈ [0, (3 − √5)/2] *)
i := 0                              (* i denotes the number of weakening steps *)
Qᵢ := Q
compute Σ_Qi                        (* Σ_Qi represents the set of answers to Qᵢ *)
while (Σ_Qi = ∅ and S(Mⁱ⁺¹) ⊆ 𝕍) do
      begin
          i := i+1
          Qᵢ := P⊗Mⁱ
          compute Σ_Qi
      end
if Σ_Qi ≠ ∅ then return Σ_Qi
endif.
```

Algorithm 1.

3.2 Comparison with the ν-Rather Modifier-Based Approach

Taking a deep glance on behaviors of the ν-rather modifier and fuzzy closeness-based approaches for query weakening shows that they are significantly different. Let us compare them with respect to some criteria that seem relevant from a practical point of view.

v-rather modifier-based approach:

i) the core of the predicate P = (A, B, a, b) to be weakened is not affected by the transformation;

ii) the symmetric behavior of the approach leads to a similar weakening effect in the left and right sides when a = b;

iii) it is easy to check that the maximal relaxation that can be performed in one step in the left (respectively right) side is equal to a·θ (respectively b·θ), with θ = 1. In this case, the left and right spreads of the weakened predicate are respectively a' = 2a and b' = 2b. However, no intrinsic semantic limits are provided for the weakening process when applying this approach since the weakening can be applied iteratively;

iv) the slopes in the left and right sides of the membership function are identified as the most important factor affecting the weakening effect. On the other hand, the relative position of the function in the referential does not impact the shape of the modified function as illustrated in figure 3. Furthermore, the unit associated with a domain has no effect on the weakening (for instance when the scale of the domain is expressed in meter, the weakening effect is the same as when it is expressed in km);

v) when the predicates are crisp (i.e. classical intervals), the approach is inappropriate since v-rather(P) = P.

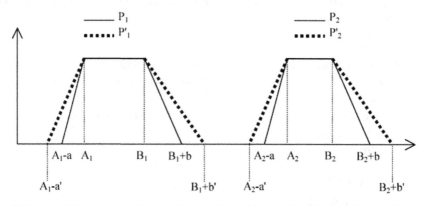

Fig. 3. Impact of the slopes and the relative position of the membership functions on the weakening mechanism when applying the v-rather modifier-based approach (a < b, a' = a/v, b' = b/v ⇒ a' < b')

Fuzzy closeness-based approach:

i) the core of the predicate P is preserved as in the previous approach;

ii) this approach is basically non symmetric. In figure 4, if $P_1 = (A_1, B_1, a, b) = (100, 180, 10, 10)$ then the weakened predicate $P'_1 = (A'_1, B'_1, a'_1, b'_1) = (100, 180, 20, 30)$ for $\varepsilon = 0.1$. Moreover, and since $\varepsilon < \varepsilon/(1 - \varepsilon)$ (for $0 < \varepsilon \leq (3 - \sqrt{5})/2] \cong 0.38$), the equality between $A \cdot \varepsilon$ (the left weakening rate) and $B \cdot \varepsilon/(1 - \varepsilon)$ (the right weakening rate) never holds, even when A = B;

iii) the maximal left (respectively right) relaxation is reached for the higher value of ε, namely $\varepsilon = \varepsilon_{max} = 0.38$. In this case, the left and right spreads of the weakened predicate are respectively $0.38 \cdot A$ and $0.61 \cdot B$. Contrary to the v-rather-based approach, this approach provides a semantic limit that may serve to stop the weakening mechanism;

iv) the relative position of the membership function on the referential is a major factor that affects the weakening effect, rather than the left and right spreads (see figure 4). On the other hand, the weakening effect is not changed when the domain unit is modified;

v) the approach is still effective for crisp predicates.

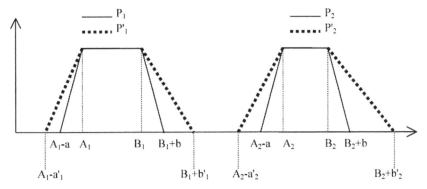

Fig. 4. Impact of the slopes and the relative position of the membership functions on the weakening mechanism when applying the closeness-based approach (a = b, $a'_1 = a + A_1\varepsilon$, $b'_1 = b + B_1\varepsilon/(1-\varepsilon)$, $a'_2 = a + A_2\varepsilon$, $b'_2 = b + B_2\varepsilon/(1-\varepsilon)$ $\Rightarrow a'_1 < a'_2$, $b'_1 < b'_2$, $a'_i < b'_i$ for $i = 1,2$)

4 Fuzzy Closeness-Based Weakening Approach for Multi-predicates Queries

For the sake of simplicity, the closeness-based weakening approach is illustrated with a conjunctive query $Q = P_1$ **and** P_2 **and** ... **and** P_k. Moreover, we will assume that the relaxation mechanism applies to each of the predicates involved in the query.

4.1 Query Weakening Strategy

Assume that a query $Q = P_1$ **and** P_2 **and** ... **and** P_k has an empty answer. To apply the fuzzy closeness-based approach for weakening Q, it is first necessary to choose a value for the parameter ε. One way (obviously, other solutions may exist) to choose this value consists in asking the user to set the maximal number of weakening steps that he authorizes. Denoting by n this number, it is easy to check that after n weakening steps, applied to a predicate P = (A, B, a, b), the resulting modified predicate P' is of the form (A, B, a + A·n·ε, b + B·n·ε/(1 − ε)). As emphasized in subsection 3.2, the maximal left relaxation provided by this approach is A·ε_{max} (with ε_{max} = 0.38) then, the following inequality $\varepsilon \le \varepsilon_{max}/n$ holds.

Choosing $\varepsilon = \varepsilon_{max}/n$, on the one hand, we increase the chances to obtain a non empty answer in a number of steps less than n and, on the other hand, we guarantee that the allowed maximal right relaxation is not violated. The same value of ε is then used to weaken all of the fuzzy terms in Q. The global weakening strategy that we advocate, is sketched in the following algorithm (where $toler^i(P_j)$ denotes the modified predicate P_j resulting from i weakening steps).

Let $Q = P_1$ and P_2 and ... and P_k
read(n)
$\varepsilon := \varepsilon_{max}/n$
$i := 0$
$Q_i := Q$
compute Σ_{Qi}
while $(\Sigma_{Qi} = \varnothing$ and $i < n)$ do
    begin
        $i := i + 1$
        for $j = 1$ to k do
                $toler^i(P_j) = \textbf{weaken}(P_j, i)$
        $Q_i := toler^i(P_1)$ and $toler^i(P_2)$ and ... and $toler^i(P_k)$
        compute Σ_{Qi}
    end
if $\Sigma_{Qi} \neq \varnothing$ then return Σ_{Qi}
endif.

function $\textbf{weaken}(P, h)$
    begin
        $M = (1, 1, \varepsilon, \varepsilon/(1 - \varepsilon))$
        $P' = P \otimes M^h$
        return P'
    end.

Algorithm 2.

4.2 An Illustrative Example

Let us consider a user who is looking for an apartment that is near the airport and not too expensive. Assume that the database of available apartments is given in table 1.

Then, let us consider the query Q: "find an apartment *near* the airport and *not too expensive*" where *near* and *not too expensive* are labels of fuzzy sets which can be represented respectively by the trapezoidal membership functions $P_1 = (0, 8, 0, 2.5)$ and $P_2 = (0, 500, 0, 100)$ pictured in figure 5. For the sake of brevity and simplicity, let us write Q under the form $Q = P_1$ **and** P_2.

Table 1. Database of apartments

Apartment	Distance between the apartment and the airport (Km)	Rent (euros)	$\mu_{P_1}(A)$	$\mu_{P_2}(A)$
A_1	13	550	0	0.5
A_2	11	700	0	0
A_3	12.5	600	0	0
A_4	11.5	670	0	0
A_5	15	500	0	1

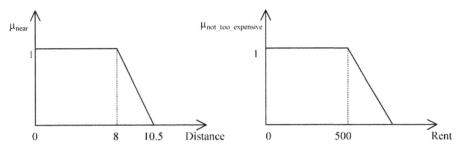

Fig. 5. The fuzzy predicates *near* and *not_too_expensive*

Assuming that the fuzzy connector **and** is modeled by the *min* operator, it is easy to check that each item of the above database gets zero for the query Q [3] with the content given in table 1, which means that none of the items satisfies the query.

Now, in order to obtain non empty answers, we propose to weaken query Q. Assume that the maximal number of weakening steps provided by the user is equal to 3 (i.e., n = 3), this leads to choose the value 0.12 for the tolerance parameter ε. Then, the weakening process will be based on the closeness relation Cl[M] with M = (1, 1, 0.12, 3/22).

By applying one weakening step, we obtain the results summarized in table 2.

Table 2. Results of one weakening step

Apartment	Distance	Rent	$\mu_{toler(P_1)}(A)$	$\mu_{toler(P_2)}(A)$	Satisfaction degree to query Q_1
A_1	13	550	0	0.70	0
A_2	11	700	0.16	0	0
A_3	12.5	600	0	0.40	0
A_4	11.5	670	0.02	0	0
A_5	15	500	0	1	0

---

[3] An item A satisfies the query Q with a degree d = min(μ_{P_1}(A), μ_{P_2}(A)). For instance for the item A_1, d = min(0, 0.5) = 0.

The weakened variant of query Q writes $Q_1 = toler(P_1)$ **and** $toler(P_2)$ where $toler$ $(P_1) = (0, 8, 0, 3.59)$ and $toler(P_2) = (0, 500, 0, 168.18)$. Unfortunately, the set of answers to Q_1 is still empty as shown in table 2. Then, a second weakening step is necessary to answer the initial user query. Since $S(M^2) = [0.77, 1.29]$ is included in $\mathbb{V}$ (which is obvious considering the choice that has bee made for ε), this step is acceptable from a semantic point of view. Now, the resulting query is $Q_2 = toler^2(P_1)$ **and** $toler^2(P_2)$ where $toler^2(P_1) = (0, 8, 0, 4.68)$ and $toler^2(P_2) = (0, 500, 0, 236.36)$. This modification leads to the results reported in table 3.

As indicated in table 3, some items of the database somewhat satisfy the weakened query Q_2. Thus, the weakening process ends successfully and returns the set of answers to the weakened query Q_2, i.e., the items A_2, A_3 and A_4 with the satisfaction degrees 0.15, 0.03 and 0.25 respectively.

Table 3. Results of the weakening process

Apartment	Distance	Rent	$\mu_{toler^2(P_1)}(A)$	$\mu_{toler^2(P_2)}(A)$	Satisfaction degree to query Q_2
A_1	13	550	0	0.78	0
A_2	11	700	0.35	0.15	0.15
A_3	12.5	600	0.03	0.57	0.03
A_4	11.5	670	0.25	0.28	0.25
A_5	15	500	0	1	0

5   Conclusion

A new fuzzy approach for generating more tolerant queries addressed to a relational database is proposed. It is based on the fuzzy semantics underlying the notion of a relative closeness relation. It constitutes a natural appropriate way to weaken a fuzzy query since it replaces a query Q by the best modification Q' in the sense that Q' remains semantically close to Q. Besides, the approach offers an efficient rational tool, which uses a single parameter M, for dealing with the stopping condition of the weakening process. The two principal characteristics of this mechanism reside in: i) the preservation of the core of the initial predicate and ii) the non symmetric nature of the left and right relaxations (due to the very notion of closeness between values). The use of a fuzzy closeness relation constitutes a new approach to predicate weakening, in particular it significantly differs from the v-rather based method presented in subsection 2.1.

Two directions of future work can be foreseen. First, we envisage to study the behavior of the weakening mechanism when using an absolute proximity, i.e., a fuzzy relation whose membership function is expressed in terms of a difference rather than a ratio. Second, some experimentations on large practical examples are needed for a deep comparison between the different approaches. Then, a guide enabling the user to choose which approach is the most suitable, could be carried out.

References

1. Andreasen T., Pivert O., On the weakening of fuzzy relational queries. 8th Int. Symp. on Meth. For intell. Syst., Charlotte, USA, pp. 144-51, 1994.
2. Andreasen T., Pivert O., Improving answers to failing fuzzy relational queries. 6th Int. Fuzzy Syst. Assoc. World Congress, IFSA, São Paulo, Brazil, pp. 345-348, 1995.
3. Bosc, P., Pivert O., Some approaches for relational databases flexible querying. J. of Intell. Inf. Syst., 1, pp. 323-354, 1992.
4. Bouchon-Meunier B., Yao J., Linguistic modifiers and imprecise categories. J. of Intell. Syst., 7, pp. 25-36, 1992.
5. Dubois D., Prade H., Tolerant Fuzzy Pattern Matching: An Introduction. In: Fuzziness in Database Management Systems (Bosc P. and Kacprzyk J., Eds), Physica-Verlag, Heidelberg, 1995.
6. Dubois D., Prade H., Fundamentals of Fuzzy Sets. The Handbooks of Fuzzy Sets Series (Dubois D., Prade H., Eds), Vol. 3, Kluwer Academic Publishers, Dordrecht, Netherlands, 2000.
7. HadjAli A., Dubois D., Prade H., Qualitative reasoning based on fuzzy relative orders of magnitude. IEEE Transactions on Fuzzy Systems, Vol. 11, No 1, pp. 9-23, 2003.
8. Motro A., SEAVE: A mechanism for verifying user presuppositions in query systems. ACM Trans. on Off. Inf. Syst., 4(4), pp. 312-330, 1986.

Querying Data Sources
in a SuperPeer Data Management System

Hélène Jaudoin[1], Michel Schneider[2], and Frédéric Vigier[1]

[1] Cemagref,
24 avenue des landais, BP 50085
F-63172 Aubière , France
{helene.jaudoin,frederic.vigier}@cemagref.fr
[2] Université Blaise Pascal,
Laboratoire d'Informatique et de Modélisation des Systèmes , ISIMA
F-63172 Aubière, France
schneider@isima.fr

Abstract. Numerous data integration systems have been proposing powerful query mechanisms of data sources. However these systems do not facilitate the evolution of existing schemas or the integration of new schemas. Many applications induce the continual arrival of data sources and thus of new schemas. These applications require more flexible systems. The PDMS (Peer Data Management Systems) supply an interesting alternative. In this paper we propose a SuperPeer Management System allowing local interoperability in a SuperPeer cluster and permitting global cooperation between the SuperPeers. We define first the architecture components and the query processing in terms of description logics. The descriptions of queries and of data source capabilities can be annotated with constraints on the attribute values domain in order to improve the data sources discovery process. We then propose a solution for query processing in such systems by adapting an existing algorithm.

1 Introduction

The popularization of computer science and of Internet has facilitated the development of computerized systems and has induced new needs for cooperation between these systems. However making interoperable computerized systems is a difficult research problem because of their heterogeneity. The database research community has proposed numerous data integration systems ([14], [5]) in order to solve this problem.

A data integration system is defined by a triple $< \mathcal{G}, \mathcal{S}, \mathcal{M} >$ [9], where $\mathcal{G}$ is the global schema, $\mathcal{S}$ the data sources and $\mathcal{M}$ the semantic mapping between $\mathcal{G}$ and $\mathcal{S}$. The first generation of data integration systems comprises federated databases ([14]) and mediation of data sources (for example the Tsimmis project [5]). In the first generation $\mathcal{M}$ is defined by the GAV (Global As View) approach i.e. the global schema is espressed as a set of views over the data sources. The federated databases allow the cooperation of a set of databases whether they

H. Christiansen et al. (Eds.): FQAS 2004, LNAI 3055, pp. 54–67, 2004.

have heterogeneous schemas or not. The cooperation is achieved by the integration of exported schemas. The mediation of data sources is based on the notion of mediator and of wrappers. These systems are based on a unique global schema, the mediated schema (see [7] for recalls about mediation architecture). All the data sources refer to this global schema through semantic links. Because the global schema is defined for the entire system, any modification is likely to fail the system. These systems are defined as tightly coupled systems. The second generation of data integration systems is based on a LAV (Local as View) approach, i.e. the data sources are defined as views over the global schema. A LAV approach permits a more easily departure and arrival of data sources.

Apart from this research problem, P2P systems receive great attention ([12], [16]) due to their interesting properties of flexibility. A P2P system is a virtual network which allows for resources to be shared between autonomous systems without using a global schema. These autonomous systems are also called peers. P2P networks are able to handle a variety of actors and heterogeneous schemas. Moreover P2P systems allow for incremental network extensions. There are three kinds of P2P architecture. In a decentralised approach or pure P2P, a peer sends its query to its neighbours; these neighbours transmit it to their neighbours, and so on, until the authorized number of hops is reached or until the query obtains an answer. In the centralised approach the metadata concerning the sharable files are centralised on a server Peer, called the SuperPeer. All the peers are linked to the unique SuperPeer. In the SuperPeer approach, there are several SuperPeers, a SuperPeer being responsible for a set of peers (cluster). [16] propose a redundant SuperPeer to improve the stability of the network. A SuperPeer, when it has no answer to a query, forwards it to its Superpeer neighbours. However P2P systems do not cater for complex queries. They have no means to describe the semantics of the data, to formulate complex queries and process them. Only keywords queries are handled by such systems.

The database research community has been taking advantage of P2P properties in order to supply flexibility to the data integration systems. [8], [10], [11] define a third generation of data integration systems. They are called Peer Data Management Systems (PDMS). PDMS are P2P systems to which some administration and conceptualization capabilities have been added. These capabilities are inspired by the mediation approach. The administration capabilities consist in defining how expressing and processing queries. The conceptualization capabilities consist in defining how the knowledge is specified and who handles knowledge, and in specifying the semantic relations between data sources and the knowledge. The semantic mapping $\mathcal{M}$ is designated as a GLAV approach in order to specify that the links between peers can be a LAV link or a GAV link. With the systems proposed in [8], [10], [11] it is possible to have the cooperation of several databases without using one single schema in a totally decentralized architecture.

However some application domains require more structured systems. For example our application domain, the sustainable land and water management domain, is naturally made up of many communities. The application domain is continually in extension: supplementary communities are likely to be defined and added to the application domain. A community consists in a set of data sources relative to the community knowledge. For regulatory purposes the data sources in a community and between communities have to cooperate. The community knowledge is quite stable. Moreover the users of such data sources are not specialized in computer science. We have to preserve them as much as possible from administration tasks. This kind of application domain needs a structured but flexible data integration system. It is for this reason that we present here a PDMS which is based on a SuperPeer approach in order to integrate more structure in the PDMS. We call it SPDMS for SuperPeer Data Management System. The SuperPeer approach allows us to centralize some administration and conceptualization tasks. At the same time, the SuperPeer approach provides extension possibilities by adding other SuperPeers. SPDMS supplies local interoperability in a SuperPeer cluster and global cooperation between the SuperPeers. A data integration system is also characterized by the semantic mapping $\mathcal{M}$ between SuperPeers and between Peers and SuperPeers. $\mathcal{G}$ and $\mathcal{S}$ are here specified via the description logics with the possibility to add domain integrity constraints.

In this paper we propose a processes to rewrite a query with domain integrity constraints in terms of views which may have constraints in a SPDMS. More especially we give a way to rewrite the constrained part of a query and to combine the resulting rewriting with the rewriting of the query remaining part. We briefly present the description logics in section 2. The SPDMS architecture described in the section 3 is an adaptation of the proposal of [8]. Our solution for the rewriting of queries with constraints is presented in section 4.

2   Preliminaries

Description Logics (DL) were developed in order to describe complex structures and reason with them. DLs allow to describe an application domain through concepts (unary predicate) and roles (binary predicate). A DL is defined by a set of constructors. Constructors used in this paper define the $\mathcal{FL}_0 + \{\geq n\}$ language. The syntax of the constructors is given in table 1, column 2. A concept description is an expression formed with constructors. Example of concept descriptions are:

. CulturalParcel, a concept name,
. PesticideArea $\sqcap$ FertilizerArea, formed using concept conjunction constructor,
. CulturalParcel $\sqcap$ $\forall$ BelongTo.Farm, formed using the concept conjunction and universal quantifier constructor,
. CulturalParcel $\sqcap$ $\geq$ 1 BelongTo $\sqcap$ $\forall$ BelongTo.Farm, formed using the concept conjunction, at least number restriction and universal quantifier constructors.

DLs are associated to semantics which is defined by an interpretation $\mathcal{I}=(\Delta^{\mathcal{I}}, .^{\mathcal{I}})$ where $\Delta^{\mathcal{I}}$ is the interpretation domain and $.^{\mathcal{I}}$ is an interpretation function.

Table 1. Syntax and semantics of $\mathcal{FL}_0 + \{\geq n\}$ language

$Constructors Name$	$Syntax$	$Semantics$
Concept Name	$\mathcal{P}$	$\mathcal{P}^{\mathcal{I}}$
Top	$\top$	$\Delta^{\mathcal{I}}$
Conjunction	C⊓D	$C^{\mathcal{I}} \cap D^{\mathcal{I}}$
Universal Quantifier	$\forall \mathcal{R}.C$	$\{x \in \Delta^{\mathcal{I}} | \forall y : (x,y) \in \mathcal{R}^{\mathcal{I}} \rightarrow y \in C^{\mathcal{I}}\}$
Atleast Number Restriction	$(\geq n\mathcal{R})$, $n \in N$	$\{x \in \Delta^{\mathcal{I}} | \sharp\{y | (x,y) \in \mathcal{R}^{\mathcal{I}}\} \geq n\}$

A concept is interpreted as a subset of $\Delta^{\mathcal{I}}$ and roles as subsets of $\Delta^{\mathcal{I}} \times \Delta^{\mathcal{I}}$. Furthermore the semantics of an arbitrary description must verify the conditions presented in column 3 of table 1. Semantics of some concept descriptions are below:

. PesticideArea ⊓ FertilizerArea points out the class of individuals which are both PesticideArea and FertilizerArea.
. CulturalParcel ⊓ ∀ BelongTo.Farm designates the class of individuals which are CulturalParcel and which belongs to a Farm.
. CulturalParcelBelongingToAFarm $\doteq$ CulturalParcel ⊓ ≥ 1 BelongsTo ⊓ ∀BelongsTo.Farm denotes the cultural parcels belonging to at least one farm.

An interpretation $\mathcal{I}$ is a model for a concept C if $C^{\mathcal{I}}$ is non-empty.

With respect to this semantics, the subsumption and equivalence reasoning are defined as follows:

Let C and D be two concept descriptions then

 − C is subsumed by D (C⊑D) iff $C^{\mathcal{I}} \subseteq D^{\mathcal{I}}$ for all interpretation $\mathcal{I}$.
 − C is equivalent to D (C≡D) iff $C^{\mathcal{I}} = D^{\mathcal{I}}$ for all interpretation $\mathcal{I}$.

The DL provide intensional descriptions (T-Box). The T-Box, also called terminology, is a set of concept definitions (A $\doteq$ C where A is a concept name and C is a concept description), such that each concept name occurs, at most, once in the left-hand side of a definition. A is called a defined concept. In this paper, we assume that the terminology is acyclic (i.e. a concept is not referred to itself, directly or indirectly in its definition). An interpretation $\mathcal{I}$ is a model for a T-Box if $\mathcal{I}$ is a model for each statement of the T-Box.

3   SPDMS Architecture Overview

To face the needs of sustainable land and water management, and more particularly related to agricultural activities, the agricultural players need to record all their practices via software or data management systems. These autonomous computerized systems have to cooperate in order to collect and to analyse the practices and to verify their conformity with the ministerial regulations. We thus

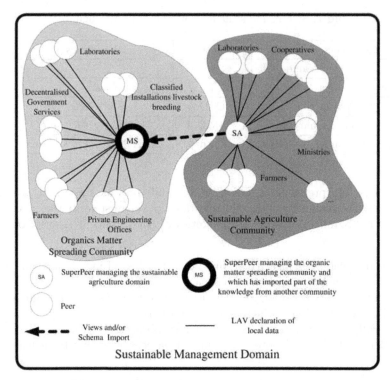

Fig. 1. SPDMS for the communities cooperation

consider a general domain compound of all the computerized systems relative to
the sustainable management of land and water (figure 1). We propose to structure the whole system in communities. A community is defined by a common
and more specific interest. The common interest is represented by community
knowledge. Because other communities are likely to extend the general domain,
and because there are so many of these communities, we cannot define global
knowledge for the domain. However several communities are likely to cooperate
either because their knowledge is similar or because they require complementary
information. For example a community dedicated to one kind of operation on
parcels in the south of France could be interested by the flooding area in the
south of France in another community. In a community, numerous computerized
systems could have the same conceptual description of their content. However
the computerized systems do not store the same data instances. A mean to distinguish them is to detail some concept attributes by specifying their allowed
values.

We now give a definition of a community and present the SPDMS peer relations inside a community and next between communities.

– A community is a set of peers gathered around a SuperPeer. A peer corresponds to a computerized system. The SuperPeer is responsible for a community. It administers the community knowledge (or SuperPeer Schema)

and the declarations of peer contents. The SuperPeer schema, called $\mathcal{T}_{\mathcal{SP}}$, is defined a priori by the human experts and is represented by a terminology of concept definitions. The set of declarations of peer contents is specified by a terminology of concept definitions, the terminology of views, called $\mathcal{T}_V$. $\mathcal{T}_V$ is built in terms of $\mathcal{T}_{SP}$. In this way peer contents are views over $\mathcal{T}_{SP}$. A community is thus considered as a mediator with LAV mapping between the SuperPeer schema and the Peer contents. Figure 2 gives an example of terminology of views. A view consists of two parts: a description in $\mathcal{FL}_0$ + $\{\geq n\mathcal{R}\}$ language and domain integrity constraints[1]. The view V1 of the figure 2 represents the cultural parcels which are in at least one organics matter spreading parcel, and whose the culture year is Y1998 or Y2000, and which are managed by a farm whose identification number is F1 or F10. The two constraints farm indentification number and culture year, are denoted with C1(V1) and C2(V1) of figure 2. The constraints allow to specify that only cultural parcels defined for some culture years and in some farms are stored by the peer associated to V1.

– Let SP1, SP2, SP3 be three SuperPeers, $\mathcal{T}_{V1}$, $\mathcal{T}_{V2}$, $\mathcal{T}_{V3}$ their relative terminologies of views and $\mathcal{T}_{SP1}$, $\mathcal{T}_{SP2}$, $\mathcal{T}_{SP3}$ their schemas.
  • Consider that SP1 and SP2 communities are similar, i.e. $\mathcal{T}_{SP1}$ is the same as $\mathcal{T}_{SP2}$. SP1 and SP2 can cooperate in order to improve the query processing. SP1 could be interested in some peer contents in SP2 and vice versa. In this case SP1 (resp. SP2) can import some views of $\mathcal{T}_{V2}$ (resp. $\mathcal{T}_{V1}$). These "external views" sustain a third terminology of views. We call $\mathcal{T}_{E1}$ the terminology of external views. The data relative to these views remain in SP2.
  • Consider now SP1 and SP3. Their knowledge has several basic concepts in common, but they are different. For example the SP1 community is dedicated to the organic matter spreading plans. The SP3 community is interested in sustainable agriculture. The SP1 community can estimate that it is important to know if the parcels which have received organic matter spreading come under a contract. Here Parcel is a common concept to SP1 and SP3. To cooperate with SP3, SP1 must proceed in two steps. First SP1 must update its schema $\mathcal{T}_{SP1}$ by adding concepts stemming from the SP3 schema. Secondly, SP1 must add external views in $\mathcal{T}_{E1}$ concerning the added schema part. The external views are issued in $\mathcal{T}_{V3}$.

We now explain the general principle of query processing. A query is expressed in terms of one SuperPeer schema. Q as the views can have a constraint part. Let Q be a query sent by a peer belonging to the SuperPeer SP. SP is responsible for answering the query. Q is a $\mathcal{FL}_0$ + $\geq n$ concept formed with the concept names of $\mathcal{T}_{SP}$. The SuperPeer must answer Q by using a combination of views of $\mathcal{T}_V$ and $\mathcal{T}_E$.
  • If the views of $\mathcal{T}_V$ answer Q totally, then only community peers are invoked.

---

[1] Adding integrity constraints amounts to allow the **OneOf** constructor in the decsription logics [2, 4, 13].

$V1 \doteq$	D(V1): CulturalParcel $\sqcap \geq 1$ CultureYear $\sqcap \forall$CultureYear.Integer $\sqcap \geq 1$ In $\sqcap \forall$In.OMSpreadingParcel $\sqcap \geq 1$ ManagedIn $\sqcap \forall$ManagedIn.(Farm $\sqcap \geq 1$ NumFarm $\sqcap \forall$NumFarm.Integer)
	C1(V1) : $\forall$ManagedIn.$\forall$NumFarm.Integer $\in \{$F1, F10$\}$
	C2(V1) : $\forall$CultureYear.Integer $\in \{$Y1998, Y2000$\}$
$V2 \doteq$	D(V2): CulturalParcel $\sqcap \geq 1$ CultureYear $\sqcap \forall$CultureYear.Integer $\sqcap \geq 1$ In $\sqcap \forall$In.OMSpreadingParcel $\sqcap \geq 1$ ManagedIn $\sqcap \forall$ManagedIn.(Farm $\sqcap \geq 1$ NumFarm $\sqcap \forall$NumFarm.Integer)
	C1(V2) : $\forall$ManagedIn.$\forall$NumFarm.Integer $\in \{$F2, F5$\}$
	C2(V2) : $\forall$CultureYear.Integer $\in \{$Y1998$\}$
$V3 \doteq$	D(V3): ≥ 1 CultureYear $\sqcap \forall$CultureYear.Integer $\sqcap \geq 1$ ManagedIn $\sqcap \forall$ManagedIn.(Farm $\sqcap \geq 1$ NumFarm $\sqcap \forall$NumFarm.Integer)
	C1(V3) : $\forall$ManagedIn.$\forall$NumFarm.Integer $\in \{$F8, F2$\}$
	C2(V3) : $\forall$CultureYear.Integer $\in \{$Y2000$\}$
$V4 \doteq$	D(V4): CulturalParcel $\sqcap \geq 1$ CultureYear $\sqcap \forall$CultureYear.Integer ≥ 1 ManagedIn $\sqcap \forall$ManagedIn.(Farm $\sqcap \geq 1$ NumFarm $\sqcap \forall$NumFarm.Integer)
	C1(V4) : $\forall$ManagedIn.$\forall$NumFarm.Integer $\in \{$F2, F4, F5$\}$
	C2(V4) : $\forall$CultureYear.Integer $\in \{$Y1998, Y1999, Y2000$\}$
$V5 \doteq$	D(V5):CulturalParcel $\sqcap \geq 1$ CultureYear $\sqcap \forall$CultureYear.Integer $\sqcap \geq 1$ In $\sqcap \forall$In.OMSpreadingParcel $\sqcap \geq 1$ ManagedIn $\sqcap \forall$ManagedIn.(Farm $\sqcap \geq 1$ NumFarm $\sqcap \forall$NumFarm.Integer)
	C1(V5) : $\forall$ManagedIn.$\forall$NumFarm.Integer $\in \{$F3, F7, F12$\}$
	C2(V5) : $\forall$CultureYear.Integer $\in \{$Y1997, Y1998, Y1999$\}$
$V6 \doteq$	D(V6):CulturalParcel $\sqcap \geq 1$ CultureYear $\sqcap \forall$CultureYear.Integer $\sqcap \geq 1$ In $\sqcap \forall$In.OMSpreadingParcel $\sqcap \geq 1$ ManagedIn $\sqcap \forall$ManagedIn.(Farm $\sqcap \geq 1$ NumFarm $\sqcap \forall$NumFarm.Integer)
	C1(V6) : $\forall$ManagedIn.$\forall$NumFarm.Integer $\in \{$F5$\}$
	C2(V6) : $\forall$CultureYear.Integer $\in \{$Y1997$\}$
$V7 \doteq$	≥ 1 With $\sqcap \forall$With.Contract

Fig. 2. Terminology of views: $\mathcal{T}_V \cup \mathcal{T}_E$

- If some views of $\mathcal{T}_E$ are necessary to answer a part of Q, then this part is forwarded towards the corresponding SuperPeers. In this case the SuperPeers collaborating with the query processing are known.
- If a part of the query has no answer, this part is forwarded randomly towards the other SuperPeers.

The next section is devoted to the query processing illustration in such a context and a proposition of solution.

4   Query Processing

4.1   General Principle

Let $\mathcal{T}_{SP}$ be the schema of a SuperPeer SP, $\mathcal{T}_V$ and $\mathcal{T}_E$ be the terminologies of views of the SP community and Q be a query in terms of $\mathcal{T}_{SP}$, processing a query amounts to a query rewriting problem. The views and the queries are made up of a conjunction of atoms. Some atoms can be constrained by some values (domain integrity constraint). We propose to proceed in two steps. First we take care of the rewriting of the constrained atoms with relevant views. A view is relevant for the Q constraints rewriting if:

a) the set of constrained atoms in the view is not disjoined of the set of constrained atoms in Q, and
b) the allowed values of its constraints is not disjoined of the values allowed by the Q's constraints.

The rewriting of the constrained atoms is a combination of views such that the allowed values of the combination is contained in the set of values allowed by Q's constraints, and such that the allowed values of the combination are as close as possible to Q allowed values.

The rewriting of the constraints is likely to supply other atoms than constrained atoms. In this way the rewriting of the constraints can supply the rewriting of a large part of Q. We must then only compute the remaining part of the query. Secondly the remaining part relative to the description logics can be solved with Best Cover algorithm (BCov) [3]. The final rewriting of Q is a combination of the two rewritings by conjunction.

Let Q be a query which seeks for the cultural parcels defined in 1998 or 2000, belonging to an organics matter spreading parcel, managed in the farms identifed by {F1, F2, F10}, which are included in organics matter spreading plans, and which have a contract. Its description is the following:

$$D(Q) \doteq \text{CulturalParcel} \sqcap \geq 1 \text{ CultureYear} \sqcap \forall \text{CultureYear.Integer}$$
$$\sqcap \geq 1 \text{ With} \sqcap \forall \text{With.Contract} \sqcap \geq 1 \text{ In}$$
$$\sqcap \forall \text{In.OMSpreadingParcel} \sqcap \geq 1 \text{ ManagedIn} \sqcap \forall \text{ManagedIn.(Farm}$$
$$\sqcap \geq 1 \text{ NumFarm} \sqcap \forall \text{NumFarm.Integer)}$$
$$\sqcap \geq 1 \text{ IncludedIn} \sqcap \forall \text{ IncludedIn.OMSpreadingPlans}$$
$$C1(Q) : \forall \text{ManagedIn.}\forall \text{NumFarm.Integer} \in \{F1, F2, F10\}$$
$$C2(Q) : \forall \text{CultureYear.Integer} \in \{Y1998, Y2000\}$$

4.2   Handling Constraints

If a constraint C of a view is not specified but corresponding atoms or others constrained atoms appear in the description part, then we consider that the view allows all value for C. We use the following notations in the sequel:

- n is the number of constraints in Q.
- $C_i(Q)$.values is the set of the allowed values of the constraint $C_i(Q)$.
- n_V is the number of views in $\mathcal{T}_V \cup \mathcal{T}_E$.
- n_j is the number of constraints of the view V_j.
- $C_i(V_j)$ is the constraint i of the view V_j.
- $C_i(V_j)$.values is the set of the allowed values of the constraint $C_i(V_j)$.

Step 1: Selecting the relevant views

If a view V does not verify one of the Q's constraints, V is not candidate to the rewriting. The sets of allowed values $C_{1,i}(V1)$.values, $C_{2,i}(V2)$.values, $C_{3,i}(V3)$.values, $C_{4,i}(V4)$.values ($i \in \{1..2\}$), join one of the sets of values $C_1(Q)$ .values and $C_2(Q)$.values. V1, V2, V3, V4 are thus candidate. V5, V6, V7 are not candidate. Indeed there exist i_5, i_6 and i,j such that the sets ($C_{5,i_5}(V5)$.values $\cap\, C_i(Q)$.values) and ($C_{6,i_6}(V6)$.values $\cap\, C_j(Q)$.values) are empty set. V7 is not candidate because V7 has no common constraint with Q. Figure 3 gives an algorithm of relevant views selecting. The worst complexity of view selecting is $o(m^3)$ where m = $\max(n, n_V, \max_{j\in\{1..n_V\}}(n_j))$.

```
input: 𝒯_V∪𝒯_E, Q
output: 𝒯_candidate
rew := Bottom
For each view V_j of 𝒯_V∪𝒯_E
    participate := true; commonconstraint := false;
    For each constraint C_{j,k}(V_j)
        For each constraint C_i(Q)
            If (C_{j,k}(V_j).attrname = C_i(Q).attrname) and
            (C_{j,k}(V_j).values ∩ C_i(Q).values = ∅) Then
              participate := false
            EndIf
            If (C_{j,k}(V_j).attrname = C_i(Q).attrname) then
              commonconstraint := true
            EndIf
        EndFor
    EndFor
    If (participate = true) and (commonconstraint = true) then
        𝒯_candidate := 𝒯_candidate ∪ V_j
    Endif
EndFor
```

Fig. 3. Step 1: Relevant views selecting

Step 2 : Rewriting the constrained atoms

Rewriting constrained atoms implies to process all constrained atoms in the same time. Consider the Q constraints $C_1(Q)$ and $C_2(Q)$ and two views V´ and V¨ described respectively by:

V´ $\doteq$ ∀ManagedIn.∀NumFarm.Integer ⊓ ∀CultureYear.Integer
   with C_1(V´): ∀ManagedIn.∀NumFarm.Integer $\in$ {F2} and
   with C_2(V´): ∀CultureYear.Integer $\in$ {Y1998, Y2000}
V¨ $\doteq$ ∀ManagedIn.∀NumFarm.Integer ⊓ ∀CultureYear.Integer
   with C_1(V¨): ∀ManagedIn.∀NumFarm.Integer $\in$ {F1,F2,F10} and
   with C_2(V¨) ∀CultureYear.Integer $\in$ {Y1998}

Try to rewrite the constraints separately. V¨ is candidate to the rewriting of ∀ManagedIn.∀NumFarm.Integer ∈ {F1,F2,F10}. V´ is candidate to the rewriting of ∀CultureYear.Integer ∈ {Y1998, Y2000}. $C_1(Q)$ and $C_2(Q)$ are thus separately rewrited ($C(V´)$ and $C(V¨)$ are contained in $C_1(Q)$ and $C_2(Q)$ respectively; $C(V´)=C_1(Q)$ and $C(V¨)=C_2(Q)$). However V´ ⊓ V¨ is not close to the Q constrained part. Indeed V´ ⊓ V¨ ≐ ∀ManagedIn.∀NumFarm.Integer ⊓ ∀CultureYear.Integer with: ∀ManagedIn.∀NumFarm.Integer ∈ {F2} and ∀CultureYear.Integer ∈ {Y1998} is not very close to Q allowed values but V´ ⊓ V¨ can form a part of rewriting. In this way the constrained atoms have to be taken into account all together.

Instead of dealing with constraints separately, we consider them as an only one. A naïve solution consists in computing the cartesian product of the values allowed by the constraints, for the query and for each view. We generate thus a set of n-uples by view (if the number of Q's constraints and view constraints is n). In the same way, we generate the set of tuples from the values allowed by Q's constraints. We denote this set $S(Q)$. The ith value of a n-uple belongs to the allowed values of the ith constraint. Each set of n-uples from a view, contained in $S(Q)$ implies the candidature of the view to the Q rewriting. Some sets of n-uples stemming from views of $T_{candidate}$ are not contained in $S(Q)$. If the view alone, can not rewrite the constraints, using a part of the view can be required. We can combine them with other views by conjunction, as long as their conjunction is not contained in the $S(Q)$. Let S´ be a set of n-uples stemming from views or from conjunctions of views, contained in Q's constrained atoms. The constrained atoms rewriting amounts to find the union of S´ elements which covers $S(Q)$.

The problem can be expressed in the following way:
Let $\{S(V_i)\}$, $i \in \{1..n_V\}$ be the sets of n-uples generated from the allowed values of the V_i's constraints where $V_i \in T_{candidate}$. Rewriting the constrained atoms amounts then to cover $S(Q)$ with the combination of sets issue of $\{S(V_i)\}$, $i \in \{1..n_V\}$ by using the ⊓ and ∪ operations.

---

1. Compute the conjunctions of $S(V_i)$ until the resulting set is contained in $S(Q)$.
  . STOP when it is impossible to generate other sets or
  when all the generated sets are included in $S(Q)$
    . Remove the conjunctions of size n (it is made up of n conjuncts of kind $S(V_i)$) contained in the conjunctions of size n-1.
    . Remove the conjunctions equivalent to the empty set.
  Let S´ be the set of the generated conjunctions.
2. Cover $S(Q)$ by the union of elements of S´.

Fig. 4. Step 2: A simple proposition for rewriting constraints

We can apply the proposition to the example of the figure 2:
There are two constraints. We generate thus sets of 2-uples. Q accepts three values for the first constraint and two values for the second. We generate thus (2×3) 2-uples.

$\mathcal{T}_{candidate} = \{$V1, V2, V3, V4$\}$

S(Q) = {F1 Y1998, F2 Y1998, F10 Y1998, F1 Y2000, F2 Y2000, F10 Y2000}

S(V_1) = {F1 Y1998, F10 Y1998, F1 Y2000, F10 Y2000} $\subseteq$ S(Q)

S(V_2) = {F2 Y1998, F5 Y1998}

S(V_3) = {F2 Y2000, F8 Y2000}

S(V_4) = {F2 Y1998, F2 Y1999, F2 Y2000, F4 Y1998, F4 Y1999, F4 Y2000, F5 Y1998, F5 Y1999, F5 Y2000}

Next we generate the conjunctions of size 2 with S(V_i) not contained in S(Q).

S(V_2)∩S(V_3) = $\emptyset$

S(V_2)∩S(V_4) = {F2 Y1998, F5 Y1998} $\subseteq$ S(Q)

S(V_3)∩S(V_4) = {F2 Y2000} $\subseteq$ S(Q)

It is not possible to generate other sets. S′ is thus made up of {S(V_1), S(V_2)∩S(V_4), S(V_3)∩S(V_4)}.

A cover of S(Q) with the element of S′ is S(V_1) $\cup$ (S(V_3)∩S(V_4)). {F2 1998} is not covered.

The rewriting of the constrained atoms is $V_1 \sqcup (V_3 \sqcap V_4)$).

Step 3 : Rewriting Q being given the rewriting of its constrained atoms

Let rew$_{constraints}$ be the rewriting of the constrained atoms. Since rew$_{constraints}$ is a combination of views, rew$_{constraints}$ may contain other descriptions than constraints. It is then redundant to compute the rewriting of the Q's part already answered by rew$_{constraints}$. We propose then to compute the difference [15], between Q and each disjunction of rew$_{constraints}$. The difference operation is possible to achieve by considering each disjunction of rew$_{constraints}$ separately. In this way the used language remains the $\mathcal{FL}_0$ + ≥n language and the computing of the difference is possible. For each disjunction of rew$_{constraints}$ (i.e. for V_1 and $V_3 \sqcap V_4$), we obtain:

Q - V_1 = ≥ 1 With $\sqcap$ ∀ With.Contract

Q - ($V_3 \sqcap V_4$) = ≥ 1 With $\sqcap$ ∀ With.Contract $\sqcap$ ≥ 1 In $\sqcap$ ∀ In.OMSpreading Parcel $\sqcap$ ≥ 1 IncludedIn $\sqcap$ ∀ IncludedIn.OMSpreadingPlans

The concepts (Q - V_1) and (Q - ($V_3 \sqcap V_4$)) are transmitted as query input to BCov algorithm [3] briefly presented in next section. The output of BCov with Q - V_1 (resp. with ($V_3 \sqcap V_4$)) is combined to V_1 (resp. ($V_3 \sqcap V_4$))) by conjunction.

4.3   Elaborating the Combination with BCov [3]

BCov algorithm computes the best cover of a query being given a terminology (here $\mathcal{T}_V \cup \mathcal{T}_E$) and a concept definition Q. BCov outputs a "combination of views that contains as much as possible of common information with Q and as less as possible of extra information (the miss) with respect to Q". Here we do not consider the miss. However we use the rest of Q given by BCov, interesting in our P2P context. The rest is the part of Q which is not covered by the views. The rest can be forwarded towards other communities for a later processing. The BCov problem is translated into an equivalent problem : the minimal transversal computing of a Hypergraph $\mathcal{H}$. Each vertex of the hypergraph matches with a $\mathcal{T}_V \cup \mathcal{T}_E$ axiom. The edges defined for each clause of Q are a set of vertices. A vertex composes an edge if the edge clause belongs to the set of the least common subsumers between Q and (primitive or defined) concepts specified by the vertex. Finding the best cover amounts to the computing of minimal transversals of a hypergraph. The rest consists in the conjunction of the clauses whose relative edge is empty. BCov must be adapted in order to not choose the views which are not satisfiable with the views of $rew_{constraints}$.

The edges of the hypergraph builded from $\mathrm{BCov}(\mathrm{Q} - (\mathrm{V}_3 \sqcap \mathrm{V}_4), \mathcal{T}_V \cup \mathcal{T}_E)$ are:

$w_{\geq 1In} = \{\mathrm{V}1, \mathrm{V}2, \mathrm{V}5, \mathrm{V}6\}$
$w_{\forall In.OMSpreadingParcel} = \{\mathrm{V}1, \mathrm{V}2, \mathrm{V}5, \mathrm{V}6\}$

V5 and V6 must be not considered because V5 and V6 do not verify the Q's constraints. V1, V2 are not retained because they kill the constraints rewriting obtained with $(\mathrm{V}_3 \sqcap \mathrm{V}_4)$.

$w_{\geq 1In}$ and $w_{\forall In.OMSpreadingParcel}$ are thus empty.

$w_{\geq 1With} = \{\mathrm{V}7\}$
$w_{\forall With.Contract} = \{\mathrm{V}7\}$
$w_{\geq 1IncludedIn} = \{\emptyset\}$
$w_{\forall IncludedIn.OMSpreadingPlans} = \{\emptyset\}$

The rest of $\mathrm{BCov}(\mathrm{Q} - (\mathrm{V}_3 \sqcap \mathrm{V}_4), \mathcal{T}_V \cup \mathcal{T}_E)$ is ($\geq$ 1 In $\sqcap$ $\forall$ In.OMSpreadingParcel $\sqcap \geq$ 1 IncludedIn $\sqcap$ $\forall$ IncludedIn.OMSpreadingPlans). Indeed they correspond to the empty edges. The rewriting computed by BCov for Q - $(\mathrm{V}_3 \sqcap \mathrm{V}_4)$ is V7.

In the same way we obtain V7 as rewriting of Q - V_1, and ($\geq$ 1 IncludedIn $\sqcap$ $\forall$ IncludedIn.OMSpreadingPlans) as rest.

The final rewriting of Q is then: $(\mathrm{V}1 \sqcap \mathrm{V}7) \sqcup (\mathrm{V}3 \sqcap \mathrm{V}4 \sqcap \mathrm{V}7)$.

5 Conclusion

This paper deals with two points concerning data integration systems: the architecture based on a SuperPeer approach, the formalization of the query processing problem in this context and its resolution.

There are many works interested in the Peer-to-Peer networks in order to add flexibility to data integration systems ([8], [10], [11]). Our proposition is a SuperPeer Data Management System (SPDMS). If it is less generic than the approach proposed in [8], the SPDMS has the advantage to supply both structure and extensibility possibilities. In this way the SPDMS is well adapted to the application context which require structure but which is in continual extension. Our contribution stems from the formal specification of the peer contents and of the knowledge holded by the SuperPeer, and from the semantical relations specification between Peers and SuperPeer, and between SuperPeers. The knowledge and the semantic relations between peers are described using description logics.

In our architecture each peer is considered as a potential data source. The peers publish their content through views via the SuperPeer knowledge. The resolution of a query amounts to the problem of query rewriting with views. The conceptualization of such a problem is the object of many works notably [6], [1] and [3]. We ground the query processing on BCov presented in [3]. Here we propose to add integrity constraints over the descriptions of the peers and the views, in order to improve the query processing. First the constraints allow to avoid the peer invocations when their contents is interesting but not their extensions. Second our application context is made up of lots of similar peer contents. We propose a simple solution for taking into account the constraints. Here we only point out a proposition of rewriting so that the rewriting is as close as possible to the query constraints. We propose to combine the BCov results with the constraints rewriting. It would be interesting to integrate the constraint handling in BCov algorithm by representing the constraints with the OneOf constructor. Our actual work consists in studying the rewriting problem with integrity constraints in the maximally-contained rewriting case.

Acknowlegments

We would like to thank Farouk Toumani for its suggestions and usefull discussions about topics presented here. We thank François Goreaud for its comments on earlier versions of this paper.

References

1. F. Baader, R. Küsters, and R. Molitor. Rewriting concepts using terminologies - revisited. Technical Report LTCS-Report-99-12, Aachen University of Technology Research Group for Theoretical Computer Science, 2000.
2. Franz Baader, Diego Calvanese, Deborah McGuinness, Daniele Nardi, and Peter F. Patel-Schneider, editors. *The Description Logic Handbook: Theory, Implementation, and Applications*. Cambridge University Press, 2003.
3. B. Benatallah, M-S. Hacid, C. Rey, and F. Toumani. Request Rewriting-Based Web Service Discovery. In Dieter Fensel, Katia Sycara, and John Mylopoulos, editors, *International Semantic Web Conference (ISWC 2003), Sanibel Island, FL, USA*, volume 2870 of *LNCS*, pages 242–257. Springer, October 2003.
4. A. T. Borgida and P. F. Patel-Schneider. A semantics and complete algorithm for subsumption in the classic description logic. *Journal of Artificial Intelligence Research*, 1:277–308, 1994.
5. H Garcia-Molina, Y Papakonstantinou, D Quass, A Rajaraman, Y Sagiv, J Ullman, V Vassalos, and J Widom. The tsimmis approach to mediation: Data models and languages. *Journal of Intelligent Information Systems (JIIS)*, 8(2):117–132, 1997.
6. A Halevy. Answering queries using views: A survey. *VLDB*, 2000.
7. A Halevy. Data integration : A status report. In *German Database Conference BTW-03*, Leipzig, Germany, 2003. Invited Talk.
8. A Y Halevy, Z G Ives, D Suciu, and I Tatarinov. Schema mediation in peer data management systems. In *International Conference on Data Engineering (ICDE'2003)*, Bangalore, India, 2003.
9. M Lenzerini. Data integration : A theoretical perspective. In *PODS*, Madison, Wisconsin, 2002.

10. W S Ng, B C Ooi, K-L Tan, and Aoying Zhou. Peerdb: a p2p-based system for distributed data sharing. In *International Conference on Data Engineering (ICDE'2003)*, Bangalore, India, 2003.
11. B C Ooi, Y Shu, and K-L Tan. Relational data sharing in peer-based data management systems. In *Sigmod Record special issue on P2P*, 2003.
12. B C Ooi, K-L Tan, H Lu, and A Zhou. P2p: Harnessing and riding on peers. In *The 19th National Conference on Data Bases*, 2002.
13. Andrea Schaerf. Reasoning with individuals in concept languages. *Data and Knowledge Engineering*, 13(2):141–176, 1994.
14. A P Sheth and J A Larson. Federated database systems for managing distributed, heterogeneous, and autonomous databases. *ACM Computing Surveys*, 22(3):183–236, 1990.
15. G Teege. Making the difference : A substraction operation for description logics. In *KR-94*, pages 540–550, Bonn, Germany, 1994.
16. B. Yang and H. Garcia-Molina. Designing a super-peer network. In *IEEE International Conference on Data Engineering*, 2003.

Logic-Based Integration
of Query Answering and Knowledge Discovery

Marcelo A.T. Aragão and Alvaro A.A. Fernandes

Department of Computer Science
University of Manchester
Oxford Road, Manchester M13 9PL, UK
{m.aragao,a.fernandes}@cs.man.ac.uk

Abstract. There is currently great interest in integrating knowledge discovery research into mainstream database systems. Such an enterprise is nontrivial because knowledge discovery and database systems are rooted in different paradigms, therefore foundational work needs to be carried out and a candidate unified syntax and semantics needs to be proposed. Elsewhere we have indeed carried out such foundational work and used it to propose a unified syntax and semantics for integrating query processing and knowledge discovery. We refer to the resulting class of database systems as *combined inference database systems* (CIDS), since they are a class of logic-based databases and the integration is anchored by a view of query answering as deductive inference and of knowledge discovery as inductive inference. The most important novel capability of CIDS is that of evaluating expressions which seamlessly compose query answering and knowledge discovery steps. This gives rise to increased flexibility, usability and expressiveness in user interactions with database systems, insofar as many relevant and challenging kinds of information needs can be catered for by CIDS that would be cumbersome to cater for by gluing together existing, state-of-the-art (but, syntactically and semantically, heterogeneous) components. In this paper, we provide an overview of CIDS, then we introduce two motivating applications, we show how CIDS elegantly support such challenging application needs, and we contrast our work with other attempts at integrating knowledge discovery and databases technology.

1   Introduction

In both science and industry, data stocks have grown so large and varied as to give rise to one of the defining challenges of modern computing, viz., how to extract from such stocks the most valuable information that they support.

Areas in science in which this challenge is very well characterized include post-genomic biology, climatology, and astrophysics and particle physics, among many others. In industry, businesses are everywhere concerned with deriving from their data stocks information that is likely to give them competitive advantage, with customer relationship management being perhaps the most prominent

H. Christiansen et al. (Eds.): FQAS 2004, LNAI 3055, pp. 68–83, 2004.

example of that. In spite of the outstanding success of database technology, extracting the most valuable kinds of information to be obtained from data stocks is beyond their traditional capabilities. The realization of this fact has given impetus to research on knowledge discovery and data mining.

For the purposes of this paper, we observe that query answering (the paradigmatic database task) retrieves *information in extensional form*, i.e., as (potentially large) collections of individual, specific items of information. For example, the answer to the question "Who has participated in which project?" would enumerate (i.e., extensionally present) individual, specific people who have participated in individual, specific projects. In contrast, the goal of knowledge discovery is to retrieve *information in intensional form*, i.e., as a few, general, characteristic statements that are supported by the data. For example, the answer to the question "Who can participate in some project?" would summarize (i.e., intensionally present) in one statement (or, possibly, a few) the constraints and conditions for people (in general) to participate in projects (also in general).

The above remarks make it clear that query answering and knowledge discovery are complementary information management technologies and that it would be beneficial to integrate them. In spite of this, reconciling query answering and knowledge discovery is nontrivial, since their roots lie somewhat apart (query answering in the intersection of logic and computer science, knowledge discovery in machine learning and the problem-solving-as-search paradigm in artificial intelligence). Thus, any attempt at integration must address this foundational issue before a unified syntax and semantics for the combined task can be proposed.

In [5] such foundational work was indeed carried out, giving rise to a proposed unified syntax and semantics for integrating query processing and knowledge discovery. The resulting class of database systems is referred to as *combined inference database systems* (CIDS). Our motivation for this is twofold: CIDS are a class of logic-based databases and the integrated approach to query answering and knowledge discovery that they support is founded on a view of query answering as deductive inference and of knowledge discovery as inductive inference. CIDS evaluate expressions which seamlessly compose query answering and knowledge discovery steps by compiling them to a database calculus that is then mapped to a database algebra and, in this form, optimized, before being passed on to a concrete database engine for evaluation. Thus, CIDS hold the promise of providing users with flexible, effective and efficient means for extending the range of information management tasks that they can seamlessly carry out. We believe that the benefits of that flexibility are pervasive and we indicate this with a discussion, and examples, of CID deployability.

The remainder of the paper is structured as follows. Section 2 contributes an introduction to CIDS. It introduces technical background used to define CIDS as formal constructs and shows how the syntax and semantics of tasks that combine query answering and knowledge discovery arises from that definition. Section 3 then describes two application scenarios in which information needs that require integrated query answering and knowledge discovery steps are currently largely uncatered for. Section 4 contrasts our work with other attempts at integrating knowledge discovery and databases technology and indicates where CIDS are novel and uniquely useful. Finally, Section 5 lists the main contributions of the results reported and indicates the directions for our future work.

2   An Overview of Combined Inference Database Systems

The main technical goal in the proposal of CIDS was to establish a unified formal foundation for both query answering and knowledge discovery. The approach we have taken to achieve that is logic-based [19]. The main motivations for this choice were the established views of query answering as a deductive task [7] and of knowledge discovery as an inductive one [10]. The nontrivial challenge that CIDS are unique in responding to is, roughly, that of combining deductive and inductive processes in a single formalism to which a database-centric operational semantics can be assigned. In this section, we review, within the prevailing space constraints, the technical development that, for reasons of space, we have only reported in detail elsewhere [5].

Logical Framework. The logical formalism underlying CIDS is *parametric Datalog* (p-Datalog, for short) [15], for increased clarity in the context of this paper, we adapt. This represents a choice of interpretation for the parameters of the logical system in [15]. p-Datalog extends Datalog [7] to contexts where absolute validity is no longer a requirement of the logical system. In [15], the presentation context is that of uncertain reasoning, but other contexts are admissible. In any case, in this paper, what our interpretation of p-Datalog provides is a principled treatment of the validity requirement when absolute validity is too stringent. Syntactically, the extensions manifest themselves in two annotations to each clause: one assigns a *validity assessment* to the clause, the other assigns to the clause a triple of functions, referred to as *validity combinators* that, taken together, determine precisely how the validity assessment of the clause is propagated in p-Datalog derivations in which the clause is used as a premiss. Semantically, the extensions are shown to lead to a logic that enjoys the same desirable metalogical properties as Datalog (e.g., a proof-theoretic, a model-theoretic and a fixpoint semantics that coincide) and of which Datalog (and hence relational databases) are a special case.

A *p-Datalog clause* is a Datalog clause annotated with a validity assessment C and with a triple of validity combinators $\langle f^\wedge, f^\leftarrow, f^\vee \rangle$. The validity assessment can be interpreted (e.g., as it is in [15]) as the degree of certainty associated with the clause, but in CIDS there is no (and there is no need to have any) such specific commitment. The validity combinators determine, respectively, how the validity of the literals in the body are to be combined, how the validity of the body is assigned to the clause as a whole, and how the different validities associated with the different clauses that share the same predicate name are to be combined into a single validity assessment. Thus, if $p(X,Y) \leftarrow q(X,Z), p(Z,Y)$ is a Datalog clause, then one could annotate it with a validity assessment and validity combinators to yield, e.g., the following p-Datalog clause: $p(X,Y) \leftharpoonup \top \vdash q(X,Z), p(Z,Y) \langle min, min, max \rangle$. If we let $\top$ denote the largest possible validity assessment and *min* and *max* denote the functions that return, respectively, the smallest and the largest value in a set, then, if we so annotate every clause, p-Datalog reduces to Datalog.

In CIDS, use is made of validity assessments and validity combinators to reconcile in a single logical formalism the derivation of deductive and inductive consequences in a principled manner. In particular, since p-Datalog terms, literals, clauses and clause sets are the only primitive types, closure is ensured, but for compositionality to be also ensured, there is a need to reconcile the fact that query answering, being deductive, is truth-preserving while knowledge discovery, being inductive, is not. Compositionality goes beyond closure in requiring not only that the outputs of one task are syntactically acceptable as inputs to subsequent ones but, also, that they are semantically so. CIDS rely on the clause annotations of p-Datalog to underpin its principled treatment of these semantic concerns. In particular, many specific instantiations of CIDS (including those referred to in this paper) are proved (in [5]) to preserve the classically desirable metalogical properties of p-Datalog (and hence, of Datalog).

CIDS as Deductive Database Systems. A **combined inference database** (CID) $\mathcal{D}$ is a pair $\langle IDB, EDB \rangle$ where IDB is a set of p-Datalog rules, referred to as the *intensional database*, and EDB is a set of p-Datalog ground facts, referred to as the *extensional database*. The clauses in IDB and in EDB are constrained to belong to a given language $\mathcal{L_D}$, i.e., $(IDB \cup EDB) \subseteq \mathcal{L_D}$. A *CID schema* defines the lexicon for $\mathcal{L_D}$ and may include relation names whose extent is not defined either extensionally in EDB or intensionally in IDB. These undefined relation names are, precisely, those whose definition may be computed by inductive inference, thus characterizing the discovery of knowledge. Constraints [7] imposed on a Datalog-based deductive database are also imposed on a CID, viz., clauses must be range restricted, and predicate symbols occurring as relation names in IDB must not occur in EDB, and vice-versa. The constraints [15] imposed on p-Datalog programs are also imposed on CIDs but these are not particular relevant here (see [5] for details).

Unlike a Datalog-based deductive database, in which the inferential apparatus is fixed (and, classically, based on resolution [7]), in the technical construction of CIDS we consider their inferential apparatus separately. Thus, a CID system is a pair $\langle \mathcal{D}, \mathcal{I_D} \rangle$ where $\mathcal{D}$ is a CID and $\mathcal{I_D}$ is a non-empty set of inference rules. A CID inference rule takes as premises, and infers as consequences, p-Datalog clauses in the language $\mathcal{L_D}$. CID inference rules are either deductive (in which case they have facts, i.e., information in extensional form, as consequences), or inductive (in which case they have rules, i.e., information in intensional form, as consequences). In either case, it is part of the definition of a CID inference rule that it specifies precisely which validity assessment it annotates its consequences with, given the validity assessments and combinators that annotate the premises involved in the inference.

A single underlying logic and a unified inferential apparatus, taken together, reconcile deductive inference and inductive inference in a principled manner. Thus, compositionality arises, as expected, as the characteristic property of processes that combine CID inference rules in arbitrarily complex formal derivations over the p-Datalog clauses in a CID. More specifically, combinations of inference rules in $\mathcal{I}_\mathcal{D}$ can capture particular combinations of query answering and knowledge discovery, as described below.

CIDS as Classical Database Systems. In addition to the model-theoretic and fixpoint semantics that we extend and adapt from [15], an operational semantics has been defined for CIDS that is based on a database calculus and algebra such as underpin mainstream query processing engines. The benefits of this technical move is to ensure that CIDS admit of an implementation strategy in which they emerge as mainstream database systems, unlike, e.g., the many approaches to deductive databases surveyed in [19]. Recall that the combined inference tasks that a CIDS evaluates are combinations of inference rules in $\mathcal{I}_\mathcal{D}$. Now, every CID inference rule in $\mathcal{I}_\mathcal{D}$ is a comprehension expression, in the Fegaras-Maier monoid calculus [11], over p-Datalog clauses in $\mathcal{L}_\mathcal{D}$. It follows that every combined inference task that is expressible in a given CIDS can be compiled into a monoid calculus expression, and this, in turn, can be translated into an equivalent, optimizable, concretely implementable monoid algebra (using the results in [11] and, e.g., a physical algebra such as in [23]).

Figure 1 depicts six monoid comprehensions that are CID inference rules. For the full details of how to interpret the expressions in Figure 1, we refer the reader to [5] and, on the monoid calculus and algebra, to [11]. For reasons of space, we can only briefly describe their meaning here. Firstly, we need to introduce some technical background, as follows.

The Monoid Approach to Query Processing. In abstract algebra, a **monoid** is a triple $\langle \mathbb{T}_\oplus, \oplus, \mathcal{Z}_\oplus \rangle$ consisting of a set $\mathbb{T}_\oplus$ together with a binary associative operation $\oplus : \mathbb{T}_\oplus \times \mathbb{T}_\oplus \rightarrow \mathbb{T}_\oplus$, called the *merge* function for the monoid, and an identity element $\mathcal{Z}_\oplus$ for $\oplus$, called the *zero* element of the monoid. Monoids may also be commutative or idempotent. Some monoids are on scalar types and are referred to as **primitive monoids**. Examples of primitive monoids are $\langle int, +, 0 \rangle$, $\langle int, max, 0 \rangle$, $\langle boolean, \wedge, true \rangle$, and $\langle boolean, \vee, false \rangle$. Monoids on collection types are referred to as **collection monoids**. Collection monoids require an additional function $\mathcal{U}_\oplus$, referred to as the *unit* function, so that it is possible to construct all instances of the collection type. An example of a collection monoid is $\langle set, \cup, \{\}, \lambda x.\{x\} \rangle$, where $\mathcal{U}_\oplus = \lambda x.\{x\}$ is the function that given any x returns the singleton $\{x\}$. Thus, to construct the set of integers $\{2, 7, 5\}$ one could write $(\mathcal{U}_\oplus(2) \oplus (\mathcal{U}_\oplus(7) \oplus \mathcal{U}_\oplus(5)))$ which gives, for $\oplus = \cup$ and $\mathcal{U}_\oplus = \lambda x.\{x\}$, the set $\{2\} \cup (\{7\} \cup \{5\}) = \{2, 7, 5\}$. Other examples of collection monoids are bags $\langle bag, \uplus, \{\!\{\}\!\}, \lambda x.\{\!\{x\}\!\} \rangle$ and lists $\langle list, +\!\!+, [\,], \lambda x.[x] \rangle$, where a $\uplus$ denotes union without duplicate removal and $+\!\!+$ denotes list append, and $\{\!\{\}\!\}$ and $[\,]$ denote the the empty bag and the empty list, respectively. Crucially for this paper, collections (e.g., set, bags and lists) of p-Datalog clauses are also monoids. This fact underpins the closure property of CIDS.

A *monoid comprehension* over a monoid $\oplus$ is an expression of the form $\oplus\{e \,[\![\, w_1, w_2, \ldots, w_n\,\}$, $n > 0$. The merge function $\oplus$ is called the *accumulator* of the comprehension and the expression e is called the *head* of the comprehension.

$eep(IDB,EDB) \equiv$ $\uplus\{\ substitute((h \leftarrowtail C' \vdash), \theta)\ [\![$ $\quad (h \leftarrowtail C_0 \vdash l_1, \ldots, l_n)\ \leftarrow\ IDB,$ $\quad (r_1 \leftarrowtail C_1 \vdash)\ \leftarrow\ EDB,$ $\quad \ldots,$ $\quad (r_n \leftarrowtail C_n \vdash)\ \leftarrow\ EDB,$ $\quad \theta \equiv mgu([l_1, \ldots, l_n], [r_1, \ldots, r_n]),$ $\quad \theta \neq \triangledown,$ $\quad C' \equiv f^\leftarrow(C_0, f^\wedge(C_1, \ldots, C_n))$ $\}$	$query\_answer(Q, \langle IDB, EDB \rangle) \equiv$ $\quad \Phi(eep(\{Q\}, (EDB \cup eep(IDB,EDB))))$
(a) Elementary Production [7]	**(b) Bottom-Up Naive Evaluation** [7]
$decision\_rules(L, \langle O^+, O^- \rangle, S, M^+, M^-) \equiv$ $\cup\{\ h \leftarrowtail C' \vdash l_1, \ldots, l_n\ [\![$ $\quad (h \leftarrow l_1, \ldots, l_n)\ \leftarrow\ L,$ $\quad X \equiv query\_answers((h \leftarrow l_1, \ldots, l_n), S),$ $\quad |O^+ \cap X| \geq M^+,$ $\quad |O^- \setminus X| \geq M^-,$ $\quad C' \equiv \frac{|O^+ \cap X| + |O^- \setminus X|}{|O^+ \cup O^-|}$ $\}$	$classification\_rules(L, O^*, S, M^+, M^-) \equiv$ $\quad decision\_rules(L, O_1^+, (O^* \setminus O_1^+),$ $\quad\quad S, M^+, M^-)\ \cup$ $\quad decision\_rules(L, O_2^+, (O^* \setminus O_2^+),$ $\quad\quad S, M^+, M^-)\ \cup\ \ldots\ \cup$ $\quad decision\_rules(L, O_k^+, (O^* \setminus O_k^+),$ $\quad\quad S, M^+, M^-)$
(c) Concept Learning [22]	**(d) Classification** [22]
$taxon(L, E, S, T_0, d_{intra}, d_{inter}) \equiv$ $max\{\ t(T_0, T_1, T_2) \leftarrowtail C' \vdash\ [\![$ $\quad (t(T_1, \_, \_) \leftarrowtail C_1 \vdash)\ \leftarrow\ E,$ $\quad (t(T_2, \_, \_) \leftarrowtail C_2 \vdash)\ \leftarrow\ E,$ $\quad T_1 \neq T_2,$ $\quad \wedge\{t(\_, T_1, \_) \neq I \wedge t(\_, \_, T_1) \neq I\ [\![\ I \leftarrow E\},$ $\quad \wedge\{t(\_, T_2, \_) \neq I \wedge t(\_, \_, T_2) \neq I\ [\![\ I \leftarrow E\},$ $\quad C' \equiv \frac{1}{1 + d_{inter}(T_1, T_2, S)}$ $\}$	$taxonomy(L, E, S, N, d_{intra}, d_{inter}) \equiv$ $\quad \circ\{\lambda R.taxon(L, R, S, T, d_{intra}, d_{inter}) \cup R\ [\![$ $\quad T \leftarrow N\}(E)$
(e) Cluster Formation [13]	**(f) Conceptual Clustering** [13]

Fig. 1. Examples of CID Inference Rules

Each term w_i is called a *qualifier*, and is either a *generator* of the form $v \leftarrow D$, where v is a *range variable* and D is a *generator domain* (i.e., an expression that denotes a collection or a nested comprehension expression); a *filter* t, where t is a predicate over a range variable in scope; or a *binding* of the form $v \equiv \alpha$, where v is a new range variable and α is an expression that defines possible values for v (i.e., binding is a notational convenience with textual replacement semantics). Monoid comprehensions have a simple procedural interpretation, in which generators give rise to nested loops and multiple filters give rise to a conjunction of predicates. For example, a monoid comprehension of the form $\oplus\{e\ [\![\ v \leftarrow D, p(v)\}$ denotes a result R computed as follows:

```
R := Z⊕                    //where, e.g., Z⊕ is ∅ if ⊕ is ∪
for each v in D :
  if p(v) then
    R := R ⊕ U⊕(e) //where, e.g., U⊕(e) is {e} if ⊕ is ∪
return R
```

CID Inference Rules as Monoid Comprehensions. With these definitions in place, we can now give a brief explanation of the semantics of the CID inference rules in Figure 1. Note that each one is a monoid comprehension that specifies a particular query answering or knowledge discovery task. Firstly, as far query answering is concerned, (a) is a monoid comprehension that characterizes the inference rule known as *elementary production*, upon which the query evaluation procedure known as *bottom-up naive evaluation*, in (b), can be defined. Secondly, as far as knowledge discovery is concerned, (d) builds upon (c) (and, respectively, (f) upon (e)) to characterize *classification* (respectively, *hierarchical conceptual clustering*) as an inferential task.

The inference rule denoted by *eep*, in (a), exploits the close structural similarity between the procedural definition of elementary production [7] and the procedural semantics of a monoid comprehension. So, the generators denote scans of *IDB* and *EDB* that yield candidate premises. These are filtered to ensure that they have a most general unifier (with ▽ denoting that the *mgu* function failed to find one). Those premises that satisfy the filter justify the ejection of the corresponding consequence, which is constructed by applying the substitution θ to the head of the first premise. The only significant difference lies in the use of validity combinators to compute the validity assessment that annotates the consequence from those asserted to the premises (in the last line in *eep*). The use of the bag monoid (⊎) is necessary for the sound application of disjunctive combinators [15] because they are defined over bags of validity assessments. Then, the inference rule denoted by *query_answer*, in (b), simply applies *eep* taking premises from a singleton whose element is the query (represented as a clause) and from the set of all *eep*-inferrable consequences of $IDB \cup EDB$. The monoid comprehension Φ in (b) (see [5]) enforces the constraint embodied in the disjunctive combinators of [15].

The inference rule denoted by *decision_rules*, in (c), begins by choosing a candidate rule from the language L. A language L is an enumerable set of Datalog clauses, which is assumed given and which can be specified by alternative, compact formalisms, e.g., one based on definite clause grammars (DCGs), such as [9]. Then, the candidate rule, interpreted as query, is posed, using the *query_answers* comprehension defined in (b), against the background data and knowledge S. The result is the set X of *eep*-inferrable consequences generated by augmenting S with the candidate rule. A candidate rule r is considered to have matched the requirements for ejection if it results in a number $|O^+ \cap X|$ of true positives and a number $|O^- \setminus X|$ of true negatives that are above the stipulated thresholds M^+ and M^-. The validity assessment for the ejected consequence r is computed, in the last line of *decision_rules*, as the *success ratio* of r [13]. Now, rule-based classifiers typically discover models for one target class at a time, and this is also the approach used in CIDS. Thus, the inference rule denoted by *classification_rules*, in (d), operates by associating to each target class its corresponding partition in the given set of positive examples. The negative examples for a target class are (in this formulation) the complement of the positive ones.

The inference rules denoted by *taxon* and *taxonomy*, in (e) and (f), respectively, cooperate to specify the iterative, agglomerative induction of (a binary tree denoting) the subset relation over a set of individuals. So, the induced tree is interpreted as a taxonomy, where nonleaf nodes are taxa, and a directed edge (x, y) can be read as x *is_a_kind_of* y expressed as a fact in the extent of a database relation with schema *t(taxon_id, left_subtree, right_subtree)*. Thus, the induced model constitutes a conceptual model that can be used to assign a degree of similarity based on the attribute values of the relation from which elements were drawn to seed the agglomerative strategy. A taxon is obtained in (e) as the merge of the two closest child taxa. The chosen candidate taxon maximizes the validity assessment that is computed for it in the last line of *taxon* (i.e., it minimizes the intercluster distance between its left and right subtaxa). The two nested ∧-monoid expressions ensure that a candidate parent always has children that have not been merged before. The taxonomy itself is characterized, in (f), by an outer function-composition (denoted by ∘) monoid comprehension that expresses the bounded $n - 1$ iteration to merge n leaf nodes.

CID Tasks as Compositions of Inference Steps. Having defined some concrete CID inference rules, we can show how to compose them and specify tasks for a CID system to perform. Note, first, that the monoid calculus allows the formation of composite comprehensions. An inner monoid comprehension can be referred to anywhere that a variable of the same monoid type might occur in the outer monoid comprehension, viz., in the head, in the domain of a generator or of a binding, and in a filter. For example, the inner *query_answers* is nested into *decision_rule* in Figure 1 (c). Comprehension nesting underpins the closure property of CID inference rules. To see that, observe the general signatures of the deductive and of the inductive CID inference rules in Figure 1. Notice that *query_answers* maps a *query* to *answers* with respect to an *intensional* and an *extensional* database. Likewise, *decision_rules*, *classification_rules* and *taxonomy* all map some *evidence* into a *model* constrained by a *language bias* and with respect to some *background data* and some *background knowledge*. These abstractions can be graphically represented, as in Figure 2, the deductive case to the left, the inductive to the right. Notice further that the type of E, A, D and O is 'set of ground CID clauses', the type of Q, I, B, L and M is 'set of CID rules'. These observations establish the typing rules for composing the left and the right subgraphs into arbitrarily complex graphs. The interpretation is that an overlap of two arrows denotes variable binding (equivalently, comprehension nesting). For example, observe that one would typically want to use answers to a query as evidence for the induction of a model. In terms of Figure 2, this would mean composing the left and right parts with the A-arrow from the left overlapping with the O-arrow from the right, denoting the binding A ≡ O. The complex graphs that result from such compositions depict well-formed combinations of deductive and inductive inferential steps (captured as applications of CID inference rules in monoid form), which we refer to *CID tasks*. The textual form of CID tasks can be gauged by reference to Figure 1. The prototype evaluators we have built (as described in [5]) evaluate CID tasks in such textual form.

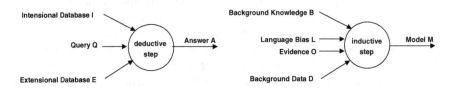

Fig. 2. Deductive and Inductive Steps as CID Task Graphs

We have stressed that CIDs display a *closure* property (as a result of the unified representation language) and a *compositionality* property (as a result of the compositionality of monoid comprehensions onto which CID tasks map). There are two further implications of the remarks above. Firstly, CIDS display a property that we refer to as *seamless evaluation*. Recall that CID tasks are arbitrary compositions of deductive and inductive tasks, nonetheless any CID task can be evaluated by a database engine based on the monoid calculus and algebra, and we are currently involved in implementing several of these, most recently one for the Grid [2]. Secondly, CIDS display a property that we refer to as *extensibility*, insofar as new deductive and inductive tasks can be performed provided that they can be expressed as described above. Once this is done, modulo the need for specific optimization strategies, the new task can be evaluated by the underlying engine without further ado.

3   The Need for Combined Inference Database Systems

The notion of a *virtual organization* (VO) [20] describes and explains the opportunistic, on-demand formation of, often short-lived, alliances between independent businesses to pounce on opportunities that would be beyond the reach of any member acting in isolation. This notion encompasses such concepts as that of a task force, a community of practice, or an advisory body, whose members are not so much independent businesses but independent experts, each in their specific domains. One diagnostic feature of VOs is that they are information businesses, both in the sense that information is often their primary raw material and primary product but, also, that asset without which they might not form at all, and, if they form, might not survive without. VOs depend on information management tools whose degree of sophistication is still only barely met by the most advanced research prototypes. Thus, it is our contention in this paper that, by their very nature, VOs are a prime source of usage scenarios in which CIDS can be shown to make a significant difference in practice, as we describe and motivate below.

Assume that a governmental health agency responds to an epidemic by setting up a task force that brings together several experts, say, medical doctors and scientists from different hospitals, universities and industrial labs. This task force is set up as a VO. Experts become members on the strength of their track record, which, in turn, comprises data about affiliation to institutions, publication, professional recognition and past participation in similar endeavours.

The virtual nature of the task force and its need to react quickly to events pose particular challenges for information management. For example, the time and effort that can be thrown at solving a problem are at a premium because, like most VOs, the task force cannot rely on ground support and infrastructure, of the kind that institutions such as those the experts are affiliated to often have at their disposal. Thus, for one example, if a problem arises that requires the deployment of sophisticated information management techniques for which support exists only in the form of a disparate, heterogeneous collection of tools, each independently developed and supplied, the resources may not be available with which to glue them together in time. Although businesses learn to cope with this kind of problem in their day-to-day activities, the extreme conditions under which a VO operates often cause this kind of problem to become mission-critical.

As an example of a problem of this kind in the hypothetical VO we are assuming, consider how candidate replacements for an expert might be procured efficiently and effectively. Efficiency is critical here because budgets are always limited and time is of the essence in responding to an epidemic: ideally one would want to produce a shortlist with the smallest possible effort. Effectiveness is also critical here because the success of the response depends on appropriate expertise deployed on the appropriate aspect of the epidemic: ideally one would want to produce a shortlist that homes in into the fewest best candidates.

Clearly, the solution to the problem requires more than simple querying of data stocks. There must exist a model of expertise that provides the background for any inference, by querying, as to who is competent in what. Likewise, there must exist a model of similarity of expertise that can rank and compare identified experts. In most cases, the two models alluded to would most likely only exist as tacit knowledge shared by a community of practice, which would be consulted about candidate replacements. Notice, however, the extreme conditions under which a VO operates may make that infeasible.

Now, the field of knowledge discovery in databases has as one of its main aims precisely that generation of explicit knowledge from data. The question then arises as to whether the tacit knowledge alluded to might be discoverable in the data held by the VO. Since the model of expertise can be represented as a classification model and the similarity model can be represented as a taxonomy, and since there are tools for the generation of both such models, it should be possible to elicit the required knowledge. So, a solution would be the more desirable the better it were to rely on integrating query answering and knowledge discovery steps. In particular, with respect to the computing infrastructure for solving the problem, it would ideally offer a flexible way of integrating query answering and knowledge discovery steps without resorting to extra programming. From the end-user viewpoint, the transition from performing one kind of step to performing the other should be as seamless as possible.

Most issues that prevent the identified solution to be readily deployed can be related to lack of closure, compositionality, seamless evaluation and extensibility. As we have indicated in Section 2, CIDS respond to the challenges arising from these issues with specific capabilities that arise from their very design at both the foundational and the deployment level. As a result of this, a CID task can be specified that solves the given problem as shown by the CID task graph in Figure 3, which can be interpreted as follows: (1) apply *decision_rules* (in Figure 1 (c)) to derive an intensional definition of a new relation that captures intensionally the notion of competence; then (2) apply *taxonomy* (in Figure 1 (f)) to derive an intensional definition of a new relation that models research profile similarities, taking the relation induced in (1) as background knowledge; finally, (3) apply *query_answers* (in Figure 1 (b)) to retrieve, based on the original data and the knowledge acquired in (2), a set of answers for the query 'Which candidate Y can replace which expert X, given the currently-held models of expertise and of expertise similarity?' We refer the reader to [5] for a detailed description of how the specified CID task is expressed as a monoid comprehension, then compiled into its equivalent monoid algebra, optimised, mapped into a physical algebra which an iterator-based evaluation engine then execute. In addition, [5] also prints the full execution log for the above task.

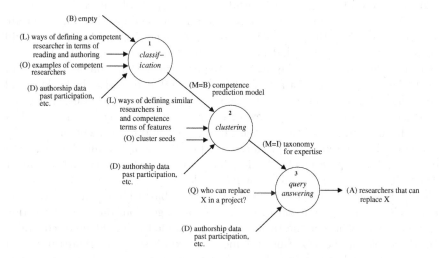

Fig. 3. Procuring Candidate Replacements for an Expert

It can therefore be seen that a CID system is a flexible platform to deploy combinations of query answering and knowledge discovery capabilities with benefits that generalise over a a wide range of applications. We have also developed case studies in which CIDS were deployed to solve problems in web-service substitutivity, functional annotation of genes, and identification of malpractice in foreign currency markets. This range of applications show how CID tasks do exhibit flexibility and expressiveness.

For illustration purposes, consider one more concrete scenario. In most open economies, banks hold on to foreign currency stocks resulting from their customers' trade. This leads to an interbank market, regulated and monitored by a *bank supervising authority* (BSA), where foreign currency surpluses and deficits are traded. This market acts to promote a balance between currency supply and demand, created by imports and exports, respectively, and provides banks with profit opportunities due to fluctuations in currency prices. BSAs set limits and margins which banks must conform themselves to so that risks are managed as stipulated in international agreements. However, in their attempt to maximize profits, banks often resort to speculative practices that can lead to severe losses if the market shifts suddenly. Since, in the limit, such practices may undermine the economic stability of entire countries and linked economies, BSAs monitor the market and intervene to coerce, possibly by reviewing the regulations. However, these practices are hard to spot, because they arise by composition of several individually-legitimate transactions.

BSAs have inspectors sifting through daily-updated transactional data, so as to shortlist those banks whose pratice merit closer scrutiny. Due to the sheer volume of transactions, automated support for the inspectors is crucial. Moreover, banks roughly know (or attemp to guess) where inspection might focus, and if the intention to do so is present, so is the ability to cover signals that could be identified extensionally, i.e., by query answering alone. Thus, from the viewpoint of the inspectors, the target is a moving one: they must learn and then learn again and again what practices are being deployed that may merit intervention. In other words, in trying to keep abreast with constantly changing pratices, BSA inspectors would benefit from CIDS, since CID tasks compose knowledge discovery with query answering steps. Figure 4 is a CID task graph combining clustering, association analysis [1] and querying. The problem it is meant to solve is that of identifying violations of the assumptions that transactions between medium-sized banks with similar business profile are often similar. Violation of this assumption raises the suspicion of collusion between the transacting banks, referred to, in this case, as (often volatile) *close partners*. BSA inspectors are after sophisticated speculative practice in which volatile close partnerships are formed between several banks. Identifying such episodes provides a good target for closer scrutiny, while knowledge of legal regulation helps exclude legitimate (often stable) partnerships. In short, the ad-hoc, intuition-guided, knowledge-intensive, but time-constrained, nature of the BSA inspection brief precludes the engineering of long-lived software solutions. For this reason, the capabilities designed into CIDS seem particularly appropriate. Preliminary experiments we have conducted were successful in identifying one speculative pratice known to have been actually employed in the past.

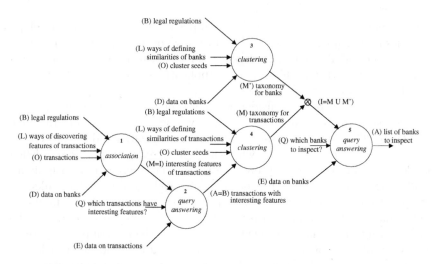

Fig. 4. Identifying Speculative Practices in Foreign Currency Markets

4   Related Work

Some extensions of SQL or some new SQL-like languages with constructs that can refer to mining algorithms have been proposed [14, 12, 18, 21]. Since these approaches involve hard-wired knowledge discovery functionalities, they deliver modest results in terms of closure, compositionality and seamlessness. Other researchers [6, 17, 16] have proposed integrating knowledge discovery capabilities into database systems. These proposals have in common the lack of a foundation which reconciles query answering and knowledge discovery of the kind that CIDS provide. Thus, the use of inductive inference in deductive databases to derive information in intensional form (first suggested in [6]) provides scant indication of how the combined functionality might be realized, and to the best of our knowledge that seminal work was not pursued further. In another approach, [17] hints at the idea of combining data and knowledge stocks into a class of information management tools called *inductive databases*, but again the few published details warrant no speculation as to how this class of systems might be formalized or realized in practice. Finally, the proposal in [16] uses version spaces to induce, from databases, strings of boolean propositions that capture simple forms of knowledge. It is, once more, difficult to be specific as to the relevant contrasts with CIDS as the published detail is not plentiful. However, it is possible to argue that, in general, the lack of a reconciliation of the inductive and deductive methods into a unified foundation has led, at the user level, all of [6, 17, 16] to somewhat ad-hoc emphases, lack of flexibility and of a clear route for incorporation into mainstream database technology.

In contrast to the above, [8] is a well-founded, Prolog-embedded, constraint-based meta-interpreter that can perform deductive and inductive inference. Unlike CIDS, for which a clear route to incorporation into mainstream database technology already stems from their formal operational semantics, the proposal in [8] relies on top-down SLDNF resolution which, as argued, e.g., in [25], is not likely to scale sufficiently for the class of applications we have described.

Perhaps more closely related to this aspect of our contributions is our own previous work on applying combinations of distinct query answering and knowledge discovery techniques. For example, a prototype implementation of some ideas based on the inductive relations of [6] was applied as a knowledge management platform [4] and later used to characterize web-services substitutivity [3]. When compared to CIDS, the implementation that underpins the contributions reported in [4] and [3] falls short in terms of closure, and seamless evaluation. The failure to deliver on closure (and hence, on compositionality) is caused by the inability to represent syntactically the distinction between outcomes with different validity assessments (also a feature, e.g., of [8]). Instead, in [4] and [3] we relied on explicit, user-defined assimilation policies to circumvent the need for propagating outcomes with non-uniform validity assessments. In the work reported here, we have chosen to treat such questions in the underlying logic instead of delegating the task to users via the assimilation policies of [4] and [3]. In terms of seamless evaluation, the implementation used in [4] and [3] does not have a database-centric operational semantics, and in this respect resembles [8].

The capabilities that CIDS make available are not matched by commercial database and data-mining systems. Modulo user-interfacing facilities, the state-of-the-art for commercial database systems is to equate data mining algorithms to user-defined functions invokable in SQL queries. In particular, IBM Intelligent Miner allows classification and clustering models coded in XML to be deployed and applied to row sets. Microsoft SQL Server with OLE DB DM allows classification models to be specified as special kind of SQL table. The model is built by inserting tuples (interpreted as training data) into it. Once built, such a model can be used in a query by a joining the corresponding table to a (normal) table through a specialized operator, referred to as a *prediction join*. In both, beyond the most trivial case, closure is restricted, and, as a result, so is compositionality. In the data-mining market, SPSS Clementine provides *application templates* that can compose data preparation, mining, and visualization steps, but *not* more than mining step. Moreover, Clementine is not a database engine, therefore evaluation is plagued by impedance mismatches, rather than seamless as in CIDS. This is because different kinds of tasks are supported by different components and the corresponding switched in execution context give rise to impedance. The prevailing levels of coupling, be it between internal components or with independent tools, are often so loose that significant engineering effort is required for interoperation to be possible.

5   Conclusions and Future Work

The main contributions of this paper are: (1) an overview of CIDS, i.e., a new class of flexible, expressive database systems, based on combining inference strategies, that can seamlessly evaluate tasks expressed involving query answering and knowledge discovery steps; and (2) the description and discussion of typical applications where combined query answering and knowledge discovery capabilities are needed and currently uncatered for, for which CIDS offer an elegant, flexible solution.

Although we have built a prototype CID system (described in some detail in [5]), much work remains to be done to render CIDS truly efficient. In the short term, we plan to investigate user-interfacing issues (e.g., a strutcured query syntax, graphical interfaces) and to identify and study in detail optimization opportunities (beyond those already described in [5]) so as to devise concrete data structures and algorithms that capitalize on that. In the medium term, we plan to deploy CIDS as a conservative extension to OGSA-DQP [2], a distributed query processor for the Grid which we have developed jointly with colleagues, and which uses the same monoid-based query processing approach that give CIDS their operational semantics. In the long term, we aim to deploy this implementation of CIDS in ongoing work in e-Science, specifically in post-genomic bioinformatics [24], in which we are involved and of which the current OGSA-DQP is already a component.

References

1. R. Agrawal and R. Srikant. Fast algorithms for mining association rules. In *Proc. VLDB'94*, pages 487–499. Morgan Kaufmann, 1994.
2. M. Alpdemir, A. Mukherjee, A. Gounaris, N. Paton, P. Watson, A. Fernandes, and D. Fitzgerald. OGSA-DQP: Service-based distributed querying on the grid. In *Proc. EDBT 2004*, volume 2992 of *LNCS*, pages 858–861. Springer, 2004.
3. M. A. T. Aragão and A. A. A. Fernandes. Characterizing web service substitutivity with combined deductive and inductive engines. In *Proc. ADVIS'02*, volume 2457 of *LNCS*, pages 244–254. Springer, 2002.
4. M. A. T. Aragão and A. A. A. Fernandes. Inductive-deductive databases for knowledge management. In *Proc. ECAI KM&OM'02*, pages 11–19, 2002.
5. M. A. T. Aragão and A. A. A. Fernandes. Combining query answering and knowledge discovery. Technical report, University of Machester, 2003.
6. F. Bergadano. Inductive database relations. *IEEE TKDE*, 5(6):969–971, 1993.
7. S. Ceri, G. Gottlob, and L. Tanca. *Logic Programming and Databases*. 1990.
8. H. Christiansen. Automated reasoning with a constraint-based metainterpreter. *Journal of Logic Programming*, 37(1-3):213–254, 1998.
9. L. Dehaspe and L. D. Raedt. Dlab: A declarative language bias formalism. In *Proc. ISMIS'96*, volume 1079 of *LNCS*, pages 613–622, 1996.
10. S. Džeroski and N. Lavrač, editors. *Relational Data Mining*. Springer, 2001.
11. L. Fegaras and D. Maier. Optimizing object queries using an effective calculus. *ACM TODS*, 25(4):457–516, 2000.
12. J. Han, Y. Fu, W. Wang, J. Chiang, O. R. Zaïane, and K. Koperski. DBMiner: interactive mining of multiple-level knowledge in relational databases. In *Proc. SIGMOD'96*, pages 550–550, 1996. ACM Press.
13. D. J. Hand, H. Mannila, and P. Smyth. *Principles of Data Mining*. MIT, 2001.
14. T. Imielinski and A. Virmani. MSQL: A query language for database mining. *DMKD*, 3(4):373–408, 1999.

15. L. V. S. Lakshmanan and N. Shiri-Varnaamkhaasti. A parametric approach to deductive databases with uncertainty. *IEEE TKDE*, 13(4):554–570, 2001.
16. S. D. Lee and L. de Raedt. An algebra for inductive query evaluation. In *Proc. ICDM'03*, 2003.
17. H. Mannila. Inductive databases and condensed representations for data mining. In *Proc. ILP'97*, volume 13, pages 21–30. MIT Press, 1997.
18. R. Meo, G. Psaila, and S. Ceri. A new SQL-like operator for mining association rules. In *Proc. VLDB'96*, pages 122–133, 3–6 1996. Morgan Kaufmann.
19. J. Minker. Logic and databases: A 20 year retrospective. In *Proc. LID'96*, LNCS 1154, pages 3–58, 1996.
20. A. Mowshowitz. Virtual organizations. *CACM*, 40(9):30–37, 1997.
21. A. Netz, S. Chaudhuri, U. M. Fayyad, and J. Bernhardt. Integrating data mining with sql databases: OLE DB for data mining. In *Proc. ICDE'01*, pages 379–387, 2001. IEEE Computer.
22. J. R. Quinlan. Learning decision tree classifiers. *ACM Computing Surveys*, 28(1):71–72, 1996.
23. S. Sampaio, N. W. Paton, J. Smith, and P. Watson. Validated cost models for parallel OQL query processing. In *Proc. OOIS'02*, LNCS, pages 60–75, 2002.
24. R. D. Stevens, A. J. Robinson, and C. A. Goble. myGrid: personalised bioinformatics on the information grid. *Bioinformatics*, 19(1), 2003.
25. J. D. Ullman. Bottom-up beats top-down for datalog. In *Proc. 8th ACM SIGACT-SIGMOD-SIGART PODS'89*, pages 140–149, 1989. ACM Press.

Discovering Representative Models in Large Time Series Databases

Simona Rombo[1] and Giorgio Terracina[2]

[1] DIMET, Università di Reggio Calabria
Via Graziella, Località Feo di Vito, 89060 Reggio Calabria, Italy
rombo@ing.unirc.it
[2] Dipartimento di Matematica, Università della Calabria,
Via Pietro Bucci, 87036 Rende (CS), Italy
terracina@mat.unical.it

Abstract. The discovery of frequently occurring patterns in a time series could be important in several application contexts. As an example, the analysis of frequent patterns in biomedical observations could allow to perform diagnosis and/or prognosis. Moreover, the efficient discovery of frequent patterns may play an important role in several data mining tasks such as association rule discovery, clustering and classification. However, in order to identify interesting repetitions, it is necessary to allow errors in the matching patterns; in this context, it is difficult to select one pattern particularly suited to represent the set of similar ones, whereas modelling this set with a single model could be more effective. In this paper we present an approach for deriving representative models in a time series. Each model represents a set of similar patterns in the time series. The approach presents the following peculiarities: *(i)* it works on discretized time series but its complexity does not depend on the cardinality of the alphabet exploited for the discretization; *(ii)* derived models allow to express the distribution of the represented patterns; *(iii)* all interesting models are derived in a single scan of the time series. The paper reports the results of some experimental tests and compares the proposed approach with related ones.

Keywords: Time Series, Frequent Pattern Discovery.

1 Introduction

In the literature, several approaches have been developed for efficiently locating previously defined patterns in a time series database (i.e., query by content) [1, 7, 10, 14, 15, 20]. However, a challenging issue is the discovery of previously unknown, frequently occurring patterns; indeed, in most cases, the patterns that could be of interest are unknown. As an example, some relevant medical problems are today faced by processing electrical signals detected on the human body; tests, such as the Electroencephalogram (EEG) or the Electrocardiogram (ECG) produce complex, large and analog signals allowing to perform diagnosis and/or prognosis. In this context, the discovery of frequently occurring patterns could

H. Christiansen et al. (Eds.): FQAS 2004, LNAI 3055, pp. 84–97, 2004.

be exploited to both identify disease-characterizing patterns and to foretell the risk of being subject to a disease.

Some approaches have been already proposed in the literature for discovering frequent patterns [17, 19] or periodicities [4, 21] in time series. The knowledge discovery approaches for time series can be subdivided in two main categories: those ones working directly on the original time series and those ones requiring a discretized representation of them. Generally the former approaches are very precise but more complex, since they require the application of complex mathematical operators, whereas the latter ones are more efficient but their precision and performance are constrained by the number of symbols (the *alphabet*) exploited in the discretization.

A first contribution of this paper is the proposal of a technique exploiting a discrete representation of the time series but whose complexity does not depend on the size of the alphabet used for the discretization; this allows to preserve efficiency of discrete techniques yet maintaining a good accuracy of the results.

The discovery of frequent patterns can play a relevant role both in the computation of time series similarities [2] and in several data mining tasks, such as association rule discovery [8, 13], clustering [9] and classification [16]. However, given a set of patterns characterized by a high similarity degree, it is difficult to select from them one representative pattern. This problem is even more relevant when the pattern must be exploited as a reference within different time series [2]. Some approaches exploit fitness measures [5] to select the most suited pattern; however, their effectiveness could be biased by the distribution of the patterns and the exploited fitness measure.

A second contribution of this paper consists in the construction of *models* for frequent patterns appearing in a time series. Intuitively, a model is a pattern that may never be present in the time series which represents a set of patterns characterized by a high similarity degree. The construction of models provides two main benefits: *(i)* The recognition of characterizing features (i.e., representative patterns) from a time series is not biased by the relative differences among its patterns; indeed, approaches selecting one representative pattern from a set of similar ones need to determine the best pattern, among those in the set. On the contrary, the model generation phase is independent from the relative differences among the similar patterns. *(ii)* Models simplify the comparison of characterizing features among different time series; this is important, for instance, in time series similarity detection approaches [2].

In this paper we carefully introduce the definition of model, we show the relationship between a model and the represented patterns and we present an algorithm for determining the K models best characterizing a time series.

Finally, it is worth pointing out that the main problems arising in the discovery of frequent patterns in a time series are caused by both the length of the time series and the difficulty of efficiently computing the distance between the set of candidate frequent patterns and the portions of the time series. Indeed, a time series might contain up to billions of observations; as a consequence, minimizing the number of accesses to its values is mandatory. Moreover, the computation of distances between portions of the time series generally requires the construction of (possibly large) matrices and a number of comparisons which, in some cases, could be quadratic in the length of the time series [3, 18].

A *third contribution* of this paper consists in the definition of an approach which derives all interesting models in a single scan of the time series (thus minimizing the number of accesses to its values) and which exploits models to significantly simplify the identification of similar patterns.

The plan of the paper is as follows: in Section 2 we provide some preliminary definitions and formally state the addressed problem. Section 3 describes the model extraction algorithm in detail whereas, Section 4 is devoted to present some results of experiments we have conducted on real data sets. In Section 5 we relate our proposal with existing ones pointing out similarities and differences among them; finally, in Section 6 we draw our conclusions.

2   Preliminaries

In this section we provide some preliminary definitions needed to describe our algorithm and we formally state the addressed problem.

Definition 1. *Time Series*: A time series $T = t_1, \ldots, t_m$ is a sequence of m values captured from the observation of a phenomenon.   □

Usually, time series regard very long observations containing up to billions of values. However, the main purpose of knowledge discovery on time series is to identify small portions of the time series characterizing it in some way. These portions are called subsequences.

Definition 2. *Subsequence*: Given a time series $T = t_1, \ldots, t_m$ a subsequence s of T is a sequence of l contiguous values of T, that is $s = t_q, \ldots, t_{q+l}$, for $1 \leq q \leq m - l$.   □

As we have pointed out in the Introduction, we require the input time series to be discretized. Our approach is quite independent from the discretization technique and any of the approaches already proposed in the literature (e.g., [7, 17, 15, 20]) can be exploited.

Definition 3. *Discretized Time Series*: Given a time series $T = t_1, \ldots, t_m$ and a finite alphabet Σ, the discretized time series D, obtained from T by applying a discretization function f_Σ, can be represented as a sequence of symbols $D = f_\Sigma(T) = \alpha_1, \ldots, \alpha_n$ such that $\alpha_i \in \Sigma$ and $n \leq m$.   □

Obviously, the accuracy of the discretization heavily depends on both the dimensionality reduction and the cardinality of Σ. As we will see in the following, the complexity of our approach does not depend on Σ; as a consequence, we may work on very accurate representations yet guaranteeing good performances.

Analogously to what we have done for subsequences, we can introduce the concept of word.

Definition 4. *Word*: Given a discretized time series $D = \alpha_1, \ldots, \alpha_n$, a word w of D is a sequence of l contiguous symbols in D, that is $w = \alpha_q, \ldots, \alpha_{q+l}$, for $1 \leq q \leq n - l$.   □

In this context, determining if two subsequences are similar, may correspond to determining if the associated words are equal. However, considering exact matches between words may produce too restrictive comparisons in presence of highly accurate discretizations. For this reason, we introduce the concept of distance between two words and of word similarity as follows.

Definition 5. *Distance*: Given two words w_1 and w_2, w_1 is at an Hamming distance (or simply at distance) e from w_2 if the minimum number of symbol substitutions required for transforming w_1 in w_2 is e.   □

Definition 6. *Similarity*: Given two words w_1 and w_2 and a maximum distance e, w_1 and w_2 are similar if the Hamming distance between them is less than or equal to e.   □

It is worth pointing out that the distance measure defined above is quite different from the Euclidean distance usually exploited for time series [7, 15, 20]; however, as we will show, this definition is one of the key features allowing our technique to have a complexity independent from the alphabet exploited in the discretization. In Section 3.2 we characterize the relationship between the distance defined above and the euclidean distance between two subsequences that are considered similar; moreover, in Section 4 we provide experimental results showing that this notion of distance allows to effectively identify sets of patterns sufficiently similar each other.

Example 1. Consider the words $w_1 = bcabb$ and $w_2 = baabc$. By exploiting Definition 5 we say that w_1 is at distance $e = 2$ from w_2.   □

Given a word w of length l, a time series may contain a set of up to $\sum_{i=1}^{e} \binom{l}{i}(|\Sigma| - 1)^i$ distinct words at a distance less than or equal to e from w. However, none of them can be considered the most suited to represent this set. It is, therefore, necessary to refer to this set with one single word which is not present in the time series but correctly represents the whole set. We call this word a model for that set. In order to specify how models can be described, the following definition is important.

Definition 7. *Don't care Symbol*: Given an alphabet Σ, the "don't care" symbol X is a symbol not present in Σ and matching, without error, all the symbols in Σ.   □

Example 2. Consider the words $w_1 = bcabb$ and $w = baabc$; both of them match exactly the word $w_M = bXabX$.   □

Now, consider a generic word w_M containing some don't care symbols. This can be used to represent the set WS_M of words in the time series exactly matching all the symbols of w_M. As a consequence, we may say that w_M represents or *models* WS_M. Note that, for each pair of words $w_i, w_j \in WS_M$, the maximum distance between w_i and w_j equals the number of don't care symbols present in w_M. Therefore, the number of don't care symbols in a model can be exploited as the maximum distance considered acceptable for indicating that two words are similar.

Finally, if we associate each don't care symbol in the model with the list of symbols in Σ it must be substituted with for obtaining words in WS_M, we are able to allow the model to express the distribution of the words in WS_M. More formally:

Definition 8. *e-model*: Given a discretized time series D and a maximum acceptable distance e, an e-model w_M for D is a tuple of the form $w_M = \langle w, \sigma_1, \ldots, \sigma_e \rangle$ such that $w \in \{\Sigma \cup X\}^+$ is a word which contains e don't care symbols and matches at least one word in D; each σ_i is a *list of substitutions* $[a_{i_1}|...|a_{i_s}]$ indicating the symbols that can be substituted to the ith don't care symbol of w to obtain a word in D.   □

Example 3. Consider the discretized time series D=aabccdaddabbcadcaadbcad and a maximum distance $e = 2$. The tuple $\langle aXbcXd, [a|b|d], [a|c] \rangle$ is an e-model for D; indeed, it represents the words {aabccd, abbcad, adbcad} in D.   □

When this is not confusing, we will represent the e-models in the more compact form $aX[a|b|d]bcX[a|c]d$ or, simply, $aXbcXd$. Moreover, when it is not necessary to specify the number of don't care symbols characterizing an e-model, we will use the terms e-model and model interchangeably.

We are now able to formally state the problem addressed in this paper.

Definition 9. *Statement of the Problem*: Given a discretized time series D, a maximum acceptable distance e and an integer K, our algorithm derives the K best e-models for D, that is the K e-models representing the maximum number of words in D.   □

Consider now a word w_1; from Definition 8 we have that it can be modelled by $\binom{l}{e}$ different e-models, each one given by different positions of its e don't care symbols. We call each of these models an *e-neighbor* of w_1, because it allows to represent a set of words at distance e from w_1.

Definition 10. *e-neighbor set*: Given a word w, the set of e-models representing it is called the e-neighbor set of w.   □

Example 4. Consider the word $w = abcd$ and a maximum allowed distance $e = 2$. We have that the e-neighbor set of w is $\{abXX, aXcX, aXXd, XbcX, XbXd, XXcd\}$ □

Note that the e-neighbor set of a word w_2 at distance e from w_1 is only partially overlapped to the e-neighbor set of w_1. In this case, the overlapping models can be considered more representative than the other ones, since they represent more words. The following example illustrates this important concept.

Example 5. Consider a distance $e = 1$ and the words $w_1 = aab$ and $w_2 = abb$. The e-neighbor set of w_1 is $\{aaX, aXb, Xab\}$ whereas the e-neighbor set of w_2 is $\{abX, aXb, Xbb\}$. Only the e-model aXb represents both w_1 and w_2 and, therefore, it is more representative than the other ones. The complete representation of this model is $\langle aXb, [a|b] \rangle$ from which both w_1 and w_2 can be derived.   □

3   The Model Discovery Algorithm

The main idea underlying our approach is that of deriving the models during one single scan of the time series and minimizing the number of comparisons between candidate models. Indeed, the main problems arising in the discovery of frequent patterns in a time series are due to both the length of the time series and to the difficulty of efficiently computing the distance between the candidate patterns and the portions of the time series. As for the former problem, minimizing the number of accesses to the time series is important because this can contain up to billions of elements. As far as the latter one is concerned, classical approaches require the construction of (possibly large) matrices for the computation of distances and a number of comparisons which, in some cases, is $O(n^2)$ [3, 18].

In our approach, the role of models and, in particular, of don't care symbols, is fundamental for solving both problems mentioned above. In particular, we scan the time series with a sliding window of length l and, for each extracted word we compute its e-neighbor set[1]. Each e-model in the e-neighbor set is suitably stored and associated with a counter indicating the number of words it represents in the time series; each time a model is generated, its number of occurrences is incremented (the first time it occurs, its counter is set to 1). Moreover, when a model is stored, also the word it has been generated from is taken into account for updating its lists of substitutions (see Definition 8). At the end of the computation, only the K most frequent models are taken into account.

From the description above, it should be clear that one important point in our approach is the efficient storage/update of the models. In order to solve this problem, we exploit a compact *Keyword Tree* [11] as support index structure for improving the efficiency of the algorithm. Keyword trees are tree-based structures which allow to efficiently store and access a set of words by representing their symbols as arc labels in the tree; each leaf node corresponds to the word that can be obtained by concatenating the symbols in the path from the root to that leaf node. The compact representation is obtained by collapsing chains of unary nodes into single arcs; words sharing the same prefixes share also the corresponding nodes and arcs in the tree. It is worth observing that: *(i)* if l is the length of the words stored in the tree, l is the maximum depth of the tree; *(ii)* the space required by a compact keyword tree is $O(n_w)$, where n_w is the number of distinct words it represents; this is motivated by the fact that, in the compact representation, each word insertion requires the creation of at most one

---

[1] Recall that the e-neighbor set of a word is the set of e-models representing it.

internal node in the tree; *(iii)* common prefixes of different words share the same arcs, this allows sensible space savings; *(iv)* with the growing of the word lengths lower branches of the tree are mainly constituted by collapsed chains of unary nodes; in other words, this situation corresponds to an actual average depth of the tree lesser than l.

A pseudocode of our model discovery algorithm is given next:

Input: A discretized time series D, and three integers l, e and K, representing, respectively, the length of the models to extract from D, the maximum distance considered acceptable and the number of best models to derive for D.
Output: a set *ResultSet* containing the K best models for D.
Type
    WordSet: Set of Words;
var
    w, m: words;
    e-neighborSet, *ResultSet*: WordSet;
    T: Keyword Tree;
    p_{leaf}: pointer;
    i,j: integer;
begin
    ResultSet:= $\emptyset$;
    for i:=1 **to** *Lenght(D)* $-\ l\ +\ 1$ **do begin**
        w:=*Subword(D,i,l)*;
        e-neighborSet:=*Extract_e-neighbors(w)*;
        for each $m\ \in$ *e-neighborSet* **do begin**
            p_{leaf}:=*Insert(T,m,w)*;
            IncrementOccurrences(p_{leaf});
        end;
    end;
    ResultSet:=*FillResult(T,K)*;
end;

Here, function *Lenght* receives a discretized time series D as input and yields as output its lenght.

Function *Subword* receives a time series D and two integers i and l and returns the word of lenght l starting from position i in D.

Function *Extract_e-neighbors* derives the e-neighbor set of a word w. Obtained e-neighbors are stored in the set *e-neighborSet*.

Function *Insert* receives a Keyword Tree T and two words m (representing a model) and w (representing the word the model has been derived from); it inserts m in T and returns the pointer to the leaf node of T associated with the last symbol of m. If m was not already present in T its number of occurrences is set to 0. The function *Insert* exploits w to update the lists of substitutions associated with m; in particular, the symbol a_i of w corresponding to the ith don't care symbol of m is added to the list of substitutions σ_i associated with m.

Function *IncrementOccurrences* receives a pointer p_{leaf} and increments the number of occurrences stored in the node pointed by p_{leaf} and corresponding to the last inserted model.

Function *FillResult* receives a Keyword Tree T and an integer K as input and yields as output the set of K most representative models for D.

3.1 Complexity Issues

As far as the computational complexity of our approach is concerned, the following considerations can be drawn. All the models are derived during one single scan of the time series; in particular, for each of the n symbols in the time series the following operations are carried out: *(i)* The e-neighbors of the word of length l starting from that position are computed. These are $\binom{l}{e}$ and their construction, carried out by procedure *Extract_e-neighbor*, costs $O\left(\binom{l}{e}\right)$. *(ii)* Each e-neighbor is inserted in the keyword three and its number of occurrences is updated. In the worst case, the insertion of an e-neighbor is performed in $O(l)$, whereas updating its number of occurrences can be performed in constant time.

Finally, the last step of the computation is the selection of the best K models. Efficient implementations allow to perform this task in a time linear in the number of generated models which, in the worst case, is $n\binom{l}{e}$; note, however, that this number of models occurs only if all the generated models are different, which is mostly a theoretical case.

Summarizing, the overall complexity of our algorithm is $O\left(nl\binom{l}{e}\right)$. It is important to point out that: *(i)* Generally $l << n$ i.e., the length of models of interest is very small w.r.t. the total length of the time series. *(ii)* e is usually low; generally $e \leq 10 - 15\%$ of l to limit the differences among patterns to be considered similar. *(iii)* The computational complexity does not depend on the cardinality of the alphabet exploited for representing the discretized time series. This allows to have fine-grained representations of both the time series and the models yet maintaining good performances. *(iv)* The derivation of the set of similar patterns described by the same model is not performed by computing the distance between the patterns, but by counting the number of exact matches between the models representing each pattern. This allows to sensibly simplify the comparison between the patterns and to reduce the number of comparisons. Indeed, several approaches measure the distance between each pattern and a set of "promising candidate" patterns by applying matrices-based nearest-neighbor techniques [6, 18]. However, they require to compute and maintain up to date distance matrices which can have dimensions up to $O(n^2)$. On the contrary, we need to check, for each word, only $\binom{l}{e}$ exact matches.

3.2 Discussion

In our approach it is important to clarify the relationship existing between the maximum distance e allowing to identify if two words are similar (as defined in Definition 6) and the maximum euclidean distance δ_{max} existing between two subsequences represented by the same model.

Given the time series T, its discretized representation D, the alphabet Σ, the length l of the models and the maximum distance e, in what follows we give an upper bound to the maximum euclidean distance between two subsequences in T represented by the same model. Two extreme situations must be considered: *(i)* the model is of the form $m_1 = a_1 X a_2..a_p X a_{p+2}..a_q X a_{q+2}$, i.e. each don't care symbol is isolated and *(ii)* the model is of the form $m_2 = a_1..a_p X..X a_{p+e+1}..a_r$, i.e. it is characterized by e consecutive don't care symbols.

In both cases, the $(l - e)$ portions of the models different from X indicate that the discretized patterns must match exactly those portions to be represented by that model; the maximum euclidean distance between these portions is determined by the discretization step, i.e. by the size of the interval of values represented by each symbol in the discretization phase. Let us call this quantity π.

Consider now case *(i)*, the maximum euclidean distance among subsequences in T represented by models of this form is $\delta_1 = \sqrt{(l - e)\pi^2 + e f_1(D)}$, where:

$f_1(D) = max\{(a_i - a_j)^2 \mid a_{i-1} a_i a_{i+1}, a_{j-1} a_j a_{j+1}$ are words in D and $a_{i-1} = a_{j-1}, a_{i+1} = a_{j+1}\}$.

As for case *(ii)*, the maximum euclidean distance among subsequences in T represented by models of this form is $\delta_2 = \sqrt{(l - e)\pi^2 + f_2(D, e)}$, where:

$f_2(D, e) = max\{\Sigma_{k=1}^e (a_{i_k} - a_{j_k})^2 \mid a_{i_0} a_{i_1}..a_{i_{e+1}}, a_{j_0} a_{j_1}..a_{j_{e+1}}$ are words in D and $a_{i_0} = a_{j_0}, a_{i_{e+1}} = a_{j_{e+1}}\}$.

From the reasoning above, we can conclude that the maximum euclidean distance δ_{max} between two subsequences in T represented by the same model is $\delta_{max} = max\{\delta_1, \delta_2\}$. As we will see in the following, this number could be effectively exploited for choosing the most suited values of $|\Sigma|$ and e.

4   Experiments

In order to verify the effectiveness of our approach we have performed several tests on real application data. In particular, we have considered several time series resulting from electromyographic (EMG) signals. These kinds of signals are widely used as a suitable means to have access to physiological processes involved in producing joint movements. For simplicity, we have considered time series fitting in main memory (we plan to address efficient disk-based algorithms in future work).

A first series of experiments has been carried out to asses the performances of the approach with alphabets of different cardinalities. In particular, we have exploited alphabets containing from 4 to 80 symbols and we have measured the execution time for each of these alphabets. Then we have averaged results obtained on several time series data. Figure 1 shows obtained values. The figure confirms that the approach performances are actually independent from Σ. This result is important because our approach guarantees a good accuracy in the comparison of the interesting patterns and a fine-grained representation of the models yet maintaining good execution times.

A second series of experiments have been conducted for verifying the relationship existing between the euclidean distance characterizing two subsequences

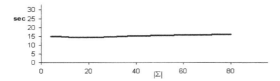

Fig. 1. System performances with various alphabets

represented by the same model m and the distance e exploited to build the models. First we have computed the theoretical upper bounds (δ_{max}) to these distances, as explained in Section 3.2. Table 1(a) shows these values for the considered time series and different combinations of e and $|\Sigma|$. Note that these values could be exploited for helping the user in the selection of the most suited values for e and $|\Sigma|$.

Table 1. (a) Values of δ_{max} for various Σ and e; (b) Maximum euclidean distances among subsequences represented by the same models

<table>
<tr><td colspan="6" align="center">(a)</td><td colspan="6" align="center">(b)</td></tr>
<tr><td>$|\Sigma|$</td><td>4</td><td>10</td><td>15</td><td>25</td><td>40</td><td>$|\Sigma|$</td><td>4</td><td>10</td><td>15</td><td>25</td><td>40</td></tr>
<tr><td>e</td><td></td><td></td><td></td><td></td><td></td><td>e</td><td></td><td></td><td></td><td></td><td></td></tr>
<tr><td>1</td><td>58.27</td><td>29.72</td><td>20.73</td><td>15.32</td><td>13.89</td><td>1</td><td>36.56</td><td>17.97</td><td>12.49</td><td>8.28</td><td>5.51</td></tr>
<tr><td>2</td><td>75.88</td><td>43.17</td><td>31.40</td><td>28.09</td><td>26.23</td><td>2</td><td>43.40</td><td>24.04</td><td>22.95</td><td>13.46</td><td>10.46</td></tr>
<tr><td>3</td><td>92.61</td><td>58.67</td><td>44.75</td><td>41.05</td><td>34.10</td><td>3</td><td>56.88</td><td>39.94</td><td>35.13</td><td>26.35</td><td>22.76</td></tr>
<tr><td>4</td><td>105.60</td><td>81.69</td><td>75.51</td><td>70.04</td><td>69.16</td><td>4</td><td>78.93</td><td>70.52</td><td>62.74</td><td>60.59</td><td>59.26</td></tr>
</table>

After this, we have performed several runs of our algorithm with values of e ranging from 1 to 4 and with alphabets of cardinality ranging from 4 to 40. For each of these experiments we have measured the maximum and the average euclidean distances among the subsequences represented by the same models. Results are shown in Table 1(b) and 2.

Table 2. Average euclidean distances among subsequences represented by the same models

$|\Sigma|$	4	10	15	25	40
e					
1	8.73	4.90	3.48	2.17	1.36
2	8.64	4.72	4.03	2.18	1.51
3	9.00	5.38	5.05	2.81	2.20
4	10.50	7.97	6.56	5.66	4.87

From the analysis of these tables it is possible to observe that: *(i)* the distances among similar patterns significantly decreases with the growing of the alphabet; this result is important because the user can chose the alphabet best fitting the accuracy of results she/he needs without compromising the performances of the algorithm (recall that the algorithm complexity is not influenced by the cardinality of the alphabet). *(ii)* The distances increase with the growing of e; this is directly implied by the definition of model and proves the direct correlation between e and the euclidean distance. *(iii)* Theoretical values of δ_{max}

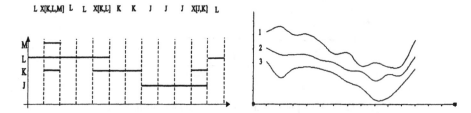

Fig. 2. Example of an interesting model discovered by our algorithm

approximate particularly well the real maximum distances observed among the derived patterns; this is important because these upper bounds can be effectively exploited to relate the values of e and $|\Sigma|$ to the desired cut-off euclidean distance.

Finally, we have run our algorithm to verify its ability to identify interesting patterns. In particular, we have applied it on a EMG time series registering finger movements; within the observation period, one specific movement was randomly repeated. Our algorithm has been able to correctly locate this repeated movement. The corresponding model, along with the plot of some of the represented portions in both the discretized and the original time series are shown in Figure 2.

5   Related Work

The problem of locating previously known patterns in a time series received much attention in the literature and can be regarded as a solved problem [1, 7, 10, 14, 15, 20]. The more interesting problem of finding previously unknown, frequently occurring patterns is still regarded as a difficult problem and received less attention in the literature.

In [4] an approach for discovering weak periodicities in time series has been presented. By "weak periodic" signals, the Authors refer to partial and approximate periodicities. The Authors exploit autocorrelation functions to extract partial periodicities; this allows the approach to automatically discover the period length.

The approach of [4] and our own are similar because both of them look for approximate repetitions of patterns; however, several differences hold between them. Indeed: *(i)* [4] look for a particular class of repetitions, namely periodicities that are signals periodically occurring, whereas our approach finds different kinds of frequent repetitions; *(ii)* [4] apply complex Fast Fourier Transforms to discover periodicities, whereas our approach counts exact occurrences of models; *(iii)* the computational complexity of [4] is $O(|\Sigma|n\log n)$; it is worth observing that it increases linearly with the cardinality of the alphabet, whereas our approach is independent from the alphabet size; moreover, the dependency of our approach from n is linear.

An approach, called EMMA, for finding the K most frequently repeated patterns (called motifs) from discretized time series is presented in [17]. In EMMA, candidate motifs of fixed length l are first rearranged into an hash table of $l^{|\Sigma|}$ addresses. This organization is used as a heuristic for motif search based on the assumption that the hash function groups similar patterns into the same locations. Then, the most frequent motifs are obtained by measuring the distances between candidate motifs; to this purpose, the Authors exploit a variant of the ADM algorithm [18] for computing sequence distances.

The two approaches address quite similar problems; indeed: *(i)* both of them work on discretized time series; *(ii)* both of them look for general pattern repetitions, without considering periodicity or trend information, and *(iii)* both of them allow for errors in the pattern repetitions. However, several differences hold between them; indeed: *(i)* EMMA derives the K most frequently repeated patterns, i.e. patterns from the time series, whereas our approach builds models, i.e. patterns *representing* portions of the time series; *(ii)* the approach of EMMA is based on an hash table with $l^{|\Sigma|}$ addresses and, as a consequence, its performances significantly depend on the cardinality of the alphabet, whereas our approach exploits keyword trees and e-neighbors allowing it to be independent from the alphabet; *(iii)* in EMMA the occurrences of the patterns are counted by considering the distances between candidate motifs; this could be a computationally heavy task when repeated for all the candidate motifs, even if the Authors improve previously proposed approaches. On the contrary, in our approach, pattern repetitions are counted by looking at exact matches of models, which is an easier task.

In [19] the Authors present an approach for finding frequent patterns in multi-dimensional time series. In particular, the Authors first use the Principal Component Analysis to transform multi-dimensional time series to one dimensional time series; then, based on the Minimum Description Length principle, they discover the optimum period length of interesting patterns. Finally, they apply a simplified version of the EMMA [17] algorithm to find motifs of the optimum length.

The approach of [19] and our own can be considered orthogonal; indeed, we could apply [19] to discover the optimal model length to search, whereas our approach could be exploited by [19] as an approach alternative to [17] being independent from the alphabet size and providing more general models.

In [21] an approach to discover periodic patterns from time series with trends is presented. The approach is based on time series decomposition; in particular, the time series is first decomposed in three components: *seasonal*, *trend* and *noise*. Then, an existing partial periodicity search algorithm is applied to find either partial periodic patterns from trends without seasonal component or partial periodic patterns for seasonal components. The main difference between the approach of [21] and our own resides in the kind of patterns to be derived; moreover, [21] decompose the time series, whereas we work on the whole time series.

The discovery of frequently repeated patterns has been also exploited to solve the problem of measuring time series similarity. As an example, the Authors of [2] consider two sequences similar if they have enough non-overlapping time-ordered pairs of subsequences that are similar. Atomic subsequence matches are considered; moreover, subsequences are indexed with an R^+-$Tree$ [12] structure. In our opinion, our approach could be effectively exploited in this context to solve the problem of efficiently finding similar portions between the two time series into consideration.

6   Conclusions

In this paper we have presented an approach for deriving representative models in time series. The main contributions of the paper are: *(i)* the proposal of a technique exploiting discretized time series whose complexity does not depend from the exploited alphabet; this allows to obtain both good efficiency and good accuracy of the results; *(ii)* the exploitation of models for locating the most representative portions of the time series; *(iii)* the derivation of all interesting models in one single scan of the time series and *(iv)* the exploitation of the concept of e-neighbor to simplify the identification of similar patterns.

We have carried out several experiments to assess the performances of the proposed approach and we have compared our proposal with related ones, highlighting similarities and differences among them.

As for future work, we plan to extend our approach to the identification of variable length models and models having more complex structures. As an example, in biomedical time series it would be of interest the identification of "causality" patterns, that are patterns composed by two portions always repeated in the same order and indicating that the presence of an "event" at the time instant t foretells the probable presence of a related event in the future. This would give more insights to the study of cause-effect events in biomedical time series.

References

1. R. Agrawal, C. Faloutsos, and A. Swami. Efficient similarity search in sequence databases. In *Proc. of the 4th International Conference on Foundations of Data Organization and Algorithms*, pages 69–84, Chicago, IL, 1993.
2. R. Agrawal, K.I. Lin, H.S. Sawhney, and K. Shim. Fast similarity search in the presence of noise, scaling, and translation in time-series databases. In *Proc. of the Twenty-First International Conference on Very Large Data Bases*, pages 490–501, Zurich, Switzerland, 1995. Morgan Kaufmann.
3. H. Andre-Jonsson and D. Badal. Using signature files for querying time-series data. In *Proc. of the 1st European Symposium on Principle of Data Mining and Knowledge Discovery*, pages 211–220, Trondheim, Norway, 1997.
4. C. Berberidis, I. Vlahavas, W.G. Aref, M. Atallah, and A.K. Elmagarmid. On the discovery of weak periodicities in large time series. In *Proceedings of the 6th Pacific-Asia Conference on Advances in Knowledge Discovery and Data Mining (PAKDD 2002)*, pages 51–61, Taipei, Taiwan, 2002.
5. A. Brazma, I. Jonassen, I. Eidhammer, and D. Gilbert. Approaches to the automatic discovery of patterns in biosequences. *Journal of Computational Biology*, 5(2):277–304, 1998.

6. W.A. Burkhard and R.M. Keller. Some approaches to best-match file searching. *Communications of the ACM*, 16(4):230–236, 1973.
7. K. Chan and A.W. Fu. Efficient time series matching by wavelets. In *Proc. of the 15th IEEE International Conference on Data Engineering (ICDE'99)*, pages 126–133, Sydney, Australia, 1999. IEEE Computer Society Press.
8. G. Das, K. Lin, H. Mannila, G. Renganathan, and P. Smyth. Rule discovery from time series. In *Proc. of 4th International Conference on Knowledge Discovery and Data Mining*, pages 16–22, New York, 1998. ACM Press.
9. U.M. Fayyad, C. Reina, and P.S. Bradley. Initialization of iterative refinement clustering algorithms. In *Proc. of 4th International Conference on Knowledge Discovery and Data Mining*, pages 194–198, New York, 1998. ACM Press.
10. X. Ge and P. Smyth. Deformable markov model templates for time-series pattern matching. In *Proc. of the 6th ACM SIGKDD International Conference on Knowledge Discovery and Data Mining*, pages 81–90, Boston, MA, 2000.
11. D. Gusfield. *Algorithms on Strings, Trees and Sequences: Computer Science and Computational Biology*. Cambrige University Press, 1997.
12. A. Guttman. R-trees: a dynamic index structure for spatial searching. In *ACM SIGMOD*, pages 47–57, Boston, Massachusetts, 1984.
13. F. Höppner. Discovery of temporal patterns - learning rules about the qualitative behaviour of time series. In *Proc. of the 5th European Conference on Principles and Practice of Knowledge Discovery in Databases*, pages 192–203, Freiburg, Germany, 2001.
14. K. Kalpakis, D. Gada, and V. Puttagunta. Distance measures for effective clustering of ARIMA time-series. In *Proc. of the 2001 IEEE International Conference on Data Mining*, pages 273–380, San Jose, CA, 2001.
15. E.J. Keogh, K. Chakrabarti, M.J. Pazzani, and S. Mehrotra. Dimensionality reduction for fast similarity search in large time series databases. *Journal of Knowledge and Information Systems*, 3(3):263–286, 2001.
16. E.J. Keogh and M. Pazzani. An enhanced representation of time series which allows fast and accurate classification, clustering and relevance feedback. In *Proc. of 4th International Conference on Knowledge Discovery and Data Mining*, pages 239–241, New York City, NY, 1998. ACM Press.
17. P. Patel, E.Keogh, J.Lin, and S.Lonardi. Mining motifs in massive time series databases. In *Proceedings of IEEE International Conference on Data Mining*, pages 370–377, Maebashi City, Japan, December 2002.
18. D. Shasha and T. Wang. New techniques for best-match retrieval. *ACM Transaction on Information Systems*, 8(2):140–158, 1990.
19. Y. Tanaka and K. Uehara. Discover motifs in multi-dimensional time-series using the principal component analysis and the mdl principle. In *Prooc. of the Third International Conference on Machine Learning and Data Mining in Pattern Recognition (MLDM 2003)*, pages 252–265, Leipzig, Germany, 2003. Lecture Notes in Computer Science, Springer Verlag.
20. B.K. Yi and C. Faloutos. Fast time sequence indexing for arbitrary lp norms. In *Proceedings of the 26th International Conference on Very Large Databases*, pages 385–394, Cairo, Egypt, 2000.
21. J. Xu Yu, M.K. Ng, and J. Zhexur Huang. Patterns discovery based on time-series decomposition. In *Proceedings of the 5th Pacific-Asia Conference on Advances in Knowledge Discovery and Data Mining (PAKDD 2001)*, pages 336–347, Hong Kong, China, 2001.

A New Approach for Mining Association Rules in Data Warehouses

Marcela Xavier Ribeiro[1,*] and Marina Teresa Pires Vieira[1,2]

[1] Department of Computer Science, Federal University of São Carlos, São Carlos, SP, Brazil
{marcela,marina}@dc.ufscar.br
[2] Faculty of Mathematics, Natural Sciences and Information Technology,
Methodist University of Piracicaba, Piracicaba, SP, Brazil
mtvieira@unimep.br

Abstract. Interesting patterns can be revealed by applying knowledge discovery processes in data warehouses. However, the existing data mining techniques only allow one to extract patterns from a single fact table of a data warehouse. Since each fact table contains data about a subject, the existing techniques do not allow multiple subjects of a data warehouse to be related. In this paper, we propose a new technique for mining association rules in a data warehouse, which allows items from multiple subjects of a data warehouse to be related. The rules mined through this technique are called *multifact association rules* because they relate items from multiple fact tables. We propose a new efficient algorithm called *Connection* to mine such rules. The proposed algorithm can process each fact table in parallel, resulting in improved performance.

1 Introduction

A trend in KDD (Knowledge Discovery in Databases) is the joint use of data warehousing and data mining technologies. The mining of association rules is one of the most commonly performed data mining tasks. This task finds interesting relations among items of a dataset. Data warehouses store data about manufacturing, distribution, sales and other business processes. When subjected to a data mining process, the warehouse's data can reveal patterns that are useful in many applications and may be particularly valuable for large companies' decision making processes. Each data warehouse's subject is represented by a fact table. Thus, if a data warehouse contains information on more than one subject, it will have more than one fact table. The joint analysis of those multiple fact tables can reveal interesting patterns relating multiple subjects.

Traditional association rule mining techniques require data to be transferred to a single table. However, when analyzing multiple fact tables, the data transferring process leads to loss of information and involves high costs. Fact tables of a data warehouse often have a very large amount of data and these data are replicated when they are combined. One form of solving this problem is to analyze each fact table separately.

---

* Holds a CAPES/Brazil scholarship

H. Christiansen et al. (Eds.): FQAS 2004, LNAI 3055, pp. 98–110, 2004.
© Springer-Verlag Berlin Heidelberg 2004

The need of algorithms for mining multiple data tables separately was emphasized in [6]. A technique for mining association rules in multiple relations of a deductive database was proposed in [4]. The original technique involved performance limitations and was subsequently improved in [14]. In [17] it is explored the mining process involving transactions whose attributes were distributed in two different sets of data.

In this paper, we introduce a new technique that allows rules relating multiple fact tables to be mined; we have called these rules multifact association rules. A multifact association rule associates items from distinct fact tables that are indirectly related through common dimension tables. For example, consider a data warehouse containing academic information, with information regarding tests and assignments of the same set of students stored in distinct fact tables. The joint analysis of these two fact tables can be very useful. It would be interesting, for example, to analyze how scores given for home assignments influence test scores and vice versa.

1.1 Organization of the Paper

This paper is organized as follows. Section 2 presents the basic concepts of data warehouses and the traditional association rule mining task. Section 3 discusses the question of mining multifact association rules and the *Connection* algorithm, which implements this kind of mining. Section 4 gives examples and results of the application of the *Connection* algorithm. Finally, section 5 sets forth our conclusions and lists future work to be done in this area.

2 Basic Concepts

2.1 Data Warehouses

Data warehouses are often used to store huge quantities of pre-processed historical data. Each subject of a data warehouse is stored in a fact table and its dimension tables. The fact constellation schema (or multifact schema) is used to design data warehouses when information must be stored about more than one subject. This schema has two or more fact tables that share several dimensions. A fact table contains measures identified by pointers to the dimension tables [7]. An example of a fact constellation schema is shown in Figure 1.

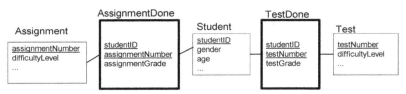

Fig. 1. Example of a data warehouse with two fact tables

The data warehouse of Figure 1 stores information about test scores and scores given for home assignments. This data warehouse has two fact tables, *Assignment-Done* and *TestDone*, representing the main subjects of the data warehouse. These fact tables share the dimension table *Student*, but do not share the dimension tables *Assignment* and *Test*. Currently, an OLAP operation called *Drill Across* [13] can combine two or more fact tables sharing the same dimension tables in a single report. To avoid a misleading report, however, only common columns or dimensions can be used. Thus, a desirable report relating columns of two non-shared dimensions (for example, *Assignment* and *Test* in Figure 1) cannot be produced. However, this analysis can be accomplished using the technique presented herein.

2.2 Association Rule

The problem of mining association rules in a table can be defined as follows [1]: Let I = $\{i_1,.., i_n\}$ be a set of literals called items. A set $X \subseteq I$ is called an *itemset*. An itemset X with k elements is called a *k-itemset*. Let R be a table with transactions t involving elements that are subsets of I. A transaction t *supports* an itemset X if $X \subseteq t$. The *support* of an itemset X is the ratio between the number of transactions of R that support the itemset X and the total number of transactions of R. An itemset X is called a *frequent itemset* if its support value is greater than or equal to the minimum support specified by the user. An *association rule* is an expression of the form $X \rightarrow Y$, where X and Y are itemsets; the rule's *support* is the ratio between the number of transactions of R that contain X and Y and the total number of transactions of R. *Confidence* is the ratio between the number of transactions containing X and Y and the number of transactions containing X. A well-known example of an association rule involving market basket data is: "70% of the purchases that contain diapers also contain beer and 4% of all purchases contain these two items". In this example, 70% is the rule's *confidence* and 4% is the rule's *support*. The mining of association rules consists of finding association rules that satisfy the restrictions of minimum *support* and *confidence* specified by the user. These rules are called *strong rules*.

The problem described above is also known as the problem of mining Boolean association rules because it involves mining categorical data. This paper explores the mining of Boolean association rules involving items originating from multiple fact tables.

3 Mining Multifact Association Rules

3.1 Definition of the Problem

In this work, a fact table refers to any data involving a fact table and its dimensions. Thus, a fact table here can contain not only data about its own attributes but also the data of its dimension attributes.

The purpose of a multifact association rule is to relate items from different fact tables, as stated by *Definition 1*.

Definition 1: Let $F = \{F_1, F_2,..., F_n\}$ be a set of fact tables of a data warehouse, and let $S_1, S_2 \subseteq F$ be sets of fact tables. Let $t_{ji} \in R_j$ be a tuple from a table $R_j \in S_i$. A multifact association rule is an expression of the form $X \rightarrow Y$, where X and Y are itemsets, so that $X \subseteq \cup_{j=1}^{m} t_{j1}$, $m=|S_1|$; $Y \subseteq \cup_{j=1}^{p} t_{j2}$, $p=|S_2|$, and $S_1 \cap S_2 = \phi$. [1]

---

[1] Tuples t_{j1} and t_{j2} are been considered sets of values instead of ordered lists of values, since the order of values is not important here.

Example

Consider the following rule that could be obtained from the data warehouse shown in Figure 1.

Rule 1: "assignmentNumber=1", "assignmentGrade=A" → *"testNumber=2", "testGrade=A"*

In *rule 1*, itemset $X=\{$"AssignmentNumber=1", "AssignmentGrade=A"$\}$ comes from the fact table $S_1=AssignmentDone$, and itemset $Y=\{$"testNumber=2", "test-Grade=A"$\}$ comes from $S_2=TestDone$, meaning that the occurrence of itemset X in S_1 leads to the occurrence of the itemset Y in S_2. Therefore, *rule 1* is an example of a multifact association rule. Note that the example considers S_i as being a unique table; however, S_i can represent a set of fact tables, according to *Definition 1*.

The fact tables of a set F are related if a set of dimension tables D shared among all fact tables $F_i \in F$ exists, so that $|D| \geq 1$. Thus, it is possible to relate transactions from the different fact tables through the primary keys of the shared dimensions of D. For the discussion below, consider **PK(D)** as an union of the primary key attributes of every dimension $D_i \in D$. The attributes $PK(D)$ are common to every fact table $F_i \in F$ and their values identify a set of transactions in a fact table called **block**. A *block*, whose definition is given below, is the unit of analysis of multifact mining processes.

*Definition 2: Let $ID(t_j)$ be the value of attributes $PK(D)$ of a transaction $t_j \in F_i$. The set of transactions $b=\{t_1,t_2,...,t_m\}$ belonging to F_i, such that $ID(t_k)= ID(t_j)$, $\forall k, j \mid 1 \leq k, j \leq m$, is called a **block** of F_i.*

Blocks from different fact tables, having the same values for the $PK(D)$ attributes, are related through the process of mining multifact association rules. This set of blocks is called a **segment**. A more formal definition of *segment* is given below.

*Definition 3: Let $ID(b_j)$ be the value of the attributes $PK(D)$ for a block b_j. The set of blocks $B=\{b_1,b_2,...,b_n\}$ is called a **segment** of F if $ID(b_i)=ID(b_j)$, $\forall i, j \mid 1 \leq i, j \leq n$, $b_i \in F_i$, $b_j \in F_j$ and $n=|F|$.*

Similarly to the way that the traditional mining of association rules reveals the tendency for items to occur in the transactions of a table, multifact mining reveals the tendency for items to occur in the segments of a set F of fact tables.

Example

Consider the data of fact tables *TestDone* and *AssignmentDone* of Figure 1 illustrated in Figure 2.

The fact tables *TestDone* and *AssignmentDone* share the dimension table $D_1 =$ Student, where PK(*Student*) = {*studentID*}. Figure 2 shows the *blocks* of each fact table in alternating colors for $F = \{TestDone, AssignmentDone\}$. The set of connected blocks forms a *segment*. The *blocks* whose data appear in bold do not form segments. Consider the multifact association rule:

"assignmentNumber=1", "assignmentGrade=A" → *"testNumber=2", "testGrade=A"*

This rule means that students who get a grade *"A"* for their first assignment are likely to get a grade *"A"* on their second test.

studentID	testNumber	testGrade
S1	2	A
S1	3	C
S2	2	A
S2	5	B
S3	2	A
S5	5	B
S5	3	A
S6	4	D
S6	2	E
S7	5	B
S7	4	A
S8	5	B

Fact Table TestDone

studentID	Assignment Number	Assignment Grade
S1	1	A
S1	2	D
S2	1	A
S3	4	D
S3	6	B
S4	6	D
S5	3	C
S6	3	C

Fact Table AssignmentDone

Fig. 2. Example of blocks and segments

One aspect involved in the mining of multifact association rules is how to quantify the interest of a multifact rule. Although the literature proposes several parameters that quantify the interest of a rule [3, 5, 8, 9, 11, 15], none of them is directly applicable to multifact association rules. Therefore, we have adapted the parameters of *support* and *confidence* to be applied in cases involving data from multiple fact tables (definitions 4 to 6) and introduced a new measurement of interest called *weight*. In the definitions of these measurements of interest, *F* represents the set of fact tables, while *X* and *Y* represent itemsets of *F*.

Definition 4: The ***support'*** *of an itemset X is the ratio between the number of segments of F in which X occurs and the total number of segments of F.*

Definition 5: The ***support'*** *of a multifact association rule X→Y of F is the ratio between the number of segments in which X and Y occur together and the total number of segments of F .*

Definition 6: The ***confidence'*** *of a multifact association rule X→Y of F is the ratio between the number of segments in which X and Y occur together and the number of segments of F in which X occurs.*

The values of *support'* and *confidence'* consider only the data of *blocks* that form *segments* of *F*. However, the segments do not cover all the information contained in the original fact table. The interesting measure *weight*, given in definitions 7 and 8 below, quantifies how much significant are the occurrences of the itemsets in the related data in comparison with their occurrences in the whole data.

Definition 7: The ***weight*** *of an* ***item*** $i_j \in F_i$, *where* $F_i \in F$, *is the ratio between the number of segments of F in which* i_j *occurs and the number of blocks of the fact table* F_i *in which* i_j *occurs.*

Definition 8: A rule A satisfies the minimum ***weight*** *if all its items satisfy the minimum* ***weight*** *specified by the user.*

The *weight* of an item i_j which belongs to a rule *A*, indicates the percentage of occurrences of i_j that was used in the mining process to calculate the *support'* and *confidence'* of rule *A*.

Example

In the fact tables shown in Figure 2, the *weight* of item *"testGrade=B"* of the table *TestDone* is 2/4, where the value 2 is the number of segments in which *"test-Grade=B"* occurs, and 4 is the number of blocks of table *TestDone* in which the item *"testGrade=B"* occurred. The *support'* of *"testGrade=B"* is 2/5, where 5 is the total number of segments, and 2 is the number of segments where the item *"testGrade=B"* occurs. Now let us consider the rule *"assignmentGrade=A"* → *"testGrade=C"*. The *support'* of this rule is 1/5, which corresponds to the support of the itemset *{"assignmentGrade=A", "testGrade=C"}*. The *confidence'* of this rule is 1/2, where 1 is the number of segments that contain the itemset *{"assignmentGrade=A", "testGrade=C"}* and 2 is the number of segments that contain the itemset *{"assignmentGrade=A"}*.

The definitions of *frequent'* itemsets and *strong'* multifact association rules are presented below.

*Definition 9: If an itemset X satisfies the minimum support' and all its elements satisfy the minimum weight, then X is a **frequent'** itemset.*

*Definition 10: If a rule A satisfies the minimum values established for confidence', support' and weight, then this rule is a **strong'** rule.*

The problem of mining multifact association rules consists in finding all the *strong'* rules in a set *F* of two or more fact tables.

Based on the above definitions, the next subsection discusses a new algorithm called *Connection* for mining multifact association rules in a data warehouse.

3.2 The Connection Algorithm

In traditional mining of association rules, the problem of mining rules is divided into two steps: first, find all the frequent itemsets; second, generate all the strong rules. Many algorithms have been developed to improve the performance of the first step, which is the most complex of the two. Some algorithms use breadth-first search to determine the frequent itemsets, while others use depth-first search [12]. Breadth-first searching algorithms determine the frequent k-itemsets before they determine the frequent k+1-itemsets, while depth-first searching algorithms do not follow this order. One way of determining the support of an itemset is to count directly the occurrences of it in the database. Another way is to determine the support by intersecting tidlists, which are lists of identifiers of transactions that support the itemset. These strategies are used to determine the support in the existing association rule mining algorithms, as for example, in the algorithms *Apriori* [2], *Partition* [16] and *FP-Growth* [10], and can also be adapted for mining multifact association rules. The *Connection* algorithm, similarly to the *FP-Growth* algorithm, uses depth-first search and direct support counting to determine the *frequent'* itemsets of each fact table. Moreover, similarly to the *Partition* algorithm, it uses intersection of *tidlists* but, in this case, the tidlists are used to determine the global itemsets, i.e., the ones that involve items from different fact tables.

The *Connection* algorithm uses the values of minimum *support'*, minimum *confidence'* and minimum *weight* to mine multifact association rules of interest, using a structure called MFP-tree. This structure allows the *frequent'* itemsets of a fact table to be found by scanning it just twice. The MFP-tree is a structure based on the FP-tree [10] modified as follows:

- In the MFP-tree, two fields, one to store the tidlist and the other storing the value of the *weight* of each item, are added to the elements of the *Header* table of the original FP-tree structure.

- Instead of storing the support, as in the FP-tree, the nodes of the MFP-tree, which represent items, store the number of occurrences of the respective item in the transactions of **segments**.

Each node of the MFP-tree corresponds to a *frequent'* item and each branch corresponds to an itemset found in one or more transactions of the segments of a fact table.

Basically, the *Connection* algorithm finds the *frequent'* itemsets of each fact table using the MFP-tree and obtains the tidlists of these itemsets. The *frequent'* itemsets originating from distinct fact tables are then combined to form the global itemsets, and their tidlists are intersectioned allowing to calculate the *support'* of the global itemsets found. The global *frequent'* itemsets are then used to generate the *strong'* rules. The *Connection* algorithm is illustrated in Figure 3.

Algorithm: *Connection*

Input: The set of fact tables F, values of minimum *support'* s', minimum *confidence'* c', and minimum *weight* w

Output: The set C of multifact association rules mined

Function Connection (R,s',c',w) {

1. $T=\{ ID(b_i) \mid ID(b_i)=ID(b_j), b_i \in F_i, b_j \in F_j, \forall i,j \mid 1 \leq i \leq |F|$ and $1 \leq j \leq |F|\}$

2. M= ϕ

3. R = ϕ

4. for each fact table $F_i \in F$ **do** {

5. M_i = *Build MFP-tree of* F_i

6. R_i = *Find the frequent' itemsets of the MFP-tree* M_i

7. $M = M \cup M_i$

8. $R = R \cup R_i$

9. }

10. G = *Find the global frequent' itemsets using the sets M and R*

11. C = *Generate the multifact association rules from G*

Fig. 3. Connection Algorithm

The set of *segments of F* is found on **line 1**. In order to find this set, all the fact tables $F_i \in F$ are scanned, and the $ID(b_i)$ (identifier of each *block* b_i), which is present in all the fact tables $F_i \in F$, is added to T. T has all the identifiers of segments of F.

On **lines 2** and **3**, the *Connection* algorithm initializes two sets, M and R. These sets are used to store the MFP-trees M_i and the set of *frequent'* itemsets R_i of all the fact tables $F_i \in F$.

All the fact tables F_i in the loop of **lines 4** to **9** are scanned. The MFP-tree M_i of the fact table F_i is built on **line 5**. The construction of the MFP-tree is similar to the construction of the FP-tree [10] with some changes. The fact table F_i is scanned once and the *support'* and *weight* are calculated for each itemset found. Only the items that satisfy the minimum *support'* and minimum *weight* are considered to construct the MFP-tree. The field *weight* of an element of the *Header* table is initialized with the value of *weight* of the item that it represents. To fill out the MFP-tree M_i only data originating from blocks $b_j \in F_i$ such that $ID(b_j) \in T$ are processed, unlike the FP-tree, in which all the F_i data are considered. Furthermore, $ID(b_j)$ is added to the tidlist of all the elements of the *Header* table that represents the items found in block b_j.

On **line 6** the MFP-tree M_i is used to determine the set R_i (the superset of all the *frequent'* itemsets of the fact table F_i). Let us consider that *ntuples(X)* and *nsegments(X)* are, respectively, the number of occurrences of itemset X in tuples of the segments and the number of occurrences of itemset X in the segments *of F*. The algorithm scans the *MFP-tree* M_i, adding all the itemsets X to the set R_i, such that *ntuples(X)* $\geq s' \times |T|$, where s' is the minimum *support'* established and $|T|$ is the number of segments. Because an itemset X of the MFP-tree M_i is *frequent'* if *nsegments(X)* $\geq s' \times |T|$ and *ntuples(X)* $\geq$ *nsegments(X)*, the set R_i is a superset that contains all the *frequent'* itemsets of the fact table F_i. On **lines 7** and **8** the MFP-trees M_i and the sets R_i are added, respectively, to the M and R set.

On **line 10** the sets M and R are used by the algorithm to determine the set G of global *frequent'* itemsets. Let $n = |F|$ be the number of fact tables analyzed, R_i is the set containing all the *frequent'* itemsets of the fact table F_i returned in the previous step of the algorithm, and r_i is an itemset belonging to R_i. The tidlist of an itemset r_i is obtained by intersecting the tidlists of each element of an itemset r_i. The process of determining the set of global *frequent'* itemsets G consists of finding all the itemsets $g = r_1 \cup r_2 ... \cup r_n$, such that $|r_1.tidlist \cap r_2.tidlist,..., \cap r_n.tidlist|/|T| \geq s'$, where s' is the user-specified minimum *support'*. On **line 11** the set G is used by the algorithm to generate the set of multifact association rules C. The algorithm generates all the X and Y combinations that satisfy the restriction of *definition 1*. The set C of multifact association rules is returned by the algorithm on **line 12**.

Example

Consider the values of minimum *support'* $s'=0.4$, minimum *confidence* $c'=0.8$ and minimum *weight=0.6*. The MFP-trees M_1 and M_2, shown in Figure 4 and 5, are obtained by executing the *Connection* algorithm over the set of fact tables F= *{Test-Done, AssignmentDone}*. The abbreviations "assg" and "nbr" indicate "assignment" and "number". Each node of the MFP-tree consists of an item's name followed by the number of occurrences of the item in transactions of segments.

The mined rules for the set of fact tables F=*{TestDone, AssignmentDone}* are given below, where *sr* and *cr* indicate, respectively, the *support'* and *confidence'* values of a rule. The *weight* value of each item *i* of a rule is indicated in wr(*i*).

"assgNbr=1" → *"testNbr=2"*
sr=0.4, cr=1, wr("assgNbr=1") = 1, wr("testNbr=2") = 1

"assgNbr=1" → *"testGrade=A"*
sr=0.4, cr=1, wr("assgNbr=1") = 1, wr("testGrade=A")= 4/5

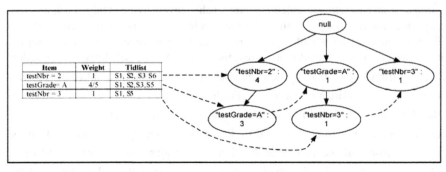

Fig. 4. MFP-tree M_1 of fact table *TestDone*

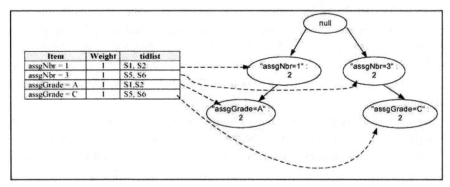

Fig. 5. MFP-tree M_2 of fact table *AssignmentDone*

"assgGrade=A" → *"testNbr=2"*
sr=0.4, cr=1, wr("assgGrade=A") = 1, wr("testNbr=2") = 1

"assgGrade=A" → *"testGrade=A"*
sr=0.4, cr=1, wr("assgGrade=A") = 1, wr("testGrade=A")= 4/5

"assgNbr=1" → *"testNbr=2", "testGrade=A"*
sr=0.4, cr=1, wr("assgNbr=1") = 1, wr("testNbr=2") = 1, wr("testGrade=A")= 4/5

"assgGrade=A" →*"testNbr=2", "testGrade=A"*
sr=0.4, cr=1, wr("assgGrade=A") = 1, wr("testNbr=2") = 1, wr("testGrade=A")= 4/5

"assgNbr=1", "assgGrade=A" → *"testNbr=2"*
sr=0.4, cr=1, wr("assgNbr=1") = 1, wr("assgGrade=A") = 1, wr("testNbr=2") = 1

"assgNbr=1", "assgGrade=A" → *"testGrade=A"*
sr=0.4, cr=1, wr("assgNbr=1") = 1, wr("assgGrade=A") = 1, wr("testGrade=A")= 4/5

"assgNbr=1", "assgGrade=A" → *"testNbr=2", "testGrade=A"*
sr=0.4, cr=1, wr("assgNbr=1") = 1, wr("assgGrade=A") = 1, wr("testNbr=2") = 1,
wr("testGrade=A")= 4/5

Consider the mined rule *"assgGrade=A"* → *"testGrade=A"*. The *support'* value of 0.4 indicates that the itemset *{"assgGrade=A", "testGrade=A"}* is present in 40% of the segments. The *confidence'* value of 1 indicates that item *"testGrade=A"* is present in 100% of the segments that contain item *"assgGrade=A"*. The *weight* values, *wr("assgGrade=A")=1* and *wr("testGrade=A")=4/5*, indicate that 100% of the occurrences of *"assgGrade=A"* in *AssignmentDone* and 80% of the occurrences of *"testGrade=A"* in *TestDone* were used to calculate the *support'* and *confidence'* of the rule in the mining process.

The results would be different if the fact tables were joined and an association rule mining algorithm were applied to the resulting table, because the data from the original tables are replicated during the joining operation, leading to incorrect calculations of *support* and *confidence* thresholds.

To calculate *support'* and *confidence'* values correctly, our approach keeps the data from multiple tables separated, leaving the original transactional structure intact and avoiding replications. This is done by using the units of *block* and *segments* that represent the units of relationships between the tables. The use of *blocks* and *segments* to count the *support'* enables these thresholds to represent the relationships between the tables more accurately than the traditional *support* and *confidence* measures.

4   Experimental Results

This section presents the results of tests applied on real data involving a data warehouses R_A that is described next. The experiments were performed on an 800 MHz Pentium-III PC with 256 megabytes of main memory, running on Microsoft Windows/XP. The *Connection* algorithm was written in Java programming language.

The data warehouse R_A shown in Figure 6 is derived from the *Academic System* of a Brazilian university.

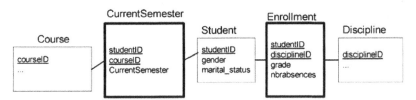

Fig. 6. Data Warehouse R_A

The dimension table *Student* contains information about all the students that have attended the university, while the fact table *Enrollment* contains information about the students' performance in the various disciplines. The fact table *CurrentSemester* holds information about the students' current semester. For our analysis, the following joining operation was executed in the data warehouse R_A, resulting in the *StudentSemester* table:

StudentSemester ← *Student * CurrentSemester*

where * represents the *Natural Join* operation from Relational Algebra.

Table 1 shows the number of tuples of the fact tables of the data warehouse R_A used in the experiments.

An example of the mined rule applying the *Connection* algorithm on the set *F={Enrollment, StudentSemester}* of fact tables is shown below, where the values of the attribute *grade* ∈ *[0..10]* were discretized into intervals of *2* units, and "AG" represents the discipline Analytical Geometry.

"gender=male, marital_status=single → disciplineID=AG, grade=[7..8];
support'= 36%; confidence'= 70%;
weight(gender=male)= 21%; weight(marital_status=single")=22%
weight(disciplineId=AG) =93%; weight(grade=[7..8])= 93%"

The above rule shows that single male students tend to get grades of 7 to 8 in Analytical Geometry. The *support'* value indicates that *36%* of the students are male, single, and enrolled in the discipline of *AG* and also have a grade of 7 to 8 in this subject. The *confidence'* of the rule shows that *70%* of the single male students are enrolled in *AG* and have grade of 7 to 8 in this subject. Since only related data were considered to calculate *support'* and *confidence'* in the mining process, the percentage of occurrences of the items *gender=male, marital_status=single, disciplineId=AG and grade=[7..8]* considered to calculate the *support'* and *confidence'* were, respectively, *21%, 22%, 93%* and *93%*. This rule could only be mined because the transactions of each student were grouped in the fact tables, which allowed the rules' support to be above the minimum user-specified support value. The multifact association rules reveal interesting patterns which cannot be discovered using the traditional association rule mining algorithms.

Table 1. Number of Transactions

Data Warehouse	Fact Table	Number of Transactions
R_A	*StudentSemester*	22592
	Enrollment	215219

To check the performance, the *Connection* algorithm was applied to the set of fact tables of the data warehouse R_A.

The execution time of the *Connection* algorithm mainly depends on the variation of the user-specified minimum *weight*. The graphs presented in Figure 7 illustrate the variation in the number of rules generated and the execution time according to the minimum *weight* used by the *Connection* algorithm to analyze the sets of fact tables of the data warehouse R_A.

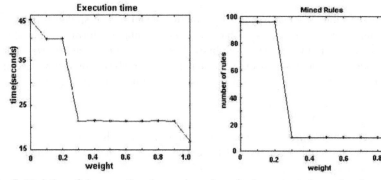

Fig. 7. Variation of the execution time and number of rules generated as a function of minimum *weight for R_A*

As can be seen in the graphs of Figure 7, as the *weight* factor increases, there is a tendency for the number of mined rules and the mining time to decrease until a constant value is reached. The mining time decreases as the value of the minimum *weight* increases because the minimum *weight* restriction eliminates of the search space the elements that do not satisfy it. Eliminating the items that do not satisfy the restriction of interest of minimum *weight* causes the number of rules to decrease as well, allowing only rules of interest to be mined.

The performance of algorithm *Connection* can be improved through parallel processing when different processors find the *frequent'* itemsets of the fact tables separately and a central processor finds the set of global *frequent'* itemsets and the *multifact* association rules.

5 Conclusions and Future Work

The main contribution of this work is to provide a method for mining multifact association rules in data warehouses, relating data from multiple fact tables. Although the method proposed here requires a little more processing effort than the traditional methods, the rules it produces are absolutely new and allow one to relate multiple fact tables.

We have demonstrated that a data mining algorithm relating multiple fact tables can be applied without the data migrating to a single table. The technique proposed here considers the original structure of data during the mining process. No preprocessing is required to combine the data. Because it respects the structure of data, the method proposed herein can be used in a variety of applications, such as mining involving multiple tables of a relational database and mining data from object-oriented databases.

Based on the results of this work, future research could take several directions, e.g., expanding the mining techniques described here involving categorical data to mining quantitative data. Another future effort might be to create multifact mining methods for other types of data mining, such as the detection of sequential patterns.

References

1. Agrawal, R.; Imielinski, T.; Swami, A. *Mining association rules between sets of items in large databases.* In Proc. of the ACM SIGMOD Int'l Conf. on Management of Data, Washington, D.C., USA, 1993
2. Agrawal, R.; Srikant, R. *Fast algorithms for mining association rules.* In Proc. of the Int'l Conf. on Very Large Databases, Santiago de Chile, Chile, 1994
3. Bayardo, R.; Agrawal, R. *Mining the most interesting rules.* In Proc. of the ACM SIGKDD Int'l Conf. on Knowledge Discovery and Data Mining, San Diego, CA, USA, 1999
4. Deshape, L.; Raedt, L. *Mining association rules in multiple relations.* In Proc. of the 7th International Workshop on Inductive Logic Programming, Prague, Czech Republic, 1997
5. Dong, G.; Li, J. *Interestingness of Discovered Association Rules in Terms of Neighborhood-based Unexpectedness.* In Proc. of the Second Pacific-Asia Conference on Knowledge Discovery and Data Mining (PAKDD'98), Melbourne, Austrália, 1998

6. Dzeroski, S.; Raedt, L. *Multi-relational Data Mining: a Workshop Report.* ACM SIGKDD Explorations Newsletter, vol. 4, 2002
7. Elmasri, R.; Navathe, S. *Fundamentals of Database Systems.* Addison-Wesley, 2000
8. Freitas, A. *On Objective Measures of Rule Surprisingness.* In Proc. of the Second European Conference on the Principles of Data Mining and Knowledge Discovery (PKDD'98), Nantes, França, 1998
9. Freitas, A. *On rule interestingness measures.* Knowledge-Based Systems, vol. 12, 1999
10. Han, J.; Pei, J.; Yin, Y. *Mining frequent patterns without candidate generation.* In Proc. of the ACM SIGMOD Int'l Conf. on Management of Data, Dallas, Texas, USA, 2000
11. Hilderman, R.J.; Hamilton, H.J. *Knowledge discovery and interestingness measures: a survey.* Technical Report CS 99-04, Department of Computer Science, University of Regina, Canada, 1999
12. Hipp, J.; Güntzer, U.; Nakhaeizadeh, G. *Algorithms for Association Rule Mining - A General Survey and Comparison.* SIGKDD Explorations, vol. 2, 2000
13. Kimball, R. *Data Warehouse Architect,* in *DBMS and Internet System, http://www.dbmsmag.com/9603d05.html.* 1996. p. 14-19.
14. Nijssen, S.; Kok, J. *Faster Association Rule for Multiple Relations.* In In Proc. of the 7th International Joint Conference on Artificial Intelligence (IJCAI 2001), Seattle, USA, 2001
15. Omiecinski, E. *Alternative interest measures for mining associations in databases.* IEEE Transactions on Knowledge and Data Engineering, vol. 15 no. 1, January/February 2003
16. Savarese, A.; Omiecinski, E.; Navathe, S. *An Efficient Algorithm for Mining Association Rules in Large Databases.* In Proc. of the 21st Conf. on Very Large Databases (VLDB'95), 1995
17. Vaidya, J.S.; Clifton, C. *Privacy Preserving Association Rule Mining in Vertically Partitioned Data.* In Proc. of the 8th ACM SIGKDD Int'l Conf. on Knowlegde Discovery and Data Mining, Edmonton, Alberta, Canada, 2002

Query Rewriting in Itemset Mining

Rosa Meo, Marco Botta, and Roberto Esposito

Dipartimento di Informatica, Università di Torino, Italy
{meo,botta,esposito}@di.unito.it

Abstract. In recent years, researchers have begun to study *inductive databases*, a new generation of databases for leveraging decision support applications. In this context, the user interacts with the DBMS using advanced, constraint-based languages for data mining where constraints have been specifically introduced to increase the relevance of the results and, at the same time, to reduce its volume.
In this paper we study the problem of mining frequent itemsets using an inductive database[1]. We propose a technique for query answering which consists in rewriting the query in terms of union and intersection of the result sets of other queries, previously executed and materialized. Unfortunately, the exploitation of past queries is not always applicable. We then present sufficient conditions for the optimization to apply and show that these conditions are strictly connected with the presence of functional dependencies between the attributes involved in the queries. We show some experiments on an initial prototype of an optimizer which demonstrates that this approach to query answering is not only viable but in many practical cases absolutely necessary since it reduces drastically the execution time.

1 Introduction

The problem of mining association rules and, more generally, that of extracting frequent sets from large databases has been widely investigated in the last decade [1, 21, 15, 23, 4, 18, 24]. These researches addressed two major issues: on one hand, performance and efficiency of the extraction algorithms; on the other hand, the exploitation of user preferences about the patterns to be extracted, expressed in terms of constraints. For instance, Ng et al. [15] proposed a constrained frequent set mining framework within which the user can use a rich set of constraints that must be satisfied by the searched rules and that include SQL-style aggregate and non-aggregate predicates. These constraints can be exploited to guide the mining process, by pushing them deeply in the mining algorithms, in order to prune the search space of frequent itemsets as early as possible.

Constraints are widely exploited also in data mining languages, such as in [10, 14, 8, 23, 24] where the user specifies in each data mining query, not only the constraints that the items must satisfy, but also different criteria to create groups

---

[1] This work has been funded by EU FET project cInQ consortium on discoverying knowledge by Inductive Queries (IST-2000-26469).

of tuples from which itemsets will be extracted. Constraint-based mining languages are also the main key factor of inductive databases proposed by Mannila and Imielinski in [9], in order to leverage decision support systems. These new promising approaches to mining will become really effective only when efficient optimizers for the mining languages will be available, i.e., if it will be possible to execute a query exploiting the available information in the database, such as the constraints in the schema, the indices or the results of previously executed queries.

In this paper, we introduce a very generic constraint-based language for the extraction of frequent itemsets and study the conditions under which query rewriting in the constraint-based mining language is possible.

By query rewriting we mean the determination of a relational expression on a set of queries whose result is equivalent to the result of a given query for every database on the same schema. Query rewriting is usually performed by query optimizers because the execution plan of the DBMS for the query in the rewritten form is better in terms of execution costs than for the original query. In the past, query rewriting has been widely used in relational databases, in data warehouses and in statistical database systems [3, 7, 6, 11, 25, 17]. In these works, query rewriting of a query computing aggregate functions is performed in terms of union of other queries whose results have already been materialized. In particular, [25] suggests that the choice of the materializations (the summaries) should be made according to the user frequent requests. We also make this assumption for the choice of the data mining materializations. Interestingly, [6] introduces iceberg queries and observes that a query which searches for itemsets is an example of this kind of queries. Iceberg queries are generally very expensive to compute since they require several scans of huge relations. As a consequence, in order to speed up the execution time, it makes sense to try to factorize the effort already done by the DBMS. [13, 11] search for the conditions under which query rewriting of queries with aggregate functions is possible. In [16] the problem of recognizing equivalent queries in multidimensional databases has been addressed.

1.1   Storage and Exploitation of the Results of Other Queries

We imagine that we can store the result sets of some query in the database. We do this because our aim is to reduce as much as possible the computational times of the data mining engine since, nowadays, the storage space is critic to a lesser extent.

Furthermore, we suppose to work in an environment similar to a data warehouse, in which database content updates occur rarely and in known periods of time. Thus, previous results are considered up to date and can be usefully exploited to speed up the execution of current queries. Suppose, for instance, that the optimizer recognizes that the current query is equivalent to a previous one whose result is available in the database. This allows the system to completely avoid huge computational effort: the exploration of the lattice search space of the frequent itemsets, and several scans of the database which are needed to compute the aggregate functions on the itemsets (notably support count). In Section 4, we show that this approach is feasible and advantageous, by means of some experiments with a prototype optimizer. At the moment, the implemented optimizer recognizes equivalent queries, and exploits such equivalences to avoid heavy computations. However, it can be easily extended to recognize when the result of the current query is contained in a materialized result, thus saving computation in this case as well.

In this paper, of course, we start answering a little part of the complex and interesting issues arisen by the usage and maintainance of materializations in data mining. We start finding conditions under which the composition by means of set union and intersection of previous query results gives the solution of a current query. Not surprisingly, these conditions are related to the existence of functional dependences between the attributes on which itemsets are defined and the attributes on which the constraints are expressed. These results are similar, but more general than those presented in [20, 19] where the problem of query decomposition in inductive databases has been studied in terms of convex version spaces and seems to be linked to the monotonicity property of constraints.

1.2 Item Dependent and Context Dependent Constraints

In all the previous works in constraint-based mining, a somewhat implicit assumption has always been made: properties on which users define constraints are functionally dependent on the item to be extracted, i.e., the property is either always true or always false for all the occurrences of a certain item in the database. In this case, it is possible to establish the truth of the constraint considering only the properties of the item itself, that is, separately from the context of the database in which the item is found (e.g., the purchase transaction). In this paper, we will characterize the constraints that are functionally dependent on the item extracted and call them *item dependent*. The exploitation of these constraints proves to be extremely useful from the viewpoint of the optimization of languages for data mining. In fact, the result set of queries that are constrained only on item dependent properties can be directly derived by the result set of related queries. In particular, if an optimizer can decompose the query into sub-queries that have been already executed by the system, the system can drastically reduce the workload by means of relational operations on the previous results.

In contrast to item dependent constraint, we present a new class of constraints for which the assumption of functional dependence is not valid; in other words, constraints whose satisfaction depends on the transactions in the database. We call these constraints, *context dependent*. We believe that these constraints are very difficult to manage. Indeed, they still might show the same properties of monotonicity and anti-monotonicity studied so far in literature but still cannot be embedded in algorithms as already done in the literature [15, 12].

Then, we will characterize a kind of queries which can possibly contain context dependent constraints and do not present any negative impact on the proposed optimization method.

The rest of the paper is organized as follows. Section 2 presents some preliminary definitions such as item dependent and context dependent constraints. Section 3 states the main results of the paper: sufficient conditions for query rewriting based on the materialization of other queries. Finally Section 4 shows some experimental results. These results further motivate the proposed approach. Section 5 draws some conclusions.

2   Preliminary Definitions and Notation

Let us consider a database instance D and let T be a database relation having the schema $TS=\{A_1, A_2, \ldots, A_n\}$. A given set of functional dependencies Σ over the attribute domains $dom(A_i)$, $i = 1..n$ is assumed to be known.

For the sake of exemplification, let us also consider a fixed instance of the application domain. In particular, we will refer to a market basket analysis application in which T is a `Purchase` relation that contains data about customer purchases. In this context, TS is given by {tr, date, customer, product, category, brand, price, qty}, where: `tr` is the purchase transaction identifier, `customer` is the customer identifier, `date` is the date in which the purchase transaction occurred, `product` is the purchased product identifier, `category` is the category to which the product belongs, `brand` is the manufacturer of the product, `price` is the product price, and `qty` is the quantity purchased in transaction `tr`. The Σ relation is {product→price, product→category, product→brand, {tr, product}→qty, tr→date, tr→customer}. It should be noted, however, that the validity of the framework is general, and it does depend on neither the mining query language nor the running database example.

Of course, the above schema could also be represented over a set of relations and dimensions adopting the usual data warehouse star schema. Nonetheless, we keep the database in this non normalized form since it is very usual to mine data from the result of a pre-processing step of the whole data warehouse content (by means of selection and join over fact relation and one or more dimension relations).

The following equivalence relation will prove to be useful for the forthcoming discussion:

Definition 1. *Grouping equivalence relationship: two sets of attributes K_1 and K_2 are said to be* grouping equivalent *if and only if for any relation T defined on TS:*

$$\forall t_1, t_2 \in T : t_1[K_1] = t_2[K_1] \Leftrightarrow t_1[K_2] = t_2[K_2]$$

where $t_1[K_1]$ is the projection of the tuple t_1 on the attributes in K_1.

Sets of attributes that are grouping equivalent form a grouping equivalence class E. Each set of attributes belonging to the same grouping equivalence class partitions a database relation T in the same groups. We assume to know about a set of grouping equivalence classes $E_1 \ldots E_j$.

Example 1. In the `Purchase` example, the following non trivial equivalence class may be found: $E_1 = \{\{\text{tr}\}, \{\text{date}, \text{customer}\}, \{\text{tr}, \text{date}\}, \{\text{tr}, \text{customer}\}, \{\text{tr}, \text{date}, \text{customer}\}\}$.

Let us denote by $X \rightarrow Y$ a functional dependency (FD) between two attribute sets X (LHS) and Y (RHS) in the database schema TS.

Definition 2. *A* dependency set *of a set of attributes X contains all the possible RHS that can be obtained from X following a FD in Σ (direct or transitive) such that there is no $X' \subset X$ such that $X' \rightarrow Y$.*

As we did for equivalence classes, we assume to know about a set of dependency sets.

Example 2. The dependency set of $\{\text{product}\}$ is $\{\text{category}, \text{price}, \text{brand}\}$. The dependency set of $\{\text{tr}\}$ is $\{\text{customer}, \text{date}\}$ while the dependency set of $\{\text{tr}, \text{product}\}$ is $\{\text{qty}\}$.

In writing a mining query, the user must specify the following parameters:

- The *item attributes*, a set of attributes whose values constitute an item, i.e., an element of an itemset.
- The *grouping attributes* needed in order to decide how tuples are grouped for the formation of each itemset.
- The *mining constraints* which may be based either on the values of any of the attributes in TS (e.g., kind of product, price or quantity) or on aggregate values (e.g., sum of prices of products in an itemset)
- An expression over a number of *statistical measures* used to reduce the size of the result set and to increase the relevance of the results. This evaluation measures are evaluated only on the occurrences of the itemsets that satisfy the mining constraints.

Usually in market basket analysis, when the user/analyst wants to describe by means of itemsets the most frequent sales occurred in purchase transactions, the grouping attribute is `tr` (the transaction identifier) and the itemsets are formed by the projection on `product` of sets of tuples selected from one group. However, for the sake of generality and of the expressive power of the mining language, grouping can be decided differently in each query. For instance, if the analyst wants to study the buying behavior of customers, grouping can be done using the `customer` attribute, or if the user wants to study the sales behaviour over time he/she can group by `date` or by week or month in the case these attributes were defined.

Users may exploit the mining constraints in order to discard uninteresting itemsets and to improve the performances of the mining algorithm.

By summarizing, a mining query may be described as

$$Q = (T, G, I, \Gamma(M), \Xi)$$

where T is the database relation, G is the set of grouping attributes, I is the set of item attributes, Γ is a boolean expression of atomic predicates over a set M

of attributes (the *mining attributes*) with $M \subset TS$, and Ξ is an expression on some statistical measures used for the evaluation of each itemset.

An atomic predicate can be any of the following:

1. $A_i \theta v_{Ai}$
2. $\text{agg}(A_i) \theta v$

where θ is a relational operator such as $<, <=, =, >, >=, <>$, v_{Ai} is a value from the domain of attribute A_i, $\text{agg}(A_i)$ is the result of an aggregate function on the set of values of A_i which appear in the tuples from which the itemset has been extracted, v is a value from the natural or rational domain. Finally, Ξ is a boolean expression in which each term has the form

$$\xi(\nu) \theta v$$

where ξ is a statistical measure for the itemset evaluation and θ and v are defined as above. We require that the evaluation measure $\xi : \mathbb{N} \rightarrow \mathbb{R}$ of an itemset J is a function applied to the number of the groups in which J satisfies the constraints.

Examples of ξ are **support count** and **frequency**. The support count is the counting of the distinct groups containing the itemset. The itemset frequency is computed as the ratio between the itemset support count and the total number of database groups.

A mining engine, takes a query Q defined on an input relation T and generates a result set R [2].

Example 3. The query

$$Q = (\text{ Purchase}, \{\text{tr}\}, \{\text{product}\},$$
$$\text{price} > 100 \wedge \text{count}(\text{product}) >= 2, \text{support count} >= 20)$$

over the **Purchase** relation (first parameter) extracts itemsets formed by products (third parameter), where all the products in the itemset have been sold in the same transaction (second parameter). Moreover, each product in the itemset must have price greater than 100 and the itemset must contain at least two products (aggregate function $\text{count}(\text{product}) >= 2$ on the candidate itemset). Finally, support count of the returned itemsets must be at least 20.

Example 4. The following query over the **Purchase** relation extracts itemsets formed by occurrences of products in sales grouped by date where the selected products are sold in a low quantity (less than 10 units each) and where the itemset support count is at least 30.

$$Q = (\text{Purchase}, \{\text{date}\}, \{\text{product}\}, \text{qty} < 10, \text{support count} >= 30)$$

Now that we have seen how constraint-based mining queries are formed, let us define two particular types of predicates in constraints: the *item dependent* constraints and the *context dependent* ones.

---

[2] In particular, the mining engine stores R on the same DB from which R was mined as a pair of normalized relations R_{summary} and R_{detail}. R_{summary} has the schema {Itemset_id, Ξ} where Itemset_id is the identifier of the itemset and Ξ is its statistical evaluation expression. The second relation R_{detail}, over the schema {Itemset_id, I}, contains the detail of each itemset in terms of its constituting items.

Definition 3. *Let us consider the query*
$$Q = (T, G, I, \Gamma(M), \Xi)$$
An atomic predicate P(A$_i$) $\in \Gamma(M)$, A$_i \in M$ *is defined as an* item dependent constraint *if and only if A_i belongs to the dependency set of at least one attribute subset of I. Otherwise, it is defined as a* context dependent constraint.

Example 5. Predicate price>100 in the query of Example 3 is an item dependent constraint because price is in the dependency set of product. Predicate support count>=20 is not an item dependent constraint because it is not applied on an attribute in the dependency set of product and also because it is not a predicate in a constrained expression, but in a statistical evaluation expression.

Example 6. Predicate qty>100 in query of Example 4 is a context dependent constraint because qty depends on either product or tr alone.

We notice that an itemset $\mathcal{I}$ satisfies an item dependent constraint either in any database group in which it occurs, or in none. This immediately implies the following:

Lemma 1. *An itemset $\mathcal{I}$ that satisfies an item dependent constraint in a mining query has a statistical measure that is a function of the total number of groups in which I occurs in the given database instance.*

On the contrary, a context dependent constraint might be satisfied by some occurrences of itemset $\mathcal{I}$, but not all of them. Then, its statistical measure is based on the number of groups in which the itemset satisfies the constraint (that might be less than the total number of groups in which it appears).

3 Query Rewriting

We suppose that a certain set S of other queries Q_i have been already executed by the inductive database management system and that their results have been stored in distinct result sets R_i.

Definition 4. *A query Q_0 on TS is rewritable in terms of a set $S' = \{Q_j\} \subseteq S$ of other queries if it is possible to rebuild the result set R_0 using only intersection and union operations of the result sets R_j and this is true regardless of the database instance.*

Certainly, the query rewriting of Q_0 on queries in S is possible for every database instance on the given schema, if certain hypothesis are fulfilled.

Definition 5. *A set of queries $S' = \{Q_i\} \subseteq S$ is a candidate rewriting of Q_0 if the following conditions hold for all $Q_i \in S'$:*

1. *G_i is in the same grouping equivalence class of G_0*
2. *I_i is in the same grouping equivalence class of I_0.*
3. *Ξ_0 and Ξ_i are logically equivalent expressions on the same statistical evaluation measures and values.*

Condition 1 guarantees that grouping attributes in Q_0 and in Q_i partition the input relation T into the same groups for every database defined on TS.

Condition 2 allows the result sets of different queries R_i, R_j to be intersected and joined even when $I_i \neq I_j$. In such a situation it is necessary to rewrite the two result sets in terms of a common element in the grouping equivalence class to which I_i and I_j both belong.

Condition 3 guarantees that any result element in R_i has been evaluated by the same statistical evaluation measures as in Q_0. If those measures were not the same for all the queries in S', it would be necessary to recompute them for each result element and this would require to access again the input relation. This should be avoided in order to save computational work, otherwise most of the benefits gained would be wasted.

Now we can establish the main result of this paper. It defines how the various query results can be composed together.

Theorem 1. *Let us consider a query Q and let $S' = \{Q_i, Q_j\}$ be a candidate rewriting of Q. If both M_i and M_j are in the dependency set of any two subsets of I, then the following relationships hold.*

$$\Gamma(M) = \Gamma_i(M_i) \wedge \Gamma_j(M_j) \Rightarrow R = R_i \cap R_j$$
$$\Gamma(M) = \Gamma_i(M_i) \vee \Gamma_j(M_j) \Rightarrow R = R_i \cup R_j$$

Proof. (sketch) We first notice that being Q_i and Q_j in a candidate rewriting of Q, then their results may be composed together since the semantics of the itemsets extracted by Q_i and Q_j are the same. Moreover, let us recall that an itemset appears in a result set iff it satisfies both the query constraints and the statistical expression. The result follows from the following considerations:

- an itemset which satisfies the conjunction (respectively the disjunction) of $\Gamma_i(M_i)$ and $\Gamma_j(M_j)$ will be included in the intersection (respectively the union) of R_i and R_j.
- the atomic predicates involved are item dependent constraints and hence, as a consequence of Lemma 1, the statistical measures associated to them does not depend on the constraints themselves. Hence, its value is the same in R_i, R_j, and R.

Item dependent constraints in a query Q guarantee that a query rewriting candidate $\{Q_i, Q_j\}$ of Q can be used for answering query Q if there is a logical equivalence between mining predicates of Q and the conjunction (disjunction) of mining predicates in Q_i and Q_j. In these cases, the itemsets found respectively in the intersection (union) of the results R_i and R_j are also in R and viceversa. This Theorem has important consequences, from the computational viewpoint, because not only we can predict which itemsets we will found in the result of query Q without coming back to the database but also the value of their statistical measures.

3.1 Query Rewriting for Mining Queries on Context Dependent Constraints

In order to explain how it is possible to do query rewriting, even for context dependent constraints, let us consider a sample query Q and one of its candidate rewritings $Q' = \{Q_i, Q_j\}$. Let J be an itemset which appears in both Q_i and Q_j, and let us denote with O_i and O_j the sets of database groups that contain J in which J satisfies the mining constraints in Q_i and Q_j respectively. As we will discuss below, O_i and O_j are not necessarily the same set and hence the set of groups which satisfy both the mining conditions $\Gamma_i(M_i)$ and $\Gamma_j(M_j)$ should be computed as $O_i \cap O_j$. The important implication of this fact is that the number of groups that satisfy both queries cannot be foretold directly from the results of Q_i and Q_j, when only the size of O_i and the size of O_j are known: one usually needs to access the database and retrieve the entire group lists O_i and O_j.

Interestingly, Theorem 1 states it is sufficient that the query constraints are item dependent for query rewriting to be possible (without making accesses to the original database relation T). Under the theorem assumptions, in fact, whether J satisfies the constraints or not uniquely depends on J itself. If J satisfies the constraints, it does it for all the groups in which J occurs. This implies that, for any item dependent constraint, the set of groups O_i and O_j are either equal or empty.

On the other hand, when a mining query is based on context dependent constraints, the occurrences of an itemset J may satisfy the mining constraints in certain database groups *but not in others*. This is the core characteristic of context dependent constraints: whether they are satisfied by an itemset depends on the database context in which the itemset occurs. As a consequence, in order to answer the mining query, it is usually necessary to retrieve all the database groups in which the itemset occurs in order to verify case by case the constraints (or typically maintaining O_i and O_j for each itemset J, and then by means of their intersection and union).

Interestingly, as it is stated below, there are situations in which this can be avoided even when context dependent constraints are involved.

Theorem 2. *Let us consider a query Q and let $S' = \{Q_i, Q_j\}$ be a candidate rewriting of Q. Let us also assume that G and I are such that an itemset appears at most once in each group. If $\Gamma_i(X) \Rightarrow \neg\Gamma_j(Y)$ (i.e., $\Gamma_j(Y)$ is always false for the itemsets that satisfy $\Gamma_i(X)$ regardless the database instance T) then the following relationships hold:*

$$\Gamma(M) = \Gamma_i(M_i) \wedge \Gamma_j(M_j) \Rightarrow R = \emptyset$$
$$\Gamma(M) = \Gamma_i(M_i) \vee \Gamma_j(M_j) \Rightarrow R = R_i \cup R_j$$

For each itemset J in R and for each statistical measure ξ_k that contributes to Ξ, the new value of $\xi_k(\nu)$ is computed by setting:

$$\nu = \nu_i + \nu_j$$

where ν_i and ν_j are the number of groups in which J appears and that satisfy the mining constraints of the query Q_i and Q_j respectively.

Proof. (sketch) We first notice that since we do not assume item dependent constraints, the statistical measure of an itemset may change accordingly to the constraints involved in the queries.

The first part of the theorem follows since $\Gamma_i(M_i) \Rightarrow \neg\Gamma_j(M_j)$ implies that an itemset in relation T cannot satisfy $\Gamma_i(M_i) \wedge \Gamma_j(M_j)$.

For the second part, the union of R_i and R_j contains all itemsets which satisfy either $\Gamma_i(M_i)$ or $\Gamma_j(M_j)$. Moreover, since any group contains at most one occurrence of a fixed itemset J and it cannot satisfy both Γ_i and Γ_j, then that group contributes either to the count of J in R_i or to its count in R_j, but not to both. Hence, the evaluation measure in R resulting from the sum of the counts in R_i and R_j is correct.

4   Experiments

The query rewriting of a query Q requires the identification of a set of queries which satisfy either Theorem 1 or Theorem 2 and the foreseen algebraic operations between their result sets. This is advantageous provided that their overall cost is less than the cost of executing the query from scratch. Indeed union and join of two results by means of SQL queries are well known to be very efficient operations provided that the needed indices are defined.

Hence, an important issue involved in the optimization problem is the identification of which queries among previous ones may be used as Q_1 and Q_2. In the most general setting, the solution to the problem is not trivial at all, since it requires to be able to recognize the equivalence of logical formulae. The problem is even more complex than this, since when Q increases in size, the number of different ways in which we can choose Q_i and Q_j increases exponentially. A complete solution to this problem is clearly out of the scope of this paper. Anyway, at the present time we already implemented an optimizer that tests for the equivalence of two, possibly complex, queries. In the forthcoming work, we plan to implement a heuristic strategy based on the greedy covering strategy in order to find approximate solutions to the general problem.

In the following we explain how the optimizer checks for the logical equivalence between a query Q and one of its candidate rewritings Q_i. In brief, the following operations are performed:

1. Rewriting of the mining constraints of the two queries in disjunctive normal form. This step is necessary in order to make it easier to identify equivalent logical expressions.
2. Substitution of some mining constraints with some other equivalent ones or elimination of redundant ones. This is done by the exploitation of the functional dependencies in the database schema.
3. Generation of a compact representation of the truth table of the two resulting expressions.
4. Check the equivalence between the two predicates expressions on the table.

Example 7. Consider queries

$Q = ($ Purchase, $\{\text{tr}\}, \{\text{product}\},$

   category $= $ 'computer' $\wedge$ brand $= $ 'XX'

   $\vee$category $= $ 'hi-fi' $\wedge$ price $< 200,$

   support count $>= 20)$

$Q_i = ($ Purchase, $\{\text{tr}\}, \{\text{product}\},$

   category $= $ 'computer' $\wedge$ $(\neg$category $= $ 'hi-fi' $\vee$ price $\geq 200)$

   $\vee$category $= $ 'hi-fi' $\wedge$ price $> 100 \wedge$ price $< 200),$

   support count $>= 20)$

and suppose that the following functional dependencies are known to hold:

- no product in category hi-fi costs less than 150 (that is category $= $ 'hi-fi' $\rightarrow$ price ≥ 150).
- all products that have 'XX' brand are in category 'computer' (that is brand $= $ 'XX' $\rightarrow$ category $= $ 'computer').

The optimizer performs the following transformations:

1. it transforms constraints in disjunctive form. Q is already in disjunctive form. Q_i becomes:

   $Q_i = ($ Purchase, $\{\text{tr}\}, \{\text{product}\},$

     category $= $ 'computer' $\wedge \neg$category $= $ 'hi-fi'

     $\vee$category $= $ 'computer' $\wedge$ price ≥ 200

     $\vee$category $= $ 'hi-fi' $\wedge$ price $> 100 \wedge$ price $< 200,$

     support count $>= 20)$

2. it exploits the known functional dependencies and some basic property of range predicates in an ordered domain. As a result query Q becomes

   $Q = ($ Purchase, $\{\text{tr}\}, \{\text{product}\},$

     category $= $ 'computer' $\vee$ category $= $ 'hi-fi' $\wedge$ price $< 200,$

     support count $>= 20)$

and query Q_i becomes

     $Q_i = ($ Purchase, $\{\text{tr}\}, \{\text{product}\},$ category $= $ 'computer'

      $\vee$category $= $ 'computer' $\wedge$ price ≥ 200

      $\vee$category $= $ 'hi-fi' $\wedge$ price $< 200),$

      support count $>= 20)$

3. it builds the truth table of the mining constraints expressions in Q and in Q_i from step 2 and verifies that they are logically equivalent. In this case this is easily checked to be true.

The time complexity of the solution is exponential in the number of distinct predicates involved; anyway, a careful implementation keeps the problem tractable for most reasonable queries. In order to test the last assertion, we

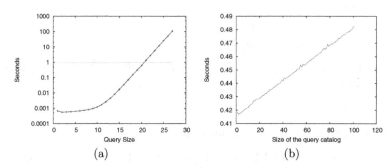

(a)   (b)

Fig. 1. Optimization times as a function of (a) number of atomic predicates and (b) the size of the query catalog.

randomly built queries of increasing length and ran the testing procedure over them. The results are reported in logarithmic scale in Figure 1 (a). It is worth noting that, even if the algorithm is clearly exponential, whenever the number of predicates involved in the queries is not larger than 20, the time spent to process the query is less than $10^{-0.2} \approx 0.63$ seconds[3]. Since typical query lengths are much smaller than 20, we can argue that in common situations the processing time for the equivalence checking is actually acceptable.

The algorithm which checks the entire database catalog of previous queries simply repeats the equivalence checking algorithm once for each past query until an equivalence is found. Hence, the complexity increases linearly with the number of previous queries as it can be seen in Figure 1 (b). Of course, a number of "cleaning" policies can be devised in order to keep the size of the query catalog relatively small.

Let us consider an experiment we made on a sample database having $\approx$ 250,000 records containing $\approx$ 10,000 sales transactions composed of 25 items on average, randomly extracted from a total of 939 items. The system took about one millisecond for the optimization steps, 12 seconds to prepare the dataset for the mining algorithm and 543 seconds to build the final result using a Partition-like algorithm (at the end, the result set contained 42 association rules).

The system ran on a setting which corresponds to a nearby of the origin of the two Figures 1 (a) and (b). The results prove the feasibility of the proposed approach since they make evident that the time saved in case the optimization succeeds is dramatically smaller than the execution time of the mining algorithm.

---

[3] The testing program was written entirely in C++. The testing machine running Linux (Kernel v.2.4) sports two Pentium III processors (1.4GHz each) and 1Gb of RAM. The mining engine connects to a MySQL server (v.3.23.53) by means of an ODBC connection.

Notice that, even in the case that the query catalog has 100 queries with 15 atomic predicates on average, the time spent by the optimizer is still less than four seconds, which is acceptable.

5   Conclusions

In this paper we studied the problem of query rewriting for queries that mine frequent itemsets. The proposed technique consists in rewriting the query in terms of union and intersection of the result sets of other queries, previously executed and materialized. We found sufficient conditions for the optimization to apply and shown by means of some experiments that this approach is viable because it reduces drastically the execution time. This seems absolutely necessary in many data mining applications.

In the future we plan to consider also fuzzy evaluation techniques for the problem of mining frequent itemset from a database. Previous results in this direction already exist (the so called condensed ϵ-adequate representations developed by Boulicaut and Rigotti in [2]) that consider approximate solutions to the identification of the statistical evaluation measure of an itemset.

References

1. R. Agrawal, H. Mannila, R. Srikant, H. Toivonen, and A. I. Verkamo. Fast discovery of association rules. In U. M. Fayyad, G. Piatetsky-Shapiro, P. Smyth, and R. Uthurusamy, editors, *Knowledge Discovery in Databases*, volume 2. AAAI/MIT Press, Santiago, Chile, September 1995.
2. J.-F. Boulicaut, A. Bykowski, and C. Rigotti. Free-sets: a condensed representation of boolean data for the approximation of frequency queries. *Data Mining and Knowledge Discovery*, 7(1):5–22, 2003.
3. S. Chaudhuri, S. Krishnamurthy, S. Potarnianos, and K. Shim. Optimizing queries with materialized views. In *Proc. of 11th ICDE*, March 1995.
4. S. Chaudhuri, V. Narasayya, and S. Sarawagi. Efficient evaluation of queries with mining predicates. In *Proc. of the 18th Int'l Conference on Data Engineering (ICDE)*, San Jose, USA, April 2002.
5. S. Chaudhuri and K. Shim. Optimizing queries with aggregate views. In *Proc. of EDBT*, 1996.
6. M. Fang, N. Shivakumar, H. Garcia-Molina, R. Motwani, and J. Ullman. Computing iceberg queries efficiently. In *Proceeding of VLDB '98*, 1998.
7. A. Gupta, V. Harinarayan, and D. Quass. Aggregate query processing in data warehousing environments. In *Proceedings of VLDB '95*, pages 358–369, 1995.
8. J. Han, Y. Fu, W. Wang, K. Koperski, and O. Zaiane. DMQL: A data mining query language for relational databases. *In Proceedings of SIGMOD-96 Workshop on Research Issues on Data Mining and Knowledge Discovery*, 1996.
9. T. Imielinski and H. Mannila. A database perspective on knowledge discovery. *Communications of the ACM*, 39(11):58–64, November 1996.
10. T. Imielinski, A. Virmani, and A. Abdoulghani. Datamine: Application programming interface and query language for database mining. *KDD-96*, pages 256–260, 1996.

11. H.-J. Lenz and A. Shoshani. Summarizability in olap and statistical data bases. In *Proceedings Ninth International Conference on Scientific and Statistical Database Management*, pages 132–143. IEEE Computer Society, August 1997.
12. C. K.-S. Leung, L. V. S. Lakshmanan, and R. T. Ng. Exploiting succinct constraints using fp-trees. *ACM SIGKDD Explorations*, 4(1):40–49, June 2002.
13. F. M. Malvestuto. The derivation problem for summary data. In *Proceedings of the ACM SIGMOD International Conference on Management of Data*, pages 82–89, 1988.
14. R. Meo, G. Psaila, and S. Ceri. A new SQL-like operator for mining association rules. In *Proceedings of the 22st VLDB Conference*, Bombay, India, September 1996.
15. R. T. Ng, L. V. S. Lakshmanan, J. Han, and A. Pang. Exploratory mining and pruning optimizations of constrained associations rules. In *Proceedings of 1998 ACM SIGMOD International Conference Management of Data*, pages 13–24, 1998.
16. W. Nutt, Y. Sagiv, and S. Shurin. Deciding equivalence among aggregate queries. In *Proceedings of ACM PODS*, pages 214–223, 1998.
17. C.-S. Park, M. H. Kim, and Y.-J. Lee. Rewriting olap queries using materialized views and dimension hierarchies in data warehouses. In *Proceeding of ICDE'01*, 2001.
18. C.-S. Perng, H. Wang, S. Ma, and J. L. Hellerstein. Discovery in multi-attribute data with user-defined constraints. *ACM SIGKDD Explorations*, 4(1):56–64, 2002.
19. L. D. Raedt. A perspective on inductive databases. *ACM SIGKDD Explorations*, 4(2):69–77, December 2002.
20. L. D. Raedt, M. Jaeger, S. D. Lee, and H. Mannila. A theory of inductive query answering. In *Proceedings of IEEE International Conference on Data Mining*, pages 123–130. IEEE Computer Society, December 2002.
21. R. Srikant, Q. Vu, and R. Agrawal. Mining association rules with item constraints. In *Proceedings of 1997 ACM KDD*, pages 67–73, 1997.
22. D. Srivastava, S. Dar, H. V. Jagadish, and A. Y. Levy. Answering queries with aggregation using views. In *Proceeding of VLDB '96*, 1996.
23. D. Tsur, J. D. Ullman, S. Abiteboul, C. Clifton, R. Motwani, S. Nestorov, and A. Rosenthal. Query flocks: A generalization of association-rule mining. In *Proceedings of 1998 ACM SIGMOD International Conference Management of Data*, 1998.
24. H. Wang and C. Zaniolo. User defined aggregates for logical data languages. In *Proc. of DDLP*, pages 85–97, 1998.
25. X. S. Wang and C. Li. Deriving orthogonality to optimize the search for summary data. *Information Systems*, 24(1):47–65, 1999.
26. Y. Zhao, P. M.Deshpande, J. F. Naughton, and A. Shukla. Simultaneous optimization and evaluation of multiple dimensional queries. In *Proceedings of ACM SIGMOD '98*, pages 271–282, 1998.

Query Answering
Based on Collaboration and Chase

Zbigniew W. Raś[1,2] and Agnieszka Dardzińska[3,1]

[1] UNC-Charlotte, Department of Computer Science, Charlotte, N.C. 28223, USA
[2] Polish Academy of Sciences, Institute of Computer Science, Ordona 21, 01-237
Warsaw, Poland
[3] Bialystok Technical Univ., Dept. of Mathematics, ul. Wiejska 45A, 15-351
Bialystok, Poland

Abstract. Query Answering System (QAS) for a Distributed Information System (DIS) which is based on collaboration and *Chase* is presented in this paper. Collaboration among systems is driven by the QAS
requests for knowledge needed to resolve, so called, non-local queries at
a client site. As the result of these requests, knowledge in the form of
definitions of incomplete or locally foreign attribute values is extracted
at a number of sites in DIS and next exchanged between all of them.
The final outcome of this step is a new knowledge-base KB created at
the client site. Now, the chase process will begin: each incomplete slot
in a column corresponding to attribute listed in a query, let us say d, is
chased with respect to rules from KB describing d. All other incomplete
attributes listed in a query are processed the same way. When the chase
process ends, the query is handled by QAS in a standard way.

1 Introduction

Distributed information system is a system that connects a number of information systems using network communication technology. In this paper, we assume
that these systems are autonomous and incomplete. Incompleteness is understood by allowing to have a set of weighted attribute values as a value of an attribute. Additionally, we assume that the sum of these weights has to be equal 1.
The definition of an information system of type λ and Distributed Information
System (DIS) proposed in this paper is a modification of definitions given by
Raś in [13] and used later by Raś and Dardzińska in [14] to talk about semantic inconsistencies among sites of DIS from the query answering point of view.
The type λ is introduced mainly to monitor the weights assigned to values of
attributes by *Chase* algorithm, if they are greater than or equal to λ. If the
weight assigned by *Chase* to one of the attribute values is less than the allowed
threshold value, then this attribute value has to be ruled out. Semantic inconsistencies are due to different interpretations of attributes and their values among
sites (for instance one site can interpret the concept *young* differently than other
sites). Different interpretations are also due to the way each site is handling
null values. Null value replacement by a value suggested either by statistical or

H. Christiansen et al. (Eds.): FQAS 2004, LNAI 3055, pp. 125–136, 2004.

some rule-based methods is quite common before a query is answered by QAS. Ontologies ([9], [10], [16], [17], [18], [2], [3], [19], [7]) are widely used as a sort of semantical bridge between information systems built independently so they can collaborate and understand each other. In [14], the notion of the optimal rough semantics and a method of its construction was proposed. The rough semantics can be used to model and nicely handle semantic inconsistencies among sites due to different interpretations of incomplete values. Distributed chase is a chase algorithm [1] linked with a site S of DIS, called a client, which is similar to $Chase1$ [6] and $Chase2$ [4] with additional assumption concerning the creation of knowledge bases at all sites of DIS involved in the process of solving a query submitted to S. The knowledge base at the client site contains rules extracted from S and also rules extracted from information systems at its remote sites. The structure of the knowledge base and its properties are the same as properties of the knowledge bases used in $Chase1$ or $Chase2$ algorithms. The difference only lies in the process required to collect these rules. In a distributed framework, these rules are extracted from the local and remote sites, usually under different semantics. Although the names of the attributes are often the same among sites, their granularity levels may differ from site to site. As the result of these differences, the knowledge base has to satisfy certain properties in order to be used by $Chase$. The same properties are required by the query answering system based on $Chase$ and will be given in this paper.

2   Query Processing with Incomplete Data

In real life, data are often collected and stored in information systems residing at many different locations, built independently, instead of collecting them and storing at only one single location. In this case we talk about distributed (autonomous) information systems. It is very possible that an attribute is missing in one of them while it occurs in many others. Also, in one information system, an attribute might be strongly incomplete, while in other systems the same attribute is either complete or close to being complete. Saying that attribute is strongly incomplete, we mean that the value of this attribute is either unknown or only partially known for most of the objects. Assume that user submits a query to one of the information systems (called a client), which rather would prefer not to answer it (we assume that the query answering system for the client site is possessing some intelligence) due to the fact that some of the attributes used in a query are missing or strongly incomplete at the client site. In such a case, network communication technology is used to get definitions of these unknown or strongly incomplete attributes from other information systems (called servers). All these new definitions form a knowledge base which can be used to chase that missing or strongly incomplete attributes at the client site. But, before any chase algorithm, called *rule-based chase*, can be applied, semantic inconsistencies among sites have to be somehow resolved. For instance, it can be done by taking rough semantics [Raś & Dardzińska], mentioned earlier.

Definition 1:   We say that $S = (X, A, V)$ is a partially incomplete information system of type λ, if S is an incomplete information system and the following three conditions hold:

- $a_S(x)$ is defined for any $x \in X$, $a \in A$,
- $(\forall x \in X)(\forall a \in A)[(a_S(x) = \{(a_i, p_i) : 1 \leq i \leq m\}) \rightarrow \sum_{i=1}^{m} p_i = 1]$,
- $(\forall x \in X)(\forall a \in A)[(a_S(x) = \{(a_i, p_i) : 1 \leq i \leq m\}) \rightarrow (\forall i)(p_i \geq \lambda)]$.

Now, let us assume that S_1, S_2 are partially incomplete information systems, both of type λ. The same set X of objects is stored in both systems and the same set A of attributes is used to describe them. The meaning and granularity of values of attributes from A in both systems S_1, S_2 is also the same. Additionally, we assume that $a_{S_1}(x) = \{(a_{1i}, p_{1i}) : 1 \leq m_1\}$ and $a_{S_2}(x) = \{(a_{2i}, p_{2i}) : 1 \leq m_2\}$.

We say that containment relation Ψ holds between S_1 and S_2, if the following two conditions hold:

- $(\forall x \in X)(\forall a \in A)[card(a_{S_1(x)}) \geq card(a_{S_2(x)})]$,
- $(\forall x \in X)(\forall a \in A)[[card(a_{S_1}(x)) = card(a_{S_2}(x))] \rightarrow$
$$[\sum_{i \neq j} |p_{2i} - p_{2j}| > \sum_{i \neq j} |p_{1i} - p_{1j}|]].$$

Instead of saying that containment relation holds between S_1 and S_2, we can equivalently say that S_1 was transformed into S_2 by containment mapping Ψ. This fact can be presented as a statement $\Psi(S_1) = S_2$ or $(\forall x \in X)(\forall a \in A)[\Psi(a_{S_1}(x)) = \Psi(a_{S_2}(x))]$. Similarly, we can either say that $a_{S_1}(x)$ was transformed into $a_{S_2}(x)$ by Ψ or that containment relation Ψ holds between $a_{S_1}(x)$ and $a_{S_2}(x)$.

So, if containment mapping Ψ converts an information system S to S', then S' is more complete than S. Saying another words, for a minimum one pair $(a, x) \in A \times X$, either Ψ has to decrease the number of attribute values in $a_S(x)$ or the average difference between confidences assigned to attribute values in $a_S(x)$ has to be increased by Ψ.

To give an example of a containment mapping Ψ, let us take two information systems S_1, S_2 both of the type λ, represented as Table 1 and Table 2.

It can be easily checked that the values assigned to $e(x_1)$, $b(x_2)$, $c(x_2)$, $a(x_3)$, $e(x_4)$, $a(x_5)$, $c(x_7)$, and $a(x_8)$ in S_1 are different than the corresponding values in S_2. In each of these eight cases, an attribute value assigned to an object in S_2 is less general than the value assigned to the same object in S_1. It means that $\Psi(S_1) = S_2$.

3   Query Processing with Distributed Data and Chase

Assume now that $L(D) = \{(t \rightarrow v_c) \in D : c \in In(A)\}$ (called a knowledge-base) is a set of all rules extracted initially from $S = (X, A, V)$ by $ERID(S, \lambda_1, \lambda_2)$, where $In(A)$ is the set of incomplete attributes in S and λ_1, λ_2 are thresholds for minimum support and minimum confidence, correspondingly. $ERID$ is the

Table 1. Information System S_1

X	a	b	c	d	e
x_1	$\{(a_1,\frac{1}{3}),(a_2,\frac{2}{3})\}$	$\{(b_1,\frac{2}{3}),(b_2,\frac{1}{3})\}$	c_1	d_1	$\{(e_1,\frac{1}{2}),(e_2,\frac{1}{2})\}$
x_2	$\{(a_2,\frac{1}{4}),(a_3,\frac{3}{4})\}$	$\{(b_1,\frac{1}{3}),(b_2,\frac{2}{3})\}$		d_2	e_1
x_3		b_2	$\{(c_1,\frac{1}{2}),(c_3,\frac{1}{2})\}$	d_2	e_3
x_4	a_3		c_2	d_1	$\{(e_1,\frac{2}{3}),(e_2,\frac{1}{3})\}$
x_5	$\{(a_1,\frac{2}{3}),(a_2,\frac{1}{3})\}$	b_1	c_2		e_1
x_6	a_2	b_2	c_3	d_2	$\{(e_2,\frac{1}{3}),(e_3,\frac{2}{3})\}$
x_7	a_2	$\{(b_1,\frac{1}{4}),(b_2,\frac{3}{4})\}$	$\{(c_1,\frac{1}{3}),(c_2,\frac{2}{3})\}$	d_2	e_2
x_8		b_2	c_1	d_1	e_3

Table 2. Information System S_2

X	a	b	c	d	e
x_1	$\{(a_1,\frac{1}{3}),(a_2,\frac{2}{3})\}$	$\{(b_1,\frac{2}{3}),(b_2,\frac{1}{3})\}$	c_1	d_1	$\{(e_1,\frac{1}{3}),(e_2,\frac{2}{3})\}$
x_2	$\{(a_2,\frac{1}{4}),(a_3,\frac{3}{4})\}$	b_1	$\{(c_1,\frac{1}{3}),(c_2,\frac{2}{3})\}$	d_2	e_1
x_3	a_1	b_2	$\{(c_1,\frac{1}{2}),(c_3,\frac{1}{2})\}$	d_2	e_3
x_4	a_3		c_2	d_1	e_2
x_5	$\{(a_1,\frac{3}{4}),(a_2,\frac{1}{4})\}$	b_1	c_2		e_1
x_6	a_2	b_2	c_3	d_2	$\{(e_2,\frac{1}{3}),(e_3,\frac{2}{3})\}$
x_7	a_2	$\{(b_1,\frac{1}{4}),(b_2,\frac{3}{4})\}$	c_1	d_2	e_2
x_8	$\{(a_1,\frac{2}{3}),(a_2,\frac{1}{3})\}$	b_2	c_1	d_1	e_3

algorithm for discovering rules from incomplete information systems, presented
by Dardzińska and Raś in [5]. The type of incompleteness in [5] is the same as
in this paper but we did not provide there a threshold value λ for the minimal
confidence of attribute values assigned to objects. The algorithm *ERID* works
the same way for incomplete information systems of type λ, since the knowledge
discovery process in *ERID* is independent from the largeness of parameter λ.
Assume now that a query $q(B)$ is submitted to system $S = (X, A, V)$, where B
is the set of all attributes used in $q(B)$ and that $A \cap B \neq \emptyset$. All attributes in
$B - [A \cap B]$ are called foreign for S. If S is a part of a distributed information
system, definitions of foreign attributes for S can be extracted at its remote sites
(see [14]). Clearly, all semantic inconsistencies and differences in granularity of
attribute values among sites have to be resolved first. To simplify the problem,
we take the same assumption as in [14]. It mean that we only allow different
granularity of attribute values and different semantics related to different interpretations of incomplete attribute values among sites. In [14], it was shown that

we can process a query of the type $q(B)$ at site S by discovering definitions of values of attributes from $B - [A \cap B]$ at remote sites for S and use them to answer $q(B)$.

Foreign attributes for S, can be seen as attributes entirely incomplete in S, which means values (either exact or partially incomplete) of such attributes have to be ascribed to all objects in S. Stronger the consensus among sites on a value to be ascribed to x, *better* the result of the ascription process for x can be expected. Assuming that systems S_1, S_2 are storing the same sets of objects and using the same attributes to describe them, system S_1 is *better* than system S_2, if $\Psi(S_2) = S_1$. So, clearly *the best* information system will be the one which is complete. The question remains, if the values predicted by the imputation process are really correct, and if not, how far they are (assuming that some distance measure can be set up) from the correct values which clearly are unknown? Classical approach, to this kind of problems, is to start with a complete information system and remove randomly from it, let's say, 10 percent of its values and next run the imputation algorithm on the resulting system. The next step is to compare the descriptions of objects in the system which is the outcome of the imputation algorithm with descriptions of the same objects in the original system. But, before we can continue any further this discussion, we have to decide first on the interpretation of functors *or* and *and*, denoted in this paper by $+$ and $*$, correspondingly. We will adopt the semantics of terms proposed by Raś & Joshi in [15] as their semantics has all the properties required for the query transformation process to be semantically correct [see [15]]. It was proved that, under their semantics, the following distributive property holds: $t_1 * (t_2 + t_3) = (t_1 * t_2) + (t_1 * t_3)$.

So, let us assume that $S = (X, A, V)$ is an information system of type λ and t is a term constructed in a standard way (for predicate calculus expression) from values of attributes in V seen as *constants* and from two functors $+$ and $*$. By $N_S(t)$, we mean the standard interpretation of a term t in S defined as (see [15]):

- $N_S(v) = \{(x, p) : (v, p) \in a(x)\}$, for any $v \in V_a$,
- $N_S(t_1 + t_2) = N_S(t_1) \oplus N_S(t_2)$,
- $N_S(t_1 * t_2) = N_S(t_1) \otimes N_S(t_2)$,

where, for any $N_S(t_1) = \{(x_i, p_i)\}_{i \in I}$, $N_S(t_2) = \{(x_j, q_j)\}_{j \in J}$, we have:

- $N_S(t_1) \oplus N_S(t_2) =$
  $$\{(x_i, p_i)\}_{i \in (I-J)} \cup \{(x_j, p_j)\}_{j \in (J-I)} \cup \{(x_i, max(p_i, q_i))\}_{i \in I \cap J},$$
- $N_S(t_1) \otimes N_S(t_2) = \{(x_i, p_i \cdot q_i)\}_{i \in (I \cap J)}.$

The incomplete value imputation algorithm *Chase*, given below, converts information system S of type λ to a new more complete information system $Chase(S)$ of the same type. Our algorithm is entirely new in comparison to known strategies for chasing incomplete data in relational tables because of the assumption about partial incompleteness of data (sets of weighted attribute values can be assigned to an object as its value). This forced us to develop a new discovery algorithm, called *ERID*, which can extract rules from this type of incomplete data (see [5]) so it can be used in the *Chase* algorithm given below.

Algorithm Chase$(S, In(A), L(D))$;
    Input   System $S = (X, A, V)$,
                    set of incomplete attributes $In(A) = \{a_1, a_2, ..., a_k\}$ in S,
                    set of rules $L(D)$ discovered from S by $ERID$.
    Output System $Chase(S)$
    begin
    S':= S;
    $j := 1$;
    while $j \leq k$ **do**
    begin
    $S_j := S$;
    for all $x \in X$ **do**
        $q_j := 0$;
        begin
        $b_j(x) := \emptyset$;
        $n_j := 0$;
        for all $v \in V_{a_j}$
        begin
        if $card(a_j(x)) \neq 1$ and $\{(t_i \rightarrow v) : i \in I\}$
            is a maximal subset of rules from $L(D)$
            such that $(x, p_i) \in N_{S_j}(t_i)$ **then**
            if $\sum_{i \in I}[p_i \cdot conf(t_i \rightarrow v) \cdot sup(t_i \rightarrow v)] \geq \lambda$ **then**
            begin
            $b_j(x) := b_j(x) \cup \{(v, \sum_{i \in I}[p_i \cdot conf(t_i \rightarrow v) \cdot sup(t_i \rightarrow v)])\}$;
            $n_j := n_j + \sum_{i \in I}[p_i \cdot conf(t_i \rightarrow v) \cdot sup(t_i \rightarrow v)]$
            end
        end
        $q_j := q_j + n_j$;
        end
    if $\Psi(a_j(x)) = [b_j(x)/q_j]$ **then** $a_j(x) := [b_j(x)/q_j]$;
    $j := j + 1$;
    end
    $S := \bigcap\{S_j : 1 \leq j \leq k\}$; /definition of $\bigcap\{S_j : 1 \leq j \leq k\}$ is given below/
    if $S \neq S'$ **then** $Chase(S, In(A), L(D))$
    end

Information system $S = \bigcap\{S_j : 1 \leq j \leq k\}$ is defined as:
    $a_S(x) = \{a_{S_j}(x)$: *if* $a = a_j$ *for any* $j \in \{1, 2, ..., k\}\}$
                      for any attribute a and object x.

Still, one more definition is needed to complete the presentation of the algorithm *Chase*. Namely, we say that:
    $[b_j(x)/p] = \{(v_i, p_i/p)\}_{i \in I}$, if $b_j(x) = \{(v_i, p_i)\}_{i \in I}$.

Algorithm *Chase* converts any incomplete or partially incomplete information system S to a new information system which is more complete. At each recursive call of *Chase*, its input data including S, $L(D)$, and from time to time $In(A)$ are changing. So, before any recursive call is executed, these new data have to be computed first.

Now, we give the time complexity $(T - Comp)$ of the algorithm *Chase*. Assume first that $S = S(0) = (X, A, V)$, $card(In(A)) = k$, and $n = card(X)$. We also assume that $S(i) = Chase^i(S)$ and
$n(i) = card\{x \in X : (\exists a \in A)[a_{S(i)}(x) \neq 1]\}$, both for $i \geq 0$.

Clearly, $n(0) > n(1) > n(2) > ... > n(p) = n(p+1)$, because information system $Chase^{i+1}(S)$ is more complete than information system $Chase^i(S)$, for any $i \geq 0$.

$$T - Comp(Chase) = \bigcirc[\textstyle\sum_{i=0}^{p}[k \cdot [n + n(i) \cdot card(L(D)) \cdot n] + n(i)]] =$$
$$\bigcirc[\textstyle\sum_{i=0}^{p}[k \cdot [n(i) \cdot card(L(D)) \cdot n]]] = \bigcirc[k^2 \cdot n^3 \cdot m].$$

The final worst case complexity of *Chase* is based on the observation that p can not be larger than $k \cdot n$. We also assume here that $m = card(L(D))$.

Explanation. Algorithm *Chase* is called recursively p times (this is why we have $\sum_{i=0}^{p}$). Each recursive call has to improve minimum one slot in S, otherwise algorithm will stop. How large is p depends on the additional threshold for *Chase* which defines the acceptable improvement for a slot in S so the algorithm does not stop. For instance, if we set up the threshold in a way that maximum 10 improvements per slot in S can take place, then $10 \cdot In(S)$ is the worst value for p (where $In(S)$ is the number of incomplete slots in S). In practice, the value p is usually low. Now, for each incomplete attribute in $In(A)$, where $card[In(A)] = k$, we identify which slots have incomplete values (the total number of incomplete slots in $Chase^i(S)$ is equal to $n(i)$). It takes $n \cdot k$ steps to do that. For each row in S, which has an incomplete slot, we identify all rules in $L(D)$ supported by that row. It takes $n(i) \cdot card(L(D))$ steps to do that. For all these rules, we calculate their confidence and support. So, the worst number of steps needed to achieve that in i-iteration of *Chase* will be $n(i) \cdot card(L(D)) \cdot n$.

Now, let us assume that the client site is represented by a partially incomplete information system S of type λ. When a query is submitted to S, its query answering system QAS will replace S by $Chase(S)$ and next will solve the query using, for instance, the strategy proposed Raś & Joshi in [15]. Clearly, we can argue here why the resulting information system obtained by *Chase* can not be stored aside and reused when a new query is submitted to S? If S does not have many updates, we can do that by keeping a copy of $Chase(S)$ and next reuse that copy when a new query is submitted to S. The original information system S has to be kept so when user wants to enter new data, they can be stored in the original system. System $Chase(S)$, if stored aside, can not be reused by QAS when the number of updates in the original S exceeds a given threshold value. It means that the newest information system S has to be chased by our *Chase* algorithm before any query is answered by QAS.

4   Distribution, Inconsistency, and Distributed Chase

If rules in $L(D)$, called the knowledge base and used by algorithm *Chase*, are extracted from many information systems in DIS, including the client S, the possibility to have the data updated in on of them is greatly increasing. This means that the possibility of reusing $Chase(S)$ by QAS for a longer time is automatically decreasing.

As we already pointed out, the knowledge base $L(D)$, contains rules extracted locally at the client site (information system queried by user) as well as rules extracted from information systems at its remote sites. Since rules are extracted from different information systems, inconsistencies in semantics, if any, have to be resolved before any query can be processed. There are two options:

- a knowledge base $L(D)$ at the client site is kept consistent (in this scenario all inconsistencies have to be resolved before rules are stored in the knowledge base),
- a knowledge base at the client site is inconsistent (values of the same attribute used in two rules extracted at different sites may be of different granularity level and may have different semantics associated with them).

In general, we assume that the information stored in a local system ontology and in a global ontology (if they are provided) is sufficient to resolve inconsistencies in semantics of all sites involved in *Chase*. Inconsistencies related to the confidence of conflicting rules stored in $L(D)$ do not have to be resolved at all (algorithm *Chase* does not have such a requirement).

The fact that rules stored in $L(D)$ are often extracted at different sites and under different interpretations of incomplete values is not pleasant, if we want to use them in *Chase*. As we have already shown in [14], the rough semantics (see [14]) is very useful to handle inconsistencies related to different interpretations of incomplete values. Following the same approach as in [14], we can apply rough semantics to rules in $L(D)$ when information system S has to be chased by *Chase* algorithm.

One of the problems related to an incomplete information system $S = (X, A, V)$ is a freedom how new values are constructed to replace incomplete values in S, before any rule extraction process begins. This replacement of incomplete attribute values in some of the slots in S can be done either by *Chase* or/and by a number of available statistical methods (see [8]). This implies that semantics of queries submitted to S and driven (defined) by the query answering system QAS based on *Chase*, will often differ. Following the approach in [14], rough semantics can be also used by QAS to handle this problem.

In this paper we only concentrate on granularity-based semantic inconsistencies. Assume first that $S_i = (X_i, A_i, V_i)$ is an information system for any $i \in I$ and that all of them form a Distributed Information System (DIS). Additionally, we assume that, if $a \in A_i \cap A_j$, then only the granularity levels of a in S_i and S_j may differ but conceptually its meaning, both in S_i and S_j is the

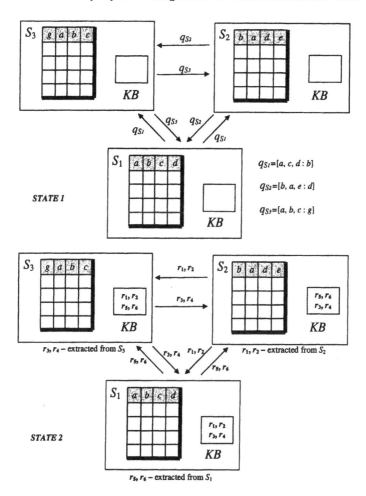

Fig. 1. Global extraction and exchange of knowledge

same. Assume now that $L(D_i)$ is a set of rules extracted from S_i, which means that $D = \bigcup_{i \in I} L(D_i)$ is a set of rules which can be used by *Chase* algorithm associated with any of the sites of DIS. Now, let us say that system S_k, $k \in I$ is queried be a user. *Chase* algorithm, to be applicable to S_k, has to be based on rules from D which satisfy the following conditions:

- attribute value used in the decision part of a rule from D has the granularity level either equal to or finer than the granularity level of the corresponding attribute in S_k.
- the granularity level of any attribute used in the classification part of a rule from D is either equal or softer than the granularity level of the corresponding attribute in S_k.
- attribute used in the decision part of a rule from D either does not belong to A_k or is incomplete in S_k.

These three conditions are called distributed *Chase* S_k-applicability conditions. Let $L_k(D)$ denotes the subset of rules in D satisfying these three *Chase* S_k-applicability conditions.

Assuming now that a match between the attribute value used in the description of the tuple t and the attribute value used in a description of a rule $s \to d \in L_k(D)$ is found, the following two cases should be considered:

- an attribute involved in matching is the decision attribute in $s \to d$. If two attribute values, involved in that match, have different granularity, then the decision value d has to be replaced by a softer value which granularity will match the granularity of the corresponding attribute in S_k.
- an attribute a involved in matching is the classification attribute in $s \to d$. If two attribute values, involved in that match, have different granularity, then the value of attribute a has to be replaced by a finer value which granularity will match the granularity of a in S_k.

The new set of rules, constructed from $L_k(D)$ following the above two steps, is called granularity-repaired set of rules. So, the assumption that $L_k(D)$ satisfies distributed Chase S_k-applicability conditions is sufficient to run *Chase* successfully on S_k using this new granularity-repaired set of rules.

In Figure 1, we present two consecutive states of a distributed information system consisting of S_1, S_2, S_3.

In the first state, all incomplete attributes in all three information systems have to be identified. System S_1 sends request q_{S_1} to the other two information systems asking them for definitions of its incomplete attributes. Similarly, system S_2 sends request q_{S_2} to the other two information systems asking them for definitions of its incomplete attributes. Finally, system S_3 sends request q_{S_3} to the other two information systems asking them also for definitions of its incomplete attributes. Next, rules describing the requested definitions are extracted from each of these three information systems and sent to the systems which requested them. So, the set $L(D_1)$ is sent to S_2 and S_3, the set $L(D_2)$ is sent to S_1 and S_3, and the set $L(D_3)$ is sent to S_1 and S_2.

The second state of a distributed information system, presented in Figure 1, shows all three information systems with the corresponding $L(D_i)$ sets, $i \in \{1, 2, 3\}$, all abbreviated as KB. Now, the *Chase* algorithm is run independently at each of our three sites. Resulting information systems are: $Chase(S_1)$, $Chase(S_2)$, and $Chase(S_3)$. Now, the whole process is recursively repeated. It means, all incomplete attributes in all three new information systems are identified again. Next, each of these three systems is sending requests to the other two systems asking for definitions of its incomplete attributes and when these definitions are received, they are stored in the corresponding KB sets. Now, *Chase* algorithm is run again at each of these three sites. The whole process is repeated till some fixed point is reached (all 3 systems have to become stable). When this step is accomplished, a query submitted to any S_i, $i \in \{1, 2, 3\}$, can be processed in a standard way.

We believe, that our query processing strategy for incomplete information systems guarantees the most accurate results because the incomplete values at all information systems have been replaced by new values representing the consensus of all sites. Our initial testing results for QAS based on distributed $Chase$ are quite promising.

References

1. Atzeni, P., DeAntonellis, V. (1992) Relational database theory, The Benjamin Cummings Publishing Company
2. Benjamins, V. R., Fensel, D., Pérez, A. G. (1998) Knowledge management through ontologies, in *Proceedings of the 2nd International Conference on Practical Aspects of Knowledge Management (PAKM-98)*, Basel, Switzerland.
3. Chandrasekaran, B., Josephson, J. R., Benjamins, V. R. (1998) The ontology of tasks and methods, in *Proceedings of the 11th Workshop on Knowledge Acquisition, Modeling and Management*, Banff, Alberta, Canada
4. Dardzińska, A., Raś, Z.W. (2003) Rule-Based Chase Algorithm for Partially Incomplete Information Systems, in **Proceedings of the Second International Workshop on Active Mining (AM'2003)**, Maebashi City, Japan, October, 2003, 42-51
5. Dardzińska, A., Raś, Z.W. (2003) On Rules Discovery from Incomplete Information Systems, in **Proceedings of ICDM'03 Workshop on Foundations and New Directions of Data Mining**, (Eds: T.Y. Lin, X. Hu, S. Ohsuga, C. Liau), Melbourne, Florida, IEEE Computer Society, 2003, 31-35
6. Dardzińska, A., Raś, Z.W. (2003) Chasing Unknown Values in Incomplete Information Systems, in **Proceedings of ICDM'03 Workshop on Foundations and New Directions of Data Mining**, (Eds: T.Y. Lin, X. Hu, S. Ohsuga, C. Liau), Melbourne, Florida, IEEE Computer Society, 2003, 24-30
7. Fensel, D., (1998), *Ontologies: a silver bullet for knowledge management and electronic commerce*, Springer-Verlag, 1998
8. Giudici, P. (2003) Applied Data Mining, Statistical Methods for Business and Industry, Wiley, West Sussex, England
9. Guarino, N., ed. (1998) Formal Ontology in Information Systems, IOS Press, Amsterdam
10. Guarino, N., Giaretta, P. (1995) Ontologies and knowledge bases, towards a terminological clarification, in *Towards Very Large Knowledge Bases: Knowledge Building and Knowledge Sharing*, IOS Press
11. Pawlak, Z. (1991) Rough sets-theoretical aspects of reasoning about data, Kluwer, Dordrecht
12. Pawlak, Z. (1991) Information systems - theoretical foundations, in **Information Systems Journal**, Vol. 6, 1981, 205-218
13. Raś, Z.W. (1994) Dictionaries in a distributed knowledge-based system, in **Concurrent Engineering: Research and Applications**, Conference Proceedings, Pittsburgh, Penn., Concurrent Technologies Corporation, pp. 383-390
14. Raś, Z.W., Dardzińska, A. (2004) Ontology Based Distributed Autonomous Knowledge Systems, in **Information Systems International Journal**, Elsevier, Vol. 29, No. 1, 2004, 47-58
15. Raś, Z.W., Joshi, S. Query approximate answering system for an incomplete DKBS, in **Fundamenta Informaticae Journal**, IOS Press, Vol. 30, No. 3/4, 1997, 313-324

16. Sowa, J.F. (2000a) Ontology, metadata, and semiotics, in B. Ganter & G. W. Mineau, eds., *Conceptual Structures: Logical, Linguistic, and Computational Issues*, LNAI, No. 1867, Springer-Verlag, Berlin, 2000, pp. 55-81

17. Sowa, J.F. (2000b) Knowledge Representation: Logical, Philosophical, and Computational Foundations, Brooks/Cole Publishing Co., Pacific Grove, CA.

18. Sowa, J.F. (1999a) Ontological categories, in L. Albertazzi, ed., *Shapes of Forms: From Gestalt Psychology and Phenomenology to Ontology and Mathematics*, Kluwer Academic Publishers, Dordrecht, 1999, pp. 307-340.

19. Van Heijst, G., Schreiber, A., Wielinga, B. (1997) Using explicit ontologies in KBS development, in *International Journal of Human and Computer Studies*, Vol. 46, No. 2/3, 183-292.

Construction of Query Concepts in a Document Space Based on Data Mining Techniques

Youjin Chang[1], Minkoo Kim[2], and Iadh Ounis[3]

[1] Graduate School of Information & Communication, Ajou University,
San 5 Wonchon-dong Paldal-gu Suwon, Republic of Korea
xaritas@ajou.ac.kr
[2] Department of Computer Engineering, Ajou University,
San 5 Wonchon-dong Paldal-gu Suwon, Republic of Korea
minkoo@ajou.ac.kr
[3] Department of Computing Science, University of Glasgow,
Glasgow, G12 8QQ, UK
ounis@dcs.gla.ac.uk

Abstract. We discuss the issue of reformulating the user's initial query to improve the retrieval performance. We propose to refine the query by adding a set of *query concepts* that are meant to precisely denote the user's information need. To extract the most probable *query concepts*, we first extract a set of features from each document using summarization, and classify the extracted features into a set of predefined categories from Yahoo!. Finally, we cluster these features into primitive (basic) concepts. For a new query, we select its most associated primitive concepts and generate all possible interpretations of the query. The most probable interpretations are chosen as *query concepts* and are added to the initial query during the reformulation process. Our experiments are performed on the TREC 8 collection. The experimental evaluation shows that our query concept approach is as good as current query reformulation approaches, while being particularly effective for poorly performing queries. We also show that various data mining techniques could be helpful to generate the primitive concepts more effectively.

1 Introduction

The information explosion has made it difficult for common users to easily find their information needs. Information Retrieval (IR) systems intend to relieve the users from these difficulties by retrieving relevant documents, while filtering out the non-relevant documents. Many existing retrieval systems adopt a keyword-based retrieval approach, as this approach makes easy the expression of queries, while allowing for a fast retrieval procedure to take place. However, this method has a disadvantage for searching relevant documents. Indeed, since it filters every document which has the same words as the initial queries, the results are sometimes too many or too few. Moreover, most people are not good at making effective queries right away, leading to ill-defined initial queries which cause a poor retrieval performance.

H. Christiansen et al. (Eds.): FQAS 2004, LNAI 3055, pp. 137–149, 2004.
© Springer-Verlag Berlin Heidelberg 2004

To solve these problems, many researchers have tried to find some appropriate solutions for representing user's interest correctly [2, 3, 10, 14]. One of these solutions is query reformulation, which consists in query terms reweighting and/or expansion. In query terms expansion, they have used the user's relevance judgment or a well-defined knowledge base, such as a thesaurus to add relevant terms to the initial query. While relevance feedback is most effective when relevance information about retrieved documents is provided by users, this information is not always available. On the other hand, the concept-based retrieval approach takes into account the domain knowledge to determine an appropriate interpretation of the initial query. However, it does not work well in general as the relationship captured in a thesaurus is not always valid in the context of a given user query. Nevertheless, the concept-based retrieval can be remarkable in that it starts from the considerable interest in bridging the gap between the terminology used in defining initial queries and the terminology in representing documents. It treats those query words not as literal strings of letters, but as concepts [14]. Therefore, the concept-based retrieval approach could retrieve relevant documents even if they do not necessarily contain the specific words used in the initial query.

In our approach, we define a set of appropriate terms that denote the user's information needs adequately as *query concepts*. These *query concepts* are constructed by pre-processing the concepts which are directly extracted from a document space. Since it is impossible to make an optimal thesaurus for every field of study, we try to construct the domain knowledge, called the *primitive (basic) concepts,* not from a thesaurus but from a document collection which is considered to be not only the subject of retrieval, but also a domain which includes latent semantics (meaning) at the same time. Therefore, our research focuses on two issues; how to construct primitive concepts from a document space nicely and how to properly form *query concepts* from these primitive concepts.

In Section 2, we describe some methods which construct primitive concepts from a document space. In Section 3, we discuss how to construct *query concepts* by combining primitive concepts. The experiments and results are presented in Section 4. In the experimental tests, we evaluate our query concept method with previous approaches such as Rocchio's relevance feedback. TREC 8 collection is used in order to compare the results. The results show that our proposed method is very promising, especially for poorly performing queries.

2   Extracting Primitive Concepts from a Document Space

We suppose that there are primitive concepts, also called *basic concepts,* which are able to represent the salient and important meaning of a document and document collection. These primitive concepts could be used as the domain knowledge in the retrieval process. We use the vector space model to represent documents, queries, and concepts. We define these concepts as a set of terms that are different from a set of synonyms in a thesaurus. Attributes of primitive concepts should be orthogonal to each other in a document, and simultaneously, be distinct and prominent in a document space. It is important that the primitive concepts are orthogonal. Indeed, generally, a document and an initial query contain multiple meanings. We could break the initial query and/or the document into several singular meanings, for representing their associated content. This idea, which divides an object into several atomic units, is related to the classical vector decomposition, which assumes that the dimensions of a vector are independent. For instance, in the vector representation, we could decompose a vector to several unit-vectors. Mathematically, each unit vectors has different direction, i.e. they are orthogonal to each other. In the same manner, if primitive concepts have orthogonal attributes, we can represent the main topics of a document and/or a query by combining these primitive concepts, adequately.

The problem is how to construct primitive concepts which have orthogonal and distinctive properties. If we assume that the document collection is a large observational dataset, which has latent meanings, then we can find those concepts through global modeling and local pattern discovery. Mannila [13] stated that data mining is the analysis of observational data sets to find unsuspected relationships and to summarize the data in novel ways that are both understandable and useful to the data analyst. Following this idea, in order to extract the primitive concepts, we propose to identify the distinctive features of each document by using a two-layer analysis. First we summarize each document and extract its significant features (i.e. local analysis), then we cluster the resulting features of the whole document collection (i.e. global analysis). From now on, we look into each of these two layers in generating the primitive concepts.

2.1 Local Analysis: Extracting Feature Vectors from a Given Document by Summarization

First, we aim to extract features (in the form of a vector) that are distinctive to each document. We propose to extract salient contents by selecting the significant sentences in a document. For this purpose, we adopt simple and well-known summarizing techniques [11,16] to extract the feature vectors from each document. The earlier research of Lam-Adesina and Jones [11] mentioned that summary generation methods seek to identify document contents that convey the most "important" information within a document. Thus, following Lam-Adesina and Jones's approach, we select the significant sentences of each document using Luhn's keyword cluster method [12], the title term frequency method [11], the location method suggested by Edmundson [7], and the ratio of significant terms in a sentence.

However, summarization is not enough to generate the orthogonal features of a document. Indeed, we need to merge the selected sentences that have overlapping terms among them. Therefore, we partition the significant sentences into several orthogonal feature vectors that do not share common terms. For example, assume that we represent a sentence as a vector of terms with their associated TF/IDF weight values in the document. Thus, for each document, we can consider a set of vectors $S = \{s_1, s_2, ..., s_{ms}\}$, where ms, i.e. *measure of significance* [11], is the number of selected significant sentences for a given document (e.g. see Figure 1). In this case, *ms* is 4. To build the feature vectors of the illustrated document d_1, we partition S as follows. First, s_1 is assigned to feature f_1. Since s_2 has a common term 'computer' with s_1, s_2 is also assigned to f_1. On the other hand, s_3 is assigned to the new feature f_2 in that it has no overlapping terms with the first two sentences. The sentence s_4 is merged into f_1 because of the shared term 'information'. As a result, this process makes two feature vectors which are orthogonal to each other.

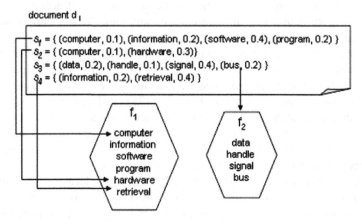

Fig. 1. The procedure of partitioning significant sentences into feature vectors

This idea of partitioning is devised by constructing maximally connected components in graph representation [5]. Each vector s_i is a subgraph, such that the vertices of the subgraph are the terms of the vector and the edges connect the terms which are in the same sentence s_i. After the partitioning process, each feature vector f_i will be seen as a maximally connected component as described in Figure 2.

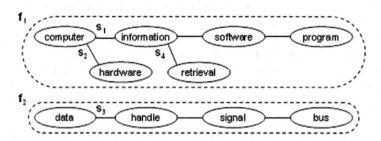

Fig. 2. The partitioned sentences represented by maximally connected components

In Figure 1 and 2, it is easy to see that f_1 and f_2 are orthogonal, in other words, there is no overlapping term between these two feature vectors. In our previous research [4], we used all terms in sentences to extract the feature vectors from a given document (We label this approach as *Approach 1* in our experiments). However, we observed that some insignificant words that occur very often as connectors between sentences in the TREC 8 collection, lead to a situation where all sentences of a given document are merged to one. To remove unnecessary unification, we took only the significant terms, which have their TF/IDF weight value above a threshold θ fixed empirically to 0.3 in our experiments. Only those terms are considered in the feature vector (We label this approach as *Approach 2*). This refinement could lead to a loss of information depending on the value of the used threshold. Indeed, if some sentences are selected as significant sentences by the used summarization scoring method [11], but they have no term with a weight value above the threshold, then these sentences are removed. As a result, we built 665,981 feature vectors using the *Approach 1* case and only 571,672 feature vectors using the *Approach 2* case.

2.2   Global Analysis: Clustering the Feature Vectors into Primitive Concepts

The summarization approach allows us to find local patterns in a given document. While the extracted feature vectors in a given document have orthogonal attributes, we cannot guarantee that they are orthogonal with the feature vectors in other documents. For example, consider the *Relation A* and the *Relation B* in Figure 3. The *Relation A*, defined on the same document d_1, is definitely orthogonal following our approach in Section 2.1. However, the *Relation B* could reference the same feature. In other words, feature f_1 and feature f_4 in Figure 3 could be similar, including common terms. Indeed, summarization methods discover only local patterns in the document space. To alleviate this problem, we adopt a clustering method, which is generally used for descriptive modeling [13], to generate primitive concepts that are approximately orthogonal.

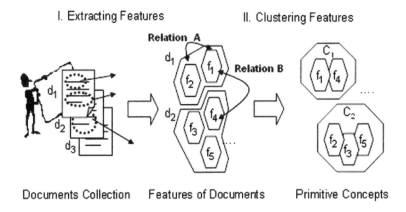

Fig. 3. The procedure of constructing primitive concepts

Many effective and efficient clustering algorithms could be used to implement this task. In order to cluster feature vectors into primitive concepts, we could apply existing clustering methods such a K-means [1]. However, since our feature vectors are extremely sparse, we preferred to device a clustering algorithm that better suits our objective. This algorithm is similar to the single pass and reallocation method used in early work in cluster analysis [9]. Therefore, we divided the clustering procedure into two steps: (1) Clustering feature vectors to concept vectors using single pass method, (2) Reallocate the concept vectors.

In the first step of clustering, if more than $u\%$ (e.g. 80%) of terms in a feature vector f_i are contained in the centroid vector of a cluster C_j, we put f_i into C_j and recompute the centroid vector of C_j such that $C_j = (C_j + f_i) / 2$. If between $u\%$ (e.g. 80%) and $v\%$ (e.g. 20%) of terms in f_i are contained in C_j, then we ignore f_i. If less than $v\%$ of terms in f_i are contained in C_j, we keep trying to put f_i into other clusters. If f_i is not assigned to any cluster, we create a new cluster that contains f_i. Therefore, we adopt the algorithm given below. The complexity of the proposed algorithm is $O(N^2)$. After the first step, we get m clusters called primitive concept vectors. In the reallocation step, we re-compare the features to the generated centroid vectors and reassign these features to the concept vectors accordingly. Parameters u and v were set experimentally to 80 % and 20% respectively.

```
Algorithm

Let f1, ..., fN be feature vectors,
m the number of generated clusters,
and u and v are controlled parameters.

m = 1;
Cm = f1;
for i = 2 to N
{
    done = FALSE;
    j = 1;
    while(j <= m and not done) {

        if fi is more than u% overlapped with Cj then {
            Cj  = (Cj + fi) / 2;
            done = TRUE;        /* assign fi to Cj */
        }
        else if fi is more than v% overlapped with Cj then
            done = TRUE;        /*  ignore fi */
        else
            j = j + 1;
    }

        if (not done) then {
            m = m + 1;
            Cm  = fi;                /* Create a new cluster */
        }
}
```

2.3   Reinforcement of the Global Analysis by Classification

We propose to refine the generated primitive concepts by adopting a classification method before the application of the clustering process. The classification method is usually used for learning a function that maps an item into one of several predefined classes [13]. We propose to apply the classification method prior to the clustering process in order to discriminate the ambiguity of an individual word or phrase which could be used (in different contexts) to express two or more different meanings (*polysemy*). Polysemy causes a problem in the clustering procedure. Terms having two or more different meanings are called 'ambiguous terms'. For example, assume that the document d_2 is about transportation and the feature vector f_3 in d_2 is represented by $f_3 = \{(car, 0.4), (bus, 0.4), (handle, 0.2), (signal, 0.3)\}$. Comparing the feature vector f_3 with the feature vector f_2 of document d_1 in Figure 1, we can notice that those features look similar to each other, but f_1 and f_2 represent different meanings. While 'handle', 'signal', and 'bus' in f_2 represent a process of computer hardware, those terms in f_3 mean an operation of transportation. Generally, one solution to discriminate a *polysemy* is to consider the other words surrounding the *polysemy* (e.g. 'data' in f_2 vs. 'car' in f_3).

Instead of training our classification procedure on TREC 8, we used a predefined classifier. Indeed, we have chosen to classify the feature vectors into the 12 categories of the Yahoo![1] website (art, business & economy, computers, education, entertainment, government, health, recreation, reference, science, social science, and advice). Therefore, we used the 12 directory pages of Yahoo as classifiers. We calculated the cosine similarity between all the feature vectors and the classifiers. Then, we assigned the feature vectors to the most similar class. If one feature vector was not assigned to any class, this feature vector will be allocated to a special class named 'Etc.'. As a result, we classified the feature vectors into 13 classes (See Table 1).

Table 1. The number of classified feature vectors according to Yahoo category

Category	Approach 1	Approach 2
Art	28085	12333
Business & Economy	53427	12380
Computers	80032	19386
Education	48122	13499
Entertainment	26165	6130
Government	56460	13988
Health	29161	5059
Recreation	43636	17722
Reference	50986	14101
Science	23194	9178
Social science	13367	3629
Advice	29639	8763
Etc.	183707	435504
Total	665981	571672

[1] http://www.yahoo.com

Once the features are classified, we apply the clustering process defined in Section 2.2. on each resulting category (or class). The clustering of each category will generate a set of primitive concepts. We consider two different options. The first option consists in merging the primitive concepts resulting from all classes excepting the 'Etc.' class (*Classification 1*). This is done in order to obtain a more robust set of primitive concepts. On the other hand, as a second option, we merge the primitive concepts of all resulting classes including the 'Etc' class (*Classification 2*). Table 2 lists the resulting number of primitive concepts.

Table 2. The number of primitive concepts from all cases

Concept	Process for Generating Primitive Concepts	The number of Primitive Concepts
PC1	Approach 1 / No Classification	7532
PC2	Approach 2 / No Classification	16253
PC3	Approach 1 / Classification 1	2781
PC4	Approach 2 / Classification 1	2707
PC5	Approach 1/ Classification 2	13077
PC6	Approach 2 / Classification 2	16460

3 Information Retrieval Using *Query Concepts*

For a new query, we select its most associated primitive concepts with the initial query and generate all possible interpretations of the query. The most probable interpretations are chosen as *query concepts* and are added to the initial query during the reformulation process. The primitive concepts, which are seen to be surrogates of the domain knowledge, are extracted as discussed in Section 2.

We propose to reformulate the ill-defined initial queries that have multiple meanings by using the following methodology:

(1) Select first top N primitive concepts (usually between 5 concepts and 10 concepts) that are similar to the initial query q_0, using cosine similarity.
(2) Generate all possible combination of primitive concepts under a DNF (Disjunctive Normal Forms) form. These are called candidates *query concepts.*
(3) Choose the DNF that is most similar to the initial query q_0 using the cosine measure. The chosen DNF is called QC_{best}
(4) Choose k terms (usually between 5 terms and 10 terms) from the selected $QC_{best}.$
(5) Construct the enhanced query $q' = \alpha q_0 + \beta QC_{best}$, where $0 \leq \alpha \leq 1$ and $\beta = 1 - \alpha$. α and β are called weighting constants.

We use MAX operation for the OR connective in the DNFs that are generated in step (2) above. For example, let the selected primitive concepts be $C_1, C_2, ..., C_{10}$ (when $N = 10$) and the initial query q_0. We can generate all possible DNFs as follows:

$C_1, C_2, ..., C_{10} (single)$,
$C_1 \vee C_2, C_1 \vee C_3, ..., C_9 \vee C_{10} (pair)$
$C_1 \vee C_2 \vee C_3, C_1 \vee C_2 \vee C_4, ..., C_8 \vee C_9 \vee C_{10} (triple)$

From all possible DNFs, we select the one that is most similar to q_0 as the best query concept. Suppose that $C_1 \vee C_3$ is the DNF that is most similar to the initial query q_0. Then $C_1 \vee C_3$ becomes the QC_{best}. Among the terms in the $QC_{best} = C_1 \vee C_3$, we choose k high-frequency terms (usually between 5 terms to 10 terms) for constructing the enhanced query q'. Then, we added these selected high-frequency terms to the initial query. Finally, we construct the enhanced query $q' = \alpha q_0 + \beta QC_{best}$ [4]. Figure 4 shows this process graphically.

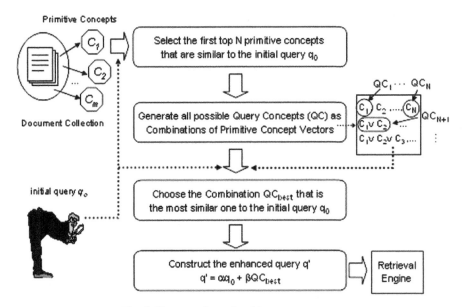

Fig. 4. The procedure of making *query concepts*

4 Experiments

For the evaluation procedure, we used the TREC 8 ad hoc dataset. It contains about 521,251 documents distributed on two CD-ROM disks (TREC disks 4 and 5) taken from the following sources: Federal Register (FR), Financial Times (FT), Foreign Broadcast Information Service (FBIS), and LA Times (LAT). 50 topics (topic 401-450) were chosen to evaluate the performance of the IR system. Each topic consists of three parts: title, description and narrative. It is said that the different parts of the TREC topic allow investigation of the effect of different query lengths on retrieval performance [11]. The user's initial query is usually incomplete. Thus, we only used the title field of the topics.

Now, we describe our experimental results in a series of comparisons as follows. First of all, we built a Baseline using the vector space model without relevance feedback. Then, we performed the Rocchio's relevance feedback method (RRF) [15]. In RRF, we assume that the top three retrieved documents are relevant to the initial query. Then, we selected twenty terms from those documents as relevant (expanded) terms. Secondly, we conducted experiments using our proposed Query Concept Method (QCM) and applied RRF on top of QCM (RRF-QCM). The QCM is to expand initial query with *query concepts* generated by the process described in Section 3. As shown in Table 2, we have used 6 approaches of primitive concepts, PCi (i=1 to i=6). We have built an enhanced query with these 6 primitive concepts approaches, reweighting and/or expanding terms in the query. We have experimented thoroughly with the 6 proposed QCM approaches, and PC3, which consists in classifying and merging the twelve classes, was the most efficient and effective approach. Therefore, due to space limitation, in this paper, we only include the results obtained using PC3 (See Table 3). Our weighting constants for the enhanced query q' were set experimentally to $\alpha=0.8$ and $\beta=0.2$.

Table 3. Retrieval Performance of Baseline, RRF and QCM variations. All QCM variations are based on PC3. C-QCM is the combined strategy which applies the QCM method to the poorly performing queries and only the Baseline for the remaing queries

Recall-Precision	BASELINE	RRF	QCM	RRF-QCM	C-QCM
at 0.00	0.532	0.406	0.526	0.450	0.552
at 0.10	0.275	0.272	0.274	0.270	0.293
at 0.20	0.237	0.213	0.235	0.222	0.248
at 0.30	0.198	0.179	0.199	0.184	0.209
at 0.40	0.175	0.143	0.175	0.153	0.181
at 0.50	0.118	0.102	0.116	0.107	0.126
at 0.60	0.079	0.068	0.073	0.071	0.080
at 0.70	0.049	0.034	0.043	0.042	0.049
at 0.80	0.040	0.015	0.032	0.022	0.040
at 0.90	0.024	0.013	0.023	0.012	0.024
at 1.00	0.006	0.012	0.007	0.007	0.006
Ave Precision	0.138	0.118	0.135	0.123	0.143
5 docs:	0.320	0.256	0.316	0.244	0.340
10 docs:	0.280	0.240	0.272	0.232	0.288
15 docs:	0.256	0.217	0.256	0.223	0.279
20 docs:	0.226	0.198	0.229	0.214	0.245
30 docs:	0.208	0.181	0.209	0.197	0.221
R-Precision	0.193	0.163	0.189	0.175	0.202

On the other hand, we split the 50 topics into two groups: the group of good queries and the group of poor queries. The split is based on the average precision achieved by our baseline. If the average precision is above 0.1, we consider the query to be good. On the other hand, thirty-four queries with an average precision under 0.1 were considered to be poor. The idea is that good queries do not need to be enhanced by the *query concepts*. Therefore, we have adopted a combined strategy, where the QCM approach is applied only for poor queries (C-QCM in above Table 3). Good queries will be run with the Baseline only. Table 3 shows that our C-QCM combined method overcomes the baseline (0.143 vs. 0138). Note that the RRF methods are worse than the Baseline. If only the 34 poorly performing queries are used, we find that our approach performed better than the baseline. Table 4 shows that our methods perform consistently well and the average precision of the QCM methods is better than the RRF approach.

Finally, generally, query reformulation consists of term reweighting and/or term expansion. We reweight the terms of the initial query if the selected primitive concepts has the same terms as in the initial query. The weighting value is decided by the weighting constants described in step (5) of Section 3. The query term reweighting with query term expansion showed better results than query term reweighting only (See Table 4). In addition, the *Approach 2* case was not good for defining *primitive concepts*. This is perhaps due to the loss of information. Therefore, we only list in Table 4 those PCi corresponding to *Approach 1*.

Table 4. Retrieval Performance of Baseline, RRF and QCM variations for the 34 poorly performing queries. QTR means query term reweighting and QTE means both query term reweighting and query expansion

Recall-Precision	Baseline	RRF	QTR			QTE		
			PC1	PC3	PC5	PC1	PC3	PC5
at 0.00	0.373	0.276	0.395	0.364	0.358	0.385	0.366	0.422
at 0.10	0.101	0.137	0.100	0.099	0.091	0.124	0.118	0.113
at 0.20	0.061	0.083	0.057	0.058	0.054	0.072	0.068	0.072
at 0.30	0.039	0.065	0.039	0.040	0.035	0.050	0.051	0.047
at 0.40	0.031	0.054	0.029	0.029	0.027	0.033	0.034	0.031
at 0.50	0.012	0.028	0.012	0.012	0.011	0.022	0.015	0.014
at 0.60	0.009	0.021	0.009	0.009	0.005	0.011	0.012	0.012
at 0.70	0.000	0.013	0.000	0.000	0.000	0.000	0.005	0.004
at 0.80	0.000	0.010	0.000	0.000	0.000	0.000	0.000	0.000
at 0.90	0.000	0.009	0.000	0.000	0.000	0.000	0.000	0.000
at 1.00	0.000	0.009	0.000	0.000	0.000	0.000	0.000	0.000
Ave-Precision	0.039	0.053	0.038	0.038	0.035	0.044	0.041	0.043
5 docs:	0.159	0.147	0.159	0.153	0.152	0.181	0.127	0.188
10 docs:	0.132	0.141	0.135	0.124	0.124	0.141	0.133	0.165
15 docs:	0.112	0.128	0.118	0.112	0.109	0.140	0.119	0.145
20 docs:	0.103	0.118	0.106	0.103	0.097	0.128	0.111	0.125
30 docs:	0.099	0.111	0.099	0.099	0.095	0.116	0.112	0.116
R-Precision	0.085	0.089	0.087	0.085	0.080	0.096	0.096	0.097

5 Conclusion

We proposed a new framework for automatically enhancing initial queries using *query concepts*. The *query concepts* are meant to denote the users' information needs. The *query concepts* are based on the extraction of features from a document space and classifying/clustering these features into primitive concepts. While our query enhancing approach is particularly efficient when applied to the poorly performing queries, it still achieves results that are as good as the classical reformulation approaches for all queries. The best improvement over the baseline is achieved when the queries are classified according to their performance. However, to be practical, this optimal setting requires the prediction of the quality of the initial query [6], which is still an open research question as asserted by the new TREC2003 Robust track[2]. Another interesting future direction would be the effective construction of *query concepts* not from document collection but from the retrieved documents. Indeed, as the size of the document collection increases, the generation of primitive concepts becomes more time-consuming. Hence, we are considering other methods not only for constructing primitive concepts from a document space, but also for generating probable *query concepts*.

Acknowledgement

This work was partially supported by National Research Laboratory on Korea Institute of Science and Technology Evaluation and Planning (KISTEP) (M10302000087-03J0000-04400) and by the Brain Korea 21 Project in 2003.

References

1. Baeza-Yates, R., Ribeiro-Neto, B.: Modern information retrieval. Addison Wesley (1999) 117-134
2. Bookman, L., Woods, W.: Linguistic Knowledge Can Improve Information Retrieval. Proceedings of ANLP-2000, Seattle, WA, May 1-3 (2000) 1-9
3. Chang, C., Hsu, C.: Integrating query expansion and conceptual relevance feedback for personalized web information retrieval. Computer Networks and ISDN Systems, 30(1-7) (1998) 621-623
4. Chang, Y., Choi, I., Choi, J., Kim, K., Raghavan, V.V.: Conceptual Retrieval Based on Feature Clustering of Documents, Workshop on Mathematical/Formal Methods in Information Retrieval at the 25th Annual International ACM SIGIR Conference on Research and Development in IR, in Tampere, Finland, August 15 (2002) 89-104
5. Cormen, T. H., Leiserson, C. E., Rivest, R. L., Stein, C.: Introduction to algorithm. Second Edition. The MIT Press (2001) 498-501
6. Cronen-Townsend, S., Zhou, Y., Croft, B. W.: Predicting query performance, Proceedings of the 25th annual international ACM SIGIR Conference on Research and Development in IR, in Tampere, Finland, August 15 (2002) 299-306
7. Edmundson, H. P.: New Methods in Automatic Abstracting. Journal of the ACM, 16(2) (1969) 264-285
8. Fellbaum, C.: WordNet: An Electronic Lexical Database. The MIT Press (1998)
9. Frakes, W. B., Baeza-Yates, R.: Information Retrieval: Data Structures and Algorithms. Prentice Hall, Englewood Cli#s, NJ (1992)

---

[2] http://trec.nist.gov

10. Kim, M., Lu, F., Raghavan, V. V.: Automatic Construction of Rule-based Trees for Conceptual Retrieval. In Proceedings of SPIRE2000, A Coruna, Spain, IEEE Computer Society Press (2000) 153-161
11. Lam-Adesina A. M, Jones, F.J.G.: Applying summarization techniques for term selection in relevance feedback. In Proceedings of the 24th Annual International ACM SIGIR Confer-ence, ACM press (2001) 1-9
12. Luhn, H. P.: The automatic creation of literature abstracts. IBM journal of research & development, 2 (2), April. (1958) 159-165
13. Mannila, H.: Global and local methods in data mining: basic techniques and open problems. ICALP 2002, 29th International Colloquium on Automata, Languages, and Programming, (c) Springer-Verlag, Malaga, Spain, July (2002) 57-68
14. Qiu, Y., Frei, H.P.: Concept based query expansion. In Proceedings of the 16th annual international ACM SIGIR conference on Research and Development in Information Retrieval, ACM Press (1993) 160-170
15. Rocchio, J. J.: Relevance feedback in information retrieval in the SMART system. Prentice Hall (1971) 313-323
16. Tombros, A., Sanderson, M.: Advantages of Query Biased Summaries in Information Retrieval. In Proceedings of the 21st ACM SIGIR (1998) 2-10
17. TREC Web Corpus: WT10g, http://www.ted.cmis.csiro.au/TRECWeb/wt10g.html (visited March 18th, 2004)

Towards Formal Ontologies Requirements with Multiple Perspectives

Ahmed Arara and Djamal Benslimane

LIRIS, Université Lyon 1, 69622 Villeurbanne, France
{ahmed.arara,djamal.benslimane}@iuta.univ-lyon1.fr

Abstract. Ontology is very promising in constructing a conceptual data model that can be very close to reality. Ontologies, as an explicit specification of conceptualization, play an essential role in information exchange and integration. Due to the facts that different perceptions, views, and abstractions, we end up having several representations of the same real world entity. The multi-representation problem is commonly known in the discipline of spatial databases and object-oriented modeling and different solutions have been proposed. Multi-representation ontologies are expected to become crucial due to the increasingly demand of multi-represented concept shareability among different applications and user communities in the same domain of interest. In this paper, we consider the notion of context as an abstraction mechanism to deal with multi-representation ontologies (contextual ontologies). A formal representation language based on modal description logics is proposed to comply with the requirements of multiple perspectives of domain ontology.The proposed representational language will provide constructs that deal with the multi-perspectives needs, and consequently queries can be formulated to deal with the multi-represented entities.

1 Introduction

Large ontologies are becoming an essential component of many domains and areas of interests such as the Web, e-commerce, medical applications, and government agencies. Many standardized ontologies have emerged such as UMLS [10] in medicine, and UN/SPSC [1] in goods and services. Large ontologies are found in enormous applications to support content-based search and navigation techniques. Furthermore, ontologies are being used more to support querying and reasoning tasks in areas such as databases, configuration and intelligence tasks.

Ontologies are exploded and became so large that it is not so easy for users in the same domain with different interests to allocate some concepts that are relevant to their needs. Each ontology user has his/her own need and expectation from existing large ontology. Using user profiles to query large ontologies will provide a view of the ontology that corresponds to each user profile. Some research has been dedicated to the information filtering based on user profiles [3, 7].

H. Christiansen et al. (Eds.): FQAS 2004, LNAI 3055, pp. 150–160, 2004.

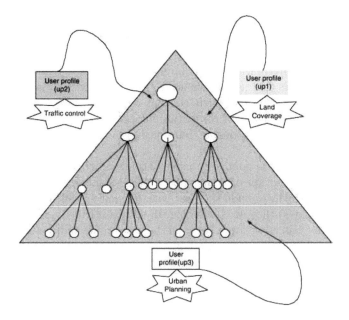

Fig. 1. Example of accessing large ontologies based on user profiles

For a given large ontology (LO) and a set of user profiles (UP), the following can be stated (see figure 1):

- Not all concepts in LO are relevant for a particular user profile (up). This is to say that some concepts should be hidden, and cannot be part of this particular profile. For example, a concept "ROAD" will be irrelevant to a user with profile (up_1) interested in land coverage. To such user, the information of green areas and built-up areas is rather sufficient. Another user with traffic control profile (up_2) will be interested in the concept "RoadSign". A third user with profile (up_3) has an interest in computing the built-up areas for a specific region and has no interest in the sub-concept that may belong to concepts: "Roads", "Building" and "ParkingLots". The concepts "Land-Cover", "Built-upArea", "GreenArea" , "Road", "Building", "parkingLots", "RoadSign", and others form part of large ontologies.
- Not all attributes and relations among concepts are relevant to all user profiles $(up_1, \cdots, up_n)$. For example, up_2 will be interested in attributes such as number of lanes but not road thickness or type of asphalt used in building the road. Also, relations among concepts may be significant for some user profiles and irrelevant for others. For example, sub-concepts such as "Roas-Sign" and "TrafficLaw" are important for user profile up_2 and not for up_1. Making some attributes and relations invisible is considered by manipulating user profiles to provide the end user with what he just needs.

Large ontologies are so difficult to be manipulated and queried by users. Ontology users, however, are interested only in small set of concepts or sub-

ontologies from that huge ontology. A user of specific profile browses the large
ontology in order for him to retrieve only concepts that are relevant to his interests and/or applications. The problem with this is that the user needs to know
more of contextual information about large ontologies that guides him/her to
filter out only concepts that satisfy his need. In fact, all existing large ontologies
are context-free with respect to their concept representations. In other words,
there is no explicit description of contextual information that may guide user to
efficiently retrieve the set of concepts, relationships, and attributes that fulfil his
exact need.

Our idea is to propose contextualizing ontological concepts and attributes
by incorporating the notion of context to the large ontology contents. Hence,
contextual ontology will provide the user with explicit specification of concepts
and to what context(s) they are belonging. In this case, when querying context-
dependent ontology an association between the user profile and the contextual information supplemented by contextual ontology is performed, and consequently
this association will allow the retrieval of only concepts that have contextual
match to the user profile.

The main characteristics of the proposed contextual ontology are:

- Information visibility. Information should be seen from one context or a set
  of contexts. To satisfy this need, context manipulation and context operations should provide information filtering by suppressing or augmenting
  information due to contextual operations such as negation, disjunction, and
  conjunction of contexts.
- Information zooming. To attain this feature, the notion of granularity or
  levels of information detail should enable the user to zoom in or zoom out
  by going from coarse-grain level to fine-grain one and vice versa.
- Navigation features are essentially important to view the structure of any
  concept and its relationships with other concepts. In contextual ontologies,
  it should be noted that a concept is allowed to occur in different nodes of
  taxonomies depending on the context to which it refers.

Our objective is to focus on how a context-dependent ontology can be formally represented and queried based on contextual information conveyed by
various user profiles. Description logics have become de facto of formalizing ontology. Modal description logics (MDLs) is found to be expressive and suitable
to the need of contextual ontology. MDLs are description logics augmented by
modal operators namely: (i) the necessity operator to express that a concept
holds in all worlds that are accessible from the world where it exists, and (ii) the
possibility operator to express a concept holds in some worlds accessible from
the world where it exist. In this paper, we intend to present a formalism based on
modal description logics that uses the notion of context to multi-represent information elements in domain ontology. Context-based description logic language
is proposed to meet the requirement specifications of the proposed contextual
ontologies. The following Section gives an overview of modal description logics.
Section 3 presents the syntax and semantics of the proposed contextual language and presents some very simple examples. Section 4 briefly surveys some

other works that are relevant to the issue of multiple viewpoints or perspectives. Finally, section 5 concludes the paper.

2   Modal Description Logics

2.1   Generality

Modal logics are a formalism used to express dynamic aspects of knowledge such as beliefs, judgments, intuitions, obligations, time, actions, etc. In modal logic, the semantics of expressions or formula is defined in terms of the truth of things in different worlds or contexts. This contrasts with classical description logic, where things are just true or false, and not true in one context and false in another. Modal logics distinguish modes of truth. For the generalized modal logic, modes of truth are explained by referring to (abstract) worlds namely: truth in all (accessible) worlds, truth in this world, and truth in some (accessible) world. The diversified modal logic systems with several modal operators make them very appealing to deal with all sorts of relational structures among worlds. For example, in classical DLs a faithful wife is the one who loves here husband we express as:

$$\textbf{faithfulWife} = \textbf{wife} \sqcap \exists \textbf{loves.husband} \tag{1}$$

If we would like to emphasize the fact that a faithful wife always loves her husband, we need to express the same concept as:

$$\textbf{faithfulWife} = \textbf{wife} \sqcap \exists [\textbf{always}] \textbf{loves.husband} \tag{2}$$

Note that we augmented [**always**] as a temporal operator to emphasize that being faithful wife is to always love her husband. Temporal description logic has been investigated by [5] and it has been applied to several applications where time (viewed as context) is crucial.

Another example in standard description logic, we may define a concept "Goodcomputer" to be a computer with large screen as:

$$\textbf{Goodcomputer} = \textbf{computer} \sqcap \textbf{part.largescreen(1)} \tag{3}$$

But if we need to represent the knowledge that only the secretary believes that a good computer is the one with large screen but her boss has a totally different view of a good computer. Hence, we express formula (3) above as:

$$[\textbf{Secretary} - \textbf{believes}](\textbf{3}) \sqcap \neg[\textbf{boss} - \textbf{believes}](\textbf{3}) \tag{4}$$

Modalities in modal logics can take different forms. The first example illustrates the use of the temporal operator "[**always**]" the second example uses modality to express belief "[**Secretary Believes**]" and "[**boss believes**]". In this last example, two different views are expressed of the same concept but viewed by two different people. The simple examples are meant only to whisper that many modalities can be explored to represent requirements of many application disciplines, that are becoming more and more complex and they may call out for more expressive description logics languages. The strategy is that logics are tailored to the application problem by augmenting new logical constructs to deal with new demands of language expressivity. The expressiveness of DLs languages, however, is a tradeoff between expressive power and computational tractability. This tradeoff issue has been the ultimate concerns in logics by the research community. The $ALCN_M$ family of DL language is the basic representation language for the non-contextual information. It is a combination of clasical DLs and modal logics. A brief discussion of the syntax and semantics is given in the subsection below.

2.2 $ALCN_M$ Language-Syntax and Semantics

The basic elements of a concept language are concepts, roles and objects. A concept is a class that is used to describe a set of objects with common properties. Roles are used to describe binary relationships between objects. The syntax of modal ALCN is defined in definition 1. The syntax consists of the classical ALCN constructs and the modal operators ($\Box_i C, \Diamond_i C$) known as necessity and possiblity operator respectively). According to the syntax rules of definition 1, modal ALCN concepts (C and D) are constructed from primitive concept (A), roles (R), and from modal operators ($\Box_i C, \Diamond_i C$) defined in the last two lines of definition 1. The formal semantics of modal ALCN language are interpreted by: (i) the conventional Tarski model, where an interpretation is a pair $(\triangle^I, .^I)$, such that the set ($\triangle^I$ is the interpretation domain and $.^I$ is the interpretaion function that maps every concept to a subset of ($\triangle^I$) and every role to a subset of ($\triangle^I$ x $\triangle^I$). (ii) Kripke model where concepts are interpreted with respect to a set of worlds or contexts denoted by S. If $|S| = 1$ then our interpretation becomes the classical interpretation of Tarski-Model described in (i) above. Having a set of contexts or worlds $S = s_1, ..., s_n$, our model of interpretation of concepts will require a kripke structure $< S, \nabla >$, where ∇ denotes an accessible or structural binary relation between contexts. Thus, We say s_2 is accessible from s_1 through the realtion $(s1 \nabla s2)$. Our interpretation model requires a mapping function denoted by $I(s) = < \triangle^{I(s)}, R_0^{I(s)} ..., C_0^{I(s)}, ..., a_0^{I(s)}, ... >$ where:

$\triangle^{I(s)}$ an interpretation domain in context s $\in$ S.

$R_0^{I(s)}$ set of roles that are interpreted in context s.

$C_0^{I(s)}$ set of concepts that are interpreted in context s.

$a_0^{I(s)}$ set of objects that are interpreted in world s.

Definition 1. (syntax)   *The syntax of our extended modal ALCN is given below:*

$$C, D \longrightarrow A \mid$$

$A \mid$	(atomic concept)
$\top \mid \perp \mid$	(top, bottom)
$C \sqcap D \mid$	(conjunction)
$C \sqcup D \mid$	(disjunction)
$\neg C \mid$	(complement)
$\forall R.C \mid$	(value restriction)
$\exists R.C \mid$	(existential quantification)
$(\leq nR) \mid$	(at most number restriction)
$(\geq nR) \mid$	(at least number restriction)
$(\Box_i C) \mid$	("necessity" $\leftrightarrow$ for all contexts)
$(\Diamond_i C)$	("possibility" $\leftrightarrow$ for some contexts)

Definition 2. (Semantics)   *The semantics of our extended modal ALCN is given below:*

$$A^{I(s)} = A^{I(s)} \subseteq \Delta^{I(s)}$$
$$(C \sqcap D)^{\mathcal{I}(\mathfrak{I})} = C^{\mathcal{I}(\mathfrak{I})} \cap D^{\mathcal{I}(\mathfrak{I})}$$
$$(C \sqcup D)^{I(s)} = C^{I(s)} \cup D^{I(s)}$$
$$(\neg C)^{I(s)} = \Delta^{I(s)} \setminus C^{I(s)}$$
$$(\exists R.C)^{I(s)} = \{a \in \Delta^{I(s)} \mid \exists y : (a,b) \in R^{I(s)} \wedge b \in C^{I(s)}\}$$
$$(\forall R.C)^{I(s)} = \{a \in \Delta^{I(s)} \mid \forall b : (a,b) \in R^{I(s)} \longrightarrow b \in C^{I(s)}\}$$
$$(\leq nR)^{I(s)} = \{a \in \Delta^{I(s)} \mid \ \|\{b \mid (a,b) \in R^{I(s)}\}\| \leq n\}$$
$$(\geq nR)^{I(s)} = \{a \in \Delta^{I(s)} \mid \ \|\{b \mid (a,b) \in R^{I(s)}\}\| \geq n\}$$
$$s \models \Box_i C \ iff \ \forall t \nabla s \ t \models C$$
$$s \models \Diamond_i C \ iff \ \exists t \nabla s \ t \models C$$

The second definition (definition 2) shows the interpretation (formal semantics) of constructs used by modal ALCN language. The interpretation of the constructors is based on the mapping function I(s) that associates concepts C with sets $C^{I(s)}$, roles R with their binary relations $R^{I(s)}$, objects a_0 with the set $a_0^{I(s)}$, and with the restriction that these concepts, roles and objects are interpreted in world $s \in S$.

3   Adaptation of Modal Description Logics to Contextual Ontologies – $C - DL$

Contextual ontologies are certainly formal ontologies with the constraint of being context-dependent. In this respect, we assume that concepts may be shared by several applications (of the same domain) but with different interests and purposes. Hence, a context-based description logics language supported by the existing expressive and efficient language $ALCN_M$ is feasible to represent contextual ontology and to meet its requirements. In the classical DLs, new constructs are proposed to allow for expressing contextual concepts, and roles. In Modal logics, the notion of modality is introduced [11] to allow for the occurrence of concepts in different contexts (S). In the following, we present the some design parameters associated with the proposed language:

- Modal operators are applied in front of concepts to form complex ones (i.e. $\Diamond C$ and ($\Diamond (C \sqcap D$).
- Non-rigid designators of objects. The object names whose interpretation is not fixed in contexts.
- The accessibility relation between contexts is reflexive, asymmetric, and transitive.
- Increasing domain assumption. Given two contexts s and t and context t is accessible from context s. We apply the increasing domain assumption where we have $\Delta^{I(s)} \subseteq \Delta^{I(t)}$. In this case, accessible means that there are $n \geq 1$ contexts $(s_1, \cdots, s_n)$ such that $s = s_1$ and $t = s_n$ for all i $(1 \leq i \leq n)$, there exists contextual modality such that $(s_i, s_{i+1}) \in \nabla$. The advantage of this model is that the domain elements that have been introduced in s can also be referred to in all contexts that are accessible from s.

3.1   Syntax and Semantics of Contextual ALCN

Definition 3. (Syntax of concept terms) *Let $s_1, \cdots, s_n$ be a set of context names. Classical and Contextual concept terms C and D can be formed by means of the following syntax:*

$$C, D \longrightarrow A \,|$$ (atomic concept)

$\qquad\quad \top \,|\, \bot \,|$ (top, bottom)

$\qquad\quad C \sqcap D \,|$ (conjunction)

$\qquad\quad C \sqcup D \,|$ (disjunction)

$\qquad\quad \neg C \,|$ (complement)

$\qquad\quad \forall R.C \,|\, \forall_{\mathbf{s_1}, \cdots, \mathbf{s_n}} \mathbf{R.C} \,|$ (classical and contextual value restriction)

$\qquad\quad \exists R.C \,|\, \exists_{\mathbf{s_1}, \cdots, \mathbf{s_n}} \mathbf{R.C} \,|$ (classical and contextual existential quantification)

$\qquad\quad (\leq nR) \,|\, (\leq_{\mathbf{s_1}, \cdots, \mathbf{s_n}} \mathbf{nR})$(classical and contextual at most number restriction)

$\qquad\quad (\geq nR) \,|\, (\geq_{\mathbf{s_1}, \cdots, \mathbf{s_n}} \mathbf{nR})$(classical and contextual at least number restriction)

Definition 4. (Syntax of contextual terminology axioms) *Let $\mathcal{A}$ be a concept name and let $\mathcal{D}$ be a classical/contextual concept term. Also, let $s_1, \cdots, s_n$ be a set of context names. A contextual terminology axioms $C - TBox$ is a finite set $\mathcal{T}$ of the two following terminology axioms:*

1. *$\mathcal{A} = \mathcal{D}$ (Classical defined-as axiom)*

2. *$\mathcal{A} =_{s_1, \cdots, s_n} \mathcal{D}$ (Contextual defined-as axiom)*

The $C - TBox$ constitutes the so called multirepresentation ontologies.

Definition 5. (Semantics of contextual concept terms) *The semantics of the contextual part of the language is given by a contextual interpretation defined in a context j over $\mathcal{S}$. A context j is either a simple context name belonging to $\mathcal{S}$ or a composed context defined as a conjunction of simple contexts[1]. A contextual interpretation $\mathcal{CI} = (\mathcal{I}_0, \mathcal{I}_1, \cdots, \mathcal{I}_j, \cdots, \mathcal{I}_t)$ is obtained by associating to each context j a non-contextual interpretation $\mathcal{I}_j = (\Delta^{\mathcal{I}}, \cdot^{\mathcal{I}^j})$, which consists of an interpretation domain $\Delta^{\mathcal{I}}$, and an interpretation function $\cdot^{\mathcal{I}^j}$. The interpretation function $\cdot^{\mathcal{I}^j}$ maps each atomic concept $A \in \mathcal{C}$ to a subset $A^{\mathcal{I}}j \subseteq \Delta^{\mathcal{I}}$ and each role name $R \in \mathcal{R}$ to a subset $R^{\mathcal{I}}j \subseteq \Delta^{\mathcal{I}} \times \Delta^{\mathcal{I}}$. Let $Co(j)$ be a function which returns a set of all context names appearing in a simple/composed argument context j [2]. The extension of $\cdot^{\mathcal{I}^j}$ to arbitrary concepts is inductively defined as follows:*

$(\exists_{s_1, \cdots, s_m} R.C)^{\mathcal{I}}j = \{x \in \Delta^{\mathcal{I}} \mid \exists y : (x, y) \in R^{\mathcal{I}}j \wedge y \in C^{\mathcal{I}}j \wedge Co(j) \cap \{s_1, \cdots, s_m\} \neq \emptyset\}$

$(\forall_{s_1, \cdots, s_m} R.C)^{\mathcal{I}}j = \{x \in \Delta^{\mathcal{I}} \mid \forall y : (x, y) \in R^{\mathcal{I}}j \rightarrow y \in C^{\mathcal{I}}j \wedge Co(j) \cap \{s_1, \cdots, s_m\} \neq \emptyset\}$

$(\leq_{s_1, \cdots, s_m} nR)^{\mathcal{I}}j = \{x \in \Delta^{\mathcal{I}} \mid Co(j) \cap \{s_1, \cdots, s_m\} \neq \emptyset \wedge \quad \|\{y \mid (x, y) \in R^{\mathcal{I}}j\}\| \leq n\}$

$(\geq_{s_1, \cdots, s_m} nR)^{\mathcal{I}}j = \{x \in \Delta^{\mathcal{I}} \mid Co(j) \cap \{s_1, \cdots, s_m\} \neq \emptyset \wedge \quad \|\{y \mid (x, y) \in R^{\mathcal{I}}j\}\| \geq n\}$

$(C \sqcap_{s_1, \cdots, s_m} D)^{\mathcal{I}}j = \{x \in \Delta^{\mathcal{I}} \mid x \in C^{\mathcal{I}}j\} if Co(j) \cap \{s_1, \cdots, s_m\} = \emptyset,$

$= \{x \in \Delta^{\mathcal{I}} \mid x \in C^{\mathcal{I}}j \cap D^{\mathcal{I}}j\} if Co(j) \cap \{s_1, \cdots, s_m\} \neq \emptyset$

---

[1] $j = s_1$ and $j = s_1 \wedge s_2$ are two examples of simple context and composed context respectively.

[2] $Co(s_1 \wedge s_2) = \{s_1, s_2\}$ and $Co(s_1) = \{s_1\}$ are two examples of the function Co.

3.2   Some Very Simple Examples

In the following, we briefly describe contextual constructors accompanied by simple examples.

The contextual value restriction constructor $(\forall_{s_1,\cdots,s_m} R.C)$: It will define a new concept all of whose instances are related via the role R only to the individuals of class C and in the contexts s_1 to s_m. For example, in two contexts s_1 and s_2, the concept Employee is defined as individuals with either an attribute EmployeeNumber in context s_1 or an attribute LastName in context s_2. The concept is expressed as it follows:

$$Employee = \forall_{s_1} EmployeeNumber.Number \sqcup \forall_{s_2} LastName.String$$

Outside of the two contexts s_1 and s_2, the concept *Employee* corresponds to an empty set.

The contextual existential quantification constructor $(\exists_{s_1,\cdots,s_m} R.C)$ will construct a new concept all of whose instances are related via the role R to at least one individual of type C and only in contexts s_1 to s_m. For example, the following expression describes that student is an individual that has at least one graduation diploma in context s_1 and in the same time participates in at least one course in context s_2:

$$Student = \exists_{s_1} Diploma.Graduate \sqcap \exists_{s_2} Register.Course$$

It should be noted that the interpretation of the expression Student in the context s_1 or s_2 separately will give us an empty concept. On the contrary, the interpretation of Student in the context $(s_1 \wedge s_2)$ will correspond to some individuals satisfying the two conditions of the expression.

The contextual number (at most, at least) restriction constructors $(\leq_{s_1,\cdots,s_m} nR, \geq_{s_1,\cdots,s_m} nR)$: They specify the number of role-fillers. The $\leq_{s_1,\cdots,s_m} nR$ is used to indicate the maximum cardinality whereas, the expression $\geq_{s_1,\cdots,s_m} nR$ indicates the minimum cardinality in the given contexts s_1 to s_m. The following example illustrates two cardinalities in different contexts: context s_1 where a man is allowed for at most one wife at one period of time, and context s_2 where he is allowed to have at most four wives at the same time. In the two contexts s_1 and s_2, the type of $NumberOfWife$ is $Number$.

$$Man = (\leq_{s_1} 1NumberOfWife \sqcup \leq_{s_2} 4NumberOfWife) \sqcap$$
$$\forall_{s_1,s_2} NumberOfWife.Number$$

The contextual conjunction $(C \sqcap_{s_1,\cdots,s_m} D)$: It will define either a concept resulting of the conjunction of the two concepts C and D in the defined contexts s_1 to s_m, or a concept equivalent to concept C outside of all the given contexts $(s_1$ to $s_m)$. For example, the following expression decsribes a Manager as being a person of sex female and who either has at least one responsability in the context s_1 or manages at leat one project in the context s_2. Outside of the two contexts s_1 and s_2, Manager is only defined as being a person of sex female and nothing else.

$$Manager = (Person \sqcap \forall Sex.Female) \sqcap_{s_1,s_2}$$
$$(\exists_{s_1} Responsability.String \sqcup \exists_{s_2} Manage.Project)$$

4   Related Work and Discussion

In the following, a brief discussion of how this paper is related to other approaches that deal with the issue of modeling and reasoning about conceptual schemas in various contexts.

Contextualized Ontology (C-OWL). A theoretical framework and a concrete language for contextualized local ontology was proposed by [9]. In this research, the notions of contexts and ontologies are combined and are considered complementary. Their definition of contextual ontology is "... to keep its contents local but they put in relation with contents of other ontologies via context mappings". The approach considers autonomous representation and management of local ontologies. The OWL language is extended with respect to its syntax and semantics to meet the requirements of contextualized ontology. The new C-OWL language is augmented with rules (or as they are called bridge rules) that allow for relating (syntactically and semantically) concepts, roles, and individuals of different ontologies. In the view of Bouquet et al. [9], there is a need for explicit representation of meanings to enhance services like search, knowledge and service integration, and knowledge discovery. To cope with the problem of semantic heterogeneity, they argue that imposing a single schema will always cause a loss of information. Their theoretical framework considers the following:

- Different conceptualizations provide a set of local ontologies that can be autonomously represented and managed,
- Inter-relationships between contextualized ontologies can be discovered and represented, and
- The relationships between contextualized ontologies can be used to give semantic-based services and preserving their local "semantic identity". The approach focuses on the import feature of OWL to support mapping between objects, concepts, and roles between two local ontologies.

Modal Description Logics. The classical description logics are not intended to deal with the dynamic aspects of knowledge representation such as spatial, temporal, beliefs, obligations, etc [12]. Modal descriptions logics, however, are adequate to represent such notions. Modal description logics can be defined as description logics (DLs) augmented by some modal operators like (a) necessity to express that a concept holds in some given worlds (i.e. all worlds in the future), (b) possibility to express the existence of a world in which a concept holds. Different modal description logics have been proposed to deal with this dynamic aspect of concepts. As a matter of fact, we found out that temporal logics are the most suitable and closely related to our approach. In temporal description logics, some temporal operators (for example Until and Since) are introduced to define a concept in the past, present and future tense [4]. In a similar manner, we can consider the tense in general (past, present and future) as a characterization of a context. According to such characterizing criteria, the temporal description logics give us the evolution feature of the whole concept from one context to another. Hence, this work is different from ours in the sense that it does not give us the ability to explicitly designate context names of contexts as in the temporal case where a precise time is given.

RDF Context. Resource Description Framework (RDF) is an emerging standard for the representation and exchange of metadata in the semantic web. RDF and RDF schema (RDFS) have been exploited in a variety of applications only to name few: resource discovery, cataloguing, digital libraries,etc. Recently, RDF(S) has become a good candidate for ontological knowledge representation. RDFS, as an ontology language, however, suffers from the power of expressivity and automated reasoning. A. Delteil and C. Faron-Zucker have proposed in [8] an extension of RDFS to go beyond the existing triple RDF statement-that is: the resource (subject), the property (predicate) and the value (object). They suggested a Defined Resource Description Framework (DRDFS) that enables the definition of class, property, and axiom definition to express contextual knowledge on the Web. The approach is based on the conceptual graph (CG) features. In this work, contextual annotations are proposed using extended RDF primitives namely *context*, *isContextOf*, and *referent*. The problem with this approach is that: it considers a context as a whole cluster of RDF statements (annotations). Moreover, rules based on the translation of CG graphs are needed to construct RDF contexts. In our approach, we consider a concept that may coexist in several contexts but with variable sets of properties.

Topic Maps. Topic Maps (TMs) [2] are an emerging new tool used for organization, management, and navigation of large and interconnected corpora of information resources. TMs collect key concepts of information sources and tie them together. The key concepts in topic maps are topics, associations, and occurrences. A topic is a resource within the computer that stands in for (or 'reifies') some real-world subject. An association is a link used to tie related topics. Occurrences are a set of information resources that may be linked to a topic. Topics can have base name, and variants of base names. This naming scheme allows the applicability of different names to be used in different specific contexts or scopes such as for multilingual representations. Topics have types expressed by class-instance relation (Rome is instance of a city). Topic types are also topics according to TMs standard (ISO/IEC 13250-2000). The notion of scope (the limit of validity) in TMs is one of the key distinguishing features of the topic maps paradigm; scope makes it possible for topic maps to incorporate diverse worldviews. In a given context, a topic has a specific scope. Different TMs can form different layers above the same information pool and provides us with different views of it. In fact, TMs capture contextual validity through the aspects of scope. Another filtering mechanism used in TMs is the facet which is used to assign metadata to the information resources. Thus, facets are based on the properties of information resources whereas scope is based on the properties of the topics.

5   Conclusion

In this paper, we have presented a solution to the problem of multirepresentation ontologies. In this respect, we have illustrated how an ontological concept may be represented in several facets/contexts according to its intended uses.

A contextual ontology language is presented. It is based on modal description logic. Specific constructors are adapted from the existing ones to deal with the multirepresentation aspect.

As future work, we aim at finalizing and implementing the proposed constructs. Further, we intend to validate and test the proposed language in the domain of urbanism where we expect a wide range of contexts like transportation, land use, urban planing, etc. A link with existing standard ontology languages based on description logic (OWL) will be established in the future. Finally, we intend to adapt the class-based logic query language [6] to deal with the need of browsing and searching concepts in large multirepresentation ontologies.

References

1. United nations standard product and services classification (unspsc) code organization. In), http:/www.unspsc;org/home.htm.
2. ISO 13250. Information technology - sgml applications - topic maps(. Technical report, International Organization for Standardization, ISO/IEC 13250, 1995.
3. David Abrams, Ronald Baecker, and Mark H. Chignell. Information archiving with bookmarks: Personal web space construction and organization. In *Proceedings of ACM SIGCHI'98*, pages 41–48, 1999.
4. Alessandro Artale and Enrico Franconi. A temporal description logic for reasoning about actions and plans. *Journal of Artificial Intelligence Research (JAIR)*, 9:463–506, July 1998. December 1998.
5. Alessandro Artale, Enrico Franconi, and Federica Mandreoli. Description logics for modelling dynamic information. *citeseer.nj.nec.com/570199.html*, 1999.
6. Djamal Benslimane, Mohand-Said Hacid, Evimaria Terzi, and Farouk Toumani. A class-based logic language for ontologies. In *In the proceedings of the Fifth International Conference on Flexible Query Answering Systems. October 27 - 29, 2002, Copenhagen, Denmark. Proceedings. Lecture Notes in Computer Science 1864 Springer 2000, ISBN 3-540-67839-5*, pages 56–70, October 2002.
7. Jie-Mein Goh Danny POO, Brian Chn. A hybrid approach for user profiling. In *Proceedings of the 36th Hawii International Conference On System Sciences (HICSS'0)*, 2003.
8. A. Delteil and catherine Faron-Zucker. Extending rdf(s) with contextual and definitional knowledge. In *In Proceedings of the IJCAI Workshop on E-Business and the intelligent Web, Seattle, 2001.*, 2001.
9. P. Pouquet et al. C-owl: Contextualizing ontologies. *In Proceedings of the 2nd International Semantic Web Conference (ISWC2003), 20-23 October 2003, Sundial Resort, Sanibel Island, Florida, USA.*, Oct 2003.
10. A.T. McCray and S.J. Nelson. The representation of meaning in the umls. *Methods of information in medicine*, 34:193–201, 1995.
11. Wolter and M. Zakharyaschev. Multi-dimensional description logics. In *Proceedings of IJCAI'99)*, pages 104–109, USA, 1999. Morgan Kaufmann.
12. F. Wolter and M. Zakharyaschev. Satisfiability problem in description logics with modal operators. In *In Proceedings of the 6th Int. Conf. on Knowledge Representation and Reasonning, KR'98, Trento, Italy, June 1998.*, pages 512–523, 2001.

A Unifying Framework for Flexible Information Access in Taxonomy-Based Sources*

Yannis Tzitzikas[1], Carlo Meghini[2], and Nicolas Spyratos[3]

[1] Information Technology, VTT Technical Research Centre of Finland
ext-yannis.tzitzikas@vtt.fi
[2] Istituto di Scienza e Tecnologie dell' Informazione [ISTI], CNR, Pisa, Italy
meghini@isti.cnr.it
[3] Laboratoire de Recherche en Informatique, Universite de Paris-Sud, France
spyratos@lri.fr

Abstract. A taxonomy-based source consists of a taxonomy and a database storing objects that are indexed in terms of the taxonomy. For this kind of sources, we describe a *flexible* interaction scheme that allows users to retrieve the objects of interest without having to be familiar with the terms of the taxonomy or with the supported query language. Specifically we describe an *interaction manager* whose functionality unifies several well-known interaction schemes including query by example, answer enlargement/reduction, query relaxation/restriction, index relaxation/contraction, feedback and adaptation mechanisms.

1 Introduction

A taxonomy-based source consists of a taxonomy and a set of objects that are indexed with respect to the taxonomy. Given a taxonomy-based source a user can find the desired objects by either browsing or querying the source. In this paper we propose an interaction scheme whose objective is to make the desired objects easy to find for the user, even if the source has a query language which is *unknown* to the user. The proposed scheme is actually a generalization of the interaction schemes that are currently used. The proposed interaction manager supports several kinds of interaction, including query by example, index relaxation/contraction, query relaxation/restriction, answer enlargement/reduction, "relevance" feedback, and adaptation facilities, in a uniform manner. This interaction manager is actually a specialization of the interaction manager of the generalized interaction scheme that was proposed in [16]. According to [16], the interaction of a user with an information source is viewed as a sequence of *transitions* between *contexts* where a context is a consistent "interaction state". The user has at his/her disposal several ways to express the desired transition. The traditional query-and-answer interaction scheme is only one kind of transition. Then, it is the interaction manager that has to find (and drive the user to) the

---

* Work supported by ERCIM and the DELOS NoE in Digital Libraries, Contract No G038-507618

H. Christiansen et al. (Eds.): FQAS 2004, LNAI 3055, pp. 161–174, 2004.

new context. Methods allowing the user to specify a transition relatively to the current context are also provided. Furthermore, methods for restricting the set of transitions to those that can indeed lead to a context were described. That work [16] gave the foundations of this interaction manager from a mathematical point of view, in terms of an abstract view of an information source that generalizes information retrieval bases [1], databases and knowledge bases [17]. The current paper specializes this framework for taxonomy-based sources and shows how the corresponding computational tasks can be performed.

The paper is organized as follows. Section 2 introduces taxonomy-based sources and Section 3 recalls the more essential parts of the generalized interaction scheme proposed in [16]. Subsequently, Section 4 describes how this scheme can be applied on taxonomy-based sources. Finally, Section 5 concludes the paper and identifies issues for further research.

2 Taxonomy-Based Sources

Taxonomies is probably the oldest and most widely used conceptual modeling tool still used in Web directories (e.g. in Google and Yahoo!), Content Management (hierarchical structures are used to classify documents), Web Publishing (many authoring tools require to organize the contents of portals according to some hierarchical structure), Web Services (services are typically classified in a hierarchical form), Marketplaces (goods are classified in hierarchical catalogs), Personal File Systems, Personal Bookmarks for the Web, Libraries (e.g. Thesauri [9]) and in very large collections of objects (e.g. see [13]). Although more sophisticated conceptual models (including concepts, attributes, relations and axioms) have emerged and are recently employed even for meta-tagging in the Web, almost all of them have a backbone consisting of a subsumption hierarchy, i.e. a taxonomy.

We view a taxonomy-based source S as a quadruple $S = \langle T, \preceq, I, Q \rangle$ where:

- T is terminology, i.e. a finite set of names called *terms*, e.g. `Canaries`, `Birds`.
- $\preceq$ is a reflexive and transitive binary relation over T (i.e. a pre-order) called *subsumption*, e.g. `Canaries` $\preceq$ `Birds`,
- I is a function $I : T \rightarrow 2^{Obj}$ called *interpretation* where Obj is a finite set of objects called *domain*. For example $Obj = \{1, ..., 100\}$ and $I(\texttt{Canaries}) = \{1, 3, 4\}$, and
- Q is the set of all queries defined by the grammar $q ::= t \mid q \wedge q' \mid q \vee q' \mid \neg q \mid (q)$ where t is a term in T.

The pair $(T, \preceq)$ is the taxonomy of S.

We assume that every terminology T also contains two special terms, the *top term*, denoted by $\top$, and the *bottom term*, denoted by $\bot$. The top term subsumes every other term t, i.e. $t \preceq \top$. The bottom term is strictly subsumed by every other term t different than top and bottom, i.e. $\bot \preceq \bot$, $\bot \preceq \top$, and $\bot \prec t$, for every t such that $t \neq \top$ and $t \neq \bot$. We also assume that $I(\bot) = \emptyset$ in every interpretation I.

Query answering in a source S is based on the notion of model. An interpretation I is a *model* of a taxonomy $(T, \preceq)$ if for all t, t' in T, if $t \preceq t'$ then $I(t) \subseteq I(t')$. Given an interpretation I of T, the model of $(T, \preceq)$ *generated* by I, denoted $\bar{I}$, is given by: $\bar{I}(t) = \bigcup\{I(s) \mid s \preceq t\}$.

An interpretation I can be extended to an interpretation of queries as follows: $I(q \wedge q') = I(q) \cap I(q')$, $I(q \vee q') = I(q) \cup I(q')$, and $I(\neg q) = Obj \setminus I(q)$.

Given a source $S = \langle T, \preceq, I, Q \rangle$ and a query $q \in Q$, the answer of q is the set $\bar{I}(q)$, also denoted by $S(q)$.

Figure 1 (below at Section 4) illustrates two taxonomy-based sources. Objects are represented by natural numbers, the membership of an object to the interpretation of a term is indicated by a dotted arrow from the object to that term, subsumption of terms is indicated by a continuous-line arrow from the subsumed term to the subsuming term. We do not illustrate the top and bottom terms and we illustrate only the transitive reduction of the subsumption relation.

3   The Generalized Interaction Scheme for Information Access

This scheme is described in terms of an abstract view of a source. Specifically, a source S is viewed as a function $S : Q \rightarrow \mathcal{A}$ where Q is the set of all queries that S can answer, and $\mathcal{A}$ is the set of all answers to those queries, i.e. $\mathcal{A}=\{ S(q) \mid q \in Q\}$. As we focus on retrieval queries, we assume that $\mathcal{A}$ is a subset of $\mathcal{P}(Obj)$, the powerset of Obj, where Obj is the set of all objects stored at the source.

Let $\mathcal{S}$ be the set of all sources that can be derived by "updating" the source S (e.g. for adapting it), but for the moment let us suppose that $\mathcal{S}$ is the set of all functions from Q to $\mathcal{P}(Obj)$.

Let $\mathcal{U}$ denote the set of all triples in $\mathcal{S} \times Q \times \mathcal{A}$, i.e. $\mathcal{U} = \mathcal{S} \times Q \times \mathcal{A}$. A triple $c = (S, q, A) \in \mathcal{U}$ is called an interaction context, or *context* for short, if $S(q) = A$. Let $\mathcal{C}$ denote the set of all contexts, i.e. $\mathcal{C}= \{ (S, q, A) \in \mathcal{U} \mid S(q) = A\}$. Given a context $c = (S, q, A)$, S is called the *source view* of c, q is called the *query* of c and A is called the *answer* of c. The interaction between the user and the source is carried out by a software module called *Interaction Manager* (IM). The interaction of a user with the source is viewed as a sequence of *transitions* between contexts. At any given time, the user is in one context, the *focal context*. At the beginning of the interaction with the system the user starts from the initial context $(S, \epsilon, \emptyset)$ where S is the stored information source, ϵ is the empty query and $\emptyset$ is the empty answer[1]. However, any context of $\mathcal{U}$ could serve as the initial context, e.g. the context $(S, \top, Obj)$. There are several methods the user can use for moving from one context to another, i.e. for changing the focal context. For example, in the traditional query-and-answer interaction scheme, the user actually "replaces" the current query q by formulating a new query q' and the "interaction manager" drives him to the new context (S, q', A') where

---

[1] We assume that $S(\epsilon) = \emptyset$ therefore $(S, \epsilon, \emptyset)$ is a context.

$A' = S(q')$. However this is only one way of changing the focal context. Several other ways will be presented below.

3.1   Context Transition Specifications (CTSs) through Replacements

Suppose that the user can *replace* one component of the focal context (i.e. either S, q or A) by explicitly providing another component (resp. S', q' or A'). So we can have three kinds of replacements: (a) query replacements, denoted by $[q \rightarrow q']$, (b) answer replacements, denoted by $[A \rightarrow A']$, and (c) source view replacements, denoted by $[S \rightarrow S']$.

As the user should always be in a context i.e. in a triple (S, q, A) where $S(q) = A$, after any of the above kinds of replacement, the IM should try to reach a context c' by changing one (or both) of the remaining two components of the focal context. Instead of leaving the IM to decide, it is the user that indicates to the IM the component(s) to be changed after a replacement. A replacement plus an indication of the above kind, is a *Context Transition Specification (CTS)*. Below we list the CTSs that we consider and discuss in brief the motivation beneath.

- $[q \rightarrow q'/A]$. Here the answer A must be changed. This is the classical query-and-answer interaction scheme: when the user replaces the current query q with a new query q', the user is given a new answer (i.e. an A' such that $A' = S(q')$). Thus we can write: $[q \rightarrow q'/A](S, q, A) = (S, q', S(q'))$.
- $[S \rightarrow S'/A]$. This is again a classical interaction scheme: whenever the source changes (e.g. after an update) the answers of queries change as well, i.e. here we have $A' = S'(q)$.
- $[A \rightarrow A'/q]$. Here the query must be changed. This interaction scheme may help the user to get acquainted with the query language of the source. It can be construed as an alternative query formulation process. The user selects a number of objects (i.e. the set A') and asks from the IM to formulate the query that "describes" these objects. Subsequently the user can change the query q' in a way that reflects his/her information need. Roughly this resembles the Query By Example (QBE) process in relational databases. It also resembles the relevance feedback mechanisms in Information Retrieval systems. For example, the user selects a subset A' of the current answer A consisting of those elements of A which the user finds relevant to his/her information need. Subsequently, the IM has to change appropriately the query.
- $[S \rightarrow S'/q]$. Here the query q must be changed. This resembles the way that a relational database management system changes the query q that defines a relational view, after an update of the database, in order to preserve the contents (tuples) of the view.
- $[A \rightarrow A'/S]$. Here the source view S has to be changed. Here the user wants A' (instead of A) to be the answer of q. The IM should try to *adapt* to the desire of the user by changing the source view from S to an S' such that $S'(q) = A'$. So this is a flexible and easy-to-use method that allows users to express their demand for source adaptation.

- $[q \rightarrow q'/S]$ Here again the source view S must be changed. This means that the user replaces the current query q by a query q', because the user wants the current answer A to be the answer of q', not of q. The IM should try to *adapt* to the desire of the user by changing the source view from S to an S' such that $S'(q') = A$.

The second column of Table 1 lists each kind of CTS that can be applied on a focal context $c = (S, q, A)$. Given a context c and a context transition specification R, the role of the IM is to find the desired target context $R(c)$, if one exists. The third column shows the target context after each kind of CTS where boldface is used to indicate the component that the IM has to compute in order to reach that context, assuming that only one of the remaining two components of the focal context can be changed. The notations $n_S(A')$ and $n_{S'}(A)$ denote queries that will be explained in detail in the next section.

Table 1. Context Transitions Specifications

CTS num	CTS notation	$R(c)$	evaluation of $R(c)$
(1)	$[q \rightarrow q'/A]$	$(S, q', \mathbf{S}(\mathbf{q'}))$	relies on query evaluation
(2)	$[S \rightarrow S'/A]$	$(S', q, \mathbf{S'}(\mathbf{q}))$	relies on query evaluation
(3)	$[A \rightarrow A'/q]$	$(S, \mathbf{n_S}(\mathbf{A'}), A')$	relies on naming functions
(4)	$[S \rightarrow S'/q]$	$(S', \mathbf{n_{S'}}(\mathbf{A}), A)$	relies on naming functions
(5)	$[A \rightarrow A'/S]$	$(\mathbf{S'}, q, A')$	relies on source adaptation
(6)	$[q \rightarrow q'/S]$	$(\mathbf{S'}, q', A)$	relies on source adaptation

3.2 Finding the Target Context

In CTSs (1) and (2) of Table 1, the IM has to change the answer in order to reach to a context. These cases are relatively simple as the target context always exists and the desired answer A' can be derived using the query evaluation mechanism of the source. However, the cases in which the IM has to find a new query (i.e. in CTSs (3) and (4)) or a new source view (i.e. in CTSs (5) and (6)) are less straightforward as the target context does not always exist.

In CTS (3) and (4) the IM has to find a $q \in Q$ such that $S(q) = A$ for given S and A. Supporting these cases requires having a "naming service", i.e. a method for computing one or more queries that describe (name) a set of objects $A \subseteq Obj$. Ideally we would like a function $n : \mathcal{P}(Obj) \rightarrow Q$ such that for each $A \subseteq Obj$, $S(n(A)) = A$. Having such a function, we would say that the query $n(A)$ is an exact name for the object set A. Note that if S is an *onto* function then the naming function n coincides with the inverse relation of S, i.e. with the relation $S^{-1} : \mathcal{P}(Obj) \rightarrow Q$. However, this is not always the case, as more often than not, S is not an onto function, i.e. $\mathcal{A} \subset \mathcal{P}(Obj)$. Furthermore, if S is onto and one-to-one, then S^{-1} is indeed a function, thus there is always a unique q such that $S(q) = A$ for each $A \subseteq Obj$ [2]. As S is not always an onto function, "approximate" naming functions are introduced, specifically a *lower* naming function n^- and an *upper* naming function n^+, defined as follows:

$$n^-(A) = lub\{ q \in Q \mid S(q) \subseteq A\}$$
$$n^+(A) = glb\{ q \in Q \mid S(q) \supseteq A\}$$

where lub stands for least upper bound and glb for greatest lower bound. If A is a subset of Obj for which both $n^-(A)$ and $n^+(A)$ are defined (i.e. the above lub and glb exist), then $S(n^-(A)) \subseteq A \subseteq S(n^+(A))$ and $n^-(A)$ and $n^+(A)$ are the best "approximations" of the exact name of A. Note that if $S(n^-(A)) = S(n^+(A))$ then both $n^-(A)$ and $n^+(A)$ are exact names of A.

Let us now return to CTS (3) and (4). If a naming function n_S is available for source S, then the target contexts exist and they are the ones shown in the third column of Table 1. If only approximate naming functions are available, then two "approximate" next contexts exist:

$$- [A \to A'/q](S, q, A) = \begin{cases} (S, n_S^-(A'), S(n_S^-(A'))) \\ (S, n_S^+(A'), S(n_S^+(A'))) \end{cases}$$

$$- [S \to S'/q](S, q, A) = \begin{cases} (S', n_{S'}^-(A), S'(n_{S'}^-(A))) \\ (S', n_{S'}^+(A), S'(n_{S'}^-(A))) \end{cases}$$

Notice that in the above cases, IM does not change only q, but also the answer. In the case $[A \to A'/q]$, the new context has an answer, say A", which is the closest possible to the requested (by the user) answer A'. In the case $[S \to S'/q]$, the new context has an answer A' which is the closest possible to the current A.

In CTS (5) and (6) the IM is looking for a $S \in \mathcal{S}$ such that $S(q) = A$ for given q and A. Clearly, the sought source S always exists if and only if $\mathcal{S}$ is the set of all functions from Q to $\mathcal{A}$. The process of finding the desired S', which we shall hereafter call *source adaptation*, cannot be described within this abstract framework. However, the restricted relative replacements and the source relaxation/contraction mechanisms that are introduced in the sequel, can be exploited for finding the target context even if source adaptation is not supported.

3.3   Relative Replacements and Relative CTSs

Relative replacements allow the user to specify the desired replacement without having to provide explicitly the new component but by defining it relatively to the current. These methods can be very helpful for the user during the interaction with the system. Relative replacements are based on the three partially ordered sets (posets) that are associated with each source, namely:

---

[2] Usually, sources are not one-to-one functions. For instance, the supported query language may allow formulating an infinite number of different queries, while the set of all different answers $\mathcal{A}$ is usually finite (e.g. $\mathcal{P}(Obj)$).

- The poset of answers $(\mathcal{P}(Obj), \subseteq)$
- The poset of queries $(Q, \leq)$. Given two queries q and q' of Q, we write $q \leq q'$ iff $S(q) \subseteq S(q')$ in every possible source S in $\mathcal{S}$. We write $q \sim q'$ if both $q \leq q'$ and $q' \leq q$ hold. Let $Q_\sim$ denote the set of equivalence classes induced by $\sim$ over Q.
- The poset of sources $(\mathcal{S}, \sqsubseteq)$. Given two sources S and S' in $\mathcal{S}$, $S \sqsubseteq S'$ iff $S(q) \subseteq S'(q)$ in every query $q \in Q$.

For every element x of the above lattices, let
$Br(x)$ denote the elements that are greater than or equal to x,
$Nr(x)$ the elements that are less than or equal to x,
x^+ a component that covers x, and x^- a component that is covered by x [3] in the corresponding poset. Note that there may not always exist a unique x^+ or a unique x^-. Specifically, we may have zero, one, or more x^+'s and x^-'s for a given x.

These partial orders can be exploited by the IM for moving to a component (answer, query, or source) that covers, or is covered by, the current component. Let $Up(x)$ denote a component among those greater than x and that the IM can compute (ideally $Up(x) = x^+$), and let $Down(x)$ denote a component among those less than x and that the IM can compute (ideally $Down(x) = x^-$). These relative replacements can be used within context transition specifications. A CTS defined by a relative replacement will be called *relative CTS*. Table 2 lists all possible relative CTSs.

Table 2. Relative Context Transitions Specifications

CTS num	CTS notation	description
(1r)	$[q \to Up(q)/A]$	query relaxation resulting in answer enlargement
(1r)	$[q \to Down(q)/A]$	query contraction resulting in answer reduction
(2r)	$[S \to Up(S)/A]$	source relaxation resulting in answer enlargement
(2r)	$[S \to Down(S)/A]$	source contraction resulting in answer reduction
(3r)	$[A \to Up(A)/q]$	answer enlargement resulting in query relaxation
(3r)	$[A \to Down(A)/q]$	answer reduction resulting in query contraction
(4r)	$[S \to Up(S)/q]$	source relaxation resulting in query contraction
(4r)	$[S \to Down(S)/q]$	source contraction resulting in query relaxation
(5r)	$[A \to Up(A)/S]$	answer enlargement resulting in source relaxation
(5r)	$[A \to Down(A)/S]$	answer reduction resulting in source contraction
(6r)	$[q \to Up(q)/S]$	query relaxation resulting in source contraction
(6r)	$[q \to Down(q)/S]$	query contraction resulting in source relaxation

Relative CTSs can enhance flexibility during information access by the user. Also note that they can very easily been reflected at the user interface layer of the system. Indeed, the user interface can have two buttons, "Up" and "Down", for

---

[3] An element x is covered by y (or y covers x) if $x < y$ and there is no z such that $x < z < y$.

every component of the focal context. By pressing a button, the corresponding relative replacement is specified. An additional option control can allow the user to indicate to the IM the component (S, q, or A) that should be changed in order to reach the new context.

3.4   Restricting the Relative CTSs

The three partial orders mentioned earlier (and their interrelationships) can be exploited in order to restrict the set of relative CTSs to those for which the IM can indeed compute the target context.

In particular, we can restrict $Up/Down(A)$ so that to support CTS (3) even if naming functions are not available (or if they are available, but there is no exact name for A'). This can be achieved by defining:

$$Up(A) = S(Up(q)) \quad \text{and} \quad Down(A) = S(Down(q))$$

We can restrict $Up/Down(A)$ so that to support CTS (5) even if source adaptation is not available. This can be achieved by defining $Up(A)$ and $Down(A)$ as follows:

$$Up(A) = Up(S)(q) \quad \text{and} \quad Down(A) = Down(S)(q)$$

We can restrict $Up/Down(q)$ so that to support CTS (6) even if source adaptation is not available, but naming functions are available. This can be achieved by defining $Up(q)$ and $Down(q)$ as follows:

$$Up(q) = n_{Down(S)}(A) \quad \text{and} \quad Down(q) = n_{Up(S)}(A)$$

4   Application on Taxonomy-Based Sources

For applying on taxonomy-based sources the interaction scheme just described, we have to find a method for computing the target context after every kind of CTS. The CTSs that require computing a new answer, can be supported using the query evaluation method already described in Section 2. So we only have to focus on the cases where the IM after a CTS has to find a new query or a new source view. The first case relies on naming functions and the second on source adaptation. Below we show that naming functions and source adaptation are possible for taxonomy-based sources.

Naming functions. Given a source S and an answer A, we seek for a query q' such that $S(q') = A$. Finding q' requires defining the naming functions n^- and n^+ for taxonomy-based sources. Naming functions for taxonomy-based sources were first described in [15] where they were exploited for creating automatically inter-taxonomy mappings. Before describing them, let us first introduce an auxiliary definition. Given an object $o \in Obj$, we shall use $D_I(o)$ to denote the query obtained by taking the conjunction of all terms t such that $o \in I(t)$, i.e. $D_I(o) = \bigwedge \{t \in T \mid o \in I(t)\}$. For keeping our notations simple, we shall also sometimes use $D_I(o)$ to denote the set $\{t \in T \mid o \in I(t)\}$. It can be easily proved that if we exclude from our consideration the queries that contain negation, then the naming functions are defined as follows:

$$n^-(A) \sim \bigvee \{ D_I(o) \mid o \in A, \ S(D_I(o)) \subseteq A\}$$

$$n^+(A) \sim \bigvee \{ D_I(o) \mid o \in A\}$$

The proofs of the above two propositions can be found in Appendix A. It is important to note that the evaluation of the above formulas is a computationally tractable task. Indeed, the time complexity for computing $n^-(A)$ is $O(|Obj|^2 * |T|)$, while the time complexity for computing $n^+(A)$ is $O(|Obj| * |T|)$. As an example, consider the source shown in Figure 1.(a). Here we have: $n^-(\{1,2,3\}) = a$ and $n^+(\{1,2,3\}) = a \vee b$. Now the set $\{1,2,4\}$ has an exact name, i.e. $n^-(\{1,2,4\}) = n^+(\{1,2,4\}) = a \vee (b \wedge c)$.

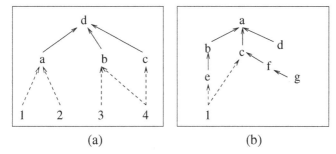

(a)   (b)

Fig. 1. Two taxonomy-based sources

Source adaptation. Given a query q and an answer A, here we seek for a source S such that $S(q) = A$. We first need to define the set of sources $\mathcal{S}$ that we assume and their ordering. Let $S = \langle T, \preceq, I, Q \rangle$ be the original stored source. We will consider that all sources in $\mathcal{S}$ have the same taxonomy, i.e. the taxonomy $(T, \preceq)$, and the same query language Q. So two sources S and S' of $\mathcal{S}$ may differ only in their interpretation, so we assume that $S = \langle T, \preceq, I, Q \rangle$ and $S' = \langle T, \preceq, I', Q \rangle$. If $\mathcal{I}$ denotes the set of all interpretations of T over Obj, then we can define the set of all sources $\mathcal{S}$ as follows: $\mathcal{S} = \{ \langle T, \preceq, I, Q \rangle \mid I \in \mathcal{I}\}$. For defining the ordering over $\mathcal{S}$, let us first introduce an auxiliary definition. Given two interpretations I and I' of T we write $I \sqsubseteq I'$ if and only if $I(t) \subseteq I'(t)$ for every $t \in T$. One can easily see, that if S and S' are sources of $\mathcal{S}$, then $S \sqsubseteq S'$ iff $I \sqsubseteq I'$.

Let us now return to the problem at hand. Specifically, let us consider CTS (5), i.e. $[A \rightarrow A'/S]$. Here we seek for a S' such that $S'(q) = A'$. Let $A^+ = A' \setminus A$ and $A^- = A \setminus A'$, so A^+ is the set of objects that have to added to the current answer, and A^- is the set of objects that have to deleted from the current answer in order to reach A', i.e. we can write $A' = (A \cup A^+) \setminus A^-$. Below we explain how source adaptation can be achieved by considering each form that the query q may have.

At first, suppose that $q = t$ where $t \in T$. For reaching the desired S' we have to update the interpretation I of S. Note that $\bar{I}(t)$ must no longer contain the set A^-, but it has to contain the set A^+. Recall that an object o may belong to $\bar{I}(t)$ either because $o \in I(t)$ or because $o \in I(t')$ where $t' \preceq t$. So in order to exclude from $\bar{I}(t)$ an object o of A^- we have to delete it from the interpretations of all terms that are narrower than t, specifically from the terms $\{t' \in D_I(o) \mid t' \preceq t\}$. So for each $t' \in D_I(o)$ such that $t' \preceq t$ we must set $I'(t') := I(t') \setminus \{o\}$ Now in order to add to $\bar{I}(t)$ an object o of A^+ we can just add it to the interpretation of t. So we must set $I''(t) := I'(t) \cup A^+$.

Now suppose that q is a conjunction $q = t_1 \wedge ... \wedge t_k$. One can easily see that the set A^+ must be somehow added to each $\bar{I}(t_i)$ for $i = 1, ..., k$. However we don't necessarily have to delete the set A^- from each $\bar{I}(t_i)$, as it suffices to delete each object of A^- from only one $\bar{I}(t_i)$. In this case, we need a criterion for selecting the term whose interpretation we are going to reduce. Among the several possible criteria, we select to delete an object o of A^- from the interpretation of the term to which this deletion causes the less perturbation to the interpretation I. Let us now define formally the minimal perturbation criterion. Let $Nr(t) = \{t' \mid t' \preceq t\}$ and $Br(t) = \{t' \mid t \preceq t'\}$ We can now define the perturbation of deleting o from the interpretation of a term t as follows:

$$pertDel(o, t) = |Nr(t) \cap D_{\bar{I}}(o)|$$

For example, consider the source shown in Figure 1.(b). In this source we have $D_I(1) = \{e, c\}$ and $D_{\bar{I}}(1) = \{a, b, c, e\}$. Some examples follow:
$pertDel(1, c) = |Nr(c) \cap D_{\bar{I}}(1)| = |\{c, f, g\} \cap \{a, b, c, e\}| = |\{c\}| = 1$
$pertDel(1, b) = |Nr(b) \cap D_{\bar{I}}(1)| = |\{b, e\} \cap \{a, b, c, e\}| = |\{b, e\}| = 2$
$pertDel(1, a) = |Nr(a) \cap D_{\bar{I}}(1)| = |\{a, b, c, d, e, f, g\} \cap \{a, b, c, e\}| = |\{a, b, c, e\}| = 4$
Also note that if $o \notin \bar{I}(t)$ then $pertDel(o, t) = 0$.

Now suppose that q is a disjunction of terms, i.e. $q = t_1 \vee ... \vee t_k$. It is evident that here the set A^- must be excluded from each $\bar{I}(t_i)$, $i = 1, ..., k$. On the other hand, we don't have to add the objects of A^+ to all $\bar{I}(t_i)$, as it suffices to add each object of A^+ to only one term of t. We can again adopt a minimal perturbation criterion for selecting the appropriate term of q. Specifically, we can define the perturbation of adding an object o to the interpretation of a term t as follows:

$$pertAdd(o, t) = |Br(t) \setminus D_{\bar{I}}(o)|$$

Some examples over the source of Figure 1.(b) follow:
$pertAdd(1, d) = |Br(d) \setminus D_{\bar{I}}(1)| = |\{a, d\} \setminus \{a, b, c, e\}| = |\{d\}| = 1$
$pertAdd(1, f) = |Br(f) \setminus D_{\bar{I}}(1)| = |\{a, c, f\} \setminus \{a, b, c, e\}| = |\{f\}| = 1$
$pertAdd(1, g) = |Br(g) \setminus D_{\bar{I}}(1)| = |\{a, c, f, g\} \setminus \{a, b, c, e\}| = |\{f, g\}| = 2$
Also note that if $o \in \bar{I}(t)$ then $pertAdd(o, t) = 0$.

Now the queries that contain all boolean connectives can be handled analogously. Specifically, Table 3 sketches the needed algorithms for each kind of queries. The table includes the case of queries in CNF (conjunctive normal form). Note that any query with logical connectives can be converted to CNF by using one of the existing algorithms (e.g. see [8]).

Table 3. Source Adaptation

query form	algorithm
$q = t$	(a) for each $o \in A^-$ do $\quad\quad$ Delete(o, t) (b) $I'(t) := I'(t) \cup A^+$
$q = \neg t$	(a) for each $o \in A^+$ do $\quad\quad$ Delete(o, t) (b) $I'(t) := I'(t) \cup A^-$
$q = t_1 \vee ... \vee t_k$	(a) for each $o \in A^-$ do $\quad\quad$ for each $i = 1, ..., k$ do $\quad\quad\quad\quad$ Delete(o, t_i) (b) for each $o \in A^+$ do $\quad\quad m =$arg$_i$ min $\{pertAdd(o, t_i) \mid i = 1, .., k\}$; $\quad\quad I'(t_m) := I(t_m) \cup \{o\}$ $\quad\quad$ end for
$q = t_1 \wedge ... \wedge t_k$	(a) for each $i = 1, ..., k$ do $\quad\quad I'(t_i) := I(t_i) \cup A^+$ (b) for each $o \in A^-$ do $\quad\quad m =$arg$_i$ min $\{pertDel(o, t_i) \mid i = 1, .., k\}$; $\quad\quad$ Delete(o, t_m) $\quad\quad$ end for
$q = d_1 \wedge ... \wedge d_m$ where $d_j = t_{j1} \vee ... \vee t_{jn_j}$	(a) add each object of A^+ to each disjunction of q (b) delete each object of A^- from the disjunction that causes the less perturbation
	algorithm Delete(o, t) $\quad\quad$ for each $t' \in D_I(o)$ such that $t' \preceq t$ do $\quad\quad\quad\quad I'(t') := I(t') \setminus \{o\}$ end algorithm

In order to define relative CTCs for taxonomy-based sources we have to show how source relaxation/contraction and query relaxation/contraction can be achieved. For relaxing and contracting a source S we shall use two operations: one for relaxing and one for contracting the interpretation of S. Hereafter with I, we shall denote a model of the taxonomy. For relaxing (resp. contracting) a model I, we will use an operation $\cdot^+$ (resp. $\cdot^-$) defined as follows:

$$I^+(t) = \bigcap \{I(t') | t \prec t'\}$$

$$I^-(t) = \bigcup \{I(t') | t' \prec t\}$$

The $\cdot^+$ operation was first introduced in [11] and it is founded on *abduction* [6]. So, if $S = \langle T, \preceq, I, Q \rangle \in \mathcal{S}$, then $Up(S) = \langle (T, \preceq), I^+, Q \rangle$ and $Down(S) = \langle (T, \preceq), I^-, Q \rangle$.

Another remark, is that the above operators can give us an alternative solution to the source adaptation problem in the special case where A' is a subset or a superset of the current answer A. Specifically, if $A \subset A'$ then our search space is $Br(S)$. We can apply iteratively the operator $\cdot^+$ on S until reaching to a source

S' such that $S'(q) \supseteq A'$ or until reaching the fixed point of $\cdot^+$. If $S'(q) = A'$ then we have found the solution, while if $S'(q) \supset A'$ then there is no exact solution. In the last case we can define only "approximate" solutions. Analogously we can treat the case where $A \supset A'$. In particular, if $A \supset A'$ then the search space is $Nr(S)$ and we can search it by applying iteratively the operator $\cdot^-$ on S until reaching to a source S' such that $S'(q) \subseteq A'$ or until reaching the fixed point of $\cdot^-$.

Concerning relative query replacements, given a query $q \in Q$ we need to define $Up(q)$ and $Down(q)$. Note that $Up(q)$ and $Down(q)$ do not necessarily have to correspond to q^+ and q^- respectively. Due to reasons of space we do not describe these functions in detail. Besides, mechanisms for query relaxation have already been proposed for several kinds of sources, including relational [7], semi-structured [4], Description-Logics-based [12, 3] and Web sources [10]. We only note that the answer of the query $Up(q)$ (resp. $Down(q)$) should be bigger (resp. smaller) than the current, and that intentional query containment does not always implies extensional subsumption, e.g. if $I(a) = \{1\}$ and $I(b) = \{1\}$ then although a is intentionally contained by $a \vee b$, here we have $I(a) = I(a \vee b)$.

In conclusion, we have just showed that the generalized interaction scheme is feasible for taxonomy-based sources. Although we have not reported refined complexity results, it is evident that all associated computational tasks have polynomial complexity.

5   Concluding Remarks

In this paper we specialized the unified generalized framework for information access that was proposed in [16] for the case of taxonomy-based sources. The resulting model captures several kinds of interaction that are more complex than those that are currently supported. We described the algorithms and showed that these tasks are computationally tractable.

Further research includes specializing the generalized interaction scheme for sources with conceptual models that allow representing the relationships that may hold between the individual objects of the domain. Specifically we plan to elaborate the case where sources employ Description Logics (DL) [5] knowledge bases, as DL is the knowledge representation language of the Semantic Web [2]. We strongly suspect that this specialization is again feasible because we can view a DL source as a taxonomy-based source. Indeed, there are several approaches for constructing in polynomial time the taxonomy of concepts of a DL knowledge base (e.g. see [14]).

References

1. Ricardo Baeza-Yates and Berthier Ribeiro-Neto. *"Modern Information Retrieval"*. ACM Press, Addison-Wesley, 1999.
2. Tim Berners-Lee, James Hendler, and Ora Lassila. "The Semantic Web". *Scientific American*, May 2001.
3. Alain Bidault, Christine Froidevaux, and Brigitte Safar. "Repairing Queries in a Mediator Approach". In *Proceedings of the ECAI'00*, pages 406–410, Berlin, Germany, August 20-25 2000.

4. Lee Dongwon. *"Query Relaxation for XML Model"*. PhD thesis, University of California, 2002.

5. F.M. Donini, M. Lenzerini, D. Nardi, and A. Schaerf. "Reasoning in Description Logics". In Gerhard Brewka, editor, *Principles of Knowledge Representation*, chapter 1, pages 191–236. CSLI Publications, 1996.

6. T. Eiter and G. Gottlob. The complexity of logic-based abduction. *Journal of the ACM*, 42(1):3–42, January 1995.

7. Terry Gaasterland. "Cooperative Answering through Controlled Query Relaxation". *IEEE Expert: Intelligent Systems and Their Applications*, 12(5), 1997.

8. Antony Galton. *"Logic for Information Technology"*. John Wiley & Sons, 1990.

9. International Organization For Standardization. "Documentation - Guidelines for the establishment and development of monolingual thesauri", 1986. Ref. No ISO 2788-1986.

10. Wen-Syan Li, K. Selçuk Candan, Quoc Vu, and Divyakant Agrawal. "Query Relaxation by Structure and Semantics for Retrieval of Logical Web Documents". *IEEE Transactions on Knowledge and Data Engineering*, 14(4), 2002.

11. Carlo Meghini and Yannis Tzitzikas. "An Abduction-based Method for Index Relaxation in Taxonomy-based Sources". In *Proceedings of MFCS 2003, 28th International Symposium on Mathematical Foundations of Computer Science*, pages 592–601, Bratislava, Slovak Republic, August 2003. Springer Verlag.

12. E. Mena, V. Kashyap, A. Illarramendi, and A. Sheth. "Estimating Information Loss for Multi-ontology Based Query Processing". In *Proceedings of Second International and Interdisciplinary Workshop on Intelligent Information Integration*, Brighton Centre, Brighton, UK, August 1998.

13. Giovanni M. Sacco. "Dynamic Taxonomies: A Model for Large Information Bases". *IEEE Transactions on Knowledge and Data Engineering*, 12(3), May 2000.

14. S. Sanner. "Towards practical taxonomic classification for description logics on the Semantic Web". Technical Report KSL-03-06, Stanford University, Knowledge Systems Lab, 2003.

15. Yannis Tzitzikas and Carlo Meghini. "Ostensive Automatic Schema Mapping for Taxonomy-based Peer-to-Peer Systems". In *Seventh International Workshop on Cooperative Information Agents, CIA-2003*, pages 78–92, Helsinki, Finland, August 2003. (Best Paper Award).

16. Yannis Tzitzikas, Carlo Meghini, and Nicolas Spyratos. "Towards a Generalized Interaction Scheme for Information Access". In *Procs of the 3rd Intern. Symposium on Foundations of Information and Knowledge Systems,FoIKS'2004*, Vienna Austria, February 2004.

17. Jeffrey D. Ullman. *"Principles of Database and Knowledge-Base Systems, Vol. I"*. Computer Science Press, 1988.

A   Proofs

Prop. $\bigvee_{o \in A} D_I(o) \sim n^+(A)$
Proof:
It suffices to prove the following two:
(a) The query $\bigvee_{o \in A} D_I(o)$ is a lower bound of $\{ q \mid S(q) \supseteq A \}$.
(b) $\bigvee_{o \in A} D_I(o) \in \{ q \mid S(q) \supseteq A \}$

(proof of (a))
Let x denote the query $\bigvee_{o \in A} D_I(o)$. We will prove that x is a lower bound of the set $\{ q \mid S(q) \supseteq A \}$, i.e. we will prove $x \leq y$ for each $y \in \{ q \mid S(q) \supseteq A \}$. Since $A \subseteq \bar{I}(y)$, for each $o \in A$, $o \in \bar{I}(y)$. Recall that each $o \in A$ is indexed under the set of terms $D_I(o)$. This implies that it must be $y \geq D_I(o)$ otherwise o would not be an element of $\bar{I}(y)$. Thus $y \geq \bigvee_{o \in A} D_I(o)$, i.e. $y \geq x$.

(proof of (b))
Each $o \in A$ is an element of $I(t)$ for each $t \in D_I(o)$. Thus o is an element of $I(D_I(o))$. This implies that $A \subseteq \bigcup \{ I(D_I(o)) \mid o \in A \} = I(\bigvee_{o \in A} D_I(o))$. Since $I \sqsubseteq \bar{I}$, we infer that $I(\bigvee_{o \in A} D_I(o)) \subseteq \bar{I}(\bigvee_{o \in A} D_I(o))$, thus $\bigvee_{o \in A} D_I(o) \in \{ q \mid S(q) \supseteq A \}$.

Since (according to (a)) the query $\bigvee_{o \in A} D_I(o)$ is a lower bound of $\{ q \mid S(q) \supseteq A \}$ and (according to (b)) it is an element of $\{ q \mid S(q) \supseteq A \}$, it follows that this query is the glb of $\{ q \mid S(q) \supseteq A \}$. ⋄

Prop. $\bigvee \{ D_I(o) \mid o \in A, \ S(D_I(o)) \subseteq A \} \sim n^-(A)$

Proof: If suffices to prove the following two:
(a) The query $\bigvee \{ D_I(o) \mid o \in A, \ S(D_I(o)) \subseteq A \}$ is an upper bound of $\{ q \mid S(q) \subseteq A \}$.
(b) $\bigvee \{ D_I(o) \mid o \in A, \ S(D_I(o)) \subseteq A \} \in \{ q \mid S(q) \subseteq A \}$

(proof of (a))
Let x denote the query $\bigvee \{ D_I(o) \mid o \in A, \ S(D_I(o)) \subseteq A \}$. We will prove that x is an upper bound of the set $\{ q \mid S(q) \subseteq A \}$, i.e. we will prove $x \geq y$ for each $y \in \{ q \mid S(q) \subseteq A \}$. Suppose that there is an object $o \in \bar{I}(y)$ such that $o \notin \bar{I}(x)$. Since o is indexed under the set of terms $D_I(o)$, it must be $y \geq D_I(o)$ otherwise o would not be an element of $\bar{I}(y)$. If $S(D_I(o)) \subseteq A$ then certainly o would be an element of $\bar{I}(x)$ by the definition of x. So, let us suppose that $S(D_I(o)) \not\subseteq A$. In this case $y \geq D_I(o) \Leftrightarrow \bar{I}(y) \supseteq S(D_I(o))$. As $S(D_I(o)) \not\subseteq A$ we infer that $\bar{I}(y) \not\subseteq A$ which is a contradiction. Thus the hypothesis $o \notin \bar{I}(x)$ is not valid, hence x is an upper bound of $\{ q \mid S(q) \subseteq A \}$.

(proof of (b))
If $S(D_I(o)) \subseteq A$ then $\bigcup \{ S(D_I(o)) \mid o \in A, \ S(D_I(o)) \subseteq A \} \subseteq A$. Thus $\bigvee \{ D_I(o) \mid o \in A, \ S(D_I(o)) \subseteq A \} \in \{ q \mid S(q) \subseteq A \}$.

Since (according to (a)) the query $\bigvee \{ D_I(o) \mid o \in A, \ S(D_I(o)) \subseteq A \}$ is an upper bound of $\{ q \mid S(q) \subseteq A \}$ and (according to (b)) it is an element of $\{ q \mid S(q) \subseteq A \}$, it follows that this query is the lub of $\{ q \mid S(q) \subseteq A \}$. ⋄

Interactive Schema Integration with Sphinx

François Barbançon and Daniel P. Miranker

Department of Computer Sciences, 1 University Station C0500
The University of Texas at Austin, Austin TX 78712-0233 USA
{francois,miranker}@cs.utexas.edu

Abstract. The Internet has instigated a critical need for automated tools that facilitate integrating countless databases. Since non-technical end users are often the ultimate repositories of the domain information required to distinguish differences in data types, we suppose an effective solution must integrate simple GUI based data browsing tools and automatic mapping methods that eliminate technical users from the solution. We develop a meta-model of data integration as the basis for absorbing feedback from an end-user. The schema integration algorithm draws examples from the data and learns integrating view definitions by asking a user simple yes or no questions. The meta-model enables a search mechanism that is guaranteed to converge to a correct integrating view definition without the user having to know a view definition language such as SQL or even having to inspect the final view definition. We show how data catalog statistics, normally used to optimize queries, can be exploited to parameterize the search heuristics and improve the convergence of the learning algorithm.

1 Introduction

Integrating data from a given set of databases requires making choices about the nature and validity of potential semantic relationships between elements in the database schemas. When the semantic structure of the databases is fully declared, it is possible to derive semantically correct view definitions and schema mappings to federate those databases [14]. On the other hand, omissions, or uncertainties about underlying semantic properties of the data can result in several competing view definitions, each of them corresponding to a different interpretation of the underlying data representation. We postulate that end-users, through domain expertise, intuitively possess the necessary knowledge to discriminate between competing interpretations.

Many problems in heterogeneous database integration can already be resolved by encompassing user interaction in a point and click interface. This is the case with the specification of attribute mappings in the schema mapping problem, and with building synonym correspondences and unit conversions for a data dictionary. This is not the case for schema integration (data deriving from more than one table). In addition to the above, schema integration requires the specification of query-operators including JOIN and/or higher-order query constructs [12], which have not admitted simple GUI interfaces. We propose a prototype system named Sphinx, designed to extract this knowledge without requiring any abstraction skills from the user.

The reader may recognize that the Clio system [29] entails a similar problem definition and Sphinx, like Clio, will combine both user interface and machine learning

H. Christiansen et al. (Eds.): FQAS 2004, LNAI 3055, pp. 175–190, 2004.

techniques. Clio's learning component examines possible join paths in the query graph and ranks possible view definitions by estimating their likelihood. Clio then uses data examples to help the user decide between alternative mappings. The user examines a set of illustrative examples as well as the output of the system for the top-ranked view definitions. The user examines those examples and renders judgment as to whether it has converged on a correct transformation. If it hasn't, the user can provide further assistance through an interaction with the system, based on a range of operators which help guide its convergence to the correct result: "Clio helps the user understand the results of the mappings being formed and allows the user to verify that the transformations that result are what she intended" [29].

Our work is distinguished from Clio by having first developed a linguistic meta-model of integrating view definitions enabling an active learning algorithm. The benefits include the guarantee that through a simple, question-based, interaction, Sphinx will converge to a correct result and report to the user when it has done so. Further, the user will not need to verify or refine the resulting view definition.

Sphinx extends the Version Spaces learning algorithm to represent a meta-model of all possible view definitions. We detail the Version Space model by considering, syntactically, a subset G of SQL, which may appear in the learned view definition. The generated language L(G) has few semantic limitations, but the limitations we do place allow us to contain the size of the search space within tractable bounds. We feel we do so without significantly compromising the language's practical expressiveness.

The active learning system seeks to learn a representative instance in L(G) by generating data examples chosen to maximize information gain, and to reduce the total number of examples viewed by the user. In addition to identifying and ordering heuristics by virtue of our own knowledge of data integration problems, the system chooses a heuristic based on a cost function parameterized by using system catalog statistics in a manner analogous to optimizing query costs.

Coupling Version Spaces with sample selection from an existing database required us to extend the paradigm. In particular, a new kind of rule for *missing examples* is introduced to deal with ambiguities introduced by various functional dependencies and constraints that occur in schemas and data sets.

2   Defining an Intentional View

Consider two sources: Product Reviews and Supplier Catalog, with overlapping content. In order to make information from both those sources simultaneously accessible from a single search interface, we define a federated schema. By expressing a federated view as a query over the source data, we fully specify the underlying data integration.

A mapping of attributes from the source schema to the target (federated) schema is immediately apparent (Figure 1). Each arrow shows a correspondence between fields in the source and the target schema. This schema mapping process is natural and intuitive given the clear correspondences in our example. However this schema mapping is not sufficient to unambiguously define a federated view over the source data. Several questions must be answered hinging on the nature of semantic relationship between elements in the source schema.

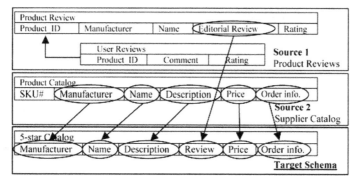

Fig. 1. Federating Product, and Review catalogs.

Identical products between the **Product Review** and the **Supplier Catalog** tables should be matched with a join operation in order to populate the target schema with product listings and their corresponding reviews. There are three main possibilities to join **Product Review** and **Product Catalog**: (SKU# → Product_ID), (Name → Name) and (Manufacturer, Name → Manufacturer, Name). A fourth possible join is a right outer join, which will map products listed in the catalog, even if no matching reviews can be found. Further, as the name '5-star Catalog' indicates, only products with '5-star' ratings in their reviews should populate the target schema.

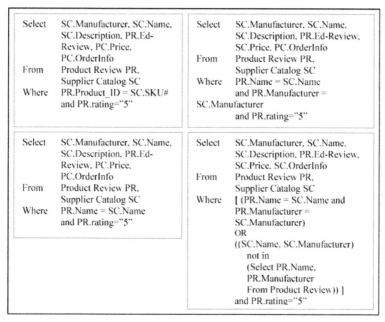

Fig. 2. Four possible view definitions.

Consider four of the many possible view definitions (Figure 2). To determine which of those alternatives is correct is to precisely answer the questions raised above about the nature of the join between **Product Reviews** and **Supplier Catalog**.

3 Search Space for Query Discovery

Sphinx explores a hypothesis space, containing all the possible queries under consideration. The exploration of this space will yield the correct query. We propose two methods to initialize this search. The first method we present allows us to merge an initial set of possible view definition into a covering space. This space will contain each of those view definitions, as well as points in between representing combinations. We also present a method, which initializes a default search space starting from a user defined data-mapping example, rather than an initial set of view definitions.

3.1 Initialization by Query Merging

Let us consider a set of view definitions VD_1, VD_2, ..., VD_n. We write each of those view definitions as an algebra sentence using projections, selections and a Cartesian product. We assume that all those view definitions are compatible with the same attribute to attribute schema mapping (such as in Figure 1). In practice this assumption means that each of those view definitions has the same projection operator to the target view $\Pi(a_1, ..., a_t)$, and that the attributes involved originate from the same set of relations. Taking into account the bag semantics of the Cartesian product, we can perform a bag maximum operation [10] of the Cartesian products in all view definitions, so that each VD_1, VD_2, ..., VD_n can be rewritten using a common Cartesian product $O_1 x O_2 x ... O_c$ as shown in (1). In a calculus (or SQL) sentential form, the projected attributes will then originate from the same variable assignment.

$$VD_1 = \Pi(a_1, ..., a_t) (\sigma_{1,1} \, o \, \sigma_{1,2} \, o \, ... \, o \, \sigma_{1, \lambda(1)} (O_1 x O_2 x ... x O_c))$$
$$VD_2 = \Pi(a_1, ..., a_t) (\sigma_{2,1} \, o \, \sigma_{2,2} \, o \, ... \, o \, \sigma_{2, \lambda(2)} (O_1 x O_2 x ... x O_c)) \tag{1}$$
$$...$$
$$VD_n = \Pi(a_1, ..., a_t) (\sigma_{n,1} \, o \, \sigma_{n,2} \, o \, ... \, o \, \sigma_{n, \lambda(n)} (O_1 x O_2 x ... x O_c))$$

$$VD(F_1, F_2, ..., F_{pf}) = \Pi(a_1, ..., a_t)$$
$$(F_1 \sigma_{1,1} \, o \, F_2 \sigma_{1,2} \, o \, ... \, o \, F_{\lambda(1)} \sigma_{n, \lambda(n)} \tag{2}$$
$$F_{\lambda(1)+1} \sigma_{2,1} \, o \, F_{\lambda(1)+2} \sigma_{2,2} \, o \, ... \, o \, F_{\lambda(1)+\lambda(2)} \sigma_{2, \lambda(2)}$$
$$...$$
$$F_{\Sigma\lambda(i)+1} \sigma_{n,1} \, o \, F_{\Sigma\lambda(i)+2} \sigma_{n,2} \, ... \, F_{pf} \sigma_{n, \lambda(n)} (O_1 x O_2 x ... x O_c))$$

$$VD_1 = VD(F_1=True, F_2=True, ..., F_{\lambda(1)}=True, False, False, ..., False)$$
$$VD_2 = VD(False, ..., False, F_{\lambda(1)+1}=True, ..., F_{\lambda(1)+\lambda(2)}=True, False, ..., False) \tag{3}$$
$$...$$
$$VD_n = VD(False, ..., False, F_{\Sigma\lambda(i-1)}=True, ..., F_{\Sigma\lambda(i)}=True)$$

In (2), we merge those view definitions into a formula parameterized by Boolean variables F_1, F_2, ..., F_{pf}. Each of those Boolean variables F_i is combined with a selection operator σ_i, such that σ_i is omitted if and only if F_i is false. In (3), each of the original view definitions is expressed using the new formula, for some Boolean assignment of the variables F_i.

The resulting formula: $VD(F_1, ..., F_{pf})$ represents the search space of possible view definitions. The learning algorithm will seek to converge by finding the correct assignments to each Boolean variable (also called feature) $F_1, F_2, ..., F_{pf}$.

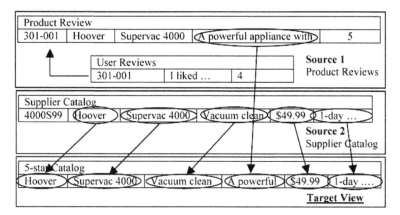

Fig. 3. A data-mapping example.

3.2 Default Initialization

A search space can also be initialized using an initial data mapping as shown in Figure 3. That data-mapping example is constructed from data values taken in displayed source tables using a QBE-like, point and click interface. This does not require any abstraction skills from the user. However we assume that as a domain expert, the user knows and understands the data sufficiently to produce a correct mapping. This data mapping immediately gives us the schema mapping of attributes from source to target. However, it also contains more information than the schema mapping, because it is grounded with actual data instances from each source. This enables us to initialize a search space for query discovery.

With the following steps, we define a parameterized Boolean formula (**4**), which will represent the initialized search space:

$$VD(F_1,..., F_{pf}) = \Pi(a_1, ..., a_t) (F_1\sigma_1 \text{ o } ... \text{ o } F_{pf}\sigma_{pf} (O_1 \times O_2 \times ... O_c)) \tag{4}$$

Steps:

1. Introduce a Cartesian product between all the tables $(O_1, O_2, ..., O_c)$, which appear in the data-mapping example.
2. Introduce the projections necessary to form the federated (target) view from the Cartesian product: $\Pi(a_1, ..., a_t)$.
3. Create equality selection predicates $\sigma_1, \sigma_2, ..., \sigma_k$ for every value in the data mapping.
4. Create equality join predicates $\sigma_{k+1}, \sigma_{k+2}, \sigma_{pf}$ for every pair of values in the data mapping which are in distinct tables and are equal.

We detail these steps for the data-mapping example illustrated in Figure 3:

- The Cartesian product is **Product Reviews** x **Supplier Catalog**
- It follows that the projection operator is $\Pi_{(SC.Manufacturer,\ SC.Name,\ SC.Description,}$ $_{PR.Ed.Review,\ SC.Price,\ SC.Orderinfo.)}$
- The selection predicates are σ_1: "PR.SKU = '301-001'", σ_2: "PR.Manufacturer = 'Hoover'", ..., σ_{11}: "SC.Orderinfo = '1-day shipping'".
- The join predicates σ_{12}: "PR.Manufacturer = SC.Manufacturer" and σ_{13}: "PR.Name=SC.Name".

This data-mapping example immediately excludes a join on attributes Product_ID and SKU# and no corresponding predicate is created.

The default search space defined in (**4**), while fairly general, is not complete. All legal equality predicates consistent with the initial data mapping are generated but any other arbitrary predicates are not. Selection predicates are preferred to self-joins. This has been sufficient for applications in both e-commerce and bioinformatics, due to the nature of the mappings between databases in similar domains [17]. As determined by ongoing experience, additional features may be added directly to the initialization of the search space or by expansion of the user interface (we expect outer-joins and query paths may be added to the learnable feature set without greatly expanding the search space). Learning inequality predicates with arbitrary threshold values is likely to be intractable, or even undecidable [18], and thus such functionality must be added by expanding the user interface.

4   User Interaction Algorithm

Many types of mappings necessary to perform database integration can be represented easily in a user interface. This is the case with the mappings in previous sections, but also with synonym mappings, and unit conversions. Building such dictionaries can be fastidious, but the basic process is simple and can be grasped by anyone familiar with the data. The goal of Sphinx is to propose a user interaction model for those semantic properties, which cannot be easily expressed in a simple user interface format. Sphinx does not ask the user to understand abstract specifications of view definitions, whether they are expressed in an abstract language (such as SQL) or expressed as symbols in a diagram. To solve the query discovery problem, Sphinx will limit its interaction to a simple and rigid framework. The only kind of interaction permitted with the user is showing several elements of input data combined together to form a row of output (e.g. Figure 3). The user must simply examine the output data instance and decide if it belongs to the target view.

4.1   User Interaction Model

Our user interaction framework takes away from the user the burden of making complex or abstract decisions. In particular, it is the active learning, which will construct and choose new data instances to submit them to the user. The Versions Spaces model will keep track of the search space exploration, allowing the learning algorithm decide when the correct view definition has been derived and end the process. The performance of the system is measured in terms of the burden imposed on the user, by counting the number of examples, or questions submitted before termination.

4.2   Question and Answers Game

We leave all formal expositions of the Sphinx algorithm to the full version of this text [2]. Instead, we will seek to illustrate here, with a simple question and answer game, how Sphinx modifies Version Spaces. The reader familiar with Mitchell's Version Spaces [19] will recognize some of the concepts exposed here.

Consider a database containing descriptions of a group of people, where each person has exactly three characteristics: first name, married or single, and male or female. This constitutes a source database. The user chooses a target group of people, for which the system will try to state a definition. A set of features will characterize the target group's definition. The system tries to deduce what those features are by asking if certain individuals in the database are in the target group.

The user starts by declaring that John, single, male is an individual in the target group. The system builds a search space, inventing a predicate for each feature F_1, F_2 and F_3. F_1 has "name = John", F_2 has "is single", F_3 has "is male". These are the only 3 *equality* predicates, which may filter the target group from the database without excluding John. We define a feature vector of size 3, for queries q on the database: (q_1, q_2, q_3). Our search space is illustrated in Figure 4(a): there are 8 delimited areas. Each area corresponds to a truth assignment of the feature vector and a possible target group.

As the question and answers game progresses, possibilities for the target group's feature vector are eliminated. There are only three situations, which can lead to a reduction in the size of the search space. We illustrate each with an example.

4.2.1 Positive Example Convergence Rule
The system asks the user if 'Mary, single, and not male' is in the target group and the user answers yes. The system deduces that F_1 and F_3 are not in the target group's feature vector. Either of those features would eliminate Mary from the target group, so they are excluded. In Figure 4(b), the excluded areas for the target group are grayed out. The search space is reduced to the non-gray areas: its size is now 2, since the only possibilities left for the target group's feature vector are (0, 1, 0) and (0, 0, 0).

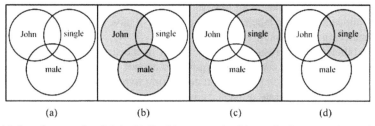

(a)   (b)   (c)   (d)

Fig. 4. (a) Search space for Q&A. (b) Positive example: Mary, single, not male. (c) Negative example: Mary, single, not male. (d) Cannot find a married person in the database.

4.2.2 Negative Example Convergence Rule

Assume the game is in its initial state again, and that the system asks the user if 'Mary, single, and not male' is in the target group and the user answers no. The system can deduce that either F_1 or F_3 must be in the target group's feature vector. The exclusion of both would put Mary in the target group. In Figure 4(c), the excluded areas for the target group are grayed out. The search space is reduced to size 6, since the only possibilities excluded for the target group were (0, 1, 0) and (0, 0, 0)

4.2.3 Missing Example Convergence Rule

Assume the game is again in its initial state. Sample selection, limits the system to asking questions about people who are listed in the source database. Assume that the system discovers that all the people in the database are single. In that case we can say that feature F_2 is indifferent. The feature is indifferent because its inclusion in the target group's feature vector makes no difference as to the final composition of the target group: there are no married people to be included or excluded from the target group. Since F_2 is indifferent, we decide to eliminate all possibilities in the search space, which do not include F_2. Any correct definition of the target group which does not include F_2, will remain correct when F_2 is added. As illustrated in Figure 4(d), this halves the size of the search space to 4.

We arbitrarily excluded 4 *example feature vectors*: (0, 1, 0), (0, 1, 1), (1, 1, 0), (1, 1, 1) for which no instances could be exhibited. Those 4 example feature vectors are labeled missing, and together, those four lead to a reduction of search space from 8 to 4 possible definitions of the target group.

5   Correctness and Limitations

The Question & Answer game mirrors the user interaction process used in Sphinx. The target group the system is trying to learn represents the federated view definition (the target or target query) and the people used as examples represent the data-mapping examples, which the user will label as positive or negative. It should be apparent to the reader that the Question&Answer game above is sure to converge to a correct result within a finite number of steps, provided that the correct view definition was in its initial search space. In the general case, we prove in extenso, that with its modifications to Versions Spaces, Sphinx remains a consistent learner [2]. Further, because of the three convergence rules, progress is guaranteed, since every possible vector in the hypothesis space can always be assigned one of three labels. When all 2^{pf} vector values have been labeled, the algorithm will have converged, which guarantees termination in a finite number of steps.

Missing labels are the result of dependencies in the data: examples necessary to discriminate between two competing hypothesis cannot be instantiated with existing data. When we identify such cases when competing hypothesis cannot be disambiguated, it is possible to generate a trigger equivalent to the disambiguating example. If the trigger is activated by changes in the underlying data sources, then the conflicting example can be submitted to the user. The target concept will be disambiguated and the trigger removed. This does not require a new initialization of the learning algorithm, but rather supposes a simple additional user interaction step.

Adopting the Version Spaces model limits Sphinx to learning queries which can be represented by a vector of binary features. However, it is possible to represent any arbitrary predicate, as long as the WHERE clause of the query is formed by a conjunction of such predicates (i.e. expressed in CNF). On the other hand, SQL queries represented with Version Spaces have no flexibility in their SELECT and FROM clauses: competing schema mappings cannot be evaluated since the projection operator must remain a common denominator when queries are merged. For this reason, view definitions with competing aggregation/sorting operators or with nested sub-queries cannot be handled by Sphinx, unless those operators and nested queries appear exclusively within a predicate in the WHERE clause. In Figure 2, one of the queries contains an outer join, which is represented using a nested sub-query inside of a predicate. Effectively Sphinx can represent both an inner and an outer join simultaneously, and will treat them as competing hypotheses, finding examples to discriminate between the two. Although disjunctions may appear inside query predicates, Version Spaces representation does not handle UNION on the same level as conjunctive predicates. Likewise there is no explicit handling of negation.

6 Sample Selection

The search space considered by Sphinx is always finite, and we guaranteed that the algorithm would converge to a result in a finite number of steps. However the size of the search space is 2^{pf}, where pf is the cardinality of the potential feature set. Thus, the challenge is to limit the number of examples (positive or negative) presented to the user during the search. To a lesser degree limiting missing examples is also important since they require computation time. Thus we look at the active learning and sample selection strategy, which is the part of the system selecting the questions in the Q&A game.

Any strategy wishing to conclude the Q&A phase quickly, will select examples, which shrink the search space by as much as possible. As illustrated earlier, there is a tremendous difference in value between positive, negative and missing examples. To be precise, a positive example negating k features, reduces the size of the search space from 2^{pf} to 2^{pf-k}. In contrast reducing the search space from 2^{pf} to 2^{pf-1} requires exactly 2^{pf-1} missing examples. It can be shown that a strategy collecting no positive examples would require 2^{pf} examples (missing or negative) to converge: an ineffective method. Thus any strategy must focus on finding at least one, possibly several, examples labeled *positive* by the user.

In order to obtain a positive example, the system should seek to present to the user an example where only a very unlikely set of features are negated. By negating only a set of very unlikely features, the system can effectively bet that it has produced a positive example. Drawing an analogy in our Q&A game, assume the system can estimate that "Name= John" is unlikely to be a defining feature of the target group. In that case, the system would try to obtain a positive example by asking the user if "Paul", single, male is in the target group. The rationale here is that "Paul" or "John", the first name is unlikely to determine membership in the target group.

6.1 Join Feature Bias

In the rest of our analysis we proceed to motivate and experiment with heuristics to explore the initial default search space in particular, rather than one built by query merging. This allows us to use Sphinx as a standalone system. And, as the goal is to explore a large space with an acceptable amount of user interaction, the search space generated by default presents a greater challenge, because of all the extraneous predicates, which are generated in the default method. Query merging, producing search spaces containing far fewer features, represents the less challenging of the two problems.

A simple count shows that the overwhelming majority of the potential features are selection predicates (Table 1). Most production databases contain a very large number of attributes, and for each of those, a selection predicate is generated. A join feature is created only when supported by the initial data-mapping example: a relationship exists between two objects in the data mapping.

An accidental match between a "9.99" as the price $9.99 and a "9.99" as September 99 is possible, but is an unlikely event given any pair of objects chosen at random by the user. Thus almost all join features observed in the data-mapping example are not flukes and do represent existing semantic relationships. Thus two factors combine here to privilege join features: a pure Cartesian product without a join predicate is a very unlikely operation, and most observed join features between objects belonging to different tables are not accidental.

We elaborate a baseline strategy S_b based on this observation. In its initial phase S_b searches for positive examples by choosing sub-goals that do not negate any potential join predicates. Instead, strategy S_b will search for examples, which negate a small given set of selection predicates (never more than 10). The search progresses by modifying the set until a positive example is found or the algorithm converges. The small set of negated selection features is chosen with an initial randomization and modified in an incremental and randomized search pattern (the choice of the latter having no observed effect on the success of the search). Once positive examples have been found, S_b enters its second phase, and searches for examples in which both join and selection predicates will be negated.

It should be observed that in addition to its bias for join features vs. selection features, strategy S_b possesses another built-in bias: it consistently bets that of all the potential features (a large number), only a very small number are likely to appear in the *Where* clause of the target query. This is consistent with our ad-hoc observation in the course of solving schema integration problems, that federating view definitions rarely contain selection predicates, if at all.

6.2 Information Gain Bias

We make the observation that not all features are equally likely. Consider the following feature predicate: "Name = 'Supervac 4000'". It is unlikely to appear in a view definition because few rows in the source, perhaps only one, will fulfill that predicate. On the other hand a feature such as "Rating = '5-star'" is more likely. A significant portion of the rows may well fall in the '5-star' category and building a view with those rows might be of use.

Using catalog statistics, we can measure for each selection predicate their information gain. The basic assumption is that the information gain will serve to estimate the likelihood of a predicate. A selection predicate with very low information gain will split the rows in the database in two groups, one of which is very small (only a few rows), the other very large (all the other rows). A selection predicate with very high information gain will split the rows into groups of comparable size. The information gain is maximal for a predicate, which splits the rows into two groups of equal size. A comparable bias could be introduced to estimate the likelihood of individual join predicates, however the overall small number of join predicates precludes the need.

We introduce a new strategy S_c, a refinement of S_b based on this information gain bias. This strategy does not require likelihood estimations to be accurate. The likelihood function should, above all, cluster predicates into two major categories: the most unlikely predicates (very low information gain), and the other predicates (low to high information gain). This clustering will replace the random process used in S_b.

6.3 Experiments

We implemented a prototype system with a graphic-user interface. This prototype handles the kind of data mapping instances presented here, as well as mappings, in which meta-data elements are mapped to data [12]. This small higher-order generalization allows for a broader range of restructuring queries across schematically disparate sources, without any substantial changes to the overall system.

We chose four domains to experiment with data integration. The first three problems were actual internet database integration tasks conducted under contract, in an ad-hoc fashion by a web services consulting firm. Almost all source data was derived from live websites in HTML form. The source sites were wrapped to produce structured results. Those schema integration tasks are created by experimenting with Sphinx, and are ranked in Table 1, by increasing level of empirical complexity. In the first domain the target queries populate a Healthcare provider directory database merging two data sources. The second domain is based on a sport statistics databases for web publishing. The third domain is the '5 Star Catalog' for electronics and comes from the area of online price monitoring for B2B merchandise distributors. A simplified version of that schema is used as an illustrative example throughout this exposition. The fourth domain is based on a bioinformatics integration effort to combine the functionalities of two application platforms for handling microarray data: SMD (Stanford Microarray Database) and BASE (BioArray Software Environment). Both these production systems carry out the analysis of gene expression microarrays in various laboratories throughout the world.

Each test set includes source databases, a target schema, and two interesting target queries populating different tables of the target schema. The number of features (i.e. Selection and Join predicates) appearing in the *Where* clause of each query is shown (e.g. 1J, 0S: 1 Join and no Selection predicates) in the *Query Size* column (Table 2). The number of examples Sphinx requires to reach the target query is averaged over ten runs for each query and shown in Table 2. The decimal averages are a product of random factors present in both heuristics and sample selection.

Table 1. Selection vs. Join Features.

		Potential Features	Potential Selection Features	Potential Join Features
Healthcare	Query 1	14	14	0
Directory	Query 2	15	15	0
Sports	Query 3	25	24	1
Statistics	Query 4	25	24	1
5 Star	Query 5	30	28	2
Catalog	Query 6	30	28	2
SMD →	Query 7	57	57	0
Base	Query 8	35	33	2

Table 2. Active learning experiments with Sphinx.

	Query Size	Potential Features	Strategy S_c			Strategy S_b		
			Number of Examples			Number of Examples		
			Total	Pos.	Neg.	Total	Pos.	Neg.
Query 1	0J, 0S	14	2.2	2.2	0.0	1.4	1.4	0.0
Query 2	0J, 1S	15	4.7	2.0	2.7	5.5	2.5	3.0
Query 3	1J, 0S	25	4.9	3.7	1.2	2.5	1.5	1.0
Query 4	1J, 1S	25	4.8	1.8	3.0	11.4	1.6	9.8
Query 5	2J, 0S	30	5.9	3.2	2.7	4.0	2.0	2.0
Query 6	2J, 1S	30	8.9	2.7	6.2	11.7	2.0	9.7
Query 7	0J, 0S	57	4.5	4.5	0.0	x	x	x
Query 8	1J, 0S	35	3.2	2.2	1.0	3.0	2.0	1.0

x – interactive search did not complete in a reasonable amount of time

Table 2 results show the randomized strategy S_b is sometimes slightly more successful than the refined strategy S_c for target queries which do not have a selection predicate in their *Where* clause. The performance of S_b degrades quickly when the target query contains even a single selection predicate and can fail in large search spaces. S_c shows more stability, its performance slowly decreases when the complexity of the target query increases. This is because S_c uses data catalog statistics to differentiate among the selection features, and picks those which can be excluded from the target query with high probability.

Table 3 compares the performance of both active learning strategies for Sphinx with two experiments in which Sphinx is hobbled to become a passive learning system. These two experiments do not represent valid strategies but are designed to identify bounds, both lower (oracle) and upper (random) on the number of examples an active learning algorithm may require. In these passive learning experiments, the user carries the burden of constructing data mapping examples as well as labeling them. Sphinx merely indicates when the system has converged to a target query. To measure a lower-bound, an omniscient user (us), constructed an optimal sequence of examples to converge Sphinx as quickly as possible. To measure an upper-bound a naive user chooses examples at random from the set of possible data mappings. At each step there is an equal probability of a positive or a negative example being chosen. Each example is picked randomly from its respective population of positive or negative examples. Unlike the oracle the random user is not in a feedback loop with the learning system, and does not know which examples need to be picked next in order to finish converging the system.

We observe that the number of required examples spikes when predicates are added to the target query, and that regardless of the number of potential features, the simplest target queries require a small number of examples. These experiments suggest that even with imperfect heuristics, the observed complexity is mostly correlated with the size and complexity of the target query rather than with the number of potential features. This is an unusual result for a machine-learning algorithm, due to the extremely specific and well-defined nature of our target concepts.

Table 3. Active learning vs. Passive learning.

	S_c	S_b	Oracle			Random		
	Total	Total	Total	Pos.	Neg.	Total	Pos.	Neg.
Query 1	2.2	1.4	1	1	0	26	13	13
Query 2	4.7	5.5	2	1	1	26	13	13
Query 3	4.9	2.5	2	1	1	7.5	3.5	3.0
Query 4	4.8	11.4	3	1	2	22	11	11
Query 5	5.9	4.0	4	1	3	12	5.5	6.0
Query 6	8.9	11.7	5	1	4	42	21	21

7 Related Work

Mediator-based architectures to federate heterogeneous databases have drawn a lot of interest [7], [8], [15], [25], [26], [28] to cite a few. In these systems, the basic assumption is that some highly qualified engineers may become domain experts and in one form or another write the specifications that will drive the data integration. In that line of work, several general-purpose query languages for specifying heterogeneous data integration include SchemaSQL and SchemaLog [13], and XQuery [27]. As shown by Krishnamurthy, Litwin and Kent [14], such languages must possess higher order features to bridge schematic heterogeneities across data sources [11], [28]. Semantic schema integration methods take into account semantic relationships represented as first order assertions, and correspondences between schema elements [1], [9], [12], [20], [22], [26] or can be built into meta-dictionaries of data and meta-data elements [3]. In both cases federated schema integration can be derived from semantic descriptions.

With the maturation of those systems, the problem of generating semantic specifications to federate data sources garnered more attention. Milo and Zohar [17] observe that the vast majority of mappings between schema elements in heterogeneous databases are trivial and lend themselves to automation. Thus, automated schema matching tools were developed with the goal of helping an engineer cope with the plethora of domain information, which must be reconciled to federate heterogeneous databases. Most mappings can be derived automatically, and user expertise can be saved for a smaller number of truly complex mappings. Rahm and Bernstein [21] offer a taxonomic survey of these automated schema-matching tools. While they often have high accuracy, these tools cannot guarantee that a correct mapping has been derived. A database specialist with domain expertise must examine the system's final output to verify the correctness. The average non-technical user cannot be expected to use the advanced query or semantic modeling languages commonly used to express those mappings. Thus because their founding principles in terms of input and expected output (as well as projected application) are so radically different from the approach proposed by Sphinx and Clio, it is impossible to compare the performance of those systems with ours by any measure.

In machine learning, the Version Spaces algorithm [19] is often associated with domains where the input data is noiseless. To our knowledge, we are the first to exploit it in the context of databases. Cohn, Atlas and Ladner [4] proposed a practical approach where the learning algorithm controls the selection of labeled examples that it is learning from. This approach greatly improves the algorithm's capacity to learn from a fixed number of examples, and has been applied to other machine learning systems [5], [15], [16], [24]. The exploration of formal learning theory related to this active form of learning has also been the subject of much work [6], [23].

8 Conclusion

Many challenges of data integration such as attribute correspondence and unit conversion can be solved with point and click interfaces. If this were enough to solve the general problem of database integration the subject would be closed. Sphinx addresses the open issue of schema integration where both simple and potentially complex queries over multiple data sources are required to populate the federated views.

We built a Version Spaces model for query discovery by example and developed the Sphinx learning algorithm, by adding a new kind of label and a new learning rule to the two labels and the two rules in the original Version Spaces algorithm. This new algorithm allows full and accurate verification by a user of potential mappings of semantic relationships. This is accomplished entirely by example, where only the initial data-mapping example needs to be supplied by the user. The active learning and sample selection system incorporated in Sphinx generate additional examples, which are labeled positive or negative by the user. We present a search heuristic, which is greatly improved by the use of catalog statistics to minimize the number of examples submitted to the user.

Ongoing work can quickly address a wide range of practical issues in schema integration within the framework we established. Currently Sphinx relies entirely upon the user to provide semantic knowledge and does not seek to derive it from context or from existing data. This strict split between the user's and system's responsibilities was motivated by our specific goals. However, by incorporating additional user interaction, Sphinx could easily initialize a more sophisticated default search space producing a more complete set of view definitions. Simultaneously, by incorporating more data mining and reverse engineering techniques, Sphinx could exploit better heuristics in order to navigate the resulting expanded search space.

Future work could also seek to address those features, which cannot be handled by the current Version Spaces framework. While not strictly necessary, the inclusion of a

UNION operator would significantly expand the ability of Sphinx to handle a large set of real world problems. As for handling xml data, nested relational queries with competing levels of nesting cannot be compared with Sphinx. They require the introduction of the NEST and UNNEST operators in the algebra, which is beyond the expressive power of the current Boolean representation.

References

1. Arens Y., C. Knoblock, WM. Shen (1996): Query Reformulation for Dynamic Information Integration. JIIS 6(2/3): 99-130.
2. Barbançon F., D. Miranker (2004): Active Learning of Schema Integration Queries. The University of Texas at Austin, Dept. of Computer Sciences Tech. Report CS-TR-04-23 (submitted for publication).
3. Chen Y., W. Benn: Building DD to Support Query Processing in Federated Systems. KRDB 1997: 5.1-5.10.
4. Cohn D., L. Atlas, R. Ladner: Improving Generalization with Active Learning. Machine Learning 15(2): 201-221 (1994).
5. Dagan I., S. Engelson: Committee-Based Sampling for Training Probabilistic Classifiers. ICML 1995:150-157.
6. Gasarch W., C. Smith: Recursion Theoric Models of Learning: Some Results and Intuitions. Annals of Mathematics and Artificial Intelligence, 15:151-166 (1995).
7. Garcia-Molina H., Y. Papakonstantinou, D. Quass, A. Rajaraman, Y. Sagiv, J. Ullman, V. Vassalos, J. Widom: The TSIMMIS Approach to Mediation: Data Models and Languages. JIIS 8(2): 117-132 (1997).
8. Haas L., D. Kossman, E. Wimmers, J. Yang: Optimizing Queries Across Diverse Data Sources. VLDB 1997: 276-285.
9. Johannesson P.: Using Conceptual Graph Theory to Support Schema Integration. ER 1993: 283-296.
10. Kent W. (1992): Profile Functions and Bag Theory. Hewlett-Packard Company. Technology Department, Hewlett-Packard Laboratories. Palo Alto, California.
11. Kent W.: Solving Domain Mismatch and Schema Mismatch Problems with an Object-Oriented Database Programming Language. VLDB 1991: 147-160.
12. Krishnamurthy R., W. Litwin, W. Kent: Language Features for Interoperability of Databases with Schematic Discrepancies. SIGMOD Conference 1991: 40-49.
13. Lakshmanan L., F. Sadri, I. Subramanian: SchemaSQL - A Language for Interoperability in Relational Multi-Database Systems. VLDB 1996: 239-250.
14. Levy A., A. Rajaraman, J. Ordille: Querying Heterogeneous Information Sources Using Source Descriptions. VLDB 1996: 251-262.
15. Lewis D., J. Catlett: Heterogeneous Uncertainty Sampling for Supervised Learning. ICML 1994:148-156.
16. Liere R., P. Tadepalli: Active Learning with Committees for Text Categorization. AAAI 1997: 591-596.
17. Milo T., S. Zohar: Using Schema Matching to Simplify Heterogeneous Data Translation. VLDB 1998: 122-133.
18. Miranker D., M. Taylor, A. Padmanaban: A Tractable Query Cache by Approximation. SARA 2002: 140-151.
19. Mitchell T.: Version Spaces: A Candidate Elimination Approach to Rule Learning. IJCAI 1977: 305-310.
20. Mitra P., G. Wiederhold, M. Kersten: A Graph-Oriented Model for Articulation of Ontology Interdependencies. EDBT 2000: 86-100.

21. Rahm E., P. Bernstein: A survey of approaches to automatic schema matching. VLDB Journal 10(4): 334-350 (2001).
22. Spaccapietra S., C. Parent, Y. Dupont: Model Independent Assertions for Integration of Heterogeneous Schemas. VLDB Journal 1(1): 81-126 (1992).
23. Stephan F.: Learning via Queries and Oracles. COLT 1995:162-169.
24. Thompson C., M. Califf, R. Mooney: Active Learning for Natural Language Parsing and Information Extraction. ICML 1999: 406-414.
25. Tomasic A., L. Raschid, P. Valduriez: Scaling Heterogeneous Databases and the Design of Disco. ICDCS 1996: 449-457.
26. Vassalos V., Y. Papakonstantinou: Describing and Using Query Capabilities of Heterogeneous Sources. VLDB 1997: 256-265.
27. XML Query: http://www.w3.org/TR/Xquery.
28. Yan L., M. Özsu, L. Liu: Accessing Heterogeneous Data Through Homogenization and Integration Mediators. CoopIS 1997: 130-139.
29. Yan L., R. Miller, L. Haas, R. Fagin: Data Driven Understanding and Refinement of Schema Mappings. SIGMOD Conference 2001.

On Querying Ontologies and Databases

Henrik Bulskov, Rasmus Knappe, and Troels Andreasen

Department of Computer Science,
Roskilde University,
P.O. Box 260, DK-4000 Roskilde, Denmark
{bulskov,knappe,troels}@ruc.dk

Abstract. This paper concerns the motivation for and subsequently the analysis of proposed additions, in the form of new operators, to a concept language ONTOLOG for use in querying a content-based text retrieval system. The expressiveness of the proposed query language introduces the possibility for querying both objects in the base but also mechanisms for direct querying of the ontology, and it furthermore enables the end-user to tailor the evaluation principle of the system by influencing query expansion in the ontology.

1 Introduction

In working with ontology-based information retrieval systems, one important aim is to utilize knowledge from a domain-specific ontology to obtain better and closer answers on a semantical basis, thus to compare concepts rather than words. Within this field our primary focus has been on representation of the ontology, description of the searchable objects, and on how to compare concepts and measure the similarity between them.

In this paper we want to shift our focus in the direction of query formulation and specifically on how to use the description language, ONTOLOG, to formulate queries. Over the years most users have learned to formulate queries as sets of words, as handled by most search engines. This works very well for many purposes, especially with the new generation of search engines developed during the last couple of years. One major problem with query formulation as sets of words is the limited expressiveness, and therefore the lack of opportunities for rewriting or expanding queries. If the first try does not work, it can be difficult to find alternatives.

In ontology-based information retrieval systems, queries are formulated using concepts, spanning from simple sets of concepts, like the sets of terms used in classical information retrieval, to sets of compound concepts extracted from natural language by some kind of natural language processing.

Even if the query formulation is done using natural language then rewriting, for most people, is extremely difficult without detailed knowledge about the domain and the evaluation principle used by the querying system. One possible solution is for the system to perform query expansion using a ontology-based similarity measure.

H. Christiansen et al. (Eds.): FQAS 2004, LNAI 3055, pp. 191–202, 2004.

Query expansion of this type is typically hidden from the end-user and one could argue that experienced users, domain experts and knowledge engineers have a specific need for more sophisticated control over the query expression in order to query both the text objects in the database, but also to pose queries directly to the structure of the ontology. This facilitates the need for the introduction of a conceptual query language with enhanced expressiveness. We propose to achieve this by extending the concept language ONTOLOG used for description of queries and conceptual indexing of text objects in the database, to form a query language.

The paper is organized as follows. Firstly we introduce and formally define the concept language used for describing the semantics of queries and objects in the database. Secondly we describe the ontology-based similarity measure in use for comparing concepts. And finally we extend the concept language for use as a query language, based on an analysis identifying the need for enhanced expressiveness. Conclusions are given in Section 5.

2   Concept Language

The purpose of the ontology is to define and relate concepts that can be used in descriptions. The ontology framework is generative in the following sense. A basic ontology defines a set of atomic concepts and situates these in a concept inclusion lattice, which basically is a taxonomy over single or multi-word concepts that are treated as atomic in the modelling of the domain. In combination with a given basic ontology, a concept language (description language) defines a set of well-formed concepts.

The concept language in focus here, ONTOLOG[9], defines a set of semantic relations which can be used for "attribution" (feature-attachment) to form compound concepts. The suitable number of available relations may vary with different domains, but among the more general relations that probably will be present in most domain modelings are WRT (With-respect-to), CHR (Characterized-by), CBY (Caused-by), TMP (Temporal), LOC (Location).

Expressions in ONTOLOG are descriptions of concepts situated in an ontology formed by an algebraic lattice with concept inclusion (ISA) as the ordering relation.

Attribution of concepts, combining atomic concepts into compound concepts by attaching attributes, can be written as a feature structures. Simple attribution of a concept c_1 with relation r and a concept c_2 is denoted $c_1[r\colon c_2]$.

We assume a set of atomic concepts $\mathbf{A}$ and a set of semantic relations $\mathbf{R}$, as indicated with $\mathbf{R}=\{$WRT, CHR, CBY, TMP, LOC, ... $\}$. Then the set of well-formed concepts $\mathbf{L}$ of the ONTOLOG language is recursively defined as follows.

- if $x \in \mathbf{A}$ then $x \in \mathbf{L}$
- if $x \in \mathbf{L}$, $r_i \in \mathbf{R}$ and $y_i \in \mathbf{L}, i = 1, \ldots, n$
  then $x[r_1\colon y_1, \ldots, r_n\colon y_n] \in \mathbf{L}$

It appears that compound concepts can be built from nesting, for instance $c_1[r_1\colon c_2[r_2\colon c_3]]$ and from multiple attribution as in $c_1[r_1\colon c_2, r_2\colon c_3]$. The attributes of a multiple attributed term $T = x[r_1: y_1, \ldots, r_n: y_n]$ is considered as a set, thus we can rewrite T with any permutation of $r_1: y_1, \ldots, r_n: y_n$.

The basis for the ontology is a simple taxonomic concept inclusion relation ISA$_{\text{KB}}$, which is atomic in the sense that it defines a relation over the atomic concepts **A**. It is considered as domain or world knowledge and may for instance express the view of a domain expert. We distinguish this (knowledge base) relation ISA$_{\text{KB}}$ because concepts are assumed to be related by specific knowledge over the domain. For that reason we cannot expect the relation ISA$_{\text{KB}}$ to be transitively closed or reduced and therefore define the relation ISA as the transitive closure of ISA$_{\text{KB}}$ and the relation ISA$_{\text{REDUC}}$ as the transitive reduction of ISA$_{\text{KB}}$.

Based on ISA, the transitive closure of ISA$_{\text{KB}}$, we can generalize into a relation over all well-formed concepts of the language **L** by the following.

- if x ISA y then $x \leq y$
- if $x[\ldots] \leq y[\ldots]$ then also
    $x[\ldots, r: z] \leq y[\ldots]$, and
    $x[\ldots, r: z] \leq y[\ldots, r: z]$,
- if $x \leq y$ then also
    $z[\ldots, r: x] \leq z[\ldots, r: y]$

where repeated ... in each inequality denotes identical lists of zero or more attributes of the form $r_i: w_i$.

Take as an example the sentence: *"the black dog is making noise"* which can be translated into this semantic expression *noise[CBY: dog[CHR: black]]*.

Descriptions of text expressed in this language describe semantics and goes beyond simple keyword descriptions. A key question in the framework of querying is of course the definitions of similarity or nearness of terms, now that we no longer can rely on simple matching of keywords.

3   Similarity

For the purpose of devising a ontology-based similarity measure, we can utilize the intuitive notion that similar concepts have much in common, and thereby derive similarity as being proportional to how much concepts share or how close they are in the ontology. In doing so we have to consider computational complexity, as is required by any large scale query evaluation environment. We therefore produce a similarity measure by firstly restricting the possible number of concepts we have to take in consideration when comparing any given pair of concepts, and secondly we derive similarity from "reasoning" within this restricted set of concepts.

3.1   Similarity Graphs

The restriction on the possible number of concepts to be considered, is established by constructing a so-called similarity graph [8] covering the subset of the ontology that contributes to overall similarity between the concepts being compared. A similarity graph can be viewed as a subpart of the ontology represented as a graph with a subset of concepts as nodes and relations connecting these as edges.

We can therefore define a similarity graph for any set of one or more concepts and specifically use this notion as a basis for similarity based on graph computations. The similarity between two concepts can thus be derived from a similarity graph covering these concepts.

To include in the definition of similarity graphs we first define the term-decomposition $\tau(c)$ and the upwards expansion $\omega(c)$ of a concept term c. The term-decomposition is defined as the set of all terms appearing in c. If we for a concept $c = c_0[r_1 : c_1, \ldots, r_n : c_n]$, where c_0 is the atom attributed in c and $c_1, \ldots, c_n$ are the attributes (which are atoms or further compound concepts), define:

$$subterm(c) = \{c_0, c_1, \ldots, c_n\}$$

and straightforwardly extend *subterm* to be defined on a set of concepts $C = \{c_1, \ldots, c_n\}$, such that

$$subterm(C) = \cup_i subterm(c_i)$$

then we can obtain the term-decomposition of c as the closure by subterm, that is, by repeatedly applying *subterm*:

$$\tau(c) = \{c\} \cup \{x | x \in subterm^k(c) \text{ for some k}\}$$

As an example the term $noise[\text{CBY}: dog[\text{CHR}: black]]$ decomposes to the following set of concepts:

$\tau(noise[\text{CBY}: dog[\text{CHR}: black]]) =$
$\{noise[\text{CBY}: dog[\text{CHR}: black]],$
$noise, dog[\text{CHR}: black], dog, black\}$

The upwards expansion $\omega(C)$ of a set of terms C is then the transitive closure of C with respect to ISA_{KB}.

$$\omega(C) = \{x | x \in C \vee y \in C, y \text{ ISA } x\}$$

This expansion thus only adds atoms to C.

Now a similarity graph $\gamma(C)$ is defined for a set of concepts $C = \{c_1, \ldots, c_n\}$ as the graph that appears when decomposing C and connecting the resulting set of terms with edges corresponding to the ISA_{KB} relation and to the semantic relations used in attribution of elements in C. We define the triple (x, y, r) as the edge of type r from concept x to concept y.

$$\gamma(C) = \cup \begin{array}{l} \{(x, y, \text{ISA}) | x, y \in \omega(\tau(C)), x \text{ ISA}_{\text{REDUC}} y\} \\ \{(x, y, r) | x, y \in \omega(\tau(C)), r \in \mathbf{R}, x[r : y] \in \tau(C)\} \end{array}$$

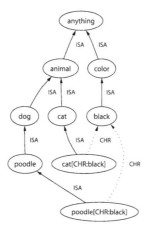

Fig. 1. An example of a similarity graph for the concepts *cat*[chr: *black*] and *poo-dle*[chr: *black*]

Figure 1 shows an example of a similarity graph covering two terms.

The primary purpose of a similarity graph is thus to form the basis for measuring similarity on the restricted set of concepts that contributes to overall similarity between a given set of concepts.

3.2   Evaluation

A time-honored and obvious approach to calculating the similarity between concepts is to reflect what connects them in the ontology. Rada et al. [10] measures similarity as proportional to the number of ordering (ISA) edges between the concepts in question in the ontology. Resnik [11] uses the same taxonomic structure as starting point, but augments the nodes by empirical probability estimates to compensate for non-uniform distance in the ontology, and points out that similarity can be derived using for example another partial (part-of) ordering relation. Another approach, as presented in previous work [6] calculates similarity by using a shortest path, considering both ordering and semantic edges.

As raised in [7, 4] the shortest path approach to similarity lacks the influence of an important aspect that has to do with multiple connections between concepts. We may for instance have concepts connected directly through inclusion and in addition through an attribute dimension, as $cat[CHR : black]$ and $poodle[CHR : black]$. Taking all possible paths connecting two concepts x and y solves this problem, but involves an increase in complexity. If we can reflect the multiple connections phenomenon without traversing all possible paths, we may have a more realistic means of similarity derivation. One option in this direction is to put emphasis on the nodes "shared" by x and y in the similarity graph covering both x and y.

With $\alpha(x)$ [7] as the set of nodes (upwards) reachable from x, we have $\alpha(x) \cap \alpha(y)$ as the reachable nodes shared by x and y, which thus obviously is an indication of what's common between x and y.

This notion can be transformed into a normalized measure, as described in [5], by using a set of major properties that improves a given function's accordance with the semantics of the ontology and used these to guide the choice of function.

The selected similarity function, as described in [5] is a weighted average, where where $\rho \in [0,1]$ determines the degree of influence of both the nodes reachable from both x and y.

$$sim(x,y) = \rho \frac{|\alpha(x) \cap \alpha(y)|}{|\alpha(x)|} + (1 - \rho) \frac{|\alpha(x) \cap \alpha(y)|}{|\alpha(y)|}$$

As illustration consider the subontology in fig. 1. The similarities for *poodle* $[CHR : black]$ and the other concepts included in the subontology are, when collected in a fuzzy subset of similar concepts (with $similar(x) = \Sigma sim(x,y)/y$) and $\rho = \frac{4}{5}$ the following:

$similar(poodle[CHR : black]) =$
$1.00/poodle[CHR : black] + 0,66/poodle + 0,59/cat[CHR : black] +$
$0,54/dog + 0,54/black + 0,43/animal + 0,43/color + 0,36/cat + 0.31/anything$

The purpose of similarity measures in connection with querying is of course to look for similar rather than for exactly matching values, that is, to introduce soft rather than crisp evaluation.

In addition to the problem of finding a useful measuring principle, a challenge is to device a principle of similarity-based evaluation that is realistic in connection with query processing.

To this end the principle of similarity expansion is an obvious improvement. Instead of calculating similarities in connection with every matching of two values during evaluation, one of these can be expanded and similarity matching becomes a matter of value to set comparison. As indicated through the example above we can introduce similar values by expanding a crisp value into a fuzzy set including also similar values.

4   Concepts, Queries and Answers

The framework shortly described above and in more detail covered in [5], is initially aimed at a query-answering mechanism where NL-queries are posed to a base of text objects and where ontology-based descriptions, that are expressions in a concept language, are derived through shallow NL parsing and matched by means of ontology-based similarity. In this context concepts, conceptual-based descriptions, ontology, and similarity are (or may be) all hidden from the user who poses a textual query and receives a textual answer. While this may well serve the naive end-users needs it is probably not satisfactory for skilled users such as domain experts, knowledge engineers, and super-users. Typically, skilled users prefer control over the query expression rather than the ease of automatic evaluation from textual expressions. Furthermore, domain and ontology engineers obviously need to pose queries for evaluation against the ontology rather than against the base of text objects.

In other words, there is a need for an optional evaluation of queries against the ontology rather than against the text base, and for a conceptual query language. We discuss below aspects concerning evaluation against the ontology - intensional evaluation - and introduce a conceptual query language.

Obviously, the presented framework can be extended to support the concept language, applied in descriptions, used directly as a query language since queries are transformed into descriptions. A query such as *"large dog"* maps to a description such as *"dog[CHR:large]"* and the latter can as well be used as a query.

4.1   Querying the Ontology

An obvious extension to a framework where evaluation of queries to database objects involves interpretation of the query based on an ontology, is a means for querying the ontology concepts directly rather than the database objects. Evaluation of an ontology query can namely be considered as an intermediate step in the evaluation of queries for objects.

The answer to a single concept query[1] can be given an interpretation simply by the function *similar* defined above. So for a given concept ϕ we can set $queryanswer(\phi) = similar(\phi)$, so with the ontology described in figure 1 we have (for a given similarity setting):

$queryanswer(poodle) =$
$1.00/poodle + 0,91/poodle[CHR : black] + 0,80/dog + 0,60/animal +$
$+0,53/cat + 0,47/cat[CHR : black] + 0,30/color$

Aggregation for multiple concept queries can be done in several ways with one simple option being fuzzy union. This topic is further discussed in [1, 2, 12].

When considering ontology queries, the question is whether an interpretation purely against the generative ontology is the most obvious. For any query the result of the ontology interpretation can be further evaluated in the database whereby the result of the text object interpretation will be obtained. Thus the text object interpretation reflects the database while the ontology interpretation does not.

An alternative to evaluation in the generative ontology is an evaluation in the "extensional ontology" reflecting the database.

We define the extensional ontology as the subontology O_{DB} reflecting the database extension as follows. O_{DB} is the subontology of the generative ontology covering the set of (atomic and compound) concepts used or referred to in the descriptions in the database and any generalizations of these. Thus O_{DB} is a precise reflection of the database content, it is finite and it is non generative.

---

[1] A query with a single concept description.

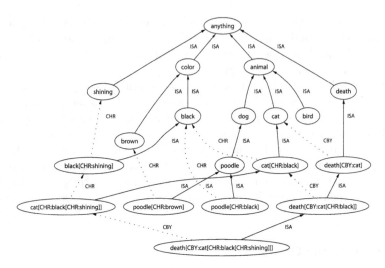

Fig. 2. An example of an extensional ontology for a database with object descriptions listing the concepts *bird*, *poodle*[**chr: brown**], *poodle*[**chr: black**] and *death*[**cby:cat**[**chr: black**[**chr: shining**]]]

Consider as an example a database consisting of the text objects:

- The two dogs are a black poodle and a brown poodle
- The bird and the death caused by the shining black cat

The descriptions for these objects may be respectively {*poodle*[CHR : *brown*], *poodle*[CHR : *black*]} and {*bird, death*[CBY: *cat*[CHR: *black*[CHR: *shining*]]]}. Assuming a set of more general concepts, an example of an extensional ontology corresponding to this database is shown in figure 2.

The advantage of interpreting concepts in the extensional ontology is that the evaluation does not include any concepts not indexed in the base, and we thereby restrict the concepts we have to take into consideration when evaluating queries.

4.2   Querying by Description Expressions

Another obvious extension to the framework is to allow queries posed directly as expressions in the concept language (using the concept language as query language). Thus in place of an NL-query "Some black cat" to support a description query "*cat[CHR:black]*".

Let us consider ontology queries and assume an extensional ontology interpretation. Thus the answer to a single concept query is a set of concepts appearing in the (descriptions of) objects that are most similar to the query concept.

Take as an example the query Q = "*cat[CHR:black]*" evaluated using $similar_\alpha(Q)$ where α is a threshold limiting the set of similar concepts to those with a membership grade (i.e. similarity) $\geq \alpha$. The query is evaluated in the extensional ontology shown in figure 2, resulting in the following similar concepts.

$similar_{0.6}(cat[CHR : black]) =$
$1.00/cat[CHR : black] + 0.93/cat[CHR : black[CHR : shining]] +$
$0.93/death[CBY : cat[CHR : black]] +$
$0.89/death[CBY : cat[CHR : black[CHR : shining]]] +$
$0.65/poodle[CHR : black] + 0.60/black + 0.60/cat$

This type of querying may by applicable in cases where the user knows the ontology and the database content well and has a rather specific intention. Without knowledge about the ontology, however, it may be difficult in any case to pose concept queries and likewise with only brief knowledge about the database content posed queries will probably often give unsatisfactory or empty answers.

Posing an NL-query is leaving the control and responsibility for a satisfactory conceptual representation of the query intention to the system. With a concept query the user gains control, but may face problems exploiting this control.

Take as an example the query where the user is interested objects about "colored dogs in general or any specific type of colored dog". This query is problematic because it cannot be expressed using pure concept language.

With special attention to experienced users and domain experts it appears that there is a need for a query language with a broader type of encirclement in query expressions than what can be expressed with pure concept language. For instance a "very large black dog" object will only to some (if any) extent belong to the answer to the query "large pet". The explanation here is the similarity based evaluation of queries, which in turn motivates the introduction of more expressiveness to the query language.

4.3   Query Language

Now a concept as a query maps to a set of similar concepts, and similarity is influenced by distance in the ontology. The extension to the concept language introduced here is specialization/generalization operators to cope with a quite useful notation for disjunctions along specialization and/or generalization, and thus avoid reduced similarity over paths of specialization and/or generalization.

Given the concept language $\mathbf{L}$ based on the set of atomic concepts $\mathbf{A}$ and the set of semantic relations $\mathbf{R}$, as described above, we define an extension of $\mathbf{L}$ to a query language $\mathbf{QL}$ as follows.

- $\mathbf{L} \subseteq \mathbf{QL}$
- $* \in \mathbf{QL}$
- if $c \in \mathbf{L}$ then $c_> \in \mathbf{QL}$ and $c_< \in \mathbf{QL}$
- if $c \in \mathbf{QL}$, $r_i \in \mathbf{R}$ and $c_i \in \mathbf{QL}, i = 1, \ldots, n$
  then $c[r_1 : c_1, \ldots, r_n : c_n] \in \mathbf{QL}$

The interpretation of this extended language is the following. $*$ denotes any well-formed concept in $\mathbf{L}$. $c_>$ denotes any specialization of c while $c_<$ denotes any generalization of c. A query involving the operators $<, >$ and $*$ can be considered a disjunctive query over the set of denoted concepts.

With the ontology in figure 2, we have that $dog_<$ denotes all of $\{dog, animal, anything\}$ and $dog_>$ denotes all of $\{dog, poodle, poodle[CHR : brown], poodle$

$[CHR : black]\}$. The set of denoted concepts for a query is obviously the crisp answer to the query when evaluated in the extensional ontology. Thus a query like "Do we have dogs", with the interpretation "Give me a dog or some specialization of that" can be expressed in the query $dog_>$ and the answer provides a conceptual description of the kinds of dogs that are currently contained in the database without specification of actual dogs and without cardinalities. The reading in the answer is something like "We have poodles here in colors black and brown".

Also with the ontology in figure 2, we have that $cat[CHR : black_<]$ denotes all of $\{cat[CHR : black], cat[CHR : color], cat[CHR : anything]$ while $cat[CHR : black_>]$ denotes $\{cat[CHR : black], cat[CHR : black[CHR : shining]]\}$.

Concepts that are not part of the extensional ontology such as $animal[CHR : black]$ can of course also be used in queries. We have that $animal[CHR : black_<]$ denotes $\{animal[CHR : black], animal[CHR : color], animal[CHR : anything]\}$ and $animal[CHR : black_>]$ denotes $\{animal[CHR : black], animal [CHR : black[CHR : shining]]\}$.

In some cases the combination of disjunction from expression as above with similarity may confuse the picture. If for instance we want a conceptual answer to $dog_>$ we probably prefer to reveal only what are the different kinds of dogs and have no interest in adding what may be similar to some kind of dogs. On the other hand, if we consider for instance $cat[CHR : black]$ we may prefer an interpretation where specializations of the property $black$ are considered equally fulfilling properties so that we get an answer corresponding to

$$similar_{0.6}(cat[CHR : black_>]) =$$
$$1.00/cat[CHR : black] + 1.00/cat[CHR : black[CHR : shining]] +$$
$$0.93/death[CBY : cat[CHR : black]] + 0.89/death[CBY : cat[CHR : black[CHR : shining]]]$$
$$0.65/poodle[CHR : black] + 0.60/black + 0.60/cat$$

One reasonable question related to the introduction of specialization/generalization-queries is to what extend such aspects are already covered by the pure concept language. What is the need of an expression such as $animal[CHR : *]$ to represent "Animal characterized by just anything"[2] when we already can express $animal[CHR : top]$ which basically denotes the same thing. The most important argument for the extension is that we have to cope with side-effects from introducing similarity and especially also consider graduate decrease in similarity over longer paths of specialization. We consider $animal$ to have dog as a more similar concept and $poodle[CHR : brown]$ as less similar concept.

5   Conclusion

One important aspect in working with ontology-based information retrieval systems, concerns the utilization of knowledge from domain-specific ontologies to obtain better and closer answers on a semantical basis.

---

[2] Notice that $animal[CHR : *]$ and $animal[CHR : Top_>]$ are equivalent.

In this context a major problem concerns query formulation in general concerns, due to the limited expressiveness of the query language, and therefore the lack of opportunities for rewriting or expanding queries. If the first try does not work, it can be difficult to find alternatives. Rewriting of queries is therefore extremely difficult without detailed knowledge about the domain and the evaluation principle used by the querying system. One possible solution is to enhance the control the end-user has over the query language.

We have therefore introduced additions, in the form of new operators, to the concept language ONTOLOG for use as query language. This has introduced the possibility for querying both objects in the base but also mechanisms for direct querying of the ontology. Experienced users, domain experts, and knowledge engineers can thereby browse the structure the ontology for use in both querying the system, but also for use in ontology engineering and re-construction. The additional operators can furthermore be used to guide the expansion of concepts in the ontology, and can thereby allow the end-user to tailor the evaluation principle to favor more general or more specific answers to a given query. The use of the concept language ONTOLOG as query language therefore seems to indicate a usable theoretical and practical foundation for querying and browsing of ontology-based querying systems.

Acknowledgments

The work described in this paper is part of the OntoQuery[3] [3] project supported by the Danish Technical Research Council and the Danish IT University.

References

1. Andreasen, T.: On knowledge-guided fuzzy aggregation, 9th International Conference on Information Processing and Management of Uncertainty in Knowledge-Based Systems, IPMU'2002, Annecy, France, July 1-5 , 2002, Proceedings
2. Andreasen, T.: Query evaluation based on domain-specific ontologies. 20th IFSA / NAFIPS International Conference Fuzziness and Soft Computing, NAFIPS'2001, pp. 1844-1849, Vancouver, Canada, 2001, Proceedings
3. Andreasen, T., Jensen, P. Anker, Nilsson, J. Fischer, Paggio, P., Pedersen, B. Sandford & Thomsen, H. Erdman: Ontological Extraction of Content for Text Querying, NLDB'2002, Stockholm, Sweden, 2002.
4. Andreasen, T., Bulskov, H. and Knappe, R.: On ontology-based querying, to appear in Eighteenth International Joint Conference on Artificial Intelligence, August 9-15, Acapulco, Mexico, Proceedings
5. Andreasen, T., Bukskov, H., and Knappe, R.: Similarity from Conceptual Relations, pp. 179-184 in Ellen Walker (Eds.): 22nd International Conference of the North American Fuzzy Information Processing Sociaty, NAFIPS 2003, Chicago, Illinois USA, July 24-26, 2003, Proceedings

---

[3] The project has the following participating institutions: University of Copenhagen, The Technical University of Denmark, Copenhagen Business School, and Roskilde University.

6. Bulskov, H., Knappe, R. and Andreasen, T.: On Measuring Similarity for Conceptual Querying, LNAI 2522, pp. 100-111 in T. Andreasen, A. Motro, H. Christiansen, H.L. Larsen (Eds.): Flexible Query Answering Systems 5th International Conference, FQAS 2002, Copenhagen, Denmark, October 27-29, 2002, Proceedings
7. Knappe, R., Bulskov, H. and Andreasen, T.: On Similarity Measures for Content-based Querying, International Fuzzy Sysytems Association, World Congress, Istanbul, Turkey, June 29-July 2, 2003, Proceedings
8. Knappe, R., Bulskov, H. and Andreasen, T.: Similarity Graphs, LNAI 2871, pp. 668-672 in N. Zhong, Z.W. Ras, S. Tsumoto, E. Suzuki (Eds.): 14th International Symposium on Methodologies for Intelligent Systems, ISMIS 2003, Maebashi, Japan, October 28-31, 2003, Proceedings
9. Nilsson, J. Fischer: A Logico-algebraic Framework for Ontologies - ONTOLOG, in Jensen, P. Anker & Skadhauge, P. (eds.): Proceedings of the First International OntoQuery Workshop - Ontology-based interpretation of NP's, Department of Business Communication and Information Science, University of Southern Denmark, Kolding, 2001
10. Rada, Roy, Mili, Hafedh, Bicknell, Ellen, Blettner, Maria: Development and Application of a Metric on Semantic Nets, IEEE Transactions on Systems, Man, and Cybernetics, Volume 19, 1989
11. Resnik, Philip: Semantic Similarity in a Taxonomy: An Information-based Measure and its Application to Problems of Ambiguity in Natural Language, Journal of Artificial Intelligence, pp. 95-130, 1999
12. Yager, R.R.: A hierarchical document retrieval language, in Information Retrieval vol 3, Issue 4, Kluwer Academic Publishers pp. 357-377, 2000.

On the Discovery of the Semantic Context of Queries by Game-Playing

Alessandro Agostini and Paolo Avesani

ITC-IRST Trento
Via Sommarive 18, 38050 Povo, Trento, Italy
{agostini,avesani}@irst.itc.it

Abstract. To model query answering, a question arises out of how the meaning of a user's query is functional to get a valuable answer. In this paper, (1) we investigate the question within an existing peer-to-peer architecture for knowledge exchange – called KEx, (2) we extend the query answering functionality of KEx by a co-evolutive process based on the user's preference information, (3) we model query answering as a language game.

Keywords: formal modeling of query answering, search, self-organization, language games, coordination.

1 Introduction

Responses to queries may not contain the information the user really wants. If we are to build information systems that meet users' expectations, it is necessary to determinate what it means for an answer to be appropriate. To this aim, Grice's maxims of cooperative conversation [9] provided a starting point for the field of cooperative answering. For answers to be appropriate, or relevant, the user of databases and information systems in general must ask the appropriate queries in order to arrive at the desired information [8]. To do so, the user must know something about the information source's schema, namely, the way the information is stored and classified. This is often hard to happen in real-world scenarios. Following [26], moreover, a system "is not user-friendly when it requires a detailed knowledge of the database structure, especially in the presence of large amounts of heterogeneous data" (p. 356). But cooperative answering systems are expected to be user-friendly, and users "usually have [only] a high-level knowledge of the database structure, based on their natural perception of data correlations" (p. 357). The lack of knowledge about the database structure "does not preclude the need to enforce specific selection criteria on the results" (*ibidem*). To build information systems that meet users' expectations, we agree with [26] on the tradeoff between allowing natural queries and receiving relevant answers it may be well obtained by using an interactive, cooperative and adaptive query modeling.

In this paper, we present a model whereby the ability to do appropriate queries and provide useful answers emerges as the result of a complex, dynamic and co-evolutive interaction.

H. Christiansen et al. (Eds.): FQAS 2004, LNAI 3055, pp. 203–216, 2004.

1.1   Motivation: Knowledge Exchange

An increasingly common technique to solve a user's query on the web is "guess-ing" its context – that is, the semantic content, conceptualisation or meaning of the query from the user [11]; see also [14]. Rather than explicitly requiring the user either to directly enter context information or know something about the information source's schema, this technique guesses when such context may be relevant to the user. The problem here is that few of the results returned may be *valuable* to the user [4, 13]. Which documents are valuable to the user depends on the semantic content of the user's query. Under such premises, guessing relevance in such *semantic context discovery* problem becomes a true challenge.

As far as we know, today search techniques "by guessing" are limited to cases where potential contexts can be identified based on the keyword query; cf. [11]. Unfortunately, these cases rarely happen in the highly distributed environment of the Web, where users can manage huge amount of data and use several kinds of queries. Appropriate queries, in short, are difficult to ask. In this paper, we face the problem of appropriate query formulation in KEx.

KEx (for "Knowledge Exchange", see [6, 5]) is a distributed, knowledge man-agement system implemented as a peer-to-peer architecture, where: "(i) each peer (called K-peer) provides all the services needed to create and organize local knowledge from an individual's or a group's perspective, and (ii) social struc-tures and protocols of meaning negotiation are introduced to achieve semantic coordination among autonomous peers" [6, from the *Abstract*]. Roughly speak-ing, (i) involves the representation of the knowledge of each K-peer and the services provided by the system – KEx as a whole, in order to manage such knowledge. On the other hand, (ii) involves the representation of the knowledge and reasoning mechanisms or services that each K-peer uses to communicate. So, KEx provides each individual peer or the community of peers with the way to represent, organize and communicate local knowledge according to its goals and interpretative perspective.

In the current version, KEx contains a main research problem. It is indeed possible and very common that the meaning of a query, advanced by a user selecting some "seeker" from a set of available peers, is conceptualised by the seeker in a even very different way from the potential providers suitable to re-spond. In other words, the query and the potential answer may refer to different "contexts." A "context" in KEx is a main data structure used to represent local knowledge. Local knowledge, in particular, is the knowledge available to the user to organize the meaning of a query.

Now, suppose that meaning conceptualization, or context, affects query for-mulation. For example, this would happen to a user who looks at the names of her data directories to decide the query expression to use. A question then arises out of how query meaning and query evolution and refinements are functional to achieve query success. In this paper, we investigate this question. We claim that a robust solution will need a module to incrementally learn synonyms and abbreviations from linguistic mappings that are performed over time.

The cooperative model we propose is based on the philosophy of language games [27], the methodology and seminal extensive work by Steels on discrimination games [17], guessing games [22, 24, 21] and classification games [23], and some of the ideas about advertising games [1, 3]. To illustrate such philosophy and methodology, we briefly rely on the following background.

Originally, Wittgenstein [27] introduced the concept of language "games" to emphasize the role of language speaking in everyday life. Among a large number of games, Wittgenstein defined the game of "describing an object through features," for instance the external shape or dimension. As we will see, relevant answers to a query about an object – think of a document, sometimes correspond to discover the features by which the document was classified by the questioner.

Wittgenstein's language games have been used and modified successively to study natural language semantics by experimental use of visually grounded robots in a distributed group [18, 20]. The problem was to determine the systematic relations between language forms ("words"), their meanings ("concepts") – expecially local meaning assigned to words by a single agent, and their referents ("instances," "objects").

A major sub-problem is "naming," that is, how vocabulary and meanings are learned individually and a shared lexicon eventually emerges in a group of agents. The problem of naming may be expressed in game-theoretical terms, and was extensively studied since the *naming games* [18]. In short, each "player" from an uniform set of agents has a set of words and a set of objects, and randomly associates a word to an object, called "the topic," to form *his local* lexicon. It is assumed that all the agents gain a positive payoff in cooperating "but only if they use the same language" [18]. A naming game is a coordination game in the sense of game theory (see for instance [15]), and it is repeatedly played among randomly chosen pairs of players. Thus, a naming game involves a different couple of agents at each repetition of playing. By definition a naming game is adaptive, in the sense that the players in the game change their internal state. A reason for changing is to be more successful in playing future games. Of course, naming is a crucial issue in query answering.

There are several variations and extensions of a naming game. Among others are the *guessing games* [22, 24, 21]. In contrast with the naming games, instead of playing directly the topic, in a guessing game a speaker explicitly plays to a hearer just a linguistic hint. Then, the hearer guesses the topic through the verbal description ("verbalisation") provided by the speaker. The game ends in success just in case the hearer's guess is equal to the topic. The game ends in failure otherwise. In this paper, we propose a kind of guessing game that, we believe, is appropriate and suitable to model query answering interaction.

From now on we proceed as follows. The main components of our model, basically seekers and providers, are defined in Section 2. The algorithm that determines the main steps of query answering ("query-answering game") is advanced in the details and discussed in Section 3. The functionality of the algorithm in a real application like KEx is presented in Section 4. We end this paper with some related work (Section 5) and the conclusion (Section 6).

2   Seekers and Providers

We image that a system ("community") of agents, or "peers," is available to a user. The user may employ a peer to play the role of the seeker or the provider. Intuitively, a peer in the role of the seeker incorporates the functions dealing with knowledge management and query making. These functions allow the user to perform some manipulation of documents, mainly to create clusters by using distinctive features of its documents and compare documents to judge their similarity, and do queries. In particular, this paper focuses on the ability of a seeker to make *queries by example*. On the other hand, a peer in the role of the provider has the same organizational structure of the seeker – both are "peers" – plus the ability to answer queries by example.

The peers have reasoning abilities. We illustrate these abilities along the basic components, terminology and notation of our framework.

The "knowledge domain," or domain of data, is a set of documents – called the universal set of documents. We denote this set by $\mathcal{D}$. One might consider a document as any object provided with a textual content. For example, a document may be a web page, a journal article, any finite string of terms written in a previously specified language. For the aim of this paper, however, what matters is the interpretation of a document, say its semantics, and the local classification of the document, as we will see below. Each peer p has a repository consisting of a proper[1] subset of the universal set of documents, denoted by: $\mathcal{D}_p$.

The peers share a minimal language $\mathcal{L}$, defined as follows. Let Text $(\cdot)$ be a text extraction function. We refer to the keywords extraction function of [25, Sec. 4]. Given a document d, Text (d) lists all the keywords in d, precisely, the most frequent terms that were found in a list of frequent (Italian) terms. Thus, Text $(\cdot)$ combines simple statistical measures with elementary linguistic knowledge. Applied to a document d, Text $(\cdot)$ produces a set Text (d) of **words**. We call Text (d) the (textual) **semantics of** d [2].

Definition 1. Let Text $(\cdot)$ and $\mathcal{D}$ be given. We define $\mathcal{L} = $ Text $(\mathcal{D})$, where Text $(\mathcal{D}) = \bigcup_{d \in \mathcal{D}}$ Text (d).

Of course, each peer in the system may have an additional set of words to express autonomous concepts and queries (labels of nodes of a context and keywords in [6], respectively). We denote peer p's language by $\mathcal{L}_p$. In this paper, we deal with words from natural language without further specification. The use of more abstract languages, however, does not change the basic features of our approach.

Remark 1. Although much of the initial work in cooperative answering focused on natural language and dialogue systems (see [8] for references) and, on the other hand, language games were originally thought of to study natural language semantics – see for instance [27, 18, 19, 23], the tenets of a cooperative

---

[1] We note that if p's repository and $\mathcal{D}$ coincide, then it would not make sense for p to play the role of the seeker, because no documents to seek would exist in this case.

[2] Other text extraction functions are ammissible in our framework. Although important, a specific treatment of keywords extraction is out of the scope of this paper.

query-answering system ought to be universal to queries themselves, regardless of whether the queries are cast in natural language, in formal logic, or what else.

Documents may be organized by the peers in "clusters." In particular, documents may be aggregated by individual peers according to a general schema, or similarity measure, which is applied by each peer p locally to classify its documents repository $\mathcal{D}_p$. Informally, a cluster is a set of similar documents. To define a cluster formally, we rely on the following terminology and notation.

A peer manages and classifies its documents by using "features" and preferences over its "lexicon" (see subsection 2.1). Intuitively, a feature of a document is a pair composed by a (key)word in the document, to be thought of as a standardized text from procedure $\mathsf{Text}\,(\cdot)$ of text extraction, and a relative value. For example, think to the frequency of occurrence of that word in the document. Following [25], given a document d we rank a word $w \in \mathsf{Text}\,(d)$ on the basis of a slighly better method than just counting the number of occurrences of the word in the document. More precisely, we use the inverse document frequency [12].

Definition 2. Let peer p, document repository $\mathcal{D}_p$ and word $w \in \mathsf{Text}\,(d)$ for document $d \in \mathcal{D}$ be given. We define the **weight of** w **in** d **for** p as follows.

$$\mathsf{W}_p[w,d] = N[w,d] \cdot log\frac{Card(\mathcal{D}_p)}{\mathsf{doc}_p[w]},$$

where $N[w,d]$ is the total number of occurrences of w in d, $Card(\mathcal{D}_p)$ is the number of documents in $\mathcal{D}_p$ ($\mathcal{D}_p$'s cardinality), and $\mathsf{doc}_p[w]$ is the total number of documents in $\mathcal{D}_p$ containing w. Note that $\mathsf{W}_p[w,d]$ is a real number, so $\mathsf{W}_p[\cdot,\cdot]$ is a function from $\mathcal{L} \times \mathcal{D}$ to R.

$$log\frac{Card(\mathcal{D}_p)}{\mathsf{doc}_p[w]}$$

is called **inverse document frequency of** w **for** p, in symbols: $\mathsf{IDF}_p[w]$.

The intuitive meaning of $\mathsf{IDF}_p[\cdot]$ is that terms which rarely occur over a collection of documents in peer p's repository are the most relevant. The importance of each term is assumed to be inversely proportional to the number of documents that contain the term. Since $\mathsf{IDF}_p[\cdot]$ represents word specificity in the view of a peer p, it is expected to improve the precision of p's classification of documents. In particular, it has been proved (Salton and Yang, 1973; see [12]) that the combination $\mathsf{W}_p[w,d]$ of term frequency of a word in a document $N[w,d]$ with the inverse document frequency $\mathsf{IDF}_p[w]$ of Definition 2 better characterizes documents' content than term frequency[3].

We are now ready to define the "features of a document for a peer."

Definition 3. Let peer p and document $d \in \mathcal{D}$ be given. The **features set of** d **for** p is the set $F_{p,d} = \{(w,v) \mid w \in \mathsf{Text}\,(d), v = \mathsf{W}_p[w,d]\}$. The **features set for** p is the set $F_p = \bigcup_{d \in \mathcal{D}_p} F_{p,d}$.

---

[3] We refer the interested reader to [12] for further discussion.

We call the pair (w, v) a **feature** (of d for p). We say that w is the attribute (or name) of the feature (w, v), and that v is its value. Some features are "distinctive." Informally, features are distinctive when refer to the same attribute with different values. We rely on the following definition.

Definition 4. Let features (w_1, v_1), (w_2, v_2) for a peer p be given. We say that (w_1, v_1) and (w_2, v_2) are **distinctive** if $w_1 = w_2$ and $v_1 \neq v_2$.

We use distinctive features to distinguish documents. Intuitively, two documents are similar if they have similar content. To be more precise, we need some notation. Given peer p and document $d \in \mathcal{D}_p$, let V_d denote the finite sequence over real numbers – we call it **feature vector**, obtained by listing the value of each feature of d for p. That is, given $d \in \mathcal{D}_p$, we define feature vector $\langle v_1, v_2, \ldots, v_k \rangle$, where v_i for $i = 1, 2, ..., k = Card(F_{p,d})$ is the value of the ith feature of d for p.

For all peers in the system, we now define $\mathsf{Sim}^p(\cdot, \cdot)$ to be a similarity measure defined over "normalized feature vectors." To normalize two feature vectors, we order the attributes of each feature in each vector according to the same ordering relation, and extend the shortes vector by adding zeros. (See references in [25].)

Definition 5. Let peer p and documents $d, d' \in \mathcal{D}$ be given. We define

$$\mathsf{Sim}^p(d, d') = \frac{< V_d, V_{d'} >}{\| V_d \| \cdot \| V_{d'} \|},$$

where $< V_d, V_{d'} >$ denotes the result of the scalar product of normalized feature vectors V_d and $V_{d'}$, and $\| V_d \| \cdot \| V_{d'} \|$ is the product of the vectors' norm[4]. (See also [25, Sec. 5].)

Note that function $\mathsf{Sim}^p(\cdot, \cdot)$ is partial recursive. We say that documents d, d' have similar content, or that are **similar for** peer p just in case $\mathsf{Sim}^p(d, d') \neq 0$. We say documents d, d' are **similar** if d, d' are similar for some peer. Note that $\mathsf{Sim}^p(d, d') \in [0, 1]$; also compare function $\mathsf{Sim}^p(\cdot, \cdot)$ to the *Cosine* similarity measure [16].

Remark 2. The similarity measure $\mathsf{Sim}^p(\cdot, \cdot)$ provides the peer p with the main mechanism to update clusters, in the sense that only retrieved documents similar to the document $d \in C$ taken by p as the example to support the query ("query by example") are added to the cluster C. Moreover, $\mathsf{Sim}^p(\cdot, \cdot)$ is defined according to the user needs for all peers p. Thus, we assume that whenever a peer p is selected by a user u to play the role of the seeker – in other words, u has employed p to search some documents – , we have $\mathsf{Sim}^p(\cdot, \cdot) \equiv \mathsf{Sim}^u(\cdot, \cdot)$. As an obvious consequence, a user with a similarity measure that differs from that considered in Definition 5 is supposed to be unable to employ p as the seeker suitable to pursue the query.

A "distinctive feature set" is a set of features distinguishing a document from a set of other documents. In a system of peers, as our system, we need

---

[4] Recall that $\| V \| = Sqr(< V, V >)$.

to associate a distinctive feature set to peers, so that a distinctive feature set becomes a kind of local "ontology" used by a peer to classify its documents. We will see the relationship between distinctive feature sets and clusters once we have defined these two concepts. We begin to define a "distinctive feature set of a document for a peer with respect to a set of documents," in symbols: $D_{p,d}^C$.

Definition 6. Let peer p, document $d \in \mathcal{D}$, set of documents $C \subseteq \mathcal{D}_p$ and features set $F_{p,d}$ be given. We define:

$$D_{p,d}^C = \{(w,v) \in F_{p,d} \mid \forall d' \in C, \; \not\exists (w',v') \in F_{p,d'} \; w' = w \text{ or } \exists (w,\tilde{v}) \in F_{p,d'} \; \tilde{v} \neq v\}.$$

Note that $D_{p,d}^C \subseteq F_{p,d}$, $D_{p,d}^{\{d\}} = \emptyset$, and $D_{p,d}^{\emptyset} = F_{p,d}$. Thus, the elements of $D_{p,d}^C$ are all features suitable by p to distinguish a document d from other documents in C. Of course, a distinctive feature set is a feature set.

We now are ready to define clusters of documents by distinctive features. Given a peer p, we denote the **relative complement** $\mathcal{D}_p \setminus C$ of a set C by $\overline{C_p}$.

Definition 7. Let peer p be given. A **cluster of** p is the set $C \subseteq \mathcal{D}_p$ such that for all $d, d' \in C$, the distinctive feature sets of d and d' for p with respect to $\overline{C_p}$ are defined, and

$$D_{p,d}^{\overline{C_p}} = D_{p,d'}^{\overline{C_p}}.$$

As will be clearer by the next definition, we use distinctive feature sets to label clusters. Definition 7 has an important consequence on this, as it allows us to define a way to assign a "name" to a cluster by using preferences over documents' distinctive features. Whenever d in Definition 7 is "the example of a query" (see also Step 2 in Section 3), we say that cluster C is the **query cluster**.

We need some notation.

Given a peer p, let $\mathsf{Pref}^p(\cdot, \cdot)$ be a total function from $\mathcal{L}_p \times (pow(F_p) \cup pow(\mathcal{D}_p))$ to integers (denoted by Z). Positive, negative and neutral preferences are possible. Note that Definition 7 implies that for all peers p, all words w in p's language, and for every set of documents $C \subset \mathcal{D}_p$, $\mathsf{Pref}^p(w, D_{p,d}^{\mathcal{D}_p \setminus C}) = \mathsf{Pref}^q(w, D_{p,d'}^{\mathcal{D}_p \setminus C})$ for all $d, d' \in C$. This is equivalent to say that a peer's preferences over feature sets that distinguish a document from the complement of a cluster do not depend on the choice of the document. So the next definition is sound and gives a way to decide how to name a cluster.

Definition 8. Let peer p, cluster C of p and word $w \in \mathcal{L}_p$ be given. We define:

$$\mathsf{Pref}^p(w, C) = \mathsf{Pref}^p(w, D_{p,d}^{\mathcal{D}_p \setminus C}),$$

if there is $d \in C$ such that $\mathsf{Pref}^p(w, D_{p,d}^{\mathcal{D}_p \setminus C})$ is defined, and $\mathsf{Pref}^p(w, \emptyset) = 0$. Otherwise, $\mathsf{Pref}^p(w, C)$ is undefined.

We say that C **is labelled with** w **by** p just in case $\mathsf{Pref}^p(w, C)$ is maximum, that is, $\mathsf{Pref}^p(w', C) \leq \mathsf{Pref}^p(w, C)$ for every $w' \in \mathcal{L}_p$ with $w' \neq w$.

2.1   Lexicon

Each agent has a "lexicon." Given a peer p, we denote the lexicon of p by Lx_p. Informally, a peer's lexicon is a set of pairs, where the first component is a word, or "label," build from the peer's language, and the second component is a feature set for the peer. Formally, we define the lexicon of peer p as follows:

$$Lx_p = \{(w, F_{p,d}) \mid w \in \mathcal{L}_p,\, d \in \mathcal{D}_p,\, \mathsf{Pref}^p(w, F_{p,d}) \text{ defined}\}.$$

A lexicon may be either empty or incomplete, that is, there may be some word with no associated feature set or some feature set with no associated word. Notice that there is not one lexicon for all peers, but each peer has its local lexicon.

Each peer p in the system has two functions, denoted by $query(\cdot, \cdot)$ and $answer(\cdot, \cdot)$. Informally, $query(\cdot, \cdot)$ provides a peer in the role of the seeker with the way to translate the local knowledge about a document – i.e., the document used as the example for a query, into a language suitable to express the query. For simplicity, from now on we assume that each peer has a *finite* language.

Definition 9. Let peer p and $d \in \mathcal{D}_p$ be given. We define $query(F_{p,d}, Lx_p)$ to be the finite sequence $\langle w_1, w_2, \ldots, w_n \rangle$ over $\mathcal{L}_p$ such that $(w_i, F_{p,d}) \in Lx_p$ ($i = 1, 2, \ldots, n$), and for all $i, j \leq n$, if $i \leq j$ then $\mathsf{Pref}^p(w_i, F_{p,d}) \geq \mathsf{Pref}^p(w_j, F_{p,d})$.

We call the finite sequence $\langle w_1, w_2, \ldots, w_n \rangle$ **query expression**. Informally, by using $query(F_{p,d}, Lx_p)$ the peer p exploits and communicate existing high-level knowledge of the user about the document d.

Clusters' names and function $query(\cdot, \cdot)$ are employed by peers to convey clusters' meaning to query language. How a cluster's name may be used to export some of the cluster's meaning to a query is the content of the next theorem.

Theorem 1. Suppose that a nonempty cluster C is labelled with w by peer p. Then there is a document $d \in C$ such that $query(D_{p,d}^{\overline{C_p}}, Lx_p) = \langle w, w_2, \ldots, w_n \rangle$ for arbitrary $w_2, \ldots, w_n$.

Proof: Let C be a nonempty cluster of p and let C be labelled by w. Then there is $d \in C$ such that $\mathsf{Pref}^p(w, D_{p,d}^{\mathcal{D}_p \setminus C})$ is defined, hence $(w, D_{p,d}^{\overline{C_p}}) \in Lx_p$ and $query(D_{p,d}^{\overline{C_p}}, Lx_p)$ is defined. Moreover, $\mathsf{Pref}^p(w, D_{p,d}^{\mathcal{D}_p \setminus C})$ is maximum over $\mathcal{L}_p$, so $query(D_{p,d}^{\overline{C_p}}, Lx_p)$ is of the form $\langle w, \ldots \rangle$. ⊣

Answering by using $answer(\cdot, \cdot)$ allows a peer in the role of the provider to interpret a query, according to the provider's lexicon. We rely on the following definition. (Recall that $\mathcal{L}$ denotes the universal system language, see Def. 1. Let Λ denote the set of peers in the system.)

Definition 10. Let peer p and finite sequence $\langle w_1, w_2, \ldots, w_n \rangle$ over $\bigcup_{q \in \Lambda} \mathcal{L}_q \cup \mathcal{L}$ be given. We define $answer(\langle w_1, w_2, \ldots, w_n \rangle, Lx_p)$ to be the set of feature sets $F \subset F_p$ for p such that for all $i = 1, 2, \ldots, n$ there is a feature of the form $(w_i, \cdot)$ such that $(w_i, \cdot) \in F$ and $(w_i, F) \in Lx_p$.

So, each w_i is used by the peer as the input to find ("guess") the cluster (if any) suitable to answer to the query expression $\langle w_1, w_2, \ldots, w_n \rangle$.

3   Interactive Querying Algorithm

In normal operation, the user selects "the seeker" from the system of peers. The seeker selects one or more providers as the target peers for a query. We called **context** the semantic content, conceptualisation, or meaning, of the user query. The user, the seeker and the target provider(s) continuously go through a loop performing the following actions:

Step 1. A context $\mathcal{C}$ for the user is delineated (by the user itself). The context consists of a set of documents from the user's document repository currently in the field of attention of the user. Without loss of generality, we assume $\mathcal{C} = \mathcal{D}_u = \mathcal{D}_s$ (u = the user, s = the seeker).

Step 2. One document d in the context is chosen (by the user) according to the user's distinctive feature sets, which determine the **query cluster**[5]. The document may be thought of as "the example" of the user's query.

Step 3. The selected cluster C is labelled by the seeker with a word w in the seeker's language. The seeker's action is performed with maximum preference $\mathsf{Pref}^s(w, C)$. Intuitively, w is the recommended name of the cluster provided (with preference $\mathsf{Pref}^s(w, C)$) by the seeker to the user.

Step 4. The seeker sends to the target provider(s) the sequence $\langle w_1, w_2, \ldots, w_n \rangle$ ("query expression") produced by applying function $query(\cdot, \cdot)$ to the seeker's "knowledge" about d. Precisely, $\langle w_1, w_2, \ldots, w_n \rangle = query(F_{s,d}, Lx_s)$, where $F_{s,d}$ is the user's distinctive feature set distingushing d from all other documents in the context which are not in the query cluster. The query expression is a kind of recommended query to the user.

Step 5. An attempt is made by the target provider(s) to find possible features distinguishing the document-example d from the set of all documents in its document repository. In other words, an attempt is made by the target provider(s) to find possible distinctive feature sets on the basis of the received query expression. The question the provider p poses itself is, roughly: "there are a cluster C' of p, some document(s) $d' \in \mathcal{D}_p$ and a distinctive feature set $D_{p,d'}^{\mathcal{D}_p \setminus C'}$ such that $D_{p,d'}^{\mathcal{D}_p \setminus C'} \neq \emptyset$ and $D_{p,d'}^{\mathcal{D}_p \setminus C'} \in answer(\langle w_1, w_2, \ldots, w_n \rangle, Lx_p)$?" If the answer is yes, then C' is the **answering cluster** of the provider that hopefully matches with the query cluster C of the seeker.

Step 6. The provider p sends document(s) $d' \in \mathcal{D}_p$ to the seeker, who evaluates it againts the example d by using $\mathsf{Sim}^s(d, d')$. If the provider's result is relevant, that is, $\mathsf{Sim}^s(d, d') > \delta$ for some fixed, user dependent relevance parameter δ, preferences over the peers' lexicon are updated to success. Otherwise, preferences over the peers' lexicon are updated to failure.

On the basis of the foregoing steps, that we refer to as the rules of the **query-answering game** $\mathcal{G} = \langle u, s, p, d, \mathcal{C} \rangle$, a number of query formation or query refinement situations arise. (In the following, C denotes the query cluster produced in Step 2.)

---

[5] For simplicity, we assume that a nonempty distinctive feature set suitable to form a cluster of similar documents exists. Otherwise, we may think to extend the model to allow more features that those of the form (w, v) we have considered in this paper.

1. *The seeker is unable to express the example d by words* (Step 4 fails): Either the seeker's lexicon Lx_s is not developed enough or the seeker's naming function $query(\cdot, \cdot)$ is undefined over $(D_{s,d}^{\mathcal{D}_s \backslash C}, Lx_s)$. The seeker (possibly by interacting with the user) then creates a new element $(w, D_{s,d}^{\mathcal{D}_s \backslash C})$ in its lexicon with preference $\mathsf{Pref}^s(w, D_{s,d}^{\mathcal{D}_s \backslash C}) = 0$.

2. *The provider is unable to interpret the query from the seeker* (Step 5 fails): Either the provider is unable to find possible features distinguishing the example from the set of all documents in its database or the provider does not understand the query expression from the seeker. In the first case, the game ends in failure – the provider's response is an empty set of documents together with a message error[6]. In the second case – suppose that the provider has found at least a set of distinguishing features, the provider extends its lexicon and creates associations between the seeker's query expression and each suitable set of features. More precisely, the following actions are done. (Let $\langle w_1, w_2, \ldots, w_n \rangle$ be the query expression from the seeker and let $D_{p,d'}^{\mathcal{D}_p \backslash C'}$ denote a set of distinguishing features found by the provider, cf. Step 5. Observe that such set depends on d' and C', so many distinguishing features sets may be found.) Then, for all $i = 1, \ldots, n$:

   - the provider adds the new element $(w_i, D_{p,d'}^{\mathcal{D}_p \backslash C'})$ to its lexicon with fixed preference:
   $$\mathsf{Pref}^p(w_i, D_{p,d'}^{\mathcal{D}_p \backslash C'}) = 0.$$

3. *The seeker is able to send a query expression for the example and the provider is able to interpret it* (Step 6; no linguistic failures arise): We distinguish two cases, that are also the possible outcomes of the query-answering game $\mathcal{G}$.

   (a) *The provider's response is compatible ("relevant") with the seeker's query.* This means that $\mathsf{Sim}^s(d, d') > \delta$ for a fixed, previously defined, user dependent relevance parameter δ. The query succeeds, the game ends in success. Note that it is possible, indeed probable at the beginning of the game, that the query cluster and the answering cluster are labelled with different words and that the seeker and the provider(s) use different feature sets. The seeker increases the value of its lexicon preferences over the winning associations $(w_i, D_{s,d}^{\mathcal{D}_s \backslash C})$ and decreases lexicon preferences over competing associations $(w, D_{s,d}^{\mathcal{D}_s \backslash C})$ for all words w not present in the query expression. The seeker's motivation to adapt preferences is to update cluster label.

   Similarly, the provider increases lexicon preferences over winning associations $(w_i, D_{p,d'}^{\mathcal{D}_p \backslash C'})$ and decreases preferences of competing associations $(w_i, D_{p,d'}^{\mathcal{D}_p \backslash \hat{C}'})$ in its lexicon.

---

[6] At this stage of the game, it would be possible for the provider to create new features to distinguish the example of the seeker from the provider's documents. Our model development at now, however, does not allow to do this. We have planned to extend our model to deal with features out of the form (w, v). We leave it for future work.

(b) *The provider's response is not compatible with the seeker's query.* This means that $\mathsf{Sim}^s(d, d') \leq \delta$. The query fails, the game ends in failure.

4   KEx Integration: Similar Documents Service

We now describe the functionality of the algorithm, which allows us to add a new service to KEx – we call it *Similar Documents Service* (SDS). The Similar Documents Service can be used for many purposes, the most important to the aim of this paper is the following. Suppose that the user likes a particular document's content, but wish it had more to say. Then, Similar Pages & Documents can find documents with similar content with which the user may be unfamiliar. If the user is interested in researching a particular area or topic, say information about a particular concept or "meaning," Similar Pages & Documents can help to find a large number of resources very quickly, without having to worry about selecting the right keywords. These are automatically generated ("recommended") as the most successful names for the concept under attention. The more specialized a document is, the fewer results our algorithm will be able to find.

As a consequence of the algorithm' structure, the Service provides the user with a document retrieval semi-automatic "strategy". On the most practical said, when the user clicks on the *Similar Pages & Documents* link for a search result – say "give me a set of documents related to document d" –, after a finite training period KEx automatically scouts the system of peers, or a subset of previously selected (available, preferred, etc.) peers, for documents that are related (i.e., similar in the sense of Definition 5) to this result. In general, the similarity measure used by the user depends on the seeker employed to query the system – recall Remark 2.

A critical step to the integration is the notion of "context." In fact, in this paper we have defined a context be a set of documents from the user's document repository currently in the field of attention of the user. However, in KEx "contexts" are the main data structures used to represent local knowledge. Local knowledge is the knowledge available to autonomous agents. KEx provides each individual agent or community with the mechanisms to represent and organize local knowledge according to its goals and interpretative perspective. Contexts are used to this aim. Precisely, contexts are used to conceptualize data according to three main components: an "unique identifier," or context name; a set of "explicit assumptions," that provide meta-information about the context (e.g., the context's owner); and an "explicit representation." Among possible reference models to explicitly represent a context's content (e.g., first-order logic, description logics, graphs), KEx used concept hierarchies (see for instance [7]) also known as terminological ontologies. For lack of space, we refer the reader to [2] for a thoughtful discussion on the role of context *à la* KEx in our model.

5   Related Work

Our approach to query answering is related to clustering of search results, as performed by Northern Light (*www.northernlight.com*), for example. Northern Light dynamically clusters search results into categories previously defined. These may be changed by new interactions to the user, who may narrow search results to any of these categories. More generally, there is a growing tendency of clustering techniques being used in web search (the system user - search engine is a query answering system, although not always cooperative!) to present the user with some query refinement options alongside the matching documents, that is, the documents supposed by the engine/provider to be relevant to the user. Other examples are Teoma (*www.teoma.com*) and AltaVista (*www.altavista.com*). However, an inherent problem of these techniques is naming of the clusters – that is, to select the right word or label to convey the cluster's meaning or to select useful expressions that can serve as query refinement terms. A recent work [10] studies this problem in the specific case of document collections being searched are domain-specific or limited in size.

6   Conclusion

We have presented a model whereby the ability to do appropriate queries emerges as the result of a complex, dynamic and co-evolutive interaction among peers, where each peer may play the role of the user-seeker or the provider. Our model is adaptive. We have argued that adaption, as basically influenced by the language usage, is not distinct from the categorization process behind query answering. In order to investigate the dynamic refinement of a query and query flexibility, we have advanced a model in which queries and answers are a consequence of language evolution and meaning construction. To determinate what it means for an answer to be appropriate, however, it is necessary but not sufficient to build information systems that meet users' expectations. Then, we must determine how to build information systems that exhibit cooperative answering behavior. The result of this paper is a specific cooperative technique aimed at identifying, after a finite number of steps, the most relevant answer with respect to the user's intentions and queries' meaning. Our aim was the tight coupling of knowledge discovery and classification with query processing and evolution, as a mean to provide the user with the most relevant possible answer. For doing this, we have exploited existing high-level knowledge of the user and low-level text retrieval techniques.

As main directions of research, we mention experimental evaluation of the Interactive Querying algorithm and "semantic matching of seekers and providers." In fact, the functionality of query-answering described provides a mapping between the seeker and the provider. The mapping is a "matching" between the contexts used, respectively, by the seeker who makes the query and by the provider who attempts to solve it. The problem, that we leave here for future work, is to make the relation between query-answering and context matching clearer. A first answer is proposed in [2, Remark (16)].

Acknowledgments

This work was partially supported by the *Provincia Autonoma di Trento* Project EDAMOK ("Enabling Distributed and Autonomous Management of Knowledge") under deliberation number 1060-4/5/2001.

References

1. A. Agostini and P. Avesani. Advertising games for web services. In R. Meersman, Z. Tari, and D. Schmit, editors, *Proceedings of the Eleventh International Conference on Cooperative Information Systems (CoopIS-03)*, pages 93–110, Berlin Heidelberg, 2003. Springer-Verlag LNCS 2888.
2. A. Agostini and P. Avesani. Adaptive querying to knowledge exchange. Technical report, ITC-IRST, Trento, Italy, January 2004.
3. P. Avesani and A. Agostini. A peer-to-peer advertising game. In M. Orlowksa, M. Papazoglou, S. Weerawarana, and J. Yang, editors, *Proceedings of the First International Conference on Service Oriented Computing (ICSOC-03)*, pages 28–42, Berlin Heidelberg, 2003. Springer-Verlag LNCS 2910.
4. C. L. Barry. *The Identification of User Criteria of Relevance and Documents Characteristics: Beyond the Topical Approach to Information Retrieval*. PhD thesis, Syracuse University, 1993.
5. M. Bonifacio, P. Bouquet, G. Mameli, and M. Nori. KEx: A Peer-to-Peer solution for distributed knowledge
management. In *Proceedings of the Fourth International Conference on Practical Aspects of Knowledge Management (PAKM-02)*, pages 490–500, Heidelberg, 2002. Springer-Verlag LNAI 2569.
6. M. Bonifacio, P. Bouquet, G. Mameli, and M. Nori. Peer - mediated distributed knowledge management. In *Proceedings of AAAI Spring Symposium on Agent Mediated
Knowledge Management (AMKM-03)*, Stanford, CA, 2003. Stanford University.
7. A. Büchner, M. Ranta, J. Hughes, and M. Mäntylä. Semantic information mediation among multiple product ontologies. In *Proceedings of the 4th World Conference on Integrated Design and Process Technology (IDPT-99)*, 1999.
8. T. Gaasterland, P. Godfrey, and J. Minker. An overview of cooperative answering. *Journal of Intelligent Information Systems*, 1(2):123–157, 1992.
9. H. Grice. Logic and Conversation. In P. Cole and J. Morgan, editors, *Syntax and Semantics*.
Academic Press, New York, 1975.
10. U. Kruschwitz. An adaptable search system for collections of partially structured documents. *IEEE Intelligent Systems*, 18(4):44–52, 2003.
11. S. Lawrence. Context in Web Search. *IEEE Data Engineering Bulletin*, 23(3):25–32, 2000.
12. C. D. Manning and H. Schtze, editors. *Foundations of Statistical Natural Language Processing*. The MIT Press, Cambridge, MA, 1999.
13. S. Mizzaro. Relevance: The whole history. *Journal of the American Society for Information Science*,
48(9):810–832, 1997.
14. R. Navarro-Prieto, M. Scaife, and Y. Rogers. Cognitive strategies in web searching. In *Proceedings of the Fifth Conference on Human Factors & the Web (HFWEB-99)*. NIST, 1999.
15. M. J. Osborne and A. Rubinstein. *A Course in Game Theory*. The MIT Press, Cambridge, MA, 1994.
16. G. Salton and M. McGill. *Introduction to Modern Information Retrieval*. McGraw-Hill, New York, NY, 1983.
17. L. Steels. Perceptually grounded meaning creation. In Y. Demazeau, editor, *Proceedings of the Second International Conference on Multi-agent Systems (ICMAS-96)*, pages 338–344, Los Alamitos, CA, 1996. IEEE Computer Society.

18. L. Steels. Self-organizing vocabularies. In C. Langton and T. Shimohara, editors, *Proceedings of the V Alife Conference*, Cambridge, MA, 1996. The MIT Press.
19. L. Steels. The synthetic modeling of language origins. *Evolution of Communication*, 1(1):1–34, 1997.
20. L. Steels. The origins of syntax in visually grounded robotic agents. *Artificial Intelligence*, 103:133–156, 1998.
21. L. Steels. Language games for autonomous robots. *IEEE Intelligent Systems*, 16(5):16–22, 2001.
22. L. Steels and F. Kaplan. Situated grounded word semantics. In T. Dean, editor, *Proceedings of the Sixteenth International Joint Conference on Artificial Intelligence (IJCAI-99)*, pages 862–867, San Francisco, CA, 1999. Morgan Kaufmann.
23. L. Steels and F. Kaplan. AIBO's first words. The social learning of language and meaning. *Evolution of Communication*, 4(1):3–32, 2002.
24. L. Steels, F. Kaplan, A. McIntyre, and J. Van Looveren. Crucial factors in the origins of word-meanings. In A. Wray, editor, *The Transition to Language*, pages 214–217. Oxford University Press, Oxford, UK, 2002.
25. P. Tonella, F. Ricca, E. Pianta, and C. Girardi. Using keyword extraction for web site clustering. In Ken Wong, editor, *Proceedings of the Fifth International Workshop on Web Site Evolution (WSE-03)*, pages 41–48, Amsterdam, The Netherlands, September 22, 2003. IEEE Computer Society.
26. A. Trigoni. Interactive query formulation in semistructured databases. In T. Andreasen, A. Motro, H. Christiansen, and H. L. Larsen, editors, *Proceedings of the Fifth International Conference on Flexible Query Answering Systems (FQAS-02)*, pages 356–369, Berlin Heidelberg, 2002. Springer-Verlag LNAI 2522.
27. L. Wittgenstein. *Philosophical Investigations*. Blackwell, Oxford, UK, 1953.

Information Retrieval System for Medical Narrative Reports

Lior Rokach[1], Oded Maimon[1], and Mordechai Averbuch[2]

[1] Department of Industrial Engineering, Tel-Aviv University, Tel-Aviv, Israel
[2] Tel-Aviv Sourasky Medical Center and Faculty of Medicine, Tel-Aviv University, Tel-Aviv, Israel

Abstract. This paper presents a novel information retrieval system designed specifically for medical case finding applications. The proposed system begins by extracting medical information from free-text narrative reports and storing it in a predefined relational clinical data mart. The extraction is performed using a medical thesaurus and a regular expression pattern match. Following the extraction phase, inclusion/exclusion criteria are provided to the system using a physician-friendly user interface. The system converts the entered criteria into a single SQL command which can be then executed on the relational data mart. In order to achieve the appropriate response time required for on-line analysis, the system implements several caching mechanisms. The proposed system has been examined on real-world database. The performance of the system has been compared to the results obtained manually by a physician. The comparison indicates that the proposed system can be used for non-critical case-finding applications such as: finding appropriate patients for clinical trials.

1 Introduction

In a 1973 review the chief of the Computer Research Branch at the National Institutes of Health asserted that the data underlying the patient care process "are in the large majority nonnumeric in form and are formulated almost exclusively within the constructs of natural language" [12]. Today, more than 30 years later, much of the data stored in hospital information systems are still stored in free-text format, including history and physical exams, pathology reports, operative reports, discharge summaries, and radiology reports. Databases containing free-text medical narratives often need to be searched to find relevant information for clinical and research purposes.

Although there are vast of applications involving dedicated input forms that enable storing and arranging medical data in relational databases, these applications are still not fully installed. Physicians and other medical personnel do not readily accept the need to invest time to use such applications and prefer to use less time-consuming methods, such as transcription services (physician vocally records its finding, which is then dictated manually into free-text files). Consequently plenty of useful data is still stored in free-text medical narrative which makes it difficult to search for a set of patients that fulfill certain criteria.

H. Christiansen et al. (Eds.): FQAS 2004, LNAI 3055, pp. 217–228, 2004.

Medical narratives present some unique problems that are not normally encountered in other domains. When a physician writes an encounter note, a highly telegraphic form of language may be used. There are often very few (if any) grammatically correct sentences, and acronyms and abbreviations are frequently used. Very few of these abbreviations and acronyms can be found in a dictionary and they are highly idiosyncratic to the domain and local practice. Often misspellings, errors in phraseology, and transcription errors are found in dictated reports.

Extraction of relational medical data from free-text has been studied for a long time (see for instance [14]). More specifically many researchers have proposed various methods for mapping text to UMLS metathesaurus concepts [5], [7], [10].

Medical narratives present some unique problems that are not normally encountered in other domains. When a physician writes an encounter note, a highly telegraphic form of language may be used. There are often very few (if any) grammatically correct sentences, and acronyms and abbreviations are frequently used. Very few of these abbreviations and acronyms can be found in a dictionary and they are highly idiosyncratic to the domain and local practice. Often misspellings, errors in phraseology, and transcription errors are found in dictated reports.

Even if the issue of extraction medical information from free-text reports is solved, an appropriate system still needs to enable users easily writing medical queries and handle these queries efficiently. Due to the ambiguity, interconnectedness and complex relationships of medical data, SQL per-se is insufficient for providing a rigorous answer except for the most simple of queries. For instance the simple query "retrieve all patients that have been diagnosed with cancer" involve many diagnosis codes, making it difficult writing the appropriate SQL command explicitly as well as executing this command in reasonable time. Consequently major IT resources are required on regular basis to handle these requests.

It would be highly advantageous to have a method for easy extraction of medical information from free-text reports with minimum loss of information. This paper presents a suitable system that has been developed in the last three years that attempts to accomplish this goal.

2   System Description

2.1   Overview

Figure 1 illustrates the block diagram of the proposed system. The input for the process is a free-text report such as discharge summary. The Medical Free-Text ETL (Extraction Transformation Loading) extracts the relevant medical information from the report and loads into the relational clinical data mart. Then using Query Composition Module, a physician writes a medical query, which is processed by the Medical Query Processor to output a list of appropriate patients.

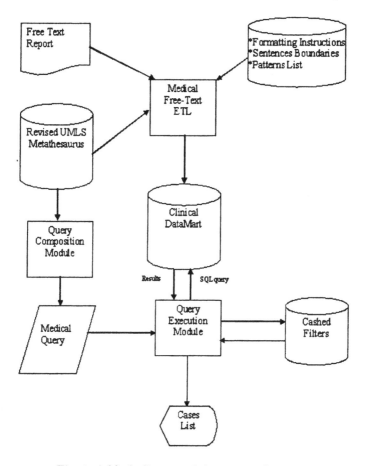

Fig. 1. A block diagram of the proposed system

2.2   Revised UMLS Metathesaurus

In 1986, the National Library of Medicine began a long term and vast research and development project to build a Unified Medical Language System (UMLS). The purpose of the UMLS is to aid the development of systems that help health professionals and researchers retrieve and integrate electronic biomedical information from a variety of sources. The UMLS contains from three knowledge sources: metathesaurus, lexicon and semantic network. The metathesaurus provides a uniform, integrated distribution format from over 60 biomedical vocabularies and classifications, and links many different names for the same concepts. The lexicon contains syntactic information for many terms, component words, and English words, including verbs that do not appear in the metathesaurus. The semantic network contains information about the types or categories (e.g., "Disease or Syndrome", "Virus") to which all Metathesaurus concepts have been assigned and the permissible relationships among these types (e.g., "Virus" causes

"Disease or Syndrome"). The proposed system uses the UMLS [11] revised as following:

The concepts have been organized in new simplified medical categories which reflect the structure of the clinical data mart. The categories are: Diagnosis, Medication, Lab, Procedures, Allergens, Food, Gender, Units and Other. An effort has been made to classify each concept to exactly one category. However there are still few concepts that belong to more than one category.

Unreliable or unused synonyms have been removed. For instance all synonyms denoted as "suppressed" have been removed. All Non-English synonyms have been removed.

Some missing synonyms have been added. For instance uncovered brand names for existing medications have been added to the Metathesaurus.

"Case sensitive" indication has been added to some synonyms. Namely these synonyms should be matched only if the case has been kept. This feature can be used to resolve ambiguities (like in the case of COLD which is abbreviation of "Chronically Obstructive Lung Disease" and cold which represent "common cold") or to be able to handle abbreviation that represents words in English (for instance the upper case LET represents "Linear Energy Transfer" or upper case PIE represents "Pulmonary Eosinophilia").

All relations other than the hierarchical relationship have been removed. Relations between concepts from different categories have been removed. Furthermore the hierarchical relationships: Broader (RB), Narrower (RN), Parent (PAR) and Child (CHD) have been transformed into a Directed Acyclic Graph that contains only relations between concepts and their immediate children. In order to obtain the acyclic structure, contradictions between the hierarchical relationships of different source vocabularies have been resolved by using voting mechanism when possible. Namely given two concepts denoted as a and b, if the relation "a parent of b" appears in more source vocabularies than the relation "b parent of a" then the first relation is chosen as the correct one. In case of equality a manual arbitration has been performed.

2.3   Medical Free-Text ETL

The Medical Free-Text ETL performs several operations on each narrative that is being fed to the system as described in the following subsections.

Formatting. Initially the medical record undergoes a formatting step, a process whereby amongst other:

- Numbers written in text (e.g. "twenty two") are replaced with corresponding digits ("22");
- Dates are converted to a uniform format, for example the ISO 8601 standard form. For example the dates "June 23, 1998", "23 June 1998", "06/23/1997" and "23.6.1997" are all replaced with 1998-06-23;
- Redundant spaces are removed; and

"This is a 66 year old woman status post coronary artery bypass graft in 1989-06-23 with coronary artery disease, hypertension, diabetes mellitus, peripheral vascular disease, kidney stones. She was complaining of nausea and dizziness when she began to ... "

ID	Extracted data	Types	Concept Key (CUI)
1	66	Number	N/A
2	woman	Gender	10043209
3	coronary artery bypass graft	Procedure	10010055
4	1989-06-23	Date	N/A
5	coronary artery disease	Diagnosis	10010054
6	hypertension	Diagnosis, symptoms	10020538
7	diabetes mellitus	Diagnosis	10011849
8	peripheral vascular disease	Diagnosis	10085096
9	kidney stones	Diagnosis	10022650
10	nausea	Symptoms	10027497
11	dizziness	Symptoms	10012833

This is a <0_number> year old <1_gender> status post <2_procedures> in <3_date> with <4_diagnosis>, <5_diagnosis_symptoms>, <6_diagnosis>, <7_diagnosis>, <8_diagnosis>. She was complaining of <9_symptoms> and <10_symptoms> when she began to ...

Fig. 2. Illustration of extraction and tagging

- A "find and replace" procedure is performed using a suitable list of prede-termined "finds" and corresponding "replaces". For instance it is used for replacing the strings like "1/2" with "0.5". The actual content of this stage is project dependent, namely each health institution may have different con-tent.

Extraction and Tagging. Formatting is followed by an extraction and tagging procedure. In this phase the system identifies phrases and tokens in the text, extracts their values and stores them in a suitable table together with their meta-thesaurus concept identifier (CUI) (if applicable). Then the original substring is replaced with a category tag (or tags) to which it belongs together with a suitable ordinal number. The text replacement is required for easing the pattern matching phase (see below).

Figure 2 illustrates the extraction and tagging phase on a simple narrative. It begins with a formatted text. It extracts the important facts into a suitable table. Then it generates a new text including the appropriate tags. Currently am-biguities are not resolved. For instance the abbreviation "DM" will be extracted as Dermatomyositis as well as Diabetes Mellitus.

```
INPUT: T - The Free Text
OUTPUT: RESULT - Is a table presenting the extracted data
DO
  t ← Next Token in T
  IF t ∉ STOPWORD THEN
   List← ∅
   IF t ∈ CACHE THEN
    List←CACHE(t)
   ELSE
    List <- Select phrases in MRCON with first token=t order by length
    IF List=∅ THEN
     Add t to STOPWORD using LRU strategy.
    ELSE
     Add List to CACHE using LRU strategy.
    END IF
   END IF
   FOR each phrase pᵢ in List
    IF current position in T contains pᵢ THEN
     Add pᵢ to Result
     Replace the pᵢ in T with a tag.
     Promote the position in T accordanly.
     EXIT FOR
    END IF
   END FOR
  END IF
UNTIL no more tokens
RETURN Result
```

Fig. 3. Pseudo-code for extraction and tagging module

Figure 3 describes the pseudo-code for extraction and tagging medical phrases in the text based on the meta-thesaurus. As the meta-thesaurus is stored in a database table (known as MRCON in UMLS), and this table contains many entries, it will be desirable that the number of queries will be minimized as much as possible. In order to achieve this goal the following measures have been added:

– Stopword - Any word which appears in the Stopwords table (such as "the", "in") will not be searched for. The Stopwords is based on a fixed size hash table. This table is updatable (see below) based on LRU strategy. Nevertheless several basic words can be permanent members of this table and can not be removed.
– In order to improve database querying performance an attribute that contains the first word and an attribute the represents the phrase length (in characters) have been added to the MRCON table.
– A caching mechanism is used in order to avoid querying the database with the same query in adjacent times. Each entry in this cache represents a list of phrases beginning with the same token sorted by phrase length. This cache is managed as LRU hash table, where the first token is used as the key and the list of phrases is used as the stored item.

Lemmatization. The lemmatization process converts each word to its uninflected form; the singular form in the case of a noun, the infinitive form in the case of a verb, and the positive form in the case of an adjective or adverb. The Lemmatization was performed by using WORDNET's morphology library functions [8].

Sentences Boundaries Identification. Sentences boundaries are identified by searching for terminating signs. For each project a different termination may be provided usually it contains at least the following strings: Termination = { ".", "?", "!" }. However using this naive approach for detecting sentence boundaries is not sufficient in case of medical narratives as periods and other signs are frequently used inside sentences (for instance: "Patient was discharged on Lopressor 25 milligrams p.o. b.i.d.").

The above problem can be resolved by providing an exception list. This list specifies the circumstances in which a termination string will not be treated as a sentences separator. The exception list is described as a list of regular expressions. Table 1 illustrates a suitable list written using the Perl notation.

Table 1. Regular Expressions for Sentences Boundaries

$(b|t|q)\.i\.d\.?$	$p\.o\.?$	$\.,$and
$p\.r\.n$	$q\.d\.?$	$\.of$
$q\.h\.s$	$\sq\.$	$(Dr\.)(\s?)(\w+)$

For convenience purposes, the sentence boundaries are also tagged, specifically the termination token is replaced with the tag: <END_OF_SCENTENCE>.

2.4   Pattern Matching

The resulting text is analyzed by a pattern searching protocol aimed to understand the context of the extracted data items and the relation between the various items. This step is performed based on a supplied list of patterns. The patterns consist of a regular expression and mapping instructions. The regular expression is used to define what to search in the text, while the mapping instruction describes how the matched text should be mounted in the clinical data mart. Regular expressions have been used before in medical data for identifying negated [2]. For example the following regular expression is used to identify diagnosis and its suitable date.

<[0-9]+_Diagnosis> (in|on) <[0-9]+_Date>

Notice that the "[0-9]+" has been added in order to match the identifier counter used in tags (whose value can be any number).

For example the following regular expression is used to identify negative diagnosis:

<[0-9]+_Diagnosis>[.]{1,100}(excluded|ruled out|r/o)

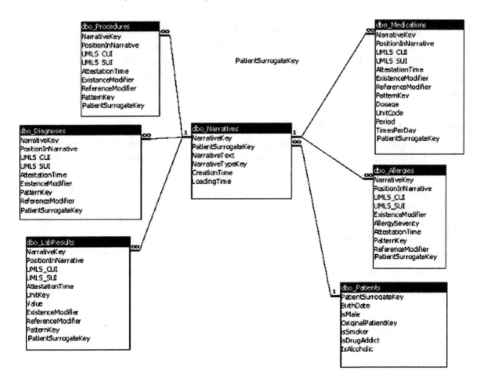

Fig. 4. Relational schema of the clinical data mart

The last regular expression looks for the diagnosis tag, whenever it is followed by the words excluded, ruled out or r/o (limited to 100 characters).

After the regular expression has been matched, the extracted values participating in the expression should be inserted in the database based on the mapping instruction provided. The mapping instruction indicates the appropriate field and table in which each data items should be stored. The simplest way to represent the mapping definition is to use SQL Statement, specifically an insert Statement. It is important to note that it is preferred that there be no updating of data, that is old records and entries are not amended, changed or erased. Rather, new data is added as a new record. It has been found that the consequent redundancy has only a minimal negative effect on database integrity.

2.5   Clinical Data Mart

The medical information extracted in the previous stages is stored in a Clinical Data Mart. Figure 4 illustrates the relational schema of the clinical data mart. For the sake of simplicity only part of the schema is presented. Each patient has exactly one entry in the patients table. In order to reduce the dependency to the source system, we used a newly created surrogate key for identifying the patients. Each patient may have several narratives and each narrative may relate to several entries in the tables: Diagnoses, Procedures, Medications, Lab Results

Table 2. A list of predefined clauses structures used in the proposed system

#	Clause Structure	Category
1	(Is/Is not) allergic to {Allergens}	Allergies
2	(Has/Has not) family member that is allergic to {Allergens}	Allergies
3	Is (Male/Female)	Demographic
4	Is at (minimum/maximum) [1-100] years old	Demographic
5	(Is/Is not) diagnosed with {Diagnoses} within the last [1-365] (Days/Weeks/Months/Years)	Diagnosis
6	(Has/Does not have) family history of {Diagnoses}	Diagnosis
7	(Was/Was not) in pregnant during the last [1-365] (Days/Weeks/Months/Years)	Diagnosis
8	(Is/Is not) diagnosed with {Diagnoses}	Diagnosis
9	Is diagnosed with {Specific Diagnosis} but has no other {General Diagnosis}	Diagnosis
10	Patient record (contains/does not contain) following words: {words}	General
11	Height is (Greater/Lesser) than [Number]	General
12	Weight is (Greater/Lesser) than [Number]	General
13	Patient (Is/Is not) a smoker	Habits
14	Patient (Is/Is not) a drug addict	Habits
15	Patient (Is/Is not) alcoholic	Habits
16	(Current/Previous/Any) {Lab Exam} is between [Number] and [Number]	Lab
17	(Current/Previous/Any) {Lab Exam} is (Positive/Negative)	Lab
18	(Current/Previous/Any) {Lab Exam} is (Greater/Lesser) than [Number]	Lab
19	Current {Lab Exam} has changed from previous by (More than/Less than) [Number] (Units/Percent)	Lab
20	(Is/Is not) currently taking {Medications}	Medication
21	(Is/Is not) taking {Medications} for the last [1-365] (Days/Weeks/Months/Years)	Medication
22	(has/has not) undergone {Procedures} within the last [1-365] (Days/Weeks/Months/Years)	Procedure
23	(has/has not) undergone {Procedures}	Procedure

and Allergies. All clinical data could be stored in a single table. Nevertheless in order to boost the system performance we decomposed it into several tables. It is possible to further improve performance by de-normalizing the proposed schema, for instance by adding the PatientSurrogateKey to other table and avoid join operations.

Query Composition Module. The unique characteristics of the presented system allow accurate responses to complex medical queries. In general a query is a list of inclusion or exclusion criteria and the response to a query is list patients that suit that criteria.

In the proposed system a query is made up of one or more clauses. A clause represents a simple condition. For example "patient is taking insulin" is a clause. Table 2 describes a list of predefined clauses used in the proposed system. We used the notation of round parentheses to represent multiple-selection, curly brackets to represent text input and square brackets to represent numeric input. Most of the clauses are self-explained. Nevertheless clause number 9 requires some explanation. This clause is used to represent clauses such as: "The patient is diagnosed with Adenocarcinoma of lung but has no other Malignant Neoplasm". A plural form has been used to indicate cases where several optional medical terms might be used. For instance clause number 8 can be used to represent clauses such as: "Patient is diagnosed with Hypertension OR Diabetes Mellitus"

One or more clauses are added together to make up one criterion. For example, "patient is taking Insulin AND patient is diagnosed with Hypertension". Between clauses there is either the AND operator or the OR operator. One or more criteria typically make up the inclusion criteria. Similarly a different set of criteria makes up the exclusion criteria.

It is important to note that this query structure is exceptionally convenient as it reflects the structure of queries provided by persons in the field of medical data inquiries.

Query Execution Module. The query provided by the user is converted into a SQL statement. This process is usually straightforward. The only issue that requires clarification is how to select medical concepts that are generalization of more specific medical concepts. For instance the medical concept "Malignant Neoplasm" is the parent of many other medical concepts such as "Carcinoma of lung" which is the parent of other concepts, etc. In order to avoid recursive queries, we create in advance a table named ChildrenFull that is populated with all connections (direct and indirect) that exist between concepts. The table has two attributes ParentCUI and DescendantCUI. Each path between two concepts is represented by a single entry in this table.

In order to reduce the execution time of the SQL statements it is possible to store certain results in cached tables and avoid the necessity to execute them. The most straightforward way to implement this idea is to store the list of patients that has a certain medical concept in their medical history. The caching keeps a suitable table for each of medical concept that was chosen to be cached. The decision of which concept to cache depends on several factors:

- FREQ: How frequently this concept has been used as it appears in the queries that have been entered by the user. If a certain concept has been used 10 times and a different concept has been used 5 times, we will prefer to cache the first concept.
- TIME: The execution time required to get the results for this concept if the query is executed from scratch. This measure is a good indication for the time that can be saved by caching this concept. Usually concepts that have more descendants require more time to execute.
- SPACE: The space required to store the cached results.

Given that there is a certain space allocated for caching we sort the concepts according the following index:

$$Caching\_Index = \frac{FREQ \cdot TIME}{SPACE}$$

The caching space is populated with the concepts having the highest caching index.

Experimental Study

The potential of the proposed system for use in real word applications was studied. The study was conducted on a database obtained from Mount Sinai Hospital in New York. This database contains 4,129 fully de-identified discharge summaries from the Internal Medicine department.

The most commonly used evaluation measures for information retrieval systems are recall and precision [1]. Recall is the proportion of relevant documents in a collection that are retrieved (sensitivity). Precision is the proportion of retrieved documents in a search that are relevant (positive predictive value). Recall and precision are often measured using a test collection of known queries, documents, and relevance judgments.

Table 3. Results Summary of queries used in the experiment

Trial Source	Precision	Recall
[4]	90.85%	98.17%
[3]	87.33%	100%
[9]	91.35%	96.53%
[6]	90.74%	94.72%
[16]	89.28%	97.87%
[13]	92.66%	94.48%

Table 3 presents the results obtained for 6 queries that have been used in this experiment. All these queries have been obtained from clinical trials protocols presented in the literature in the recent years. These protocols represent a real life medical queries that consist of complicated inclusion and exclusion criteria. The precision and recall have been evaluated by comparing the system results to the results obtained by a two physicians, assuming that these manual results are error-free. As it can be seen the system achieved very high recall values (96.96% on average) but less notable precision values (90.37%). Moreover the variance of the results is relatively small although the queries are very different. This fact may indicate that the proposed system is not sensitive to the query complexity. Nevertheless additional experiments are required for establishing this hypothesis.

3   Conclusions

This paper presented a new system for retrieving medical narrative reports. The system enables the physician to enter complicated medical queries using English-like sentences. The system has been examined on a real-world database using real-world queries. The results indicate that the proposed system can be used for non-critical case-finding applications such as: finding appropriate patients for clinical trials.

References

1. M. Buckland and F. Gey. The relationship between recall and precision. Journal of the American Society for Information Science, 45(1):12-19, 1994.
2. Chapman W. W., Bridewell W, Hanbury P, Cooper GF, Buchanann BG. A Simple Algorithm for Identifying Negated Findings and Diseases in Discharge Summaries. Journal of Biomedical Informatics 2001: 34: 301-310.
3. Cohn J.N., Tognoni G. A randomized trial of the angiotensin-receptor blocker valsartan in chronic heart failure. New Engl J Med December 6, 2001;345:1667-75.
4. Doshi S. N., McDowell I. F., Moat S.'J., Folic acid improves endothelial function in coronary artery disease via mechanisms largely independent of homocysteine lowering. Circulation. 2002;105:22-26.
5. Hersh W. R., Hickam D. D., Leone T. J., Words, concepts, or both: Optimal indexing units for automated information retrieval. Frisse ME (ed.) Proceedings of the 16th Annual SCAMC, 644-648, 1992.
6. Israel E, Banerjee T. R., Fitzmaurice G. M., et al. Effects of inhaled glucocorticoids on bone density in premenopausal women. N Engl J Med. 2001;345:941-947.
7. Lin R, Lenert L, Middleton B and Shiffman S. A free-text processing system to capture physical findings: Canonical phrase identification system (CAPIS). In Clayton PD (ed) Proceedings of the 15th Annual SCAMC, 168-172, 1991
8. Miller G. A., WORDNET: A Lexical Database for English. Communications of the ACM, 38(11):39-41, 1995.
9. Mohr JP, Thompson J. L. P., Lazar R. M., et al, for the Warfarin-Aspirin Recurrent Stroke Study Group. A comparison of warfarin and aspirin for the prevention of recurrent ischemic stroke. N Engl J Med. 2001;345:1444-1451.
10. Nadkarni P, Chen R, Brandt C. UMLS concept indexing for production databases: a feasibility study. J Am Med Informatics Assoc. 8:80-91, 2001.
11. NLM. UMLS Knowledge Sources, 13th Edition, 2002.
12. Pratt A. W., Medicine, computers, and linguistics. Advanced Biomedical Engineering 1973: 3:97-140.
13. Roy D., Talajic M., Dorian P., Connolly S., Eisenberg M. J., Green M. et al. Amiodarone to prevent recurrence of atrial fibrillation. Canadian Trial of Atrial Fibrillation Investigators. N Engl J Med 2000;342:913-20.
14. Sager N., Hirschman, L., Grishman, R., and Insolio, C. (1977). Transforming Medical Records Into a Structured Data Base. In D. Waltz, Natural Language Interfaces, ACM-SIGART Newsletter, No. 61 (Feb. 1977), pp. 38-39.
15. Van Rijsbergen, C. J. Information Retrieval. 2nd edition, London, Butterworths, 1979.
16. White H. D., Simes J., Anderson N. E., Hankey G. J., Watson J. D., Hunt D., et al. Pravastatin therapy and the risk of stroke. N Engl J Med 2000;343:321-327.

PHEASANT: A PHysicist's EAsy ANalysis Tool

Vasco Amaral*, Sven Helmer, and Guido Moerkotte

Fakultät für Mathematik und Informatik Universität Mannheim
{amaral,helmer,moer}@pi3.informatik.uni-mannheim.de

Abstract. We present Pheasant, a framework for the analysis process in High Energy Physics (HEP). It uses PheasantQL, the first domain specific visual query language for HEP analysis. This allows us to express complex decay queries easily with no programming efforts, abstracting the storage and optimization details. The currently existing tools overburden users with many complex details and intricacies. A small scale assessment conducted with a prototype demonstrates the effectiveness of our technique.

1 Introduction

Currently, data analysis in High Energy Physics (HEP) is often a tedious, inefficient, and cumbersome chore. Physicists face several obstacles during this process, be it as end users or as developers.

At the moment, the adopted tools do not distinguish between different layers of abstraction. This means, that physicists who want to analyze data have to learn many different details that are totally unrelated to physics. As examples we mention the storage layout of the data, interfaces of many different utility libraries, programming languages following diverse paradigms (procedural, object-oriented, etc.). As a consequence, scientists are distracted from their actual work. Every time they change from one experiment to another, they face a steep learning curve when familiarizing themselves with the tools used in the new experiment.

The major goal of our work is to optimize the HEP analysis process. One important aspect of performance is increasing the user productivity. We can simplify a user's interaction with an analysis framework and make it more flexible for incorporating changes by introducing different layers of abstraction. In the ideal case we want to be able to separate the user's point of view (conceptual layer) from the data representation (logical layer) and this in turn from the actual data storage (physical layer).

We propose an *unifying framework* for analysis, called Pheasant (PHysicist's EAsy ANalysis Tool), that distinguishes between the conceptual, logical, and the physical layer of the data and presents the same view to the user for each analysis

---

* This work is supported by the Portuguese Fundação para a Ciência e a Tecnologia (FCT) through a research scholarship ref. SFRH/BD/8918/2002, and by Laboratório de instrumentação e Física experimental de Partículas (LIP)

H. Christiansen et al. (Eds.): FQAS 2004, LNAI 3055, pp. 229–242, 2004.

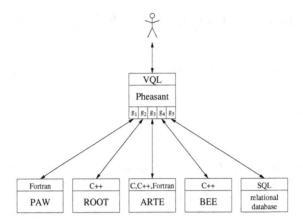

Fig. 1. *Unifying* framework - The user views his particular analysis framework in the same way as others.

framework he is working with. On the conceptual level (upper part of Figure 1) this framework features the first declarative *domain specific visual query language* (DSVQL) for HEP analysis called PheasantQL in which physicists are enabled to construct queries using familiar concepts, opening up a new application area. Not having to know implementation details or certain programming skills makes it much easier for a user to become acquainted with the framework.

On the logical level (middle part of Figure 1) we provide a more detailed representation of the data in form of a logical schema. However, this representation still hides implementation details. The visual language queries are mapped onto an algebra, which operates on the logical schema.

On the physical level (lower part of Figure 1) different (existing) tools can be plugged into our framework via code generation modules (represented by g_i). A code generation module translates the algebraic form of the query into the appropriate syntax of the corresponding tool. In this way, developers may introduce changes on the physical layer without affecting the user and can even extend the framework quite elegantly. (Note that our framework provides no information integration facilities, it just acts as a wrapper to different tools.)

The paper is organized as follows. In Section 2 we are going to give a very brief introduction to High Energy Physics. We present an overview over our framework in Section 3. This is followed by a description of the data model and the visual language in Sections 4 and 5. A small scale assessment is given in Section 6. Finally, Section 7 concludes our paper.

2   A Short Overview on High Energy Physics (HEP)

An in depth review of HEP is beyond the scope of this paper. A good introduction to the subject can be found in [12] and [13]. Generally speaking, physicists discover new, short-lived particles and their properties in order to develop a model of the real world at a subatomic level. They do this with the help of large accelerators in which particles collide with other particles. An accelerator supplies the particles, which are grouped into *bunches*, with energy taking them close to the speed of light. As soon as the system stabilizes, a period of data acquisition, a so called *run* begins. The time span during which two bunches collide is called an *event*. Large detectors record the results of these events. Unfortunately, in any current big experiment it is technically infeasible to gather all information of all collisions (due to the sheer volume of data), so the physicists filter the data with several levels of triggers. The resulting data is initially stored on tape.

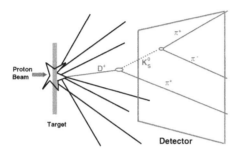

Fig. 2. Colliding the beam of particles against a target.

The reconstruction and investigation of decays and decay chains of short-lived particles is one of the main tasks of the data analysis after collecting the data. Physicists have to reconstruct segments of the trajectories of particles, match them with other segments to reproduce full tracks, extract further properties and deduce complete decay chains. An example decay is depicted in Figure 2.

3   Our Solution

In this section we give an overview of our solution: the *unifying* framework Pheasant. Before delving into details on Pheasant we explain the basic concepts of Visual Query Languages and Domain Specificity that inspired our approach. This is followed by a short description of the framework architecture.

3.1   Preliminaries

Current Visual Query Languages are mostly used to simplify the user's manipulation of the logical storage level. This features languages that usually have a one-to-one direct mapping of their notation to textual query language blocks. The main reason for this is to keep expressivity and flexibility. These languages are mostly aimed at programmers who are used to the concepts underneath.

With the goal to reach the user's conceptual level, metaphor-based visual query languages appeared (like CIGALES[14] for GIS applications). Meant to be used by inexperienced end-users, they are characterized by being easy to learn but very difficult to build since, very often, ambiguity, lack of flexibility, and inappropriate metaphors led to the failure of these projects.

Domain specific engineering methodology comes into play when a family of applications in a specific domain has to be developed by users, who are not necessarily software engineers. It focuses on generating a language that gives the user the possibility to concentrate on what to compute in contrast on how to compute it.

Domain Specific Languages lead to the reduction of time and cost involved in the development and modification of a family of tools in a certain domain. To design them requires a mature domain knowledge and involves software reuse.

The combination of both VQL and DSL concepts are Domain Specific Visual Query Languages (DSVQL). There exist very few of them, examples can be found in ALGOVISTA[19] for algorithms search and AIGLE-CIGALES[15] for GIS domain.

3.2   The Framework Description

As said before, both DSL and VQL concepts inspired us to develop the first declarative DSVQL for HEP analysis called PheasantQL.

We believe that declarative DSVQL is ideal for this application area because of the following reasons. The reason for being declarative is that no programming logic is involved. It is visual to be more intuitive, easy to use and learn, and reduce the error rate. It is domain specific because in this complex domain where users have to code their queries hundreds of times, it is justified to develop a solution that gathers the patterns into conceptual notations of domain of speech, and automate the generation of query code. The other reason is that General Purpose Languages (GPL) have shown to be difficult for the user in this domain.

In our framework queries can be constructed from elements representing concepts taken from the HEP domain, not the coded implementation space. This makes it easier for the user to become acquainted with the system.

The final queries are automatically generated from these high-level specifications with a domain-specific code generator into the target analysis framework (see Figure 3(a) for the rough architecture of Pheasant).

This approach will mean to the user that nobody has to know the physical layout of data, since all queries are formulated on a logical level. If the need for extension of the language arises, (i.e. to add new algorithms for advanced users), the modularity of this approach helps on re-usage of code and keeping the programming activities controlled. Also, optimizations and re-implementations on the physical level are completely hidden from ordinary users.

We have implemented a prototype with an intuitive interface that models the world as a physicist sees it (see Figure 3(b), which shows a decay chain query). The interfaces of our unifying framework consists of an interface that implements a DSVQL and several code generation modules.

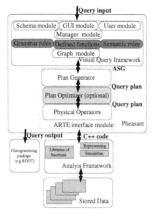

(a) Architecture of Pheasant

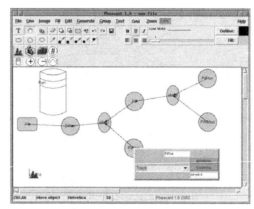

(b) Pheasant visual layout

Fig. 3. Different views of Pheasant.

As a first step we conducted a requirements analysis to determine the physicists demands as thoroughly as possible. We then proceeded by modeling the HEP data analysis environment.

Following this initial stages we had the proper ground to start with the design of the Visual Language by identifying the common patterns in the analysis code. Based on that, the language was proposed and the it's formalization by defining the grammar and semantics was fulfilled.

The architecture of the framework was delineated and the implementation using a prototype engineering life-cycle was started.

Due to the modularity of our approach an experienced user can apply our framework merely as a front-end to such tools as ARTE [1], BEE [10], ROOT[16], or PAW [18]. With this front-end he or she can rapidly generate code (e.g. SQL or C++) for the conventional tools and modify this code in the usual way.

4   Data Model

We have modeled the semantic model of the HEP analysis data in an ER diagram that is depicted in Figure 4. It consists of three major entities: **Run**, **Event** and **Particle**. The attributes of the entity **Run** define the parameters of the experiment, e.g. the setup of the detectors, the time span during which data acquisition took place and general quality issues. As events can only exist within a run, they are modeled as a weak entity (dependent on the entity **Run**). Its attributes describe properties of particle bunches involved in an event. The remainder of the diagram consists of various entities for describing particles. We have particles that actually leave traces in the detector. These are described by their tracks. Particles reconstructed by computations, i.e. whose existence has been derived from the data, are called vertices. We also have to be able to store

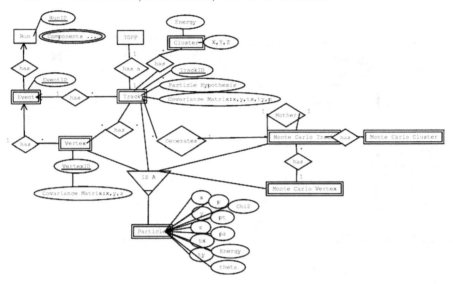

Fig. 4. Patterned ER model of the HEP analysis data, which excludes detector related data.

simulation results. These are the Monte Carlo entities. With the data gained from simulations the plausibility of the measured results is verified.

5   Description of Our Visual Language

In designing a consistent VQL, we took into account – based on previous works in the area of VL [7] – that it should satisfy three major user activities: understanding the structure of the data, query formulation and result set visualization. In HEP analysis, the structure of the data does not change much, so we refrained from explicitly showing the whole domain, like in other VLs. We hide the schema to avoid a confusing layout of the interface, as we expect the users to be very familiar with it. This means that each operator contains browsable and editable data, which usually is not visible.

5.1   Informal Description of the Syntax

We are going to introduce the basic building blocks of our language with the help of a running example. (More details on the formal specification, including transformational semantics into relational algebra, can be found in [2].) Let us start with the theoretical thoughts of a physicist doing analysis. Figure 5 shows the schematics of a typical decay chain that can be the center of an investigation. Particle D^+ (on the left hand side) eventually decays into particles Π^+ and Π^- (on the right hand side). A typical query of medium complexity is to find the D^+ particle with the highest energy level for each event. The particles on the right hand side are the ones whose presence is directly recorded by a detector. Physicists use these as a starting point to search for the original particles, which are too short-lived or too small to be detected.

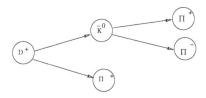

Fig. 5. Example of D^+ decay schematics.

We are now going to translate these thoughts into a query. First of all we have to decide which run and event data to use. This is the task of the collection operator, which is represented by a small disk symbol (see Figure 6(a)). Associated with this operator is a list of attributes and a list of filter predicates. Assume for a moment that we are only interested in the data from the third run, so in a first step, we have a collection operator that selects this data for us. Collections can be combined using the standard set operators $\cap, \cup$, and $\setminus$.

(a) Collecting the data in step 1   (b) Selection, Aggregation, Transformation

Fig. 6. Some basic operators.

For the second step we need three more operators: Selection, Aggregation, and Transformation (see Figure 6(b) for their symbols). Selection works on the data retrieved by a collection operator and selects actual particles detected during these runs and events according to predicates that refer to particles. Aggregation and Transformation operators work on the results of selection operators. An aggregation sums up information on particles per event, i.e. we get one result for each event. Transformation combines the results of two (or more) selections according to predicates that refer to attributes of all participating selections. Usually this results in the construction of a particle higher up in the decay chain. So, the transformation operator creates new particle objects with the data from previous selections.

We now need a way to connect the objects. For this we use simple lines with arrows that describe the data flow from one operator to another.

Our language supports two more complicated primitives to relate selection objects: the comparison and the minimal distance operators, (see Figure 7). Both of them relate two different selection objects and apply a restrictive selection based on a criteria given by the user.

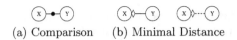

(a) Comparison   (b) Minimal Distance

Fig. 7. Comparison and Minimal Distance operators.

The first one, basically compares attribute values of one selection object to those of another selection object.In doing so, it filters out particles that do not satisfy the condition of the comparison operator.

The second case is the Minimal Distance operator. In contrast to the comparison operator the minimum distance operator is directed. It operates in two modes mandatory and non-mandatory, which are symbolized by a solid and a broken line, respectively. The operator does two things. First of all, all particles in A are matched to the nearest (corresponding) particle in B. Then, if the distance between the two is larger than a user-defined threshold, the particles are filtered out. In mandatory mode all particles in A not finding a partner are also filtered out (in non-mandatory mode, they are allowed to pass).

Fig. 8. Result Set Specification:1D,2D,3D,Value Result and operator omission.

And last, but not least, we have to describe how to visualize the result of the query in the third step. We provide four different operators for the description of the result (see Figure 8): three operators to create one-, two-, and three-dimensional histograms, and one operator to output numeric values.In case of absence of a result operator,(in this case we will represent it textually by $\perp$), the result will be a set of tuples that match the decay description.

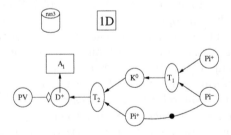

Fig. 9. Example of a Complete Query: the D^+ decay.

Figure 9 shows the complete query. The two operators in the upper part of Figure 9 tell the system that we are interested in the data from the third run and want a one-dimensional histogram output of the result. We begin on the right hand side with extracting all Pi$^+$ and Pi$^-$ particles from the events of the third run. With the help of a transformation operator (T_1) we reconstruct a $\overline{K}^0$ particle. Another transformation operator (T_2) helps us find D^+ particles. One condition operator was inserted contains the condition expression that guarantees that Pi$^+$ and Pi$^-$ have the same mass. A minimal distance operator is used to select the selection object PV, (primary vertex in physics jargon), that is closer to the computed D^+ particle, if none exists, the decay chain is also not selected. Finally an aggregation operation filters out the particles with the maximal energy level for each event.

Implicit graph structures. There are some non-visible implicit operators in our language that we will specify in this section.

There is an implicit data flow from Collection objects to all operators that have no apparent source. Another implicit data flow goes from all operators having no obvious output to a Result object.

There are also object references with which physicists are able to connect measured data to simulated data (e.g. tracks to Monte Carlo tracks). The references are depicted by an arrow labeled with the keyword *ref*. In the mandatory mode ($\bigcirc \xrightarrow{mand.ref} \bigcirc$) an object will be selected, if and only if the corresponding reference exists (otherwise it will be filtered out). In non-mandatory mode ($\bigcirc \xrightarrow{ref} \bigcirc$) objects not referencing other objects are kept.

5.2   The Grammar

In order to proceed with the definition of the syntax of our language, we have to describe how symbols may be formed into valid phrases of the language.

Comparing our diagrammatic language operators with graphs and edges, we make use of a graph grammar to define our visual query language (see Figure 10). This grammar is context-sensitive since it allows left and right graphs of a production to have an arbitrary number of nodes and edges.

We define PheasantQL's grammar as constituted of four parts $\langle \Sigma, N, P, S \rangle$ where:

- Σ is the finite set of terminal symbols. We decided to use the symbols of the language itself as terminals in the grammar, so there is no problem to recognize the components introduced in the last section.
- N is the finite set of nonterminal symbols. In our description, non-terminals have a grayish background, while for the terminals the regular background is used.
- P are the production rules stated in Figure 10. They are represented as $LHS ::= RHS$ where productions with the same LHS (left hand side), separate the different RHSs (right-hand sides) by |.
- S is the start symbol λ or null graph.

Let us give some extra explanatory notes. In our production rules we define a and b as connection points to the rest of the graph, and they are used to keep

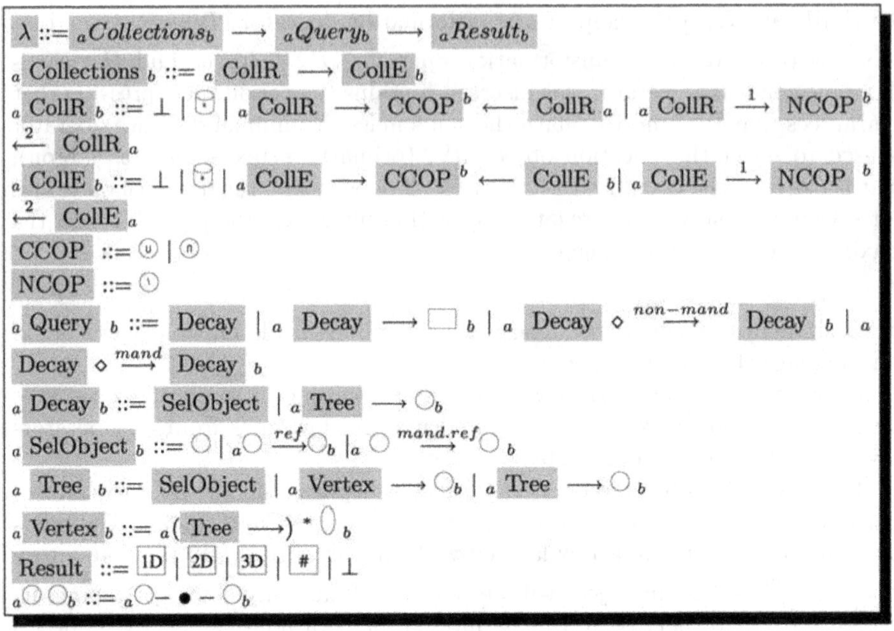

$\lambda ::= {}_a Collections_b \longrightarrow {}_a Query_b \longrightarrow {}_a Result_b$

${}_a$ Collections ${}_b ::= {}_a$ CollR $\longrightarrow$ CollE ${}_b$

${}_a$ CollR ${}_b ::= \perp \mid \boxdot \mid {}_a$ CollR $\longrightarrow$ CCOP ${}^b \longleftarrow$ CollR ${}_a \mid {}_a$ CollR $\xrightarrow{1}$ NCOP ^{b} $\xleftarrow{2}$ CollR ${}_a$

${}_a$ CollE ${}_b ::= \perp \mid \boxdot \mid {}_a$ CollE $\longrightarrow$ CCOP ${}^b \longleftarrow$ CollE ${}_b \mid {}_a$ CollE $\xrightarrow{1}$ NCOP ^{b} $\xleftarrow{2}$ CollE ${}_a$

CCOP $::= \ⓤ \mid \ⓝ$

NCOP $::= \ⓥ$

${}_a$ Query ${}_b ::=$ Decay $\mid {}_a$ Decay $\longrightarrow \square {}_b \mid {}_a$ Decay $\diamond \xrightarrow{non-mand}$ Decay ${}_b \mid {}_a$ Decay $\diamond \xrightarrow{mand}$ Decay ${}_b$

${}_a$ Decay ${}_b ::=$ SelObject $\mid {}_a$ Tree $\longrightarrow \bigcirc_b$

${}_a$ SelObject ${}_b ::= \bigcirc \mid {}_a \bigcirc \xrightarrow{ref} \bigcirc_b \mid {}_a \bigcirc \xrightarrow{mand.ref} \bigcirc_b$

${}_a$ Tree ${}_b ::=$ SelObject $\mid {}_a$ Vertex $\longrightarrow \bigcirc_b \mid {}_a$ Tree $\longrightarrow \bigcirc_b$

${}_a$ Vertex ${}_b ::= {}_a ($ Tree $\longrightarrow)^* \bigcirc_b$

Result $::= \boxed{1D} \mid \boxed{2D} \mid \boxed{3D} \mid \boxed{\#} \mid \perp$

${}_a \bigcirc_b ::= {}_a \bigcirc - \bullet - \bigcirc_b$

Fig. 10. Grammar of Visual elements of PheasantQL.

the graph orientation after applying the rule (meaning that the data flow goes from a to b).

Associated with each operator is some additional data, like attribute lists and condition lists. During query construction, this information is hidden most of the time. It can be easily accessed and edited by means of pop-up menus, like the one in Fig. 3(b). We describe this hidden data associated with each operator with the symbol ::$\propto$ (see Figure 11).

Furthermore, we distinguish between two different collection types: run collections and event collections. When no collections are given in a query, the query considers all available data. If we define a run collection, only data from the selected runs will be considered. We can restrict this further by additionally supplying a description of an event collection. Then only a subset of the events of the run collection will be taken into account. When specifying an event collection without any run collection, we regard the relevant events from all runs. When connecting collections via set operators, we have to differentiate between commutative operators $(\cup, \cap)$ and non-commutative operators $(\backslash)$.

The language has been designed considering the need of the user to extend the expression, conditions and transformation functions with his own ones (otherwise it would be very restrictive). We make use of the terms UDF, meaning set of user-defined functions, the corresponding subsets are: UDSFs (user defined scalar functions); UDAFs (user-defined aggregate functions), and UDTFs (user defined table functions). For instance, users can integrate their own aggregation

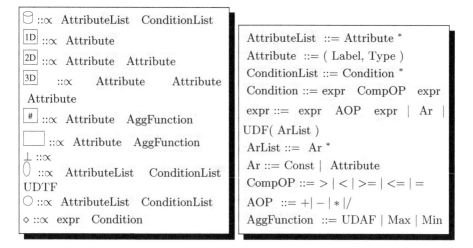

Fig. 11. Definition of terminals (and associated non-terminals).

functions (the system currently provides a max- and min-function UDAF) into an aggregation operator. To connect selection objects via a transformation operator, the user can also supply his or her own transformation function (usually a function to reconstruct vertices UDTF). Some expressions and conditions can also be composed by UDFs.

6   Usability Evaluation

In order to support our claims that Pheasant and its language really improves the HEP analysis process, we conducted a small scale assessment. In doing so, we compared the Pheasant prototype to an actually employed C++ framework, BEE [10].

6.1   Evaluation Procedure

In our evaluation we followed the guidelines given by the ISO92141-11 standard. In this standard, usability is defined as: **Effectiveness -** accuracy and completeness; **Efficiency -** resources spent to complete a query **Satisfaction in use -** the convenience in use (as perceived personally).

We have planned our assessment to follow six major steps: subject recruitment, task preparation, pilot session (in order to uncover any eventual bugs in the tasks), training session, evaluation session and result analysis.

Three types of persons were chosen: informed programmers (Inf-P), uninformed programmers (N-I-P), and non-programmers (N-P). Programmers are those familiar with computers and regular users of programming languages. This group can be subdivided in informed (if they have already programmed with the present analysis framework) or uninformed (if they have not. Non-programmers

Non-P	C++ BEE	Pheasant
Training time (hours:minutes)	2:15	1:05
Mean total exam time (hours:minutes)	> 2 : 00	1:35
Mean confidence/query (5 very/0 not)	1	3,5
Non-I-P	C++ BEE	Pheasant
Training time (hours:minutes)	1:20	1:15
Mean total exam time (hours:minutes)	> 2 : 00	0 : 40
Mean confidence/query (5 very/0 not)	2	4
Inf-P	C++ BEE	Pheasant
Training time (hours:minutes)	0:20	1:35
Mean total exam time (hours:minutes)	2 : 00	0 : 35
Mean confidence/query (5 very/0 not)	3.5	4,5

Fig. 12. Time analysis.

BEE/C++	N-P	N-I-P	Inf-P	Pheasant	N-P	N-I-P	Inf-P
Correct				Correct	87.5	80	87.5
Minor data Error			12.5	Minor data Error			
Minor language error		20	50	Minor language error		20	12.5
Essentially correct	0	20	62.5	Essentially correct	87.5	100	100
Wrong answer	37.5	20	25	Wrong answer	12.5		
Invalid	25	20	12.5	Invalid			
Not attempted	37.5	20		Not attempted			
Totally incorrect	100	60	37.5	Totally incorrect	12.5	0	0

Fig. 13. Error analysis.

are those familiar with computers and operating systems, but having little programming experience.

6.2   Results

From our time analysis (Figure 12), we can confirm a tendency for more time spent learning and using C++ and BEE as opposed to Pheasant. This can be justified by the complexity of C++ and the BEE library. At the same time the test subject had less confidence in the quality of his/her query (see also Figure 12). This subjective impression was confirmed by the huge error rate when using BEE (see Figure 13).

In Figure 14 we have given an excerpt of a list of features needed in HEP analysis. The test subjects were supposed to rate how they were satisfied with the realization of each feature in the corresponding framework. Our goal was to identify potential weaknesses of each framework.

Let us now summarize our evaluation. In terms of **Effectiveness**, Pheasant provides the user with a tool that is more accurate and complete. When looking at **Efficiency** the present running approaches, we have a clear evidence that less time is used to achieve the same goal. Generally, the **Satisfaction in use** was

Pheasant / BEE	Non-P	Non-I-P	Inf-P	Mean
Structuring the query	5/1	5/1	4/4	4.7/2
Dealing with different structures of data (schema)	3.5/1	3/1	3.5/3	3.3/1.7
Expressing a decay	5/1	5/2	4.5/2	4.8/1.7
Expressing filter conditions	5/1	5/2	5/4.5	5/2.5
Expressing and using Vertexing	5/1	5/2	5/4	5/2.3
Expressing and using User defined functions	4.5/1	3/3	3.5/5	3.7/3
Referencing objects	5/3.5	5/2	3/5	4.3/3.5
Expressing the result set	5/1	5/ 2	5/3.5	5/2.2
Mean	4.8/1.3	4.5/1.9	4.2/3.9	

Fig. 14. Language Constructs analysis: Subject evaluation. Scale from 1(worst) to 5(best).

higher with Pheasant. The only exception to this were expert users, who feel very familiar with their day-to-day tool.

7   Conclusion and Outlook

We have introduced the concept of DSVQL to the domain of HEP for the first time by providing a flexible framework helping in the analysis process. This opens a new research area for DSL.

Presently, we have designed the query language (by specifying the syntax and formal semantics). For the prototype we have implemented the interface, the algebraic operators layer, and integrated ROOT histogramming for result visualization. We can already map simple queries to the algebraic layer, the full mapping mechanism is under construction. A first assessment of Pheasant by real users has encouraged us to continue working on improving our framework.

For the near future we want to deal with user query versioning and storage, support for multiple users, and document generation. After doing a full assessment of Pheasant we expect changing some of the elements in the language to become even more user intuitive and include concepts that were not included in the first prototype.

References

1. H. Albrecht, "The computing Model for HERA-B", CHEP'97, Berlin,Proceedings edited by DESY Hamburg, Germany,1997
2. V. Amaral, S. Helmer, G. Moerkotte "Pheasant: A Physicist's Easy Analysis Tool" Technical Report of the University of Mannheim: 8/03, 2003
3. V. Amaral, S. Helmer, G. Moerkotte, "A Domain Specific Visual Query Language for the High Energy Physics Environment", Proc. 3rd OOPSLA Workshop on Domain-Specific Modeling (DSM), Anaheim, 2003: 9-16
4. "Designing and Implementing a New Abstraction Layer to Optimize the HEP Analysis Process", V. Amaral, S. Helmer, G. Moerkotte, IEEE Conference of Nuclear Sciences NSS, Conference Record N26-104, Portland, 2003

5. "A Visual Query Language for HEP Analysis", V. Amaral, S. Helmer, G. Moerkotte, IEEE Conference of Nuclear Sciences NSS, Conference Record N26-105, Portland, 2003
6. V. Amaral, S. Helmer, G. Moerkotte "Pheasant: Usability Evaluation" Technical Report of the University of Mannheim: 2004
7. T. Catarci, M. Costabile, S. Levialdi, C. Batini, "Visual Query Systems for Databases: A Survey", Journal of Visual Languages and Computing, 1995
8. S. Cluet, G. Moerkotte "Nested Queries in Object bases" Workshop in Computing, 1993, Springer
9. L. Fegaras, D. Maier "Optimizing Object Queries Using an Effective Calculus" ACM Transactions on Database systems, Vol. 25, N 4, December 2000,pp. 457-516
10. T. Glebe, "Clue - The BEE event model library", HERA-B Note 01-138, Software 01-019, 2001
11. M. Jaedicke, B. Mitschang, "User-Defined Table Operators: Enhancing Extensibility for ORDBMS", 25th VLDB Conference, Edinburg,Scotland,1999
12. D. Malon,E. May, "Critical Database Technologies for High Energy Physics", proceedings of the 23rd VLDB Conference Athens, Greece, 1997
13. D.Perkins, "Introduction to High Energy Physics", Addison-Wesley, 1982
14. A. Portier. Grasp: A graphical system for statistical databases. In *CIGALES: un langage graphicque d'interrogation de Systémes d'Information Géographiques*, Ph.d Thesis. University of Paris, 1992.
15. A. Lbath, M. Portier, R. Laurini, Using a Visual Language for the Design and Query in GIS customization. International IEEE Conference on Visual Information Systems (VISUAL'97), San Diego, pp197-204.
16. F. Rademakers, R. Brun, "ROOT: An Object-Oriented Data Analysis Framework", Linux Journal, 1 of July 1998
17. HERA-B: http://www-hera-b.desy.de
18. PAW: http://wwwasd.web.cern.ch/wwwasd/paw/
19. ALGOVISTA:http://cgi.cs.arizona.edu:8080/algovista/servlet/algovista

Combining Knowledge-Based Methods to Refine and Expand Queries in Medicine

Lina F. Soualmia[1] and Stéfan Jacques Darmoni[2]

[1] CISMeF & L@STICS, Rouen University Hospital, 76031 Rouen, France
[2] PSI Laboratory - FRE CNRS 2645, INSA-Rouen, 76131 Mont-Saint Aignan, France
{lina.soualmia,stefan.darmoni}@chu-rouen.fr

Abstract. Information retrieval remains problematic in spite of the numerous existing search engines. It is the same problem for health information retrieval. We propose in this paper to combine three knowledge-based methods to enhance information retrieval using query expansion in the context of the CISMeF project (Catalogue and Index of French-speaking Medical Sites) in which the resources are indexed according to a structured terminology of the medical domain and a set of metadata. The first method consists of building and using morphological knowledge of the terms. The second method consists of extracting association rules between terms by applying a data mining technique over the indexed resources. The last method consists of formalizing the terminology using the OWL-DL language to benefit from its powerful reasoning mechanisms. We describe how these methods could be used conjointly in the KnowQuE prototype (Knowledge-based Query Expansion) and we give some preliminary results.

1 Introduction

The amount of health information available on Internet is considerable. Information retrieval remains problematic: users are now experiencing huge difficulties in finding precisely what they are looking for, among the tons of documents available online. Generic search engines (for example Google[1]) or generic catalogues (for example Yahoo[2]) cannot solve this problem efficiently because they usually offer a selection of documents that turns out to be either too large or ill-suited to the query. Free text word-based (or phrase-based) search engines typically return innumerable completely irrelevant hits requiring much manual weeding by the user and might miss important information resources. Free text search is not always efficient and effective: the sought page might be using a different term (synonym) that points to the same concept; spelling mistakes and variants are considered as different terms; search engines cannot process HTML *intelligently*.

We propose in this paper to combine three knowledge-based methods (natural language processing, knowledge discovery in databases and formal reasoning) in the KnowQuE (Knowledge-based Query Expansion) [1] prototype to precise and expand a user query submitted over the CISMeF[3] [2] catalogue (acronym of Catalogue and

---

[1] http://www.google.com
[2] http://www.yahoo.com
[3] www.chu-rouen.fr/cismef

H. Christiansen et al. (Eds.): FQAS 2004, LNAI 3055, pp. 243–255, 2004.

Index of French-speaking Medical Sites). CISMeF has been developed since 1995 to help health professionals, as well as students and the general public, during their search for electronic health information. All the resources (documents and Web sites) indexed in the CISMeF catalogue are described by the librarians by using the vocabulary of a structured terminology that is similar to ontology of the medical domain, and a set of metadata founded on the Dublin Core.

The first KnowQuE module is composed by a morphological knowledge base that has been built according to the terminology. Recent works [3-5] show the contribution of morphological processing for information retrieval in French. For example for a query on *'astmatic child'* the module should retun documents on *'children with asthma'*. Lexical resources (in French) are needed for the medical vocabulary. The second module is founded on association rules [6] between terms, extracted from the indexed resources by a data mining technique. These association rules are used in the information retrieval process. For example the association rule *'prevention of breast cancer → mammography'* is extracted because *'prevention of breast cancer'* and *'mammography'* are frequently used conjointly to index the resources. Applying the association rule, a query on *'mammography'* should return documents on *'prevention of breast cancer'*. The third component use terminological reasoning. It is composed by a formal terminological knowledge base built by automatic translation of the terminology into the OWL DL-based language [7] and the resources of the catalogue into instances (or individuals) of the OWL concepts and roles (or classes and relations). Reasoning mechanisms are involved here to verify the knowledge-base consistency and mainly to answer queries.

We briefly introduce in section 2 the CISMeF catalogue (the metadata elements set and the structure of the terminology) in which our experimentations are carried out. As the main contribution of the paper is the combination of methods for query expansion, the KnowQuE architecture and its three modules are described in section 3. We give some preliminary results for morphological processing and association rules mining and we detail the modeling strategies used to convert the terminology into a formal knowledge base. We conclude and give future work in section 4.

2   The CISMeF Metadata and Terminology

The CISMeF catalogue was developed since 1995 to assist the health professionals (physicians, dentists, pharmacist…), the students and the general public in their search for health information on the Web. As opposed to Yahoo, CISMeF is a quality-controlled health gateway, cataloguing the most important and quality-controlled sources of institutional health information in French in order to allow end-users to search them quickly and precisely. The CISMeF catalogue describes and indexes a large number of health information resources ($n=12{,}891$) and has three main topics: guidelines for health professionals, teaching material for students in medicine, and consumer health information. A resource can be a Web site, Web pages, documents, reports and teaching material: any support that may contain health information. Metadata and a terminology "oriented" ontology are used to describe the selected resources.

Metadata is data about data or specifically in the context of the Web, it is data describing Web resources. Several sets compose the CISMeF metadata. Among them Dublin Core (DC) [8] metadata set. DC is not a complete solution; it cannot be used to describe the quality or location of a resource. To fill these gaps, CISMeF uses its own elements to extend the DC standard. The user type is taken into account thanks to additional fields in the resources intended for health professionals and those intended to students in medicine [9]. The metadata format was the HTML language in 1995. In 2000, in order to allow interoperability with other platforms the XML language became the metadata format. Since December 2002, the format used is RDF a basic Semantic Web language [10], within the EU-project MedCIRCLE framework [11] in which CISMeF is a partner.

A particular field of the metadata is the *description*. The catalogue resources are indexed according to the CISMeF terminology, which is based on the MeSH [12] concepts and its French translation provided by the INSERM[4] (National Institute of Health and Medical Research). Approximately 22,000 keywords (e.g.: *abdomen, hepatitis*) and 84 qualifiers (example: *diagnosis, complications*) compose the MeSH thesaurus in its 2003 version. These concepts are organized into hierarchies going from the most general at the top of the hierarchy to the most specific at the bottom of the hierarchy. For example, the keyword *hepatitis* is more general than the keyword *hepatitis viral A*. The qualifiers, also organized into hierarchies, can be used to specify which particular aspect of a keyword is addressed. For example the association of the keyword *hepatitis* and the qualifier *diagnosis* (noted *hepatitis/diagnosis*) restrict the *hepatitis* to its *diagnosis* aspect.

The heterogeneity of Internet health resources and the great specificity of MeSH keywords (which make it difficult to refer broadly to a medical specialty) led the CISMeF team to introduce two new concepts, respectively *metaterms* and *resource types*. The keywords and qualifiers in CISMeF are gathered according to *metaterms*. Metaterms (n=66) concern medical specialties. The *resource types* (n=127) describe the nature of the resource (e.g.: *teaching material, clinical guidelines*). The metaterms and resource types enhance information retrieval into the catalogue when searching "*guidelines in cardiology*" or "*databases in virology*", where *cardiology* and *virology* are metaterms and *guidelines* and *databases* are resource types.

Many ways of navigation and information retrieval are possible in the catalogue. The most used is the *simple search* (free text interface). It is based on the subsumption relationships. If the query (a word or an expression) can be matched with an existing term, then the result of the query is the union of the resources that are indexed by the term, and the resources that are indexed by the terms it subsumes, directly or indirectly, in all the hierarchies it belongs to. For example a query on *Hepatitis* will return as answer all the resources indexed with the descriptor *Hepatitis* but also those indexed with *Hepatitis A, Hepatitis B*...etc. If the query cannot be matched, the search is done over the other fields of the metadata and in a worse case a full-text search is carried out. But it is not an optimized solution and this kind of search requires a good knowledge of the medical domain.

The CISMeF terminology has the same structure as a terminological ontology [13]:
- The vocabulary, that describes major terms of the medical domain, is well known by the librarians and the health professional.
- Each concept has:
  - a preferred term (Descriptor) to express it in natural language.
  - a set of properties.

---

[4] http://dicdoc.kb.inserm.fr:2010/basimesh/mesh.html

- a natural language definition that allows to differentiate it from the concepts it subsumes and those that it subsumes.
- a set of synonyms.
- a set of constraints to apply on the qualifiers. For example the qualifier *'Complications'* could only be used for the *'Diseases'* arborescence and not for the *'Anatomy'*.
- a set of equivalences. For example the association *'Hepatitis/chemically induced'* is equivalent to the keyword *'Hepatitis, toxic'*.

Nevertheless, the consistency of the terminology has not yet been studied and some incoherencies arise. For example, in the *'Anatomy'* arborescence, some keywords are organized hierarchically according to the *'part of'* relationships, but it is wrongly considered as a *'is a'* relationships. As a consequence, a query on *'headache'* returns also documents on *'mouth pain'*, *'eye pain'* and *'ear pain'* among others. A formal representation is needed to verify the terminology consistency (§ section 3.3.).

3   KnowQuE to Enhance Information Retrieval

The submitted queries over the search engine are seldom matched to the vocabulary. We have extracted and analyzed the kind of queries of the http server and their associated number of answers between the 15th August 2002 and the 6th February 2003. 1,552,776 queries were extracted. Among them 892,591 (58.62%) were submitted via the *simple search* interface and 365,688 (40.97% of the simple queries) had no answer. To enhance this kind of information retrieval, which is largely used over the catalogue, we have developed the KnowQuE prototype founded on morphological processing, association rules mining and terminological reasoning.

3.1   Morphological Processing

A major task in information retrieval is to match a query with a document. It could be realized by query normalization (lemmatization by reducing a word to its lexeme, stemming by reducing a word to its root form) or by query enrichment (by adding inflexions or derivations). In the Web, the user queries are frequently composed by few words. Many works have addressed 'terminological variation', which can be processed at different levels: characters [14] (spelling and accenting mistakes, case variants), words and their morphological variants [15-17], syntax [17], or concepts with general-language [18]. Phonemic matching is yet another method to match words based on their pronunciations. Finally, recent works [3-5] show the contribution of morphological processing for information retrieval in French. The general observation is that lemmatization brings a statistically significant improvement and that stemming additionally improves the results, but in a non-statistically significant way.

3.1.1 Principles
To reduce the silence of the system and the number of empty answers, the morphological processing in the first KnowQuE module is founded on the following operations.

Query segmentation: the query is segmented into words by using string tokenizers (for example: * $,!§;|@).

Character normalizations: we apply two types of normalization at this step.

(1) *Lowercase conversion*: all the uppercased characters are replaced by their lowercase version;

(2) *Deaccenting*: all accented characters (*e.g. "éèêë"*) are replaced by non-accented (*"e"*). (words in the French MeSH are not accented, and words in queries can be accented or not, or wrongly accented (*"athlètisme"*).

Stop words: we eliminate the stop words (such as *the, and, when*).

Exact expression: we use regular expressions to match the exact expression of each word of the query with the terminology. For example '*accident*' will be matched with the term '*circulation accident*' (but not with '*accidents*' and '*chute accidentelle*').

Morphological knowledge: we replace each word by its *root* in the morphological family. The root is generally the simple form of the term. A morphological family of a term is composed by its *inflexions* (for example {*accident, accidents*}) and *derivations* (for example {*probability, probabilistic*}). If the user query is *"children with asthma"* it will be replaced by the Boolean query *"child [keyword] AND asthma [keyword]"*. The problem is that this kind of knowledge base doesn't yet exist for the French medical language [19].

3.1.2 Extracting Derivations and Expanding Queries

To build a morphological knowledge-base according to the CISMeF terminology, we have used a general-domain lexical resource [20]. It is not specific to the medical domain but it allowed us to obtain 2,732 morphological families of keywords (total of 9,401; 3,388 are composed by 1 word), 55 families of qualifiers (total 84; 55 of 1 word) and 28 families of resource types (total 127; 28 of 1 word). In this first step we have only considered the terms that are composed by 1 word. The root of a morphological family is the matched keyword with the terminology (resp. qualifier and resource type) even if it is not in its simple form. By analyzing the other terms composed by 2 or more words, we have found that 1,935 terms (1,899 keywords; 8 qualifiers; 22 resource types) are *semi-matched*. We consider that a term is *semi-matched* when at least one of the words that compose it is matched. For example the keyword *"accidents"* has as family: {*accident, accidents, accidenté, accidentées, accidentel, accidentels, accidentelle, accidentelles, accidentellement, accidenter*}. Therefore, the keyword *"accident circulation"* is semi-matched because *accident* is matched and not *circulation*. The semi-matching is useful for the *exact expression* step.

Table 1. Covering the vocabulary

	Keywords	Qualifiers	Resource Types	Terms
Nb terms matched	2 732	55	28	2 815
1 word matching	80.64%	100%	100%	81.33%
Semi-matching	4 631	63	50	4 750
TOTAL	48.80%	75%	39.37%	**49.11%**

We have implemented the algorithm in Java with an ODBC connection to the CISMeF Oracle 8.i database. The different functions of the algorithm (Segmentation,

Normalization, Stop Words, Exact Expression and Morphological Knowledge) were expressed using SQL queries and regular expressions.

For preliminary results, we have tested the algorithm on a set of 77,382 queries with empty answers, which correspond to 48,255 distinct queries. The size of the queries is small. 12,974 queries (26.89%) are composed by 1 word; 16,347 (33.88%) by 2 words; 10,972 (22.74%) by 3 words; 4,360 (9.03%) by 4 words; 3,602 are composed by more than 4 words (7.46%).

The 48,255 null queries were segmented into 121,958 words. By applying the different steps of our algorithm, a total of 92,887 terms (76.16%) were matched with the terminology and the morphological base, but 29,071 terms remain unknown (23.84%) (Table 2). Many of the unknown words are spelling errors but, in addition to morphological knowledge, semantic knowledge is necessary, for example *heart* and *cardiac* are semantically related and a syntactic analysis is not adapted.

Table 2. Matching the queries

	Matched terms	**%**
Segmentation	12 579	10.31%
Normalization	20 447	16.77%
Stop Words	21 022	17.24%
Exact Expression	28 837	23.64%
Morphological knowledge	10 002	8.20%
TOTAL	**92 887**	**76.16%**

We have done a quantitative analysis to match the null queries of the users with the terminology enriched by a morphological knowledge base. As in [3] the ongoing qualitative evaluation is realized by the medical librarian.

3.2 Data Mining

The second KnowQuE module is founded on *Association Rules* mining. We apply this data mining technique on the CISMeF database. Our first goal is to extract knowledge in the form of new and interesting association rules between couples of (keyword/qualifier) from the indexed resources. The second gal is to exploit these association rules in the query expansion process. Association rules were initially used in data analysis and in data extraction from large relational databases [6]. We are interested in the discovery of Boolean association rules.

3.2.1 Definitions
A Boolean association rule (AR) is expressed as:

$$AR : i_1 \wedge i_2 \wedge \ldots \wedge i_j \Rightarrow i_{j+1} \wedge \ldots \wedge i_n \tag{1}$$

This formula states that if an object has the items $\{i_1,\ldots, i_j\}$ it tends also to have the items $\{i_{j+1}, \ldots, i_n\}$. To evaluate an association rule, there exist objective measures (founded on statistics) and subjective measures (founded on human expertise).

The AR *support* (2) represents its utility. This measure corresponds to the proportion of objects that contains at the same time the rule antecedent and consequent.

$$Support\ (AR) = |\{i_1, i_2,..., i_n\}| \tag{2}$$

The AR *confidence* (3) represents its precision. This measure corresponds to the proportion of objects that contains both antecedent and consequent among those containing the antecedent.

$$Confidence\ (AR) = |\{i_1, i_2,..., i_n\}|/|\{i_1, i_2,..., i_j\}| \tag{3}$$

3.2.2 Knowledge Extraction Process

The knowledge extraction process is realized in several steps: the data and context preparation (objects and items selection), the extraction of the frequent itemsets (compared with a minimum support threshold), the generation of the most informative rules using a Data Mining algorithm (compared with a minimum confidence threshold), and finally the interpretation of the results.

An extraction context is a triplet $C= (O, I, R)$ where O is the set of objects, I the set of all the items and R a binary relation between O and I. An itemset is frequent in its context C if its support is higher than the minimal threshold initially fixed (by the user). The extraction problem of frequent itemsets has an exponential complexity in size of n, the number of the potential frequent itemsets is 2^n. The itemsets form a lattice [21] which construction is time and space consuming. The most known algorithm used to extract frequent itemsets is Apriori [6]. In our case we use the A-Close algorithm, which calculates the *closed frequent itemsets* [22] using the semantic based on the closure of the Galois connection [23], reducing by that itemsets space size studied. The algorithm calculates the generators of the frequent closed itemsets. The generators of a closed itemset I_{close} are the itemsets of maximal size which closure is equal to I_{close}. New bases for association rules are deduced from the closed frequent itemsets and their generators. These bases consist of minimal non-redundant association rules [22].

In our case, the extraction context is the following: the objects are the annotations used to describe the indexed resources O={annotations}. The relation R represents the indexing relation between an object and an item with I={(Keyword/Qualifier)}, the couples of (keyword/qualifier). We have implemented the A-Close algorithm in Java and tested it on several sets of resources by fixing the support to 10 documents and the confidence to 100% (exact rules) to have an objective measure.

Table 3. Number of resources and rules extracted for 10 specialties

Specialty	Nb Resources	Nb Rules
Environment	1 254	53
Neurology	1 137	25
Pediatrics	906	57
Diagnosis	883	33
Therapeutic	782	18
Oncology	644	20
Cardiology	558	2
Psychiatrics	515	3
Allergy	509	36
Gastroenterology	501	13

3.2.3 Evaluation

All the extracted rules (260) were evaluated by an expert (medical librarian) (Table 4). An interesting association rule is one that confirms a hypothesis or states a new hypothesis. In our case, there may be several cases of interesting association rules in function of the existing relationships between the terms of the terminology. It could associate:

– a (in)direct son and its father in the hierarchy (FS)
– two terms that belong to the same hierarchy (same (in)direct father) (B)
– a See Also relationship that exists in the terminology (SA)
– a new relationship judged interesting (NW).

Among the 260 rules, 142 (54.61%) were judged interesting by our expert:

breast cancer/diagnostic ⇒ *mammography* (support=25 documents, confidence=1)
aids/prevention and control ⇒ *condom* (support=10 documents; confidence=1)

Among the interesting rules we have obtained:

– 68.31% new rules (NW)
– 14.49% See Also relationships (SA)
– 10.56% Brother relationships (B)
– 05.63% Father-Son relationships. (FS)

Table 4. NW: new rules, SA: see also, B: brothers, FS: father-son, OT: other (not interesting)

Specialty	NW	SA	B	FS	OT
Environment	13	4	7	5	24
Neurology	8	4	1	0	12
Pediatrics	0	2	2	1	52
Diagnosis	26	3	0	1	3
Therapeutic	3	3	2	0	10
Oncology	17	1	1	0	1
Cardiology	0	0	0	0	2
Psychiatrics	0	1	0	0	2
Allergy	26	3	2	1	4
Gastroenterology	4	1	0	0	8

The Father-Son relationships are already used in the information retrieval process. The other types of interesting association rules could be used to expand the users' queries. A set of elements (keywords and couples (keyword/qualifier)) deduced from the association rules are proposed (Figure 1) to the user who may expand its query by choosing and adding some of them. For example the query *'mammography'* may be replaced by *'(mammography) [keyword] OR (breast cancer/prevention and control) [keyword/qualifier]'*.

3.3 Formal Representation of Knowledge

The third component of the KnowQuE prototype is founded on terminological reasoning. Reasoning requires a formal and logic-based representation of the concepts and their relationships. We chose the OWL-DL language [7] to represent the CISMeF terminology. The advantage of using terminological logic is the possibility of advanced inferencing services (satisfiability, subsumption, classification, consistency, instanciation, realization and retrieval), which can contribute to maintaining a consistent terminological system and to enhanced possibilities for querying.

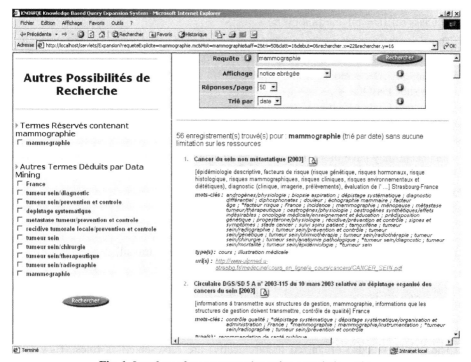

Fig. 1. Interface of query expansion using association rules

There are numerous works concerning the UMLS (Unified Medical Language System) Semantic Network representation with a formal language [24-27], but the MeSH (a component of the UMLS metathesaurus developed since 1960) has not been studied before. It suffers from its size, its numerous incoherencies, cycles and ambiguities concerning the medical concepts. For example, *'diagnosis'* is a medical specialty and also a qualifier. The MeSH has been enhanced by introducing new concepts (metaterms, resource types) in CISMeF but it is not sufficient. We propose here to:

- distinct between the *'pat-of'* and the *'is-a'* relationships (the *Anatomy, Biological Sciences* and *Geographic Locations* hierarchies are treated separately)
- distinct between the notions (specialty, keyword, qualifier, resource type)
- represent the restrictions on the qualifiers
- represent the equivalences between keywords and couple of (keyword/qualifier)
- evaluate the consistency of the obtained terminological knowledge base.

The terminological knowledge base is composed by a TBox containing the concepts and relations of the terminology, and an ABox (under construction) containing the instances of the TBox, i.e. the indexed documents. The terminology, stored in a relational database, is automatically translated into an OWL-DL ontology using Java and PL-SQL programs. The constructors we have used are the following ones:

The keywords, metaterms (specialties) and resource types are represented as concepts. When two classes have the same label but correspond to distinct notions, we add *mt_label* and *tr_ label* as prefixes. The metaterms are sub-concepts of Top. For example in OWL the metaterm *cardiology* is represented as:

```
<owl:Class rdf:ID="mt_cardiology"/>
```

The *'is-a'* relations between concepts are represented as subsumption. For example *'accident domestique'* is a subconcept of *'accidents'*.

```
<owl:Class rdf:ID="accident_domestique">
   <rdfs:subClassOf>
       <owl:Class rdf:about="#accidents" />
   </rdfs:subClassOf>
 </owl:Class>
```

A concept may have more than one super-concept. It is represented using intersection between concepts.

```
<owl:Class rdf:ID="accident_radiation">
   <rdfs:subClassOf>
       <owl:Class>
               <intersectionOf rdf:parseType="Collection">
                       <owl:Class rdf:about="#accident_travail" />
                       <owl:Class rdf:about="#accidents" />
               </intersectionOf>
       </owl:Class>
   </rdfs:subClassOf>
 </owl:Class>
```

The qualifiers (also organized hierarchically) are represented as roles. They are prefixed by *qu_lablel* and have a *domain_qu_label* as domain. We have no information concerning the range of a relation.

```
<owl:ObjectProperty rdf:ID="qu_contre-indications">
   <rdfs:domain rdf:resource="#domain_qu_contre-indications" />
   <rdfs:subPropertyOf>
       <intersectionOf rdf:parseType="Collection">
               <owl:ObjectProperty rdf:about="#qu_pharmacologie" />
               <owl:ObjectProperty rdf:about="#qu_usage_therapeutique" />
       </intersectionOf>
   </rdfs:subPropertyOf>
</owl:ObjectProperty>
```

The domain of the qualifiers is represented as union of concepts.

```
<owl:Class rdf:ID="domain_qu_contre-indications">
   <owl:unionOf rdf:parseType="Collection">
       <owl:Class rdf:about="#anesthesie_et_analgesie" />
       <owl:Class rdf:about="#intervention_chirurgicale" />
       <owl:Class rdf:about="#produits_chimiques_inorganiques" />
       ...
   </owl:unionOf>
</owl:Class>
```

An association between a keyword and a qualifier is represented as a concept:

```
<owl:Class rdf:ID="hepatite_qu_diagnostic">
    <rdfs:subClassOf>
        <owl:Class>
            <owl:Restriction>
                <owl:onProperty rdf:resource="#qu_diagnostic" />
                <owl:someValuesFrom rdf:resource="#hepatite" />
            </owl:Restriction>
        </owl:Class>
    </rdfs:subClassOf>
</owl:Class>
```

The size of the TBox is large 9,767 concepts (9, 491keywords; 65 metaterms; 127 resource types; 84 domains) and 85 relations (84 qualifiers and 1 relation part-of). The instances (13,000 resources) have not yet been included. For each one, the corresponding descriptors must be represented in the OWL ontology. The instances will be treated as primitive concept definitions and for each individual new primitive concept will be added. For example if a resource is indexed with *'hepatitis/diagnostic'* and *'viral vaccines'*, this resource is an instance of the concept C = ∃diagnostic.hepatitis ∩ viral_vaccines.

The query processing will be done thanks to the retrieval terminological service.

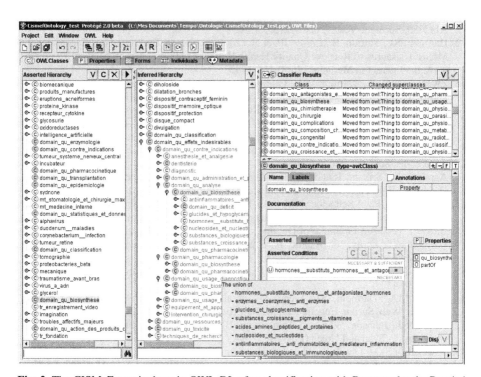

Fig. 2. The CISMeF terminology in OWL-DL after classification with Racer under the Protégé 2000 editor

4   Conclusion and Future Work

We have proposed in this paper to use conjointly three knowledge-based components for query expansion in the context of the CISMeF catalogue. Morphological processing gave good quantitative results in the case of automatic query expansion. The morphological knowledge base should be completed by treating the terms of 2 (and more) words. The qualitative evaluation is under realization by the medical librarians. Morphological processing is useful due to the size of the queries. Data mining enabled to find interesting association rules. The evaluation of the contribution of this technique will be made by a set of users that will assess the *utility* of this kind of (interactive) query expansion, with a Likert 4-value scale. The terminological knowledge base is under construction. For concept descriptions we have used few constructors. For query processing, a user query will be translated into a concept description and the answer will be the union of all the instances (resources) of this concept. This third method will allow inferencing during query answering. The problem we expect here is related to the size of the terminology.

References

1. Soualmia, LF., Barry, C., Darmoni, SJ. (2003). Knowledge-Based Query Expansion over a Medical Terminology Oriented Ontology. Dojat, Keravnou, Barahona (Eds.), LN in AI#2780, Springer-Verlag, p.209-213.
2. Darmoni, SJ., Thirion, B., Leroy, JP. et al. (2001). A Search Tool based on 'Encapsulated' MeSH Thesaurus to Retrieve Quality Health Resources on the Internet. Medical Informatics & the Internet in Medicine, 26(3):165-178.
3. Zweigenbaum, P., Darmoni, SJ., Grabar, N. (2001) The contribution of morphological knowledge to French MeSH mapping for information retrieval. JAMIA 2001, 8:796–800.
4. Gaussier, E., Grefenstette, G., Hull, D., Roux, C. (2000) Recherche d'information en français et traitement automatique des langues. Journal TAL, 41(2):473–493.
5. Savoy, J.(2002) Morphologie et recherche d'information. Cahier de recherche en informatique CR-I-2002-01, Université de Neuchatel, Division économique et sociale, Faculté de Droit et des Sciences Économiques.
6. Agrawal, R., Srikant, R. (1994) Fast Algorithms for Mining Association Rules in Large Databases. Proceedings VLDB Conference, 478-499.
7. Horrocks, I., Patel-Schneider, PF., van Harmelen, F. (2003) From SHIQ and RDF to OWL: The making of a web ontology language. Journal of Web Semantics, to appear.
8. Baker, T. (2000) A Grammar of Dublin Core. Digital-Library Magazine, vol 6 n°10.
9. Darmoni, SJ., Leroy, JP., Baudic, F., et al. (2000) CISMeF: a structured Health resource guide. Methods Informatics in Medicine, 39(1):30-35.
10. Berners-Lee, T., Heudler, J., Lassila, O. (2001). The Semantic Web. Scientific American, 284(5):34-43.
11. Mayer, MA., Darmoni, SJ., Fiene, M., et al. (2003). MedCIRCLE Modeling on the Semantic Web. Surjan, Engelbrecht, McNair (Eds) Stud. Health Technol. Inf. 95:667-672.
12. Nelson, SJ., Johnson, WD., and Humphreys, BL. (2001) Relationships in Medical Subject Headings. In Bean and Green (Eds)., 171-184.
13. Sowa, JF. (2000) Ontology, Metadata and Semiotics. B.Ganter, G.W.Mineau (Eds), Conceptual Structures: Logical, Linguistic, and Computational Issues, LN in AI #1867, 55-81.
14. Lovis, C., Baud, R. (2000) Fast Exact String Pattern-Matching Algorithms Adapted to the Characteristics of the Medical Language. JAMIA 2000, 7(4):378–391.

15. McCray, AT., Srinivasan, S., Browne, AC. (1994) Lexical Methods for Managing Variation in Biomedical Terminologies. In: Proc 18th Annu Symp Comput Appl Med Care, 235–239.
16. Lovis, C., Michel, PA., Baud, R., Scherrer, JR.(1995) Word Segmentation Processing: a way to Exponentially Extend Medical Dictionaries. Greenes, Peterson, Protti, (Eds.) Proc 8th World Congress on Medical Informatics, 28–32.
17. Jacquemin, C., Tzoukermann, E. (1999) NLP for Term Variant Extraction: A Synergy of Morphology, Lexicon, and Syntax. Strzalkowski (Ed) NLP and IR, 25–74.
18. Hamon, T., Nazarenko, A., Gros, C. (1998) A Step Towards the Detection of Semantic Variants of Terms in Technical Documents. Proc 17th ACL-COLING, 498–504.
19. Zweigenbaum, P., Baud, R., Burgun, A., et al. (2003) Towards a Unified Medical Lexicon for French. Stud. in Health Technol. Inf. 95:415-420.
20. New, B., Pallier, C., Ferrand, L. and Matos R. (2001) Une Base de Données Lexicales du Français Contemporain sur Internet: LEXIQUE, L'Année Psychologique, 447-462.
21. Davey, BA., Priestley, HA.(1994) Introduction to Lattices and Order. Cambridge University Press.
22. Pasquier, N., Bastide, Y., Taouil, R. and Lakhal, L. (1999) Efficient Mining of Association Rules Using Closed Itemset Lattices. Information Systems, 24(1):25-46.
23. Ganter, B., Wille R. (1999) Formal Concept Analysis: Mathematical Foundations. Springer-Verlag.
24. Schulz, S. Hahn, U.(2001) Medical Knowledge Re-engineering – converting major portions of the UMLS into a terminological knowledge base. IJMI, 64(2-3):207-221.
25. Horrocks, I., Rector, A. (1997) Experience Building a Large, Re-usable Medical Ontology using a Description Logic with Transitivity and Concept Inclusions. Workshop on Ontological Engineering AAA Spring Symposium.
26. Cornet, R., Abu-Hanna, A. (2002) Usability of Expressive Description Logics – A Case Study in UMLS. Proceedings of the AMIA 2002 Annual Symposium, 180-184.
27. Kashyap, V., Borgida, A. (2003) Representing the UMLS Semantic Network using OWL. Proceedings of the 2nd International Semantic Web Conference.

WS-CatalogNet:
Building Peer-to-Peer e-Catalog

Hye-young Paik[1,*], Boualem Benatallah[2], and Farouk Toumani[3]

[1] School of Information Systems, Queensland University of Technology, Brisbane, Australia
h.paik@qut.edu.au
[2] School of Computer Science, University of New South Wales, Sydney Australia
boualem@cse.unsw.edu.au
[3] LIMOS, ISIMA, University Blaise Pascal, France
ftoumani@isima.fr

Abstract. One of the key issues in product catalogs is how to efficiently integrate and query large, intricate, heterogeneous catalogs. We propose a framework for building a dynamic catalog portals using catalog communities and semantic peer relationships between them. The aim is to facilitate distributed, dynamic and scalable integration of e-catalogs. Our approach is based on Peer-to-Peer architecture. Peers in our system serve as data integration mediators having individual schema to support semantically rich queries. Connections between peers are established based on domains and the relationships they represent. Schema and relationships in peers are used for routing queries among peers.

1 Introduction

Behind every *product portal* such as Amazon.com, there exists diverse, potentially large number of product catalogs which have to be *integrated and queried*. We highlight two main problems in current product portals: (i) The integration is centralised and based on a single categorisation server. It is not suited for the dynamic Web based environment where catalogs are added or removed frequently, and the content/capabilities of existing catalogs may change over time. Conventional approaches where the development of an integrated catalogs require the understanding of each of the underlying catalog are inappropriate. (ii) Modern Web catalog portals have very limited search capabilities. In fact, they mostly rely on information retrieval technology, where a keyword is searched against entire content. Instead of centralised integration, we aim to facilitate distributed, dynamic and scalable catalog integration. We make the following contributions:

- We propose the concept of *catalog community* as a means to architect the organi-sation and integration of a potentially large number of dynamic product catalogs. A catalog community is a container of catalogs which offer products of a common domain (e.g., Laptops, PCGames). It provides a description of desired products without referring to actual sellers (e.g., a seller of IBM Laptops). In order to be accessible through a community, product sellers (providers) need to register their catalogs with it. Catalog providers can join or leave any community of interest at any time. Catalog communities may newly form or disappear.

---

* This paper was written when the author was at CSE, University of New South Wales.

H. Christiansen et al. (Eds.): FQAS 2004, LNAI 3055, pp. 256–269, 2004.

- We propose a metadata indexing model for querying the catalog community also, for representing semantics of relationships among peer catalog communities. Query routing between the communities is done via such relationships (even with no or minimal knowledge of the schema about the other party).
- We implemented a prototype named *WS-CatalogNet*. The prototype is a web service-based [3] tool for (i) building catalog communities, (ii) creating memberships between a catalog provider and a community, and (iii) defining peer relationships between communities.

The paper is organised as follows. Section 2 introduces catalog communities and how they are used in integrating/organising product catalogs as peers. In section 3, we explain how a community processes a query (both locally and collaboratively with other peer communities.). The implementation of the proposed system is discussed in section 4. Section 5 discusses related work. Finally, section 6 concludes the paper with some remarks on the ongoing work.

2   Design Overview

An online product catalog contains a set of *categorised* products that can be browsed and searched electronically. Our observations showed that most portal sites provide customers with two ways of searching: browsing via categories, searching using keywords. The two approaches can also be combined by restricting keyword searches to a category. In general, the portal will return a product as a "match", if any part of the description of the product contains the keyword. Answering queries based on keywords has obvious short-comings [8, 10]. The query model in current web portals (e.g., Amazon.com) does not allow users to query precisely using rich descriptions of the products. For example, users can only ask for "*products related to laptop*", rather than "*a laptop with SONY as a manufacturer, more than 2 year warranty*".

This section explains how we utilise the concept of catalog communities and peer relationships between them to meaningfully organise the available information space. Each catalog community is specialised in a single domain of products and defines a set of attributes that effectively describes the domain (e.g. attributes in domain of Laptops could be brand, CPU, size of RAM, size of HDD, weight, network capabilities etc). Using the attributes of the community, a query like "Give me a list of laptops made by Sony with at least 250 MB memory and 40GB HDD and more than 1 year warranty" becomes a trivial task. Some existing portal sites would serve this kind of query as an *advanced search* feature, where the customers use a form that lists supported searchable fields. However, for portals to provide such advanced search features, they would have to maintain (centrally) different sets of attributes for different types of products, and provide corresponding search interfaces for each type. This makes it very difficult, if not impossible, for the portal sites to provide semantically rich query. In our approach, community designer/provider maintains their own set of attributes.

2.1   Catalog Communities

A catalog community is a *container* of product catalogs of the same domain (e.g., community of Laptops). It provides a description of desired products without referring to actual sellers (e.g., `www.laptopworld.com`). A community maintains a set of categories that describe the domain it supports. For example, the community of `Laptops` in Figure 1 (A) has categories which organise the products as `Used Laptops`, `Super Fast Laptops` and `Ultra Portable`. Each category in a community is associated with a set of attributes that are used in describing the products. There are a set of attributes defined for the community as a whole (the `default` category), plus attributes that are specific to each category. For example, the default category of the community of `Laptops` may have {`Name, Brand, CPU, RAM, HDD, DisplaySize, Display-Type, Price`}. The category `UsedLaptop` in community `Laptops` has extra attributes that are specific to the category such as `YearUsed, Condition`, etc.

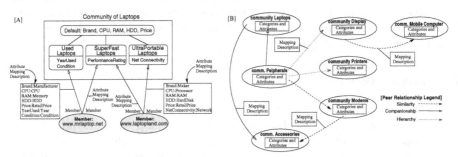

Fig. 1. (A) Community of Laptops, (B) Peer Relationships Between Communities

For a catalog to be accessible through a community, the catalog provider must register the catalog with the community. In registration, the provider associates his catalog with one or more categories of the community. Also, during registration, the provider supplies a description of how its local product attributes are mapped to the the attributes in the associated categories of the community. By registering, the catalog provider becomes a member of the community

Example 1. **Community of Laptops** Consider a community that describes laptops. Figure 1 (A) shows the community of `Laptops` which has three product categories `Used Laptops`, `SuperFast Laptops`, `UltraPortable Laptops`. It has default attributes that apply to all categories, and some category specific attributes. Let us assume that a catalog provider `www.mrlaptop.net` can provide products that belong to categories `Used Laptops` and `SuperFast Laptops`. To become a member, the catalog provider associates his catalog with categories `UsedLaptops` and `SuperFast Laptops` and provide attribute mappings between the local catalog description and the category description of the community. Here, the mapping can be incomplete, meaning that the catalog provider may not have all attributes that specified in categories of the community.

2.2   Peering Catalog Communities

A single community by itself is a fully functional, *integrated*, domain specific product catalog. It can serve semantically rich queries regarding their own domain. These individual communities collaborate with each other by forming peer-to-peer relationships (peer relationship in short). We consider three types of peer relationship:

- **Hierarchy:** the domain of one community is a specialisation/generalisation of the other (e.g., community `Printers` is a specialisation of community `Peripherals`).
- **Similarity:** the domain of one community is similar to another, in the sense that the two have common categories that are considered analogous, or interchangeable (e.g., category `CD-RW Drives` in community `SonyRetailers` and category `CD-RW/DVD` in community `CheapCDRom`).
- **Companionship:** the domain of two communities compliments each other (e.g., the user who buys a CD burner from `SonyRetailers` may want to look at some blank CDs from a community `BlankCDMedia`).

Figure 1 (B) shows a few catalog communities and peer relationships among them. Defining relationships determines how communities interact with each other. We assume that between two communities there only be one peer relationship.

Forming Peer Relationships. Let us assume that community C_1 wants to form a relationship with C_2 [1]. Since the terms used to define categories and attributes are different from one community to another, the administrator of C_1 needs to express how C_2's categories and attributes are mapped to C_1 for the collaboration to happen. We consider three possible ways of describing these mappings.

- **Full support:** C_1 provides explicit, one-to-one mapping of between the attributes in C_1 (respectively, in categories) and those in C_2. Therefore, the query expressed in C_1's terms can be fully translated into C_2's.
- **Category support:** C_1 does not disclose the attributes, but provide what kind of categories are available C_1. In this case, the mapping only expresses which category in C_1 maps to which is category in C_2.
- **No Disclosure:** C_1 does not define any mapping regards to C_2's categories and attributes. In this case, no mapping is explicitly described. It is left to C_2 to figure out how to answer C_1's queries.

Communities are used to divide a vast information space into meaningful, manageable spaces. By doing so, it is much easier to agree on the global attributes (i.e., within the community) for product descriptions, because a community represents products from a single domain that would have shared, common properties. By defining the peer relationships, individual communities discover other communities in the available space and know how to collaborate with them.

3   Query Processing in *WS-CatalogNet*

Two Stage Search. In our approach, users can engage in two-stage information seeking activities: (i) start looking for information in general terms, (ii) then get into specific information. In the first stage (*metadata search stage*), users explore communities and

---

[1] For space reasons, we will not discuss how C_1 discovers C_2 in details, but WS-CatalogNet provides metadata search facility for discovering other communities in WS-CatalogNet.

their relationships in WS-CatalogNet. Metadata queries are used to discover communities. Typical examples are *"List all communities that sell DVDs"* or *"What are the related communities of Laptop"*, etc. Once the user locates a community of interest, the user is now in the second stage (*product search stage*) where a more specific query is submitted to the community. In this paper, we focus on the second stage and look at how individual communities process the queries. Also, we discuss how a community collaborate with other communities (known via peer relationships) to process a query.

To submit a query to a community interest, the user examines the defined categories and attributes of the community and formulating a query using them. We assume that the query can be expressed in a simple SPJ form. For example, for the community of Laptops, the user can submit a query like the following: *SELECT Brand, CPU, HDD, Price FROM Category_UsedLaptop WHERE YearUsed < 3 AND Price < 2000*. Note that FROM part of the query is a name of the category. That is, the query is specifically directed to a category (e.g., Category_UsedLaptop).

Since the community does not store the product data locally, every query submitted to a community is re-directed to its members for processing. Also, the community can ask other communities to process the query by forwarding it to peers (depending on what the user want). Before we explain how the above query would be processed by the community, we look the elements involved in the query forwarding.

3.1   Query Forwarding among Catalog Communities

When a community forwards a query to other communities, it considers two elements: Metadata indices on the category/attributes mappings and a query forwarding policy.

Metadata Indices. A community use a metadata index on the category/attribute mapping description to decide to which members (respectively, peers) the query will be forwarded to. Two types of metadata indices are used: *intra-community index* and *inter-community indices*.

Intra-community Index. The intra-community index is used for routing queries to local members of the community. When the members register, they provide descriptions regard to how their local product attributes are mapped to attributes in the community. This index is built based on which categories (respectively attributes) are supported by which member. The first level index key is on the name of the categories (including the default). The value of the key refers to a second level index key, which is on the name of attributes of the category. The value of second level key refers to a list of members that can serve the attribute in a query (i.e., a member has specified a mapping for the attributes). A member can be registered with one or more categories. Figure 2 (A) illustrates the intra-community index.

Inter-community Indices. The inter-community index is used for routing queries to peers. A community may need to forward a query to peers in situations like the following:

– When no matches to the query is found, rather than returning an empty result, the community may forward the query to other communities.

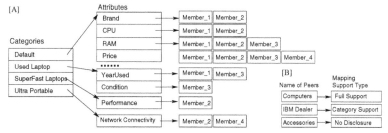

Fig. 2. In Community of Laptops: (A) Intra-Community Index, (B) Peers/SupportType Index

- The relationships between communities are formed on the basis of hierarchy, similarity or companionship semantics. Communities use these relationships to expand the size of results, or to offer the users alternatives products to what was originally requested.
- When the community temporarily unable to process the query (e.g., undergoing some changes), rather than returning a message that says "unavailable", it might be beneficial to forward the query to other communities.

There are two types of inter-community indices:

- *Peer/SupportType Index:* This type of index is used to find out what type of mapping is supported in a peer. An example in Figure 2 (B) shows that the community of Laptop has full mapping description of the community of Computers, only category mapping description of the community of IBM Dealer and so on.
  If C_1 is in *full support* type with C_2, the query from C_1 can freely be translated in C_2's terms. If C_1 has only category mapping description of C_2, C_1 knows to which category in C_2 the query can be forwarded. However, it still needs a way of resolving attribute names mismatch. (e.g., BookName in C_1 could be Title in C_2). When C_1 has no mapping description (i.e., no disclosure) of C_2, it is up to C_2 to address the mismatch problem before processing the forwarded query.
- *Attr-Category/Synonym Index:* To help communities solve mismatch problem, we use synonym-based matching approach. As can be seen in Figure 3 (A), an index of synonyms is kept in a community. In this type of index, a list of synonyms for each attribute (respectively, category) defined in the community is constructed For example, for the attribute CPU, synonyms are {processor, chipset, chip}. These synonyms are used, between communities, to find an alternative terms for the attributes/category used in a query.

Query Forwarding Policy. Query forwarding is controlled by two elements: *peer selection* and a *forwarding policy*.

- *Peer selection:* It may not be efficient for a community to forward a query to every peer. Then the question is "how do we select peers for forwarding?". We use the different types of relationships among peers as a basis for the selection process, namely; hierarchy, similarity and companionship (see Section 2.1). If the purpose

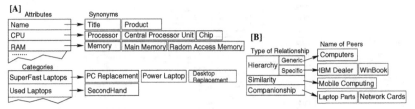

Fig. 3. In Community of Laptops: (A) Attr-Category/Synonym Index, (B) Relationship/Peer Index

of forwarding process is to expand the size of result, we may choose peers with similarity or hierarchy. If the purpose is to find alternative or complimentary products to what is was originally requested, peers with companionship relationship will be useful. In our approach, we currently make a simplified assumption that the user decides the type of relationships that she wants to use in forwarding. At the time of submitting a query, as a preference, she indicates which type of relationships is relevant to what she is expecting in the query forwarding. A type of index called *Relationship/Peer index* is used to identify the peers in each type of relationship. Figure 3 (B) shows an example of such index we use. The index key is on the type of relationships and the value of the key refers to names of peers.

– *Forwarding policy:* A forwarding policy dictates whether the forwarding is allowed or not, when the forwarding should be initiated and permitted hop count for subsequent forwarding. The basic structure of a `forward policy` is as follows:

```
forward policy: when empty|expand|always
                hop n
```

The policy requires two attributes to be specified: `when` and `hop`. The `when` is used to decide when the forwarding should be initiated. If it is *empty*, the query is forwarded when the result from local members is empty (i.e., no match) whereas *expand* sets it so that the query is forwarded even if the results from the local member is not empty. This can be useful if the community wishes to obtain larger number of tuples in the results. If the attribute `when` is set to *always*, it means that the community is currently overloaded with other requests, or temporarily undergoing changes, hence the query will be automatically forwarded without being processed locally. `hop` is used to set the limit as to how many subsequent forwarding can happen. Consider the following example:

```
forward policy: when empty
                hop 3
```

This policy allows forwarding of the query, when the result from local members is empty. The subsequent forwarding should end when the hop count reaches 3.

3.2 Query Processing

Intra-community Query Processing. Let us look at how a query is processed within a single community. At a community, the user can choose to submit a query only to a specific category or to the entire community. Assume a query Q(C, A, Condt), where C is a community, A is a set of of selected attributes and Condt is a set of conditions. Let V denote all attributes that appear in A and Condt. For each attribute a_i in V, a set M_i is identified, which contains the members that support a_i (i=1..number of attributes in V). The decision on where to forward the query to is made after the members that exists in every M_i are found. Consider the following two queries:

```
SELECT Brand, CPU, Price        SELECT Brand, Price
FROM Category_Default           FROM Category_UsedLaptop
WHERE RAM > '250MB'             WHERE YearUsed < 2
```

In the first query, V = {Brand, CPU, Price, RAM}. According to Figure 2, {Member_1, Member_2} are candidates for answering the query. In the second query, V = {Brand, Price, YearUsed}. According to Figure 2, {Member_1} should be considered for query forwarding.

Inter-community Query Processing. Let assume two communities C_1 and C_2. C_1 wants to forward a query to C_2 via the peer relationship. An example query Q.1 is composed as follows using attributes in C_1:

```
Q.1)   SELECT Brand, PerformanceRating
       FROM    Category_SuperFastLaptops
       WHERE   price < 3000
```

- **Full Support:** C_1 has the full description as to how attributes (respectively, categories) in itself are mapped to C_2. In this case, before forwarding, Q.1 is translated so that it uses terms understood by C_2.
- **Category Support:** When C_1 only has mappings for categories, C_1 translate Q.1 so that the category name is understood by C_2. Then, attach the synonym list for each attribute in Q.1. C_2 will use the synonyms to match the attributes. Q.2 is the result of the category translation and attachment of the synonym lists.

```
Q.2)
SELECT Brand (title, product), PerformanceRating (rating, review)
FROM    Category_PowerLaptop
WHERE   price (retail price, listed price) < 3000
```

- **No Disclosure:** When there is no mapping available, synonyms for attributes (respectively for categories) are identified and attached to Q.1 before forwarding (as in Q.3).

```
Q.3)
SELECT Brand (title, product), PerformanceRating (rating, review)
FROM    Category_SuperFastLaptops (PowerLaptop, PCReplacement)
WHERE   price (retail price, listed price) < 3000
```

C_2 refers to the synonyms to find alternative attribute/category names to match the terms in the query with C_2's own.

4   *WS-CatalogNet* Implementation

WS-CatalogNet is a web service based environment for building catalog communities. It consists of a set of integrated tools that allow catalog providers to create communities,

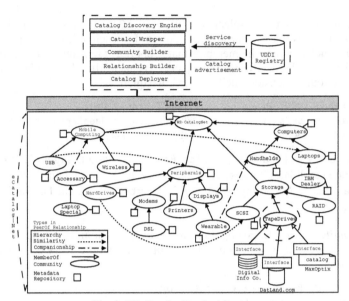

Fig. 4. *WS-CatalogNet* Architecture

member relationships (between a catalog provider and community) and peer relationships (between communities). It also allows users to access the communities and send
queries to them. In *WS-CatalogNet*, both product catalogs and communities are represented as web services [3]. The UDDI (Universal Description, Discovery and Integration) registry is used as a repository for storing web services' information. In UDDI
registry, every web service is assigned to a tModel. The tModel provides a classification
of a service's functionality and a formal description of its interfaces. We design specific
tModels for product catalogs (see Table 1) and for communities (see Table 2). These
two specific tModels are WSDL document types of tModel.

Table 1. operations in tModel for product catalog members

Operations for Member, M	Return Type	Description
Query(String query)	String	Query M
GetGeneralInfo()	HashMap	Get metadata about M
GetAttributes()	HashMap	Get product attributes of M

Figure 5 illustrates each step involved in building a catalog community (respectively
a catalog member) as a web service. Overall, the prototype has been implemented using
Java. The discovery engine is implemented using the IBM Web Services Development
Kit 5.0 (WSDK). WSDK provides several components and tools for Web service development (e.g., UDDI, WSDL (Web Service Description Language), and SOAP (Simple
Object Access Protocol)). In particular, we used the UDDI Java API (UDDI4J) to access a private UDDI registry (i.e. hosted by the *WS-CatalogNet* platform), as well as

Table 2. Operations in tModel for catalog communities

Operations for Community, C	Description
`String Query(String queryS)`	`Query C with queryS`
`HashMap GetGeneralInfo()`	`Get metadata of C`
`HashMap GetAttributes()`	`Get product attributes of C`
`String ForwardedQuery(String originComm,int hopLeft, String query)`	`Process forwarded query from originComm to C`
`Int Register(String membName,HashMap generalInfo,HashMap attributeMapping)`	`Register member MembName to C`
`Int Deregister(String membName)`	`Deregister member membName from C`
`Vector GetMemberNames()`	`Get member names registered to C`
`ECatalogInfo GetMemberInfo(String membName)`	`Get member's details (general information, product attributes and the attribute mappings between the member and community C)`
`Int AddPeer(String peerName, HashMap,generalInfo, HashMap attributes,HashMap attributeMapping)`	`Add a peer community`
`Int RemovePeer(String peerName)`	`Remove a peer`
`Vector GetPeerNames()`	`Get peer names of C`
`ECatalogInfo GetPeerInfo(String peerName)`	`Get peer community's details`

the WSDL generation tool for creating the WSDL documents and SOAP service descriptors required by the catalog discovery engine. *WS-CatalogNet* is composed of the following modules: *catalog discovery engine, catalog builder, community builder, relationship builder*, and *catalog deployer* (see Figure 4).

Catalog Discovery Engine. It facilitates the registration and location of product catalogs and catalog communities. When a catalog (respectively community) registers with a discovery engine, a UDDI SOAP request is sent to the UDDI registry. After the registration, the catalog (respectively community) can be located by sending the UDDI SOAP request (e.g., service name) to the UDDI registry.

Catalog Wrapper. It assists catalog providers to create a web service by wrapping the existing catalog. It provides a step-by-step process to create new catalog web service, starting from the creation of WSDL document to the registration of the WSDL to UDDI registry.

Community Builder. It assists catalog providers in the creation and maintenance of catalog communities. Like the catalog builder, it provides a step-by-step process to create new catalog communities, starting from the creation of WSDL document to registration of WSDL to UDDI registry.

When building a community, the community provider has to download a special class named `QueryProcessor` which is provided our system. The class provides meth-

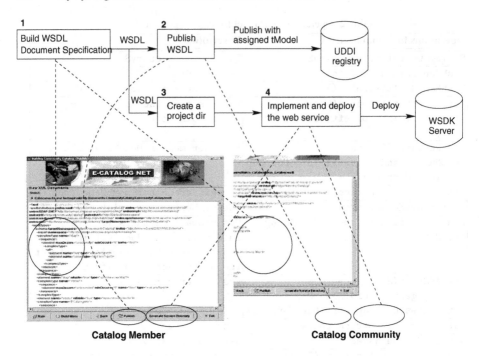

Fig. 5. Steps to build a catalog community (respectively a catalog member) using Web Services

ods for processing query requests for each catalog community. It relies on metadata about members and peers (i.e., intra and inter-community indices). The metadata is generated during the creation of membership or peer relationship, and stored as XML documents. This class is lightweight and the only infrastructures that it requires are standard Java libraries, a JAXP-compliant XML parser, and a SOAP server. In the current implementation, we use Oracle's XML parser 2.0 and IBM's Apache Axis 1.0.

Relationship Builder. It allows to create relationships between the communities (respectively between a community and its members). The relationship builder provides functionality to discover catalog communities (respectively product catalogs) stored in UDDI registry. Once a community (respectively a catalog) is found, the relationship builder allows the community administrator to add/remove peer link between two communities (respectively, add/remove member from a community). It also maintains (i.e., insert or delete) the metadata documents about intra, inter-community indices whenever a change occurs (e.g., a member is added, a peer is removed, etc.)

Catalog Deployer. The catalog deployer is responsible for generating a *service implementation binding directory*. The web service implementation-binding directory contains all the necessary files for web services to be deployed in WSDK server. The directory also includes the implementation files for the new service. WSDL2WebService is a tool in WSDK which generates a fully deployable *service implementation-binding directory* from a single WSDL document. One of the files generated by the tool is a template for the actual implementation of the new service. The template has default implementation of the operations in the service. In the case of product catalogs, It is up to the catalog providers to provide the actual implementation and link it to the web service.

5   Related Work

We identify two major areas to discuss related work, namely product catalog integration and peer-to-peer systems. Most existing work in integration of online catalogs use a schema integration approach. For example, [11] uses synonym set which contains a list of synonyms for source catalog schema attributes. Using 'intersection' of the synonym sets, an integrated global schema is derived. [7] suggests a logical integration model, in which all categories of products are organised in a single graph structure and each leaf links to source catalog's product attribute tree which represent local catalog's product classification scheme. However, construction of product attribute tree for each product of a source catalog is not a trivial exercise. [4] considers the product catalog integration as content management issue. They use information extraction techniques to derive a structured, integrated schema from a set of *documents* containing unstructured product description. Most approaches result in static integration which can not easily scale up (e.g., to accommodate new catalogs). The specific issue of integrating large number of dynamic catalogs is not considered.

The area of Peer-to-Peer systems has attracted many researchers over the past few years. The first breed of systems such as Gnutella, Napster and other systems alike has focused on sharing files (e.g., music, video clips). These systems only support limited set of metadata and offer limited querying functionality (such as keyword based search, IR-style content matching). Such limitation may be acceptable for simple file sharing purposes, but there also is need for structured querying to exploit the inherent semantics in data ([2, 10]). Our work focuses on the similar issue, therefore, we concentrate the discussion mainly on current efforts that leverage database query paradigm in P2P environment. Most work in this area deal with the semantic interoperability between peers. For example, [9] uses metadata (schema description and keywords) which is associated with every relation, and candidate peers for query forwarding are selected based on the comparison result of metadata. [6] proposes use of mapping tables which map data *values* between two peers. Such mapping tables are constructed by domain experts. These approach assume no knowledge about underlying schema of the peers when forwarding a query, but bear efforts of users to identify the correct mappings.

In [1], new schema mappings are learned from existing mappings by a way of transivity in a *mapping graph* which is formed under an assumption that a group of peers that may have agreed on common semantics. Some approaches use data integration techniques. [5] propose schema mediation language in peer-to-peer setting. Each peer contains storage descriptions which specify what kind of data is stored by relating its relation to one or more peer relations. It uses two main techniques (local-as-view, global-as-view) used for schema mediation in data integration systems. Also, [2] uses the Local Relational Model (LRM) to translate general queries to the local queries with respect to the schema of the peer. Both work assume all peers employ relational data model.

[10] propose a framework for distributed query processing through mutant query plans (MQP) and multi-hierarchy namespaces. A query plan includes verbatim XML encoded data, references to actual resource locations (URL) and references abstract resource names (URN). A peer can mutate an incoming query plan by either resolving URN to URL, or substituting a sub-plan with the evaluated XML encoded data. The authors of [8] have proposed super-peer based routing[2] in RDF-based peer-to-peer setting. We use similar concept to construct routing indices.

Our work is unique from the other related approaches in the following aspects: (i) peers are used as a small scale, domain specific data integration medium, (ii) we consider types of the relationships between peers. This is intended to give flexibility to communities when they establish peer relationships. Such flexibility means a peer can decide what kind of interaction it wants with the others. The metadata for routing queries also reflect the flexibility in peer relationships, (iii) we cater for situations where there is be no (or partly complete) description of mappings, but peers still can forward queries.

6   Conclusion and Future Work

We have proposed a scalable integration framework which can deal with potentially large number of product catalogs. The framework follows peer-to-peer paradigm, but unlike simple file sharing systems, each peer has capability to serve semantically rich queries and such queries can be expanded by forwarding to other peers regardless of the level of knowledge about the schema of other peers. Having this framework enables us to embark on more interesting problem which is restructuring of the relationships between peers or the peers themselves. The dynamic nature of the environment we are facing with, makes it critical that the system is able to adapt to necessary changes and do self-monitoring in terms of detecting the needs for such changes automatically. For example, if certain user query is not served quickly, or not served at all, the community might look at its members to see whether it needs more providers to serve users' demand, or need more peers to forward queries. Our ongoing work concerns developing and evaluating the self-monitoring, restructuring, adaptation mechanism in WS-CatalogNet.

References

1. K. Aberer, P. Cudre-Mauroux, and M. Hauswirth. The Chatty Web: Emergent Semantics Through Gossiping. In *Proc. of the 12th International World Wide Web Conference (WWW 2003)*, Budapest, Hungary, May 2003.
2. P. Berstein, F. Giunchigiloa, A. Kementsietsidis, J. Mylopoulos, L. Serafini, and I. Zaihrayeu. Data Management for Peer-to-Peer Computing: A Vision. In *Proceedings of the Fifth International Workshop on the Web and Databases (WebDB 2002)*, pages pp. 89–94, Madison, Wisconsin, June 2002.
3. F. Curbera, M. Duftler, R. Khalaf, W. Nagy, N. Mukhi, and Sanjiva Weerawarana. Unraveling the Web Services Web: An Introduction to SOAP, WSDL, and UDDI. *IEEE Internet Computing*, 6(2):pp.86–93, 2002.

---

[2] The idea of super-peer is also discussed in [12].

4. D. Fensel, Y. Ding, and B. Omelayenko. Product Data Integration in B2B E-Commerce. *IEEE Intelligent Systems*, Vol. 16, Issue 4:pp. 54–59, Jul/Aug 2001.
5. A. Halevy, Z. Ives, D. Suciu, and I. Tatarinov. Schema Mediation in Peer Data Management Systems. In *Proc. of 19th International Conference on Data Engineering (ICDE 2003)*, Bangalore, India, March 2003.
6. A. Kementisietsidis, M. Arenas, and R.J. Miller. Mapping Data in Peer-to-Peer Systems:Semantics and Algorithmic Issues. In *Proc. of ACM SIGMOD 2003 Conference*, San Diego, CA, June 2003.
7. S. Navathe, H. Thomas, M. Satits A., and A. Datta. A Model to Support E-Catalog Integration. In *Proc. of the IFIP Conference on Database Semantics*, Hong Kong, April 2001. Kluwer Academic Publisher.
8. W. Nejdl, M. Wolpers, W. Siberski, C. Schmitz, M. Schlosser, I. Brunkhorst, and A. Lser. Super-Peer-Based Routing and Clustering Strategies for RDF- Based Peer-To-Peer Networks. In *Proc. of the 12th International World Wide Web Conference (WWW 2003)*, Budapest, Hungary, May 2003. ACM Press.
9. W.S. Ng, B.C. Ooi, K.L. Tan, and A. Zhou. PeerDB: A P2P-based System for Distributed Data Sharing. In *Proc. of the 19th International Conference on Data Engineering (ICDE 2003)*, pages pp. 633–644, Bangalore, India, March 2003.
10. V. Papadimos, D. Maier, and K. Tufte. Distributed Query Processing and Catalogs for Peer-to-Peer Systems. In *Proc. of the First Biennial Conference on Innovative Data Systems Research (CIDR 2003)*, Asilomar, CA, January 2003.
11. G. Yan, W. Ng, and E. Lim. Product Schema Integration for Electronic Commerce–A Synonym Comparison Approach. *IEEE Transactions on Knowledge and Data Engineering*, 14(3), May/June 2002.
12. B. Yang and H. Garcia-Molina. Designing a Super-Peer Network. In *Proc. of 19th International Conference on Data Engineering (ICDE 2003)*, Bangalore, India, March 2003.

A Flexible Data Processing Technique for a Tele-assistance System of Elderly People

Alberto Tablado, Arantza Illarramendi,
Miren I. Bagüés*, Jesús Bermúdez, and Alfredo Goñi**

University of the Basque Country, Donostia, Spain

Abstract. In this article we present the main features of the data processing technique defined for a system called AINGERU, that provides a new kind of tele assistance service for elderly people. The purpose of developing AINGERU has been to overcome the main constraints that tele assistance services nowadays present by making an extensive use of new advances in PDAs (Personal Digital Assistants), wireless communications, and, semantic web and agent technologies.

Concerning the defined data processing technique, the main advantages that it presents are the following:

flexibility - for accessing and managing different types of data by using specialist agents; and for allowing external actors to request the system data through the developed web services.

expressivity - due to the development of a domain ontology that describes states of illnesses that elderly people can suffer from as well as specific states generated by the values captured by the sensors.

interoperability - due mainly to the development of a task ontology that facilitates the communication of the system agents with agents of other systems at a semantic level.

1   Introduction

Most of tele assistance services offered nowadays are based on hardware equipment located at the elderly person home which is connected to the wired public phone network. There is also a kind of medallion that the person wears on the wrist or around the neck, and a system (software and hardware) located at the company office that provides the tele assistance service. When the person feels bad (physically or emotionally) she presses the medallion and a conversation link is established with a person of the tele assistance company. This operator decides the measures to take.

These tele assistance services, although they accomplish an interesting and necessary function, present the following main shortcomings:

* This work is supported by a grant of the Basque Government.
** All authors are members of the Interoperable DataBases Group, online at http://siul02.si.ehu.es. This group is part of the Department of Computer Languages and Systems, at the University of the Basque Country in Spain. This work is mainly supported by the University of the Basque Country and Diputación Foral de Gipuzkoa (cosupported by the European Social Fund).

H. Christiansen et al. (Eds.): FQAS 2004, LNAI 3055, pp. 270–281, 2004.

- They are *passive*, i.e., they mainly react only when the user requires it.
- Their *coverage is limited*, normally constrained to the person's home and within a radius of some meters around the home.
- They *do not monitor* automatically vital signs that, in some situations, may have repercussion on the person's life.

Having as a goal to overcome the previous weaknesses, we are developing the system AINGERU[1], that is our proposal for a new way of tele assistance for elderly people. AINGERU takes benefit from the new advances in the areas of networking (wireless communications), mobile computing (Personal Digital Assistants) and semantic web and agent technologies to accomplish its goal.

Hence, apart from supporting the functionalities provided by current tele assistance services, AINGERU also:

- offers an *active assistance* by using agents that behave in the face of anomalous situations without a direct human intervention.
- offers an *anywhere and anytime* assistance by using wireless communications and PDAs.
- and allows *to monitor* vital signs by using sensors that capture the values of those signs and feed a decision support system that analyzes them and generates an alarm when necessary.

In this article our goal is not to make a detailed description of the global AINGERU system. Instead, our goal is to show briefly the three main advantages that its data processing technique offers:

flexibility – for accessing and managing different types of data by using specialist agents; and, for allowing external actors to request the system data through the developed web services.

expressivity – due to the development of a domain ontology that describes states of illnesses that elderly people can suffer from as well as specific states generated by the values captured by the sensors.

interoperability – due mainly to the development of a task ontology that facilitates the communication of the system agents with agents of other systems at a semantic level.

We show through the paper how each one of those advantages is accomplished. However, in order to be able to understand in a better way those advantages we show next, the global architecture of AINGERU (see Fig. 1) and we enumerate briefly its components.

As can be observed in Fig. 1, there are six different types of components, namely: User PDAs, Control Center, Care Center, Health Center, Technical Center and External Users Devices. AINGERU supports the distributed nature of the application domain.

User PDA. Each person monitored by AINGERU carries a PDA. The PDA is a central element in AINGERU architecture and its main goal is twofold, first to

---

[1] AINGERU is the word in the Basque language for expressing the notion of guardian angel.

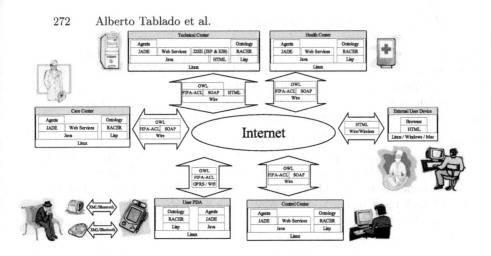

Fig. 1. Architecture of AINGERU.

monitor the user (using sensors) and then, when special circumstances require, to be the link between the person and the center (Control Center) responsible for monitoring her/him. Due to its reduced size, a PDA can be carried anywhere. Three are the basic functions of PDAs: *manual activation of an alarm* (when the user feels bad, or something is happening in his environment and he wants to notify it, he presses the button that appears in the interface and an alarm is activated in the Control Center); *automatic activation of an alarm* (the PDA receives data sent by sensors related to pulse, mobility, etc., and an agent situated at the PDA analyzes those data using a domain ontology in order to activate an alarm when an anomalous situation is detected); and *agenda services* (PDAs provide their users with classical agenda services, such as remembering when they have to visit the doctor, when they have to take their medicines, which appointments they have, etc).

Control Centers. These are the centers in charge of monitoring people. Each Control Center hosts a computer called Control Center. The number of Control Center computers depends on how many users must be monitored.

Care Centers. These are the public health centers for primary assistance. Each Care Center hosts one or more computers. Part of the AINGERU application must run in one of those computers (called Care Center) in order to provide AINGERU users with new functionalities such as: accessibility of physicians to data stored in the user PDA, direct insertion of medical appointments in the PDA, etc.

Health Centers. They correspond to hospitals. In the presence of an alarm, the Control Center could decide that the user must be transferred to a hospital. In that case, the Control Center would send information about the user to the hospital so they could be prepared when the user arrives. Due to this, part of the AINGERU application must also run in one of the Health Center computers (called Health Center) without interfering with existing applications.

Technical Center. The goal of this center is the development and support of the AINGERU application. It hosts a computer called Technical Center. This center is in charge of providing AINGERU components with new software releases, new services, and so forth.

Concerning communication aspects among the AINGERU components, in Fig. 1 we can observe the different levels that are used. At the physical level, the wired or wireless communication appears. At the transport level, FIPA is used for inter agent communications and SOAP for web services. At the application level, agents and web services communicate through ontologies described in OWL[2].

In the rest of this paper, in Sects. 2, 3 and 4 respectively we explain the main features of the advantages provided by the data processing technique: flexibility, expressivity and interoperability. Next, we present an example that shows how the advantages are applied in AINGERU. We finish with the conclusions.

2   Flexibility through the Use of Agents and Web Services

One of the goals when building AINGERU was to develop a flexible system. That means on the one hand, to facilitate the incorporation of new elements that could be used to monitor people; and, on the other hand, to establish a friendly link between the system and outside actors. In order to accomplish those aspects, agent and web service technology are used.

2.1   Agents

We have developed several agents that run in different components that are part of the AINGERU system (for example, in the PDA that the person carries, in the Control Center that is in charge of monitoring people, etc.). All the different kinds of agents that take part in the AINGERU system are described in the task ontology, with the goal of making them visible to external applications.

There are other systems that also promote applying agents in Health Care [3–9]. However, as far as we know, they are still in their initial development and they do not put special emphasis on combining the agent technology with the use of PDAs.

Each type of agent of AINGERU is a specialist in a distinct task and has a specific role in the system. Taking into account the space limitations of this article, we present in the following the description of only those agents in charge of capturing sensor data (Bluetooth Agent and Sensor Agents).

Bluetooth Agent. This agent is located in the user's PDA and is responsible for retrieving actual data from sensors and serving them to other agents. The Bluetooth agent does not interpret data; it acts as an intermediary between Sensor Agents and actual hardware. It deals with all aspects related to Bluetooth communications, giving other agents a friendly interface and so, hiding them the technical features. There are planned other types of intermediaries, like Serial

---

[2] OWL [1, 2] is an ontology representation language from the Semantic Web forum.

Agent, which can read data from sensors via serial lines. Both kind of Agents will offer the same interface to Sensor Agents, achieving a real independence of the underlying technology.

Sensor Agent. More accurately, there are different kinds of Sensor Agents. They are specialized depending on the kind of sensor they deal with. There are Pulse Sensor Agents, ECG Sensor Agents and so on. These agents are located at the user's PDA and are responsible for interpreting raw data sent by the Bluetooth Agent (if sensors send data via Bluetooth links) and making them available to other agents.

Other agents can ask Sensor Agents about the data they manage. Moreover, those data may not be only *raw* data but *high level semantic* data too. This means that, for example, if an agent requests the ECG of a person, it could get the real wave, maybe as a graphic, or the characteristics of the ECG, the P, QRS and T wave values.

2.2 Web Services

Web Services [10] are an implementation of Remote Procedure Calling that are adopted by the World Wide Web Consortium [11]. Based on XML for parameter encoding, web services have received industry support and have spread quickly throughout the web. AINGERU web services have been developed using JAXP-RPC. As examples of those web services, we can mention:

- Vital Signs: A web service exported by the Care Center. It provides information about user vital signs at real-time. Authorized actors (physicians, for example) can obtain data about the current values of the sensors that monitor the user.
- Location: A web service exported by the Technical Center. It provides information about the current location of the user. Location information is managed by the Location Agent residing in the User Agency.
- Appointments: Web services exported by the Care Center and the Technical Center. They manage the user appointments (with physicians, with relatives, etc.). The PDA will alert the user on time.
- Medical Records: Web service exported by the Care Center. It allows physicians to obtain medical records of the users.

These web services can also be invoked using an HTML access, allowing relatives and physicians related with a monitored person, using a browser, to consult data about user appointments, medicines taken, etc.

Moreover, the architecture of AINGERU allows the incorporation of public web services such as those that provide information about sports, weather forecasts, etc.

3   Expressivity through the Use of a Domain Ontology

Another goal when building AINGERU was to manage the domain knowledge in such a way that could be shared with other systems. For this reason we decided to develop the domain ontology called MedOnt (Medical Ontology). MedOnt terms describe states of illnesses that elderly people can suffer from as well as specific states generated by the values captured by the sensors. With respect to this MedOnt ontology, we follow the approach of GALEN [12] (which, in turn, is directly related to the well-known SNOMED [13] medical terminology) although we do not use the GALEN Representation and Integration Language (GRAIL [14]), we use OWL.

So far, we deal with a "toy" MedOnt ontology that we have built with the collaboration of physicians (see Fig. 2). However, it will be increased in the near future. For example, in this ontology we can observe the Temp>39 term. This term describes that the temperature of the user is above 39 degrees.

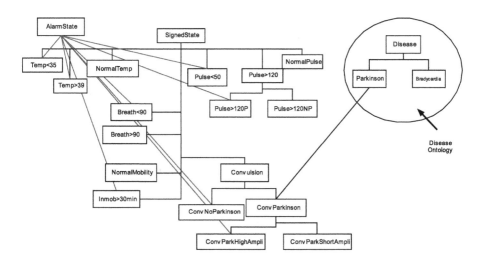

Fig. 2. Graphic representation of MedOnt.

Moreover, this term is subsumed by the term AlarmState, this means that when the corresponding sensor agent captures, for example, the value 40 for the vital sign temperature and this information is asserted in the ontology, an instance of an AlarmState is inferred and then the adequate action must be taken. RACER [15] is the reasoner we have selected to deal with the ontology.

The JohnAlarm term (see Fig. 3) illustrates the desirable customization of the MedOnt ontology loaded into each user's PDA. The JohnAlarm term is a kind of AlarmState that describes the potential anomalous situations of the user John. We consider customization a very interesting feature because every single person has peculiarities added to general symptoms; for example, the state of John, who suffers from bradycardia is not in a JohnAlarm if the pulse is below 50 but above 40. In this specific state, an AlarmState is, in fact, activated if the pulse is below 40. Notice that in the customization process the term Pulse<50 is no longer an AlarmState.

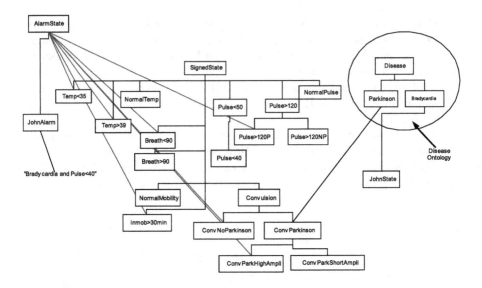

Fig. 3. Graphic representation of a fragment of a personalized MedOnt.

There are also some terms in the MedOnt ontology that describe situations combining `SignedState` detected by sensors with a state of disease. For example, the term `Convulsion` describes the situation when the Mobility Sensor reports shaking over a certain threshold and `ConvParkinson` describes the state of the kind of `Convulsion` of a person who suffers from `Parkinson`'s disease. Notice that `ConvParkinson` is not considered an `AlarmState`. By contrast, `ConvNoParkinson` describes a kind of `Convulsion` of people not suffering from Parkinson's disease, and this term is considered a kind of `AlarmState` because the person is possibly suffering from an epilepsy episode.

4   Interoperability through the Use of a Task Ontology

Another goal that we planned to reach when developing the AINGERU system was to have a semantic representation of the communication protocols used by the system actors. For that reason we developed a task ontology called OperOnt (Operational Ontology).

What we tried to obtain with that representation was to have a specification of the system that would facilitate: (i) the interoperability of AINGERU with other related systems, (ii) the understanding of AINGERU communication features by external actors, and (iii) the AINGERU evolution.

So far, the OperOnt[3] ontology is basically divided into three interrelated areas of descriptions: (i) actors, which interact using different kinds of messages, (ii) messages with different purposes and dealing with different kinds of contents

---

[3] see http://siul02.si.ehu.es/Aingeru/OperOnt.owl

and (iii) subjects representing the kinds of message contents. Next we outline each area, but we want to stress that there are axioms in the ontology that describe their interrelationships. Furthermore, it is worth mentioning that the formalism used in this approach together with the semantic web technology enable the proper integration of new areas into this ontology.

Actors. We divide this area into human agents, software agents and AINGERU web services. Human agents are classified into two groups: on one hand AINGERU users and, on the other hand all those people who are concerned with the user assistance, from sanitary people to relatives. Software agents are described taking into account their location and their goals (for instance, whether they work in a PDA or in a computer, if they are attending a sensor or interacting with an ontology, and so on). Web services are described on the basis of their functionality.

Messages. Considering the standards-compliant principle in AINGERU, we have included descriptions of messages according to their functionality in FIPA [16] protocols. Message descriptions are based on three FIPA protocols: FIPA Request Interaction Protocol, FIPA Subscribe Interaction Protocol and FIPA Query Interaction Protocol. Kinds of messages that appear in OperOnt are: `Agree`, `Cancel`, `Failure`, `Refuse`, `Query`, `Subscribe` and `Inform`.

Another feature that differentiates messages is the particular field of the message content. For example, two messages whose functionality is `Query-ref` are different kinds of messages if they differ in the kind of request (for instance, if one requests a `Location`, and the other requests some `Medicine`).

Subject of Messages. This area describes terms about the subject or the topic on which the message is centered . For example, `InputOutput`, `Location`, `Urgency`, `Emergency`, `Sensor`, `Hospital`, `Appointments`, `Medicines` and `Dump` describe different kinds of topics. Typically, conceptualization in one area is used as qualification for terms in another area. That is, different terms in one area serve as a domain or as a range for properties in the other. For example, a `Query` whose `theSubject` is a `Location` is a `LocationQuery`.

5   A Sample Scenario of the System at Work

Following is an example that shows how an external agent interoperates with the AINGERU system in order to perform a complex task. That external agent belongs to an information system of a hospital, that takes part of the AINGERU network, and its goal is to update a customized version of the MedOnt ontology, which is stored in a particular PDA (for example, to add a new term that is a specialization of an existing one).

Two are the main steps that the external agent must do to accomplish its goal: i) to discover how to communicate with AINGERU agents and ii) to contact the adequate AINGERU agent. In the first step, the OperOnt ontology plays an important role. Because the external agent does not know which is the format of the messages that it must interchange with AINGERU agents (it only knows *what it wants* to communicate but it does not know *how*), it uses OperOnt (stored at the hospital) to obtain the message formatted properly. OperOnt is also used by this external agent to understand the messages that it receives from AINGERU agents. In this step, we can observe how AINGERU favors the interoperability with external agents.

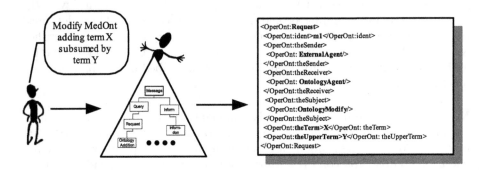

Fig. 4. Using OperOnt to build the message.

In the second step, the external agent needs to discover where the specialist AINGERU agent is. That agent is to whom the external agent must send the message obtained at step 1. There are several agencies in AINGERU that offer facilities to discover which agent offers a certain service. They are called Service Discovery facilities and are based on the DAML-S [17] Web Services Description Language. In our example, the external agent asks (to the Service Discovery at the hospital) for the particular agent that is in charge of the customization of the MedOnt ontology stored in a particular PDA.

In this step we can see the flexibility that AINGERU offers to deal with different agents.

Once the external agent knows to which agent needs to send its request (step 2) and how to do it (step 1), it establishes the communication and waits for the response. In order to understand the response, it uses OperOnt again.

Updating the MedOnt ontology is an interesting task in a real environment. Moreover, the use of ontologies to describe knowledge related to: users and system functionality, increases the expressivity level of the system.

6   Related Works

We classify tele assistance applications in two general groups. In the first group, we include those systems that provide limited coverage, such as existing tele alarms. The main features of those systems are the following: they use wired

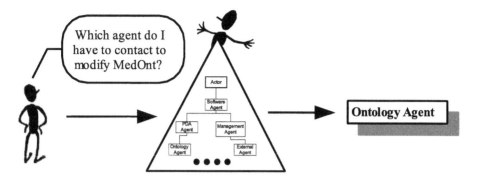

Fig. 5. Searching for the specialized agent.

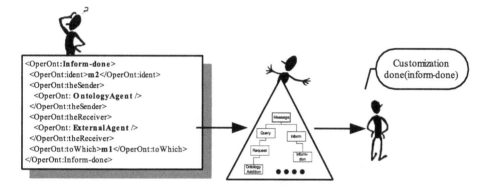

Fig. 6. Using OperOnt to understand the result.

phone communications to contact tele assistance services providers, their coverage is restricted usually to the user home and their activation is triggered by the user, generally using a button. Therefore, they do not support an *active anywhere and anytime* assistance. Moreover they do not incorporate data processing techniques.

In the second group we include more advanced systems. The coverage provided by these systems is broader, they use PDAs and take advantage of wireless communications. They provide *anywhere and anytime* assistance, but they are not *active*. PDAs are used as intermediary elements and their goal is merely reduced to transmit data from sensors to a central computer where data analysis is made. They do not take advantage of the ability of the PDAs to carry out a certain pre-analysis before sending data to the central computer. So they do not deal with data processing techniques at the PDA as we do. Notice that wireless communications are slow, expensive and unstable so, analysis made in the PDA can save communication costs and can detect anomalies earlier. Examples in this group are LifeGuard [18] (a project developed by the Stanford University and the NASA to monitor astronauts), doc@HOME [19] (A PDA stores and sends information about the user health status, putting it available to doctors and researches), Sensatex [20] (a shirt with sensors embedded that sends vital signs to a PDA and to a central computer), SILC [21] (combines sensors and GPRS transmission), or TeleMediCare [22] (sensors send data to computers that are near the user via Bluetooth).

AINGERU goes one step further by providing not only *anywhere and anytime* assistance using wireless communications, but also a *high quality assistance* that reacts automatically when circumstances require it, mainly due to the use of agents that run in the PDAs and semantic web technology.

7   Conclusions

The main contributions of AINGERU can be summarized under two different perspectives: one related to the application domain; and, the other related to the technical issues.

Concerning the application domain, AINGERU goes one step further in the tele assistance service by providing: (i) *anywhere and anytime* assistance using PDAs and wireless communications; and, (ii) a *high quality assistance* reacting in the face of anomalous situations, mainly due to the use of agents and semantic web technology.

With respect to technical issues, and in particular concerning the data processing, for the development of AINGERU we have built: (i) agents that are specialist in different tasks, that can be executed in the PDA and in computers at different centers, and that can communicate among them at the semantic level; (ii) two ontologies that allow sharing knowledge, medical and operational, with other systems; and (iii) web services that bring AINGERU closer to physicians and relatives concerned with the users of AINGERU.

Acknowledgements

The authors would like to thank Volker Haarslev and Ralf Möller for their help in carrying RACER to PDAs.

References

1. *Web Ontology Language (OWL) Guide Version 1.0*, World Wide Web Consortium Std., http://www.w3.org/2001/sw/WebOnt/guide-src/Guide.html.
2. G. Antoniou and F. van Harmelen, "Web Ontology Language: OWL," in *Handbook on Ontologies in Information Systems*, S. Staab and R. Studer, Eds.   Springer-Verlag, 2003, paper I.4, pp. 67–94.
3. (2003, July) Telecare, a multi-agent tele-supervision system for elderly care. [Online]. Available: http://www.uninova.pt/~telecare
4. H. Mouratidis, G. Manson, P. Giorgini, and I. Philp, "Modelling an agent-based integrated health and social care information system for older people," in *15th European Conference on Artificial Intelligence*, 21 July 2002.

5. S. L. Mabry, S. J. Kollmansberger, T. Etters, and K. L. Jones, "IM-Agents for patient monitoring and diagnostics," in *15th European Conference on Artificial Intelligence*, 22 July 2002.

6. A. Moreno and D. Isern, "Offering agent-based medical services within the AgentCities project," in *15th European Conference on Artificial Intelligence*, 22 July 2002.

7. D. Isern, D. Sánchez, A. Moreno, and A. Valls, "HeCaSe: an agent-based system to provide personalised medical services," in *Workshop Agentes en el tercer milenio, in Conferencia de la Asociación Española para la Inteligencia Artificial*, 2003, pp. 30–39.

8. L. M. Camarinha-Matos and H. Afsarmanesh, "Virtual Communities and Elderly Support," *Advances in Automation, Multimedia and Video Systems, and Modern Computer Science*, pp. 279–284, Sept. 2001.

9. D. Isern, D. Sánchez, A. Moreno, and A. Valls, "HeCaSe: deployment of agent-based health care services," in *Workshop Agentes en el tercer milenio, in Conferencia de la Asociación Española para la Inteligencia Artificial*, 2003, pp. 60–61.

10. (2003, Dec.) Web Services Activity. World Wide Web Consortium. [Online]. Available: http://www.w3.org/2002/ws

11. (2003, Dec.) World Wide Web Consortium. [Online]. Available: http://www.w3.org

12. (2003, Dec.) OpenGALEN: Making the impossible very difficult. [Online]. Available: http://www.opengalen.org/

13. (2003, Dec.) SNOMED International. [Online]. Available: http://www.snomed.org/

14. A. Rector and S. Bechhofer, "The GRAIL concept modelling language for medical terminology," *Artificial Intelligence in Medicine*, no. 8, pp. 139–171.

15. R. Möller and V. Haarslev. (2003, July) RACER: Renamed ABox and Concept Expression Reasoner. [Online]. Available: http://www.fh-wedel.de/~mo/racer/

16. (2003, Dec.) Foundation for Intelligent Physical Agents. [Online]. Available: http://www.fipa.org

17. (2003, July) DAML Services. [Online]. Available: http://www.daml.org/services

18. (2003, Dec.) LifeGuard, wireless personal physiological monitor. [Online]. Available: http://lifeguard.stanford.edu

19. (2003, Dec.) doc@HOME. [Online]. Available: http://www.docobo.com

20. (2003, Dec.) Sensatex. [Online]. Available: http://www.sensatex.com

21. (2003, Dec.) Supporting Independently Living Citizens. [Online]. Available: http://www.fortec.tuwien.ac.at/silcweb/SILC.htm

22. (2003, Dec.) TelemediCare. [Online]. Available: http://www.telemedicare.net

Semantic Web Services Discovery Regarded as a Constraint Satisfaction Problem

Salima Benbernou, Etienne Canaud, and Simone Pimont

LIRIS (Lyon Research Center for Images and Intelligent Information Systems)
Université Claude Bernard Lyon 1,
43 bd du 11 Novembre 69100 Villeurbanne, France
{sbenbern,ecanaud,spimont}@liris.univ-lyon1.fr

Abstract. The web services discovery is a fundamental problem in semantic web services. The problem is to find services that can be combined to form an admissible answer to a query. At the same time, constraint satisfaction is recognized as a fundamental problem in artificial intelligence. In this paper, we will investigate the connection between both problems. We will show that they are the same problem despite their very different formulation. The reason is that they can be recast as the following fundamental algebraic problem: given two relational structures A and B, is there a homomorphism $h : A \to B$? In our approach, the proposed homomorphism is a labelled graph homomorphism. The latter is based on *simple conceptual* graph which is considered as the kernel of most knowledge representation formalism built upon Sowa's model. Reasoning in this model can be expressed by a graph homomorphism.

1   Introduction

Semantic web services [1–3] constitute a new active research field which aims at combining the full power of two important research and development directions in the area of web technology: web services and semantic web. By an e-Service we mean any piece of software that makes itself available via internet technologies and interacts with its clients in order to perform a specified task. A client can be either a human user, or another e-Service. Many researches on e-services span many interesting issues such as: discovery, composition, coordination, verification [4]. In this paper, we are particularly interested in semantic web services discovery; we will use the semantic knowledge to find services that can be composed to form an admissible answer to a query. There are several research works that propose to apply semantic web technology to web services [1, 5, 2, 6, 7]. Examples of such efforts include DAML-S [8] and automatic composition of e-services [9]. This paper concentrates on the reasoning issue to automate the discovery of e-services.

At the same time, constraint satisfaction is recognized as a fundamental problem in artificial intelligence. Starting with the pioneering work of Montanari [10] researchers in artificial intelligence have investigated a class of problems that became known as *constraint satisfaction problems (CSP)*. The input to

H. Christiansen et al. (Eds.): FQAS 2004, LNAI 3055, pp. 282–294, 2004.

such problems consists of a set of variables, a set of possible values for the variables, and a set of constraints between the variables that satisfies the given constraints. The study of constraint satisfaction occupies a prominent place in artificial intelligence, because many problems that arise in different areas can be modelled as constraint satisfaction problems in a natural way.

What do semantic web services discovery and CSP problem have in common? The goal of this paper is to describe the intimate connection between constraint satisfaction and semantic web services discovery. We will show that they are the same problem despite their very different formulation. The reason is that they can be recast as the following fundamental algebraic problem: given two relational structures A and B, is there a homomorphism $h : A \rightarrow B$? Services are described by means of terminological axioms and query is represented by a constraint conjunctive clause. In order to define such a homomorphism, we transform both representations into a graph more particularly a tree. A proposed graph is based on Conceptual Graphs (CGs) which are expressive and the kernel of most knowledge representation formalism built upon Sowa's model [11]. It allows representing knowledge about an application domain in a graphical way. In knowledge representation, one is usually not only interested in *representing* knowledge, but also wants to *reason* about the represented knowledge. For CGs, one is, for example, interested in validity of the graph, and in the question of whether one graph subsumes another one or not. Then, reasoning in this model can be expressed by a graph homomorphism. In this paper we concentrate on developing such homomorphism as a labelled graph homomorphism. To the best of our knowledge, the work presented in this paper is the first one to try to make a connection between constraint satisfaction and semantic web services discovery.

The rest of the paper is structured as follows. We first present a Web Services database which is a description of Web Services using a description logic and that can query Web Services. In section 3, we recall basic definitions of constraint satisfaction problem and of CGs. Thereafter, we introduce a formalism of rooted tree in order to reason on graph homomorphism. We give a formalism to translate both description of services and web services query as a rooted tree model. In section 4, we formalize the equivalence between constraint satisfaction problem and semantic web services discovery. In the last section we will propose to extend a classical CSP using the notion of *soft constraint* in order to approximate the queries and relax the constraints.

2   Description and Query Language for Web Services

Here we specify syntax and semantic for describing and querying services.

2.1   Describing Web Services Database

The web services in our database is described using a description logic. Description logics are a family of logics that were developed for modelling complex hierarchical structures on an abstract , logical level. They are equipped with well-defined, set-theoretic semantics. Furthermore, we are interested by the subsumption reasoning problem on the web services database which is decidable for most description logics. A description logic deals with unary predicates (referred to as concepts), representing sets of objects, and binary predicates (called roles). Typically, some concepts and role names (often called primitive concepts and roles) are given, and additional concepts and roles are defined by using constructors. A knowledge base in a description logic system is made up of two components:(1) the *TBox*(Terminology Box) is a general schema concerning classes of individuals to be represented, their general properties and mutual relationships,(2) the *ABox* (Assertion Box) contains partial description of a particular situation, possibly using the concepts defined in the *TBox*. It is called a set of ground facts, because it contains descriptions of individuals, their property and their relationships [12].

Definition 1. (Syntax)
Let $\mathcal{N}_C$ be a set of concept names, $\mathcal{N}_R$ be a set of role names and $n \in \mathcal{N}$. Concepts C and D can be formed by means of the following syntax.

$$
\begin{array}{lll}
C, D \rightarrow & A & \textit{(primitive concept)} \\
& \forall R.C & \textit{(value restriction)} \\
& \exists R.C & \textit{(existential restriction)} \\
& (\geq nR)(\leq nR) & \textit{(number restriction)} \\
& P(u_1, ..., u_n) & \textit{(predicate restriction, concrete domains)} \\
R \rightarrow & P_1 \sqcap ... \sqcap P_n & \textit{(role conjunction)}
\end{array}
$$

Definition 2. (Semantic)
Given a fixed interpretation, each formula denotes a binary or unary relation over the domain. Thus we can immediately formulate the semantics of attributes and concepts in terms of relations and sets without the detour through predicate logic notation. An interpretation $\mathcal{I} = (\Delta^{\mathcal{I}}, \cdot^{\mathcal{I}})$ consists of a set $\Delta^{\mathcal{I}}$ (the domain of $\mathcal{I}$) and a function $\cdot^{\mathcal{I}}$ (the extension function of $\mathcal{I}$) that maps every concept to a subset of $\Delta^{\mathcal{I}}$, every constant to an element of of $\Delta^{\mathcal{I}}$ and every attribute to a subset of $\Delta^{\mathcal{I}} \times \Delta^{\mathcal{I}}$. Moreover, we assume that distinct constants have distinct images (Unique Name Assumption). The interpretation function can then be extended to arbitrary concepts denoted as follows:

$(\forall R.C)^{\mathcal{I}} = \{d_1 \in \Delta^{\mathcal{I}} \mid \forall d_2 : (d_1, d_2) \in R^{\mathcal{I}} \rightarrow d_2 \in C^{\mathcal{I}}\}$
$(\geq nR)^{\mathcal{I}} = \{d_1 \in \Delta^{\mathcal{I}} \mid \#\{d_2 \mid (d_1, d_2) \in R^{\mathcal{I}} \geq n\}$
$(\leq nR)^{\mathcal{I}} = \{d_1 \in \Delta^{\mathcal{I}} \mid \#\{d_2 \mid (d_1, d_2) \in R^{\mathcal{I}} \leq n\}$
$(P_1 \sqcap .... \sqcap P_m) = P_1^{\mathcal{I}} \sqcap ....P_n^{\mathcal{I}}$
$(P(u_1, ..., u_n))^{\mathcal{I}} = \{d \in \Delta^{\mathcal{I}} \mid \exists d_1, ...d_n \in \Delta^{\mathcal{I}} : u_1^{\mathcal{I}}(d) = d_1...., u_n^{\mathcal{I}}(d) = d_n$ and $(d_1, ...d_n) \in P^D\}$

Definition 3. (Subsumption) *Let C,D be concept descriptions.*
D subsumes C (for short) $C \sqsubseteq D$ iff $C^{\mathcal{I}} \subseteq D^{\mathcal{I}}$ for all interpretations.
We say that two concepts C, D are equivalent (for short $C \equiv D$) if $C^{\mathcal{I}} = D^{\mathcal{I}}$ for all interpretations $\mathcal{I}$, i.e., equivalent concepts always describe the same sets.

We say that an interpretation $\mathcal{I}$ satisfies the axiom $A \sqsubseteq C$ if $A^{\mathcal{I}} \subseteq C^{\mathcal{I}}$. If $\mathcal{T}$ is a set of axioms (terminology), an interpretation $\mathcal{I}$ that satisfies all axioms in $\mathcal{T}$ is called a $\mathcal{T}$-interpretation. A concept C is $\mathcal{T}$-satisfiable if there is a $\mathcal{T}$-interpretation $\mathcal{I}$ such that $C^{\mathcal{I}} \neq \emptyset$. We say that C is $\mathcal{T}$-subsumed by D (written $C \sqsubseteq_{\tau} D$) if $C^{\mathcal{I}} \subseteq D^{\mathcal{I}}$ for every $\mathcal{T}$-interpretation $\mathcal{I}$.

Example 1. As an example of terminology $\mathcal{T}$, Fig 1 considers a part of a web services database describing information about lodging. The services are specified as a set of terminological axioms. The statement $Hotel \sqsubseteq Accommodation$ asserts that Hotel is a subclass of the class Accommodation.

$Accommodation \sqsubseteq \forall locationPlace.GeoLocation$
$Accommodation \sqsubseteq \forall capacity.Number \sqcap (\geq 1 \; capacity)$
$Accommodation \sqsubseteq \forall rate.Number$
$Hotel \sqsubseteq Accommodation$
$Hotel \sqsubseteq \forall chain.Chain \sqcap \forall category.Number$
$Hotel \sqsubseteq \forall includeService.String \sqcap (\geq 1 \; includeService)$
$Private \sqsubseteq Accommodation$
$Private \sqsubseteq \forall surface.Number \sqcap \forall ownerContact.String$
$House \sqcap Private \sqsubseteq \; \bot$
$House \sqsubseteq \forall floors.Number$
$House \sqsubseteq \forall pool.Boolean$
...

$Flat \sqsubseteq Private$
$Flat \sqcap House \sqsubseteq \bot$
$SmallFlat \sqsubseteq Flat$ ...

Fig. 1. A part of a lodging service database

In this paper, we will reason on the abstract description of services. We do not handle the extensional part of services.

2.2   Web Services Querying Language

A query Q over web services database is expressed as a *relational description* (conjunctive descriptions) with constraints. The query has the following form

$$Q(x) \leftarrow body(x, y_i)\{c_1, ..., c_p\}$$

where x is called distinguished variable and $body(x, y_i)$ is a conjunction of unary (denoting concepts) and binary (denoting roles) atoms, and c_s are constraints over the variables of the atoms. The unary conjuncts in $body(x, y_i)$ are atoms of the form $C(z)$ where z are existential or distinguished variables. The binary atoms are of the form $r(x, y_i)$ where x is the distinguished variable and y_i is an existential variable, and the c_s are evaluable predicates.

Example 2. Let us consider the following query:

"find an accommodation with a rate less than 50 for two adults". It will be written as follows:

$Q(x) \leftarrow Accommodation(x), rate(x, y), Number(y), capacity(x, z), Number(z)$
$\{y < 50, z = 2\}$

Now let us see what do web services discovery and constraint satisfaction have in common?

3 Constraint Satisfaction Problem and Graph Homomorphism of Web Services

Intuitively, an instance of a constraint-satisfaction problem consists in a set of variables, a set of possible values, and a set of constraints on variables; the question is to determine whether there is an assignment of values to the variables that satisfies the constraints. The above informal description has been formulated by Feder and Vardi [13] by identifying the problem of the constraint satisfaction problem with the homomorphism problem: given two relational structures A and B, is there a homomorphism h from A to B? Intuitively, the structure A represents the variables and the tuples of variables that participate in constraints, the structure B represents the domain of values and the tuples of values that these constraints tuples of variables are allowed to take, and the homomorphism from A to B are precisely the assignments of values to variables satisfying the constraints. Let us define such a homomorphism by defining the relational structure A and B for the web services. We identify the structure A as the structure of the query web services and B as the relational description of the services.

3.1 Relational Structure A of the Web Services Query

The relational structure which we propose is based on the class of the simple graph as pointed in [14, 11]. For the reader's convenience let us recall the basic definitions.

Definition 4. (Support) A support is a triple $\mathcal{S} = (\mathcal{T}_C, \mathcal{T}_R, \mathcal{T}_I)$ where

- $\mathcal{T}_C = (\mathcal{N}_C, <_C)$ is a concept type hierarchy of $\mathcal{S}$. $\mathcal{N}_C$ is a set of names of concept types which contains a distinguished type $\top$ and $<_C$ is a partial ordering on $\mathcal{N}_C$ which has $\top$ as its greatest element.
- $\mathcal{T}_R = ((N_R^1, N_R^2, ...), <_R)$ is the relation type hierarchy of $\mathcal{S}$. N_R^i contains the relation symbols of arity i. $\mathcal{N}_R = \bigcup_{i \in N} N_R^i$. $<_R$ is a partial ordering on $\mathcal{N}_R$ for which relation types of different arity must be incomparable.
- $\mathcal{T}_I = (\mathcal{N}_I \cup \{*\}, <_I)$ where $\mathcal{N}_I$ is a set of individual markers and $*$ is a distinguished marker called generic. The partial ordering $<_I$ on $\mathcal{N}_I \cup \{*\}$ is defined by requiring $*$ to be the greatest element.

Definition 5. (Simple graph) Let $\mathcal{S}$ be a support. A simple graph is a tuple $g = (\mathcal{N}_C, \mathcal{N}_R, E, l)$, where

- $(\mathcal{N}_C, \mathcal{N}_R, E)$ is an undirected bipartite graph with node sets $\mathcal{N}_C$ and $\mathcal{N}_R$ and edge relation $E \subseteq \mathcal{N}_C \times \mathcal{N}_R$. $\mathcal{N}_C$ and $\mathcal{N}_R$ are called the sets of concept nodes and relation nodes of g respectively.

- *l labels the vertex as follows:*

  if $r \in \mathcal{N}_R$, $l(c) \in \mathcal{N}_R^i$ it is the type of the relation vertex.
  if $c \in \mathcal{N}_C$, $l(c)$ is the couple (type(c), ref(c)), where type(c) and ref(c) are respectively type and referent of c.

Reasoning in this simple graph can be expressed by a graph homomorphism called projection, whose semantics is usually given in terms of positive, conjunctive existential FOL (First Order Logic); for more detail see [15, 14]

In our services database application, the support defined over the database is simplified. The concept types are ordered and the binary relations are unordered.

For instance, consider a part of lodging services database introduced in example 2. An ordering of the concept types is depicted in Fig 2. The binary relations are unordered.

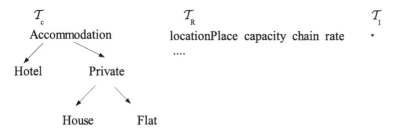

Fig. 2. An example of a support

The query graph is defined upon the simple graph defined above. Then, we reconsider the simple graph to construct the graph of the constraint query.

Definition 6. (Rooted tree) *Let $Q(x_0)$ be a query and let $\mathcal{S}$ be the simplified support , its query graph is defined as a directed, connected and acyclic graph $\mathcal{G} = (X, U, l, x_0)$, where*

- *$X = \{x_0, x_1, ..\}$ is the set of the variables in the query; each node has a label which is a concept name. x_0 is the existential variable of the query $Q(x_0)$, the graph $\mathcal{G}$ is called tree rooted on variable x_0.*
- *the set of edges $U = \{r_i(x_0, x_i), ...\}$ is a set of role names (or binary predicates) in the query.*
- *$l = \{p_1, ...\}$ is a set of unary predicate (concept name).*

For instance consider the query body of the example 2; the tree of the query is depicted in Fig 3.

Now we are interested in comparing the rooted tree of the query with the structure of the web services.

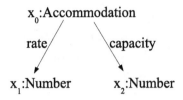

Fig. 3. A rooted tree query

3.2   The Relational Structure B of the Web Service Description

Given a web services description structure as defined in section 2.1, let us translate such a description as a rooted tree. The concept description is defined as $C \sqsubseteq \sqcap_i C_i$ (we consider only the case where C_i is not a primitive concept, we will use the primitive concept for defining the support) and the main idea underlying the translation is to represent a concept description C as a tree. Intuitively, C is represented by a tree with a root x_0 labelled by the concept name C, and each existential $\exists r.D$ in the conjunction yields a successor on r that is a root of the tree corresponding to D, and each value and number restriction yields a successor on r.

Definition 7. *(Translation from web services description to rooted tree)*
The main idea underlying the translation is to represent a concept description as a rooted tree. Intuitively, a concept C is represented by a tree with a root x_0, where every conjunction of value and number restriction $(\geq 1\ r) \sqcap (\forall r.A)$ in the top level of the conjunction yields an r-successor. Let $C \sqsubseteq \sqcap_{i=1}^{n} C_i$ be a concept description where each $C_i = (\geq 1 r_j) \sqcap (\forall r_j.C_j), i \neq j$. Formally, a translation is a tree rooted on a variable x_0 which is denoted by $T = (X, U, x_0, l)$ and is recursively defined as follows:

- *if the depth of C is 1 (all the C_j concepts are primitives) then $X = \{x_0 \bigcup_{j \leq n} x_j\}$ where each x_j corresponds to C_j, $l(x_0) = C$, $l(x_j) = C_j$ and $U = \bigcup r_i(x_0, x_{0i}), i \in [1, n]$.*
- *if the depth of $C > 1$, one builds a recursive tree $T_i = (X_i, U_i, x_{0i}, l_i)$ corresponding to C_i, where*
  - *$X = x_0 \cup \bigcup_{i \leq n} X_i$*
  - *$l(x_0) = C$, $l(x) = l_i(x)$ where $x \in X_i$*
  - *$U = \{r_i(x_0, x_{0i}) \mid i \in [1, n]\} \cup \bigcup_{i \geq 1}$*

As an example, let us consider the part of lodging service shown in example 1, the translation into rooted tree of the services is depicted in Fig 4.

The fundamental reasoning on rooted tree graph is computing subsumption relations. The subsumption relation is induced by homomorphisms between rooted trees as in [15]. The subsumption relation considered is based on the projection operation. In [15], projection is defined as a graph homomorphism between simple graph. Below, we define the definition of homomorphism between rooted trees.

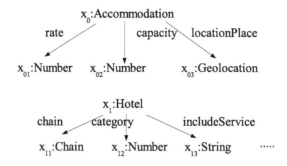

Fig. 4. A part of lodging web services translation

Definition 8. *(Homomorphism on rooted tree) Let $G = (X_G, U_G, l_G)$ and $H = (X_H, U_H, l_H)$ be two rooted trees over a simplified support S. A mapping $\varphi : X_H \rightarrow X_G$ is a homomorphism from H to G over S iff the following condition is satisfied:*
$\forall x \in H$ let $l_H(x) = P_H$ and $l_G(\varphi(x)) = P_G$ then $P_G \leq_C P_H$

Theorem 1. *Subsumption between rooted trees over a simplified support S is defined by $G \sqsubseteq H$ (H subsumes G) iff there exists a homomorphism from H to G.*

Proof (Sketch): Each concept description yields a FO formulas $\Psi_C(x)$ and each role term r is translated into a formula $\Psi_r(x, y)$. As pointed in [11], Simple Graphs are provided with first order semantics denoted by Φ. Let two simple graphs H and G over a support S, then $\Phi(S)$ is a formula corresponding to the interpretation of the partial ordering of T_C. If $G \sqsubseteq H$ then $\Phi(S) \wedge \Phi(G) \rightarrow \Phi(H)$ is valid; if $\Phi(S) \wedge \Phi(G) \rightarrow \Phi(H)$ is valid then H subsumes G [16].

Example 3. Consider the rooted trees depicted in Fig 5 . They are defined over the simplified support S given in Fig 2. The rooted tree H subsumes G, because of mapping x_i' to x_i yields a homomorphism over a support S from H to G. The state $Hotel \sqsubseteq Accommodation$, allows x_1 to inherit the rooted tree of Fig 6 .

Theorem 2. *Let G and H be rooted trees over the simplified support S. Checking whether G is subsumed by H is done in polynomial time.*

Proof (Sketch): The proof is based on a known result pointed in [17], where it has been proved that the problem of morphism is polynomial for the conceptual graph when the relation types are unordered.

4   Web Service Discovery Problem as Constraint Satisfaction Problem

This section shows that the problems of graph homomorphism, semantic web services discovery and CSP are the same problem, even they are formulated

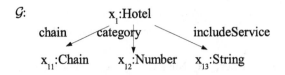

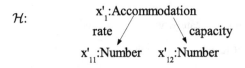

Fig. 5. Subsumption of rooted tree over the support S

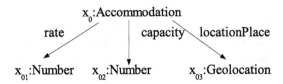

Fig. 6. Rooted tree of Concept Accommodation

in very different ways. Algorithms for building a solution or for enumerating all solutions can be directly transferred from one domain to the other one. An instance of Constraint Satisfaction Problem **CSP** is a quadruplet (X,D,C,R) consisting of:

- a set of variables $X = x_1, ..., x_n$,
- for each variables x_i, a finite set D_i of possible values (its domain) and $D = \{D_1, ... D_m\}$ in bijection with X,
- a finite set $\mathcal{C} = \{c_1, ... c_q\}$ of *constraints* restricting the values that the tuple of variables can take. We call *graph constraints* the couple (X,C),
- a set of constraint definitions, in bijection with C, $R = \{R_1, ... R_q\}$, checking for every constraint C_i: let $(x_{i1}, ... x_{ip})$ be any ordering of C_i variables, then $R_i \subseteq D_{i1} \times .... \times D_{ip}$

A *solution* of a CSP is an assignment of values to the n variables, such that all constraints are satisfied. Formally it is an application

$$\mathcal{INS} : X \rightarrow \bigcup D_i \in D$$
$$x_i \rightarrow a \in D_i$$

verifying for every constraint obtained $C_j = \{x_{j1}, ... x_{jq}\}, (\mathcal{INS}(x_{j1}, ..., \mathcal{INS}(x_{jq})) \in R_j$. (in other words that the provided uplet by replacing each variable with its instantiation is an uplet of constraint definition)

We will call CSP the associate decision problem: given a CSP P, is there a solution to P? A graph homomorphism is an application from the set of vertices to another one respecting the edges. A solution of a CSP is an application from the set of variables through a set of domain values domain respecting the constraints. Below, we will give transformation from one problem to another one.

4.1 Transformation from Web Services Graph Homomorphism to Constraint Satisfaction Problem

Let us consider two rooted trees $\mathcal{G} = (X_\mathcal{G}, U_\mathcal{G}, l_\mathcal{G}, x_\mathcal{G})$ and $\mathcal{H} = (X_\mathcal{H}, U_\mathcal{H}, l_\mathcal{H}, x_\mathcal{H})$. From $\mathcal{G}$ and $\mathcal{H}$, one constructs a CSP P=(X,C,D,R). Intuitively, there is one variable for each concept node of $\mathcal{H}$, and one constraint for each relation node of $\mathcal{H}$. The domain D_i, set of domain values is built from the concept node labels of $\mathcal{G}$. Formally a CSP P is defined as follows:

- $X = X_\mathcal{H}$
- $C = U_\mathcal{H}$
- $\forall x_i \in X_\mathcal{H}, D_i = \{y \in X_\mathcal{G} \,/label(x_i) \geq label(y)\}$. The domain D_i is a subset a possible values for the concept node y by the subsumption reasoning from $\mathcal{H}$ to $\mathcal{G}$. Then, because y is subsumed by x, we attach to x the new rooted tree corresponding to y.
- $\forall C_i$ a constraint concerning the two variables (x_i, x_j), then the definition of R is:
  $R_i = \{(y, z) \in U_\mathcal{G} \mid label(x_i, x_j) = label(y, z)\}$

It is easily to check that any subsumption graph is a solution to the CSP, and reciprocally.

Example 4. For instance, consider the homomorphism of web services depicted in Fig 5.

$X = X_\mathcal{H} = \{x_1', x_{11}', x_{12}'\}$

$D_1 = \{Hotel\}, D_2 = D_3 = \{Number\}$

As $Hotel \sqsubseteq Accommodation$ (the corresponding rooted tree of Accommodation is depicted in Fig 6), the node x_1 will inherit the children of x_0. Then the set of constraints includes two constraints $C : (x_1', x_{11}'), (x', x_{12}')$ defined by the following relations

$R(x', x_{11}')$

x'	x_{11}'
x_0	x_{01}

$R(x', x_{12}')$

x'	x_{12}'
x_0	x_{02}

Theorem 3. *The problem of subsumption of web services trees and CSP are polynomially equivalent. Moreover, every solution to one problem is a solution to the other one.*

5 Query Answering via Constraint Solving Problem Resolution

The interest of the previous transformation is not to prove that CSP and web services trees are equivalent problems. But we are interested on using some known results concerning the CSP for instance:

- Theoretical ones such as: the CSP problem is polynomial when the constraints graph is acyclic [15]. This is our case because we deal with rooted trees

- Practical ones such as some algorithmic technics to explore the solutions space.

We are more interested by the resolution methods provided by a CSP than by web services graph homomorphism. Technics based on local consistencies have been exploited and give efficient resolution algorithms [18].The graph homomorphism has some evident limitations as the classical CSP, mainly due to the lack of flexibility when facing real-web services scenarios where the knowledge is not completely available nor crisp. In such situations, the ability of stating whether an instantiation of values to variables is allowed or not is not enough or sometimes not even possible. For these reasons, ones tend to extend the classical CSP formalism. For example, CSPs have been extended with the ability to associate to each tuple of variables, or to each constraint, a level of preference, and with the possibility of combining constraints using min-max procedures. This extended formalism has been called *Fuzzy CSPs (FCSPs)*[19]. Other extensions concern the ability to model incomplete knowledge in the web services. These problems are often more faithfully represented as *soft constraints*(SCSPs). In a few words, *soft constraint* is a classical constraint, where each instantiation of its variables has an associated values belonging to a partially ordered set. The resolution process can introduce substituability or combinations of constraints, taking into account such additional values. We are also interested by the *relaxation* of the constraints whether there is no solutions for a CSP problem [20]. This is why our interest focuses on extensions of classical CSP to semantic web services discovery. Due to the space limitation, the corresponding work will be presented in another paper.

6   Related Work

We discuss here the relationship of our work to the approaches describing semantic web services discovery. Please note that the proposed frameworks are all different from ours.

The architecture of UDDI[21, 22] consists of many synchronized servers containing all the web services descriptions. One of the weak points of UDDI is the service discovery system : simple keywords with no semantic meaning will generate many unwanted answers, and no approximation is possible on these keywords. This problem also happens in systems like ebXML[23].

This is the main drawback of keyword-based descriptions : the lack of semantic often leads to ambiguity, thus making an automated handling of answers or composition of services impossible, unlike in semantic web services[24, 25].

Some propositions have been made for expending UDDI with semantic capabilities, like in [26], where DAML-S[8] data is used into UDDI records thus allowing semantic matching during services discovery.

Another approach of discovering services is given in [27], by trying to find a best cover of a query Q by subsets of a set S_T of services. The "best" solution corresponds to a coverage having the most common information with Q as well as the less extra information. The problem of discovering services in that framework is shown to be NP-hard. In [28], the approach developed presents a discovery schema that uses resolution method and a constraint-based propagation rewriting in a complementary way, where the Web services database has structural and constraint parts (represented by clauses) that is not the same description as in our approach.

7 Conclusion

We have shown that the semantic services discovery can be recast as constraint satisfaction problem. Thereby, we have used some interesting results from CGs to define a rooted tree in order to represent the knowledge, from Web Services database to the query over such databases. Subsumption of rooted tree has been characterized by labelled graph homomorphism from the subsumer to the subsumee. Starting from that labelled homomorphism of the web services, we have shown that the problem is similar to a CSP. Also, we have justified that a CSP problem is a better formalism than labelled graph homomorphism due to the extension of classical CSP. Now, we are investigating the use of the strengths of the extensional CSP on the constraint approximation and relaxation of the query during resolution.

References

1. S. McIlraith, T. C. Son, and H. Zeng. Semantic Web Services. *IEEE Intelligent Systems. Special Issue on Semantic Web*, 16(2):46–53, March/April 2001.
2. D. Fensel, C. Bussler, and A. Maedche. Semantic Web Enabled Web Services. In *Proceedings of the International Semantic Web Conference*, pages 1–2, Sardinia, Italy, June 2002.
3. D. Fensel and C. Bussler. The Web Service Modeling Framework WSMF. http://www.cs.vu.nl/~dieter/wese/publications.html.
4. S. Narayanan and S. McIlraith. Simulation, verification and automated composition of web services. In *Eleventh International World Wide Web Conference*, Honolulu, HAWAII, USA, May 2002.
5. D. Chakraborty, F. Perich, S. Avancha, and A. Joshi. DReggie: Semantic Service Discovery for M-Commerce Applications. In *Workshop on Reliable and Secure Applications in Mobile Environment, 20th Symposium on Reliable Distributed Systems*, pages 28–31, June 2001.
6. A. Bernstein and M. Klein. Discovering Services: Towards High Precision Service Retrieval. In *CaiSE Workshop on Web Services, e-Business, and the Semantic Web: Foundations, Models, Architecture, Engineering and Applications*, Toronto, May 2002.
7. Fabio Casati and Ming-Chien Shan. Dynamic and Adaptative Composition of e-services. *Information Systems*, 26(3):143–163, May 2001.
8. The DAML Services Coalition. DAML-S: Web Service Description for the Semantic Web. In *The First International Semantic Web Conference (ISWC)*, pages 348–363, June 2002.
9. D.Berardi, G.De Giacomo, M.Lenzerini, and M.Macella. Automatic composition of e-services that export their behavior. In *ICSOC 2003 1st International conference on Service Oriented Computing*, Trento, Italy, 2003.

10. U.Montanari. Networks of constraints:fundamental properties and application to picture processing. *Information Science*, 7:95–132, 1974.

11. J.F.Sowa. *Conceptual structures-Information Processing in Mind and Machine*. Addison Wesley, 1984.

12. Francesco M. Donini, Maurizio Lenzerini, Daniele Nardi, and Andrea Schaerf. Reasoning in Description Logics. In *Foundation of Knowledge Representation*. Cambrige University Press, 1995.

13. P.Kolaitis and M.Y.Vardi. Constraint satisfaction, bounded treewidth, and finite variable logics. In *CP 2002 8th International conference on Principles and Practice of Constraint Progarmming*, Ithaca, USA, September 2002.

14. F.Baader, R.Molitor, and S.Tobies. On the relation between conceptual graphs and description logics. Technical Report 98-11, AAchen University of technology Research group for Theoritcal Computer Science, 98.

15. M.L. Mugnier. Knowledge representation and reasoning based on graph homomorphism. In Springer LNAI, editor, *ICCS International Conference on Conceptual Structure*, volume 1867, pages 172–192, Darmstadt, Germany, August 2000.

16. M.L.Mugnier M.Chein. Conceptual graphs: fundamental notins. *Revue d'Intelligence Artificielle*, 6, 1992.

17. O.Brissac M.Liquiere. A class of conceptual graphs with polynomial iso-projection. In Springer LNAI, editor, *ICCS International Conference on Conceptual Structure*, 1994.

18. E.C.Freuder. Synthetizing constraint expressions. *Communication of the ACM*, 21, 1978.

19. S.Bistarelli, P.Codognet, Y.Georget, and F.Rossi. Approximation of local consistency of soft constraint. In *PADL'2000 Practical Aspects of Declarative Language*, Boston, USA, January 2000.

20. R.J.Wallace E.C.Freuder. Partial constraint satisfaction. *Artificial Intelligence*, 58, 1992.

21. F. Curbera, M. Duftler, R. Khalaf, W. Nagy, N. Mukhi, and S. Weerawarana. Unraveling the web services web: an introduction to SOAP, WSDL, and UDDI. *IEEE Internet Computing*, 6(2):86–93, Mar/Apr 2002.

22. UDDI. The UDDI Technical White Paper. http://www.uddi.org/, 2003.

23. ebXML Specifications. http://www.ebxml.org/, 2003.

24. David Trastour, Claudio Bartolini, and Javier Gonzalez-Castillo. A semantic web approach to service description for matchmaking of services. In *Proceedings of the International Semantic Web Working Symposium (SWWS)*, 2001.

25. Massimo Paolucci, Katia Sycara, and Takahiro Kawamura. Delivering semantic web services. Technical Report CMU-RI-TR-02-32, Robotics Institute, Carnegie Mellon University, May 2003.

26. M. Paolucci, T. Kawamura, T. Payne, and K. Sycara. Importing the semantic web in uddi. In *E-Services and the Semantic Web Workshop*, 2002.

27. B.Bentallah, MS.Hacid, C.Rey, and F.Toumani. Constraint propagation for web services discovery. In *WWW 2003 Workshop on E-Services and the Semantic Web (ESSW'03)*, Budapest, HUNGARY, 2003.

28. S.Benbernou, E.Canaud, MS.Hacid, and F.Toumani. Resolution and constraint propagation for web services discovery. In *RIDE 2004 14th IEEE International Workshop on Research Issues on Data Engineering, Web services for e-Commerces and e-Goverment*, Boston, USA, March 2004.

Similarity-Based Query Caching

Heiner Stuckenschmidt

Vrije Universiteit Amsterdam
de Boelelaan 1081a, 1081HV, Amsterdam
heiner@cs.vu.nl

Abstract. With the success of the semantic web infrastructures for storing and querying RDF data are gaining importance. A couple of systems are available now that provide basic database functionality for RDF data. Compared to modern database systems, RDF storage technology still lacks sophisticated optimization methods for query processing. Current work in this direction is mainly focussed on index structures for speeding up the access at triple level or for special queries. In this paper, we discuss semantic query caching as a high level optimization technique for RDF querying to supplement existing work on lower level techniques. Our approach for semantic caching is based on the notion of similarity of RDF queries determined by the costs of modifying the results of a previous query into the result for the actual one. We discuss the problem of subsumption for RDF queries, present a cost model and derive a similarity measure for RDF queries based on the cost model and the notion of graph edit distance.

1 Motivation

With the success of the semantic web infrastructures for storing and querying RDF data are gaining importance. A couple of systems are available now that provide basic database functionality for RDF data (e.g. [1]). Compared to modern database systems, RDF storage technology still lacks sophisticated optimization methods for query processing. Current work in this direction is mainly focussed on index structures for speeding up the access on triple level or for special queries (e.g. [5]). In this paper, we discuss semantic query caching [6, 4, 7, 8] as a high level optimization technique for RDF querying to supplement existing work on lower level techniques.

The idea of query caching is to reuse computed results of previously asked queries in further query processing. In order to illustrate the idea, we assume an RDF repository with information about computer science publications. A possible query is for all papers about the topic 'databases' written by researchers from the Vrije Universiteit Amsterdam. Processing this query can be done more efficiently if we already know the results of queries for all papers about 'databases', because we can evaluate the query on the result set rather than the complete repository saving the computational costs for selecting database papers from the set of all papers. Similarly, if we know the result of the query for all researchers

H. Christiansen et al. (Eds.): FQAS 2004, LNAI 3055, pp. 295–306, 2004.
© Springer-Verlag Berlin Heidelberg 2004

from the Vrije Universiteit Amsterdam, we can save costs of computing the join of papers with authors, because the result set is much smaller than the set of all authors.

In [9] we have argued for the benefits of distributed RDF repositories over centralized ones in terms of scalability and flexibility. In such a distributed setting, the benefits of query caching are even more evident: The use of a local copy of previously computed answers of a remote source instead of querying the source itself avoids communication costs which are the major cost factor in distributed query processing. Another benefit is an increase in robustness of the system, because in cases where a remote source is not available due to network problems, parts of the information is still available in the cached results.

The main function of conventional approaches to query caching, we refer to as *syntactic query caching* here is to reduce costs for network communication. In these approaches, queries to the system are completely evaluated using index structures and proxy representations. The cache is only put to use when the identifiers of results have been determined. In order to avoid costs for retrieving the complete information about the objects in the result sets, the system checks whether relevant object information is available in the cache. The access of the cached information is often organized based on the physical address of the data items to be retrieved.

Our goals as compared to syntactic caching, however, is not only to reduce network communication, but also to reduce the costs of the query processing step itself. More specifically, we don't want to execute the given query completely, but directly use previous results to avoid the need to perform selection and join operations. This is special importance for RDF query processing, because in the presence of RDF schema information query processing also involves expensive reasoning steps. Results of previous queries already contain information that has been derived in a reasoning step.

In order to be able to directly use previous results, we use the queries that have been used to produce the results in the cache as high level descriptions. When processing a new query, we first compare it to previously asked queries and determine whether there are useful results in the cache. Only if this is not the case or if we did not find all requested information in the cache we evaluate the query in the common way and retrieve the results. We refer to this strategy as *semantic query caching* (compare [8]).

In this paper, we present an approach for semantic query caching that is based on the similarity of subsuming queries. In the next section we discuss RDF querying and the notion of query subsumption. Afterward, we define a cost model for RDF querying and show how it can be used as a basis for a similarity measure used in query caching. Finally, we define the similarity of RDF queries relative to given information using the notion of graph edit distance, where the cost of edit operations is based on the cost model. We conclude with a discussion of our approach and some directions for future work.

2   RDF Queries and Subsumption

Our work on semantic caching is focussed on the special case of queries RDF data. The special characteristics of the RDF data model influences the design of different techniques used in our approach. In this section, we formally define the RDF models and queries using graph- theoretic notions. We also define the notion of query subsumption needed to make sure that we only retrieve correct answers from the cache.

A characteristic property of an RDF model is that its statements form a labelled, directed graph. The resources mentioned in the statements can be seen as nodes in such a graph (this may include properties as special kinds of resources). Subject and object of each statement are connect by a directed link labelled with the name of the property acting as predicate. RDF graphs of this kind are called *ground* graphs. Figure 1 shows such an RDF graph.

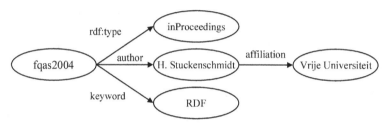

Fig. 1. Example of an RDF graph describing a publication

Based on the graph based view on an RDF model, we can characterize some properties of RDF models that are relevant for query answering. The fist basic property of RDF is the fact that a graph entails all its subgraphs. The RDF data model described above and its associated semantics provides us with a basis for defining queries on RDF models in a straightforward way. The idea that has been proposed elsewhere and is adopted here is to use graphs with unlabelled nodes as queries. The unlabelled elements in a query graph can be seen as variables of the query.

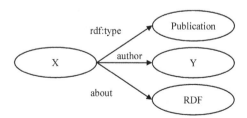

Fig. 2. An example query for publications on RDF

Figure 2 shows an RDF graph that represents a query. The nodes labelled with X and Y are unlabelled nodes in the sense of the RDF model that act as query variables. Assuming that `inProceedings` is a subclass of `Publication` and `keyword` is a subproperty of `about`, we see that the graph in figure 1 represents a result of the query in figure 2.

Using a graph based interpretation of RDF data and queries provides us with the possibility to use well established concepts from graph theory as a basis for defining important notions such as query result and query subsumption. As we will see later, representing RDF data as graphs also supports the definition of a similarity measure for comparing queries. As a basis for our investigation we use the following standard notion of graph and subgraph:

Definition 1 (Graph/Subgraph). *A graph is a 4 tuple $\langle V, E, \alpha, \beta \rangle$ where V is a finite set of vertices, $E \subseteq V \times V$ is a set of edges, $\alpha : V \to L_V$ is a function assigning labels to vertices and $\beta : E \to L_E$ is a function assigning labels to edges. A graph g' is a subgraph of a graph g denoted as $g' \subseteq g$ if $V' \subseteq V$, $E' = E \cap (V' \times V')$, $\alpha(v) = \alpha'(v)$ for all $v \in V'$ and $\beta(e) = \beta'(e)$ for all $e \in E'$.*

We can now define RDF models and queries as graphs with special labels that correspond to resources, properties and literals. In particular, we define an RDF model as a graph where all the edge labels describe RDF properties and all node labels describe resources or literals. An RDF query simply is an RDF model graph that contains unlabelled nodes and edges. These unlabelled nodes and edges correspond to query variables:

Definition 2 (RDF Model/Query Graph). *An RDF model is a graph $g = \langle V, E, \alpha, \beta \rangle$ with $L_V = R \cup L$ where R are resource IDs L are literal values and $L_E = P$ where P are property IDs.*

An RDF query graph is a RDF model graph with $L_V = R \cup L \cup \{\emptyset\}$. Nodes with $\alpha(v) = \emptyset$ correspond to variables in the query.

We can now use established concepts from graph theory for defining relations between RDF queries and models. In particular we use a modification of the notion of graph and subgraph isomorphisms. We define the notion of a relative graph match by replacing the equality conditions between node and edge labels by a specialization relation $\succeq$. The corresponding definition is the following:

Definition 3 (Relative Graph Match). *Let g and g' be graphs, then a graph match between g and g' relative to a specialization relation $\succeq$ is a bijective mapping $f : V \to V'$ if there*

- *$\alpha(v) \succeq \alpha'(f(v))$ for all $v \in V$*
- *for any edge $e = (u, v) \in E$ there exists an edge $e' = (f(u), f(v)) \in E'$ such that $\beta(e) \succeq \beta'(e')$, and for any edge $e' = (u', v') \in E'$ there exists an edge $e = (f^{-1}(u'), f^{-1}(v')) \in E$ such that $\beta(e) \succeq \beta'(e')$.*

If $f : V \to V'$ is a relative graph match between graphs g and g' and $g' \subseteq g'''$ then f is a relative subgraph match form g to g''.

It turns out that the notion of relative graph match is general enough to define conditions for an RDF model to be the answer of a query as well as conditions for an RDF query to be subsumed by another one. For this purpose, we define the specialization relation in such a way that allows us to model the use of inheritance relations and variable instantiation in querying:

Definition 4 (Query Subsumption and Query Result). *An RDF query graph g' is subsumed by a query graph g if there exists a relative subgraph match between g and g' such that*

- $\beta(e) \succeq \beta'(e')$ *iff* $\beta'(f(e)) = \beta(e)$ *or*
  $\beta'(f(e))$ `rdfs : subProprtyOf` $\beta(e)$ *can be derived.*
- $\alpha(v) \succeq \alpha'(f(e))$ *iff* $\alpha(v) = \emptyset$, $\alpha(v) = \alpha'(f(e))$ *or*
  $\alpha'(f(v))$ `rdfs : subClassOf` $\alpha(v)$ *can be derived.*

If g' is an RDF model graph, g' is called a result of g.

Based on this definition we can now explain why the graph in figure 1 is a result of the query shown in figure 2. First of all, on the structural level, we see that there is a subgraph isomorphism between the graphs. Concerning the correspondence of labels, we have

- $\emptyset \succeq fqas2004$
- $\emptyset \succeq'H.Stuckenschmidt'$
- $RDF \succeq RDF$
- $author \succeq author$
- $rdf : type \succeq rdf : type$
- $Pulication \succeq inProceedings$ because inProceedings `rdf:subClassOf` Publication
- $about \succeq keyword$ because keyword `subPropertyOf` about.

Using similar arguments, we can conclude that the query in figure 3 is subsumed by the one in figure 2.

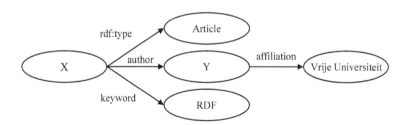

Fig. 3. Query for Articles on RDF by employees of the Vrije Universiteit which is subsumed by the query in figure 2

While the known complexity of determining subgraph isomorphisms prohibits the use of corresponding algorithms for determining query results for large information sources, the use of these algorithms for determining subsumed queries in a semantic cache is permissible because the size and number of graphs representing queries will be rather low compared to the RDF models they represent.

3   Semantic Caching and Run-Time Complexity

One of the main goals of semantic caching is the reduction of the time needed to process a given query. In order to be able to decide whether the reuse of previous results will indeed reduce the processing time, we need a cost model that enables us to estimate this time. For this purpose, we adapt the cost model proposed in [9]. We also use this cost model to argue that the reuse of partial results will indeed often lead to a reduction of the processing time.

3.1   A Cost Model for RDF Query Processing

The exact determination of the run time costs of RDF query processing depends on a number of factors as well as on our assumption about the general query processing strategy. Concerning the latter, we assume an approach, where the query processor has access to a repository that contains RDF data. This data can be accessed on the basis of single properties and returns all tuples with the respective property. Further, we assume that the data in the repository is the deductive closure of the data with respect to the model-theoretic semantic of RDF. These assumptions correspond to the design of the RDF storage and retrieval system that has been developed in cooperation with the Knowledge Representation and Reasoning Group at the Vrije Universiteit Amsterdam. Details about Sesame can be found in [1]. Under these assumptions, the overall costs of query processing is now divided into costs for accessing data in the repository and costs for performing join operations on the retrieved data.

Data Access. The first step of query processing is the retrieval of the relevant data from the repository. These access cost of instances of a property p from the repository to the query processor is modelled as $AC_p = Cinit + |p| * \|Inst\|_p * C$ where $Cinit$ represents the cost of initiating the data transmission, $|p|$ denotes the number and $\|Inst\|_p$ the average length of instances of the property p, C represents transmission cost per data unit from the repository to the query processor. In order to answer the example query from figure 2 we would have to retrieve the content of the relations `rdf:type`, `author` and `about` each time producing the costs indicated above.

Join Processing. After having retrieved the relevant data, we need to perform selection and join operations in the properties in order to compute the results of a query. The processing cost of a nested loop join of two relations p, r is defined as $NJC_{p,r} = |p| * |r| * K$, where $|x|$ denotes the cardinality of the relation x and K represents the comparison cost of two objects. Selection of tuples from a relation can be seen as a join with a relation of size 1 and therefore has a cost of $|p| * K$. For the example query, we would have to select those instances of the type relation that have Publication as an object causing costs of $|rdf:type| * K$. Further, we would have to join the result with the author relation. To compute the cardinality of intermediate results, a join selectivity measure is used. The join selectivity σ is defined as a ratio between the tuples retained by the join and those created by the Cartesian product: $\sigma = \frac{|p \bowtie r|}{|p \times r|}$. As a result, the costs for joining the author relation with the result of the selection is

$$\frac{|\text{rdf} : \text{type} \bowtie \text{'Publication'}|}{|\text{rdf} : \text{type}|} * |\text{author}| * K$$

Query Plan Costs. The overall cost of a query plan θ consists of the sum of all communication costs and all join processing costs.

$$QPC_\theta = \sum_{i=1}^{n} AC_{p_i} + PC_\theta$$

where PC_θ represents the join processing cost of all joins in the query plan θ and it is computed as a sum of recurrent applications of the formula for computing join costs. This means that the overall costs for computing the result for the query in figure 2 is the sum of the costs for accessing the three relations plus the costs for performing selections on the type and the about relations and of the costs of joining the results with each other and with the author relation.

3.2   Caching Costs vs. Querying Costs

The cost model introduced above provides us with a method to decide whether result caching provides an advantage with respect to run time complexity. In principle, we can analyze the benefits for any concrete query being asked to the systems. Due to the limited space we only discuss some general observations about the relative complexity of semantic caching as compared to traditional query processing.

The first aspect that is influenced by semantic caching are the access costs. Depending on the architecture of the overall system architecture and the implementation of the cache, the different parameters of the access costs are relevant. Concerning the initiation costs, we have to notice that normally these are higher for accessing the cache than for accessing the repository, because the costs of determining subsuming queries fall into this category. This drawback will in most cases be outranged by the savings that can be achieved on the other parameters. Already being the result of a query, the size of relations will normally be smaller in the cache, because a part of a relation is stored. While the average length of the tuples will be the same in the cache, there are cases where the transmission costs from the cache will be significantly lower that for the repository. This is for example the case when a client-server architecture is used where the repository is located at a different location and content has to be shipped over the network. Even if repository and query processor are on the same machine, the cache normally being smaller than the complete data set can be implemented as an in-memory repository that allows faster access.

The semantic caching approach also leads to potential major savings in the costs for join processing. As we cache complete query results the joins relevant for the indexing query are already computed. The fact that we use query subsumption as a criterion for selecting results from the cache makes sure that we do not miss relevant information. All that is left to do is to perform a set of additional joins and selections that would also be part of the normal query process of query answering. When we consider the queries in figures 2 and 3 we save the costs of selecting with respect to the topic and the costs for joining the type with the author relation. We still have to select the type relation with respect to Articles. Further, we have to access the keyword and the affiliation relation compute the selection with respect to the Vrije Universiteit and join the two with the cached result. The costs of the individual joins are again lower than in the normal case because the size of the cached relations is normally significantly smaller that the original ones.

4   A Cost-Based Similarity Measure for RDF Queries

In the previous section we have argued that reusing the result of subsuming queries can improve the performance of RDF querying. In real life situations, we will often have more than one relevant result set is found in the cache. In this case, we need to decide which of these result sets leads to the highest savings. We do this by defining a notion of similarity between RDF queries that reflect the amount of effort needed to compute the result of one query from the result of the other. As a consequence, the result set indexed by the query with the highest degree of similarity to the current query leads to the highest reduction and should be chosen.

4.1   Graph Edit Operations and Graph Edit Distance

There is along tradition of research on graph matching. Most of these approaches are based on the notion of subgraph isomorphisms. For determining the similarity between two graphs, often the notion of maximal common subgraph is used that also relies on the determination of an isomorphism between subgraphs [2]. These approaches are not applicable, because we do not rely on the notion of isomorphism but allow labels to be specializations of one another. An alternative approach to determine similarity between graphs in the notion of the edit distance between two graphs that is closely related to the notion of maximal common subgraphs [3] but allows for a more flexible definition of similarity. The basic idea of using the graph edit distance is to find a sequence of edit operations that transform one graph into the other. the corresponding operations are defined as follows [10].

Definition 5 (Edit Operation). *Let $\perp$ be a unique symbol different from all labels. An edit operation is written $a \to b$ where $a, b \in L_V \cup L_E \cup \{\perp\}$. An edit operation is called*

- *a node/edge relabelling if $a \neq \perp$ and $b \neq \perp$ are node/edge labels.*
- *a node/edge delete if $a \neq \perp$ and $b = \perp$*
- *a node/edge insert if $a = \perp$ and $b \neq \perp$*

Nodes can only be deleted if no edge connects to them. Edges can only be inserted between existing nodes. An edit operation $a \to b$ is undefined if $a = \perp$ and $b = \perp$, $a \in L_V$ and $b \in L_E$ or vice versa.

The similarity between two graphs can now be determined by assigning editing costs to each operation. These costs should reflect the degree of change implied and therefore the difference between the initial and the edited graph. The edit distance between two graphs is now the sum of the costs of all individual edit operations used to transform one graph into the other. In cases, where different possible sequences of operations exist, the sequence with the minimal costs is used.

Definition 6 (Edit Distance). *Let S be a sequence of edit operations $s_1, \cdots, s_k$. S transforms a graph g into a graph g' if there is a sequence of graphs $g_0, \cdots, g_k$ such that $g_0 = g$, $g_k = g'$ and g_i is the result of applying s_i to g_{i-1}. We denote this as $g \Rightarrow_S g'$.*

Let γ be a cost function that assigns to each edit operation a nonnegative real number $\gamma(s_i)$. Let further $\gamma(s_1, \cdots, s_k) = \sum_{i=1}^{k} \gamma(s_i)$ then the edit distance between two graphs g and g' is defines as

$$dist(g, g') = min\{\gamma(S)|g \Rightarrow_S g'\}$$

The notion of graph edit distance provides us with a notion of similarity between graphs, because graphs with a low edit distance can be assumed to be more similar than graphs with a high edit distance. In particular, two graphs whose edit distance in zero have similarity of one and are in fact equivalent.

4.2   Edit Operations on RDF Queries

Based on the general notion of edit operations on graphs, we can now define suitable editing operations on RDF Graphs. Edit operations on RDF graphs differ from general graph edit operations insofar, as we have to take into account the underlying data model. In particular, the triple data model does not allow us to remove edges without also removing nodes that are unconnected after removing the edge. Further, when considering query graphs, edit operations that split up the graph in two unconnected components are not permitted. In our semantic caching approach, we also only consider relabelling operations that follow the specialization relation $\succeq$. In order to avoid having to deal with operation, that do not make sense for RDF models, we define specialized edit operations on RDF graphs that correspond to the insertion, removal or replacement or triples in the underlying RDF model. In the following we define the corresponding operations as combinations of general graph edit operations that fulfill certain additional constraints:

Definition 7 (Edge Insert). *An edge insertion operation is a pair of graph edit operations $g_o \to_{s_1} g_1 \to_{s_2} g_2$ such that s_1 is a node insertion adding a node v to the graph and s_2 is an edge insertion that inserts a edge (u, v) where v is the previously inserted node and u is a node in g_0.*

The edge insertion operation above corresponds to the addition of tuple pattern to an RDF query. This operation refines the query by adding an additional constraint on the result. As we are only interested in queries that are subsumed by cached queries, we do not have to take into account the converse operation of edge deletion. The use of such a deletion operation in combination with insertion would lead to a query that is no longer subsumed by the original one. As we do not want this to happen, we can reduce the search space by only considering edge insertion in combination with refinement operations on edge and node labels as defined in the following.

Definition 8 (Edge/Node Refinement). *An edge(node) refinement operation is a graph edit operation $a \rightarrow b$ such that a is an edge(node) label in the original graph, $b \in L_E(L_V)$ and $a \succeq b$.*

The application of these special editing operations always leads to a graph that is subsumed by the original one. Based on these operations we can use the notion of edit distance provided in definition 6 to determine subsumption and, given an appropriate cost function for edit operations, compute the distance between queries in the cache and new queries submitted to the system.

4.3   Determining Editing Costs

The crucial aspect of the approach is to find a useful similarity measure for RDF queries. Relying on the edit distance of query graphs, this problem reduces to determining the costs of an edit operation that together define the edit distance. As our main goal is to reduce processing time, the costs of an edit operation should be linked to the processing costs that result from the difference between the two queries described by the operation. In section 3.2 we briefly discussed the costs of adapting cached results and compared it with the costs of processing a query in the standard way. The idea of assigning costs to edit operations is now to use the costs resulting from actually computing the results for the refined query using the results of the more general query in the cache.

For the case of an edge insertion we need to access the relation to be inserted causing costs of AC_e and to compute the join with the stored results which adds $|e| * |g| * K$ to the costs. The resulting definition of the costs of an edge insertion is the following:

Definition 9 (Insertion Costs). *Let s be an insertion operation that adds an edge $e = (u,v)$ to a query graph g. Then*

$$\gamma(s) = AC_e + |e| * |g| * K$$

Where $|e|$ denotes the number of instances of the relation $L_E(e)$ and $|g|$ denotes the number of instances of g.

For the case of an edge refinement $e \rightarrow e'$, the situation is quite similar. We have to access the relation e' that will replace a more general relation e in the query with costs AC'_e. Afterwards we also also compute the join of this relation with the results in the cache. In contrast to the insertion operation, however, we have to perform comparisons on both sides of the edge leading to addition al costs of $|e'| * |g| * 2K$. The resulting definition of the costs of an edge refinement is the following:

Definition 10 (Edge Refinement Costs). *Let s be an operation that replaces an edge label e by another edge label e' with $e \succeq e'$ then*

$$\gamma(s) = AC'_e + |e'| * |g| * 2K$$

Where $|e|$ denotes the number of instances of the relation $L_E(e)$ and $|g|$ denotes the number of results of g.

With respect to node refinement $v \rightarrow v'$ we have to distinguish two cases. The first and simpler case is the one where a label is assigned to an unlabelled node. In this case, we only have to compare every result on the cache with the value to be assigned causing costs of $|g| * K$. As we only consider replacements that change the label of a node and we claim that $v \succeq v'$, all remaining situations are cases where a class name is substituted by the name of a subclass. Consequently, we have to access the type information in the relation rdf:type causing costs of $AC_{\texttt{rdf:type}}$ and compare it with the results in the cache. This adds costs of $|\texttt{rdf:type}| * |g| * K$. The resulting definition of the costs of a node refinement is the following:

Definition 11 (Node Refinement Costs). *Let s be an operation that replaces an node label v by another edge label $v' \neq v$ with $v \succeq v'$ then*

$$\gamma(s) = \begin{cases} |g| * K & \text{if } v = \bot \\ AC_{rdf:type} + |rdf:type| * |g| * K & \text{otherwise} \end{cases}$$

As we see from the definitions, the costs of the different edit operations depend on statistics of the information in the repository and the cache. This means that if we have up-to-date statistics available, we can guarantee that our approach selects a strategy that is optimal wrt. run time costs by first simulating the query execution on the basis of the cost model before actually performing it.

5   Discussion

In this paper we describe the foundations of an approach for semantic caching of RDF queries. Our approach is a flexible one in the sense that it takes the actual information into account. In particular the same queries will have a different similarity based on the underlying information thereby ensuring that we get an optimal result wrt. the cost model. A question that we did not address in this work yet is whether the combined use of different result sets in the cache can further improve the approach. For a successful application of the approach in an RDF storage and retrieval system, a number of additional topics have to be addressed. We have to develop strategies for building and maintaining the cache. Changes in the underlying information that invalidate parts of the cached results are the main challenge here. We also need to provide indexing and retrieval methods for accessing the cache in order to avoid losing the advantages wrt. run time costs. A real system will also have to be evaluated experimentally because the implementation of the cache can significantly influence the run time behavior.

Acknowledgements

I would like to thank Richard Vdovjak for useful work on cost models for RDF query processing and Martin Schaaf for fruitful discussions about the topic of the paper.

References

1. J. Broekstra, A. Kampman, and F. van Harmelen. Sesame: A generic architecture for storing and querying rdf and rdf schema. In *The Semantic Web - ISWC 2002*, 2002.
2. H. Bunke and K. Shearer. A graph distance metric based on the maximal common subgraph. *Pattern Recognition Letters*, 19(3-4):255–259, 1998.
3. Horst Bunke. On a relation between graph edit distance and maximum common subgraph. *Pattern Recognition Letters*, pages 689–694, 1997.
4. B. Chidlovskii and U.M. Borgho. Semantic caching of web querie. *VLDB Journal*, 9(1):2–17, 2000.
5. Vassilis Christophides, Dimitris Plexousakisa, Michel Scholl, and Sotirios Tourtounis. On labeling schemes for the semantic web. In *Proceedings of the 13th World Wide Web Conference*, pages 544–555, 2003.
6. Shaul Dar, Michael J. Franklin, Bjoern Joensson, Divesh Srivastava, and Michael Tan. Semantic data caching and replacement. In *Proceedings of VLDB'96*, pages 330–341, 1996.
7. Dongwon Lee and Wesley W. Chu. Towards intelligent semantic caching for web sources. *Journal of Intelligent Information Systems*, 17(1):23–45, 2001.
8. Q. Ren, M.H. Dunham, and V. Kumar. Semantic caching and query processing. *IEEE Transactions on Knwoledge and Data Engineering*, 15(1), January/February 2003.
9. H. Stuckenschmidt, R. Vdovjak, J. Broekstra, and G.-J. Houben. Towards distributed RDF querying. *International Journal on Web Engineering and Technology*, 2004. to appear.
10. J.T.L. Wang, K. Zhang, and G.-W. Chirn. Algorithms for approximate graph matching. *Information Sciences*, 82:45–74, 1995.

Fuzzy-Spatial SQL

Gloria Bordogna[1] and Giuseppe Psaila[2]

[1] CNR – Istituto per la Dinamica dei Processi Ambientali
Sez. di Milano – Lab. di Georisorse,
via Pasubio 3/5
24044 Dalmine (BG) Italy
Tel.+390356224262
gloria.bordogna@idpa.cnr.it
[2] Università di Bergamo,
Dip. Ing. Gestionale e dell'Informazione
Viale Marconi 5
24044 Dalmine (BG) Italy
Tel +39 035 2052 355
psaila@unibg.it

Abstract. Current Geographic Information Systems (GISs) are inadequate for performing spatial analysis, since they force users to formulate their often vague requests by means of crisp selection conditions on spatial data. In fact, SQL extended to support spatial analysis is becoming the de facto standard for GISs; however, it does not allow the formulation of flexible queries. Based on these considerations, we propose the extension of SQL/Spatial in order to make it flexible. Flexibility is obtained by allowing the expression of linguistic predicates defining soft spatial and non-spatial selection conditions admitting degrees of satisfaction. Specifically, this paper proposes an extension of the basic SQL SELECT operator; proposes the definition of some spatial functions to compute gradual topological, distance, and directional properties of spatial objects; introduces a new operator for defining linguistic predicates over spatial properties, and reports the related formal semantics.

1 Introduction

For many categories of users such as planners and resource managers, the possibility to express tolerant conditions on conventional and spatial data, and to retrieve discriminated spatial information in decreasing order of relevance can greatly simplify their spatial analysis tasks which generally consists in a sequence of trial and error phases aimed at identifying spatial features of interest [0,0,0].

In this paper, we present our ideas to define a flexible spatial query language for simplifying spatial analysis when using traditional GISs. We tackle the problem having in mind the objectives of defining a language that can be easily and cheaply incorporated into existing GISs, and that can be well accepted by the GIS community.

H. Christiansen et al. (Eds.): FQAS 2004, LNAI 3055, pp. 307–319, 2004.
© Springer-Verlag Berlin Heidelberg 2004

On the one side, SQL is becoming more and more common in the GIS community, and people find it easier to learn its extensions instead of a completely novel language; in this respect there is an effort to define spatial extensions of SQL for standardisation purposes, and several proposals are now available [0,0,0,0]. However, none of there proposals allow the specification of tolerant selection conditions. Nevertheless, the need for flexible querying in GISs has been addressed by some researchers who looked at this need mainly considering the problem of representing geographic entities with unsharp boundaries, such as natural ecosystems, and of defining appropriate spatial operators for evaluating gradual topological or directional relationships between fuzzy geographic entities [0].

On the other side, fuzzy set theory [0,0] has been successfully applied to define flexible query languages for databases [0,0,0] and several approaches are now available, such as fuzzy SQL [0,0].

Based on these considerations we propose to define a fuzzy extension of SQL spatial that can be incorporated into traditional GISs. Spatial functions are proposed that make it possible to compute gradual geometrical and topological properties between crisp geographic entities, on which soft conditions can be evaluated. Then, we discuss how to personalise soft conditions based on linguistic predicates through a new SQL like operator. We will show that the resulting proposal is easy to understand, easy to use for users, provides a very high level of flexibility which is not known to other proposals, and leaves untouched the original spatial databases.

2 Related Works

Many researchers have advocated the problem of standardizing the query language for GISs and several proposals have indicated SQL as the basic language for querying geographic information [0]. There are many reasons for this choice. Basically SQL is recognized as a standard query language, it is very common and well known, and extensions can be learned faster than a completely new language.

The Spatial extensions of SQL provide syntactical means for the definition of abstract spatial data types and for the formulation of queries involving only spatial properties; queries involving thematic properties; and queries that combine both types of properties.

Several proposals of a spatial query language have been defined that extend the SQL language for dealing with spatial data [0,0,0,0]. However, none of these approaches address the problem of flexible querying. Within these approaches, the predicates of the relational calculus are extended to operate on the spatial domain, but they are still defined as crisp, i.e., binary, predicates admitting only full or no satisfaction.

On the other hand, the need for a flexible querying in GISs has been addressed by some researchers who looked at this need mainly in relation with the problem of representing geographic entities with unsharp boundaries, and of defining appropriate spatial operators for evaluating topological or directional relationships between fuzzy geographic entities 0. The problem of representing ecosystems and regions characterized by high variability whose boundary cannot be fixed exactly but can only be guessed, have brought to extend the spatial data models based on exact objects to make it possible the representation of objects with fuzzy boundary, i.e., regions with thick borders. A bunch of proposal has then come out to define spatial operators between such regions with thick boundaries [0,0,0]. Some of the proposals considered that the topological and directional relationships between regions with fuzzy boundary would be better defined as fuzzy relationships, i.e., if a degree of satisfaction of the relationship were accounted for. For example, knowing that two regions with fuzzy boundaries are overlapped is not very informative; it would be desirable to know the extent of the overlapping, i.e, to be able to distinguish if only the borders of the regions are overlapped or even their inmost parts.

In this paper, we argue that flexible spatial and not spatial operations are a useful means for simplifying spatial analysis also in the case in which the geographic entities are represented in exact way as in the classic GISs.

3   Characteristics of a Spatial Query Language

The first requirement for a spatial query language is the definition of *abstract spatial data types* for representing both spatial entities and spatial operators [0]. In the spatial extensions of SQL, the domains of relational calculus also include the spatial domain that provides an abstraction of spatial data [0]. In a relational data model, attributes of geometry type can be defined. Each geometry is associated with a spatial reference system that must be unique in the database. For example, the three relations reported in table 1 have the attribute *location* that is a spatial attributes of geometry type. Although there is still no consensus on a complete set of spatial operators to be included in a spatial query language, some fundamental and commonly used ones have been defined [0]:

Table 1. Relations with a geometry type attribute

CITIES (id: string; Name: string; population: Integer; location: polygon)
REGION (Id: string; Name: string; sales: integer; location: multi polygon)
SHOWROOMS (id: string; Name: string; sales: integer; location: point)

Geometric Functions for computing properties of spatial entities: these functions allow the computation of *area, perimeter, centroid,* etc.

Topological Binary Operators for evaluating topological relationships between pairs of spatial entities, such as *equals, disjoint, overlap, inside, contains, crossing* etc.

Metric operators for evaluating distance and direction between two spatial entities.

Set operators for creating new spatial entities, either by means of *intersection, union, difference* of two spatial entities or by means of *convex hull, Voronoi* etc. of a spatial entity.

The second requirement for a spatial query language is the *closure property* of the spatial operators. It must be possible to combine the results of queries. On the other side, there are requirements that are related to the *visualization of the query results*.

Several proposals of spatial query languages have been defined that satisfy more or less the above requirements: most of them extend the SQL language for dealing with spatial data [0,0,0,0,0]. While most extensions of SQL concentrate on representing and managing spatial data, SQL/Spatial [0] has been proposed specifically for carrying out spatial analysis. The peculiarity of SQL/Spatial is that spatial operations are incorporated into the **FROM** clause of the basic SQL query; this provides a mechanism for transmitting intermediate relations without the need of repeating spatial operations in several clauses. In facts, when using a GIS for carrying out some spatial analysis, one generally proceeds step by step. First, properties of spatial entities, i.e. attribute values, have to be accessed. Then some new spatial properties have to be computed, for example based on the evaluation of some metric or topological operator, in some cases new spatial entities must be identified based on the computations of some set operation. An intermediate relation combining all the results of spatial operations is obtained, on which the selection operation in terms of certain conditions is applied, and finally the desired attributes are projected. This procedure reflects the evaluation steps of a basic spatial SQL query:

SELECT (attribute list)
FROM (relation list) **WHERE** (condition)

in which the **FROM** clause is extended to create an intermediate single relation that is the result of some spatial operations. On this intermediate relation the *selection* in the **WHERE** clause and the *projection* in the **SELECT** clause are then applied. To achieve this goal an approach is to append new attributes derived from spatial operations to the Cartesian product of the source relations. In the **FROM** clause an SQL sub-query is nested and the spatial operations are applied in the **SELECT** clause of the sub-query producing thus the intermediate relation. For example, if the distance of each city from "*Atlanta*" has to be computed and the new spatially derived attribute *dist-from-Atlanta* has to be appended to relation *CITIES*, the following SQL/Spatial query can be formulated:

SELECT *C.name, S.name, S.sales*
FROM (**SELECT*,Distance(Centroid(***C.location***),Centroid(SELECT** *A.location*
        FROM *CITIES* **as** *A* **WHERE** *A .name="Atlanta"*)) **as** *dist-from-Atlanta*,
        Inside(*C.location, S.location***) as** *In*
        FROM *CITIES* **as** *C, Regions* **as** *S*) **WHERE** *C.population* > **80.000** AND
dist-from-Atlanta < **300** AND *S.sales* < **20.000** AND *In* =**True**

We can see that there are three nested SQL queries. The intermediate Spatial SQL query is the one that has been extended with the spatial operations **Distance** (metric operation), and **Inside** (crisp topological binary comparison operator) and is aimed at computing the single intermediate relation *INT-R:*

INT-R(C.id, C.name, C.population, C.location, S.id, S.name, S.sales, S.location, Dist-from-Atlanta, In) that is supplied as argument to the outmost SQL **FROM** clause. Notice that the topo-logical function **Inside** computes a binary value and conditions are crisp.

4 Flexible Querying in Databases

By the terms "flexible query" we mean a query allowing the expression of tolerant selection conditions, i.e., soft conditions [0]. Within fuzzy set theory crisp query con-ditions are replaced by soft conditions admitting degrees of satisfaction so that there is a gradual transition from acceptable and excluded elements. A soft condition is for-malized by means of a linguistic predicate represented by a fuzzy set. An example is the query looking for "*big* and *rich* cities".

The first definitions of flexible query languages have been done for the relational database model based on the extension of SQL [0] within the framework of fuzzy set theory [0,0]. A natural extension of a relation within fuzzy set theory is provided by the notion of fuzzy relation: given a relation r defined as a subset of $D = D_1 \times D_2 \times, ...,$ $\times D_n$ a fuzzy relation r_f is defined as a fuzzy subset of D, i.e., each tuple d of r_f has associated with it a *membership degree* $\mu_{rf}(d)$ in [0,1]. For example, given the rela-tion *CITIES* in table 1, the following fuzzy relation *CITIES$_f$* can be defined:

CITIES$_f$ (id: string; Name: string; population: Integer; location: polygon; $\mu_{CITIESf}$: [0,1])

In the context of conventional crisp databases, a flexible query formalized within fuzzy set theory takes a set of regular relations as input and produces a fuzzy relation as a result. The degree attached to each tuple is interpreted as the degree of satisfac-tion of the vague predicates in the flexible query. Notice that, in order to satisfy the closure property, a regular relation can be seen as a kind of fuzzy relation with all the tuples having the same membership degree equal to 1. Fuzzy SQL (SQLf) has been defined by extending the relational algebra [0,0,0]. The same operators defined in SQL are extended to operate on fuzzy relations. For their formal definition refer to [0]. The basic SQLf query allows first to specify a regulation mechanism of the query result in order to control the number of the desired items (tuples). This can be done by either specifying the maximum desired number **N** of tuples or a minimum threshold **T** that each tuple's membership degree must exceed to be included in the result or both of these values. Second, a **soft condition** is introduced in the **WHERE** clause at two levels: in the elementary predicates themselves and in the way they are aggregated. An SQLf query has then the following structure:

SELECT (N | T | N,T) (attribute list)
FROM (relation list) **WHERE** (soft condition)

in which **soft condition** can be defined through a simple linguistic predicate or a com-pound linguistic predicate. In most applications the membership functions of the lin-guistic predicates such as *big* and *rich* are defined by trapezoidal functions [0]. These definitions depend on both the application and the user. Soft compound conditions in the form of logical expressions of elementary conditions, for example "*big* AND *rich*", are represented by fuzzy set operations. Within a soft compound condition *pri-*

orities can be expressed by attaching *weights* to the elementary conditions [0,0]. An example of SQLf query on the relation *CITIES* is the following:

SELECT 5 0,6 *C.name*
FROM *CITIES* **as** *C* **WHERE** *C.population* **IS** *big*

in which the soft condition is expressed by *"IS big"*. It imposes the evaluation of the degree of satisfaction of the linguistic predicate "IS *big*" by the values of the attribute *C.population* of the relation *CITIES*. The intermediate fuzzy relation resulting from the evaluation of the soft condition is projected on the attribute *C.name* and the best **5** tuples over the threshold **0,6** are returned to the user as a result.

Notice that, in this fuzzy extension of SQL, linguistic values such as *big* are specified independently of the context to which they are applied. This can create problems since some linguistic values may have multiple semantics depending on the context. Further, users cannot explicitly define the semantics of the linguistic values since no SQLf operator is defined specifically for this purpose.

5   Definition of Fuzzy Spatial SQL

In this section we present our ideas for the definition of a flexible spatial query language for a conventional GIS.

A flexible spatial query language should allow the specification of preferences inside conditions involving attributes of both geometry and non-geometry type.

We adopt as starting point for defining a flexible spatial query language the SQL language and define the new language by integrating SQLf [0] and SQL/Spatial [0] presented in the previous sections, and by taking into account also practical aspects involved in the translation of information needs into a formal query. The choice of SQL/Spatial is motivated basically by the fact that we have the same objective of the designers of SQL/Spatial, i.e., the definition of a flexible spatial query language for simplifying spatial analysis. However, we relax the constraint of SQL/Spatial that does not allow spatial operations in the **WHERE** clause.

The problem of defining a generalization of the SQL language for the specification of soft conditions is faced in a way similar to one followed for SQLf, but more effective. The soft conditions are specified through linguistic predicates identifying fuzzy subsets of the attribute domains and are specified in the **WHERE** clause of the SQL query, thus producing a fuzzy relation as a result of their evaluation. However, we extend the SQLf so as to specify in the soft condition also the context of the linguistic predicates, so that it is possible to choose the proper meaning of the linguistic value.

We also define a new SQL like operator to allow users to define the term sets of the linguistic values of attributes and their semantics. In this way, the same linguistic value can be defined with a distinct meaning depending on the reference attribute.

In order to define some soft spatial conditions, i.e., soft conditions on spatially derived attributes, it is also necessary to extend the set of spatial operations defined in SQL/Spatial. We then propose a set of new and fundamental spatial functions.

5.1 Basic Query Structure

We propose the following basic structure of a Fuzzy Spatial SQL query:

SELECT ($N|T|N,T$) (A_1,A_n)
FROM (SELECT *, Spatially derived attributes FROM $R_{1,...}\ R_n$)
WHERE (Φ)

in which

N is the maximum number of desired tuples with highest membership degree, i.e., maximum query satisfaction degree;

T is the minimum value of the tuple membership degree needed for selecting a tuple;

Spatially derived attributes are attributes derived through the application of some spatial function as in SQL/Spatial; they can be either of geometry type, such as those resulting from the spatial function **Centroid,** or not, such as the result of the **Distance** function;

Φ is a soft condition composed of crisp and linguistic predicates connected by **AND, OR** and negated by **NOT**. Crisp predicates are based on the classical comparison operators applied to classical data types. Linguistic predicates have the form:

spatial tuple or *numerical-expression* **IS** *linguistic-value* **IN** *Term-set*

where a *spatial tuple* is a tuple whose elements are of geometry type, *linguistic-value* is defined in the specified *Term-set*. The *numerical-expression* can be computed by means of spatial operations. For example, the linguistic predicate:

"(**a**,*b*) **IS** *High* **IN** *Overlapping_degrees*"

in which *a* and *b* are attributes of geometry type is equivalent to

"**OVERLAPPING_DEGREE**(*a,b*) **IS** *High* **IN** *Overlapping_degrees*"

in which **OVERLAPPING_DEGREE** is a spatial function computing the degree of overlapping between *a* and *b* (see next section). In this way, the soft spatial conditions are specified in the **WHERE** clause, like in SQLf.

5.2 Definition of Linguistic Values of Spatially Derived Attributes

The definition of soft spatial conditions depends on several factors such as the application domain, the scope of the database and the user. The soft spatial conditions that can be useful in a generic spatial database are of the following type:

• *Soft Geometric conditions* on some spatially derived attribute (area, shape, contour, etc.) of spatial objects, i.e., of tuples having a geometry-type attribute. These conditions can be expressed by means of linguistic values such as *circular shaped, almost symmetric, indented contour, uneven surface, etc.*.

• *Soft Topological conditions* for evaluating soft topological relationships between pairs of spatial objects. For example, it can be useful to select the spatial objects that are more or less included in a given region.

- *Soft Metric conditions* expressed by linguistic values such as *close, far, very far, south-west, almost west, etc.*, for specifying soft distance and directional relationships between pairs of spatial objects.

The definition of the soft spatial conditions requires, as a prerequisite, the specification of the linguistic values with their meanings, i.e., their membership functions. In order to do this, the first step is the identification of membership functions and the definition of term sets (see next section). Here, we propose a set of term sets and new spatial functions, that we consider fundamental for flexibly querying spatial data.

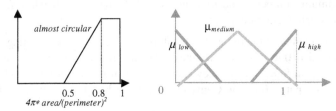

Fig. 1. Semantics of the *almost circular* (left.). Semantics of the soft topological conditions (right)

For example, consider the case of conditions on the shape of a spatial object a, i.e. **"a IS "almost circular" IN Shape_factors"**. One has first to describe the shape of the spatial objects a by a descriptor or a set of descriptors computed by some spatial function evaluating the geometry type attribute a. To clarify, the shape of a polygon can be described by a specific spatial function named **SHAPE_FACTOR**, which extends the spatial operations defined in SQL/Spatial; this function is defined as:

SHAPE_FACTOR:$D \rightarrow [0,1]$, **SHAPE_FACTOR**$(d) := 4\pi * $**Area**$(d)/($**Perimeter**$(d))^2$

in which D is a spatial domain, $d \in D$ is the spatial reference of a, and **Area** and **Perimeter** are geometric functions defined in SQL/Spatial computing the area and perimeter respectively. The linguistic value *"almost circular"* can be defined by a fuzzy subset on the domain $[0,1]$ in the term set named *shape-factor* with non-decreasing membership function $\mu_{almost\ circular}$ (see Figure 1 left).

To define linguistic topological values, two new spatial functions are necessary:

OVERLAPPING_DEGREE:$D \times D \rightarrow [0,1]$, **INCLUSION_DEGREE**:$D \times D \rightarrow [0,1]$

where D is the spatial domain. These operations extend the topological operations of SQL/Spatial, providing a means to compute two degrees in $[0,1]$ measuring the degree of overlapping and of inclusion between two spatial objects, respectively. The meanings of the topological linguistic values are then defined on the codomain $[0,1]$ of these functions. Specifically, **OVERLAPPING_DEGREE** is defined based on a similarity measure between two spatial objects as the ratio of the area of the set intersection on the area of the set union of the two spatial objects d_1 and d_2 [0]:

OVERLAPPING_DEGREE $(d_1, d_2) = $**Area**(**Intersect**$(d_1, d_2))/$ **Area**(**Union**$(d_1, d_2))$

in which **Area** computes the area of a spatial entity, **Intersect** and **Union** are set operators generating the set intersection and the set union of two spatial entities.

The linguistic topological values defined in the term set named ***OverlappingDegrees*** are *high, very high, medium, low, very low* and can be defined with membership functions non-decreasing μ_{high}, $\mu_{very\,high}$ and non-increasing μ_{low}, $\mu_{very\,low}$, and unimodal μ_{medium} on the codomain of **OVERLAPPING_DEGREE** (see Figure 1 right).

Function **INCLUSION_DEGREE** is defined based on a fuzzy inclusion measure between two spatial entities d_1 and d_2 [0]:

INCLUSION_DEGREE(d_1, d_2)=**Area**(**Intersect**(d_1, d_2))/**Area**(d_1)

The linguistic values *high, very high, medium, low, very low* can be defined by fuzzy subset on the codomain of the function **INCLUSION_DEGREE** with non decreasing and non increasing membership functions respectively (see Figure 1 right). They constitute the term set named ***InclusionDegrees.***

The basic domains of the *linguistic distance values* expressed by terms such as *far, close, very close* etc. can be defined as the domain [0,1] of a normalized distance measure (see Figure 2 left). In facts, the meaning of soft distance conditions is strongly context dependent: the meaning of *close* between two *cities* is different than between two *buildings* in the same city. For these reasons, a normalization factor of the distance that is specific of the context of the entities must be determined. For example, it can be defined as the maximum possible distance on the map between any two entities of the same context, or can be set by the user during the definition of the meaning of the term sets of linguistic values.

The definition of the meanings of the linguistic values of distance requires then the computation of the normalized distance between two spatial objects.

The *linguistic directional values* can be expressed by terms *south, south-west, on the right, etc.* and are not context sensitive. Then they can be defined by fuzzy sets with triangular membership function on the domain $[0,2\pi]$ (see Figure 2 right).

Let us formulate the following fuzzy SQL Spatial query as an example.

SELECT 5, 0.6 C.name
FROM (**SELECT** *,**Distance**(**Centroid**(C.location),
Centroid(**SELECT** A.location **FROM** CITIES **AS** A
      WHERE A.name="Atlanta")) **AS** dist-from-Atlanta,
      INCLUSION_DEGREE(C.location,S.location) **AS**
                                   inclusion-degree
FROM CITIES **AS** C, REGIONS **AS** S)
WHERE C.population IS *'big'* **IN** *CityPopulations* **AND**
      dist-from-Atlanta **IS** *'close'* **IN** *CityDistances* **AND**
      S.sales **IS** *'weak'* **IN** *Sales* **AND**
      inclusion-degree **IS** *'high'* **IN** *InclusionDegrees*

in which ***CityPopulations, CityDistances, Sales*** and ***InclusionDegrees***, are term sets of linguistic values and Distance and INCLUSION_DEGREE are spatial functions. This query retrieves the names of the cities belonging to the first 5 tuples with membership degree above 0.6. and reflecting the global satisfaction of the ANDed conditions to be big cities, close to Atlanta, highly inside a Region with weak sales.

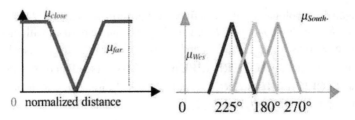

Fig. 2. Semantics of soft metric condition *close, far, West, Southwest, South*

5.3   An Operator for Defining Term Sets and Linguistic Values

In order to make the flexible spatial query language adaptable to user needs, we define a new SQL like operator for defining term sets (and the meanings of linguistic values), which can be used in the **WHERE** clause to specify linguistic predicates by means of the **IS .. IN** operator. This operator is named **CREATE TERM-SET**. This way, the semantics of linguistic predicates can be easily customized.

CREATE TERM-SET *name*
[**NORMALIZED WITHIN** (*min, max*)]
{ **EVALUATE** *expression* **WITH PARAMS** *List-of-params* }
VALUES list of Linguistic-Value-Definition

in which *name* is the name of a term set.

The set of linguistic values in the term set is defined by means of the **VALUES** clause. Each *Linguistic-Value-Definition* is a pair (*linguistic value, meaning*):

linguistic value, is a string identifying a linguistic value; for example, *'very far'*.

meaning: is a 4-tuple of ordered values in the range [0,1], and it defines the trapezoidal membership function (left bottom corner, left top corner, right top corner, right bottom corner) of the fuzzy set identified by *linguistic value*. The domain of the membership function is normalized within the range [0,1]. For example, we can define *meaning* :=(0.5, 0.75, 1, 1) for the linguistic value *'far'* (this is the trapezoidal membership function depicted in Figure 2 left) .

The possibly missing **NORMALIZED** keyword specifies if the numerical value evaluated by the **IS .. IN** operator must be normalized in the domain [0,1] of the membership functions associated with the linguistic value. In case of normalization, the range [*min, max*] is mapped to the range [0,1]; values less than (greater than) *min* (*max*) are always evaluated as *min* (*max*). If the **NORMALIZED** clause is not specified, values are always evaluated in the range [0,1].

The same term set can be evaluated by the **IS .. IN** operator over different data types. This is allowed by the non-empty list of **EVALUATE** clauses: each occurrence defines a specific function to be computed, whose values are "compared" with the linguistic values. This way, depending on the data type of the left operand appearing in the **IS .. IN** operator, the proper function is applied. Note that the **WITH PARAMS** sub-clause defines the list of formal parameters appearing in the *expression*. Consider the term set *CityDistances* to evaluate soft distance conditions.

CREATE TERM-SET *CityDistances* NORMALIZED WITHIN (0, 1000)
EVALUATE Distance (O1, O2) WITH PARAMS O1 AS Point, O2 AS Point
EVALUATE DIST WITH PARAMS DIST AS FLOAT
VALUES (*'very far'*, (0.8, 0.9, 1,1)), (*'far'*, (0.5, 0.75, 1,1)),
(*'medium_distance'*, (0.1, 0.45,0.55, 0.7)), (*'close'*, (0,0, 0.025, 0.1)),
(*'very close'*, (0,0,0.01,0.02))

Notice that distances are normalized within 0 Km and 1000 Km. This way, the term set *CityDistances* can be exploited both to directly express a conditions on two points, and to express a condition on a numerical distance. In the former case, the predefined spatial **Distance** function is evaluated, and the returned value is matched over the membership function of the linguistic values. In the latter case, the numerical value is directly matched over the membership function.

   Similarly, we can define the term set *CityQuartersDistances,* that characterizes distances between city quarters. Although similar, the concept of distance between city quarters is semantically different with respect to distance between cities. Thus, a different term set has to be defined, normalized between 0 Km and 40 Km.

CREATE TERM-SET *CityQuarterDistances* NORMALIZED WITHIN (0, 40)
EVALUATE Distance(O1, O2) WITH PARAMS O1 AS Point, O2 AS Point
EVALUATE DIST WITH PARAMS DIST AS FLOAT
VALUES (*'very far'*, (0.8, 0.9, 1,1)), (*'far'*, (0.5, 0.7, 1,1)),
(*'medium_distance'*, (0.3, 0.45,0.55, 0.7)), (*'close'*, (0,0, 0.15, 0.3)),
(*'very close'*, (0,0,0.05, 0.15))

6 Formal Semantics

Membership Function of Linguistic Values. The trapezoidal shape of the membership function of a linguistic value lv is defined by a 4-tuple (lb, lt, rt, rb), where

$$\mu_{lv}(e) = \begin{cases} \text{If } 0 \leq e \leq lb \text{ then } 0 \\ \text{If } lb < e < lt \text{ then } (e\text{-}lb)(1 + 1/(lt\text{-}lb)) \\ \text{If } lt \leq e \leq rt \text{ then } 1 \\ \text{If } rt < e < rb \text{ then } (e\text{-}rt)(1 - 1/(rb\text{-}rt)) \\ \text{If } rb \leq e \leq 1 \text{ then } 0 \end{cases}$$

The **IS .. IN** Operator. A predicate based on the **IS .. IN** operator has the form
t **IS** lv **IN** *TS*
where t is a tuple of (possibly spatial) objects, lv is a linguistic value in the term set *TS*, i.e., $lv \in$ *TS*. If the type of t matches an expression exp_i defined for *TS*, the membership function for the operator application is defined as:

$$\mu_{t \text{ IS } lv \text{ IN } TS}(t) = \mu_{lv}(exp_i)$$

Recall that the membership values generated by crisp operators are only 0 and 1.

The **WHERE** Clause. We assume that each tuple t in a source crisp spatial relation R has a membership degree $\mu(R)(t)=1$. The **WHERE** clause specifies a soft condition φ, which assigns to tuple t a new membership degree, for the purpose of selection. Applying associative properties, φ can be seen either as $\varphi = $ *sub-cond' lop sub-cond"*, where *lop* is a logical operator AND, OR, or as a negated condition $\varphi = $ NOT *(sub-cond')*, where *sub-cond'* and *sub-cond"* can be either composed conditions or simple predicates. We define the semantics of the three logical operators in accordance with the usual definition of the fuzzy AND (Min), the fuzzy OR (Max), and the fuzzy NOT (1-).

If $\varphi = $ *sub-cond'* AND *sub-cond"*, then $\mu_\varphi(t)=\text{Min}(\mu_{sub\text{-}cond'}(t), \mu_{sub\text{-}cond"}(t))$

If $\varphi = $ *sub-cond'* OR *sub-cond"*, then $\mu_\varphi(t)=\text{Max}(\mu_{sub\text{-}cond'}(t), \mu_{sub\text{-}cond"}(t))$

If $\varphi = $ NOT *(sub-cond')*, then $\mu_\varphi(t)=1 - \mu_{sub\text{-}cond'}(t)$

Then, the membership degree of a tuple t after the evaluation of φ is:

$\mu(t) = \text{Min}(\mu(R)(t), \mu_\varphi(t))$.

Finally, we define the semantics of the overall **SELECT** instruction, as far as selection is concerned. Given a source fuzzy spatial relation R (recall that the membership degree of tuples in non –fuzzy spatial relations is 1), consider the membership degree $\mu(t)$ of a tuple t after the evaluation of φ. The **SELECT** instruction generates a fuzzy spatial relations containing only tuples $t \in R$ such that $\mu(t) \geq T$, where T is the minimum threshold for membership degree specified in the **SELECT** clause.

7 Conclusions

In this paper, we proposed a solution towards the definition of a flexible spatial query language, in order to allow the expression of flexible queries on spatial data.

We start our work from existing proposals for SQL/Spatial [0], an extension of SQL for specifying spatial queries, and for SQLf [0,0], an extension of SQL for expressing flexible queries based on soft conditions and yielding fuzzy relations. The proposed language is SQL like, and extends the structure of SQL/Spatial with the concept of fuzzy relations and soft conditions derived from SQLf.

In order to express soft conditions on spatial data, a new set of fundamental spatial functions is proposed, useful for defining suitable term-sets (i.e. sets of linguistic values with their membership functions); these functions capture typical geometric, topological and metric properties of spatial objects. Based on these spatial functions, linguistic predicates can be expressed, by means of a new comparison operator, named **IS .. IN**, allowed in the **WHERE** clause of the **SELECT** operator.

This operator can be used in a very flexible way, since term sets can be freely defined by users, by means of the **CREATE TERM-SET** operator, introduced in this paper as well.

The combined use of features provided by the **CREATE TERM-SET** operator and the **IS .. IN** operator lets the user able to express complex linguistic predicates very easily and flexibly.

References

E.Bertino, G.Vantini, *Advanced Database Systems and Geographical Information Systems,* Proc. of the II Workshop on AITSES, 1-10, 1996.

P.A.Burrough, A.U.Frank, eds, *Geographic Objects with Indeterminate Boundaries,* in GISDATA series, (Taylor & Francis, 1996).

F.E. Petry, *Fuzzy Databases,* (Kluwer Academic Pub., 1996).

L. A. Zadeh, *The concept of a linguistic variable and its application to approximate reasoning, parts I, II.* Information Science, **8**, 199-249, 301-357, 1997.

L.A.Zadeh, *Fuzzy Sets as a Basis for a Theory of Possibility.* Fuzzy Sets and Systems, 1, 3-28, 1978.

P.Bosc, and H.Prade, *An Introduction to the Fuzzy Set and Possibility Theory-based Treatment of Flexible Queries and Uncertain and Imprecise Databases,* in Uncertainty Management in Information Systems: from Needs to Solutions, A. Motro and P. Smets eds, Kluwer Academic Pub., .285-324.

P.Bosc, B. Buckles, F.E.Petry, O.Pivert, *Fuzzy Databases,* in J.C.Bezdek, D.Dubois, H.Prade eds., Fuzzy sets in Approximate reasoning and information systems: the handbook of fuzzy set series, Kluwer Ac. Pub. 404-468, 1999.

P.Bosc, O.Pivert, *SQLf: a relational database language for fuzzy querying,* IEEE Trans. on Fuzzy Systems, 3, 1-17, 1995.

J.Kacprzyk, S.Zadrosny, *FQUERY for ACCESS: fuzzy querying for Windows-based DBMS,* in P.Bosc and J.Kacprzyk eds., Fuzziness in database management systems, Physica verlag, 415-433, 1995.

J.Egenhofer, *Spatial SQL: A Query and Presentation Language,* IEEE Trans. on Knowledge and Data Engineering, 6(1), 86-95, 1994.

Ng. Cary, M. Mak, A survey on Query Languages for Content-based retrieval, ???

B. Huang, H. Lin, *Design of a Query Language for Accessing Spatial Analysis in Web Environment,* Geoinformatica, 2000.

OGC.OpenGIS-*Simple Features Specification for SQL,* http://www.opengis.org/techno/specs.htm, 1998.

ArcView GIS, *Using ArcView GIS,* ESRI inc.1999.

E.Cood, *A Relational Model for Large Shared Data Banks,* Communications of the ACM, 13, 377-387, 1970.

M. Erwig, R.H.Guting, M.Schneider, M.Vazirgiannis, *Spatio-Temporal Data Types: An approach to Modeling and Querying Moving Objects,* Geoinformatica, 3(3), 269-296, 1999.

G.Bordogna, S.Chiesa, *A Fuzzy Object-Based Data Model for Imperfect Spatial Information Integrating Exact Objects and Fields,* Int. Journal of Uncertainty, Fuzziness and Knowledge-Based Systems, 11(1), 23-41, 2003.

Access to Multigranular Temporal Objects*

Elisa Bertino[1], Elena Camossi[2], and Giovanna Guerrini[3]

[1] CS Department – Purdue University
bertino@cs.purdue.edu
[2] DICO – Università di Milano
camossi@dico.unimi.it
[3] DI – Università di Pisa
guerrini@di.unipi.it

Abstract. In this paper we discuss access to object attributes in a multi-granular temporal object-oriented data model that handles the *expiration* of *dynamic attributes*, according to the age of data and their granularity [4]. Different strategies can be applied, with respect to available data and to the preferences specified by the user on either *accuracy* or *efficiency* in executing a query. We devise some properties of object access that can be applied to speed up the query process, such as the *invariance* of the queries results with respect to expiration operations, and the static detection of *unsolvability* of a query.

1 Introduction

The problem of reducing storage occupancy for temporal databases and data warehouses has been widely addressed [9, 10, 12, 13]. In such databases, a fine level of detail is often required only for just acquired data, while after a period of time only aggregated data are needed for supporting data analysis. Then, detailed data values can be removed from the database or moved to tertiary storage devices. Motivated by such considerations, we proposed T_ODMGe [4], a multi-granular temporal data model that supports *dynamic attributes*, i.e., temporal attributes whose values are maintained at different levels of detail. The levels of detail of an attribute do not only depend on the attribute semantics, rather they are also related to how recent values are. In most cases, indeed, data at a fine level of detail are useful when they are acquired, but their relevance decreases after some time. The model supports as well the specification of deletion[1] of the oldest values from the database.

In this paper we investigate the access to dynamic attributes, that will provide the core of the model query language. In particular, we define the notion of *atomic access* to a dynamic attribute value in a temporal granule. Alternative strategies can be applied to execute an access: the answer *accuracy* and the query execution *efficiency* are the parameters we take into account. In our investigation,

---

* This work has been supported by the EU under the IST Panda project.
[1] Moving of data to tertiary storage does not introduce new issues, thus we will not explicitly consider it in what follows.

H. Christiansen et al. (Eds.): FQAS 2004, LNAI 3055, pp. 320–333, 2004.

we first introduce *refinement functions*, i.e., functions for converting temporal values to finer granularities that, together with *coercion functions* [1], can be used for converting temporal values to different granularities. Then, we define the object accesses we are interested in, and the expected value returned by each one, taking into account the preference expressed by the user. We finally identify and discuss some relevant properties of the object access. Since our object access mechanism is targeted to a data model with dynamic attributes, we characterize and devise the conditions for invariance of an object access with respect to the two forms of attribute expiration considered in [4], namely *granularity evolution* and *value deletion*. Moreover, we devise the conditions for detecting *unsolvable* object accesses, i.e., by analyzing the database schema specification we can infer that they would produce no result for any database state.

The paper is organized as follows. Section 2 presents the model we extend in this paper, introducing coercion and refinement functions and discussing their properties. Section 3 presents the object accesses we consider and discusses how they can be evaluated, discussing some properties of object accesses. Finally, Section 4 discusses related work and Section 5 concludes the paper outlining future research directions.

2   Dynamic Attributes in T_ODMGe

In this section we survey the T_ODMGe model [4]. First, we introduce the basic concepts of temporal granularities, temporal types and values. Then, we formally define the functions for converting temporal attributes, formalizing some properties that are used for verifying the consistency of the access to dynamic attributes. Finally, we informally describe T_ODMGe classes and objects.

2.1   Temporal Granularities, Types and Values

According to the definition of *temporal granularity* commonly adopted by the temporal database community [2], a temporal granularity is a mapping from an ordered index set $\mathcal{IS}$ to the set of possible subsets of the *time domain*. Every portion of the time domain obtained by such a mapping is referred to as a *granule*. Granules of the same granularity cannot overlap, and must keep the same order given by the index set. *days*, *months*, *years* are examples of temporal granularities. Each non-empty granule can be represented by an index, or by a label. For example, throughout the paper, each granule of *days* is represented in the form $mm/dd/yyyy$, while granules of *months* are in the form $mm/yyyy$. When we refer to a generic granularity G, and a granule index $i \in \mathcal{IS}$, l_G^i denotes the granule label corresponding to the ith granule of granularity G. We denote with i_l the index corresponding to the granule denoted by label l. For instance, given $02/1999$ as the granule label corresponding to February 1999, with respect to granularity *months*, the corresponding index is $i_{02/1999}$. Note finally that, the order on indices induces, for each granularity G, an order on the labels of G-granules. Thus, $l_G^i > l_G^j$ will simply denote that $i > j$. Granularities used in a database schema are related by the *finer than* relationship. A granularity G is said to be *finer than* a granularity H ($G \preceq H$) if, for each index i, an index j exists such that $G(i) \subseteq H(j)$ [2] (e.g., *days* is finer than *months*). H is said *coarser than* G. The symbol "$\prec$" will be used to denote the anti-reflexive finer than relationship. A granule label is related to the labels of corresponding granule(s) in a coarser/finer granularity. In particular, if $G \prec H$, then $H(l_G^i) = l_H^j$ such that $G(i) \subseteq H(j)$; if $G \prec H$, then $G(l_H^j) = \{l_G^k \mid G(k) \subseteq H(j)\}$.

Given $\mathcal{T}$ a set of types, including class and literal types, for each type $\tau \in \mathcal{T}$, called inner type, and for each granularity $G \in \mathcal{G}$, a temporal type $temporal_G(\tau)$ is defined. A temporal value of a given temporal type $temporal_G(\tau)$ is defined as a partial function that maps G-granules to τ values. In what follows, given a type τ, either temporal or not, the notation $[\![\tau]\!]$ denotes the set of legal values for type τ. For instance, the temperature in Celsius degrees taken every day in a city could be represented by a temporal attribute of type $temporal_{days}(float)$. An example of legal value for such an attribute is $\{\langle 06/11/2003, 23.5\rangle, \langle 06/12/2003, 24\rangle, \langle 06/15/2003, 22\rangle\}_{days}$, stating that, in a given city, the temperature on the 11th of June 2003 was 23.5 degrees, on the 12th of June 2003 was 24 degrees, and so on. Let v be a value of type $temporal_G(\tau)$, we denote with $v(i)$ the value of v in the ith granule of G. Since temporal values are partial functions, given a temporal value v, an index $i \in \mathcal{IS}$ may exist such that $v(i) = \bot$. Note finally that, since we will denote granules through their labels, if v is a value of type $temporal_G(\tau)$, and l_G^i is the label of the ith granule of G, $v(l_G^i)$ equivalently denotes $v(i)$, i.e., the value of v in the granule labeled by l_G^i.

2.2   Conversion Functions

Coercion and refinement functions are used for converting a temporal value to a different granularity. Specifically, *coercion functions* have been proposed in [1] to convert temporal values to coarser granularities in a meaningful way. In [4], coercion functions are used for performing the evolution of dynamic attributes to different granularities. In [1], however, the choice of a temporal granularity for an attribute value implies establishing the *temporal precision* required by the represented information. If the attribute granularity is *months*, then for each granularity finer than *months*, e.g., *days*, the value is the same for all the days of the month (i.e., it is *downward inherited* [8]). Differently, the information should be stored at a finer granularity. This assumption does not hold any more in [4], where data are aggregated as they age and can be deleted or removed. A mechanism is needed to (re)obtain, though in an imprecise and approximate way, information at finer granularities from aggregate information stored at coarser granularities. Thus, in this paper, we introduce *refinement functions*, that convert temporal values to finer granularities. Both coercion and refinement functions will be applied when accessing dynamic attribute values. The following definition formalizes coercion and refinement functions.

Definition 1. *Let* $\tau_1 = temporal_G(\tau)$ *and* $\tau_2 = temporal_H(\tau)$ *be two temporal types such that* $G \prec H$. *A coercion function* $C : [\![\tau_1]\!] \rightarrow [\![\tau_2]\!]$ *is a total*

function that maps values of type τ_1 into values of type τ_2. A refinement function
$R : [\![\tau_2]\!] \rightarrow [\![\tau_1]\!]$ *is a total function that maps values of type τ_2 into values of*
type τ_1.   □

We consider both predefined and user-defined coercion and refinement functions. Predefined coercion functions perform selection, e.g., `first`, `last`, and aggregation, e.g., `max`, `avg`, `sum`, that correspond to the well-known SQL aggregate functions. When computing aggregation, undefined values (i.e., values at granules i such that $v(i) = \perp$) are managed as *null* values in SQL and OQL. User-defined coercion functions correspond to methods declared in the classes of the database schema. Predefined refinement functions include `restr` and `split`. Refinement function `restr` models downward inheritance [8]: if a temporal property assumes value v in a granule g, value v also refers to any granule g' of a finer granularity included in g. Thus, given the temporal types $\tau_1 = temporal_G(\tau)$ and $\tau_2 = temporal_H(\tau)$ such that $G \prec H$, and a value $v \in [\![\tau_2]\!]$, for each $j \in \mathcal{IS}$ $\mathtt{restr}(v)(j) = v(i)$, where $i \in \mathcal{IS}$ is such that $G(j) \subseteq H(i)$. Given the temporal value $v = \{\langle 01/2002, 372\rangle, \langle 02/2002, 420\rangle\}_{months}$, if we apply to v the refinement function $\mathtt{restr}_{months \rightarrow days}$, it results in the temporal value $\{\langle 01/01/2002, 372\rangle,$ $\ldots, \langle 31/01/2002, 372\rangle, \langle 01/02/2002, 420\rangle, \ldots, \langle 28/02/2002, 420\rangle\}_{days}$.

Refinement function `split`, by contrast, is suitable to attributes for which downward inheritance is not adequate. The idea is to split the value assumed by the temporal value on each granule g of the coarser granularity among the granules g' of the finer granularity included in g. This is equivalent to the uniform distribution proposed in [5]. Thus, given the above temporal types τ_1 and τ_2 and a value $v \in [\![\tau_2]\!]$, for each $j \in \mathcal{IS}$ $\mathtt{split}(v)(j) = v(i)/n$, where $i \in \mathcal{IS}$ is such that $G(j) \subseteq H(i)$ and $n = |\{h \mid h \in \mathcal{IS}, G(h) \subseteq H(i)\}|$. That is, the value of $\mathtt{split}(v)$ is obtained by splitting the value of the ith granule of H, among the G granules included in $H(i)$. Given the temporal value $v = \{\langle 01/2002, 372\rangle, \langle 02/2002, 420\rangle\}_{months}$, if we apply to v the refinement function $\mathtt{split}_{months \rightarrow days}$, it results in the temporal value $\{\langle 01/01/2002, 12\rangle, \ldots,$ $\langle 31/01/2002, 12\rangle, \langle 01/02/2002, 15\rangle, \ldots, \langle 28/02/2002, 15\rangle\}_{days}$.

Each conversion function introduced above actually corresponds to a family of functions. For instance, `sum` denotes the set of functions $\{\mathtt{sum}_{G \rightarrow H} \mid G, H \in \mathcal{G}, G \prec H\}$, where $\mathtt{sum}_{G \rightarrow H} : [\![temporal_G(\tau)]\!] \rightarrow [\![temporal_H(\tau)]\!]$. Since the behavior of each function in this set is the same, we will refer in what follows to a generic function `sum`, without explicitly specifying the granularities, if ambiguities do not arise. Note moreover that some functions are meaningful only on some attribute inner domains. For instance, `sum`, `avg` and `split` are meaningful only for numeric attributes, whereas `max` is meaningful only for attributes with ordered domains.

We devise two properties of coercion and refinement functions that influence object access. The first property refers to the *compositionality* of such functions. Given three granularities G, H, I, ordered such that $G \prec H \prec I$ (respectively, $G \succ H \succ I$), if a coercion function `f` (respectively, a refinement function) is compositional, the result of converting through `f` from G to H, and then from H to I, is the same of converting through `f` from G to I. Consider the temporal value $\{\langle 01/01/2002, 5\rangle, \langle 4/01/2002, 8\rangle, \langle 25/01/2002, 6\rangle, \langle 08/02/2002, 4\rangle,$ $\langle 28/02/2002, 15\rangle\}_{days}$. If we first apply $\mathtt{sum}_{days \to months}$, and then we apply to the obtained temporal value $\mathtt{sum}_{months \to years}$, the computation results in the temporal value $\{\langle 2002, 38\rangle\}_{years}$, as we directly apply function $\mathtt{sum}_{days \to years}$ to the temporal value at granularity *days*. Functions $\mathtt{first}$, $\mathtt{last}$, $\mathtt{max}$, $\mathtt{sum}$, and $\mathtt{restr}$ we mentioned before are compositional, whereas $\mathtt{avg}$, and $\mathtt{split}$ are not[2].

Definition 2. *Let* $\mathtt{f}$ *be a (family of) coercion function(s),* $G, H, I \in \mathcal{G}$ *be granularities such that* $G \prec H \prec I$, $\mathtt{f}$ *is* compositional *if* $\forall \tau \in \mathcal{T}$, $\forall v \in [\![temporal_G(\tau)]\!]$, $\mathtt{f}_{H \to I}(\mathtt{f}_{G \to H}(v)) = \mathtt{f}_{G \to I}(v)$. *Let* $\mathtt{f}$ *be a (family of) refinement function(s),* $G, H, I \in \mathcal{G}$ *be granularities such that* $G \succ H \succ I$, $\mathtt{f}$ *is* compositional *if* $\forall \tau \in \mathcal{T}$, $\forall v \in [\![temporal_G(\tau)]\!]$, $\mathtt{f}_{H \to I}(\mathtt{f}_{G \to H}(v)) = \mathtt{f}_{G \to I}(v)$. □

The second property refers to the *invertibility* of conversion functions. Intuitively, when converting a temporal value to a different granularity, and then performing the inverse conversion, we would expect that the original value results. Unfortunately, when converting from a finer to a coarser granularity, we loose some details that we cannot usually re-obtain by applying the inverse conversion to the finer granularity. By contrast, when converting from a coarser to a finer granularity, we introduce some details that we should be able to forget, if we are no more interested in them, then we can re-obtain the original value. This is equivalent to what happens with the cast operation in the object-oriented context. When we cast up an object to a superclass, and then recast it down to its original class, we are not able to re-obtain the details we forgot with the cast up. By contrast, if we cast down an object to a subclass, we are able to re-obtain the original object, when recasting up to its original class. The first type of conversion is captured by the notion of *quasi-inverse* functions, that takes into account that some details are lost, thus some imprecision is introduced. The second type of conversion is captured by the notion of *inverse* functions.

Definition 3. *Let* $\mathtt{f}$ *be a (family of) coercion function(s),* $\mathtt{g}$ *be a (family of) refinement function(s),* $G, H \in \mathcal{G}$ *be granularities such that* $G \prec H$. *Then,* $\mathtt{f}$ *and* $\mathtt{g}$ *are* inverse *if* $\forall \tau \in \mathcal{T}$, $\forall v \in [\![temporal_H(\tau)]\!]$, $\mathtt{f}_{G \to H}(\mathtt{g}_{H \to G}(v)) = v$. □

According to such definition, $\mathtt{sum}$ is the inverse of $\mathtt{split}$, whereas $\mathtt{restr}$ is the inverse for $\mathtt{first}$, $\mathtt{last}$, $\mathtt{max}$, $\mathtt{avg}$.

Definition 4. *Let* $\mathtt{f}$ *be a (family of) coercion function(s),* $\mathtt{g}$ *be a (family of) refinement function(s),* $G, H \in \mathcal{G}$ *be granularities such that* $G \prec H$, Δ *be a quantification of the maximum allowable error, functions* $\mathtt{f}$ *and* $\mathtt{g}$ *are* quasi-inverse *if* $\forall \tau \in \mathcal{T}$, $\forall v \in [\![temporal_G(\tau)]\!]$, $\forall i \in \mathcal{IS}$, $\mathtt{g}_{H \to G}(\mathtt{f}_{G \to H}(v))(i) = v(i) \pm \Delta$. □

The notion of quasi-inverse is meaningful only for attributes with numeric domains. Note also that, whether two functions are quasi-inverse depends on how Δ

---

[2] Some functions (e.g., $\mathtt{split}$, $\mathtt{avg}$) would be compositional if a stronger relationship than *finer-than*, such as the *periodically groups into* [2], holds among granularities.

is set. A typical setting of Δ could be, for each H-granule j, $(max_j - min_j)/n_j$ where $max_j = max\{v(h) \mid h \in \mathcal{IS}, G(h) \subseteq H(j)\}$, $min_j = max\{v(h) \mid h \in \mathcal{IS}, G(h) \subseteq H(j)\}$, $n_j = |\{h \mid h \in \mathcal{IS}, G(h) \subseteq H(j)\}|$. The global Δ could then be determined as the maximum over the Δ_j's determined in this way. With such a setting of Δ, for instance, `split` is the quasi-inverse of `sum`, whereas `restr` is the quasi-inverse of `avg`.

2.3 T_ODMGe Classes and Objects

A T_ODMGe schema[4] is given by a set of class declarations, each one identified by a name and a set of attributes. Each object has a unique identifier, and the set of its attribute values represent its state[3]. In particular, *dynamic attributes* are temporal attributes with *expiration* conditions. Expiration conditions are expressed by specifying the period of time for expiration, and the action to take when data expire: either *granularity evolution*, or *value deletion*, or both[4]. A dynamic attribute value is a tuple of temporal values at different granularities. Each value potentially represents a different temporal portion of the attribute value. The values in the tuple are ordered with respect to the temporal granularities, from the finest to the coarsest one. Let such granularities be $G_1, \ldots, G_n$, for each $i = 1, \ldots, n - 1$, $G_i \prec G_i + 1$. Specifically, the values at granularities $G_2, \ldots, G_n$ are recursively obtained starting from the first component of the tuple, through granularity evolutions, that are in turn performed by applying coercion functions. Each granularity evolution results in summarized information at a coarser granularity. Each coercion function specified for a dynamic attribute value, states how such value is obtained from the one at the immediately finer granularity. Moreover, it states how to convert the value to any coarser granularity, when accessing it.

Through value deletions, detailed values, namely the oldest ones, of dynamic attributes can be deleted from the database. Thus, each component of a dynamic attribute could represent the attribute value with respect to a different slice of time. If refinement functions are specified in a dynamic attribute definition, they state how to (re)obtain a detailed value deleted from the database, from a summarized value at a coarser granularity.

Example 1. Throughout the paper we will refer to an Accountant that stores information about tax declarations of his customers. According to the Italian laws, tax payments are performed every six months. The sum of two semester payments corresponds to an annual declaration, that must be maintained for the next five years. In order to analyze the trends of the customer payments over longer periods of time, the Accountant stores, for each customer, the average payments of the last five years. Finally, after ten years, the Accountant records only the maximal average value. Other information that are stored are the fiscal

---

[3] In [4] some constraints are formally defined ensuring that a T_ODMGe object be a valid instance of a class, requiring the object state to meet the class definition.

[4] See [4] for the detailed specification of `evolve` and `delete` clauses.

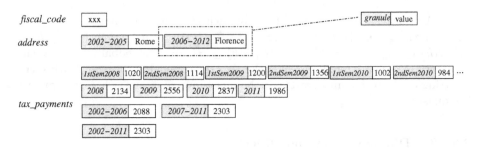

Fig. 1. Example of object state

code of the customer, that is unique for her whole life, and the history of her addresses.

Suppose that a class `taxpayer` is specified representing information about each customer of the accountant and her tax payments. In Fig. 1 an example of object state for an instance of class `taxpayer` is shown. In particular, attribute `taxes`, representing tax declarations, is dynamic. Note that the value of attribute `taxes` is a tuple of four temporal values at granularities *semesters*, *years*, *5years*, and *decades*, respectively. The temporal values at granularities *semesters* and *years* do not report values corresponding to years since 2002 to 2004, but summarized information about those tax declarations are stored at granularities *5years* and *decades*. Such situation corresponds to a definition of the attribute `taxes` specifing that tax payments information must be acquired at granularity *semesters*. Then, to such information three granularity evolutions are applied, resulting in the temporal values at granularity *years* (by applying coercion function *sum*, every year, to the temporal value at granularity *semesters*); *5years* (by applying *avg*, every 5 years, to the value at granularity *years*), and *decades* (by applying *max*, every 10 years, to the *5years* value). Finally, eldest values at granularities *semesters* and *years*, every 5 years, are deleted. Moreover, for converting such values to finer granularities, when accessing the attribute value, a tuple of refinement functions must be specified for attribute `taxes` (e.g., (*split* , *restr*, *restr*)). ◇

Note that, for each granularity G belonging to the domain of a dynamic attribute a in a class c, for each object o instance of c, two G-granules can be identified, denoting the first and the last granule for which value of attribute a of o is available at granularity G. Let l_G^F and l_G^L denote these two granules, respectively. Given the value of attribute `taxes` of Example 1, reported in Fig. 1, the first granule defined for granularity *years* l_{years}^F is 2005, whereas the last one l_{years}^L is 2011. Specifically, old values at finer granularities can be unavailable in the database, because they have already been deleted. By contrast, new values can be unavailable at a coarser granularity, because they have not been aggregated yet. Thus, considering an object o and one of its attributes a, stored at granularities $G_1, \ldots, G_n$, where $G_i \prec \ldots \prec G_n$, the relationship that holds among the various l^F and l^L is: $\forall i, 2 \leq i \leq n, l_{G_{i-1}}^L \geq l_{G_i}^L$, since values at granularity G_i are obtained from values at granularity G_{i-1}. Since we do not require that data at finer granularities are deleted before data at coarser granularities[5], the symmetric relationship among different l_G^F's does not hold.

3 Object Access

In this section we discuss how object attributes, specifically dynamic attributes, can be accessed: against an object access, different strategies can be applied, resulting in different answers. We focus on a simple form of access, requiring the value of an object attribute in a specified granule. This access denotes a non-temporal value belonging to the attribute inner domain[6]. We first discuss *unqualified object accesses*, with no conversion function specified, which rely on the semantics established in the database schema, and then *qualified object accesses*, in which a coercion or refinement function is explicitly specified and will be applied for solving the accesses, thus possibly employing a conversion semantics different from the one specified in the database schema. Finally, we discuss some properties of object accesses. First, we formalize the conditions for an access to be invariant with respect to expirations. Then, we detect the conditions according which an object access can be statically detected as unsolvable.

3.1 Unqualified Object Accesses

An *unqualified object access*, or, simply, object access, is syntactically defined as follows.

Definition 5. *Given an object identifier o, an attribute name a, and a granule label l_G^i, an* unqualified object access *is an expression of the form $o.a \downarrow l_G^i$, requiring the value of attribute a of the object denoted by o in granule l_G^i.*   □

If the inner domain of a in the class to which o belongs is τ, then the access denotes a (non-temporal) value of type τ. In solving the access we take into account the preference expressed by the user concerning whether an accurate answer is needed, or whether, by contrast, she is more interested in the efficiency in obtaining it. If no preference is specified, efficiency is privileged.

Example 2. Consider an instance i_1 of type `taxpayer` of Example 1. Suppose the value for attribute `taxes` is that reported in the object state of Fig. 1. Then, $i.\text{taxes} \downarrow 2ndSem2007$ specifies the access to the payment done during 2nd Semester of year 2007, that results in 1114 €.   ◇

The approach to solve the object access $o.a \downarrow l_G^i$ is as follows. First we check whether the requested value is directly available. This means that G is one of the granularities at which a is stored and the value of a for o at l_G^i is available. If

---

[5] In some contexts, indeed, one could be interested in keeping data at *days* detail level longer than aggregate data at *months* level [4].

[6] This access can be easily generalized to access to an object attribute value in a temporal interval, as considered in [1]. Since such extension does not introduces new issues, but it complicates the presentation, we focus on single granule object accesses.

so, such value, that is, $o.a_G(l_G^i)$, where $o.a_G$ denotes the portion of the attribute value at granularity G, is returned.

Otherwise, the requested value must be computed starting from the values stored, at different granularities, intersecting the requested granule. In this case, the access plan is dependent on the user preferences. When privileging efficiency, we minimize the number of accesses to values stored at different granularities. Specifically, the application of a refinement function to coarser values is preferred, when it is declared, since this involves a single access. Moreover, when the result must be computed by applying a coercion function to a value at a finer granularity, even a single value is sufficient for performing the computation. By contrast, when privileging accuracy, since the maximal precision is required in computing the result, the application of coercion functions take precedence, but it is performed only if all the finer values are available.

Fig. 2 summarizes the way of handling an object access $o.a \downarrow l_G^i$. In the figure, A denotes that an accurate answer is privileged (efficiency is the default). According to the algorithm reported in Fig. 2, we distinguish two different cases, whether or not G belongs to the granularities $G_1, \ldots, G_n$ at which a is stored. In the first case, i.e., a j exists such that $G = G_j$, the access strategy takes into account the relationship holding between l_G^i and l_G^F, l_G^L. Specifically, if $l_G^i \in [l_G^F, l_G^L]$, that means that the requested value has never been acquired (it cannot have been deleted, since $l_G^i > l_G^F$). Then, if an accurate answer is requested, a null value is returned, since searching for values for computing it at a finer granularity is useless. By contrast, if $l_G^i < l_G^F$, the value may have been deleted, then it could be computed from values at finer or coarser granularities. Finally, if $l_G^i > l_G^L$, the value can be present only at finer granularities.

In both cases the access is solved by applying a recursive process. Thus, when we look for the requested value at the finer granularity, this does not necessarily mean that data are available at the immediately finer granularity, rather, we may move down several granularities. Note also that, if in solving an object access, we move down or up more than one granularity, if the coercion/refinement functions are compositional, the value to be returned can be obtained by applying the function only once. If they are not compositional, by contrast, a sequence of conversions must be performed. Note finally that, in case of compositional functions, if some aggregate value are already available at an intermediate granularity, for the sake of efficiency we can directly use the already aggregate values at the intermediate granularity, rather than recompute them.

Example 3. Consider class taxpayer of Example 1, and object i_1 which state is depicted in Fig. 1. The access $i.\text{taxes} \downarrow 2002$, performed in an efficient way, results in null if no refinement function has been specified for attribute taxes for granularity $5years$, whereas if restr is specified it results in value 2088 €. By contrast, the access $i.\text{taxes} \downarrow 1stSem2005$ cannot be performed in an accurate way, but it results in 1067 € if performed efficiently with split specified for granularity $years$. Finally, the access $i.\text{taxes} \downarrow 2002 - 2021$ can be performed only if a coercion function for granularity $decades$ is specified. For example, by using max, the access results in 2088 €.   ◇

$$\text{if } o.a_G(l_G^i) \neq \perp \text{ then return } o.a_G(l_G^i)$$
$$\text{else if } \exists j, 1 \leq n, G = G_j \text{ then}$$
$$\quad \text{if } l_G^i \in [l_G^F, l_G^L] \text{ then}$$
$$\qquad \text{if A then return null}$$
$$\qquad \text{else return } R_{j+1}(o.a_{G_{j+1}})(l_G^i)$$
$$\quad \text{if } l_G^i < l_G^F \text{ then}$$
$$\qquad \text{if A then}$$
$$\qquad\quad \text{if } \forall l_{G_{j-1}}^k \in G_{j-1}(l_G^i) \text{ s.t. } o.a_{G_{j-1}}(l_{G_{j-1}}^k) \neq \perp \text{ then return } C_{j-1}(o.a_{G_{j-1}})(l_G^i)$$
$$\qquad\quad \text{else return null}$$
$$\qquad \text{else return } R_{j+1}(o.a_{G_{j+1}})(l_G^i)$$
$$\quad \text{if } l_G^i > l_G^L \text{ then}$$
$$\qquad \text{if A then}$$
$$\qquad\quad \text{if } \forall l_{G_{j-1}}^k \in G_{j-1}(l_G^i) \text{ s.t. } o.a_{G_{j-1}}(l_{G_{j-1}}^k) \neq \perp \text{ then return } C_{j-1}(o.a_{G_{j-1}})(l_G^i)$$
$$\qquad\quad \text{else return null}$$
$$\qquad \text{else if } \exists l_{G_{j-1}}^k \in G_{j-1}(l_G^i) \text{ s.t. } o.a_{G_{j-1}}(l_{G_{j-1}}^k) \neq \perp \text{ then return } C_{j-1}(o.a_{G_{j-1}})(l_G^i)$$
$$\qquad\quad \text{else return null}$$
$$\quad \text{else if } G_n \prec G \text{ then return } C_n(o.a_{G_n})(l_G^i)$$
$$\qquad \text{else if } G \prec G_1 \text{ then return } R_1(o.a_{G_1})(l_G^i)$$
$$\qquad\quad \text{else if } \exists G_j : G_j \prec G \prec G_{j+1} \text{ then}$$
$$\qquad\qquad \text{if A then}$$
$$\qquad\qquad\quad \text{if } \forall l_{G_j}^k \in G_j(l_G^i) \text{ s.t. } o.a_{G_j}(l_{G_j}^k) \neq \perp \text{ then return } C_j(o.a_{G_j})(l_G^i)$$
$$\qquad\qquad\quad \text{else return null}$$
$$\qquad\qquad \text{else return } R_{j+1}(o.a_{G_{j+1}})(l_G^i)$$
$$\qquad\qquad \text{else return null}$$

$$type(a,c) = (\tau_1, \ldots, \tau_n), \text{ s.t. } n \geq 1, \ \tau_j = temporal_{G_j}(\tau), 1 \leq j \leq n, \ G_1 \prec \ldots \prec G_n$$
$$coerc(a,c) = (C_1, \ldots, C_n) \text{ where } C_i : \tau_i \to \tau_{i+1} \forall i = 1 \ldots n-1$$
$$\qquad C_n : \tau_n \to \tau_{\succ G_n} \text{ with } \tau_{\succ G_n} = temporal_{G'}(\tau), \text{ with } G' \succ G_n$$
$$ref(a,c) = (R_1, \ldots, R_n) \text{ where } R_i : \tau_i \to \tau_{i-1} \forall i = 2 \ldots n$$
$$\qquad R_1 : \tau_1 \to \tau_{\prec G_1} \text{ with } \tau_{\prec G_1} = temporal_{G''}(\tau), \text{ with } G'' \prec G_1$$

Fig. 2. Solving the object access $o.a \downarrow l_G^i$

3.2 Qualified Object Accesses

In a *qualified object access*, a conversion function is specified. It specifies how to obtain the requested value, when it is not directly available at the specified granularity, from the values at finer/coarser granularities. A *qualified object access* is syntactically defined as follows.

Definition 6. *Given an object identifier o, an attribute name a, a granule label l_G^i, and a coercion or refinement function f, a* qualified object access *is an expression of the form $o.a \downarrow^f l_G^i$, requiring the value of attribute a of the object denoted by o in granule l_G^i, obtained through function f from the values stored for the attribute.* □

The function specified in the qualified object access will be used to compute the value, and it takes precedence over the functions specified in the schema. In particular, if f is a coercion function and an accurate result is required, a value already present in the database for the specified granule is discarded, if it was constructed with a different function. By contrast, such value will be returned if efficiency is privileged. Fig. 3 summarizes the way of handling a qualified object access $o.a \downarrow^f l_G^i$. In every case not explicitly mentioned, the access results in null. As above, A denotes that an accurate answer is privileged.

$$
\begin{aligned}
&\textbf{if } \exists k \text{ and } o.a_{G_k}(l_G^i) \neq \perp \textbf{ then} \\
&\quad \textbf{if } \mathtt{A} \textbf{ then} \\
&\qquad \textbf{if } f = C_{k-1} \textbf{ then return } o.a_{G_k}(l_G^i) \\
&\qquad \textbf{else if } f \text{ is a coercion function } \textbf{then} \\
&\qquad\quad \textbf{let } G_j = max_{\prec}\{G_k \mid 1 \leq k \leq n,\ G_k \prec G,\ \forall l_{G_k}^h \in G_k(l_G^i)\ o.a_{G_k}(l_{G_k}^h) \neq \perp \} \\
&\qquad\quad \textbf{return } f(o.a_{G_j})(l_G^i) \\
&\qquad\quad \textbf{else let } G_j = min_{\succ}\{G_k \mid 1 \leq k \leq n,\ G_k \succ G,\ \exists l_{G_k}^h \in G_k(l_G^i)\ o.a_{G_k}(l_{G_k}^h) \neq \perp \} \\
&\qquad\quad \textbf{return } f(o.a_{G_j})(l_G^i) \\
&\quad \textbf{else return } o.a_{G_k}(l_G^i) \\
&\textbf{else if } f \text{ is a coercion function } \textbf{then} \\
&\quad \textbf{if } \mathtt{A} \textbf{ then} \\
&\qquad \textbf{let } G_j = max_{\prec}\{G_k \mid 1 \leq k \leq n,\ G_k \prec G,\ \forall l_{G_k}^h \in G_k(l_G^i)\ o.a_{G_k}(l_{G_k}^h) \neq \perp \} \\
&\qquad \textbf{return } f(o.a_{G_j})(l_G^i) \\
&\quad \textbf{else let } G_j = max_{\prec}\{G_k \mid 1 \leq k \leq n,\ G_k \prec G,\ \exists l_{G_k}^h \in G_k(l_G^i)\ o.a_{G_k}(l_{G_k}^h) \neq \perp \} \\
&\quad \textbf{return } f(o.a_{G_j})(l_G^i) \\
&\textbf{else let } G_j = min_{\prec}\{G_k \mid 1 \leq k \leq n,\ G \prec G_k,\ o.a_{G_k}(l_G^i) \neq \perp \} \\
&\textbf{return } f(o.a_{G_j})(l_G^i)
\end{aligned}
$$

$$
\begin{aligned}
type(a,c) &= (\tau_1, \ldots, \tau_n),\ s.t.\ n \geq 1,\ \tau_j = temporal_{G_j}(\tau),\ 1 \leq j \leq n,\ G_1 \prec \ldots \prec G_n \\
coerc(a,c) &= (C_1, \ldots, C_n) \text{ where } C_i : \tau_i \to \tau_{i+1} \forall i = 1 \ldots n-1 \\
&\quad C_n : \tau_n \to \tau_{\succ G_n} \text{ with } \tau_{\succ G_n} = temporal_{G'}(\tau), \text{with } G' \succ G_n \\
ref(a,c) &= (R_1, \ldots, R_n) \text{ where } R_i : \tau_i \to \tau_{i-1} \forall i = 2 \ldots n \\
&\quad R_1 : \tau_1 \to \tau_{\prec G_1} \text{ with } \tau_{\prec G_1} = temporal_{G''}(\tau), \text{with } G'' \prec G_1
\end{aligned}
$$

Fig. 3. Solving the qualified object access $o.a \downarrow^f l_G^i$

Example 4. Consider the class `taxpayer` of Example 1 and object i_1 which state is depicted in Fig. 1. The qualified access $i.\mathtt{taxes} \downarrow^{restr} 2002$ results in value $2088 \, €$, while the access $i.\mathtt{taxes} \downarrow^{restr} 1stSem2008$ results in $1885€$. By contrast, the access $i.\mathtt{taxes} \downarrow^{avg} 2012$ results in $1500 \, €$ if required as efficient, in `null` if specified as accurate.   ◇

3.3   Expiration Invariance of Object Accesses

To devise the conditions aiming at ensuring access invariance against expiration, we distinguish between the two forms of expiration supported by T_ODMGe model: granularity evolution and value deletion.

Suppose that G is one of the granularities of a dynamic attribute a, specifically, $G = G_i, 1 \leq i \leq n$, and suppose that the value at granularity G for attribute a in a granule l_G^i has not been evolved yet, because the expiration condition for performing the granularity evolution to granularity G is not yet true. If an access $o.a \downarrow l_G^i$ is performed, the obtained result is the same that will be obtained if the access will be re-executed after the aggregation of attribute a in granule l_G^i, if no updates are made on $o.a_{G_{i-1}}(G_{i-1}(l_G^i))$. The access $o.a \downarrow l_G^i$ is referred as *granularity evolution invariant*. Specifically, the following result holds. The result follows from the way the access $o.a \downarrow l_G^i$ is solved when $l_G^i > l_G^L$ and efficiency is privileged, and from the way granularity evolutions are executed [4] (also refer to the definition of object consistency given in [4]).

Proposition 1. *Every object access $o.a \downarrow l_G^i$ is evolution invariant.*   □

For what concerns value deletion, suppose that the value at granularity G for an attribute a in a granule l_G^i has not been deleted, because the expiration condition is not yet true. If an access $o.a \downarrow l^i_G$ is performed, the obtained result is approximately the same, modulo an approximation Δ, that will be obtained if the access will be executed again after the deletion of attribute a in granule l^i_G, provided that $o.a_{G_{i+1}}(G_{i+1}(l^i_G))$ is defined. The access $o.a \downarrow l^i_G$ is referred as *deletion invariant*. The following result holds. The result follows from the way in which the access $o.a \downarrow l^i_G$ is solved in the case $l^i_G < l^F_G$, and from the way in which granularity evolutions are executed [4] (also refer to the definition of object consistency given in [4]), and from the definition of quasi-inverse functions.

Proposition 2. *Every object access $o.a \downarrow l^i_G$, such that the refinement and coercion functions R_i and C_i specified for granularities G_i and G_{i+1} of attribute a are quasi-inverse according to Definition 4, is deletion invariant.* □

3.4   Unsolvable Accesses

The approach discussed above to solve object accesses simply returns null if an object access cannot be solved. Actually, we can distinguish between object accesses that are (statically) known to be *unsolvable*, that is, it does not exist a database state evaluated against which they will produce a not null value, and solvable accesses that can produce null values on specific database state. Detecting object accesses that are statically unsolvable saves query execution times. Since the system knows in advance that such accesses will never return a not null answer, it does not need to execute them. Specifically, according to the way in which an object access $o.a \downarrow l^i_G$ is solved, the following result holds.

Proposition 3. *Every object access $o.a \downarrow l^i_G$ such that o is an instance of class c, $type(a, c) = (\tau_1, \ldots, \tau_n)$ with $n \geq 1$, $\tau_j = temporal_{G_j}(\tau)$, $1 \leq j \leq n$, $G_1 \prec \ldots \prec G_n$, $coerc(a, c) = (C_1, \ldots, C_n)$, $ref(a, c) = (R_1, \ldots, R_n)$, is unsolvable if one of the following conditions holds:*
- *G is not related by $\preceq$ to any of $G_1, \ldots, G_n$;*
- *$G \prec G_1$ and no R_1 has been specified [7];*
- *$G_n \prec G$ and no C_n has been specified;*
- *$G_i \prec G \prec G_{i+1}$, efficiency is privileged, and no R_i has been specified.* □

4   Related Work

Other approaches addressed the problem of efficient access to multigranular temporal data. Coercion and refinement functions we use in our approach can be considered as a particular case of semantic assumptions introduced by Bettini et al. [3], that formalize implicit information derived from temporal data stored in (relational) databases.

Our specification for refinement functions recalls *valid-time indeterminacy* introduced by Dyreson and Snodgrass in [5, 6], where probability distributions are related to a set of indeterminate time instants (or periods). The set of *standard distributions* presented in [5, 6] is totally covered by our approach, and

---

[7] This case is equivalent to the SQL specification of retaining indeterminacy of [5].

non-standard ones can be easily integrated by user-defined refinement functions. Our refinement functions, moreover, explicitly give the semantics of the applied conversion. However, the goal of both approaches is converting time instants (i.e., granules) from one granularity to another, rather than converting temporal values. In [1] conversions of temporal data to different coarser granularities are performed through coercion functions. However, such approach does not deal with the access to temporal data, different portions of which are recorded at different granularities.

The problem we address is also related to the problem of answering aggregate queries using persistent views in data warehouses [7, 11]. Such approaches, differently from ours, only consider one level of aggregation.

Yang e Widom [12] propose the *SB-Tree* indexing structure, to improve time response to queries involving temporal aggregates. The time window approach they apply considers aggregates computed with respect to a fixed temporal window that slides over time. This allows one to build, for the same attribute, several indexes, each one referring to a specific time window (that can be considered as a granularity) and to a specific aggregate (sum, count, average, minimum and maximum aggregates are considered). Such notion of granularity is different from the one we use in our approach, that is the *standard* one in the temporal database community. Moreover, aggregates at different granularities are computed considering timestamp sets, without taking into account any semantics related to sets of different cardinality. Then, such sets can be compared only in a punctual way (instant by instant). Furthermore, the aggregates are computed referring to the entire set of values an attribute takes in a relational table, and not to a single attribute value or set of timestamps. The *SB-Tree* indexing structure has been extended in [13], that, differently from our work, is oriented towards data warehouses, thus focusing on relational data and dealing with temporal granularities as datawarehouse conceptual hierarchies. The indexing approach discussed in [13] involves only aggregations (in particularly sum, but the approach is easily extensible to count and average aggregation), and all levels of detail are compressed using the same aggregation function.

5   Conclusions and Future Work

In this paper we have addressed the problem of accessing object attributes in a multigranular temporal object-oriented model supporting dynamic attributes, portions of which values are recorded at different levels of detail, depending on how recent values are. First, we have formalized how temporal values can be converted from one granularity to another through the use of coercion and refinement functions, devising some desirable properties of these functions: *compositionality* and *invertibility*. Then, we have discussed how qualified and unqualified object accesses can be solved. Finally, we have discussed some relevant properties of object accesses with respect to the model we consider: *expiration invariance* and statical *unsolvability*.

We are currently extending the work presented in the paper along different directions. First, we are developing the model query language on the basis of the access mechanism presented in this paper. Moreover, we are developing a more flexible mechanism for expiration, to take into account also information retrievable form data already stored, such as periodic trends on data values and on the amount of information stored for an attribute. The same investigation will be applied to target the access mechanism, in order to specialize the application of involved coercion and refinement functions. Finally, we are investigating the development of ad-hoc storage structures for efficient representation and access to dynamic attributes.

References

1. E. Bertino, E. Ferrari, G. Guerrini, I. Merlo. _T_ODMG: An ODMG Compliant Temporal Object Model Supporting Multiple Granularity Management. *Information Systems*, 28(8):885-927, 2003.
2. C. Bettini, C. Dyreson, W. Evans, R. Snodgrass, and X. Wang. A Glossary of Time Granularity Concepts. In *Proc. of Temporal Databases: Research and Practice*, LNCS 1399:406-413, 1998.
3. C. Bettini, X. S. Wang, and S. Jajodia. Temporal Semantic Assumptions and Their Use in Databases. *IEEE Transactions on Knowledge and Data Engineering* 10(2):277-296, 1998.
4. E. Camossi, E. Bertino, G. Guerrini, M. Mesiti. Handling Expiration of Multigranular Temporal Objects. *Journal of Logic and Computation*, 4(1):23-50, 2004.
5. C.E. Dyreson, and R. Snodgrass. Supporting Valid-time Indeterminacy. *ACM Transactions on Database Systems* 23(1):1-57, 1998.
6. C.E. Dyreson, W.S. Evans, H. Lin, and R. Snodgrass. Efficiently Supporting Temporal Granularities. *IEEE Transactions on Knowledge and Data Engineering* 12(4):568–587, 2000.
7. A. Gupta, V. Harinarayan, and D. Quass. Aggregate Query Processing in Data Warehousing Environment. In *Proc. 21st Int'l Conf. on Very Large Data Bases*, 358-369, 1995.
8. Y. Shoham. Temporal Logics in AI: Semantical and Ontological Considerations. *Artificial Intelligence* 33(1):89-104, 1987.
9. J. Skyt, and C. Jensen. Persistent Views - A Mechanism for Managing Aging Data. *The Computer Journal* 45(5):481-492, 2002.
10. J. Skyt, C.S. Jensen, and L. Mark. A Foundation for Vacuuming Temporal Databases. *Data & Knowledge Engineering* 44(1):1-29, 2003.
11. D. Srivastava, S. Dar, H. Jagadish, and A. Levy. Answering Queries with Aggregation Using Views. In *Proc. 22nd Int'l Conf. on Very Large Data Bases*, 318-329, 1996.
12. J. Yang and J. Widom. Incremental Computation and Maintenance of Temporal Aggregates. In *Proc. of 17th International Conference on Data Engineering*, 51-60, 2001.
13. D. Zhang, D. Gunopulos, V.J. Tsotras, and B. Seeger. Temporal and Spatio-Temporal Aggregation over Data Streams Using Multiple Time Granularities. *Information Systems* 28(1-2):61-84, 2003.

An Indexing Technique
for Similarity-Based Fuzzy Object-Oriented Data Model

Adnan Yazıcı, Çagrı İnce, and Murat Koyuncu

Department of Computer Engineering, METU, 06531 Ankara, Turkey

Abstract. Fuzzy object-oriented data model is a fuzzy logic-based extension to object-oriented database model, which permits uncertain data to be explicitly represented. One of the proposed fuzzy object-oriented database models based on similarity relations is the FOOD model. Several kinds of fuzziness are dealt with in the FOOD model, including fuzziness between object/class and class/superclass relations. The traditional index structures are inappropriate for the FOOD model for an efficient access to the objects with crisp or fuzzy values, since they are not efficient for processing both crisp and fuzzy queries. In this study we propose a new index structure (the FOOD Index) dealing with different kinds of fuzziness in FOOD databases and supports multi-dimensional indexing. We describe how the FOOD Index supports various types of flexible queries and evaluate performance results of crisp, range, and fuzzy queries using the FOOD index.

1 Introduction

Among the enhanced database models, despite lacking of a formal standard proposal in the past, object-oriented database models have gained a lot of interest by researchers due to the introduction of the notions of nested objects and inheritance. Despite the representational power of the object-oriented paradigm, object-oriented database models are not good at dealing with uncertain or imprecise data. However, many applications require manipulation and reasoning based on incomplete and imprecise data. Data in databases may not be accurate and users of a database may be interested in asking imprecise (fuzzy) queries. For example, an eyewitness may see the person who committed a crime but is unable to describe the person accurately. In other words, the description of the characteristics of the suspect is fuzzy. A fuzzy logic based extension to the data model is a possible solution that permits imprecise or uncertain data to be explicitly represented [7]. One of the studies on fuzzy object-oriented database modeling is a similarity-based fuzzy object-oriented data model introduced in [8]. It is later extended and named as *the Fuzzy Object-Oriented Data (FOOD) model* [14], [15]. The FOOD model permits more accurate representation of various types of uncertainty in the object-oriented data model enhanced with the fuzzy concept and fuzzy extensions. The FOOD model is a similarity-based fuzzy object-oriented model, which we consider as a reference data model throughout this study.

H. Christiansen et al. (Eds.): FQAS 2004, LNAI 3055, pp. 334–347, 2004.

Indexing techniques defined in the framework of object-oriented data models can be classified as *structural* [1], [4], [9], [10], [13] and *behavioral* [5]. Structural indexing is based on object attributes. Structural indexing proposed so far can be classified into techniques supporting nested predicates, such as the ones presented in [4], [9], [13] and techniques supporting queries issued against an inheritance hierarchy [10]. Most indexing techniques that efficiently support the evaluation of nested predicates are based on pre-computing functional joins among objects. Some of those techniques require a single-index lookup to evaluate a nested predicate. However, their update costs may be rather high. Others, such as [13], require scanning a number of indices equal to the number of classes to be traversed to evaluate the predicate. However, their update costs are not very high. Indexing techniques for queries against inheritance hierarchies are based on allocating a single index on the entire class hierarchy rather than allocating an index for each class in the hierarchy. Behavioral indexing aims at providing efficient execution for queries containing method invocations. It is based on pre-computing or caching the results of a method and storing them into an index. The major problem of this approach is how to detect changes to objects that invalidate the results of a method.

Although there are many indexing techniques for object-oriented data models, there are only a few indexing techniques for fuzzy databases. The access structure proposed in [6] uses one index per fuzzy predicate tied to an attribute. The objective is to associate each grade of a fuzzy predicate with the list of tuples that satisfy that predicate. This method only deals with homogeneous domains and assumes that the underlying relations are crisp. Another study included in [14], [16] introduces a fuzzy access structure along with a record and a file organization schema for fuzzy relational databases. In this access structure, MLGF structure is extended to index both the crisp and fuzzy attribute values together.

The first difficulty that may be encountered while investigating an indexing technique for the FOOD model is that the current crisp index structures are inappropriate for representing and efficiently accessing fuzzy data in the FOOD databases. Fuzzy querying allows one to express vague predicates represented by fuzzy sets. For this purpose, conventional access structures cannot be used directly since fuzzy predicates may not refer to entry values of the index. Therefore, an efficient indexing mechanism for the FOOD model is needed to provide fast access to the objects with crisp or fuzzy values, and processing both crisp and fuzzy queries. An efficient access structure for fuzzy data retrieval should be multi-dimensional, since both the non-fuzzy and fuzzy attributes need to be used as organizing attributes of objects for efficiently processing crisp and fuzzy queries on the same class.

In this study, we propose a new multi-dimensional indexing technique, *the FOOD Index,* in order to satisfy the needs mentioned above. The FOOD Index is a structural indexing technique, which is based on object attributes. The FOOD Index is the extension of the combination of two existing index structures, namely the Path Index [2], [3] and G-tree [11], [12]. The FOOD index adapts these index structures for the FOOD model and makes them work together.

In the rest of the paper, we first describe *the FOOD Index structure.* Section 3 includes the performance evaluations of the FOOD Index for various types of queries such as crisp exact match, crisp range and fuzzy queries. Finally, the conclusions of the study are presented in Section 4.

2 Food Index Structure

The FOOD Index is a multidimensional indexing mechanism, that is, one or more than one organizing attributes belonging to the same class can be indexed together. Selection of these attributes is usually based on types of common queries on the database and other physical database design requirements. The FOOD Index is based on the combination of G-tree Index structure and Path Index structure.

The Path Index is a data structure for indexing object-oriented databases. It provides an association between an object O at the end of a path and all instantiations ending with O and, therefore, can be used to solve nested predicates against all classes along the path. G-tree (*Grid Tree*) is a data structure designed to provide multidimensional access in databases. It combines features of both grid files and B^+-trees. It is called a G-tree because multidimensional space is divided into a grid of variable size partitions, and the partitions are organized as a B^+-tree. The partitions in the G-tree correspond to disk pages or buckets, and points are assigned to a partition until it is full. A full partition is split into two equal subpartitions, and the points in the original partition are distributed among the new partitions. Since the partitions are completely ordered, they can be stored in a B^+-tree. G-tree also has the self-balancing property of B^+-tree. For point queries, the experiments show that its retrieval and update performance is similar to that of B^+-trees independent of the data distribution. For range queries, the performance varies significantly with the data distributions. While the performance is good for two-dimensional case, it deteriorates as the number of dimensions increases.

2.1 Adaptation of Path Index Structure

Path Index structure is utilized to handle both aggregation and inheritance hierarchies in the FOOD model. Original Path Index uses B^+-tree in order to reach the stored records related with the key values searched. Search key values can be a fuzzy or a crisp value in the FOOD model. Therefore, we convert fuzzy and crisp values into a common base to form a search key. Our approach to this problem is to map fuzzy and crisp values to bit strings formed by 0's and 1's to provide a common base between those two types of values. Those bit strings are used as a search key in the tree. In this way, we adapt G-tree using these bit strings as a search key value and index both fuzzy and crisp values.

The FOOD Index, whose main structure is shown in Fig. 1, stores the path instantiations in Path Instantiation Node (PIN), which is actually a leaf node of the Path Index structure. In the case that the page size is not large enough for storing the entire path instantiations related to the same key value, the instantiations are ordered and a directory is kept at the beginning of the record. In this directory, the last instantiation in that page and the address of that page are stored for each page occupied.

As in Fig. 1, the G-tree structure is used to reach the data buckets starting from the root node of the FOOD Index. In data buckets, for each different key value there is a data bucket record. Using the key values searched, we can access to data buckets and, within those data buckets, to data bucket records related with the key values. Each data bucket record has a pointer to the PIN that stores all the path instantiations related with the key value of that data bucket record. If the path instantiations do not fit into a single page, then a directory node is utilized. Each directory record has a pointer to the next level PIN and a key path instantiation that is the last path instantiation in the next level PIN. Thus, if we look at a specific path instantiation, using directory structure, we can search the correct directory record and then access the PIN it points to.

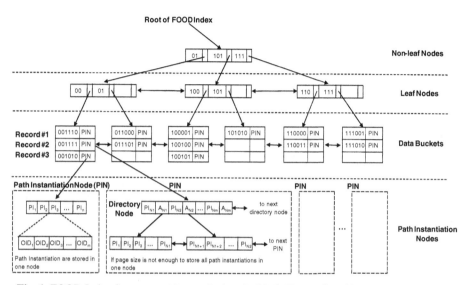

Fig. 1. FOOD Index Structure with sample data for Node Factor=3 and Data Bucket Factor=3

Within PINs, all the path instantiations, which are related with the key value of the data bucket record, are stored. Accessing those path instantiations, all the OIDs of the objects which have the nested attribute A_n with the values searched and which belongs to the target class with a membership degree greater than or equal to the threshold value of the target class are determined.

Note that, OIDs uniquely identify the objects in a FOOD database. However, OIDs do not include the class identification number since, in the FOOD model, the class that an object belongs to can be changed when attribute values of the object are changed because of fuzziness. The class information of the object is dynamically stored within the object itself.

2.2 Adaptation of G-Tree Structure

G-tree is a multidimensional data structure based on B+-tree. It uses "bit strings" for determining which path to follow in order to reach to the leaf nodes. We need to convert the fuzzy and crisp values into bit strings so that we can utilize G-tree structure in order to reach the path instantiations related with the key values searched. Since the search is guided by using the composite bit strings, we mainly concentrate on how to construct these bit strings.

Organizing attributes are a set of attributes, which are chosen from the set of all attributes to organize the data. Organizing attributes are indexed together. For example, the attributes *age* and *height* of a class *person* can be used to organize the class *person* by indexing them together in order to get answers of the queries faster.

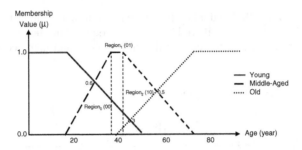

Fig. 2. Membership functions for fuzzy terms "Young", "Middle-Aged" and "Old"

A fuzzy attribute can contain either a fuzzy value or a crisp value. For example, if the fuzzy attribute is *age*, it can be a crisp value like "65" or a fuzzy term like *old*. Therefore, we need to convert the crisp values and the fuzzy terms into a single common base. The common base used in this study to represent fuzzy and crisp values is "a bit string". First of all, crisp values are converted into fuzzy values with a membership degree between [0,1] using the appropriate membership functions defined for that fuzzy term. The membership function identifies the fuzzy term to which the crisp value belongs mostly. For an accurate estimation of the fuzzy set, different membership functions are used, and, therefore, different membership values are obtained. The fuzzy set with the maximum membership degree is chosen. This value is then mapped into a bit string. For an example, membership functions for fuzzy-valued attribute *age* are given in Fig. 2, in which the regions of the fuzzy term *middle-aged* are shown.

The bit strings for different organizing attribute values must be different from each other so that we can distinguish while searching them in the index structure. Thus, constructing the bit strings, we must be sure that we obtain different bit strings for different organizing attributes values. In the FOOD index structure, the bit string structure of a fuzzy-valued attribute is as follows:

T_1	...	T_n	R_1	R_2	M_1	...	M_m	V_1	...	V_s

$T_1...T_n$: Bit string that identifies the fuzzy term. i.e. "001": young, "010": middle-aged, "100": old, "011": young AND/OR/XOR middle-aged, etc.

R_1R_2: Bit string that represents the region number that the membership value belongs to, i.e., "00": $Region_0$, "01": $Region_1$, "10": $Region_2$, "11": Fuzzy Value.

$M_1...M_m$: Bit string that identifies the membership degree represented with base 2. Using the membership functions for fuzzy terms, membership degree for crisp value is calculated. M_1 represents the integer part while the rest represent the decimal part of membership degree, i.e., for "1" μ=1.0, for "01" μ=0.5, for "011" μ=0.75 etc.

$V_1...V_s$: Bit string that represents the actual crisp value. : All 0's in case of a fuzzy value.

When we look at the graph of a fuzzy membership function (Fig. 2), we should notice that there are three main regions in the graph. In the first region, the membership value starts from 0 and increases until 1 while the value in x-axis increases. This region is called $Region_0$ and represented by "00" as a bit string. In the second region which is called Region$_1$ and represented by "01", the result membership value stays constant as 1. And in the third region which is called Region$_2$ and represented by "10", the membership value decreases from 1 to 0. The region number of the membership function that the crisp value belongs to has to be included in the bit string in order to get more precise and smaller partitions. It will also be used while the relations between fuzzy terms are being investigated. The position of the region number (R_1, R_2) in the bit string follows the fuzzy term. We note that, a region number is only valid for crisp values since fuzzy attribute value may belong to any region of the membership function. For example, fuzzy value "0.8 Tall" can belong to Region$_0$ or Region$_2$ at the same time. Thus, for fuzzy values we store "11" in a bit string as a region number.

There is no extra bit used to show whether attribute value is crisp or fuzzy since we can determine whether the attribute value is crisp or fuzzy by looking at the region number bits. If region number is "00", "01" or "10", then we can decide that the attribute value is crisp and we know that the region number is "11" when the attribute value is fuzzy. Thus crisp data is distinguished from fuzzy ones and this information is used in querying, especially for handling crisp exact-match and range queries.

If a fuzzy-valued attribute has a crisp value, then we store the original crisp value. The original crisp value as its name implies is not applicable for fuzzy attribute values and only stored for crisp attribute values. For fuzzy values, we store all 0's for those bits in the bit string.

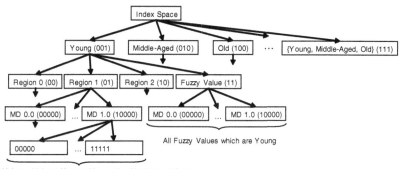

Fig. 3. Example of Index Space Partition

Note that in theory there is no limitation for the number of bits that specify the membership value in our modeling. However, after some number of bits, the membership value will distinguish records in a way that can be neglected. Therefore, we can limit the number of bits in the membership value bit string. To better understand the bit string construction, Fig. 3 shows the logical partitioning of index space for constructing bit strings for crisp and fuzzy values.

If we have only one organizing attribute of a class to be indexed, that means, we have only one dimension to index, then, we construct a bit string for that organizing attribute. However, if there is more than one organizing attributes of a class to be indexed together (multi-dimensional indexing must be used), the bit string representations of the attribute values for each dimension must be combined into one. Because we need only one bit string as an input in order to reach the leaf nodes of the FOOD Index structure. Thus, the proposed combination structure of bit strings for n dimensional indexing is as follows:

$$\boxed{B_{1,1}}\boxed{B_{2,1}} \cdots \boxed{B_{n,1}}\boxed{B_{1,2}}\boxed{B_{2,2}} \cdots \boxed{B_{n,2}} \cdots\cdots \boxed{B_{1,m}}\boxed{B_{2,m}} \cdots \boxed{B_{n,m}}$$

where $B_{i,j}$ is the jth bit of the bit string of a fuzzy-valued attribute that belongs to the ith dimension. Briefly, the combination of bit strings is obtained by combining each bits of their bit string representations one by one according to the order among the dimensions, i.e., the first bit of the first dimension, the first bit of the second dimension,..., the first bit of the ith dimension, the second bit of the first dimension, the second bit of the second dimension,..., the jth bit of the ith dimension.

2.3 Handling Object/Class and Class/Subclass Relations

An SQL type query format is used in the FOOD model. The query has three main parts: *select* clause, *from* clause and *where* clause. The conditions defined in the *where* clause is called "*where conditions*". For the fuzzy valued conditions, the threshold value for the fuzzy term takes place next to the condition in order to deal with data level fuzziness in the query. There is no need for a threshold value if the condition is crisp.

Another condition we need to deal with is "*from condition*". Because of the fuzziness in the object/class and class/subclass relations in the FOOD model, an object may not fully belong to any class but with a degree calculated by formulas. Therefore, we have to specify another threshold value for each of the classes within *from* clause of the query. The *from* clause of a query in the FOOD model says that "only deal with the objects belonging to those classes or one of their subclasses with at least the threshold levels given". The threshold values for each class takes place next to themselves in *from* clause.

And within *select* clause, the question to "what information will be retrieved as a result of the query" is answered. In the following example, the name and surname of the members who are satisfying the *from* and *where conditions* of the query are going to be retrieved as a result.

```
SELECT Member.Name_Surname FROM Native_Author (0.7), Member (0.6)
WHERE ( Author.Age =[Old] 0.8 ) and (Author.Height > 170)
```

Using the FOOD index structure, the path instantiation nodes of the attribute values which satisfy the *where conditions* of the query are searched and the path instantiations which include the target class or its subclasses are obtained. However, the objects belonging to the target class or one of its subclasses within the path instantiations are only possible results of the query, since we have not yet dealt with the factor of object/class and class/subclass relations. Different than the other object-oriented data models, since the relations are fuzzy, the objects in the FOOD model belong to the classes in database with a degree. Thus, a threshold value is defined for each of the classes specified in the *from* clause of a query. We have to check if the path instantiation satisfy the *from* condition of the query as well.

However, an object may not directly belong to the target class but to a subclass of the target class. Thus, the subclasses of the target class are also in our scope. Similar in the object/class relation, the membership degree of a class to its superclass is calculated using the similarities between the attribute values and the class range values, and the relevance of fuzzy attributes [14]. Since the class definitions do not change frequently, the membership degree of a class to its superclass may be kept in a table in order to speed up the calculations. For example, in Fig. 4, the *book* class has two subclasses of its own, *science* and *engineering*, and the membership degrees for those classes are 1. The *science* class has two subclasses, *computer science* and *computer engineering*, and the membership degrees for those classes are 1 and 0.7 respectively.

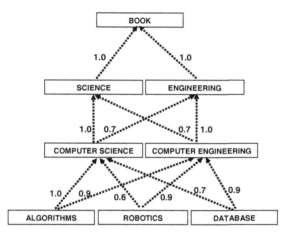

Fig. 4. Class Hierarchy for class/subclass relation

The membership degree of two classes, if there is not any direct relation between, is calculated by combining the membership degrees of the classes to their subclasses along to inheritance hierarchy into one with an operator. In this study, the operator proposed to do this is the *"minimum operator"*. For example,

$\mu_{Robotics}(Book) = Min(\mu_{Robotics}(Computer\_Engineering),$

$\mu_{Computer\_Engineering}(Engineering), \mu_{Engineering}(Book)) = Min(0.9, 1.0, 1.0) = 0.9$

However, if we look at Fig. 4, we notice that there is more than one path that can be followed from the class *Robotics* to the class *Book*, such as:

$\mu_{Robotics}(Book) = Min(\mu_{Robotics}(Computer\_Science), \mu_{Computer\_Science}(Science),$

$\mu_{Science}(Book)) = Min(0.6, 1.0, 1.0) = 0.6$

In this case, the path, which has the highest membership degree, will be considered and used.

Similarly, the membership degree of an object to any class in the same inheritance hierarchy is calculated by combining the membership degree of the object to the class for which it has the highest membership degree. For example,

$\mu_{Object}(Book) = Min(\mu_{Object}(Robotics), \mu_{Robotics}(Book)) = min(0.8, 0.9) = 0.8$

After calculating the membership degrees of the objects within the path instantiations to the index class, the path instantiations containing the objects having a membership degree less than the threshold value of the index class defined in the query are eliminated because they do not satisfy the condition given in the *from* part of the query.

Next, using the rest of the path instantiations, the OIDs of all the objects whose (nested) attribute, A_n, satisfies the *where* conditions of the query and belonging to the target class or one of its subclasses are obtained. As the last step, the attribute values of those objects defined in the *select* clause of the query are obtained and returned as the result of the query.

2.4 Retrieval Algorithm

The retrieval algorithm takes a query as argument and returns the values of the attribute(s) (specified within the *select* part of the query) of the objects belonging to the target class. The retrieval algorithm determines the type of the query such as crisp exact match, crisp range, and fuzzy queries and construct the bit string list composed of the start and stop bit string pairs. Then, it gets the objects which are in the range of the bit string pairs. In this algorithm, the critical point is the construction of the bit strings. Therefore, constructions of the bit strings are explained depending on the query types: crisp exact match query, crisp range query and fuzzy query.

Crisp Exact Match Query: We calculate the fuzzy set to which the crisp value belongs mostly, its region and its membership degree. Then, using those parameters, the start bit sting is constructed. Since exact match condition defines a point in space, the stop bit string is same as the start bit string.

For example, let's assume that the *where* condition is "*Age = 53*". Using the membership functions, we calculate the membership degrees and region numbers of the attribute value 53 as follows:

$$\mu_{young}(53) = 0.0 \qquad \mu_{middle-aged}(53) = 0.8 \qquad \mu_{old}(53) = 0.2$$
$$RegionNo = 2 \qquad RegionNo = 2 \qquad RegionNo = 0$$

Therefore, the attribute value 53 mostly belongs to the fuzzy term *middle-aged*. Then, we construct the following bit string pair for the crisp exact match condition. Note that the start and stop bit strings are the same.

No	Start Bit String	Stop Bit String
1	01010011001000000	01010011001000000

Crisp Range Query: Crisp range conditions are the conditions in the form:

indexed_attribute [>, >=, <, <=] *crisp_attribute_value*

We calculate the fuzzy set to which the crisp value belongs mostly, its region and its membership degree. Then, for each single valued fuzzy term, the start bit stings and stop bit strings are constructed using those parameters according to the range condition.

For example, let's assume that the where condition is "*age < 32*". Using the membership functions given in Fig. 2, we calculate the membership degrees and region numbers of the attribute value 32 as following:

$$\mu_{young}(32) = 0.4 \qquad \mu_{middle-aged}(32) = 0.8 \qquad \mu_{old}(32) = 0.0$$
$$RegionNo = 2 \qquad RegionNo = 0 \qquad RegionNo = 0$$

Therefore, we are interested in the following search space intervals:

No	Fuzzy Term	Region No	Membership Degree
1	Young	1	0.0 – 1.0
2	Young	2	0.2 – 1.0
3	Middle-Aged	1	0.0 – 0.8

From those search space intervals, we construct the following bit string pairs:

No	Start Bit String	Stop Bit String
1	00101000000000000	00101100000111111
2	00110001100000000	01010100000111111
3	01001000000000000	10001011001111111

Fuzzy Query: Fuzzy conditions are the conditions in the form:

$$indexed\_attribute = fuzzy\_term \ \ threshold\_value$$

The fuzzy condition contains an equality following by a fuzzy term and its threshold value. For example, "age = [tall] 0.8" and "height = [short,middle] 0.5" are fuzzy conditions in the case the attributes *age* and *height* are the indexed attributes. The threshold value eliminates undesired low-level similarities and provides flexibility for users to specify the degree of uncertainty in the result of their queries.

We calculate the similarity degrees of the fuzzy terms to the other fuzzy terms in the domain. Then, for each single or multi-valued fuzzy term, the start bit stings and stop bit strings are constructed using those parameters according to the range condition with the similarity degrees between fuzzy terms.

For example, let's assume that the where condition is "Age = [middle-aged] 0.6". We will construct bit string pairs in the case that the fuzzy term in condition is a single valued fuzzy term. Using the similarity matrix given in Table 1, we calculate the threshold values to obtain the crisp values for the previous and next fuzzy terms.

Table 1. Similarity Matrix for Fuzzy-Valued Attribute "Age"

Similarity Matrix	Young	Middle-Aged	Old
Young	1.0	0.6	0.3
Middle-Aged	0.6	1.0	0.5
Old	0.3	0.5	1.0

$$\mu_{middle-aged}(x) = 0.6 \Rightarrow \mu_{young}(x) = 0.6 * 0.6 = 0.36$$

$$\mu_{middle-aged}(x) = 0.6 \Rightarrow \mu_{old}(x) = 0.6 * 0.5 = 0.3$$

Again, using the similarity matrix, we calculate the following threshold values for any single or multi fuzzy-valued attributes.

$$\mu_{middle-aged}(x) = 0.6 \Rightarrow \mu_{young}(x) = 0.6/0.6 = 1.0$$

$$\mu_{middle-aged}(x) = 0.6 \Rightarrow \mu_{middle-aged}(x) = 0.6/1.0 = 0.6$$

$$\mu_{middle-aged}(x) = 0.6 \Rightarrow \mu_{old}(x) = 0.6/0.5 = 1.2$$

$$\mu_{middle-aged}(x) = 0.6 \Rightarrow \mu_{\{young,middle-aged\}}(x) = 0.6/0.6 = 1.0$$

$$\mu_{middle-aged}(x) = 0.6 \Rightarrow \mu_{\{young,old\}}(x) = 0.6/0.5 = 1.2$$

$$\mu_{middle-aged}(x) = 0.6 \Rightarrow \mu_{\{middle-aged,old\}}(x) = 0.6/0.5 = 1.2$$

$$\mu_{middle-aged}(x) = 0.6 \Rightarrow \mu_{\{young,middle-aged,old\}}(x) = 0.6/0.5 = 1.2$$

Therefore, we are interested in the following search space intervals in terms of fuzzy terms, region numbers and membership degrees:

No	Fuzzy Term	Region No	Membership
1	Young	2	0.0 – 0.36
2	Young	3	1.0
3	Middle-Aged	0 – 3	0.6 – 1.0
4	Old	0	0.0 – 0.3
5	{Young,Middle-Aged}	3	1.0

From those search space intervals, we construct the following bit string pairs:

No	Start Bit String	Stop Bit String
1	0011000000000000	0011000101111111
2	0011110000000000	0011110000011111
3	0100001001100000	0101110000011111
4	1000000000000000	1000000100111111
5	0111110000000000	0111110000011111

3   Performance Evaluations

The cost model for the proposed FOOD indexing is not included here due to space limitation. However, we give shortly the performance test results in this section. Since the FOOD Index is the first and only indexing technique proposed so far for the FOOD model, the FOOD index is compared with the Path Index structure, which is accepted as the most efficient index structure (according our best knowledge) for the object-oriented database model.

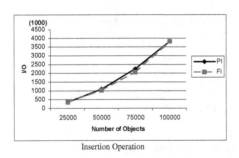
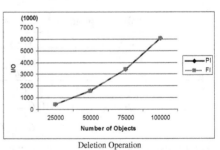

Insertion Operation   Deletion Operation

Fig. 5. Performance comparisons for insertion and deletion operations

We have done performance tests for insertion of 25000, 50000, 75000, and 100000 objects into database for FOOD Index and Path Index Structures; then we have obtained the result given in Fig. 5. The figure shows that the FOOD Index and the Path Index have similar performances for insertion operation. For deletion operation, we started with four FOOD databases that contained 25000, 50000, 75000 and 100000 objects respectively. Then, we deleted objects from databases until there were no objects at all. The objects were deleted uniformly among the classes in index path.

We have done performance tests for the FOOD Index and the Path Index structures. Fig. 5 represents the results. The figure shows that the FOOD Index and the Path Index have similar performances for deletion operation.

These are expected results since insertion and deletion operations have similar steps in both cases because both uses B$^+$-tree with some modifications, and same path instantiation node structure. However, because of the different means of handling the fuzzy attribute values, there occur some slightly differences between the FOOD Index and the Path Index.

When testing the performance of retrieval operations we consider the type of the retrieval queries. There are three types of a retrieval query: crisp exact match query, crisp range query and fuzzy query. We performed the performance tests for each type of retrieval queries. Initially, we had four FOOD databases that contain 25000, 50000, 75000 and 100000 objects. Then, we run each type of retrieval queries on the databases with the FOOD Index and the Path Index techniques using different node factors and storage types.

Crisp Exact Match Queries: We have done performance tests for crisp exact match queries of the FOOD Index and the Path Index with different number of objects and then we showed the results in Fig. 6. The figure shows that the FOOD Index and Path Index have similar performances for crisp exact match queries. Both the FOOD Index and the Path Index are very close to each other since both uses B$^+$-tree for internal nodes. Therefore, both index structures have similar performances for crisp exact match queries.

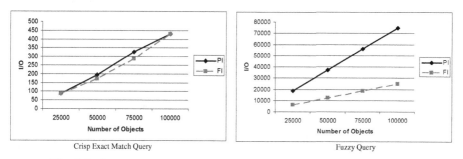

Fig. 6. Performance comparisons for crisp exact match query and fuzzy query

Crisp Range Queries: We have done performance tests for crisp range queries of the FOOD Index and the Path Index with different number of objects with respect to node factor, index dimension size and different storage types. The results show that the FOOD Index and the Path Index have similar performances for crisp range queries like crisp exact match queries.

Fuzzy Queries: We have obtained the results given in Fig. 6 for fuzzy queries. The most important thing is that the performance of the FOOD Index is almost three times better than of the Path Index. Since the FOOD Index is specially designed to handle fuzzy attribute values with crisp attribute values together, the performance of the FOOD Index is much better than that of the Path Index. Instead of using special techniques, the Path Index does a linear search between fuzzy values to determine whether they satisfy the conditions and, it costs much more as shown in Fig. 6.

How the dimension size affects a fuzzy query? First of all, the Path Index is not a multi dimensional indexing technique, thus we cannot compare it with the FOOD Index in this sense. Instead, we compare the fuzzy query performances for one and two-dimensional cases using the FOOD Index Structure. The total number of I/O operations done for retrieval of objects from database using two-dimensional index is significantly greater than that using one-dimensional index. The intuitive reason is the following: We can easily calculate that the number of different key values in two-dimensional case is the multiplication of the numbers of different key values of the first dimension and the second dimension. Thus, the number of data buckets in the two-dimensional case is more than that in the one-dimensional case. This also causes the depth of the index tree in the two-dimensional case to be more than that in the one-dimensional case. Therefore, the total number of I/O operations in the two-dimensional case is greater than that in the one-dimensional case.

4   Conclusions

A multidimensional structure that can allow both the non-fuzzy and fuzzy attribute to be indexed together will increase the effectiveness of the fuzzy database while decreasing the storage costs incurred by additional index structures. The efficient execution of queries in object-oriented databases requires the design of specific indexing techniques, to efficiently deal with predicates against nested attributes or against class inheritance hierarchies. Beyond data level fuzziness, there are other kinds of fuzziness such as object/class and class/subclass relations that need be considered in the indexing techniques.

In this study, we have proposed an indexing mechanism for both fuzzy and crisp queries. It can be used for both aggregation and inheritance hierarchies, and handles the fuzzy relations of the FOOD model. Adapting the Path Index and the G-tree structures for indexing the FOOD model resulted in the FOOD Index structure. After constructing FOOD Index structure, we have investigated the retrieval, insertion and deletion algorithms (which are not included in this paper due to the space limitation) in details.

Some performance tests are done for each database operation. In order to understand how efficient the FOOD Index mechanism is, we compared it with the Path Index structure for various types of queries. However, since Path Index is not a multi-dimensional index mechanism, we could not compare the FOOD Index with the Path Index for the two-dimensional cases.

After all the performance tests done, we conclude that the FOOD Index has similar performance to the Path Index for insertion operation, deletion operation, crisp exact match queries and crisp range queries. However, the FOOD Index performs much better for fuzzy queries that the Path Index does. The reason is that the FOOD index is specially designed to handle fuzzy queries efficiently.

References

1. Bertino, E.: An indexing technique for object-oriented databases. Proc. Seventh IEEE Int. Conf. Data Eng., Kobe, Japan, (1991)

2. Bertino, E., Catania, B., Chiesa, L.: Definition and Analysis of Index Organization for Object-Oriented Database System. Information Systems, Vol. 23, No. 2, (1998) 65-108
3. Bertino, E., Guglielmina, C.: Path-index: An approach to the efficient execution of object-oriented queries. Data & Knowledge Engineering, Vol:10, (1993) 1-27
4. Bertino, E., Kim, W.: Indexing techniques for queries on nested objects. IEEE Transaction Knowledge and Data Eng., Vol 1, No 2, (1989) 196-214
5. Bertino, E., Quarati, A.: An approach to support method invocations in object-oriented queries, Proc. Int. Workshop Research Issues in Transactions and Query Processing (RIDE-TQP), Phoenix, Ariz, (1992)
6. Bosc, P., Pivert, O.: Fuzzy Querying in Conventional Databases. In: L. A. Zadeh and J. Kacprzyk (Eds.): Fuzzy Logic for Management of Uncertainty, John Wiley and Sons Inc, (1992) 645-671
7. De Caluwe, R.: Fuzzy and Uncertain Object-Oriented Databases. World Scientific Pub. Co., (1997)
8. George, R., Srikanth, R., Petry, F. E., Buckles, B. P.: Uncertainty Management Issues in the Object-Oriented Data Model. IEEE Transactions on Fuzzy Systems, Vol:4, No:2, (1996)
9. Kemper, A., Moerkotte, G.: Access support in object bases. Proc. ACM-SIGMOD Int. Conf. Management of Data, Denver, Colo., (1991)
10. Kim, W., Kim, K. C., Dale, A.: Indexing techniques for object-oriented databases. In: W. Kim, F. Lochovsky (Eds.): Object-Oriented Concepts, Databases, and Applications, Addison-Wesley, (1989)
11. Kumar, Akhil: G-Tree: A New Data Structure for Organizing Multidimensional Data. IEEE Transactions on Knowledge and Data Engineering, Vol. 6, No.2, (1994) 341-347
12. Liu, C., Ouksel, A., Sistla, P. Wu, J., Yu, C., Rishe, N.: Performance Evaluation of G-tree and Its Application in Fuzzy Databases. Proc. of the fifth international conference on Information and knowledge management, (1996)
13. Maier, D., Stein, J.: Indexing an object-oriented DBMS. Proc. IEEE Workshop Object-Oriented DBMS, Asilomar, Calif., (1986)
14. Yazıcı, A., George, R.: Fuzzy Database Modeling. ISBN: 3-7908-1171-8, Physica-Verlag, Heidelberg, (1999)
15. Yazıcı, A, R. George, and D. Aksoy: Design and Implementation Issues in the Fuzzy Object-Oriented Data Model. Information Sciences (Int. J.), Vol. 108/1-4, (1998) 241-260
16. Yazıcı, A. and D. Cibiceli: An Access Structure for Similarity-Based Databases. Information Sciences (Int. J.), Vol. 115/1-4, (1999) 137-163

Simplification of Integrity Constraints with Aggregates and Arithmetic Built-Ins

Davide Martinenghi

Roskilde University, Computer Science Dept.
P.O.Box 260, DK-4000 Roskilde, Denmark
dm@ruc.dk

Abstract. In the context of relational as well as deductive databases, correct and efficient integrity checking is a crucial issue, as, without any guarantee of data consistency, the answers to queries cannot be trusted. To be of any practical use, any method for integrity checking must support aggregates and arithmetic constraints, which are among the most widespread constructs in current database technology. In this paper we propose a method of practical relevance that can be used to simplify integrity constraints possibly containing aggregates and arithmetic expressions. Simplified versions of the integrity constraints are derived at database design time and can be tested before the execution of any update. In this way, virtually no time is spent for optimization or rollbacks at run time. Both set and bag semantics are considered.

1 Introduction

Correct and efficient integrity checking and maintenance are crucial issues in relational as well as deductive databases. Without proper devices that guarantee the consistency of data, the answers to queries cannot be trusted. Integrity constraints are logical formulas that characterize the consistent states of a database. A complete consistency check often requires linear or worse time complexity with respect to the size of the database, which is too costly in any interesting case. To simplify a set of integrity constraints means to derive specialized checks that can be executed more efficiently at each update, employing the hypothesis that the data were consistent before the update itself. Ideally, these tests should be generated at database design time and executed before any update that may violate the integrity, so that expensive rollback operations become unneeded.

The principle of simplification of integrity constraints has been known and recognized for more than twenty years, with the first important results dating back to [24], and further developed by several other authors. However, the common practice in standard databases is still based on *ad hoc* techniques. Typically, database experts hand-code complicated tests in the application program producing the update requests or, alternatively, design triggers within the database management system that react upon certain update actions. Both methods are prone to errors and not particularly flexible with respect to changes in the schema or design of the database. This motivates the need for automated simplification

H. Christiansen et al. (Eds.): FQAS 2004, LNAI 3055, pp. 348–361, 2004.
© Springer-Verlag Berlin Heidelberg 2004

methods. Standard principles exist (e.g., *partial subsumption* [2]), but none of them seems to have emerged and gained ground in current database implementations, as all have significant limitations (see also section 4). In this paper we focus on the treatment of aggregates and arithmetic expressions in the simplification of integrity constraints, but the method we present, which extends [4], is fairly general, as summarized below.

- It uses a compiled approach: the integrity constraints are simplified at design-time and no computation is needed at run-time to optimize the check.
- It gives a pre-test: only consistency-preserving updates will eventually be given to the database and therefore no rollback operations are needed.
- The pre-test is a necessary and sufficient condition for consistency.
- The updates expressible in the language are so general as to encompass additions, deletions, changes, transactions and transactions patterns.
- It consists of transformation operators that also prove useful in other contexts, such as data mining, data integration, abductive reasoning, etc.

To be of any practical use, any simplification procedure must support aggregates and arithmetic constraints, which are among the most widespread constructs in current database technology. However, the problem of the simplification of integrity constraints containing aggregates seems, with few rare exceptions, to have been largely ignored. In fact, the most comprehensive method we are aware of [10] can only produce tests that are sets of *instances* of the original integrity constraints and does not exploit the fact that those constraints are trusted in the database state before the update.

In this paper we present a series of rewrite rules that allow the decomposition of aggregate expressions into simpler ones that can then be simplified by a constraint solver for arithmetic expressions. The practical significance of these rules is demonstrated with an extensive set of examples.

The paper is organized as follows. The simplification framework is presented in section 2, while its application to integrity constraints with aggregates and arithmetic built-ins is explained and exemplified in section 3. We review existing literature in the field in section 4 and provide concluding remarks in section 5.

2   A Framework for Simplification of Integrity Constraints

2.1   The Language

We assume a function-free first-order typed language equipped with negation and built-ins for equality ($\doteq$) and inequality ($\neq$) of terms. The notions of (typed) *terms* $(t, s, \ldots)$, *variables* $(x, y, \ldots)$, *constants* $(a, b, \ldots)$, *predicates* $(p, q, \ldots)$, *atoms*, *literals* and *formulas* in general are defined as usual. The non-built-in predicates are called database predicates, and similarly for atoms and literals.

Clauses are written in the form *Head* $\leftarrow$ *Body* where the head, if present, is an atom and the body a (perhaps empty) conjunction of literals. We assume in this paper that the clauses are not recursive, i.e., the predicate used in the head of a clause does not occur in its body (directly in the same clause, or indirectly via other clauses). A *denial* is a headless clause and a *fact* is a ground bodiless clause; all other clauses are called *rules*. Logical equivalence between formulas is denoted by $\equiv$, entailment by $\models$, provability by $\vdash$. The notation $\vec{t}$ indicates a sequence of terms $t_1, \ldots, t_n$ and the expressions $p(\vec{t})$, $\vec{s} \doteq \vec{t}$ and $\vec{s} \neq \vec{t}$ are defined accordingly. We assume that all clauses are range restricted[1], as defined below.

Definition 1 (Range restriction). *A variable in a clause is* range bound *if it occurs in the body of the clause either in a positive database literal or in an equality with a constant or another range bound variable. A clause is* range restricted *if all variables in it are range bound. A conjunction C of literals is* range restricted *if the clause $\leftarrow C$ is.*

Furthermore, the language allows built-in *arithmetic constraints* ($<$, $\leq$, $>$, $\geq$), whose arguments are arithmetic expressions. An arithmetic formula is a formula in which all the predicates are arithmetic constraints. An *arithmetic expression* is a numeric term, an aggregate term, or a combination of arithmetic expressions via the four operations ($+$, $-$, $\cdot$, $/$), indicated in infix notation. An *aggregate term* is an expression of the form $A_{[x]}(\exists x_1, \ldots, x_n F)$, where A is an aggregate operator, F is a disjunction of conjunctions of literals in which each disjunct is range restricted, $x_1, \ldots, x_n$ (the *local variables*) are some of the variables in F, and the optional x, if present, is the variable, called *aggregate variable*, among the $x_1, \ldots, x_n$ on which the aggregate function is calculated[2]. The non-local variables in F are called the *global variables*; if F has no global variables, then the argument of the aggregate, called the *key formula*, is said to be closed. The aggregate operators we consider are: Cnt (count), Sum, Max, Min, Avg (average).

Example 1. Given the person relation $p(name, age)$, $\mathsf{Avg}_y(\exists x, y\ p(x, y))$ is an aggregate term that indicates the average age of all persons, while $\mathsf{Cnt}(\exists x\ p(x, 30))$ represents the number of 30 years old persons. □

Subsumption is a widely used syntactic principle that has the semantic property that the subsuming formula entails the subsumed one. We give here a definition for denials.

Definition 2 (Subsumption). *Given two denials D_1, D_2, D_1 subsumes D_2 (indicated $D_1 \sqsubseteq D_2$) iff there is a substitution σ such that each literal in $D_1\sigma$ occurs in D_2.*

Example 2. The denial $\leftarrow p(x, y) \land q(y)$ subsumes $\leftarrow p(x, b) \land x \neq a \land q(b)$. □

In a database we distinguish three components: the *extensional database* (the facts), the *intensional database* (the rules or views) and the *constraint theory* (the integrity constraints) [16]. The constraint theory can be transformed in an equivalent one that does not contain any intensional predicates [2], and for ease of exposition we shall keep this assumption throughout the paper. For other cases

---

[1] Other texts use the terms "safe" or "allowed" to indicate the same notion.
[2] Alternatively, a number could be used instead of x to indicate the position of interest.

where intensional predicates might appear, we refer to the standard principle of *unfolding*, that consists in replacing such predicates by the extensional predicates they are defined upon. By *database state* we refer to the union of the extensional and the intensional parts only. As semantics of a database state D, with default negation for negative literals, we take its *standard model*, as D is here recursion-free and thus *stratified*. The truth value of a closed formula F, relative to D, is defined as its valuation in the standard model and denoted $D(F)$. (See, e.g., [25] for exact definitions for these and other common logical notions.)

Definition 3 (Consistency). *A database state D is* consistent *with a constraint theory Γ iff $D(\Gamma) = true$.*

The semantics of aggregates depends on the semantics underlying the representation of data. Two different semantics are of interest: set semantics, as traditionally used in logic, and bag semantics, typical of database systems. A state D contains, for every database predicate p, a relation p^D; under set semantics p^D is a set of tuples, under bag semantic a bag (or multiset) of tuples, i.e., a set of $\langle tuple, multiplicity \rangle$ pairs. Similarly, a range restricted closed formula F defines a new finite relation F^D, called its *extension*. Under set semantics the extension consists of all different answers that F produces over D; under bag semantics the tuples are the same as for set semantics and the multiplicity of each tuple is the number of times it can be derived over D. We refer to [6, 8] for formal definitions. We note that Max and Min are indifferent of the semantics; for the other aggregates, we use the notation Cnt, Sum, Avg for bag semantics and $\mathsf{Cnt_D}$, $\mathsf{Sum_D}$, $\mathsf{Avg_D}$ when referring to the set of *distinct* tuples.

The method we describe here can handle general forms of update, including additions, deletions and changes. For any predicate p in the database, we can introduce rules that determine how the extension of p is augmented and reduced, respectively indicated with p^+ and p^-, with the only restriction that p^+ and p^- be disjoint and p^+ be defined by range restricted rules.

Definition 4 (Update). *A deletion (resp. addition) referring to an extensional predicate p is a rule (resp. range restricted rule) whose head is an atom with a new name p^- (resp. p^+) having the same arity as p. A non-empty bag of deletions and additions U is an* update *whenever, for every deletion p^- and addition p^+ in the bag, $(D \cup U)(\leftarrow p^+(\vec{x}) \wedge p^-(\vec{x})) = true$ for every state D, where $\vec{x}$ is a sequence of distinct variables matching the arity of p.*

For a state D and an update U, the updated state, indicated D^U, refers to the state obtained from D by changing the extension of every extensional predicate p to the extension of the formula $(p(\vec{x}) \wedge \neg p^-(\vec{x})) \vee p^+(\vec{x})$ in $(D \cup U)$.

Note that, according to definition 4, in both set and bag semantics, when an update U determines the deletion of a tuple $p(\vec{c})$ from a relation p^D in a state D, then all of its occurrences in p^D are removed, i.e., $D^U(p(\vec{c})) = false$. We also allow for special constants called *parameters* (written in boldface: $\mathbf{a}, \mathbf{b}, ...$), i.e., placeholders for constants that permit to generalize updates into update *patterns*, which can be evaluated before knowing the actual values of the update itself. For example, the notation $\{p^+(\mathbf{a}), q^-(\mathbf{a})\}$, where $\mathbf{a}$ is a parameter, refers to the class of update transactions that add a tuple to the unary relation p and remove the same tuple from the unary relation q. We refer to [4] for precise definitions concerning parameters.

2.2   Semantic Notions

We give now a characterization of simplification based on the notion of weakest precondition [9, 18], which is a semantic correctness criterion for a test to be run prior to the execution of the update, i.e., a test that can be checked in the present state but indicating properties of the prospective new state.

Definition 5 (Weakest precondition). *Let Γ and Σ be constraint theories and U an update. Σ is a* weakest precondition *of Γ with respect to U whenever $D(\Sigma) \equiv D^U(\Gamma)$ for any database state D.*

The essence of simplification is the optimization of a weakest precondition based on the invariant that the constraint theory holds in the present state.

Definition 6 (Conditional weakest precondition). *Let Γ, Δ be constraint theories and U an update. A constraint theory Σ is a Δ-conditional weakest precondition (Δ-CWP) of Γ with respect to U whenever $D(\Sigma) \equiv D^U(\Gamma)$ for any database state D consistent with Δ.*

Typically, Δ will include Γ, but it may also contain other knowledge, such as further properties of the database that are trusted. The notion of CWP alone is not sufficient to fully characterize the principle of simplification. In [4,5], an optimality criterion is introduced, which serves as an abstraction over actual computation times without introducing assumptions about any particular evaluation mechanism or referring to any specific database state. For reasons of space, we omit this discussion and approximate optimality with syntactic minimality (minimal number of literals). We note that this is indeed an approximation: in relational databases, for example, a syntactically minimal query does not necessarily evaluate faster than an equivalent non-minimal query in all database states; the amount of computation required to answer a query can be reduced, for instance, by adding a join with a very small relation.

2.3   A Simplification Procedure without Aggregates and Arithmetic

We now describe the transformations that compose a simplification procedure for integrity constraints without aggregates and arithmetic built-ins that was introduced in [4]; we will extend it for these cases in section 3. Given an input constraint theory Γ and an update U, it returns a simplified theory to be tested before U is executed to guarantee that Γ will continue to hold after the update.

Definition 7. *For a constraint theory Γ and an update U, the notation $\mathsf{After}^U(\Gamma)$ refers to a copy of Γ in which all occurrences of an atom of the form $p(\vec{t})$ are simultaneously replaced by the unfolding of the formula:*

$$(p(\vec{t}) \wedge \neg p^-(\vec{t})) \vee p^+(\vec{t}).$$

We assume that the result of the transformation of definition 7 is always given as a set of denials, which can be produced by using, e.g., De Morgan's laws. The semantic correctness of After is expressed by the following property.

Theorem 1. *For any update U and constraint theory Γ, $\text{After}^U(\Gamma)$ is a weakest precondition of Γ with respect to U.*

Clearly, After is not in any "normalized" form, as it may contain redundant denials and sub-formulas (such as, e.g., $a \doteq a$). Moreover, the fact that the original integrity constraints hold in the current database state can be used to achieve further simplification. For this purpose, we define a transformation Optimize that exploits a given constraint theory Δ consisting of trusted hypotheses to simplify the input theory Γ. The proposed implementation [23] is here described in terms of sound rewrite rules. An application of a rewrite rule to a constraint theory always produces a smaller theory. Optimize applies the rules as long as possible and thus removes from Γ every denial that is subsumed by another denial in Δ or Γ and all literals that a restricted resolution principle, called *folding by resolution*, proves to be redundant. Undecidability issues may arise, though, to prove that the resulting theory is indeed minimal; see the end of section 3.2 and [4] for further discussion. In order to guarantee termination, we base the notion of provability, used in the conditions of applicability of the rules, on procedures searching for specific patterns, such as trivially satisfied (in)equalities, and other purely syntactic notions, such as subsumption.

Definition 8. *Given two constraint theories Δ and Γ, $\text{Optimize}_\Delta(\Gamma)$ is the result of applying the following rewrite rules on Γ as long as possible. In the following, x is a variable, t is a term, A, B are (possibly empty) conjunctions of literals, L is a literal, σ a substitution, ϕ, ψ are denials, Γ' is a constraint theory.*

$$
\begin{aligned}
\{\leftarrow x \doteq t \wedge A\} \cup \Gamma' &\Rightarrow \{\leftarrow A\{x/t\}\} \cup \Gamma' \\
\{\leftarrow A \wedge B\} \cup \Gamma' &\Rightarrow \{\leftarrow A\} \cup \Gamma' \text{ if } A \vdash B \\
\{\phi\} \cup \Gamma' &\Rightarrow \Gamma' \text{ if } \exists \psi \in (\Gamma' \cup \Delta) : \psi \sqsubseteq \phi \\
\{\leftarrow A\} \cup \Gamma' &\Rightarrow \Gamma' \text{ if } A \vdash \mathit{false} \\
\{(\leftarrow A \wedge \neg L \wedge B)\sigma\} \cup \Gamma' &\Rightarrow \{(\leftarrow A \wedge B)\sigma\} \cup \Gamma' \text{ if } (\Gamma \cup \Delta) \vdash \{\leftarrow A \wedge L\}
\end{aligned}
$$

The principle of folding by resolution is indicated in the last rule. It can be implemented, e.g., with a data driven procedure that looks in the deductive closure of $(\Gamma \cup \Delta)$ containing denials whose size is not bigger than the biggest denial in Γ.

The operators defined so far can be assembled to define a procedure for simplification of integrity constraints, where the updates always take place from a consistent state.

Definition 9. *For two constraint theories Γ and Δ and an update U, we define*

$$\text{Simp}_\Delta^U(\Gamma) = \text{Optimize}_\Delta(\text{After}^U(\Gamma)).$$

We observe that Simp preserves range restriction, as all the steps in After and Optimize do. We state now its correctness and refer to [4] for a proof.

Theorem 2. Simp *terminates on any input and, for any constraint theories* Γ, Δ *and update* U, $\mathsf{Simp}_\Delta^U(\Gamma)$ *is a* Δ-*CWP of* Γ *with respect to* U.

In the following, $\mathsf{Simp}^U(\Gamma)$ is a shorthand for $\mathsf{Simp}_\Gamma^U(\Gamma)$.

Example 3. Let $\Gamma = \{\leftarrow p(x) \wedge q(x)\}$, $U = \{p^+(\mathbf{a})\}$, where $\mathbf{a}$ is a parameter. The simplification is as follows:

$$\mathsf{After}^U(\Gamma) = \{ \leftarrow q(x) \wedge x \doteq \mathbf{a},$$
$$\leftarrow p(x) \wedge q(x) \quad \},$$
$$\mathsf{Simp}^U(\Gamma) = \{ \leftarrow q(\mathbf{a})\}. \qquad \qquad \square$$

3   Extension to Aggregates and Arithmetic

3.1   Extension of the Simplification Framework

The constraint theory output by After holds in the current state if and only if the input theory holds in the updated state. Each predicate in the input theory is therefore replaced by an expression that indicates the extension it would have in the updated state. Unsurprisingly, theorem 1 can be proven also in the presence of aggregates and arithmetic, without modifying definition 7. We always express key formulas as disjunctions of conjunctions of literals; again, this can be done by simple (bag) semantics-preserving transformations such as De Morgan's laws.

Example 4. Let $\Gamma = \{\leftarrow \mathsf{Cnt}(\exists x\, p(x)) < 10\}$, $U = \{p^+(\mathbf{a})\}$, then:

$$\mathsf{After}^U(\Gamma) = \{\leftarrow \mathsf{Cnt}(\exists x\, p(x) \vee x \doteq \mathbf{a}) < 10\}. \qquad \square$$

The new Cnt expression returned by After should indicate an increment by one with respect to the original expression. In order to determine this effect, we need to divide the expression into smaller pieces that can possibly be used during the simplification of weakest preconditions. To do that, we extend definition 8 with a set of sound rewrite rules for aggregates. Note that care must be taken when applying transformations that preserve logical equivalence on aggregates with bag semantics. Consider, for instance, $\mathsf{Sum}_x(\exists x\, p(x) \wedge x \doteq 1)$ and $\mathsf{Sum}_x(\exists x\, (p(x) \wedge x \doteq 1) \vee (p(x) \wedge x \doteq 1))$. Their key formulas are logically equivalent, but in the latter, the tuple $p(1)$ occurs twice as many times. In other words, the results may differ because the number of ways in which the key formula may succeed matters.

With regard to arithmetic constraints and expressions, we base the applicability of these rules on the presence of a standard constraint solver for arithmetic; see, e.g., [7, 19]. We use the notation $\mathcal{A} \leadsto_\mathcal{C} \mathcal{A}'$ to indicate that a constraint solver $\mathcal{C}$ reduces, in finite time, arithmetic formula $\mathcal{A}$ to a simpler formula $\mathcal{A}'$. We now extend the notion of subsumption to denials containing arithmetic constraints.

Definition 10 (Subsumption). *Let* $\mathcal{C}$ *be a constraint solver for arithmetic and* D_1, D_2 *be denials of the form* $\leftarrow C_1 \wedge \mathcal{A}_1$ *and* $\leftarrow C_2 \wedge \mathcal{A}_2$, *respectively, where* C_1, C_2 *are conjunctions of literals and* $\mathcal{A}_1, \mathcal{A}_2$ *arithmetic formulas. Then* D_1 *subsumes* D_2 *with respect to* $\mathcal{C}$ *(indicated* $D_1 \sqsubseteq_\mathcal{C} D_2$) *iff there is a substitution* σ *such that each literal in* $C_1\sigma$ *occurs in* C_2 *and* $\mathcal{A}_2 \wedge \neg \mathcal{A}_1\sigma \leadsto_\mathcal{C}$ *false.*

Example 5. Consider the following integrity constraints:

$$\phi = \leftarrow \mathsf{Cnt}(\exists x\ p(x,y)) < 10 \wedge q(y)$$
$$\psi = \leftarrow \mathsf{Cnt}(\exists x\ p(x,b)) < 9 \wedge q(b) \wedge r(z).$$

For any constraint solver $\mathcal{C}$ for which

$$\mathsf{Cnt}(\exists x\ p(x,b)) < 9 \wedge \mathsf{Cnt}(\exists x\ p(x,b)) \geq 10 \rightsquigarrow_\mathcal{C} \textit{false}$$

we have $\phi \sqsubseteq_\mathcal{C} \psi$. □

To make the definitions more readable, we introduce *conditional expressions*, i.e., arithmetic expressions written If C Then E_1 Else E_2, which indicate arithmetic expression E_1 if condition C holds, E_2 otherwise. Similarly, we introduce two binary arithmetic operators max and min and define them in terms of conditional expressions. Furthermore, we take liberties in rewrite rules to omit portions of formulas and expressions with leading and trailing ellipses $(\dots)$; they identify the same portions in both sides of the rules. Square brackets in the subscript of an aggregate indicate that the rule applies both with and without the subscript.

Definition 11. *Given two constraint theories Δ and Γ and a constraint solver for arithmetic $\mathcal{C}$, $\mathsf{Optimize}_{\mathcal{C}\,\Delta}(\Gamma)$ is the result of applying the following rewrite rules and those of definition 8 on Γ as long as possible, where x is a local variable, y a global one, $\vec{x}$ a (possibly empty) sequence of distinct local variables $x_1, \dots, x_n$ different from x, A, B, C are range restricted conjunctions of literals (C with no local variables), E_1, E_2 arithmetic expressions, $\mathcal{A}_1, \mathcal{A}_2, \mathcal{A}_3$ arithmetic formulas, t, s terms, c a constant, F a key formula, Γ' a constraint theory, σ a substitution, Agg any aggregate.*

Rules for all aggregates

$$\mathsf{Agg}_{[x_i]}(\exists \vec{x}\ A \wedge t \doteq t) \Rightarrow \mathsf{Agg}_{[x_i]}(\exists \vec{x}\ A)$$
$$\mathsf{Agg}_x(\exists \vec{x}, x\ A \wedge x \doteq x_i) \Rightarrow \mathsf{Agg}_{x_i}(\exists \vec{x}\ A\{x/x_i\})$$
$$\mathsf{Agg}_{[x_i]}(\exists \vec{x}, x\ A \wedge x \doteq t) \Rightarrow \mathsf{Agg}_{[x_i]}(\exists \vec{x}\ A\{x/t\})$$
$$\mathsf{Agg}_{[x_i]}(\exists \vec{x}\ A \wedge y \doteq t) \Rightarrow \text{If } y \doteq t \text{ Then } \mathsf{Agg}_{[x_i]}(\exists \vec{x}\ A\{y/t\}) \text{ Else } \perp^3$$
$$\mathsf{Agg}_{[x_i]}(\exists \vec{x}\ A) \Rightarrow \perp \text{ if } A \vdash \textit{false}$$

Rules for Cnt and Cnt_D

$$\mathsf{Cnt}(\exists \vec{x}\ A \vee B) \Rightarrow \mathsf{Cnt}(\exists \vec{x}\ A) + \mathsf{Cnt}(\exists \vec{x}\ B)$$
$$\mathsf{Cnt}_\mathsf{D}(\exists \vec{x}\ A \vee B) \Rightarrow \mathsf{Cnt}_\mathsf{D}(\exists \vec{x}\ A) + \mathsf{Cnt}_\mathsf{D}(\exists \vec{x}\ B) - \mathsf{Cnt}_\mathsf{D}(\exists \vec{x}\ A \wedge B)$$
$$\mathsf{Cnt}_{[\mathsf{D}]}(\exists \vec{x}\ A \wedge t \neq s) \Rightarrow \mathsf{Cnt}_{[\mathsf{D}]}(\exists \vec{x}\ A) - \mathsf{Cnt}_{[\mathsf{D}]}(\exists \vec{x}\ A \wedge t \doteq s)$$
$$\mathsf{Cnt}(\textit{true}) \Rightarrow 1$$
$$\mathsf{Cnt}_\mathsf{D}(C) \Rightarrow \text{If } C \text{ Then } 1 \text{ Else } 0$$

---

[3] Provided that t is not a local variable. The $\perp$ symbol indicates the value that applies to an empty bag of tuples (0 for Cnt, Sum, $-\infty$ for Max, $+\infty$ for Min, etc.).

Rules for Sum, Avg and $\mathsf{Sum_D}$, $\mathsf{Avg_D}$

$$\mathsf{Sum}_{x_i}(\exists \vec{x}\ A \vee B) \;\Rightarrow\; \mathsf{Sum}_{x_i}(\exists \vec{x}\ A) + \mathsf{Sum}_{x_i}(\exists \vec{x}\ B)$$
$$\mathsf{Sum}_{\mathsf{D}x_i}(\exists \vec{x}\ A \vee B) \;\Rightarrow\; \mathsf{Sum}_{\mathsf{D}x_i}(\exists \vec{x}\ A) + \mathsf{Sum}_{\mathsf{D}x_i}(\exists \vec{x}\ B) - \mathsf{Sum}_{\mathsf{D}x_i}(\exists \vec{x}\ A \wedge B)$$
$$\mathsf{Sum}_{[\mathsf{D}]x_i}(\exists \vec{x}\ A \wedge t \neq s) \;\Rightarrow\; \mathsf{Sum}_{[\mathsf{D}]x_i}(\exists \vec{x}\ A) - \mathsf{Sum}_{[\mathsf{D}]x_i}(\exists \vec{x}\ A \wedge t \doteq s)$$
$$\mathsf{Sum}_{[\mathsf{D}]x}(\exists \vec{x}, x\ A \wedge x \doteq c) \;\Rightarrow\; c \cdot \mathsf{Cnt}_{[\mathsf{D}]}(\exists \vec{x}\ A\{x/c\})$$
$$\mathsf{Avg}_{[\mathsf{D}]x}(F) \;\Rightarrow\; \mathsf{Sum}_{[\mathsf{D}]x}(F)/\mathsf{Cnt}_{[\mathsf{D}]}(F)$$

Rules for Max and Min

$$\mathsf{Max}_{x_i}(\exists \vec{x}\ A \vee B) \;\Rightarrow\; \max(\mathsf{Max}_{x_i}(\exists \vec{x}\ A), \mathsf{Max}_{x_i}(\exists \vec{x}\ B))$$
$$\mathsf{Max}_x(\exists \vec{x}, x\ A \wedge x \doteq c) \;\Rightarrow\; \text{If } \exists \vec{x}\ A\{x/c\} \text{ Then } c \text{ Else } -\infty$$
$$\mathsf{Min}_{x_i}(\exists \vec{x}\ A \vee B) \;\Rightarrow\; \min(\mathsf{Min}_{x_i}(\exists \vec{x}\ A), \mathsf{Min}_{x_i}(\exists \vec{x}\ B))$$
$$\mathsf{Min}_x(\exists \vec{x}, x\ A \wedge x \doteq c) \;\Rightarrow\; \text{If } \exists \vec{x}\ A\{x/c\} \text{ Then } c \text{ Else } +\infty$$

Rules for conditional expressions

$$\{\leftarrow \ldots \text{If } C \text{ Then } E_1 \text{ Else } E_2 \ldots\} \;\Rightarrow\; \{\leftarrow C \wedge \ldots E_1 \ldots, \; \leftarrow \neg C \wedge \ldots E_2 \ldots\}$$
$$\max(E_1, E_2) \;\Rightarrow\; \text{If } E_1 > E_2 \text{ Then } E_1 \text{ Else } E_2$$
$$\min(E_1, E_2) \;\Rightarrow\; \text{If } E_1 < E_2 \text{ Then } E_1 \text{ Else } E_2$$

Rules for the interaction with the arithmetic constraint solver

$$\{\phi\} \cup \Gamma' \;\Rightarrow\; \Gamma' \text{ if } \exists \psi \in (\Gamma' \cup \Delta) : \psi \sqsubseteq_{\mathcal{C}} \phi$$
$$\{\leftarrow A \wedge \mathcal{A}_1\} \;\Rightarrow\; \{\leftarrow A \wedge \mathcal{A}_2\} \text{ if } \mathcal{A}_1 \rightsquigarrow_{\mathcal{C}} \mathcal{A}_2$$
$$\{\leftarrow A \wedge \mathcal{A}_1, \; \leftarrow A\sigma \wedge \mathcal{A}_2\} \;\Rightarrow\; \{\leftarrow A \wedge \mathcal{A}_1, \; \leftarrow A\sigma \wedge \mathcal{A}_3\} \text{ if } \mathcal{A}_1\sigma \vee \mathcal{A}_2 \rightsquigarrow_{\mathcal{C}} \mathcal{A}_3 \;{}^{4}$$

In the remainder of the paper, we shall omit the indication of existential quantifiers when it is clear from the context that the variables they refer to are local.

Example 6. Consider the aggregates $A_1 = \mathsf{Cnt}(\exists x\ p(x) \wedge x \neq \mathbf{a})$ and $A_2 = \mathsf{Sum}_x(\exists x\ p(x) \wedge x \neq \mathbf{a})$, $\mathbf{a}$ a numeric parameter. The following rewrites apply:

$$A_1 \;\Rightarrow\; \mathsf{Cnt}(\exists x\ p(x)) - \mathsf{Cnt}(\exists x\ p(x) \wedge x \doteq \mathbf{a}) \;\Rightarrow\; \mathsf{Cnt}(\exists x\ p(x)) - \mathsf{Cnt}(p(\mathbf{a})).$$
$$A_2 \;\Rightarrow\; \mathsf{Sum}_x(p(x)) - \mathsf{Sum}_x(p(x) \wedge x \doteq \mathbf{a}) \;\Rightarrow\; \mathsf{Sum}_x(p(x)) - \mathbf{a} \cdot \mathsf{Cnt}(p(\mathbf{a})).$$

Note that the fourth Sum rule in definition 11 indicates that when the value of the aggregate variable is known, the sum will equal that value multiplied by the number of times the aggregate formula succeeds.   □

The simplification procedure can now be extended with these new rules.

Definition 12. *For two constraint theories Γ and Δ, a constraint solver for arithmetic $\mathcal{C}$ and an update U, we define*

$$\mathsf{Simpc}_{\Delta}^{U}(\Gamma) = \mathsf{Optimize}_{\mathcal{C}\Delta}(\mathsf{After}^{U}(\Gamma)).$$

The correctness of $\mathsf{Simp}_{\mathcal{C}}$ is stated as in theorem 2 for Simp, with the extra assumption that the constraint solver for arithmetic always terminates.

Theorem 3. *Given a constraint solver for arithmetic $\mathcal{C}$ that terminates on any input, $\mathsf{Simp}_{\mathcal{C}}$ terminates on any input and, for any constraint theories Γ and Δ and update U, $\mathsf{Simpc}_{\Delta}^{U}(\Gamma)$ is a Δ-CWP of Γ with respect to U.*

In the following, $\mathsf{Simpc}^{U}(\Gamma)$ is a shorthand for $\mathsf{Simpc}_{\Gamma}^{U}(\Gamma)$.

---

[4] Note that when σ is a renaming, the first produced denial is redundant and will be eliminated by the first of these three rules.

3.2   Examples of Simplification

We show now a series of examples that demonstrate the behavior of the rules and the simplification procedure in various cases; for readability, we leave out some of the trivial steps.

Example 7 (4 continued). Let $\Gamma = \{\leftarrow \mathsf{Cnt}(\exists x\, p(x)) < 10\}$, $U = \{p^+(\mathbf{a})\}$, then:

$$
\begin{aligned}
\mathsf{Simp}_\mathcal{C}^U(\Gamma) &= \mathsf{Optimize}_{\mathcal{C}\Gamma}(\{\leftarrow \mathsf{Cnt}(\exists x\, p(x) \vee x \doteq \mathbf{a}) < 10\}) \\
&= \mathsf{Optimize}_{\mathcal{C}\Gamma}(\{\leftarrow \mathsf{Cnt}(\exists x\, p(x)) + \mathsf{Cnt}(\exists x\, x \doteq \mathbf{a}) < 10\}) \\
&= \mathsf{Optimize}_{\mathcal{C}\Gamma}(\{\leftarrow \mathsf{Cnt}(\exists x\, p(x)) + 1 < 10\}) = true.
\end{aligned}
$$

The update increments the count of p-tuples, which was known (Γ) to be at least 10 before the update, so this increment cannot undermine the validity of Γ itself. The last step, obtained via subsumption, allows to conclude that no check is necessary to guarantee the consistency of the updated database state.   □

Example 8. Let $\Gamma = \{\leftarrow \mathsf{Cnt}_\mathsf{D}(\exists x\, p(x)) \neq 10\}$ (there must be exactly 10 *distinct* p-tuples) and $U = \{p^+(\mathbf{a})\}$. With a set semantics, the increment of the count depends on the existence of the tuple $p(\mathbf{a})$ in the state:

$$
\begin{aligned}
\mathsf{Simp}_\mathcal{C}^U(\Gamma) &= \mathsf{Optimize}_{\mathcal{C}\Gamma}(\{\leftarrow \mathsf{Cnt}_\mathsf{D}(\exists x\, p(x) \vee x \doteq \mathbf{a}) \neq 10\}) \\
&= \mathsf{Optimize}_{\mathcal{C}\Gamma}(\{\leftarrow \mathsf{Cnt}_\mathsf{D}(\exists x\, p(x)) + 1 - \mathsf{Cnt}_\mathsf{D}(p(\mathbf{a})) \neq 10\}) \\
&= \mathsf{Optimize}_{\mathcal{C}\Gamma}(\{\leftarrow \mathsf{Cnt}_\mathsf{D}(\exists x\, p(x)) + 1 - \mathsf{If}\ p(\mathbf{a})\ \mathsf{Then}\ 1\ \mathsf{Else}\ 0 \neq 10\}) \\
&= \mathsf{Optimize}_{\mathcal{C}\Gamma}(\{\leftarrow p(\mathbf{a}) \wedge \mathsf{Cnt}_\mathsf{D}(\exists x\, p(x)) + 1 - 1 \neq 10, \\
&\qquad\qquad\qquad \leftarrow \neg p(\mathbf{a}) \wedge \mathsf{Cnt}_\mathsf{D}(\exists x\, p(x)) + 1 - 0 \neq 10\}) \\
&= \{\leftarrow \neg p(\mathbf{a})\}.
\end{aligned}
$$

The arithmetic constraint solver intervenes in the last step using the knowledge from Γ that the original Cnt_D expression is equal to 10.   □

Example 9. When global variables occur, conditional expressions are used to separate different cases. Let $\Gamma = \{\leftarrow \mathsf{Cnt}(\exists x\, p(x,y)) > 10 \wedge q(y)\}$ (there cannot be more than 10 p-tuples whose second argument is in q) and $U = \{p^+(\mathbf{a}, \mathbf{b})\}$.

$$
\begin{aligned}
\mathsf{Simp}_\mathcal{C}^U(\Gamma) &= \mathsf{Optimize}_{\mathcal{C}\Gamma}(\mathsf{After}^U(\Gamma)) \\
&= \mathsf{Optimize}_{\mathcal{C}\Gamma}(\{\leftarrow \mathsf{Cnt}(\exists x\, p(x,y)) + \mathsf{Cnt}(\exists x\, x \doteq \mathbf{a} \wedge y \doteq \mathbf{b}) > 10 \wedge q(y)\}) \\
&= \mathsf{Optimize}_{\mathcal{C}\Gamma}(\{\leftarrow \mathsf{Cnt}(\exists x\, p(x,y)) + \mathsf{Cnt}(y \doteq \mathbf{b}) > 10 \wedge q(y)\}) \\
&= \mathsf{Optimize}_{\mathcal{C}\Gamma}(\{\leftarrow \mathsf{Cnt}(\exists x\, p(x,y)) + \mathsf{If}\ y \doteq \mathbf{b}\ \mathsf{Then}\ 1\ \mathsf{Else}\ 0 > 10 \wedge q(y)\}) \\
&= \mathsf{Optimize}_{\mathcal{C}\Gamma}(\{\leftarrow y \doteq \mathbf{b} \wedge \mathsf{Cnt}(\exists x\, p(x,y)) + 1 > 10 \wedge q(y), \\
&\qquad\qquad\qquad \leftarrow y \neq \mathbf{b} \wedge \mathsf{Cnt}(\exists x\, p(x,y)) + 0 > 10 \wedge q(y)\}) \\
&= \{\leftarrow \mathsf{Cnt}(\exists x\, p(x, \mathbf{b})) > 9 \wedge q(\mathbf{b})\}.
\end{aligned}
$$

In the last step, the second constraint is subsumed by Γ and thus eliminated.□

Example 10. We propose now an example with a complex update. Let $e(x,y,z)$ represent employees of a company, where x is the name, y the years of service and z the salary. The company's policy is expressed by

$$
\begin{aligned}
\Gamma = \{ &\leftarrow e(x,y,z) \wedge z \doteq \mathsf{Max}_{z_l}(e(x_l, y_l, z_l)) \wedge y < 5, \\
&\leftarrow e(x,y,z) \wedge z \doteq \mathsf{Max}_{z_l}(e(x_l, y_l, z_l)) \wedge y > 8) \}
\end{aligned}
$$

i.e., the seniority of the best paid employee must be between 5 and 8 years, and

$$U = \{ \ e^+(x, y_2, z) \leftarrow e(x, y_1, z) \wedge y_2 \doteq y_1 + 1,$$
$$e^-(x, y, z) \leftarrow e(x, y, z) \qquad \qquad \}$$

is the update transaction that is executed at the end of the year to increase the seniority of all employees. Note that the application of After^U to a literal of the form $e(x, y, z)$ generates

$$(e(x, y, z) \wedge \neg e(x, y, z)) \vee (e(x, y', z) \wedge y \doteq y' + 1)$$

in which the first disjunct is logically equivalent to *false* and, thus, removed by $\mathsf{Optimize}_C$. Similarly, the aggregate expression is transformed by $\mathsf{After}^U(\Gamma)$ into

$$\mathsf{Max}_{z_l}(e(x_l, y'_l, z_l) \wedge y_l \doteq y'_l + 1)$$

which is simplified by $\mathsf{Optimize}_C$ into $\mathsf{Max}_{z_l}(e(x_l, y'_l, z_l))$ and thus coincides, modulo renaming, with the original one in Γ. After the optimization steps described above, $\mathsf{After}^U(\Gamma)$ is transformed into:

$$\{ \leftarrow e(x, y', z) \wedge y \doteq y' + 1 \wedge z \doteq \mathsf{Max}_{z_l}(e(x_l, y_l, z_l)) \wedge y < 5,$$
$$\leftarrow e(x, y', z) \wedge y \doteq y' + 1 \wedge z \doteq \mathsf{Max}_{z_l}(e(x_l, y_l, z_l)) \wedge y > 8)\}.$$

The arithmetic constraint solver eliminates y and generates the arithmetic constraint $y' < 4$ for the first denial and $y' > 7$ for the second one. Then the first denial is subsumed by the first denial in Γ and we finally obtain:

$$\mathsf{Simp}_C^U(\Gamma) = \{ \leftarrow e(x, y', z) \wedge z \doteq \mathsf{Max}_{z_l}(e(x_l, y_l, z_l)) \wedge y' > 7\}. \qquad \square$$

In all the examples shown in this section the results are minimal, i.e., no smaller theory can be found that is also a conditional weakest precondition with respect to the given update. However, as mentioned in section 2.3, it might be impossible in general to determine whether the obtained result is minimal, as this seems to amount to the query containment problem in DATALOG, which is known to be undecidable. Alternatively, one could enumerate all constraint theories smaller in size than the obtained result, as the set of symbols is finite. However, the problem of determining whether a constraint theory is a conditional weakest precondition seems to be undecidable as well. Furthermore, the quality of the simplification produced by Simp_C is highly dependent on the precision of the constraint solver for arithmetic, which might be unable to reduce particular combinations of arithmetic constraints. In this respect, we found that the constraint language of constraint handling rules (CHR, [13]) seems to be particularly suitable for an implementation of the solver. Finally we note that the interaction between the solver and the simplification procedure, characterized by the last three rules of definition 11, captures many interesting cases in which arithmetic-based simplifications are possible, even across different constraints in a theory (last rule), but we cannot exclude that more complex cases escape this definition.

4 Related Works

As pointed out in section 1, the principle of simplification of integrity constraints is essential for optimizations in database consistency checking. A central quality of any good approach to integrity checking is the ability to verify the consistency of a database to be updated *before* the execution of the transaction in question, so that inconsistent states are completely avoided. Several approaches to simplification do not comply with this requirement, e.g., [24, 22, 11, 15]. Among these, we mention the resolution-based principle of partial subsumption [2, 15], which is important in semantic query optimization, although its use for simplification of integrity constraints is rather limited, as transactions are only partly allowed. Other methods, e.g., [17], provide pre-tests that, however, are not proven to be necessary conditions; in other words, if the tests fail, nothing can be concluded about the consistency. Qian presented in [26] a powerful simplification procedure that, however, does not allow more than one update action in a transaction to operate on the same relation and has no mechanism corresponding to parameters, thus requiring to execute the procedure for each update. Most works in the field lack a characterization of what it means for a formula to be simplified. Our view is that a transformed integrity constraint, in order to qualify as "simplified", must represent a minimum (or a good approximation thereof) in some ordering that reflects the effort of actually evaluating it. We propose a simple ordering based on the number of literals but we have no proof that our algorithm reaches a minimum in all cases. Most simplification methods do not allow recursion. The rare exceptions we are aware of (e.g., [22, 21, 3]) hardly provide useful simplified checks: when recursive rules are present, these methods typically output the same constraints as in the input set. None of the methods described so far can handle aggregates and only [3] considers arithmetic constraints.

The constraint solver for finite domains described in [7] and available in current Prolog systems is able to handle the arithmetic part of most of the examples and rules described in this paper (for integers). An implementation of the solver and the rules that characterize its interaction with the simplification procedure is also possible with the language of constraint handling rules [13], which is an extremely versatile tool for constraint programming. For a survey on constraint solvers and constraint logic programming in general we refer to [19].

In [10] Das extends the simplification method of [22] and applies it to aggregates. However, the hypotheses about the consistency of the database prior to the update is not exploited; consequently, the simplified test can only be a set of instances of the original constraints. In our example 7, for instance, Das' method would return the initial constraint theory, whereas we were able to conclude that no check was needed. In [8], the authors describe query optimization techniques and complexity results under set and bag semantics and introduce the important *bag-set semantics*, i.e., the semantics corresponding to the assumption that database relations are sets, but queries may generate duplicates due to projection. This semantics has been used in subsequent work, e.g., [6], to approach problems concerning queries with aggregates, such as query rewriting using views. A definition of the semantics of SQL with aggregates is given in [1], where it is shown how to translate a subset of SQL into relational calculus and algebra and general strategies for query optimization are investigated for such cases. Further investigation on the semantics of aggregates is given in [20, 12, 28]. In [14] it is shown how to optimize, by *propagation*, queries with maximum and minimum aggregates in a possibly recursive setting. User-defined and on-line aggregates are described in [27] and their use is demonstrated for data mining and other advanced database applications.

5   Conclusion

We presented a set of rewrite rules that can be applied to a set of integrity constraints containing aggregates and arithmetic expressions in order to obtain simplified tests that serve to ensure the consistency of the database before any update is made. Our approach is a first attempt to simplify aggregate expressions in a systematic way producing a necessary and sufficient condition for consistency. The rules we have presented are of practical relevance, as shown in a number of examples, and should be considered as a starting point for possibly more complete and refined simplification procedures. Although not all details were spelled out, we have shown the interaction with a constraint solver to handle combinations of arithmetic constraints. Future directions include, to name a few, the extension to aggregates with recursion and user-defined aggregates.

Acknowledgements

The author wishes to thank Henning Christiansen and Amos Scisci for many helpful comments and suggestions.

References

1. Bülzingsloewen, G. Translating and Optimizing SQL Queries Having Aggregates. *VLDB 1987*: 235–243, Morgan Kaufmann (1987).
2. Chakravarthy, U. S., Grant, J., Minker, J. Foundations of semantic query optimization for deductive databases. *Foundations of Deductive Databases and Logic Programming*: 243–273, Minker, J. (Ed.), Morgan Kaufmann (1988).
3. Chakravarthy, U., Grant, J., Minker, J. Logic-based approach to semantic query optimization. *ACM TODS* 15(2): 162–207, ACM Press (1990).
4. Christiansen, H., Martinenghi, D., Simplification of database integrity constraints revisited: A transformational approach. *LOPSTR 2003*, to appear in LNCS, Springer (2004).
5. Christiansen, H., Martinenghi, D. Simplification of integrity constraints for data integration. *FoIKS 2004*: 31–48, LNCS 2942, Springer (2004).
6. Cohen, S., Nutt, W., Serebrenik, A. Algorithms for Rewriting Aggregate Queries Using Views. *ADBIS-DASFAA 2000*: 65–78, LNCS 1884, Springer (2000).
7. Carlsson, M., Ottosson, G., Carlson, B. An Open-Ended Finite Domain Constraint Solver. *PLILP 1997*: 191–206, LNCS 1292, Springer (1997).

8. Chaudhuri, S., Vardi., M. Optimization of *real* conjunctive queries. *ACM SIGACT-SIGMOD-SIGART PODS 1993*: 59–70, ACM Press (1993).

9. Dijkstra, E.W. A Discipline of Programming. Prentice-Hall (1976).

10. Das, S. Deductive Databases and Logic Programming. Addison-Wesley (1992).

11. Decker, H., Celma, M. A slick procedure for integrity checking in deductive databases. *ICLP 1994*: 456–469, MIT Press (1994).

12. Denecker, M., Pelov, N., Bruynooghe, M. Ultimate Well-founded and Stable Semantics for Logic Programs with Aggregates. *ICLP 2001*: 212–226, LNCS 2237, Springer (2001).

13. Frühwirth, T.W. Theory and Practice of Constraint Handling Rules, *JLP* 37(1-3): 95–138 (1998).

14. Furfaro, F., Greco, S., Ganguly, S., Zaniolo, C. Pushing extrema aggregates to optimize logic queries. *Inf. Syst.* 27(5): 321–343, Elsevier (2002).

15. Grant, J., Minker, J. Integrity Constraints in Knowledge Based Systems. In *Knowledge Eng. II, Applications*: 1–25, Adeli, H. (Ed.), McGraw-Hill (1990).

16. Godfrey, P., Grant, J., Gryz, J., Minker, J. Integrity Constraints: Semantics and Applications. *Logics for Databases and Information System*: 265–306, Chomicki, J. Saake, G. (Eds.), Kluwer (1988).

17. Henschen, L., McCune, W., Naqvi, S. Compiling Constraint-Checking Programs from First-Order Formulas. *Advances in Database Theory 1982*, volume 2: 145–169, Gallaire, H., Nicolas, J.-M., Minker, J. (Eds.), Plenum Press (1984).

18. Hoare, C.A.R. (1969). An axiomatic basis for computer programming. *Commun. ACM* 12(10): 576–580, ACM Press (1969).

19. Jaffar, J, Maher, M. Constraint Logic Programming: A Survey. *JLP* 19/20: 503–581 (1994).

20. Kemp, D., Stuckey, P. Semantics of Logic Programs with Aggregates. *ISLP 1991*: 387–401, MIT Press (1991)

21. Leuschel, M., De Schreye, D. Creating Specialised Integrity Checks Through Partial Evaluation of Meta-Interpreters. *JLP* 36(2): 149–193 (1998).

22. Lloyd, J., Sonenberg, L., Topor, R. (1987). Integrity Constraint Checking in Stratified Databases. *JLP* 4(4): 331–343 (1987).

23. Martinenghi, D. A Simplification Procedure for Integrity Constraints. *World Wide Web*, http://www.dat.ruc.dk/~dm/spic/index.html (2003).

24. Nicolas, J.-M. Logic for Improving Integrity Checking in Relational Data Bases., *Acta Inf.* 18: 227–253 (1982).

25. Nilsson, U., Małuzyński, J. Logic, Programming and Prolog (2nd ed.), John Wiley & Sons Ltd. (1995).

26. Qian, X. An Effective Method for Integrity Constraint Simplification. *ICDE 1988*: 338–345, IEEE Computer Society (1988).

27. Wang, H., Zaniolo, C. User-Defined Aggregates in Database Languages, *DBPL 1999*: 43–60, LNCS 1949, Springer (2002).

28. Zaniolo, C. Key Constraints and Monotonic Aggregates in Deductive Databases. *Comput. Logic*: 109–134, LNAI 2408, Springer (2002).

QBF: A Query Broker Framework
for Adaptable Query Evaluation*

Christine Collet and Tuyet-Trinh Vu

LSR-IMAG Laboratory, INP Grenoble
B.P. 72, 38402 Saint-Martin d'Hères, France
{Christine.Collet,Tuyet-Trinh.Vu}@imag.fr

Abstract. We present QBF (Query Broker Framework), a query evaluation framework that facilitates reuse and design of flexible query processors. QBF integrates existing optimization and execution mechanisms in a uniform way. It allows the use of multiple mechanisms to efficiently and adaptively evaluate queries according to application requirements. The smallest query evaluation unit built from QBF is called a Query Broker. Query brokers can be organized in hierarchies for evaluating queries. The paper describes the QBF components and the way they interact. It also introduces one implementation of these components so as illustrating query processing strategies supported by QBF and their use.

Keywords: Query Processing, Adaptable Query Evaluation, Query Framework

1 Introduction

The increasing use of computers and the development of communication infrastructures have led to large-scale information systems also called data distribution systems (DDS) [1,2]. In such systems, querying is one of the most important functions that allows accessing and sharing data among information sources. However, processing queries in DDS is difficult because of large volumes of data distributed over networks, of heterogeneity and autonomy of underlying sources. As a result, query evaluators may use complicated techniques resolving problems related to network delays, out of memory, etc. Moreover, clients (of DDS) may have different requirements for processing data such as source preference, time limit for query evaluation, number of results being handled by a client, economic cost limit for accessing data in case of paying sources, etc. Some of them can wish to get results in brief delay even if they are not complete while others need complete and exact results. Different mechanisms [3–8] have been proposed to respond to one or several requirements previously described. However, such mechanisms have been designed and implemented for systems having specific characteristics.

---

* This work is part of the MEDIAGRID Project, supported by the french ACI Grid program.

H. Christiansen et al. (Eds.): FQAS 2004, LNAI 3055, pp. 362–375, 2004.

Providing query capabilities to a DDS can be done either using a full-functional query processing system (for short, query system) such as the one provided within database management systems (DBMS), or from scratch. In the first case, the query system often supports particular characteristics, e.g. data model, optimization strategy and criteria, etc., and is not well adapted to a large volume of heterogeneous data distributed over networks. In the second case, programming query function is hard task because it needs to integrate several mechanisms that have not been designed to work together.

Consequently, building query functions in DDS is still a very complicated and consuming-time task that is not appropriate in the concurrent age where *time-to-market* is a success factor. We do think that there is a need to provide programmers with a set of tools facilitating the design and implementation of query functions in data-intensive distributed applications. Such tools should provide a uniform way to integrate query techniques developed for different contexts so as to use them to evaluate queries according to an application requirements. Providing multiple query mechanisms that can be adapted would also reduce development efforts. However, building a generic query evaluation system able to respond to any kind of needs is difficult, even impossible because of the diversity of application requirements and the complexity of the querying mechanisms.

Therefore, we propose to abstract the functions of an expected query processor. Programmers can configure and/or extend these functions to build instances or query systems. This paper focuses on QBF, a Query Broker Framework providing the basic abstractions or components to build systems with flexible query evaluation capabilities. QBF integrates existing optimization and execution mechanisms in a uniform way. It also takes into account multiple mechanisms to evaluate queries without having knowledge of the environment. The smallest query evaluation unit built from the framework is called a Query Broker. Query brokers can be organized in hierarchies for evaluating queries. The paper concentrates on the general architecture of a query broker, the interfaces of its components and the way they interact together. Cost models and performance aspects are not considered in this first step of the work.

The rest of this paper is organized as follows. Section 2 introduces the way queries are represented within QBF. Section 3 presents the QBF components and the way they interact. Section 4 overviews the implementation of the proposed framework. It also shows how instances of the framework provide adaptive query evaluation and interactive query processing. Section 5 compares our approach with previous related works. Finally, Section 6 concludes and gives future research directions in.

2   Query Representation

Client requirements on querying a large volume of data cannot be simply what the result of a query should be but also user requirements for query processing. To support such requirements, we associate a *query context* with every *query* (plan).

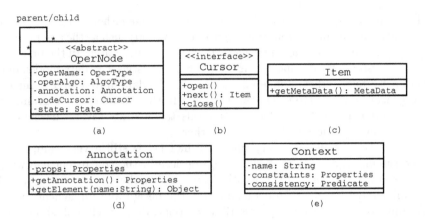

Fig. 1. Data and Query Representation

Query. The internal representation of a query in QBF is a standardized, canonical query tree or graph, so-called a *query plan*. Its nodes (defined as the OperNode abstract class, see Figure 1(a)) represent query operators such as *Select*, *Project*, *Join*, *Union*, etc. These operators consume and produce *set or sequence of items* as proposed in [4]. These items can be tuples, entities, objects or tree. They are accessed through Cursor interface (defined in Figure 1(b)). Operator nodes are annotated by their properties (Annotation, see Figure 1(d)[1]). During the cycle of life of a query, nodes can have one of the following *state*: *not-started*, *annotated*, *executing*, *stalled*, *modifying*, *halted*, *finished* (State).

Query Context. The context part of a query determines constraints that have to be checked when processing the query. It is represented as a list of parameters, i.e. couples of (name, value) (*constraints*, see Figure 1(e)). Constraints may concern users, system resources or underlying network. For example, users may wish to limit number of results (*ResultNumber*), execution time (*Timeout*) or have preference on data (*Preference*). It may exist a value-dependency among context parameters. This is represented as a propositional function (*consistency* attribute).

3   QBF Components

Figure 2 shows that QBF is comprised of six components. Each of them is designed to cope with a well-identified query evaluation concern. QueryManager provides the interface of a query evaluator. It coordinates other components to evaluate queries. PlanManager and ContextManager are responsible to provide tools for managing query plan and query context parts, respectively. BufferManager component provides storage capability for processing queries. These are base

---

[1] Properties being a list of couples (name, value), Predicate being a propositional function are data types supported in Java [9] or defined as Java classes.

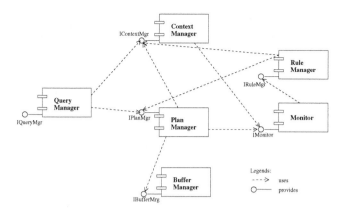

Fig. 2. QBF components

components and are indispensable for building any query evaluator. Building an adaptive query evaluator needs use of Monitor and RuleManager components. These two components allow observing the query execution (environment) and defining the way in which query evaluator behaves according to changes during query execution.

3.1 Main Components

PlanManager defines interfaces for manipulating query plans. This component is composed of Planner, Annotator, Transformer and Translator sub-components. Transformer and Translator provide possible query plan manipulations (logical and physical, respectively) which formulate the *search space* of a query. Annotator allows calculating properties of query node (**annotation**, cf. section 2) including the cost of query operation determined by a *cost model*. Planner coordinates these sub-components to enumerate equivalent query plans. It provides a *search strategy* to find an optimal query plan to execute. The separation of aspects of query optimization, ensured by PlanManager, is based on our analysis of different query optimization techniques such as [3, 10, 4]. This allows reusing the code of these sub-components to provide multiple search strategies for a query evaluation system and/or a search strategy for different query evaluation systems. The interaction between sub-components of PlanManager is defined by the sequence diagram as shown in Figure 4. It is worthy to note that, the number and the order of method calls from Planner to Annotator, Transformer and Translator are not fixed. This depends on the search strategy supported by a Planner.

ContextManager provides tools for defining and modifying contexts, i.e. instances of Context class as defined in Section 2. It defines methods for reading, writing and others processing of query contexts (e.g. **create**, **get**, **set**, **setParameter**, **compile** methods).

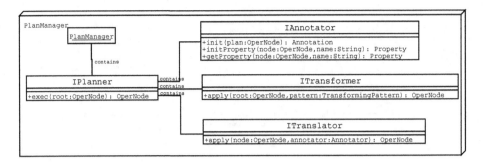

Fig. 3. Structure of PlanManager component

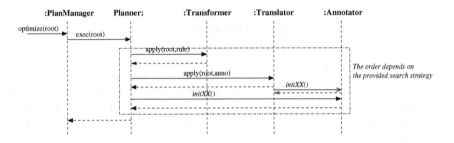

Fig. 4. Sequence diagram for query optimization

BufferManager provides interfaces for a general purpose of managing buffers (represented as Buffer instances with `get, remove, increase` methods). Buffers can be used not only to buffer I/O data but also to decouple the execution of some operators when they are inserted between query nodes. Different buffer strategies (e.g. *FIFO* vs. *LIFO*, *pull mode* vs. *push mode*) can be provided by adding new classes specializing Buffer class.

Monitor is responsible for detecting "significant" changes in the execution environment (e.g. network delays, uses of resources, query context). It keeps a list of observation elements represented by instances of `PropertyMonitor` class (see Figure 5(a)). The monitoring frequency is defined by *frequency* attribute. For each type of observation elements, `check` and `notify` methods provide code defining what is an unexpected condition of a property and how to process it. An unexpected condition is signaled by producing an *event*.

The Monitor component provides tools for creating (`create`) and managing (`remove, start, stop`) all observation elements.

RuleManager receives events produced by Monitor and launches the corresponding rule(s) to adapt the query execution to changes in the execution environment, i.e. underlying networks (e.g. delays, unaccessible data) and user's interaction (e.g. number of results limit, preference on data). Rules (cf. Figure 5(c)) define behaviors of a Query Broker towards these unexpected conditions. Rules can be of the form E-C-A (When Event If Condition Do Action) or E-A.

Fig. 5. Classes representing elements ensuring adaptivity

In receiving an event, the RuleManager applies a Strategy determining set of rules and the way they are executed. This component provides an *event listener* (the **receiveEvent** method) to communicate with the Monitor component. The RuleManager component can also support a complicated rule model or more precisely, an event model and a reaction model. A detailed description of rule manager is out of the scope of this work but can be found in [11].

QueryManager coordinates all other components of QBF. It provides methods for creating queries (**create**), modifying queries (**setxx**) and executing queries (**prepare, getData**).

3.2 Components Interaction

To understand the way components communicate, we have to consider instances of QBF, i.e. Query Brokers. As shown in Figure 7, query brokers can be organized in a hierarchy. Two kinds of dependencies can be considered: (i) query brokers intra-dependencies characterizing communication between QBF components, and (ii) query brokers inter-dependencies characterizing communication between query brokers for eventually a distributed query evaluation.

Query Broker Intra-dependencies. We can divide the interaction among components of QBF into three kinds of interactions: *query creation, query optimization* and *adaptation*.

At the beginning, a client submits a query to a QueryManager that calls the **create** operations of PlanManager and ContextManager to create query plan and query context, respectively (Figure 6(a)).

During query optimization, the query is annotated, transformed, translated and the query context is compiled to be taken into consideration during query evaluation, i.e., choosing a search strategy, adding controlled parameters driven query execution, etc. During this phase, Buffer and PropertyMonitor objects may be created and inserted into the query plan so as ensure an expected query execution (Figure 6(b)).

During execution, results are accessed through **nodeCursor** of the OperNode root while PropertyMonitor instances supervise the appropriated properties (e.g. arrival rate, producing rate, use of resources, etc.) so as to detect significant changes (events). They notify these changes by sending events to the RuleManager which launches the corresponding rules changing the evaluation strategies, e.g. re-scheduling query plan, re-optimizing query plan, etc. (Figure 6(c)).

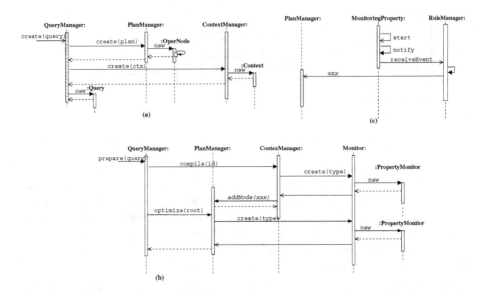

Fig. 6. Interactions among QBF components

Query Brokers Inter-dependencies. A given query can be evaluated by several distributed brokers [12]. Each broker evaluates a sub-query. The collaboration between brokers is based on message exchange. Brokers emit messages to send a query (*receive-query*), to inform the absence of data (*no-data*), to modify the context(*receive-context*), to *speed-up* or *slow-down* the input/output data stream, etc. Other messages or events can be added by application developers to satisfy particular requirements. A special type of PropertyMonitor is defined for managing the communication of query broker with its connected brokers.

The communication between brokers relies on a simple "selfish" policy: a broker cannot change the behavior of another. A broker send requests (messages) and the receiving brokers process them as they can and as they want. Brokers can send messages only to their directly connected brokers. For example, a broker can send a *speed-up* request to a connected broker which accelerates (or not) its execution depending on its own resources. If the broker decides to speed-up, it may propagate the demand to its connected brokers. If not, the initial event is not propagated. Each broker has a set of rules that define its behavior according to events coming from other brokers or clients.

4   Implementation

We developed a first prototype of our framework. We chose the Java environment as the implementation platform to exploit the high level of portability of its byte-codes. The following describes the implementation of some components considering the main concerns of an adaptive query evaluation: *query operators*, *query optimization* and *adaptation strategy*.

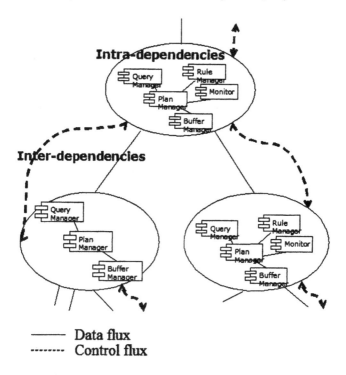

— Data flux
···· Control flux

Fig. 7. Interconnected Query Brokers

4.1   Query Operators

Query operators (*Select, Join, Union, Intersection, Difference*) are implemented
as classes SelectNode, JoinNode, UnionNode, IntersectionNode, DifferenceNode
specializing OperNode (cf. section 2). For example, the SelectNode class represents the *Select* operator having a selection condition (the `predicate` attribute).
We have also implemented WrapperNode, UnaryNode, BinaryNode as abstract
classes providing specific processes for input operators[2], unary and binary operators, respectively. All algorithms of these operators implement the Cursor
interface.

Using buffers is done by the *Buffer* operator. As a result, buffers can be inserted at anywhere in a query plan by BufferNode instances. Please note that
most of operators (except the *Buffer* operator) are implemented in *mono-thread*
mode, i.e. parent and child operators are executed in only one thread. Query
execution in *multi-thread* mode is ensured by a simple use of BufferNode in
query plan. Having storage capability, the *Buffer* operator is implemented by
two threads, one for buffer reading, i.e. corresponding to parent operator execution, and the other for buffer writing, i.e. corresponding to child operator exe-

---

[2] Input operators have no child operator.

cution. Thus, the system can choose a functional mode (mono- or multi-thread) according to available resources.

At instantiating time, programmers can provide new operators by specializing OperNode (and extending operator classes already defined). For example, we implemented SourceNode, AssignNode, ProjectNode, etc. for evaluating queries on XML data based on the algebra proposed in [13]. Figure 8 presents the query plan of a query on biological data sources GOLD, SMD, SGD giving information related to genes cartography and expression wrapped into XML format. This query aims at "looking for the organisms completely sequence and eucaryote". All non-mentioned attributes are not initialized yet.

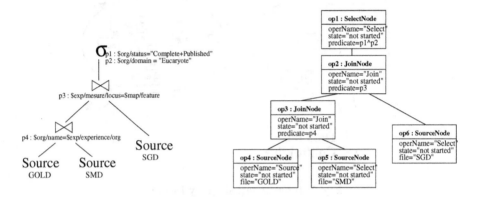

Fig. 8. Example of query

4.2   Query Optimization

The main concerns of query optimization are implemented by Transformer, Translator (*search space*), Annotator(*cost model*) and Planner(*search strategy*) sub-components of PlanManager component. Therefore, query optimization algorithm implementations are sharing among these components in using pre-defined interactions (cf. Figure 4).

The Transformer component implementation contains a set of Transforming-Pattern representing possible logical transformations of query plans. These patterns have the prioritized order and/or can be grouped into composition patterns. We implement *pushingSelection*, *pushingProjection* and *joinCommutative* for a transformative search strategy such as the one proposed in [4], *expandingJoin* for building query plans as proposed in [3]. These transformations patterns formulate the algebraic space of a query [14]. The Translator component implementation contains a set of MappedOperator representing possible logical-physical translation of query operators. We implement translation rules for every algebraic operators such as join (*MappedJoin*), select (*MappedSelect*), etc. Translations rules can also add new operators such as *sort* to query plans for enforcing data properties. The Transformer and Translator components are responsible for creating the search space of a query. The Annotator component implements mechanisms for estimating cost of operations such as presented in [15]. This annotates query operator nodes by their cost and Planner uses it for choosing the "best" query plan for execution. Please note that Annotation instance associated with nodes contains a list of properties which depend on the implemented cost model (e.g. estimated result size, time to process, uses of CPU, of memory, etc.). The Planner component provides the implementation of a search strategy within exec method. These search strategy is applied on a search space provided by Transformer et Translator and uses a cost model provided as part of Annotator to choose a optimal solution for query evaluation. Separating transformation, translation operations and cost computation make these components more reuse. The search space and cost computation can be changed without modification of search strategy and vice versa. It is possible to support multiple search strategies (Planner) on multiple search spaces (Transformer, Translator) and multiple cost models (Annotator) enable PlanManager to choose the best one depending on the input query and context. Considering an example of *transformative search strategy*, the algorithm is provided within the exec method as follows:

```
       // list of transforming patterns for generating search space in priority order
 1:    list : TransformingPattern[];
       // which computes the corresponding annotation of the cost model
 2:    annotator : Annotator;
 3:    ChoosenPlan = root;
 4:    for (int i=0; i < list.getLength(); i++){
 5:            while (true) {
 6:                    new = Transformer.apply(ChoosenPlan,list[i]);
 7:                    if (new == ChoosenPlan)
 8:                            break;
 9:                    else
10:                            ChoosenPlan = new;
11:            }
12:    }
13:    ChoosenPlan = Translator.apply(ChoosenPlan,annotator);
```

At instantiating time, programmers can add new transformation and translation rules for handling new operators. Considering the query example presented in the previous section, Figure 9 shows an example of query optimization strategy. Figure 9(a), (b), (c) are different stages of our query plan example. The last one presents the query plan already to execute.

4.3 Adaptation Strategy

The main components allowing adaptive query evaluation are Monitor and RuleManager. We implement the PropertyMonitor abstract class and its sub-classes RateMonitor, SizeMonitor and TimeMonitor to observe arrival data rate, number of data processed, and execution time, respectively. For all instances of these classes, the default value for the frequency attribute is "every 180 sec". For every PropertyMonitor sub-type, we implemented a default function (check) which

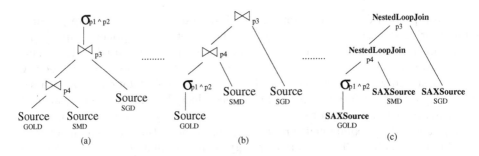

Fig. 9. Example of query optimization

determines the status of the property in which an unexpected condition must be signaled. For example, the default checking function of `RateMonitor` verifies if "the arrival rate is slower than half of predicted rate". Programmers can change *frequency* of checking and checking condition.

For the implementation of the `RuleManager` component, we use previous results of our research group on distributed active services [11]. The ADEES event service [16] has been used to build an event able to detect simple events (no composition) sent by `PropertyMonitor`. The ADRUS rule service [11] has been used to implement a ECA rule manager able to react to events detected by the event manager. The implemented rule execution model is a simple one: consumption of the triggering event, immediate E-C and C-A coupling modes, execution based on priorities, no pre-emption, etc. Note that both managers can reconfigure and adapt themselves with respect to applications requirements.

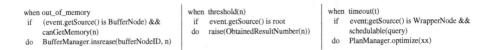

Fig. 10. Some examples of adaptation rules

Figure 10 presents some examples of adaptation rules. The first one aims at adjusting the buffer size. The second one signals that a given number of results is reached. The third one modifies query execution strategies. Adaptive query evaluation strategies implements techniques such as the ones proposed in [17, 5]. However, separation of monitoring and decision elements (Monitor and RuleManager) allow us to adapt the conditions which launches an adaptive process in a flexible way. This one can be easily adapted to input queries and/or application environment.

There is no restriction for adding new rules. Programmers can add new observation elements and adaptation rules for more adaptable query evaluation. They are responsible for ensuring the semantic of these rules. For example, to instantiate an interactive query evaluation, we must implement UserInteractionMonitor which defines all possible interaction that users can do during query evaluation, e.g. modifying query context, adding new selection condition, remove an existing selection condition, etc. Corresponding to these interactions (events), rules implement the appropriate adaptation processes for adapting query execution to new requirements.

5   Related Work

In the context of distributed systems, many efforts have been done on defining generic services such as CORBA Query Service [18]. Our work is very different from this one in proposing a more fine-grain design which consists in the separation of different concerns of query processing. This allows providing multi query evaluation strategies and extending them easily.

Some efforts have been done also on designing extensible query processing systems. The authors of [19, 4] design an optimizer generator while minimizing the assumptions on the implemented data model. As a result, the works focus on a new kind of query processing engine that can be use to query data described in any data model. Queries are represented as trees and operators consume and produce sets or sequences of items. Building query processing means providing a data model specification. In QBF, we adopted this idea of making query processing independent of data model and we characterized the different types of query plan manipulation (logical and physical levels). This facilitates reuse of code and allows providing multi query processing strategies so as to adapt to the execution context. Besides, we take into consideration needs of providing adaptive query evaluation.

Many query processing mechanisms have been proposed so as efficiently and adaptively evaluate queries. Some of them [3, 4] aim at choosing the best strategy for query execution in the statical way. For instance, [3] enumerates all alternative join trees by iterating on the number of relations joined so far pruning trees that are known to be suboptimal. However, the memory requirements and running time of this algorithm grow exponentially with query size, i.e. number of joins, so it is not suitable in the case of large queries [14]. Some recent works focalize on adaptive query evaluation in providing pipelining query operators [20, 7] or mechanisms for evaluating queries in a dynamical way [5, 8, 6]. The QBF approach allows to integrate, as adaptation rules or particular operators, these techniques so that they can work together to satisfy application requirements in different contexts and also to improve the global performance of query processing. Compared to these proposals, QBF offers the same capabilities but also integrate users interests.

The authors of [20] use the rule-based approach for adaptive query evaluation so as can integrate several adaptive query processing mechanisms like ours. However, it seems that the optimization strategy supported is unchangeable.

6   Conclusions and Ongoing Work

This paper presented QBF, a flexible query evaluation framework that allows to build Query Brokers for an adaptable evaluation of queries. We described the components of QBF or query brokers. Communication between query brokers has been introduced for showing how distributed queries may be processed. We also showed how users can specify their interests with the definition of context. We put emphasis on the reutilization and adaptability by choosing the framework approach. We implement a first prototype of QBF and use it to develop an interactive query broker for the MEDIAGRID infrastructure (http://www-lsr.imag.fr/mediagrid/) developed to provide a transparent access to biological data sources [21].

We believe our approach is significative for quickly building applications having query capabilities in different contexts. This reduces efforts to develop these applications and *time-to-market* of products. At the moment, we do not consider performance issues even though we are aware of the separation of aspects may have negative impact on performance. However, we believe that the performance can be improved with optimization code techniques which are considered in other works such as [22].

The validation of QBF is being done following two directions: (i) complexity of use of framework, i.e. how complex is it to build a new query processing system based on QBF, and (ii) performance evaluation of QBF instances, i.e. additional overheads of flexibility of framework. We will also investigate other communication protocols between query brokers for other application contexts (e.g. P2P query processing). Query optimization under constraints, checking user's interaction and aids to efficiently refine ongoing queries are other perspectives of our work.

Acknowledgments

We would like to thank Beatrice Finance and Christophe Bobineau for useful and productive discussions about our work and Genoveva Vargas-Solar for her comments on an earlier version of this paper.

References

1. Wiederhold, G.: Mediator in the Achitecture of Future Information systems. The IEEE Computer Magazine **25** (1992) 38–49
2. Domenig, R., Dittrich, K.R.: An overview and classification of mediated query systems. In: Sigmod Record. ACM (1999)
3. Selinger, P.G., Astrahan, M.M., Chamberlin, D.D., Lorie, R.A., Price, T.G.: Access path selection in a relational database management system. In: Proc. of International Conference on Management Data (SIGMOD). (1979)
4. Graefe, G., McKenna, W.J.: The volcano optimizer generator: Extensibility and efficient search. In: Proc. of International Conference on Data Engineering. (1993)
5. Kabra, N., DeWitt, D.J.: Efficient mid-query re- optimization of sub-optimal query execution plans. In: Proc. of International Conference on Management Data (SIGMOD). (1998)
6. Bouganim, L., Fabret, F., Mohan, C., Valduriez, P.: Dynamic query scheduling in data integration systems. In: Proc. of International Conference on Data Engineering (ICDE). (2000)

7. Urhan, T., Franklin, M.J.: Xjoin: A reactively-scheduled pipelined join operator. IEEE Data Engineering Bulletin **23** (2000) 27–33
8. Avnur, R., Hellerstein, J.M.: Eddies: Continuously adaptive query processing. In: Proc. of International Conference on Management Data (SIGMOD). (2000)
9. Javatm 2 platform std. ed. v1.3.1. (http://java.sun.com/j2se/1.3/docs/api/)
10. Swami, A.: Optimization of large join queries: Combining heuristics and combinatorial techniques. In: Proc. of International Conference on Management Data (SIGMOD). (1989)
11. Collet, C., Vargas-Solar, G., Grazziotin-Ribeiro, H.: Open active services for data-intensive distributed applications. In: Proc. of International Database Engineering and Application Symposium (IDEAS). (2000)
12. Vu, T.T., Collet, C.: Query brokers for distributed and flexible query evaluation. In: Proc. of RIVF. (2003)
13. Sartiani, C., Albano, A.: Yet another query algebra for xml data. In: Proc. of International Database Engineering and Application Symposium (IDEAS). (2002)
14. Ioannidis, Y.: 45. In: Query Optimization. CRC Press (2000)
15. Garcia-Molina, H., Ullman, J.D., Widom, J.: 7. In: Database System Implementation. Prentice Hall (2000)
16. Vargas-Solar, G., Collet, C.: Adees: An adaptable and extensible event based infrastructure. In: Proc. of Database and Expert Systems Applications. (2002)
17. Urhan, T., Franklin, M.J., Amsaleg, L.: Cost based query scrambling for initial delays. In: Proc. of International Conference on Management Data (SIGMOD). (1998)
18. Group, O.M.: Query service specification. http://www.omg.org/cgi-bin/doc?formal/200-06-23 (2000)
19. Graefe, G., DeWitt, D.J.: The exodus optimizer generator. In: Proc. of International Conference on Management Data (SIGMOD). (1987)
20. Ives, Z.G., Florescu, D., Friedman, M., et al.: An Adaptive Query Execution System for Data Integration. In: Proc. of International Conference on Management Data (SIGMOD). (1999)
21. Collet, C., Project, T.M.: A mediation framework for a transparent access to biological data source. In: Poster session of International Conference on Conceptual Modeling / the Entity Relationship Approach(ER). (2003).
22. Bouchenak, S., Boyer, F., Palma, N.D., Hagimont, D.: Can aspects be injected? experience with replication and protection. In: Proc. of Distributed Objects and Applications (DOA). (2003)

Retrieval Effectiveness of Written and Spoken Queries: An Experimental Evaluation

Heather Du and Fabio Crestani

Department of Computer and Information Sciences
University of Strathclyde, Glasgow, Scotland, UK
{heather,fabioc}@cis.strath.ac.uk

Abstract. With the fast growing speech technologies, the world is emerging to a new speech era. Speech recognition has now become a practical technology for real world applications. While some work has been done to facilitate retrieving information in speech format using textual queries, the characteristics of speech as a way to express an information need has not been extensively studied. If one compares written versus spoken queries, it is intuitive to think that users would issue longer spoken queries than written ones, due to the ease of speech. Is this in fact the case in reality? Also, if this is the case, would longer spoken queries be more effective in helping retrieving relevant document than written ones? This paper presents some new findings derived from an experimental study to test these intuitions.

1   Introduction and Motivations

At long last, speech is becoming an important interface between human being and machine. Computer systems, whether fixed or mobile, wired or wireless, increasingly offer users the opportunity to interact with information through speech. The conventional means of information seeking using textual queries is becoming more difficult to satisfy the desire for information access of a mobile user. Accessing information using textual queries does not work well for users in many situations, such as when users are moving around, with their hands or eyes occupied in something else, or interacting with another person. For those with visual impairment such as blindness or difficulty in seeing words in ordinary newsprint, not to mention those with limited literacy skills, speech would be the only means to satisfy their information needs. In all these cases, given the advancement of speech technology, speech enabled interface has come to the lime light of today's information retrieval (IR) research community, with the promise of enabling users to access information solely via voice.

The transformation of user's information needs into a search expression, or query is known as query formulation. It is widely regarded as one of the most challenging activities in information seeking [6]. Research on spoken query formulation and use for information access is denoted as spoken query processing (SQP).

H. Christiansen et al. (Eds.): FQAS 2004, LNAI 3055, pp. 376–389, 2004.

From 1997 (TREC-6) to 2000 (TREC-9), TREC (Text Retrieval Conference) evaluation workshop included a track on spoken document retrieval (SDR) to explore the impact of automatic speech recognition (ASR) errors on document retrieval. The conclusion draw from this three years of SDR track is that SDR is a "solved problem" [10]. This is certainly not the case for SQP.

SQP has been focusing on studying the level of degradation of retrieval performance due to errors in the query terms introduced by the automatic speech recognition system. The effect of the corrupted spoken query transcription has a heavy impact on the retrieval ranking [14]. Because IR engines try to find documents that contain words that match those in the query, any errors in the query have the potential for derailing the retrieval of relevant documents. Two groups of researchers have investigated this problem by carrying out experimental studies. One group [4] considered two experiments on the effectiveness of SQP. These experiments showed that as the query got slightly longer, the drop in effectiveness of system performance became less. Further analysis of the long queries by the other group showed that [8] the longer "long" queries are consistently more accurate than the shorter "long" queries. In general, these experiments concluded that the effectiveness of IR systems degrades faster in the presence of ASR errors when the queries are recognised than when the documents are recognised. Further, once queries are short the degradation in effectiveness becomes even more noticeable [1]. Therefore, it can be claimed that despite the current limitations of the accuracy of ASR software, it can be feasible to use speech as a means of posing questions to an IR system as long as the queries are relatively long. However, the query sets created in these experiments were artificial, being made of queries originally in textual form and dictated. Will spontaneous queries be long? Will people use same words, phrases or sentences when formulating their information needs via voice as typing onto a screen? If not, how different are written queries from spoken ones? What level of retrieval effectiveness should we expect from spontaneous spoken queries? It is a well-known fact that dictated speech is considerably different from spontaneous speech and easier to recognise [11]. It should be expected that spontaneous spoken queries would have higher levels of word error rate (WER) and different kinds of errors. Thus, the conclusions drawn from previous experimentation with spoken queries will not be valid until further empirical work is carried out to clarify the ways in which spontaneous queries differ in length and nature from dictated ones.

In this paper we present the results of an experimental study on the differences between written queries and their counterpart in spoken forms. We also present an evaluation of their respective retrieval performance effectiveness against an IR system. The paper is structured as follows. Section 2 discusses the usefulness of speech as a means of query input. Section 3 describes how we built a collection of spoken and written queries and highlights some of the differences found between the two. This collection of spoken and written queries is the test collection we will employ in our effectiveness study. The results of this study are reported in section 4. Conclusion with some remarks on the potential significance of the study and future directions of work are presented in section 5.

2   Spoken Queries

The advantages of speech as a modality of communication are obvious. It is natural just as people communicate as they normally do; it is rapid: commonly 150-250 word per minutes [3]; it requires no visual attention; it requires no use of hands.

However, ASR systems produce far from perfect transcripts, which means that there is bound to be recognition mistakes at different levels depending on the quality of the ASR systems. Queries are generally much shorter than documents in the form of both text and speech. The shorter duration of spoken queries provides less context and redundancy, and ASR errors have a greater impact on effectiveness of IR systems. Furthermore, input with speech is not always perfect in all situations. Speech is public, potentially disruptive to people nearby and potentially compromising of confidentiality. Speech becomes less useful in noisy environment. The cognitive load imposed by speaking must not be ignored. Generally when formulating spoken queries, users are not simply transcribing information but are composing it.

However, despite the unavoidable ASR errors, research shows that the classical IR techniques are quite robust to considerably high level of WER (about up to 40%), in particular for longer queries [7]. In addition, it has long been proved that voice is a richer media than written text [5]. It has more cues including voice inflection, pitch, and tone. Research shows that there exists a direct relationship between acoustic stress and information content identified by an IR index in spoken sentences since speakers stress the word that can help to convey their messages as expected [18]. People also express themselves more naturally and less formally when speaking compared to writing and are generally more personal. Thus, we would expect, as a result, that spoken queries would be longer in length than written queries. To test this hypothesis, we constructed and carried out an experiment as described in the following section.

3   Qualitative Comparison of Written versus Spoken Queries

This section summarises our previous work on an experiment we conducted to study the qualitative differences between spoken and written queries. Full description of the experimental procedure and more thorough analysis of the experimental results can be found in [9].

Our view is that the best way to assess the difference in query formulation between spoken form and written form is to conduct an experimental analysis with a group of potential users in a setting as close as possible to a real world application. We used a within-subjects experimental design [13].

3.1   Experimental Study

As retrieving information via voice is still relatively in its infancy, it would be difficult to identify participants for our study. We therefore decided to recruit from an accessible group of potential participants who is not new to the subject of Information Retrieval. 7 of our participant members were from the IR research group who have good knowledge of IR to some degree and 5 participants were research students who all have good experience of using search engines within the department of computer and information sciences, but few have prior experience with vocal information retrieval. It is worth to mention that all participants were native English speakers. There would be no language barriers for them to understand and formulate their information needs in English.

The set of topics we used for this experimental study was a subset of 10 topics extracted from TREC topic collection (topics 151-160). Each topic consists of four parts: id, title, description and narrative.

The experiment consisted of two sessions. Each session involved 12 participants, one participant at a time. The 12 participants who took part in the first session also took part in the second session. An experimenter was present throughout each session to answer any questions concerning the process at all times. The experimenter briefed the participants about the experimental procedure and handed out instructions before each session. Each participant was given the same set of 10 topics in text form. These topics were in a predetermined order and each had a unique ID. The tasks were that each participant was asked to form his/her own version for each topic in either written form or spoken form as instructed via a graphic user interface (GUI) on a desktop screen (written in Java). For session 1, each participant was asked to form his/her queries in written form for the first 5 topics and in spoken form for the second 5 topics via the GUI. For session 2, the order was reversed, that was each participant presented his/her queries in spoken form for the first half topic set and in written form for the second half topic set via the GUI. Each session lasted approximately 3 hours, which gave each participant to finish the tasks within 30 minutes and a maximum of 5 minutes time constraint was also imposed on each topic. During the course of the experiment, the written queries were collected and saved in text format. The spoken ones were recorded using close-talk microphone and saved in audio format in a wav file for each participant automatically. The data collected were used for post-experimental analysis and to test the experimental hypothesis.

3.2 Experimental Results

From this experiment, we have collected 120 written queries and 120 spoken queries that have been manually transcribed. Some of the characteristics of written and spoken queries are reported in Table 1. This table pictures clearly that the average length of spoken queries is longer than written queries with a ratio rounded at 2.48. This seems to confirm our hypothesis that spoken queries are longer than written ones. After stopwords removal, the average length of spoken queries is reduced from 23.07 to 14.33 with a 38% reduction rate and the average length of written queries is reduced from 9.54 to 7.48 with a reduction rate at 22%. These figures indicate that spoken queries contain more stopwords than written ones. This indication can also be seen from the differentials between

Table 1. Characteristics of written and spoken queries

Data set	Written queries	Spoken queries
Number of queries	120	120
Unique terms in queries	309	552
Average query length(with stopterms)	9.54	23.07
Average query length(without stopterms)	7.48	14.33
Median query length(without stopterms)	7	11

the average length and median length for both spoken and written queries. The difference between the numbers of unique terms occurred in the written query set and spoken query set is not great. This is because each participant worked on the same 10 topics and generated a written query and a spoken query for each topic, therefore there are 12 versions of written queries and 12 versions of spoken queries in relation to one topic.

The average length of written and spoken queries with/without stopwords for each topic is calculated and presented in Fig. 1. In Fig. 1, the scattered points for spoken queries always stay above the ones for written queries, which suggests the spoken queries are lengthier than the written ones. This is a case for every topic persistently. This is exactly what we would expect to see. We know from previous studies that the textual queries untrained users pose to information retrieval systems are short: most queries are three words or less. With some knowledge of IR and high usage of Web search engines, our participants have formulated longer textual queries. This is also typical of trained users. When formulating queries verbally, the ease of speech encouraged participants to speak more words.

From the above analysis, we know that spoken queries as a whole are definitely lengthier than written queries. One would argue that people with natural tendency would speak more conversationally which results in lengthy sentences containing a great deal of function words such as prepositions, conjunctions or articles, that have little semantic contents of their own and chiefly indicate grammatical relationships, which have been referred as stopwords in IR community, whereas the written queries are much terser but mainly contain content words such as nouns, adjectives and verbs, therefore, spoken queries would not contribute much than written queries semantically. However, after we remove the stopwords within both the spoken and written queries and plot the average length of spoken and written queries against their original length in one graph, as shown in Fig. 1, which depicts a very different picture. As we can see from this figure, the points for spoken queries are consistently on top of the ones for the written queries; after stopwords removal, each of them are also undoubtedly becoming shorter. Moreover, the points for spoken queries without stopwords stay above the ones for written queries without stopwords consistently across every topic. Statistically, the average spoken query length without stopwords is 14.33 and for written query, that is 7.48, which shows the spoken queries have almost doubled the length of the written ones. This significant improvement in

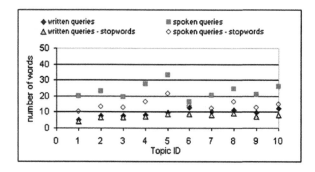

Fig. 1. Average length of queries per topic

length indicates that the ease of speaking encourages people to express not only more conversationally, but also more semantically. From IR point of view, more search words would improve the retrieval results. Ironically, for SQP, the problem is the very tool that makes it possible: the speech recognition. There are wide range of speech recognition softwares available both for commercial and research purposes. High quality speech recordings might have a recognition error rate of under 10%. The average word error rates (WER) for large-vocabulary speech recognisers are between 20 to 30 percent [15]. Conversational speech, particularly on a telephone, will have error rates in the 30-40% ranges, probably on the high end of that in general. In this case in our experiment, even if at the WER at 50%, it would not cause greater degradations on the spoken queries to make them shorter than written queries. In other word, the spoken information clearly has the potential to be at least as valuable as written material.

We also summarise the length of queries with/without stopwords for all 10 topics across all participants. The average length of queries per participant is presented in Fig. 2.

We could observe from Fig. 2 that it is the same case for every participant that his/her spoken queries are longer than written ones consistently. However, the variations of the length between spoken and written queries for some participants are very small. In fact, after we studied the transcriptions of spoken queries, we observed that the spoken queries generated by a small portion of participants are very much identical to their written ones. The discrepancies of length within written queries are very insignificant and relatively stable. All participants used similar approach to formulate their written queries by specifying only keywords. The experience of using textual search engines influenced the participants' process of query formulations. For most popular textual search engines, the stopwords would be removed from a query before creating the query representation. Conversely, the length fluctuates rapidly within spoken queries among participants.

We did not run a practice session prior to the experiment such as to give an example of how to formulate a written query and a spoken query for a topic, since we felt this would set up a template for participants to mimic later on during the course of experiment and we would not be able to find out how participants would go about formulating their queries. In this experiment, we observed that 8 out of 12 participants adopted natural language to formulate their queries which were very much like conversational talk and 4 participants stuck to the traditional approach by only speaking keywords and/or broken phrases. They said they did not want to "talk" to the computer as they felt strange and uncomfortable to speak to a machine. This suggests that participants own personalities played a key roll in the query formulation process. After stopwords removal, the spoken

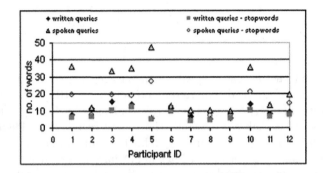

Fig. 2. Average length of queries per participant

queries are still lengthier than the written ones. Fig. 2 shows a consistency with the result of the previous analysis that people tend to use more function words and content words in speaking than writing. This is true for every participant in our experiment.

A sentence in natural language text is usually composed of nouns, pronouns, articles, verbs, adjectives, adverbs, and connectives. From IR point of view, not all words are equally significant for representing the semantics of a document. Investigating the distribution of different part of speech (POS) in the two forms of queries gives us another opportunity to shed light on the nature of the differences and similarities between spoken and written queries. Fig. 3 shows a comparison of POS between the two query sets. This figure indicates that categorematic words, primarily nouns, verbs and adjectives, i.e. words that are not function words, made up a majority of word types. There are more types of words in spoken queries than written queries. Nouns, adjectives and verbs are frequently used in both written and spoken queries. Nouns have the largest type shares in both query forms and higher percentage in written queries than spoken queries, as nouns are well known to carry more information content and therefore more useful for search purposes. Verbs are the second largest POS in spoken queries and the third largest in written queries thus they seem to play a more important role in spoken than in written queries, whereas adjectives are more common in written queries than in spoken queries. Prepositions and conjunctives are also heavily used in spoken queries. These two POS types are considered stopwords, so they would be automatically removed during the indexing procedure.

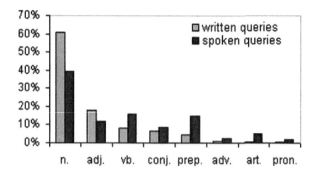

Fig. 3. Percentages of part-of-speech in written & spoken queries

4 Retrieval Effectiveness
of the Written versus Spoken Queries

This section describes the procedure and the results of an experimental analysis into the effectiveness of written versus spoken queries. In this context we assume that the spoken queries have been perfectly transcribed, that is, the speech recognition process is perfect. This is of course a gross simplification, since even well trained ASR systems make recognition mistakes. Nevertheless, we believe this study could provide the upper bound level of performance of an IR system using spoken queries.

4.1 Experimental Procedural

In order to experiment the differences in effectiveness of written and spoken queries, a suitable test environment needs to be devised. Classical IR evaluation methodology [19] suggests that such test environment should consist of the following components:

1. a collection of textual document;
2. a set of written and spoken queries with associated document relevance assessments;
3. IR system;
4. some measures of the IR system effectiveness.

The collection we used is a subset of the collection generated for TREC [20]. The collection is made of the full text of articles of the Wall Street Journal from year 1990 to year 1992. The 120 written and 120 spoken queries collected from above mentioned experiment were used. Since the two sets of queries were generated based on the 10 TREC topics, we could be able to use the corresponding set of relevant documents.

We used the Lemur IR toolkit to implement the retrieval system. Lemur has been developed by the Computer Science Department of the University of Massachusetts and the School of Computer Science at Carnegie Mellon University [16]. It supports indexing of large text collection, the construction of simple language models for documents, queries and the implementation of retrieval systems based on language models as well as a variety of other retrieval models.

The main IR effectiveness measures used in our study are the well-known measure of Recall and Precision. Recall is defined as the portion of all the relevant documents in the collection that has been retrieved. Precision is the portion of retrieved documents that is relevant to the query. Once documents are ranked in response to a query according to the retrieval status value (RSV), precision and recall can be easily evaluated. These values are displayed in tables or graphs in which precision is reported for standard levels of recall (from 0.1 to 1.0 with 0.1 increments). In order to measure the effectiveness of the IR system of written and spoken queries, a number of retrieval runs were carried out against different IR models and precision and recall values were evaluated. The results reported in the following graphs were averaged over the entire sets of 120 written queries and 120 spoken queries.

4.2   Results of the Effectiveness of Written and Spoken Queries

We ran these two sets of queries against three models implemented using the Lemur toolkit: a basic TFIDF vector space model, the Okapi, and a language modelling method that used the Kullback-Leibler similarity measure between document and query language models [12]. No relevance feedback methods were used for any of these three models. The TFIDF vector space model was implemented using standard methods in which each document and each query are represented by term frequency vectors, then the terms in those vectors are weighted using TFIDF weight, and finally the RSV value of each query-document pair is calculated as the sum of their term weights. Fig 4 depicts the effectiveness of written and spoken queries using the above TFIDF models. Naturally, we would expect the best result should be obtained for the perfect transcript, but the performances obtained for the two query sets are very similar. Like in any scientific experiment, the outcome of an IR experiment is affected by random errors. As the result, we cannot conclude that one is better than the other based on a small performance difference between two query sets. Significance tests are needed to decide whether the performance difference between two query sets is statistically significant. The paired t-test is the most widely used in IR. The general idea behind the tests is: we assume that two techniques being compared are equally good. Under the assumption, we calculate a probability (p-value) that the observed performance difference could occur by chance. The smaller is the p-value, the more significant is the difference between the two techniques. The p value derived from TFIDF retrieval was very large; this indicates that a differ-

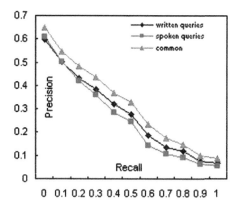

Fig. 4. P/R graph for simple TFIDF model

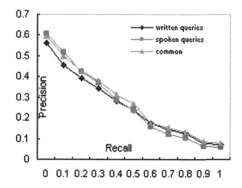

Fig. 5. P/R graph for KL & JM model

ence on system performance between spoken and written queries is statistically insignificant.

In order to identify which words were responsible for the effectiveness results, we artificially built another query set of 120 queries by using the words appearing in both written queries and spoken queries. The results obtained with this set of queries, shown in Fig 4, indicate that this query terms set obtained slightly better retrieval performance. This is an indication the important words (those responsible for the retrieval effectiveness) are present in both query sets. Those words that are present only in spoken or written queries are therefore responsible for the decrease in performance. Only slightly different results were obtained using the language model implemented in Lemur, which is based on the Kullback-Leibler similarity measure and the Jelinek-Mercer smoothing (KL&JM) [21]. Fig 5 depicts the effectiveness of the three query sets and they all had very similar performance. In fact a t-test shows that the differences are not statistically significant. It seems that the language model is not able to show the difference between the sets of spoken and written queries and the set of queries obtained

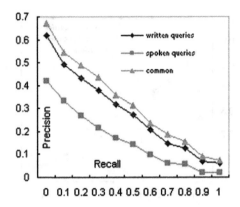

Fig. 6. P/R graph for simple Okapi model

by only considering the words these two sets have in common. Rather different results are reported in Fig 6, which shows the effectiveness of written and spoken queries against the Okapi BM25 model, implemented in Lemur using the well-known BM25 formula [17]. In this case we can observe that written queries clearly outperformed spoken ones. The t-test shows that the difference between these two performances is statistically significant. The common query terms set obtained very similar but slightly better performance as the written queries.

It is not clear to us how so different effectiveness measure were obtained for the same query sets using different models. However, it is clear that our hypothesis that spoken queries would produce better retrieval performance just because they were longer does not hold. This warrants further investigation that is still under way and that is only partially reported in the next section.

4.3   Analysis of the Experimental Results

From above Fig. 4 and Fig. 5 reporting the results of the TFIDF and KL&JM models applied to written and spoken queries, we can conclude that these two sets of queries are almost equally effective with respect to retrieval performances. This is contrary to what we expected. From the previous experiment on qualitative comparison between written and spoken queries in terms of their length, we could claim that spoken queries are more useful than written queries because they carry more content words. As far as IR performance is concerned, more content words should lead to a more effective relevant document retrieval. This fact is supported by much past research. So, where have the content words gone during the retrieval process? These two graphs also shows that the performance of the common query terms is very similar to the ones of written and spoken query sets from which it was extracted. This indicates that the words useful for retrieval purposes are those words that appear in both written queries and spoken queries. Lets us look at this result by taking a specific query. A typical user spoken query looks like the following:

"I want to find document about *Grass Roots* Campaign by *Right Wing Christian Fundamentalist* to enter the political process to further their religious agenda in the U.S. I am especially interested in threats to *civil liberties*, government stability and the *U.S. Constitution*, and I'd like to find feature articles, editorial comments, news items and letters to the editor."

Whereas its textual counterpart looks like:

"*Right wing Christian fundamentalism, grass roots, civil liberties, US Constitution.*"

Words present in both queries are reported in italic. The words appearing in the written query are more or less also present in its corresponding spoken query. Other words in spoken query include conjunctions, prepositions and articles that will be removed as stopwords. The parts such as "I want to find document about" and "I am especially interested in" are conversional and contained words that while they will not all be removed as stopwords, will definitely have very low weights (IDF or KL) and therefore would not be useful. Although there are also some nouns in the spoken query, such as "feature articles, editorial comments, news items letters editor" which specify the forms of relevant document, these words are unlikely to appear in relevant documents therefore do not contribute to the RSVs. The vocabulary sizes of these three query sets are shows in Table 2. 71% of words in written queries are in the common words whereas only 40.9% for spoken query words. The ratio of common terms over the total vocabulary sizes of written and spoken queries is 25.9%. Fig. 5 shows the effectiveness of written and spoken queries against Okapi model. Surprisingly, the BM25 formula seems to have a very bad effect on spoken queries. The written queries manage to maintain its performance, whereas the retrieval effectiveness for spoken queries gets much worse than that obtained with the TFIDF and KL&JM models. There is no clear explanation for this phenomenon. A deeper analysis needs to be carried out to study this effect, before any conclusions could be generalised.

Table 2. Vocabulary size of different query sets

Written queries	Spoken queries	Common queries terms
309	552	226

5   Conclusions and Future Work

This paper reports an experimental study on the differences between spoken and written queries in qualitative terms and in terms of their effectiveness performance, assuming perfect recognition. This study serves as the basis for a preliminary speech user interface design, to be carried out in the near future.

The results show that using speech to formulate one's information needs not only provides a way to express it naturally, but also encourages one to speak more "semantically", i.e. using more content bearing words. This means that we can come to the conclusion that spoken queries as a means of formulating and inputting information needs are utterly feasible.

IR systems are very sensitive to errors in queries, in particular when these errors are generated by applying ASR to spoken queries [2]. We are fully aware of this potential threat, therefore for future work, we are going to design robust IR models able to deal with this problem. With this goal in mind, we are going first to transcribe the recordings of the spoken queries using ASR software and identify an IR system which can be used to evaluate the effect of word error rate of spoken queries against written queries on the effectiveness of the retrieval performance. We will then study how the IR system can be made more robust to these errors. One possible way is to use on verbal information contained in speech, like for example prosodic stress, in conjunction with POS tagging to identify the most useful words on which the recognition accuracy of the ASR process should be concentrated.

As a side research, we are carrying out a similar experiment on Mandarin, a language that has a completely different semantic structure from English, to check if the results presented in this paper also hold for other languages. The topics being used for this experimental study are a subset extracted from the TREC-5 Mandarin Track and the participants are all native Mandarin speakers with good experience of using search engines.

Acknowledgements

The authors would like to thank all the participants who were from the Department of Computer and Information Sciences at the University of Strathclyde for their efforts and willingness in taking part in this experiment voluntarily.

References

1. J. Allan. Perspectives on information retrieval and speech. In *SIGIR Workshop: Information Retrieval Techniques for Speech Applications*, pages 1–10, 2001.
2. J. Allan. Knowledge management and speech recognition. *Computer*, pages 46–47, April 2002.
3. D. R. Aronson and E. Colet. Reading paradigms: From lab to cyberspace? *Behavior Research Methods, Instruments and Computers*, 29(2):250–255, 1997.
4. J. Barnett, S. Anderson, J. Broglio, M. Singh, R. Hudson, and S.W. Kuo. Experiments in spoken queries for document retrieval. In *Proceedings of Eurospeech*, volume 3, pages 1323–1326, 1997.
5. B.L. Chalfonte, Robert S. Fish, and Robert E. Kraut. Expressive richness: a comparison of speech and text as media for revision. In *proceeding of the SIGCHI conference on Human factors in computing systems: Reaching through technology*, pages 21–26, 1991.

6. C. Cool, S. Park, N.J. Belkin, J. Koenemann, and K.B. Ng. Information seeking behaviour in new searching environment. *CoLIS*, pages 403–416, 1996.
7. F. Crestani. Effects of word recognition errors in spoken query processing. In *Proceedings of the IEEE ADL 2000 Conference*, pages 39–47, Washington DC, USA, May 2000.
8. F. Crestani. Spoken query processing for interactive information retrieval. *Data and Knowledge Engineering*, 41(1):105–124, 2002.
9. H. Du and F. Crestani. Spoken versus written queries for mobile information access. In *Proceedings of Mobile HCI 2003 International Workshop on Mobile and Uniquitous Information Access*, pages 67–78, 2003.
10. J. S. Garofolo, C.G.P. Auzanne, and E. M. Voorhees. The trec spoken document retrieval track: a success story. In *Proceedings of the TREC Conference*, pages 107–130, Gaithersburg, MD, USA, November 1999.
11. E. Keller. *Fundamentals of Speech Synthesis and Speech Recognition*. John Wiley and Sons, Chichester, UK, 1994.
12. J. Lin. Divergence measures based on the shannon entropy. *IEEE Tran. on Information Theory*, 37(1):145–151, 1991.
13. S. Miller. *Experimental design and statistics*. Routledge, London, UK, second edition edition, 1984.
14. E. Mittendorf and P. Schauble. Measuring the effects of data corruption on information retrieval. In *Proceedings of the Workshop on Speech and Natural Language*, pages 14–27, Pacific Grove, CA, USA, February 1991.
15. E. Moreno, J-M. Van Thong, and B. Logan. From multimedia retrieval to knowledge management. *Computer*, pages 58–66, 2002.
16. P. Ogilvie and J. Callan. Experiments using the lemur toolkit. In *Proceedings of the 2001 Text REtrieval Conference (TREC 2001)*, pages 103–108, 2001.
17. S. Jones M.M. HancockBeaulieu S.E. Robertson, S. Walker and M. Gatford. Okapi at trec-3. In *Proceedings TREC-3, the 3 rd Text Retrieval Conference*, pages 109–127, 1995.
18. A. Tombros and F. Crestani. User's perception of relevance of spoken documents. *Journal of the American Society of Information Science*, 51(9):929–939, 2000.
19. C. van Rijsbergen. *Information Retrieval*. Butterworths, London, UK, second edition edition, 1976.
20. E. Voorhees and D. Harman. Overview of the seventh text retrieval conference (trec-7). In *Proceedings of the TREC Conference*, pages 1–24, Gaithersburg, MD, USA, 1998.
21. C. Zhai and J. Lafferty. A study of smoothing methods for language models applied to ad hoc information retrieval. In *ACM SIGIR*, 2001.

Comprehensive Comparison
of Region-Based Image Similarity Models

Zoran Stejić[1], Yasufumi Takama[2], and Kaoru Hirota[1]

[1] Dept. of Computational Intelligence and Systems Science
Interdisciplinary Graduate School of Science and Engineering
Tokyo Institute of Technology
G3-49, 4259 Nagatsuta, Midori-ward, Yokohama 226-8502, Japan
`stejic@hrt.dis.titech.ac.jp`
[2] Dept. of Electronic Systems Engineering
Tokyo Metropolitan Institute of Technology, Tokyo, Japan

Abstract. We perform a multiperspective comparison of the retrieval performance of six variants of the region-based image similarity models. Our objective is to examine the effect on the retrieval performance, of: (1) the region matching approach, (2) the region weighting strategy, and (3) the number of regions. Common for the six variants is that: (1) images are uniformly partitioned into regions (i.e., rectangular blocks of equal size), at five different resolutions; and (2) from each region, color, shape, and texture features are extracted, and used for computing the region similarity. The difference between the variants is either in the region matching approach, or in the region weighting strategy. Regarding the region matching, the correspondence between pairs of regions of the two images is established based on either: (1) their spatial closeness, (2) their visual similarity, or (3) a combination of these. Regarding the region weighting, weights, as a function of distance between corresponding regions, either: (1) decrease linearly, (2) decrease exponentially, or (3) are constant. The evaluation of the six variants is performed on 5 test databases, containing 64,339 images, in 749 semantic categories. In total, 313,020 queries are executed, based on which the average (weighted) precision, recall, rank, and retrieval time are computed. Both the number of queries and the variety of the evaluation criteria make the evaluation more comprehensive than in the case of any of the existing works, dealing with the region-based image similarity models. Results of the evaluation reveal that, contrary to the expectations, the simplest variant results in the best overall retrieval performance.

1 Introduction

Modeling image similarity is one of the most important issues in the present image retrieval research [11, 15, 4]. When asked to retrieve the database images similar to the user's query image(s), the retrieval system must *approximate the user's similarity criteria*, in order to identify the images which satisfy the user's information need.

H. Christiansen et al. (Eds.): FQAS 2004, LNAI 3055, pp. 390–403, 2004.

User's similarity criteria are represented by an *image similarity model*, which typically expresses the image similarity in terms of low-level feature (e.g., color, texture, and shape) similarities [11]. The existing image similarity models can be divided into [11]: (1) *global similarity-based* ones, with features extracted from the whole image area; and (2) *region-based* (i.e., local similarity-based) ones, with features extracted from the image regions, obtained by the partitioning (i.e., segmentation) of the image area.

Region-based image similarity models are shown to outperform the global similarity-based ones, because regions roughly correspond to the objects appearing in the images, thus giving more flexibility in capturing the image semantics [11, 15]. While many different region-based image similarity models have been recently proposed [15, 4, 3, 9, 6, 12, 1, 13], several questions – common to the majority of the region-based models, and related to their practical applications – have not been sufficiently addressed in the existing works. These **questions** are related to the *effect on the retrieval performance*, of: (1) the different model parameters; (2) the image domains being searched; and (3) the size and structure of the image database.

With the **objective** to answer these questions – particularly the first one – in this paper we perform a *multiperspective comparison of the retrieval performance of six variants of the region-based image similarity models*. The six variants include various ideas from the existing models, and cover models of varying complexity, making it possible to generalize the results to the majority of other models as well.

The evaluation of the six variants is performed on a combination of Vistex [8], Brodatz [10], and Corel [5] image databases, with over 64,000 images, in around 750 semantic categories. In total, over 300,000 queries are executed, based on which the (weighted) precision, recall, average rank, and retrieval time are computed.

The main **contributions** of the present work are: (1) we identify the questions common to the majority of the region-based image similarity models, and related to their practical applications; (2) to answer these questions, we perform the most comprehensive comparison up to date, of the region-based image similarity models – judging both by the number of queries and by the variety of the evaluation criteria; and (3) based on the comparison, we obtain some unexpected and practically important results, concerning the relation of the model complexity and the retrieval performance.

The rest of the paper is structured as follows. In Section 2, the related works are surveyed, dealing with the region-based image similarity models. Next, in Section 3, the six variants of the region-based models are introduced. Finally, in Section 4, the multiperspective comparison of the six variants is described.

2 Related Works: Region-Based Image Similarity Models

2.1 General Characteristics of Region-Based Models

In region-based image similarity models, an image is represented as a collection of regions, obtained by the partitioning (i.e., segmentation) of the image area [15,

4, 13]. Each region is represented by a collection of low-level image features (e.g., color, shape, and texture), extracted from the region [15, 13]. Given a collection of regions with their respective features, similarity of a pair of images is computed in **three steps**:

1. *establish region correspondence*: define pairs of *corresponding regions*, i.e., decide on which pairs of regions of the two images to match;
2. *match corresponding regions*: for each pair of corresponding regions, compute the region similarity, based on the similarity of their respective features;
3. *compute image similarity*: based on the computed region similarities, compute the overall image similarity.

These three steps are common for the existing image similarity models, almost without exception [15, 4, 3, 9, 6, 12, 1, 13]. Steps 1 and 2 are intermixed, since the region correspondence is frequently established based on the region similarities, which requires the regions to be (initially) matched before the region correspondence is established. We note that region similarity – in addition to the *visual similarity* expressed by the features extracted from each region – may also include the *spatial closeness* of the corresponding regions, as well as other non-local features [15].

   Parameters of the region-based model – affecting its retrieval performance – include: (1) the image partitioning (i.e., segmentation) algorithm; (2) the number of regions used to represent each image; (3) the collection of features extracted from each region; (4) the approach used to establish the region correspondence; and (5) the feature and/or region weighting strategy, used for region matching and image similarity computation.

   In Section 4 – when examining the effect of various model parameters on the retrieval performance – we focus on: (1) the number of regions; (2) the approach to establish region correspondence; and (3) the region weighting strategy.

   We do not deal with the image segmentation, since it is well-recognized that – even in the case of the state-of-the-art segmentation algorithms – the resulting regions only roughly correspond to the objects appearing in the image [11, 15]. Consequently, we assume that the number of regions has more effect on the retrieval performance than the image segmentation algorithm. Because the inaccurate segmentation is inevitable, we employ the simple and computationally efficient uniform partitioning [13], which has additional advantages, from the viewpoint of similarity computation: (1) the number of regions is the same for all images, regardless of the image content; and (2) the shape (rectangular blocks) and size of all regions are the same. We also do not address the problem of feature selection, or the related problem of feature weighting, since it is a topic on its own, not specific only to region-based image similarity models. Accordingly, we employ the commonly used image features (Section 3).

2.2   Overview of Existing Region-Based Models

Since the objective of this work is to evaluate the performance of the basic region-based image similarity model variants – rather than to propose new models –

when surveying the existing works, we focus on the evaluation part, and put less emphasis on the details of each model.

However, it is necessary to notice that majority of the existing region-based image similarity models – e.g., those in [15, 4, 3, 9, 6, 12, 1] – are more sophisticated than any of the six variants used in the experiments. Despite this, the basic steps of the image similarity computation, as well as the related issues, are conceptually similar – making it possible to generalize the experiment results to other models as well.

From the evaluation viewpoint, the main disadvantage of the existing works – e.g., [15, 4, 3, 9, 6, 12, 1] – is that, even though large-scale image collections are used in the experiments, the systematic evaluation is typically performed on only a smaller-scale collections (up to a few thousand images). *Systematic evaluation* [15, 4] refers to using each database image as a query image (Section 4.1), and averaging the performance measures over all the images in the database – in this way, a bias can be avoided, coming from the particular choice of the subset of query images. As we demonstrate in Section 4.2, results of the evaluation involving smaller-scale image collections might by very misleading.

Furthermore, what affects the retrieval performance – besides the already discussed model parameters – are the characteristics of the image collection being searched. These characteristics include the image domain(s), the size, and the structure of the image collection. Here, the structure refers to the number and variety of: (1) semantic categories covered by the collection; and (2) images in each of the semantic categories. While several works evaluate the performance of region-based models over the different image domains [13, 15, 4], very few works discuss the effects of the collection size and structure on the performance.

In Section 4 – when evaluating the retrieval performance of the six model variants – we deal with some of the mentioned issues, that have not been sufficiently addressed in the existing works.

3   Variants of Region-Based Image Similarity Models

3.1   Common Characteristics of the Six Variants

Common for the six model variants are the image partitioning and the feature extraction.

Each image is uniformly partitioned into regions (i.e., rectangular blocks of equal size), at five different resolutions – 2×2, 3×3, 4×4, 5×5, and 6×6. Accordingly, the number of regions per image is between 4 and 36, depending on the resolution. Each resolution corresponds to a different image similarity model for each of the six model variants, meaning that the **number of models** used in the experiments is: 6 model variants $\times$ 5 resolutions = 30 models.

From each region, color, shape, and texture features are extracted, and used for computing the region similarity. These are the three features most commonly used in the image retrieval [11]. Color features are represented by *color moments* [14], resulting in a 9-D feature vector. Shape features are represented by *edge-direction histogram* [2], resulting in an 8-D feature vector. Texture features

Table 1. Main characteristics of the six variants of region-based image similarity models used in the experiments. *Visual similarity* is expressed in terms of color, shape, and texture features extracted from each region, while *spatial closeness* refers to the distance between the corresponding regions, expressed in the number of regions. *Linearly/exponentially weighted* refers to the weights as a function of distance between regions. *Average* denotes the average of region similarities, weighted or not. For details, see algorithms 1 and 2.

| | Image similarity computation step | | |
Model variant	Region correspondence (established based on)	Region similarity (computed as)	Image similarity (computed as)
M-1	spatial closeness	visual similarity	average
M-2	visual similarity	visual similarity	average
M-3	visual similarity & spatial closeness	linearly weighted visual similarity	average
M-4	visual similarity & spatial closeness	exponentially weighted visual similarity	average
M-5	visual similarity	visual similarity	linearly weighted average
M-6	visual similarity	visual similarity	exponentially weighted average

are represented by *texture neighborhood* [7], resulting in an 8-D feature vector. In total, each image region is represented by a 9-D + 8-D + 8-D = 25-D feature vector. It follows that – since the number of regions per image is between 4 and 36 – the feature space has dimensionality between $4 \times 25 = 100$ and $36 \times 25 = 900$, depending on the resolution of the uniform partitioning. The feature similarity values are inversely proportional to the *distance between the corresponding feature vectors*, which are computed using the *weighted Euclidean distance* [14] for color moments, and the *city-block distance* [11] for edge-direction histogram and texture neighborhood.

3.2   Distinguishing Characteristics of the Six Variants

Details of Image Similarity Computation. The difference between the six model variants is either in the region matching approach, or in the region weighting strategy. Regarding the region matching, the correspondence between pairs of regions of the two images is established based on either: (1) their spatial closeness, (2) their visual similarity, or (3) a combination of these. Regarding the region weighting, weights, as a function of distance between corresponding regions, either: (1) decrease linearly, (2) decrease exponentially, or (3) are constant.

Table 1 summarizes the main characteristics of each variant (M-1–M-6). For all variants, similarity of a pair of images is computed following the three steps described in Section 2.1, while Table 1 outlines each step. In the following, we

---

Algorithm 1 ComputeRegionSimilarities, used in variants M-2–M-6 (see Algorithm 2, line 8). Function VisSim($Q[q], I[i]$) computes the visual similarity of a pair of image regions ($Q[q], I[i]$), expressed as the average of feature – color, shape, and texture – similarities (Section 3.1). Function SpaDis($Q[q], I[i]$) computes the spatial distance of a pair of image regions ($Q[q], I[i]$), expressed in terms of the rectangular mesh of the image blocks (Section 3.1). Finally, functions LinWgt(d) and ExpWgt(d) realize the region weighting – as the linear or exponential function of the spatial distance d between the regions, respectively.

Input: Q, I : images (e.g., a query image and a database image);
    $\{Q[q] : 1 \leq q \leq N\}$, $\{I[i] : 1 \leq i \leq N\}$: regions of images Q and I, respectively;
    method $\in \{$M-2, M-3, M-4, M-5, M-6$\}$;
Output: region similarity values $\{$RegSim($Q[q], I[i]$) : $1 \leq q, i \leq N\}$;
  1: **for** ($q \leftarrow 1$ **to** N) **do**
  2:    **for** ($i \leftarrow 1$ **to** N) **do** $\langle N \times N$ region similarity values computed $\rangle$
  3:      compute VisSim($Q[q], I[i]$);
  4:      **if** (*method* $\in \{$M-2, M-5, M-6$\}$) **then**
  5:        RegSim($Q[q], I[i]$) $\leftarrow$ VisSim($Q[q], I[i]$);
  6:      **else if** (*method* $=$ M-3) **then**
  7:        RegSim($Q[q], I[i]$) $\leftarrow$ VisSim($Q[q], I[i]$) $\times$ LinWgt(SpaDis($Q[q], I[i]$));
  8:      **else if** (*method* $=$ M-4) **then**
  9:        RegSim($Q[q], I[i]$) $\leftarrow$ VisSim($Q[q], I[i]$) $\times$ ExpWgt(SpaDis($Q[q], I[i]$));
10:      **end if**
11:    **end for**
12: **end for**

---

discuss only the distinguishing characteristics of each variant, whereas the details are given in algorithms 1 and 2.

M-1 is the simplest variant, since the region correspondence is established based on *only the spatial closeness* of the regions of the two images – meaning that pairs of regions most spatially close to each other are matched. Since the uniform partitioning results in the same regions – in terms of size, shape, and spatial location – for all images, establishing region correspondence based on the spatial closeness requires no computation: simply the regions with the same location are matched (Algorithm 2, line 4).

M-2 is the second simplest variant, with the region correspondence established based on *only the visual similarity* of the regions of the two images – meaning that pairs of regions most visually similar to each other are matched. Visual similarity of a pair of regions is computed as the average of feature – color, shape, and texture – similarities (Section 3.1). Establishing region correspondence based on the visual similarity is computationally expensive, since the similarities for all possible pairs of regions of the two images must be precomputed (Algorithm 1, i.e., Algorithm 2, line 8), in order to determine the most visually similar pairs of regions (Algorithm 2, line 12).

In terms of the criterion for establishing the region correspondence – being the spatial closeness for M-1 and visual similarity for M-2 – variants M-1 and

---

Algorithm 2 ComputeImageSimilarity, implementing the six variants (M-1–M-6). Regarding the explanation of functions $\mathsf{VisSim}(Q[q], I[i])$, $\mathsf{SpaDis}(Q[q], I[i])$, $\mathsf{LinWgt}(d)$, $\mathsf{ExpWgt}(d)$, and $\mathsf{ComputeRegionSimilarities}$, see Algorithm 1. We note that, in the case of image regions ($Q[q]$ and $I[i]$), the index (q or i) denotes the spatial location of a region, in terms of the rectangular mesh of the image blocks (Section 3.1). Consequently, the same index (e.g., $Q[i]$ and $I[i]$) means that the two regions have the same spatial location (as in line 4). The region correspondence (Section 2.1) is established in line 4 for variant M-1, and in line 12 for the remaining five variants (M-2–M-6).

Input: Q, I : images (e.g., a query image and a database image);
$\quad \{Q[q] : 1 \le q \le N\}$, $\{I[i] : 1 \le i \le N\}$: regions of images Q and I, respectively;
$\quad method \in \{\text{M-1, M-2, M-3, M-4, M-5, M-6}\}$;
Output: similarity value ImageSim of images Q and I;

 1: ImageSim $\leftarrow$ 0;
 2: **if** ($method = $ M-1) **then**
 3: $\quad$ **for** ($i \leftarrow 1$ **to** N) **do** $\langle$ N region similarity values computed, unlike in line 8 $\rangle$
 4: $\quad\quad$ compute $\mathsf{VisSim}(Q[i], I[i])$; $\langle$ regions with the same location are matched $\rangle$
 5: $\quad\quad$ ImageSim $\leftarrow$ ImageSim $+$ $\mathsf{VisSim}(Q[i], I[i])$;
 6: $\quad$ **end for**
 7: **else** $\langle$ $method \in \{\text{M-2, M-3, M-4, M-5, M-6}\}$ $\rangle$
 8: $\quad$ ComputeRegionSimilarities; $\langle$ $\mathsf{RegSim}(Q[q], I[i])$ computed, see Algorithm 1 $\rangle$
 9: $\quad$ RegionPairs $\leftarrow \{(Q[q], I[i]) : 1 \le q, i \le N\}$; $\langle$ $N \times N$ region pairs $\rangle$
10: $\quad$ MatchedPairs $\leftarrow$ 0;
11: $\quad$ **while** (MatchedPairs $< N$) **do**
12: $\quad\quad$ find maximum $\mathsf{RegSim}(Q[q], I[i])$, for all $(Q[q], I[i]) \in$ RegionPairs,
$\quad\quad\quad$ and denote the corresponding $(Q[q], I[i])$ by $(Q[q_{max}], I[i_{max}])$;
13: $\quad\quad$ RegionPairs $\leftarrow$ RegionPairs $- \big(\{ (Q[q_{max}], I[i]) : 1 \le i \le N \} \cup$
$\quad\quad\quad\quad\quad\quad\quad\quad\quad\quad\quad\quad \{ (Q[q], I[i_{max}]) : 1 \le q \le N \} \big)$;
14: $\quad\quad$ MatchedPairs $\leftarrow$ MatchedPairs $+$ 1;
15: $\quad\quad$ RegSimMax $\leftarrow \mathsf{RegSim}(Q[q_{max}], I[i_{max}])$;
16: $\quad\quad$ SpaDisMax $\leftarrow \mathsf{SpaDis}(Q[q_{max}], I[i_{max}])$;
17: $\quad\quad$ **if** ($method \in \{\text{M-2, M-3, M-4}\}$) **then**
18: $\quad\quad\quad$ ImageSim $\leftarrow$ ImageSim $+$ RegSimMax;
19: $\quad\quad$ **else if** ($method = $ M-5) **then**
20: $\quad\quad\quad$ ImageSim $\leftarrow$ ImageSim $+$ $\big($RegSimMax $\times \mathsf{LinWgt}($SpaDisMax$)\big)$;
21: $\quad\quad$ **else if** ($method = $ M-6) **then**
22: $\quad\quad\quad$ ImageSim $\leftarrow$ ImageSim $+$ $\big($RegSimMax $\times \mathsf{ExpWgt}($SpaDisMax$)\big)$;
23: $\quad\quad$ **end if**
24: $\quad$ **end while**
25: **end if**

M-2 are complementary. The remaining four variants (M-3–M-6) are inbetween M-1 and M-2, as elaborated in the following.

In variants M-3 and M-4, the region correspondence is established based on *both the visual similarity and the spatial closeness* of the regions of the two images. Concretely, the visual similarity of a pair of regions is weighted by the spatial closeness, i.e., the distance between the regions (Algorithm 1, lines 7 and 9). The difference between variants M-3 and M-4 is in the fact that region weights – as a function of distance between the regions – decrease linearly for M-3 (Algorithm 1, line 7) and exponentially for M-4 (Algorithm 1, line 9).

Finally, in variants M-5 and M-6, the region correspondence is established based on *only the visual similarity* (as in M-2), however, when computing the image similarity, the region similarities are weighted by the spatial closeness of the corresponding regions (Algorithm 2, lines 20 and 22). The difference between variants M-5 and M-6 is in the fact that region weights – as a function of distance between the regions – decrease linearly for M-5 (Algorithm 2, line 20) and exponentially for M-6 (Algorithm 2, line 22).

While pairs of variants M-3/M-4 and M-5/M-6 both employ region weighting, in variants M-3/M-4 weighting is done before the region correspondence is established, while in variants M-5/M-6 weighting is done afterwards. From the viewpoint of whether spatial closeness affects the region correspondence or not, we note that variants M-3/M-4 are closer to M-1, while variants M-5/M-6 are closer to M-2.

Regarding the computational complexity, variants M-3–M-6 are somewhat more complex than variant M-2, because of the region weighting. Similarly, variants M-3/M-4 are slightly more complex than variants M-5/M-6, since in variants M-3/M-4 *all possible ($N \times N$) pairs of regions* of the two images are weighted (Algorithm 1, lines 7 and 9), while in variants M-5/M-6 *only the (N) pairs of corresponding regions* are weighted (Algorithm 2, lines 20 and 22).

Semantics Underlying Six Variants. Common for all the six variants is that the image similarity incorporates two elements: (1) *at the region level*: local similarity of corresponding regions of the two images; and (2) *at the image level*: structural similarity, i.e., similarity of the spatial relationships among the corresponding regions of the two images. The difference between the six variants is in the amount of emphasis put on each of the two elements.

Variant M-1, by matching the regions spatially close to each other, emphasizes only the structural similarity, and is not tolerant with respect to the translation or rotation of the regions. On the contrary, variant M-2, by matching the regions visually similar to each other, emphasizes only the local similarity, thus being tolerant to any arbitrary spatial perturbation of the regions. This means that, in the case of M-2, the similarity value of a pair of images will not change after the regions are rotated or translated, as long as the regions themselves (i.e., their local similarity) remain the same.

Variants M-3–M-6 emphasize both the structural and the local similarities, thus being inbetween M-1 and M-2. However, as explained earlier, variants M-3/M-4 emphasize the structural similarity more than the local one, thus begin closer to M-1, while with variants M-5/M-6 it is the other way around, making them closer to M-2.

Among the pairs of variants M-3/M-4 and M-5/M-6, which differ only in the region weighting strategy, variants with the linear weighting emphasize the structural similarity less than variants with the exponential weighting. This gives the following ordering of the six variants, with respect to the amount of emphasis put on the structural similarity (as opposed to the local one): (1) M-1, (2) M-4, (3) M-3, (4) M-6, (5) M-5, (6) M-2. At one extreme is the M-1, emphasizing only the structural similarity, while at the other extreme is the M-2, emphasizing only the local similarity.

As described, the six variants span a range of image similarity models, including various ideas from the existing models, and covering models of varying complexity. This makes it possible to generalize the results of the experiments to the majority of other models as well.

4   Experimental Comparison of Model Variants

4.1   Experimental Setting

Test Databases. Five test databases are used, containing 64,339 images, in 749 semantic categories: (1) **Vistex-668 database** [8] contains 668 color images in 19 categories (with 12–80 images each), showing homogeneous textures. The 668 images are obtained by partitioning each of the 167 original images into 4 non-overlapping regions, as in [13]; (2) **Corel-1000-A database** [5] contains 1,000 color photographs in 10 categories (with 100 images each), ranging from natural scenes to artificial objects [15]; (3) **Corel-1000-B database** [5] contains 1,000 color photographs in 10 categories (with 100 images each), showing natural scenes; (4) **Brodatz-1776 database** [10] contains 1,776 gray-scale images in 111 categories (with 16 images each), showing homogeneous textures. The 1,776 images are obtained by partitioning each of the 111 original images into 16 non-overlapping regions; and (5) **Corel-60k database** [5] contains 59,895 color photographs in 599 categories (with 97–100 images each), ranging from naural scenes to artificial objects [15].

All the five test databases originate from the well-known image collections, used for the evaluation of the image retrieval systems [15, 4, 13]. Partitioning of each database into semantic categories is determined by the creators of the database, and reflects the human perception of image similarity. The semantic categories define the **ground truth** in a way that, for a given query image, the relevant images are considered to be those – and only those – that belong to the same category as the query image. This implies that the number of relevant images for a given query image equals the number of images in the category to which that image belongs.

The five test databases cover three different image domains: (1) color homogeneous textures; (2) gray-scale homogeneous textures; and (3) unconstrained color photographs. We note that the ratio of the database size and the number of images per category significantly differs for the different databases.

Large variance among the visual characteristics, the number of images per category and in each test database, allows for general conclusions about the performance of the tested models.

Performance Measures. The performance measures we use are: (1) precision, (2) weighted precision, (3) precision-recall curve, (4) average rank, and

(5) retrieval time. These are the five most frequently used measures of the image retrieval performance [11]. All the five performance measures are computed for each query image, based on the given ground truth. Since each image, in each test database, is used as a query, all the performance measures are averaged for each image category (category-wise average performance), as well as for each test database (database-wise average performance).

For a given query image, precision is computed as the fraction of the relevant images that are retrieved among the top-ranked K images, where K is the total number of relevant images for that query image [15, 4, 13]. Weighted precision is computed in a similar way, however, the higher a relevant image is ranked, the more it contributes to the overall weighted precision value [15]. This means that, unlike the precision, weighted precision takes into account the rank of the retrieved relevant images as well. Precision-recall curve is a sequence of precision values, at the 10 standard recall levels (10%, 20%, ..., 100%). Average rank is simply the average of the rank values for the relevant images that are retrieved among the top-ranked K images, with K as described above. Retrieval time is the computational time required to: (1) compute the similarity values between the query image and all the database images; and (2) rank (i.e., sort) the database images with respect to the query image, according to the computed similarity.

Queries. As mentioned already, each image, in each test database, is used as a query image. The exception to this is the Corel-60k database, where only 10 randomly selected images from each category are used, in order to reduce the total number of query images. Accordingly, the number of query images for Corel-60k database is: 599 categories × 10 images = 5, 990.

If each query image defines a **test case** for a given image similarity model, then a total number of test cases per model is (summing the database-wise values): $668 + 1,000 + 1,000 + 1,776 + 5,990 = 10,434$.

The total **number of queries** executed in the experiments equals the number of models (Section 3.1) times the number of test cases per model, i.e., 6 model variants × 5 resolutions × 10, 434 test cases = 313, 020. For each query, all the five performance measures are computed.

4.2   Experiment Results and Discussion

The most important results of the experiments are summarized in Table 2 and Figure 1.

On one hand, from the viewpoint of retrieval effectiveness – measured by the precision, weighted precision, and average rank – the best-performing variant is M-2, with the average retrieval precision 2% higher than that of a second-best variant, M-1. On the other hand, from the viewpoint of retrieval efficiency – measured by the retrieval time – the best-performing variant is M-1, with the average retrieval time over 14 times shorter than that of a second-best variant, M-2. Regarding the overall retrieval performance, variant M-1 – although the simplest among the six variants – is by far the best, as Table 2 and Figure 1 show.

Table 2. Average values of the different performance measures for the six model variants: (a) Retrieval precision of each variant, evaluated on the five test databases, and averaged over the five resolutions for each database. Each value in the "Average" row is an average of 5 resolutions × 10, 434 test cases = 52, 170 queries; (b) Weighted precision (W.P.), expressed in percents, and average rank (A.R.) – both averaged over the 52, 170 queries. Retrieval time (R.T.), expressed in milliseconds, evaluated on Corel-60k database, at resolution 4 × 4 (i.e., 16 regions), and averaged over 5,990 queries.

(a)

Test	Average Precision [%]					
Database	M-1	M-2	M-3	M-4	M-5	M-6
V-668	34	35	34	34	34	33
C-1000-A	47	47	43	41	37	29
C-1000-B	37	38	35	34	32	28
B-1776	55	67	62	59	61	56
C-60k	5	5	4	4	3	3
Average	36	38	36	34	34	29

(b)

Perform.	Model Variant					
Measure	M-1	M-2	M-3	M-4	M-5	M-6
W.P. [%]	49	52	48	47	46	41
A.R.	3999	4033	4188	4287	4420	4769
R.T. [ms]	123	1736	1774	1778	1755	1745

As Figure 1-b shows for Corel-60k database, it is difficult to draw general conclusions regarding the effect of the number of regions on the retrieval effectiveness. The situation is similar for the other test databases as well. However, a tendency can be seen that, in variants which do not employ region weighting (M-1/M-2), performance improves with the increase in the number of regions, while in the remaining variants the effect appears to be opposite – probably caused by the current weighting strategy. Regarding the effect on the retrieval efficiency, the retrieval time is linearly proportional to the number of regions for variant M-1, and quadratically proportional for the remaining five variants (M-2–M-6) – as a the consequence of the approach for establishing region correspondence.

Regarding the effect of the weighting scheme on the retrieval effectiveness, linear weighting (variants M-3 and M-5) outperforms the exponential one (variants M-4 and M-6). The reason is that exponential weighting imposes too strict constraints on the spatial closeness of the visually similar pairs of regions. On the other hand, weighting does not significantly affect the retrieval time.

As Table 2-a shows, the image domain has a strong effect on the retrieval performance – the ordering of the variants with respect to the average retrieval precision is very different for the domain of homogeneous textures (Vistex-668 and Brodatz-1776 databases) than for the domain of unconstrained photographs (the three Corel databases). In general, the simplest variant (M-1) performs the worst on the domain of homogeneous textures. A possible explanation is that, when the number and the diversity of images in each category is small (as is the case with Vistex-668 and Brodatz-1776 databases), the underlying similarity criteria are more specific, and thus can be better captured by the more complex variants (M-2–M-6). On the contrary, when the number and the diversity of images in each category is bigger (as is the case with the three Corel databases), the underlying similarity criteria are less-specific, i.e., more general, and thus can be better captured by the simplest variant (M-1).

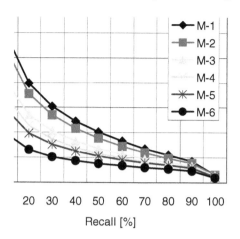

	M-1
	M-2
	M-3
	M-4
	M-5
	M-6

Recall [%]

Vari-	# Regions					Ave-
ant	4	9	16	25	36	rage
M-1	4.4	4.9	5.0	5.1	5.0	4.9
M-2	4.2	4.5	4.7	4.9	4.9	4.6
M-3	3.9	3.7	3.8	4.0	4.0	3.9
M-4	3.9	3.5	3.5	3.4	3.3	3.5
M-5	3.2	2.9	3.1	3.3	3.5	3.2
M-6	3.2	2.6	2.5	2.3	2.2	2.6

(a) Precision-recall curve   (b) Average precision [%]

Fig. 1. Performance of the six model variants on Corel-60k database: (a) Precision-recall curve, averaged over the five resolutions. Each point is an average of 5 resolutions × 5,990 test cases = 29,950 queries; (b) Average retrieval precision, in percents, for each of the five resolutions (with 2×2, 3×3, 4×4, 5×5, and 6×6 regions, respectively). Each value (except the "Average" column) is an average of 5,990 queries.

Finally, an observation about the effect of the size and structure of the image collection, on the retrieval performance. While all the six variants perform relatively well on the smaller test databases (all except the Corel-60k database), the performance radically drops on the biggest test database, with close to 60,000 images. This shows that: (1) the systematic performance evaluation – of the kind performed in this paper – is necessary to objectively estimate the performance of the image retrieval algorithms in the framework of practical applications, when large-scale image collections of complex structure are involved; and (2) the results of the evaluation involving smaller-scale image collections – of the kind performed in the existing works – might be very misleading.

At the very end, we note that the average retrieval precision of the state-of-the-art region-based image similarity model IRM [15] – on Corel-1000-A database – is 46%, while variants M-1 and M-2 both achieve 47% on the same test database. This implies that, despite their simplicity, the best-performing of the six variants do not lag behind the state-of-the-art.

5   Conclusion

We performed a multiperspective comparison of the retrieval performance of six variants of the region-based image similarity models.

Our objective was to identify and answer several questions – common to majority of the region-based image similarity models, and related to their practical applications – that have not been sufficiently addressed in the existing works.

In particular, we examined the effect on the retrieval performance, of: (1) the different model parameters; (2) the image domains being searched; and (3) the size and structure of the image database. We put particular emphasis on the model parameters.

The six model variants we compared include various ideas from the existing models, and cover models of varying complexity, making it possible to generalize the results to the majority of other models as well.

The evaluation of the six variants was performed on 5 test databases, containing 64,339 images, in 749 semantic categories. In total, 313,020 queries were executed, based on which the (weighted) precision, recall, average rank, and retrieval time were computed.

Both the number of queries and the variety of the evaluation criteria made the evaluation more comprehensive than in the case of any of the existing works, dealing with the region-based image similarity models. Results of the evaluation revealed that, contrary to the expectations, the simplest variant results in the best overall retrieval performance.

References

1. Bartolini, I., Ciaccia, P., Patella, M.: A sound algorithm for region-based image retrieval using an index. In: Proc. 11th IEEE Int. Workshop on Database & Expert Systems Applications (DEXA'00). London, UK (2000) 930–934
2. Brandt, S., Laaksonen, J., Oja, E.: Statistical shape features in content-based image retrieval. In: Proc. 15th Int. Conf. on Pattern Recognition (ICPR-2000), Vol. 2. Barcelona, Spain (2000) 1066–1069
3. Carson, C., Belongie, S., Greenspan, H., Malik, J.: Blobworld: image segmentation using expectation-maximization and its application to image querying. IEEE Trans. Pattern Analysis and Machine Intelligence. 24(8) (2002) 1026–1038
4. Chen, Y., Wang, J. Z.: A region-based fuzzy feature matching approach to content-based image retrieval. IEEE Trans. Pattern Analysis and Machine Intelligence. 24(9) (2002) 1252–1267
5. Corel Corp.: Corel Gallery 3.0. http://www3.corel.com/. (2000)
6. Deng, Y., Manjunath, B. S.: An efficient low-dimensional color indexing scheme for region-based image retrieval. In: Proc. IEEE Int. Conf. on Acoustics, Speech, and Signal Processing (ICASSP'99). Phoenix, AZ, USA (1999) 3017–3020
7. Laaksonen, J., Oja, E., Koskela, M., Brandt, S.: Analyzing low-level visual features using content-based image retrieval. In: Proc. 7th Int. Conf. on Neural Information Processing (ICONIP'00). Taejon, Korea (2000) 1333–1338
8. MIT, Media Lab.: Vision Texture Database. ftp://whitechapel.media.mit.edu/pub/VisTex/. (2001)
9. Natsev, A., Rastogi, R., Shim, K.: WALRUS: a similarity retrieval algorithm for image databases. In: Proc. ACM SIGMOD Int. Conf. on Management of Data (SIGMOD'99). Philadelphia, PA, USA (1999) 395–406
10. T. Randen: Brodatz Textures. http://www.ux.his.no/tranden/brodatz.html. (2002)
11. Smeulders, A. W. M., Worring, M., Santini, S., Gupta, A., Jain, R.: Content-based image retrieval at the end of the early years. IEEE Trans. Pattern Analysis and Machine Intelligence. 22(12) (2000) 1349–1380

12. Smith, J. R., Li, C. S.:. Image classification and querying using composite region templates. Int. Journal of Computer Vision and Image Understanding. 75(1–2) (1999) 165–174
13. Stejić, Z., Takama, Y., Hirota, K.: Genetic algorithm-based relevance feedback for image retrieval using Local Similarity Patterns. Information Processing and Management. 39(1) (2003) 1–23
14. Stricker, M., Orengo, M.: Similarity of color images. In: Proc. IS&T and SPIE Storage and Retrieval of Image and Video Databases III. San Jose, CA, USA (1995) 381–392
15. Wang, J. Z., Li, J., Wiederhold, G.: SIMPLIcity: Semantics-sensitive Integrated Matching for Picture LIbraries. IEEE Trans. Pattern Analysis and Machine Intelligence. 23(9) (2001) 947–963

Querying the SaintEtiQ Summaries – A First Attempt

W. Amenel Voglozin, Guillaume Raschia,
Laurent Ughetto, and Noureddine Mouaddib

Laboratoire d'Informatique de Nantes Atlantique, Université de Nantes
2 rue de la Houssinière, BP 92208, 44322 Nantes Cedex 3, France
{voglozin,raschia,ughetto,mouaddib}@lina.univ-nantes.fr

Abstract. For some years, data summarization techniques have been developed to handle the growth of databases. However these techniques are usually not provided with tools for end-users to efficiently use the produced summaries. This paper presents a first attempt to develop a querying tool for the SaintEtiQ summarization model. The proposed search algorithm takes advantage of the hierarchical structure of the SaintEtiQ summaries to efficiently answer questions such as "how are, on some attributes, the tuples which have specific characteristics?". Moreover, this algorithm can be seen both as a boolean querying mechanism over a hierarchy of summaries, and as a flexible querying mechanism over the underlying relational tuples.

1   Introduction

In order to handle the growth in size of databases, many approaches have been developed to extract knowledge from huge databases. One of these approaches consists in summarizing data (see for example [2, 4, 6, 9, 11]). However, summarization techniques are usually not provided with tools for end-users to efficiently use the summaries. As a consequence, users have to directly interpret the summaries, which is conceivable with a few summaries only. In other cases, tools are necessary.

In this paper, the structured data summarization model SaintEtiQ developed in our research team [11] is considered. SaintEtiQ provides a compact representation of a database, rewriting the tuples by means of linguistic variables [15] defined on each attribute, and classifying them in a hierarchy of summaries. The set of summaries, produced by the process, describes the data in a comprehensible form. Thus, each summary, expressed with fuzzy linguistic labels, symbolizes a concept that exists within the data.

This paper proposes a querying mechanism for users to efficiently exploit the hierarchical summaries produced by SaintEtiQ. The first idea is to query the summaries using the vocabulary of the linguistic variables defined in the summarization process. Although linguistic terms are used in the expression of queries, the querying process is clearly boolean. Since the querying vocabulary

H. Christiansen et al. (Eds.): FQAS 2004, LNAI 3055, pp. 404–417, 2004.
© Springer-Verlag Berlin Heidelberg 2004

is the one used within the summaries, the linguistic terms have become the attribute values in the summaries and query answers contain linguistic terms only. Then, basic queries such as "how are, on attribute(s) A_k, the tuples which are $d_{i,j}$ on A_i", can be answered very efficiently as the querying process relies on boolean operations. Moreover, the algorithm takes advantage of the hierarchical structure of the summaries, and answers are obtained rapidly. The gain is particularly important in case of a null answer, as only a small part of the summaries hierarchy has to be explored, instead of the entire relation.

Querying the summaries as explained above is interesting in order to rapidly get a rough idea of the properties of tuples in a relation. In case of null answers, it clearly saves time. In other cases, a rough answer is often not enough. Thus, the second idea is to query the database through the summaries, which would be done by retrieving tuples from the summaries obtained as an answer in the previous kind of queries. This process is then related to the "flexible querying of relational databases" trend of research. Indeed, in this case, linguistic terms are used in the expression of queries, and the answer would be composed of tuples from the summarized relation, ranked according to a degree of satisfaction to the query.

The next section describes flexible queries of databases and their features compared to classical queries. It exposes some earlier works done in this field by other researchers. Section 3 presents an overview of the SAINTETIQ model, briefly depicting the representations of summaries and the different steps of the summary building process. It also highlights the distinctive aspects of our approach. Section 4 thoroughly explains how advantage can be taken from the use of the SAINTETIQ summaries hierarchies in a flexible querying process. Expression of queries, selection of summaries and formation of results are then reviewed.

2   Regular Databases Flexible Querying

A flexible querying process operating on relational databases probes the tuples for adequacy to a query using a standard language, namely SQL. According to Larsen [8], the querying process can be divided in three steps: extension of criteria, selection of results and ordering.

The first step uses similarity between values to extend the criteria (sometimes using non-binary operators) and to find potentially interesting results. The second step, namely the selection of results, determines which data will participate in the answer to the query. These data are afterwards referred to by the term "results": the set of all results constitute the answer to a query. The last step (ordering) follows from the extension of criteria. It discriminates among the results on the basis of their relative satisfaction to the query.

The fuzzy set theory is often used in flexible querying (see [3]) because it provides a formal framework to handle the vagueness inherent to natural language. The following works, which are representative of the research on flexibility in database querying, exemplify the use of fuzzy sets. They are essentially characterized by a tuple-oriented processing, the possibility to define new terms and especially, the use of satisfaction degrees, which we have not accomplished yet.

2.1   SQLf

The querying language SQLf, proposed by Bosc and Pivert [1], is an extension of SQL aiming at "introducing fuzzy predicates into SQL wherever possible". An augmentation of both the syntax and semantics of SQL is performed in order to express elements of a query in a fuzzy form. These elements include operators, aggregation functions, modifiers (very, really, more or less), quantifiers (most, a dozen) as well as general description terms such as young or well-paid.

Evaluation of the query may be based on a particular interpretation of the query, for instance fuzzy sets crisp cardinality or Yager's ordered weighted averaging operators [14]. It occurs for each record and yields a grade of membership (of the record to the relation symbolizing the query) which is used to rank the results. An example of query in SQLf is "**select** 10 dpt **from** EMPLOYEE **group by** dpt **having** *most-of*(age = *young*) **are** *well-paid*" where standard SQL keywords are in bold face, and dpt and age are attributes from a relation named EMPLOYEE. The query selects the 10 departments which have the best satisfaction of the condition "most of the young employees are well-paid".

2.2   FQUERY

FQUERY [7] is an integration of flexible querying into an existing database management system, namely Microsoft Access. The system allows queries with vague predicates expressed through fuzzy sets. Queries may contain linguistic quantifiers and attach different levels of importance to attributes. In a such way of doing, the authors try to apply the *computing with words* paradigm and so, deal with linguistic values, quantifiers, modifiers and relations.

FQUERY uses fuzzy sets for the imprecision aspect and performs a syntax and semantics extension of SQL. Linguistic values and quantifiers are represented as fuzzy sets. The query is assimilated to a fuzzy set resulting from the combination of these sets. Accordingly, each record selected by a classical SQL query, has a matching degree used to rank that record since it indicates how well it corresponds to the query.

2.3   SummarySQL

Developed by Rasmussen and Yager [12], SummarySQL is a fuzzy query language intended to integrate summaries into a fuzzy query. The language can not only evaluate the truth degree of a summary guessed by the user but also use a summary as a predicate in a fuzzy query.

A summary expresses knowledge about the database in a statement under the form "**Q** objects in **DB** are **S**" or "**Q R** objects in **DB** are **S**". **DB** stands for the database, **Q** is a linguistic quantifier and **R** and **S** are summarizers (linguistic terms). One can obtain statements like "**most** people in **DB** are **tall**" or "**most tall** people in **DB** are **heavy**".

Predicates (summaries) and linguistic terms and are fuzzy sets in the expression that represents the selection condition. The expression is evaluated for each tuple and the associated truth values are later used to obtain a truth value for the summary. SummarySQL is used to determine whether, or to what extent, a statement is true. It can also be used to search for fuzzy rules.

3   Querying the SAINTETIQ Summaries

To concentrate flexible queries on database records may lead to prohibitive response times when a large number of records is involved, or when subqueries are expressed. Waiting for an answer for a long time is frustrating, particularly when the query fails.

Database summaries offer a means of significantly reducing the volume of input for processes that require access to the database. The response time benefits from the downsizing. Furthermore, for this querying process, performance does not depend on specific combinations of attributes, i.e., whether the attributes are indexed or not, since these summaries are general indexes for the underlying data [10]. This eliminates possible restrictions due to predefined queries tailored for efficiency.

When querying the summaries, the response time gain is made clearly at the expense of a loss of precision in the answer. This is of no importance when only a rough answer is required. But when more details about the tuples are required, querying the summaries is only a first step: the entire set of relevant tuples can be easily retrieved from the answer summaries. The querying mechanism remains efficient, and there is no loss of precision in the answer. However, the loss is in the querying language expressiveness, since for now only the linguistic variables used to build the summaries hierarchy can be used in the expression of the queries.

3.1   Summaries in SAINTETIQ

The SAINTETIQ model aims at apprehending the information from a database in a synthetic manner. This is done through linguistic summaries structured in a hierarchy. The model offers different granularities, i.e., levels of abstraction, over the data. The steps necessary to build a summary hierarchy are described below.

First, the fuzzy set theory is used to translate records in accordance with a *background knowledge* provided by the user. For each attribute, linguistic variables (which are part of the background knowledge) offer a mapping of the attribute's value to a linguistic label describing that value. For instance, with a linguistic variable for attribute INCOME (figure 1), a tuple value $t.$income $=50,000$ is expressed as $t.$income $= \{1.0/reasonable\}$ where 1.0 tells how well the label *reasonable* describes the value '$50,000'. Applying this mapping to

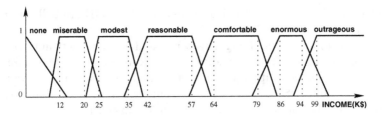

Fig. 1. Linguistic variable defined on INCOME

each attribute of a relation corresponds to a translation of the initial tuple into another expression called a *candidate tuple*.

Because one initial attribute value may be described by more than one fuzzy label (for instance, $37,000 is described by both modest and reasonable), one initial tuple may yield many translated representations, i.e., many candidate tuples. For a tuple $t = \langle v_1, v_2, \ldots, v_n \rangle$, a candidate tuple ct is under the form $ct = \langle \alpha_1/d_1, \alpha_2/d_2, \ldots, \alpha_n/d_n, \rangle$ where d_i is a fuzzy label and α_i is a satisfaction degree which tells how well v_i is described by d_i.

In a second place, comes a generalization step, allowing to represent fuzzy linguistic labels using more general labels.

Concept formation is the last step of the summary hierarchy building process. Each candidate tuple from each database record is incorporated into a tree and reaches a leaf node. This can be seen as a classification of the candidate tuple. It is important to notice that the tree is modified throughout candidate tuples incorporation: it progressively becomes a complete representation of the data. The way the tree evolves is partially controlled by learning operators. These operators discover new concepts (summaries) when necessary so that the current set of concepts reflects better the data.

For more clarity, let us mention that the tree represents the summary hierarchy and that a node represents a summary. In the hierarchy structure, the level can be associated with the relative proportion of data that is described by a summary: the deeper the summary in the tree (or the lower its level in the hierarchy), the finer the granularity. It follows that the lowest levels contain the most precise and specific summaries. The intensional expression of such summaries is similar to candidate tuples: $z = \langle \alpha_1/d_1, \alpha_2/d_2, \ldots, \alpha_n/d_n, \rangle$. There is only one label per attribute.

Inversely, the root of the tree is the most general summary view one can have over the data. The intensional expression of more general summaries may have one or more multi-labeled attributes. This depends on the labels that are present in the candidate tuples captured by the summaries. An example of such expression is $z = \langle \alpha_{11}/d_{11} + \alpha_{12}/d_{12}, \alpha_2/d_2, \ldots, \alpha_n/d_n, \rangle$.

As far as precision is concerned, the compact expression of a summary induces only an additional processing: for more details about tuples, one has to probe all of the summary's leaf nodes. No precision is lost since a candidate tuple is an exact representation of an initial tuple using the vocabulary given.

3.2   Distinctive Features

Our approach to flexible queries uses the SAINTETIQ summaries to answer questions such as "how are objects that have such and such characteristics?" (a few examples of questions can be found in Section 4.1). As the data searched by the querying process is made of summaries, it seems obvious to make results from summaries. Moving a step further, it is plain to retrieve other kinds of results such as candidate tuples or initial relational tuples.

Since one summary can be linked to candidate tuples by simply probing all its children leaves, the sort of results can be changed from summaries to candidate tuples. And one further step links candidate tuples to database records. Because the retrieval of candidate tuples or database records is immediate, in the rest of this document, results are assimilated to summaries only.

Another distinction exists in the classification step of the process: no preference is expressed as there is no evaluation of result quality with respect to the query. All results are shown to the user in a non-discriminated form and it is up to them to determine what results are better than others. As far as summaries are concerned, no ranking is performed.

4   Description of the Process

As stated in Section 2, the first step of a database flexible querying process consists in extending criteria. Thanks to linguistic variables defined for each attribute, criteria extension is already performed in SAINTETIQ. From then, we can use binary operators to identify the data to be considered as results. This section deals with all aspects of selection from the expression and meaning of a query to its matching against summaries.

To illustrate the querying process, we use a toy example based on a relation R =(thickness, hardness, temperature). R describes some imaginary steel industry materials over arbitrary features. For each attribute of R, the following descriptors are used:

- thickness: small, thin, medium, thick, huge;
- hardness: malleable, flexible, soft, medium, hard, compact, impenetrable;
- temperature: cold, low, moderated, normal, high, extreme.

4.1   Expression of a Query

This approach to flexible querying intends to answer questions such as "how are materials which are thin?" or "how are materials which are high-temperature and medium-hardness?". In the prototype developed for querying, the questions are expressed using a user-friendly interface that composes the corresponding query in an SQL-like language. For the previous questions, the queries formed are respectively:

Q_1: DESCRIBE ON temperature, hardness
   WITH thickness IN (thin)
Q_2: DESCRIBE ON thickness
   WITH temperature IN (high)
   AND hardness IN (medium)

Because an answer, for example "thin materials have a soft hardness and a low temperature", is a description of basic data (summaries, candidate tuples, database records), we consider description as an elementary operation. Embedding the DESCRIBE operator (and other operators from summary-based querying) in an extension of SQL is a future project. For a more formal expression, let:

- S be a set of attributes;
- R(S) be the relation whose tuples are summarized;
- Q be a query, for instance Q_1 or Q_2;
- A be an attribute appearing in the query ($A \in S$);
- d be a label (or descriptor) also appearing in the query.

A question explicitly defines some values (thin, high or medium) called *required characters*. In a query, descriptors embody required characters and serve as a basis for determining what data partake in the answer.

A question also defines, sometimes implicitly, the attributes for which required characters exist. The set of these input attributes for a query is denoted by X. The expected answer is a description over the other attributes, whose set is denoted by Y. Without further precision, Y is the complement of X relatively to S: $X \cup Y = S$ and $X \cap Y = \emptyset$.

Hence a query defines not only a set X of input attributes A_i but also, for each attribute A_i, the set C_{A_i} of its required characters. The set of sets C_{A_i} is denoted by C, as shown in the following example.

Example 1. Let Q_1 and Q_2 be the queries stated above.
   For Q_1, $X = \{$thickness$\}$, $Y = \{$hardness, temperature$\}$, $C_{\text{thickness}} = \{$thin$\}$ and $C = \{C_{\text{thickness}}\}$.
   For Q_2, $X = \{$hardness, temperature$\}$, $Y = \{$thickness$\}$, $C_{\text{hardness}} = \{$medium$\}$, $C_{\text{temperature}} = \{$high$\}$ and $C = \{C_{\text{hardness}}, C_{\text{temperature}}\}$.

When users formulate a question, they expect data with some characteristics to be put forward. The meaning of that question becomes arguable when many characteristics are expressed for one attribute or when conditions exist for more than one attribute.

The first case is illustrated by the question "how are materials which are flexible or soft?". Because the database records are one-valued tuples, the question is interpreted as "how are materials which hardness is one of {flexible, soft}?" and not as "how are materials which hardness is both flexible and soft?". The equivalent query for the correct interpretation is Q_3: DESCRIBE ON thickness, temperature WITH hardness IN (flexible, soft), interpreted as the condition *hardness = flexible OR hardness = soft*.

The second case is illustrated by the question "how are thick compact materials?". The querying process should put forward only data that comply with the characterization on both thickness and hardness. This precludes, for instance, thick soft materials and thin compact materials from being selected. The equivalent query for this second question is Q_4: DESCRIBE ON temperature WITH thickness IN (thick) AND hardness IN (compact). The condition of Q_4 is interpreted as *thickness = thick AND hardness = compact.*

4.2 Evaluation of a Query

This section deals with matching one particular summary against a query to decide whether it corresponds to that query and can then be considered as a result. The query is transformed into a logical proposition P used to qualify the link between the summary and the query. P is under a conjunctive form in which all descriptors appear as literals. In consequence, each set of descriptors yields one corresponding clause.

Example 2. For question q_5 "how are the materials which are thin or medium-thickness and normal or high-temperature?", the corresponding query is Q_5: DESCRIBE ON hardness WITH thickness IN (thin, medium) AND temperature IN (normal, high).

In this query, $X = \{thickness, temperature\}$, $C_{\texttt{thickness}} = \{thin, medium\}$ and $C_{\texttt{temperature}} = \{normal, high\}$. It follows that $P_5 = (thin \vee medium) \wedge (normal \vee high)$.

Let v be a valuation function. It is obvious that the valuation of P depends on the summary z: a literal d in P is positively valuated ($v(d) = \texttt{TRUE}$) if and only if d appears in z. So we denote by $v(P(z))$ the valuation of proposition P in the context of z.

Let $\mathcal{L}_{A_i}(z)$ be the set of descriptors that appear in z. An interpretation of P relatively to query Q leads to discarding summaries that do not satisfy P. But, as shown in the following example, some summaries might satisfy P and yet not match the intended semantics of the query.

Example 3. Table 1 shows the characteristics of materials covered by a summary z_0 along with z_0 itself. If z_0 is tested for conformance with Q_5 (see example 2), we can see that $v(P_5(z_0)) = \texttt{TRUE}$, but nowhere can one find a material responding to question q_5.

While confronting a summary z with a query Q, three cases might occur:

- **Case 1:** no correspondence. $v(P(z)) = \texttt{FALSE}$. For one attribute or more, z has no required character, i.e., it shows none of the descriptors mentioned in query Q.
- **Case 2:** exact correspondence. The summary being confronted with query Q matches its semantics. It is considered as a result. The following expression holds: $v(P(z)) = \texttt{TRUE}$ and $\forall i$, $\mathcal{L}_{A_i}(z) \subseteq C_i$.

Table 1. Example of descriptor combination

	thickness	temperature
ct_1	thin	extreme
ct_2	medium	extreme
ct_3	thick	high
z_0	{thin, medium, thick}	{extreme, high}

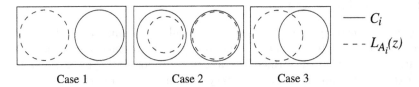

Case 1   Case 2   Case 3

——— C_i

- - - $L_{A_i}(z)$

Fig. 2. Comparison of descriptor sets $\mathcal{L}_{A_i}(z)$ and C_i

– **Case 3:** no decision can be made. There is one attribute A_i for which summary z exhibits one or many descriptors besides those strictly required (i.e., those in C_i): $\exists i, \mathcal{L}_{A_i}(z) - C_i \neq \emptyset$.
Presence of required characters in each attribute of z suggests, but does not guarantee, that results may be found in the subtree starting from z. Exploration of the subtree is necessary to retrieve possible results: for each branch, it will end up in situations categorized by case 1 or case 2. Thus, at worst at leaf level, an exploration leads to accepting or rejecting summaries; the problem of indecision is always solved.

The situations stated above reflect a global view of the confrontation of a summary with a query. They can also be interpreted, from a crisp set point of view, as a combination of comparisons, still involving $\mathcal{L}_{A_i}(z)$ and C_i, concerning one required attribute A_i. Figure 2 shows all comparisons using a set representation with $\mathcal{L}_{A_i}(z)$ symbolized by a dashed circle and C_i by a solid circle.

4.3   Selection Algorithm

This section applies the matching procedure from the previous section over the whole set of summaries organized in a hierarchy.

Since the selection should take into account all summaries that correspond to the query, exploration of the hierarchy is complete. The selection (algorithm 1) is based on a depth-first search and relies on a property of the hierarchy: the generalization step in the SAINTETIQ model guarantees that any descriptor that exists in a node of the tree also exists in each parent node. Inversely, a descriptor is absent from a summary's intension if and only if it is absent from all subnodes of this summary. This property of the hierarchy permits branch cutting as soon as it is known that no result will be found. Depending on the query, only a part

Algorithm 1 Function Explore-Select(z, Q)

$L_{res} \leftarrow \langle \rangle$ {the list for this subtree is empty}
if $\text{Corr}(z, Q) = indecisive$ **then**
    for all child node z_{child} of z **do**
        $L_{res} \leftarrow L_{res} +$ Explore-Select(z_{child}, Q)
    end for
else
    if $\text{Corr}(z, Q) = exact$ **then**
        Add(z, L_{res})
    end if
end if
return L_{res}

---

of the hierarchy is explored. In any case, all relevant results, and only relevant results, are captured.

Algorithm 1 describes the exploration and selection function with the following assumptions:

- the function returns a list of summaries;
- function Corr symbolizes the matching test reported in Section 4.2;
- operator '+' performs a list concatenation of its arguments;
- function Add is the classical constructor for lists, it adds an element to a list of the suitable type;
- L_{res} is a local variable.

4.4   Classification

The classification step is an aggregation of selected summaries according to their interpretation with respect to proposition P: summaries that have the same required characters on all attributes of the input attributes set X form a class that is denoted by B.

Example 4. Once again query Q_5 from question q_5 is considered. The proposition P_5 induced by Q_5 (see example 2) admits 9 classes that match the following interpretations where only positively valuated literals are shown: {thin, normal}, {thin, high}, {medium, normal}, {medium, high}, {thin, medium, normal}, {thin, medium, high}, {thin, normal, high}, {medium, normal, high}, {thin, medium, normal, high}.

Let z_1 and z_2 be two summaries selected for Q_5. Assume that they are described by "thin" for the thickness and "normal" for the temperature. Then, they belong to the same class {thin, normal}. Had they been described by "medium" for the thickness, "normal" and "high" for the temperature, they would have belonged to the class {medium, normal, high}.

Aggregation of summaries inside a class B is a union of descriptors (see example 5): for each attribute A_i of output set Y, the querying process supplies

Table 2. Example of selected summaries

Summary	**hardness**
z_1	flexible
z_2	soft
z_3	hard
z_4	compact

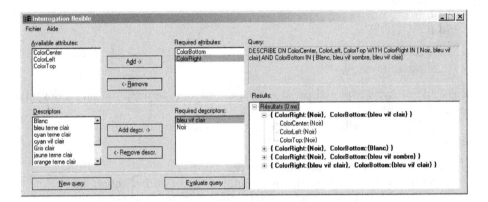

Fig. 3. Screenshot of the current implementation

a set of descriptors. This set of descriptors characterizes summaries that respond to the query through the same logical interpretation (i.e., summaries that show the same labels for input attributes).

Example 5. Table 2 lists summaries selected for class {thin, normal} along with their descriptors for attributes of Y = {hardness}. For that class, we obtain an output set C_{hardness} ={flexible, soft, hard, compact}.

The use of classes stems from the desire to provide the user with an intensional expression of results. As a response to a query, the process returns a list of classes along with a characterization of the class for each output attribute. The list is interpreted as follows: *while searching for thin or medium-thickness and normal or high-temperature materials, it turned out that:*

 — *thin normal-temperature materials are either flexible or soft;*
 — *thin high-temperature materials are hard;*
 — *...*

Figure 3 shows a screenshot of the current implementation of the querying process. The data set used for this specific screenshot describes the images of an image repository based on their color characteristics. For the expression of a query, we followed Larsen's idea that the query language should be "on the human user's condition" (see [8]). This lead to a Microsoft Access-like procedure where the user tells which attributes are required and for each of these, which fuzzy linguistic labels are wanted. The relevant query is formed by the system and displayed. The list of classes discussed in the previous paragraph can be seen on the right side of figure 3 with classes in bold face and output characterizations in normal style font.

4.5   From Summaries to Tuples in an Answer

In the summarization process, the rewriting of data into fuzzy labels produces satisfaction degrees that tell how well a label describes the data. The satisfaction degrees, which are part of a summary's intension, are not used in this paper. But the qualitative information carried by these degrees is interesting, particularly to make a better distinction between results.

A fully flexible querying process with a ranking of results can build on our approach. In a first approximation, summaries are a general index over the data used to quickly reduce the search space. Then, a second step retrieves tuples from the output summaries extension. Finally, the degrees attached to each tuple can be taken into account to compute a total satisfaction degree of the query. This second step is the subject of a future paper.

An additional enhancement would deal with a quantitative aspect. Besides satisfaction degrees, the SAINTETIQ model provides frequency and proportion data attached to descriptors and candidate tuples [10]. By using that data, we will be able to express more information in a response, for instance the response in example 5 might be "thin normal-temperature materials are either flexible or soft but only a little part of them are soft".

5   Conclusion and Future Research

In this paper, a querying tool for the summarization model SAINTETIQ has been proposed. It allows end-users to efficiently retrieve summaries, and exploits the hierarchical structure of the summaries produced by SAINTETIQ.

From a technical point of view, it performs a boolean matching between the summaries and the query on the basis of linguistic labels from a user-defined vocabulary. It is therefore a classical boolean querying tool whose novelty lies in the use of summaries and in the efficient use of a hierarchy. The querying machinery, as well as a user-friendly interface have been developed and tested on toy examples in order to validate the method.

Then, as it is easy to obtain tuples from summaries, and to rank the tuples according to their membership degree to the summaries, it has been shown that the method can also be considered as a flexible querying tool on a relational database. The flexibility entirely relies in the summarization process, and this is one of the reasons why the process is efficient.

Besides, this work is a first attempt at querying the summaries, and the richness of the framework is far from being entirely exploited. Several future developments, such as the possibility to use another vocabulary, are under consideration.

Above all, expressiveness is the main point future work will focus on as it will eventually allow imprecision in not just the representation of information but also in user queries. It might also cover preferences or priorities in queries as mentioned by Rocacher in [13].

An important concern resides in making use of the different levels of granularity that a summary hierarchy offers. For now, the selection procedure returns summaries that are at different levels in the hierarchy. As interpretation is not straightforward, we will investigate making the selection descend as far as possible, even when a summary that matches exactly the query is found on the way to leaf nodes.

From the logical or set-based expression of queries, determining the reasons of a search failure is simple (see 4.2). From then, an interaction with the user will permit us to implement one of the cooperative behaviors (corrective answers) surveyed by Gaasterland in [5]. We may display the reasons of a failure, that is the fuzzy labels in the query that cause the failure, so that the user could ask a new query based on the previous one.

References

1. Patrick Bosc and Olivier Pivert. Fuzzy queries and relational databases. In *Proc. of the ACM Symposium on Applied Computing*, pages 170–174, Phoenix, AZ, USA, March 1994.
2. Juan C. Cubero, Juan M. Medina, Olga Pons, and María Amparo Vila Miranda. Data summarization in relational databases through fuzzy dependencies. *Information Sciences*, **121 (3-4)**:233–270, 1999.
3. Didier Dubois and Henri Prade. Using fuzzy sets in database systems: Why and how? In *Flexible Query Answering Systems*, pages 45–59. Kluwer Academic Publishers, Boston, September 1997.
4. Didier Dubois and Henri Prade. Fuzzy sets in data summaries – outline of a new approach. In *Proc. 8th Int. Conf. on Information Processing and Managament of Uncertainty in Knowledge-based Systems (IPMU'2000)*, volume 2, pages 1035–1040, July 2000.
5. Terry Gaasterland, Parke Godfrey, and Jack Minker. An overview of cooperative answering. *Journal of Intelligent Systems*, 1(2):123–157, 1992.
6. Janusz Kacprzyk. Fuzzy logic for linguistic summarization of databases. In *Proceedings of the 8th International Conference on Fuzzy Systems (FUZZ-IEEE'99)*, volume 1, pages 813–818, August 1999.
7. Janusz Kacprzyk and Slawomir Zadrożny. Computing with words in intelligent database querying: standalone and Internet-based applications. *Information Sciences*, **134**:71–109, May 2001.
8. Henrik Legind Larsen. An approach to flexible information access systems using soft computing. In *Proceedings of the 32nd Hawaii International Conference on System Sciences*, volume 6, January 1999.
9. Do Heon Lee and Myoung Ho Kim. Database summarization using fuzzy isa hierarchies. *IEEE Transactions on Systems, Man and Cybernetics-Part B: Cybernetics*, **27**:68–78, February 1997.
10. Guillaume Raschia. SAINTETIQ: *une approche floue pour la génération de résumés à partir de bases de données relationnelles*. PhD thesis, Université de Nantes, December 2001.

11. Guillaume Raschia and Noureddine Mouaddib. SaintEtiQ: a fuzzy set-based approach to database summarization. *Fuzzy Sets And Systems*, **129**:137–162, 2002.

12. Dan Rasmussen and Ronald R. Yager. SummarySQL - a fuzzy tool for data mining. *Intelligent Data Analysis*, **1**:49–58, 1997.

13. Daniel Rocacher. On fuzzy bags and their application to flexible querying. *Fuzzy Sets And Systems*, **140**:93–110, November 2003.

14. Ronald R. Yager. On ordered weighted averaging aggregation operators in multicriteria decisionmaking. *IEEE Transactions on Sytems, man and Cybernetics*, **18**:183–190, 1988.

15. Lotfi A. Zadeh. The concept of a linguistic variable and its application to approximate reasoning. *Information Sciences*, **8**:199–249 & 301–357, 1975. Part III in volume **9**, pages 43-80.

Flexible User Interface
for Converting Relational Data into XML

Anthony Lo, Reda Alhajj, and Ken Barker

ADSA Lab, Department of Computer Science,
University of Calgary, Calgary, Alberta, Canada
{chiul,alhajj,barker}@cpsc.ucalgary.ca

Abstract. This paper presents VIREX (**VI**sual **RE**lational to **X**ML)
as a flexible user interface for converting a selected portion of a given
relational database into XML. VIREX works even when the catalogue
of the relational database is missing; it extracts the required catalogue
information by analyzing the database content. From the catalogue information, whether available or extracted, VIREX derives and displays
on the screen a graph similar to the entity-relationship diagram. VIREX
provides a user-friendly interface to specify on the graph certain factors
to be considered while converting relational data into XML. Such factors include: 1) selecting the relations/attributes to be converted into
XML; 2) specifying a predicate to be satisfied by the information to be
converted into XML; 3) deciding on the order of nesting between the relations to be converted into XML. All of these are specified by a sequence of
mouse clicks with minimum keyboard input. As a result, VIREX displays
on the screen the XML schema that satisfies the specified characteristics
and generates the XML documents from the relational database. Finally,
VIREX helps in optimizing the amount of information to be transferred
over a network. Also, it can be used to teach XML to beginners.

Keywords: data conversion, graphical user interface, relational database,
visual query language, XML.

1   Introduction

The problem of converting relational data into XML assumes special significance
because huge amounts of data are currently stored in relational databases which
are still dominant. There are several tools and languages out there to generate
XML documents from relational database, e.g., [8, 3]. However, most of these
approaches require users to learn a new language before they can query the
database to create the desired data files. They mainly focus on finding DTD [1]
or XML schema [2] that best describes a given relational database with a corresponding well-defined database catalogue that contains all information about
tables, keys and constraints. A disadvantage of using DTD is that it provides
very limited data types and also its very limited ability to add constraints to
data to be added into elements. XML schema allows a more sophisticated and
precise definition for both structure and data.

H. Christiansen et al. (Eds.): FQAS 2004, LNAI 3055, pp. 418–431, 2004.
© Springer-Verlag Berlin Heidelberg 2004

The Relational-to-XML conversion involves mapping the relational tables and attributes into XML elements and attributes, creating XML hierarchies, and processing values in an application specific manner. Such conversion process is systematic and mainly performed by professionals. However, we argue that it is essential to consider visual user-friendly interface because providing such an interface will definitely increase the acceptance of XML in the community and will provide an excellent training tool for XML beginners. So far, extensive research and different visual user interfaces have been successfully developed for querying relational and object-oriented databases; they are well received by naive users. However, developing user-friendly transformation tools that provide the opportunity to convert all or part of a given relational database into XML has not been considered enough.

This paper presents a flexible user interface called VIREX (**VI**sual **RE**lational to **X**ML), which facilitates converting all or a selected portion of a given relational database into XML. VIREX connects to a relational database specified by the user and uses the information from the database catalogue to derive and display on the screen a graph similar to the entity-relationship diagram (ERD). VIREX works even for circumstances where the catalogue of the underlying relational database is missing. For the latter case, VIREX extracts the required catalogue information by employing our approach described in [4] for analyzing the underlying database content. The graph simply summarizes all schema information in a pictorial interface that shows the relations, their attributes and the links between them. Certain factors may be specified on the graph to be considered while converting relational data into XML. Such factors include: 1) selecting the relations/attributes to be converted into XML; 2) specifying a filtering predicate to be satisfied by the information to be converted into XML; 3) deciding on the order of nesting between the relations to be converted into XML. The order of nesting is specified dynamically by the user dragging one node (relation) from the graph and including it inside another node. Several levels of nesting are supported, and the system allows for the nesting of only relations that have link between them. Not specifying any nesting will lead to a flat XML schema. After these three requirements are specified, VIREX displays on the screen the XML schema that satisfies the specified characteristics and generates the XML document from the underlying relational database. The user is given the opportunity to save the XML document and the corresponding schema. Finally, VIREX is essential to optimize the amount of information to be transferred over a network by giving the user the flexibility to specify the amount of relational data to be converted into XML. Also, VIREX can be used to teach XML to beginners.

The rest of the paper is organized as follows. Section 2 discusses the related work. Section 3 provides an overview of VIREX from users' perspective. The basic operations supported by VIREX are describes in Section 4. Section 5 focuses on the backend of the system, including the information kept by VIREX and the algorithms used in the conversion process. Section 6 is summary and conclusions.

2   Related Work

Visual query languages received considerable attention in the database community trying to bridge the usability gap for users. As a result, different visual query interfaces have been proposed since the start of automated databases. Query-By-Example developed by Zloof [16] is accepted as the first visual query language. A comprehensive survey about visual query systems for databases is presented in [5]. However, visual user friendly interfaces for converting relational data into XML have not received considerable attention. Hence, the work described in this paper is essential as a flexible and dynamic interactive visual approach for converting relational data into XML.

Recently there are some efforts to develop visual interfaces for XML. For instance, DataGuides [9] is a user interface for browsing XML data used in the Lore system [11]. In the current approaches described in the literature users do not have much control on how the resulting structure is achieved. Compared to this, VIREX is more flexible in allowing users to specify the structure of the XML document in terms of nesting as well as the portion of the relational data to be converted. VIREX integrates the whole process in a single flexible visual conversion tool.

XML-GL [6] and Xing [7] are visual XML query languages for querying and restructuring XML data, whereas VXT [14] is a visual XML transformation language. Xing is designed for a broad audience including end-users who wish to create queries, also expressed as rules, containing information on the structure to be queried. It is therefore significantly less expressive than XML-GL and VXT. It relies on a form-based interface which does not seem able to handle large documents, thus limiting the tool to small transformations for end-users.

The work of Shanmugasundaram et al [15] allows users to create XML data by using SQL to query the relational database; the query output is sent to some XML constructor function, which needs to be defined for each XML document. From the example given in their paper, the constructors seem to be fairly simple. Visual SQL-X [13] is a graphical tool for generating XML document from relational databases. It provides the user interface for users to edit the query and then the query can be executed later to generate XML documents. Although in their interface, they provide help for users to manage the textual query, the method is not as intuitive as visual query construction. In addition, users need to learn a new query language in order to use Visual SQL-X. BBQ [12] is a system with strong support for interactive query formulation. A tree is used in the interface to represent the tree construct of the DOM object. They allow users to perform simple operations visually on the tree in order to query, join, and filter data from the source. The XML data sources are queried and the results are presented as new XML documents and DTD. The functionality supported in BBQ and VIREX are quite similar, except that VIREX has a more flexible user interface, focuses on XML document generation from relational data, and uses XML schema instead of DTD.

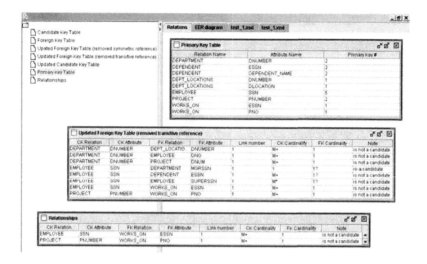

Fig. 1. The basic information extracted by analyzing database contents

3 An Overview of VIREX Front-End

VIREX connects to the relational database specified by the user and checks for the database catalogue to be used in constructing a graph similar to ERD. This graph is to be used by the user in specifying preferences regarding the portion of the database to be converted into XML. In case the database catalogue is missing, mainly for legacy databases developed using traditional programming techniques, VIREX analyzes the database content and extracts the catalogue information necessary for constructing the required ERD. The later process is performed using our approach described in [4], which generates primary and foreign keys; optimizes the foreign keys to eliminate symmetric and transitive references, which may result from a database design flaw; and finds all relationships (including n-ary) between relations. The catalogue related information is displayed on the screen as shown in Figure 1; content of any table are displayed by double clicking on its name.

ERD allows users to visualize the database model and create queries interactively. Its nodes correspond to relations in the database and the links between them represent relationships simulated by foreign keys. As shown in Figure 2, cardinalities of the links are specified and a key icon is displayed next to attribute(s) that form a primary key. Users may drag nodes of the ERD and move them around to give a nicer look for the diagram. Doing this will dynamically move the links as they are always connecting nodes of the graph. Finally, VIREX provides several operations for users to create queries visually using the ERD; these operations include selecting/unselecting relations and attributes, specifying filtering predicates, and decide on nesting. These operations are discussed next in Section 4.

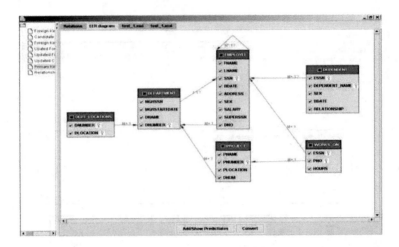

Fig. 2. ERD for the example relational database

4 Basic Operations in VIREX

VIREX provides different operations that allow users to visually convert a specific portion of a relational database into XML document and corresponding schema. These operations include selection of relations and attributes, moving relations, dragging to specify nesting of relations to be considered while converting into XML, and specifying predicates to filter relational data to be converted into XML. In this section, we discuss how these operations can help users to construct their desired XML document and schema.

The relations and attributes selection feature allows users to include relations in a query and project on certain attributes. This can be done using the checkbox next to a relation or an attribute in the ERD. Finally, when any attribute involved in a primary key (foreign key) is not selected, information about the primary key (foreign key) will not be added to the result XML schema.

Users can drag relations to dynamically nest one relation inside another as shown in Figure 3. It is a metaphor of creating a nested relation element inside another. In Figure 3, DEPT_LOCATIONS is nested inside DEPARTMENT. So, for each tuple of DEPARTMENT, a list of tuples form DEPT_LOCATIONS will be nested if they have the same value for DNUMBER.

The two operations: nesting and joining relations are actually very similar. The only difference is the format of the result because XML allows nesting, while relational data is flat. Nesting is sometimes desirable because it also improves performance of sequential scan through the XML document. VIREX allows users to nest only relations that have a link between them. It also supports multiple levels of nesting as demonstrated by the nesting PROJECT inside WORKS_ON and WORKS_ON inside EMPLOYEE as shown in Figure 3. Details about the result of nesting are discussed with illustrative examples next in Section 5.

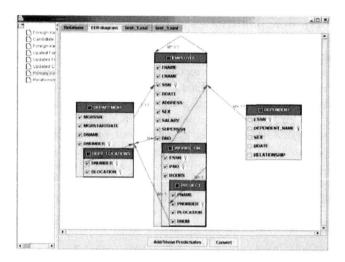

Fig. 3. Nested Relations

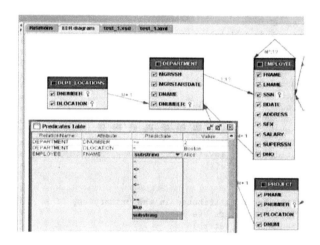

Fig. 4. Predicate construction

VIREX also allows users to specify predicates to filter the relational data to be converted into XML. A predicate is constructed using the visual interface shown in Figure 4, where users may select from drop down lists comparison operators as well as names of relations and attributes to be used in the predicate. VIREX supports the basic SQL comparison operators. Also two predicates may be connected by "and" or "or" to form another predicate.

5 Models and Algorithms

Some of the tables kept by VIREX include primary keys table, foreign keys table, and predicate-specification table. The first two tables are shown in Figure 1;

they, respectively, store primary keys and foreign keys present in the relational schema. A sample third table is shown in Figure 4. VIREX also keeps for its table a reference to its nested parent, which is set to null by default. When a relation is dragged inside another one, the reference inside the former relation is set to point to the latter relation. This information serves as input to the XML schema and document generation algorithms discussed next in this section.

There are two major algorithms used for generating the XML schema and XML document by considering user specifications on the ERD. Algorithm 51 calls some basic and simple methods for creating building blocks of the XML schema generated. These methods create XML elements which represent a primary key (key element), a foreign key (keyref element), a relation (called relation_complexType), a tuple from a relation (called tuple_complexType), etc.

Algorithm 51 *EERtoXMLSchema(DBModel, PK_Table, FK_Table)*

```
Return: XML Schema
1  dSchema <- Create the XML document and set namespace declaration
2  eSchema <- Create an XML Element
3  Set eSchema as the root element of dSchema
4  eDatabase <- Create an XML Element
5  add eDatabase to eSchema
6  for each Relation R in DBModel
7   if R is selected /* create complex type element for relation */
8    eleRC <- create_Relation_Complex(R)
9    add eleRC to eSchema
10   eleTC <- create_Tuple_Complex(R, selected_attributes(R))
11   add eleRC to eSchema
12   /* add Relationship Element for fast reference*/
13   if R is referenced in FK_Table
14     let X be the relation which references R
15     raPair <- find all relations and attributes pairs referenced by X
16     create_Relationship(R, raPair)
17     create_RelationReference(X)
18   end if
19   /* add primary key */
20   let attrs be the set of attributes in the primary key of R
21   if (all attributes in attrs are selected)
22     keyR <- create_key(R, attrs)
23     add keyR to eDatabase
24   end if
25  end if
26 end for
27 for each foreign key FK in FK_Table
28   let RF be the relation which contains FK
29   let RT be the relation which FK points to
30   let AF be the set of attributes that refers to RT
31   if (both RF and RT are selected) /*add foreign key */
32     keyrefR <- create_keyref(RF, AF, RT)
33     add keyrefR to eDatabase
34     /* add nested element if it is nested in ERD */
35     if (RF is nested under RT)
36        eNested <- create_nestedElement(RF)
37        eComplexType_RT <- find_Tuple_ComplexType_For_Relation(RT)
38        add eNested to eComplexType_RT
39     else if (RT is nested under RF)
40        eNested <- create_nestedElement(RT)
41        eComplexType_RF <-find_Tuple_ComplexType_For_Relation(RF)
```

```
42              add eNested to eCompleType_RF
43      end if
44    end if
45 end for
```

In lines 1-5 of Algorithm 51, the XML schema is created and the corresponding namespace is set. This algorithm has two major loops. The first loop (lines 6-26) creates for each selected relation the relation_complexType, the tuple_complex-Type, the key element and Relationship element, if exist. The second loop (lines 28-46) creates a keyref element for each foreign key in the selected portion of the database. For each considered foreign key, the algorithm checks whether the user specified nesting between the relations related by the foreign key; this is reflected into the XML schema by adding a reference of nested element from the nested relation to the other relation.

For creating the XML document, Algorithm 52 goes through the list of top-level and selected relations and creates for each relation a corresponding element; it calls Method 51.

Algorithm 52 *createXmlDocument(DBModel, predicateTable)*

```
Return: XML Document
1 dDocument <- create XML document and set its namespace declaration
2 eDocRoot <- create Root XML Element
3 set eDocRoot as the root element of dDocument
4 for each relation R in DBModel
5  if R is selected and is not nested under any relation
6  tuple_complexType <- find the tuple_complexType of R from dSchema
7   createRelElement(dDocument,eDocRoot,R,tuple_complexType,predicateTable)
8  end if
9 end for
```

Method 51 *createRelElement(dDocument, eDocRoot, relName, tuple_complex-Type, predicateTable)*

```
1 eRelation <- create empty Relation Element
2 queryString <- "select * from {relName}"
3 queryString_where <- emptyString
4 for each constraint in the predicateTable
5  if the constraint.relName == relName
6   if queryString_where == emptyString
7     queryString_where <- "where"
8   else
9     queryString_where <- queryString_where + "and"
10   end if
11   queryString_where <- constraint.relName + attributeName
12                      + comparison_operator + value
13  end if
14 end for
15 queryString <- queryString + queryString_where
16 ResultSet <- execute(queryString)
17 for each tuple T in ResultSet
18  eTuple <- create Relation_Tuple Element
19  create an element for each selected attribute and add it to eTuple
20  eComplexType_Tuple <- find_Tuple_ComplexType_for_Relaion(relName)
21 /* check for Relationship Element */
22  if eComplexType_Tuple has an element of type {relName}_RelationReference
23   createNaryRelationshipElement(docRoot, relName, eTuple)
```

```
24 /* check for nested Element */
25 else if (eComplexType_Tuple contains a nested element)
26    nestedElementName <- get nestedElement Name from eComplexType_Tuple
27    eComplexType_Tuple <- find Tuple_ComplexType for nestedRelName
28    eKeyRef <- find keyref between relations relName and nestedElement
29    if the nested Element references this relation
30      pKeys <- find attributes of this relation
31    else this relation refers to the nested relation
32      pKeys <- find attributes of the nested relation
33    end if
34    valueOfPKeys <- find value of pKeys from current tuple T
35    for each attribute in pKeys
36      add to predicateTable the following constraint
37      (nestedRelName, attribute, "=", valueOfPKeys)
38    end for
39    createRelElement(dDocument, eDocRoot, relName, tuple_complexType,
                       predicateTable)
40  end if
41 end for
```

The first loop in Method 51 (lines 4-14) builds a query to get tuples that satisfy the constraints in the predicate-specification table. After the query is executed, one element is created to store data of each tuple in the result set. A shortened version of the output XML document is shown in Figure 5. Then, Algorithm 52 checks if there is any relationships and nesting associated with the current relation. In case there is no relationship and no nesting, the structure of the XML document is flat. The code which handles the relationships as well as the nesting is explained next.

```
<?xml version="1.0" encoding="UTF-8"?>
<test xmlns="http://www.cpsc.ucaglary.ca/wangch/xml" xmlns:xsi="http://www.w3.org/2001/XMLSchema-instance"
xsi:schemaLocation="http://www.cpsc.ucaglary.ca/wangch/xml test_2.xsd">
 <db:DEPARTMENT_Relation xmlns:db="http://www.cpsc.ucaglary.ca/wangch/xml">
 <db:DEPARTMENT_Tuple>
 <db:MGRSSN>888665555</db:MGRSSN>
 <db:MGRSTARTDATE>1971-06-19</db:MGRSTARTDATE>
 <db:DNAME>Headquarters</db:DNAME>
 <db:DNUMBER>1</db:DNUMBER>
 </db:DEPARTMENT_Tuple>
 ...
 </db:DEPARTMENT_Relation>
 <db:DEPT_LOCATIONS_Relation xmlns:db="http://www.cpsc.ucaglary.ca/wangch/xml">
 <db:DEPT_LOCATIONS_Tuple>
 <db:DNUMBER>1</db:DNUMBER>
 <db:DLOCATION>Houston</db:DLOCATION>
 </db:DEPT_LOCATIONS_Tuple>
 ...
 </db:DEPT_LOCATIONS_Relation>
</test>
```

Fig. 5. Output Xml Document

Shown in Figure 6 is a user query where WORKS_ON represents M:N relationship between EMPLOYEE and PROJECT. The complex type which represents the EMPLOYEE relation is shown in Figure 7-a, where line 6 is a reference to the other relation connected to the WORKS_ON relationship. Note that in case of n-ary relationship where $n > 2$, there will be more elements listed in the same sequence that starts at line 5 of Figure 7-a.

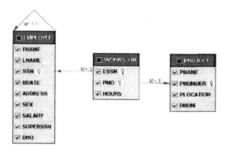

Fig. 6. Binary relationships

```
1. <xs:complexType name="EMPLOYEE_Relationship">        1. <db:EMPLOYEE_Tuple>
2. <xs:sequence>                                        2. <db:FNAME>Joyce</db:FNAME>
3. <xs:element name="EMPLOYEE_Relationship_Tuple"       3. <db:LNAME>English</db:LNAME>
   maxOccurs="unbounded">                                4. <db:SSN>453463463</db:SSN>
4. <xs:complexType>                                      5. <db:BDATE>1962-07-31</db:BDATE>
5. <xs:sequence>                                         6. <db:ADDRESS>5631 Rice, Houston,
6. <xs:element name="PNUMBER" type="xs:int"                TX</db:ADDRESS>
   maxOccurs="unbounded">                                7. <db:SEX>F</db:SEX>
7. <xs:keyref name="PROJECT.PNUMBER"                     8. <db:SALARY>25000.00</db:SALARY>
   refer="PROJECT_PrimaryKey">                           9. <db:SUPERSSN>333445555</db:SUPERSSN>
8. <xs:selector xpath="EMPLOYEE_Relation               10. <db:DNO>5</db:DNO>
   /EMPLOYEE_Tuple/PROJECT_LIST" />                     11. <db:EMPLOYEE_Relationship>
9. <xs:field xpath="PNUMBER" />                         12. <db:EMPLOYEE_Relationship_Tuple>
10. </xs:keyref>                                         13. <db:PNUMBER>1</db:PNUMBER>
11. </xs:element>                                        14. </db:EMPLOYEE_Relationship_Tuple>
12. </xs:sequence>                                      15. <db:EMPLOYEE_nAryRelationship_Tuple>
13. </xs:complexType>                                   16. <db:PNUMBER>2</db:PNUMBER>
14. </xs:element>                                       17. </db:EMPLOYEE_nAryRelationship_Tuple>
15. </xs:sequence>                                      18. </db:EMPLOYEE_nAryRelationship>
16.</xs:complexType>                                    19. </db:EMPLOYEE_Tuple>
```

(a)   (b)

Fig. 7. a) An element which represents M:N relationship; b) An employee tuple contains a binary relationship element

Method 52 *createRelationshipElement(docRoot, relName, eRelNameTuple)*

```
Return: void
1 eNary <- from eSchema a complexType with name relName_Relationship
2 raPairs <- from eNary relations and attributes involved in the relationship
3 relationship <- find from FK_Table the relation which references
                  relations & attributes in raPairs
4 queryStringA = " select "
5 queryStringB = " from "
6 queryStringC = " where "
7 for each foreign key in the relationship
8   let RF be the name of the relation of the foreign key
9   let AF be attributes of the foreign key
10  let RT be the name of relation which the foreign key points to
11  let AT be attributes in RT and correspond to AF
12  if (RT not equal relName)
13    queryStringA <= queryStringA + " {RF}.{AF}
14  else /* if RF equals to relName */
15    valueOfAttrTo <- find value of the referenced attribute
16    queryStringC <- queryStringC + "{RF}.{AF} = {valueOfAttrTo}"
17  end if
18  queryStringB = queryStringB + {relationFrom}
19 end for
20 queryString = queryStringA + queryStringB + queryStringC
```

```
21 resultSet <- execute(queryString)
22 create empty element eNaryRelation
23 add eNaryRelation to eRelNameTuple
24 for each tuple in resultSet
25   create an element for each attribute and add it to eNaryRelation
26 end for
```

Algorithm 52 creates and executes a query for each relation, and then creates a tuple element for each tuple in the query result. Then, the algorithm checks for relationships in the schema definition. Such relationships are handled by calling Method 52, where lines 4 to 21 create the query string for extracting values of the primary key that corresponds to a given foreign key. Presented in Figure 7-b is one tuple from the EMPLOYEE relation; it is related to 2 projects, and the primary key values of the projects are shown in lines 13 and 16.

Besides using the relationship element, there is another mechanism, namely nesting, which is provided for users to present data in nested structure. Although the relationships provide faster access to the project primary keys that are related to an employee record, sometimes it is desirable to get the whole tuple of the related record rather than just the primary key. Nesting allows users to nest one relation inside another. In addition, using nested elements allows data to be represented in a way where minimal references are used. For example, when users want to create an XML document with information about employees working on projects and they want the data to be accessed in a sequential manner, they can nest PROJECT inside WORKS_ON and then nest WORKS_ON inside EMPLOYEE. In the XML schema, there is an element added to represent the nested element under the complex type element defined for EMPLOYEE tuples. The element added for the nested element will have type "db:WORKS_ON_Relation". There is a similar element under WORKS_ON for its nested child PROJECT.

```
1. <xs:complexType name="EMPLOYEE_Tuple">
2. <xs:sequence>
3. <xs:element name="FNAME" type="xs:string" />
4. <xs:element name="LNAME" type="xs:string" />
5. <xs:element name="SSN" type="xs:string" />
6. <xs:element name="BDATE" type="xs:date" />
7. <xs:element name="ADDRESS" type="xs:string" />
8. <xs:element name="SEX" type="xs:string" />
9. <xs:element name="SALARY" type="xs:decimal" />
10. <xs:element name="SUPERSSN" type="xs:string" />
11. <xs:element name="DNO" type="xs:int" />
12. <xs:element name="WORKS_ON_Relation" type="db:WORKS_ON_Relation" />
13. </xs:sequence>
14. </xs:complexType>
    ...
15. <xs:complexType name="WORKS_ON_Tuple">
16. <xs:sequence>
17. <xs:element name="ESSN" type="xs:string" />
18. <xs:element name="PNO" type="xs:int" />
19. <xs:element name="HOURS" type="xs:decimal" />
20. <xs:element name="PROJECT_Relation" type="db:PROJECT_Relation" />
21. </xs:sequence>
22. </xs:complexType>
```

Fig. 8. Nested relations

Shown in Figure 9 is an employee tuple taken out from the generated XML document. This is the same employee record shown in Figure 7-b. The differ-

```
1.  <db:EMPLOYEE_Tuple>
2.  <db:FNAME>Joyce</db:FNAME>
3.  <db:LNAME>English</db:LNAME>
4.  <db:SSN>453453453</db:SSN>
5.  <db:BDATE>1962-07-31</db:BDATE>
6.  <db:ADDRESS>5631 Rice, Houston, TX</db:ADDRESS>
7.  <db:SEX>F</db:SEX>
8.  <db:SALARY>25000.00</db:SALARY>
9.  <db:SUPERSSN>333445555</db:SUPERSSN>
10. <db:DNO>5</db:DNO>
11. <db:WORKS_ON_Relation>
12. <db:WORKS_ON_Tuple>

13. <db:HOURS>20.0</db:HOURS>
14. <db:PROJECT_Relation>
15. <db:PROJECT_Tuple>
16. <db:PNAME>ProductX</db:PNAME>
17. <db:PNUMBER>1</db:PNUMBER>
18. <db:PLOCATION>Bellaire</db:PLOCATION>
19. <db:DNUM>5</db:DNUM>
20. </db:PROJECT_Tuple>
21. </db:PROJECT_Relation>
22. </db:WORKS_ON_Tuple>
23. <db:WORKS_ON_Tuple>
24. <db:HOURS>20.0</db:HOURS>
25. <db:PROJECT_Relation>
26. <db:PROJECT_Tuple>
27. <db:PNAME>ProductY</db:PNAME>
28. <db:PNUMBER>2</db:PNUMBER>
29. <db:PLOCATION>Sugarland</db:PLOCATION>
30. <db:DNUM>5</db:DNUM>
31. </db:PROJECT_Tuple>
32. </db:PROJECT_Relation>
33. </db:WORKS_ON_Tuple>
34. </db:WORKS_ON_Relation>
35. </db:EMPLOYEE_Tuple>
```

Fig. 9. A tuple for an employee relation with 2 levels of nesting

ence is that in Figure 9 there is a nested element called WORKS_ON instead of an element which represents a binary relationship in Figure 7-b. From the nested relations structure, users can get all the information about employees working on projects. Compared to the flat structure or with even the output with optimized relationships, nesting provides fastest access to related information because there is no need to perform additional scans to find tuples in other relations referenced by keyrefs. It might not make a big different for XML documents generated from small databases where the whole XML document can reside in main memory. On the other hand, it does affect the performance when larger XML documents are generated. However, the size of the result document could be larger than the one generated using flat structure. For instance, when relation B is nested inside relation A and there is M:N relationship between A and B, then there will be many tuples from relation B nested inside a tuple of relation A. In order to minimize the redundancy, some unnecessary attributes in the nested relation are removed. This is illustrated by considering line 23 in Figure 9, where there is only one child element namely "db:HOURS" in the element WORKS_ON_Tuple; WORKS_ON.ESSN and WORKS_ON.PNO are removed from the tuple since these two pieces of data are already contained in EMPLOYEE element and PROJECT element. In general, when relations are nested (as they are related by a foreign key), attribute(s) in the foreign key are removed to minimize redundancy in the generated XML document. Users should understand that the purpose of providing the nesting is to allow users to construct XML document with structures that are most suitable to the way users prefer for retrieving data. When they construct XML document from relational data, they need to decide if they want faster sequential access or smaller document size and hence decide on whether to use nesting or flat XML schema with keyrefs, respectively.

The provided nesting feature is flexible. There are no constraints on the number of levels for nesting as long as each two nested nodes are connected by a link. The illustrating example in Figure 3 shows 2 levels of nesting. Based on this, it is possible for users to restructure the ERD in a way to maximize the nesting, provided that each two nested relations are related by a foreign key. On top of this, users can also select attributes and add constraints to the predicate-specification table.

6 Summary and Conclusions

In the paper, we have proposed VIREX as a flexible visual interface for helping users to create XML documents and schemas from relational databases. Users are given the choice to convert only portion of the relational data into XML. Further, users may decide to have the result XML schema either flat or nested with arbitrary levels of nesting. Also, VIREX considers many-to-many and high-order (nary) relationships in the conversion process. Users can construct XML documents with desired structure by interacting with the ERD generated by VIREX. In addition, users can also project attributes and specify constraints for filtering out query results. VIREX simplifies the whole process of creating queries, XML schema and XML document down to a couple of mouse clicks in a flexible easy to use interactive process. Therefore, users do not need to learn new query language for constructing XML schemas and documents. The whole relational to XML conversion process is transparent to users. Currently, we are working on adding more functionality and power to VIREX.

References

1. Document Type Definition (DTD), Webpage: http://ww.w3schools.com/DTD/
2. XML Schema, Webpage: http://www.w3schools.com/schema/
3. "Creating XML Views Using Annotated XDR Schemas," Microsoft Corporation Webpage: http://msdn.microsoft.com/library/default.asp?url=/library/en-us/xmlsql/ac_mschema_5cfn.asp.
4. R. Alhajj, "Extracting the Extended Entity-Relationship Model from a legacy Relational Database," *Information Systems,* Vol.28, No.6, pp.597-618, 2003.
5. T. Catarci, et al, "Visual Query Systems for Databases: A Survey," *Journal of Visual Languages and Computing,* Vol.8, pp.215-260, 1997.
6. S. Ceri, et al, "XML-GL: a graphical language for querying and restructuring XML documents," *Computer Networks,* 31(11-16), pp.1171-1187, 1999.
7. M. Erwig, "Xing: A Visual XML Query Language," *Journal of Visual Languages and Computing,* Vol.14, No.1, pp.5-45, 2003.
8. M.F. Fernandez, W.C. Tan, and D. Suciu, "SilkRoute: Trading between Relational and XML," *Proc. of ACM WWW,* Amsterdam, May 2000.

9. R. Goldman and J. Widom, "Interactive query and search in semistructured databases," *Proc. of ACM SIGMOD WebDB Workshop,* 1998.
10. D. Lee, et al, "NeT and CoT: Translating Relational Schemas to XML Schemas using Semantic Constraints," *Proc. of ACM CIKM,* McLean, Virginia, Nov. 2002.
11. J. McHugh, et al, "Lore: A database management system for semistructured data," *SIGMOD Record,* Vol.26, No.3, 1997.
12. K. D. Munroe and Y. Papakonstantinou, "BBQ: A visual interface for browsing and querying of XML," *Proc. of IFIP Working Conf. on Visual Database Systems,* pp.277-296, 2000.
13. R. Orsini, M. Pagotto, "Visual SQL-X: A Graphical Tool for Producing XML Documents from Relational Databases," *Proc. of ACM WWW,* Hong Kong, 2001.
14. E. Pietriga and J.-Y. Vion-Dury, "VXT: Visual XML Transformer," *Proc. of IEEE Symposium on Visual/Multimedia Approaches to Programming and Software Engineering (Human Centric Computing Languages and Environments),* 2001.
15. J. Shanmugasundaram, et al, "Efficiently Publishing Relational Data as XML Documents," *VLDB Journal,* Vol.10, pp.133-154, 2001.
16. M.M. Zloof, "Query-By-Example: A Data Base Language," *IBM Systems Journal,* Vol.4, No.3, pp.324-343, 1977.

Modelling Vague Content and Structure Querying in XML Retrieval with a Probabilistic Object-Relational Framework

Mounia Lalmas and Thomas Rölleke

Department of Computer Science, Queen Mary University of London,
London E1 4NS, England, United Kingdom
{mounia,thor}@dcs.qmul.ac.uk
http://qmir.dcs.qmul.ac.uk/

Abstract. Many XML retrieval applications require relevance-oriented ranking of retrieved elements in order to capture the vagueness inherent to the information retrieval process. This relevance-oriented ranking should not only support vagueness at the content level, but also at the structural level. In this paper, we use a probabilistic object-relational framework to model representation and retrieval strategies that take into account vagueness at both content and structure level. Our approach makes use of established database technology combined with sound probability theory, thus allowing for fast and flexible prototyping of various representation and retrieval strategies.

1 Introduction

With the adoption of the XML mark-up language on the web and in digital libraries, there is the need to exploit the structural nature of XML documents for the purpose of their retrieval (e.g. [4, 8]). Searching XML documents requires query languages that support selection based on conditions with respect to *both* the content and the structure of XML documents. In addition, these query languages must take into account the intrinsic uncertainty associated with the information retrieval process to allow for a *relevance-oriented* access to XML documents.

A number of query languages for XML retrieval have been or are being proposed (e.g. [1, 7, 3, 5]). These query languages, more precisely, their evaluation, to date, provide an access to content based on string matching and regular expressions, which does not suffice for relevance-oriented search on XML documents. Examples of query languages that provide relevance-oriented search of XML documents include e.g. [9, 18]. However, only the uncertainty associated with the content of the XML documents is considered.

It is well known in information retrieval that users of retrieval systems often find it difficult to express their need for information in form of a query because they can be uncertain about the information they want, or they are unfamiliar with the document collection, thus leading to a vague formulation of the information need. For example, in the context of the world wide web, [11] shows that

H. Christiansen et al. (Eds.): FQAS 2004, LNAI 3055, pp. 432–445, 2004.

62% of queries submitted to Excite were insufficient to yield satisfactory results; these queries did not even contain structure conditions! It is therefore not realistic to assume that users can express with exactitude structure conditions when searching collections of XML documents. Even though some users may correctly express structure conditions, they may prefer to retrieve some types of elements. For example, a user may prefer to retrieve the abstracts before the conclusions of articles, and at last the articles themselves. In addition, some users may want to emphasise content condition versus structure condition, or vice versa. Representation and retrieval strategies that allow for the fact that users may not be able to appropriately express structure conditions, have preferences on the types of elements to be retrieved, and want to emphasise condition types, must consider uncertainty at both content and structure level. That is, they must provide for vague content and vague structure querying.

The INitiative for the Evaluation of XML retrieval (INEX) aims at providing an infrastructure to evaluate the effectiveness of relevance-oriented XML retrieval systems. This is done through the creation of a test collection of real world XML documents along with a set of topics and respective relevance assessments. In INEX 2002 [12], two retrieval tasks were performed: content-only queries, which are information retrieval-style user requests that ignore the document structure; and content-and-structure queries, which are requests that contain explicit references to the XML structure, either by restricting the context of interest or the context of certain search concepts. In INEX 2003[1], a third task was added, vague content-and-structure queries, where the structural constraints of a query can be treated as vague conditions. This shows the importance attached to vague structure querying for relevance-oriented XML retrieval.

In this paper, we describe relevance-oriented representation and retrieval strategies of XML documents, which consider both vague content and vague structure conditions. There are two aspects to our work: first, we introduce the concept of Boolean stemming upon which our vague structure condition is based; and second, we develop our approach for vague content and structure querying, using a probabilistic object-relational framework. The latter provides support for representing complex documents (e.g. XML documents) and describing retrieval strategies (e.g. Boolean stemming) based on generic and well-established approaches to data and information management such as relational database model, logic, and object-orientation.

Making use of established database technologies, in combination to sound probability theory for modelling uncertainty, provides the necessary expressiveness and flexibility for capturing both strict and vague content and structure querying (not just based on our concept of Boolean stemming) for accessing information from large XML repositories. In addition, it yields the flexibility, scalability and expressiveness for supporting the evaluation of the growing family and increasing complexity of XML query languages, as well as adapting to user preferences or task requirements (e.g. the level of vagueness allowed in the structure condition). Therefore, the focus of our paper is to show how our probabilistic

---

[1] See http://www.is.informatik.uni-duisburg.de/projects/inex03/.

object-relational framework is used to model representation and retrieval strategies that consider vague content and structure querying for a relevance-oriented retrieval of XML documents, based on the concept of Boolean stemming.

The structure of the paper is as follows. In Section 2, we provide a working example that will be used throughout the paper. In Section 3, we present the concept of "Boolean stemming", upon which our vague structure condition is based. In Section 4, we describe the probabilistic object-relational representation of XML documents. In Section 5, we describe the probabilistic object-relational evaluation of XML queries. We conclude and discuss future work in Section 6.

2   Working Example

We will use the (very) small XML document and the (fictitious) XPath-based query expression shown below as our working example throughout the paper. Our example document has one title, a section with a title and three paragraphs. The document has a version attribute, with value 1.0. Our query example searches for all paragraph elements in the root document element, where paragraph elements are about "sailing boats".

```
<document version="1.0">
  <title>Hello Sailing World</title>
  <section>
    <title>Sailing on the East Coast Rivers</title>
    <paragraph>Many sailing boats sail at the coast.</paragraph>
    <paragraph>Many sunny sailing days at the coast.</paragraph>
    <paragraph>Fog and drizzle are part of the game.</paragraph>
  </section>
</document>
```

```
/document//paragraph[about(., 'sailing boats')]
```

The path component "/document" expresses that the document element should be a child of the root element, and the path component "//paragraph" expresses that the paragraph element should be a descendant of the document element. If the structure condition is treated as strict (i.e. not vague), the above query would be expected to return the first paragraph before the second paragraph (since both, "sailing" and "boats" occur in the first paragraph, whereas only "sailing" occurs in the second paragraph, assuming that stemming has been performed) and no other elements. However, information that is of relevance to the user may also be contained in other elements, although the request was for paragraphs. For example, returning the section may be considered a viable result, since the section is indeed about "sailing boats".

3   "Boolean Stemming"

An XML query expression is formed by the combination of structure and content conditions. In our query example, "/document//paragraph" corresponds to the structure condition, whereas "about(.,'sailing boats')" corresponds to the content condition. The common approach is to interpret the query as a *conjunction* of the structure condition and the content condition. However, from information retrieval, we know that a conjunction of conditions is precision- rather than recall-oriented, i. e. we increase the likelihood of retrieving a higher portion of relevant documents (elements), but we increase the likelihood of missing relevant documents (elements). We also know that, from a ranking point of view, a document (an element) that fulfils many conditions will be ranked higher than a document (an element) that fulfils less conditions. It makes therefore sense to view the combination of structure and content conditions as a *probabilistic disjunction* of conditions. Rather than using the above *conjunctive* query, we formulate the following *disjunctive* query:

```
/document//paragraph $or$ //*[ about(., 'sailing boats')]
```

The same transformation can be applied to the structure condition. The path expression "/document//paragraph" is usually interpreted as a conjunction of path sub-expressions: *The element to be retrieved shall be a paragraph AND its ancestor element shall be a document AND the ancestor element shall be a child of the root element'.* By replacing the conjunction of path sub-expressions by a disjunction of path sub-expressions, we obtain the following interpretation: *The element to be retrieved shall be a paragraph OR its ancestor element shall be a document OR the ancestor element shall be a child of the root element.*

We refer to this mapping of a conjunctive expression to a disjunctive expression as *Boolean stemming*. We use the term "stemming" because we apply rules for replacing AND by OR. In our example, we used the most general rule, namely, "replace each occurrence of AND by OR". More specific rules can also be applied, for example, "replace the last occurrence of AND by OR", thus allowing for specifying various levels of vagueness as introduced later in this paper.

The replacement of AND by OR increases recall (i.e. the number of retrieved and relevant elements) at the costs of retrieving more non-relevant elements, which can have an impact on effectiveness and efficiency. With respect to effectiveness, a ranking function would ensure that the best elements are retrieved first, while at the same time allowing for vague characterisation of the structure condition. The fact that we retrieve more elements will decrease efficiency. However, we avoid join operations and complex regular expression matches that would be required for the evaluation of conjunctions.

4   Probabilistic Object-Relational Representation of XML Documents

In this section, we describe how XML documents are represented within our probabilistic object-relational framework. The representation involves two steps. XML documents are first translated into POOL programs (Section 4.1), which are then translated into PRA expressions (Section 4.2) following the so-called object-relational approach.

4.1 POOL Representation of XML Documents

POOL (which stands for probabilistic object-oriented logic) is a probabilistic representation and retrieval framework designed for representing and retrieving complex objects (see [15]). It can be used for describing the retrieval of any type of structured document standard (e.g. HTML, XML, MPEG-7). Particular to POOL is the integration of probability theory and the object-oriented paradigm. Next is an abbreviated syntax of POOL (more information can be found in [13]).

program	::= clause program
clause	::= fact | context-clause | query | rule
fact	::= proposition | probability proposition
proposition	::= term | classification | relationship
term	::= NAME
classification	::= NAME '(' NAME ')'
relationship	::= NAME '.' NAME '(' NAME ')'
context-clause	::= context | probability context
context	::= NAME '[' program ']'
query	::= '?-' subgoal-list
subgoal-list	::= subgoal | subgoal '&' subgoal-list
subgoal	::= fact-subgoal | context-subgoal
fact-subgoal	::= atom | NOT atom
atom	::= term-atom |
	classification-atom |
	relationship-atom
context-subgoal	::= context-name '[' subgoal-list ']'
rule	::= goal ':-' subgoal-list
goal	::= atom

Below we show an excerpt of the POOL program corresponding to our example document.

```
document(document1)
version.document1(1.0)
document1 [
  title(title1)
  section(section1)
  title1 [ 0.8 hello sail 0.3 world ]
  section1 [
     title1 [ sail east coast river ]
     0.2 paragraph1 [ 0.7 sail   0.4 coast   0.8 boat ]
     0.5 paragraph2 [ 0.2 sunny 0.8 sail 0.2 day 0.5 coast ]
     0.5 paragraph3 [ 0.5 fog 0.2 drizzle 0.5 part 0.3 game ] ] ]
```

"document1", "title1", etc. correspond to contexts in POOL, and model the elements "document[1]", "title[1]", etc., respectively. To express the parent-child structure between elements, POOL uses square brackets to delimit the contexts modelling the elements. For example, "section1" is a sub-context of "document1" ("section[1]" is a child element of "document[1]"), and hence, appears within "document1" context. Classifications provide the class (element) type of each element, e.g. "document", "title", "section", etc. Relationships provide attributes and their value for the elements (contexts).

Particular to POOL is the consideration of two types of uncertainty. Probabilities can be assigned at the content level (in front of a proposition) to represent how good a term[2] is at describing the content of an element; and at the structure level (in front of a context) to represent the impact an element has towards describing the content of its parent element. The probabilities assigned to "sail", "coast", "boat", etc. in a context describe how well these terms describe the content of the element modelled by that context. For example, the term "sail" is a better representation of "document[1]/section[1]/paragraph[1]" than the term "coast". These probabilities can be derived using standard term frequency (tf) information. In our example, the probabilities are fictitious (our XML document is too small to produce meaningful probability values). A probability value of 1.0 is assumed when no probability value is explicitly given.

Of particular interest to XML retrieval are the structure probabilities. In XML retrieval, the content of a parent element is often characterised as the aggregation of its content and the content of its child elements (see [8] for some examples). However, not all child elements will have the same impact in contributing to the content of the parent element. For example, an abstract may be a better reflection of what an article is about than a conclusion. This impact is modelled by assigning probabilities at the structure level. For example, in our example, "paragraph2" has a higher impact than "paragraph1" towards the content of "section1". There are no standard mechanisms to compute the structure probabilities yet: user studies could be performed to elicit these values, extensive retrieval experiments can be carried out to empirically determine optimal values, or machine learning methods could be used. This is currently a research issue.

4.2   PRA Representation of XML Documents

For evaluating POOL programs, we translate them into PRA (which stands for probabilistic relational algebra) expressions. PRA expressions representing XML documents consist of probabilistic relations, i.e., relations to which probability values are attached. In our framework, the representation of XML documents for the purpose of relevance-oriented retrieval makes use of the following four relations:

1. *instance_of(element-id, class)*: representing the type (class) of an XML element.
2. *part_of(child-id, parent-id)*: representing the child-parent structure between two XML elements.

---

[2] Probabilities can also be assigned to classifications and relationships. For simplicity, these cases are not considered in this paper.

3. *attribute(element-id, attribute-name, attribute-value)*: representing an attribute together with its value for an XML element.
4. *term(term, element-id)*: representing the content of (the terms appearing in) an XML element.

The first three relations are motivated by three of the basic pillars of object-oriented modelling, namely classification, aggregation (which we use to model the structure of XML documents) and relationships (which we use to model the attributes of XML documents). The fourth relation reflects the content dimension requires to perform relevance-oriented retrieval. The translation of our POOL program example into the above four relations is shown below:

```
instance_of(element-id, class):
(/document1, document)
(/document1/title1, title)
(/document1/section1, section)
(/document1/section1/title1, title)
(/document1/section1/paragraph1, paragraph)
(/document1/section1/paragraph1, paragraph)
(/document1/section1/paragraph1, paragraph)

part_of(child-id, parent-id):
(/document1/title1, document1)
(/document1/section1, document1)
(/document1/section1/title1, /document1/section1)
(/document1/section1/paragraph1, /document1/section1)
(/document1/section1/paragraph1, /document1/section1)
(/document1/section1/paragraph1, /document1/section1)

attribute(element-id, attribute-name, attribute-value):
(/document1, version, 1.0)

term(term, element-id):
(east, /document1/section1/title1)
(coast, /document1/section1/title1)
(sailing, /document1/section1/paragraph1)
(boats, /document1/section1/paragraph1)
...
```

The content and structure probabilities in our POOL program are associated to the "term" and the "part_of" relations, as shown below. A probability value of 1.0 is assigned to all tuples of the "instance_of" and "attribute" relations, so these relations are not shown.

term	
Prob	Tuple
1.0	(sail, /document1/title1)
0.7	(sail, /document1/section1/paragraph1)
0.4	(coast, /document1/section1/paragraph1)
0.8	(boat, /document1/section1/paragraph1)
0.8	(sail, /document1/section1/paragraph2)
...	...

termspace	
Prob	Tuple
0.562	(boat)
0.492	(east)
0.289	(coast)
0.097	(sail)
...	...

part_of	
Prob	Tuple
1.0	(/document1/title1, /document1)
1.0	(/document1/section1, /document)
0.2	(/document1/section1/paragraph1, /document1/section1)
0.5	(/document1/section1/paragraph2, /document1/section1)
...	...

classspace	
Prob	Tuple
1.0	(section)
1.0	(document)
0.64	(title)
0.43	(paragraph)

Other relations are used. For example, considering inverse document frequency (idf) together with term frequency is known to increase retrieval effectiveness. In the context of XML retrieval, considering the inverse element frequency of a term allows for discriminating between relevant and non-relevant elements. Indeed, a term that occurs in all elements, i.e has a low inverse element frequency, is not useful for describing the content of a particular element since it cannot discriminate that element from others. The inverse element frequency values in a collection are represented by a probabilistic relation. The above figure shows a relation called "termspace", which displays (the probabilistic interpretation of) the inverse element frequency values for our example program; the highest the probability, the better the term is at discriminating between relevant and non-relevant elements.

Another relation is defined to represent the importance associated to element types. The relation "classspace" above shows an example of such a relation. As for the structure probabilities, there is no standard way to obtain the type probabilities, apart from either eliciting them from users and user studies, or through extensive experimentation. In our work, and our example, we adopt the following strategy: the higher the occurrence frequency of an element type, the lowest its probability.

To recap, XML documents are transformed into POOL programs, where content, structure, element type and classification TOGETHER with their associated uncertainty are represented. POOL programs are then translated into probabilistic relations, which capture any aspect deemed necessary for the vague content and structure querying of XML documents. In the next section, we describe how the same framework is used to evaluate XML queries using these representations.

5   Probabilistic Object-Relational Evaluation of XML Queries

As for the representation of XML documents, the evaluation of XML queries is also performed in two steps. First, XML queries are translated into POOL programs (Section 5.1). It is during this translation that Boolean stemming is applied. Then POOL programs are translated into PRA expressions (Section 5.2), which access the probabilistic relations corresponding to the PRA representations of XML documents to perform retrieval.

5.1 POOL Evaluation of XML Queries

XML queries are translated into POOL queries, taking into account a vagueness level, which can be specified by a user, or set by the system for a particular application. Our current implementation allows three levels of vagueness.

vagueness level	explanation
0	no Boolean stemming
1	use a disjunction for combining structure and content criteria
2	use a disjunction for combining the path sub-expressions

Our example query is translated, using vagueness level 0, to the following POOL query:

```
retrieve(X) :- document(X) & /X[paragraph(Y) & //Y[sail]]
retrieve(X) :- document(X) & /X[paragraph(Y) & //Y[boat]]
?- retrieve(X)
```

Elements (contexts) to be retrieved are of class "paragraph", are children of the root context of class "document", and contain the terms "sail" or "boat". The first "retrieve" rule corresponds to the "sail" content condition, and the second to the "boat" content condition. Vagueness level 2 is implemented by dropping the nesting of elements and by ignoring "/" and "//". Our POOL query, using for vagueness level 2 is:

```
retrieve(X) :- document(X)
retrieve(X) :- paragraph(X)
retrieve(X) :- X[ sail ]
retrieve(X) :- X[ boat ]
?- retrieve(X)
```

Elements (contexts) to be retrieved are of class "document" or "paragraph", or contain the terms "sail" or "boat".

5.2 PRA Evaluation of XML Queries

PRA evaluation of XML queries consist of sequences of probabilistic-based standard relational algebra operations (Union, Join, Project, Select, Subtract). As described in the previous section, probability values are attached to tuples (e.g. "term" tuples, "part_of" tuples, "termspace" tuple, etc.). PRA expressions access these tuples, and their probabilities are combined to produce other probabilistic relations, until returning the retrieval results themselves, also probabilistic relations. For example, in the Project operation, when probabilistic independence is assumed among the tuples of a relation, the probabilities of duplicate tuples are added (see [10] for details). In this section, we illustrate the use of PRA to implement various retrieval strategies of the our POOL query with vagueness level 2. As an introduction, we first start with a simple POOL (content-only) query, which requests for document about "sail".

```
?- X[ sail ]
```

There are two ways to translate the above POOL query into a PRA query, depending on which relations, i.e. "term" and/or "termspace" will be accessed. The first PRA expression below uses the "term" relation only, i.e. considers term frequency information only; the second uses the two relations, i.e. considers term frequency and inverse element frequency information ($i refers to the ith column of the relation).

```
retrieve1 =  Project[$2](Select[$1=sai](term))
retrieve2 =  Project[$3](Join[$1=$1](Select[$1=sail](termspace), term))
```

In "retrieve1", selection is first applied on the "term" relation with respect to the term "sail", then a projection is applied to obtain the relevant elements. In "retrieve2", after a selection with respect to the term "sail", a join operation is performed between the "term" and the "termspace" relations (this is the equivalent to a probabilistic interpretation of the standard tf $\times$ idf in information retrieval), and then the projection is performed to obtain the retrieved elements. The retrieved elements for our XML document are shown below for the above two PRA expressions:

retrieve1 (term)	
Prob	Tuple
1.0	(/document1/title1)
1.0	(/document1/section1/title1)
0.8	(/document1/section1/paragraph2)
0.7	(/document1/section1/paragraph1)

retrieve2 (term and termspace)	
Prob	Tuple
0.097	(/document1/title1)
0.097	(/document1/section1/title1)
0.077	(/document1/section1/paragraph2)
0.068	(/document1/section1/paragraph1)

In "retrieve1", the two titles are retrieved with probability 1.0 since this is the probability assigned to "sail" in the two titles. Accordingly, the paragraphs are retrieved with probabilities 0.8 and 0.7, the probabilities assigned to "sail" in the paragraphs. In "retrieve2", the probabilities are shown for the case that the termspace probability of "sail" (0.097) is multiplied with the probability of "sail" in the elements. Though the ranking remains the same for a query with one term, the ranking might change significantly for a query with several terms. For example, a query about "sailing coast" based on an evaluation strategy without termspace retrieves the titles with 1.0 and "paragraph2" with 0.5. Considering the termspace probabilities, titles are retrieved with probability 0.097, whereas "paragraph2" is retrieved with $0.5 \cdot 0.289 \approx 0.145$; this results changes the order of retrieved elements.

Our working example POOL query with vagueness level 2 can be translated into several PRA expressions, depending on which relations described in Section 4.2 are used, which itself depends on which retrieval strategy is adopted. A translation using the "term" relation to refer to content, and to "instance_of" to refer to structure yields the following PRA query[3]:

```
retrieve_document = Project[$1](Select[$2='document'](instance_of))
retrieve_paragraph = Project[$1](Select[$2='paragraph'](instance_of))
retrieve_sail = Project[$2](Select[$1='sail'](term))
retrieve_boat = Project[$2](Select[$1='boat'](term))
retrieve = Unite(retrieve_document, retrieve_paragraph,
                 retrieve_sail, retrieve_boat)
```

"retrieve_document" selects all elements of "document" type; "retrieve_paragraph" selects all elements of "paragraph" type; "retrieve_sail" selects all elements containing the term "sail"; and similarly for "retrieve_boat". In all four relations, projection is applied to obtain the elements, which are then all united to provide the final ranking.

To consider inverse element frequency information and class frequency information, join operations are performed between the "term" and the "termspace" relations, and between the "instance_of" and the "classspace" relations, respectively. For example, the PRA equations for "retrieve_document" and "retrieve_sail" for the above PRA query are replaced by the following two PRA equations, respectively:

```
retrieve_document_classspace =  Project[$2](
      Join[$1=$2](Select[$1='document'](classspace), instance_of))

retrieve_sail_termspace = Project[$3](
      Join[$1=$1](Select[$1='sail'](termspace), term))
```

The retrieved elements for our XML document are shown below:

retrieve	
Prob	Tuple
1.000	(/document1)
0.711	(/document1/section1/paragraph1)
0.479	(/document1/section1/paragraph2)
0.435	(/document1/section1/paragraph3)
0.097	(/document1/section1/title1)
0.097	(/document1/title1)

"document1" is retrieved with 1.0 since the document element matches the vague interpretation of the structure condition, and the type "document" is rare

---

[3] The actual translation leads to a more complex expression, because translation rules are generic, and optimisation is performed. All PRA expressions in this Section are simplified for clarity.

in our small XML example. Element "paragraph1" is ranked higher than "paragraph2" since "paragraph1" contains both "sail" and "boat", whereas "paragraph2" contains only "sail", although the probability of "sail" is higher in "paragraph2" than in "paragraph1". "paragraph3" is retrieved merely because of the structure condition to retrieve paragraphs (probability of "paragraph" in "classpace" is 0.43). The titles are retrieved merely because of the content condition; here, the probability of "sail" in "termspace" leads to the element probability of 0.097, as explained above.

The above ranking illustrates a major problem: "document1" and "paragraph3" are retrieved because of the structure condition, but their retrieval probabilities are comparatively high. This is due to the probabilities in the "classpace" relation. A disjunction which assumes content and structure condition to be independent as done so far, will highly rank an element that matches one condition (structure or content) to a high degree. This leads directly to the requirement that we would like to control the degree to which the match of structure or content condition contributes to the final retrieval probabilities.

Therefore, we consider now preferences on the structure and content condition in the so-called "conditionspace" relation. Whereas we showed clear criteria for estimating the probabilities of the "termspace" and "classpace" relations, it is currently still an open question of how to estimate the probabilities of the "conditionspace" relation. In the scope of this paper, we do not discuss further the estimation, and we assume that probabilities regarding which types of conditions is important to a particular group of users is that given below. The corresponding ranking is also shown below. In our case, our group of users puts more emphasise to the content condition than the structure condition.

conditionspace	
Prob	Tuple
0.6	content
0.4	structure

retrieve	
Prob	Tuple
0.400	(/document1)
0.416	(/document1/section1/paragraph1)
0.212	(/document1/section1/paragraph2)
0.174	(/document1/section1/paragraph3)
0.058	(/document1/section1/title1)
0.058	(/document1/title1)

This result and the overall strategy with "termspace", "classpace" and "conditionspace" has now the desired properties and flexibility for modelling vague structure and content retrieval, although in this paper, for simplicity, we did not take into account the POOL probabilities that an element contributes to the content of its parent element (see [16] for this). For the result in this paper, we observe that "document1" is retrieved now with a smaller probability than "paragraph1". Although the class "document" has a maximal probability in our example, "paragraph1" is ranked higher since "paragraph1" fulfils the structure and the content conditions.

The PRA expression for joining the "conditionspace" relation with the retrieval strategy based on the "classpace" and "termspace" relations is rather complex. The overall idea is that a condition attribute column is added to the relation "retrieve" and that the following join is performed:

```
retrieve = Project[$3, 'structure'](Join[$1=$2]
              (Select[$1='document'](classpace), instance_of))
cond_retrieve = Project[$2](Join[$1=$2](conditionspace, retrieve))
```

In this paper, we do not extend further on the probabilistic assumption underlying the PRA operations. Here, we assumed independence throughout, where for the "conditionspace" relation it seems appropriate to argue a disjointness (weighted sum) assumption rather than the independence assumption applied here. This is also reflected by the choice of probabilities in the "conditionspace" relation, i.e. they sum up to 1.0. Where independence and where disjointness assumption is the better choice will be investigated experimentally (but see [14] for some initial theoretical investigation on this).

6   Summary and Outlook

A relevance-oriented ranking of XML documents must acknowledge the fact that not all users express (or retrieval tasks can have) clear structure conditions, and that users may have preferences, e.g. the types of elements to retrieve. Therefore, uncertainty must be taken into account, not only at the content level, but also at the structure level in relevance-oriented XML retrieval applications.

In this paper, we described representation and retrieval strategies that model uncertainty at both content and structure level. We used a probabilistic object-relational framework for this purpose, thus allowing fast and flexible prototyping of various representation and retrieval strategies in a uniform, comparable and elegant manner. Our approach is based on probability theory and object-relational modelling principles where neither the probability estimation, nor the relations are pre-defined. Therefore, the level of Boolean stemming, the approach we use to provide for vague structure condition, and the estimation of probabilistic parameters such as "termspace", "classspace", and "conditionspace" can be adapted according to user preferences or specific task requirements.

Our next step is to evaluate the different representation and retrieval strategies in terms of effectiveness and efficiency. This will done as part of the INEX initiative, which aims at providing an infrastructure to evaluate the effectiveness of relevance-oriented XML retrieval systems, through the creation of a test collection of XML documents [12].

Other work allowing for vague structure querying is that of e.g. [17,6,2], which can be briefly summarised as partial (uncertain) matches between the document and the query structure conditions using various simple to more complex strategies. We intend to model them in our object-relational probabilistic framework thus comparing the effectiveness and efficiency of our Boolean stemming to theirs.

References

1. S. Abiteboul, D. Quass, J. McHugh, J. Widom, J. Wiener, and J. Widom. The Lorel Query Language for Semistructured Data. *International Journal on Digital Libraries*, 1(1):68–88, April 1997.

2. S. Amer-Yahia, S. Cho, and D. Srivasta. Tree pattern relaxation. In *Proceedings of International Conference on Extended Database Technology (EDBT)*, 2002.
3. A. Berglund, S. Boag, D. Chamberlin, M.F. Fernandez, M. Kay, J. Robie, and J. Simeon. XML Path Language (XPath) 2.0. W3C Working Draft, November 2002. http://www.w3.org/TR/xpath20.
4. H. Blanken, R. Schenkel T. Grabs, and G. Weikum, editors. *Intelligent Search on XML*. Springer-Verlag, 2003.
5. S. Boag, D. Chamberlin, M.F. Fernandez, D. Florescu, J. Robie, and J. Simeon. XQuery: An XML query language. W3C Working Draft, 2002. http://www.w3.org/TR/XQuery.
6. D. Carmel, Y.S. Maarek, M. Mandelbrod, Y. Mass, and A. Soffer. Searching XML documents via XML fragments. In *Proceedings of ACM SIGIR Conference on Research and Development in Information Retrieval*, pages 151–158, Toronto, Canada, July 2003.
7. D. Chamberlin, J. Robie, and D. Florescu. Quilt: An XML query language for heterogeneous data sources. In *International Workshop on the Web and Databases (WebDB)*, pages 53–62, Texas, USA, May 2000.
8. N. Fuhr, N. Goevert, G. Kazai, and M. Lalmas, editors. *INEX: Evaluation Initiative for XML retrieval - INEX 2002 Workshop Proceedings*, DELOS Workshop, 2003.
9. N. Fuhr and K. Grossjohann. XIRQL: A query language for information retrieval in XML documents. In *Proceedings of ACM SIGIR Conference on Research and Development in Information Retrieval*, New Orleans, USA, August 2001.
10. N. Fuhr and T. Rölleke. A probabilistic relational algebra for the integration of information retrieval and database systems. *ACM Transactions on Information Systems*, 14(1):32–66, 1997.
11. B.J. Jansen, A. Spink, and T. Saracevic. Real life, real users and real needs: A study and analysis of user queries on the web. *Information Processing & Management*, 36(2):207–227, 2000.
12. G. Kazai, M. Lalmas, N. Fuhr, and N. Goevert. A report on the first year of the INitiative for the Evaluation of XML Retrieval (INEX02). *Journal of the American Society for Information Science and Technology*, 2004. In press.
13. M. Lalmas, T. Rölleke, and N. Fuhr. Intelligent hypermedia retrieval. In P. S. Szczepaniak, F. Segovia, and L. A. Zadeh, editors, *Intelligent Exploration of the Web*. Springer-Verlag Group (Physica-Verlag), 2002.
14. T. Roelleke. A frequency-based and a poisson-based probability of being informative. In *Proceedings of ACM SIGIR Conference on Research and Development in Information Retrieval*, pages 227–234, Toronto, Canada, July 2003.
15. T. Rölleke. *POOL: Probabilistic Object-Oriented Logical Representation and Retrieval of Complex Objects*. Shaker Verlag, Aachen, 1999. Dissertation.
16. T. Rölleke, M. Lalmas, G. Kazai, I. Ruthven, and S. Quicker. The accessibility dimension for structured document retrieval. In *Proceedings of the BCS-IRSG European Conference on Information Retrieval (ECIR), Glasgow*, March 2002.
17. T. Schlieder and M. Meuss. Result ranking for structured queries against xml documents. In *DELOS Workshop: Information Seeking, Searching and Querying in Digital Libraries*, Zurich, Switzerland, 2000.
18. A. Theobald and G. Weikum. The index-based XXL search engine for querying XML data with relevance ranking. In *Advances in Database Thechnology - EDBT 2002, 8th International on Extending Database Technology*, pages 477–495, Prague, Czech Republic, March 2002.

Cluster Characterization
through a Representativity Measure

Marie-Jeanne Lesot and Bernadette Bouchon-Meunier

Laboratoire d'Informatique de Paris 6
Université Pierre et Marie Curie
8 rue du capitaine Scott, 75 015 Paris, France
{Marie-Jeanne.Lesot,Bernadette.Bouchon-Meunier}@lip6.fr

Abstract. Clustering is an unsupervised learning task which provides a decomposition of a dataset into subgroups that summarize the initial base and give information about its structure. We propose to enrich this result by a numerical coefficient that describes the cluster representativity and indicates the extent to which they are characteristic of the whole dataset. It is defined for a specific clustering algorithm, called Outlier Preserving Clustering Algorithm, OPCA, which detects clusters associated with major trends but also with marginal behaviors, in order to offer a complete description of the inital dataset. The proposed representativity measure exploits the iterative process of OPCA to compute the typicality of each identified cluster.

1 Introduction

Given a set of numerical descriptions of datapoints, information extraction often consists in clustering [7, 6], i.e. decomposing the dataset into homogeneous and distinct subgroups that summarize the initial base. This learning task gives information about the data structure and highlights the major trends present in the dataset. Yet it usually overlooks [3, 9] the marginal behaviors represented by atypical points or outliers, although the latter are also necessary to characterize the dataset.

More precisely, a complete characterization should contain information both on major trends and atypical behaviors, together with knowledge about the group representativity, as illustrated by the following example: consider a device having three different modes, semantically described as "high", "low" and "abnormally low". This linguistic characterization includes the atypical behavior together with the major ones, which is indeed necessary to describe accurately the process. Moreover it indicates that the three components are not equivalent and it specifies the most important cases: the adverb "abnormally" underlines the peculiarity of the third mode and conveys information about its representativity. It is necessary to the description and, for instance, it makes it possible to distinguish this device from another one having three normal modes, described as "high", "low" and "very low".

H. Christiansen et al. (Eds.): FQAS 2004, LNAI 3055, pp. 446–458, 2004.
© Springer-Verlag Berlin Heidelberg 2004

Therefore, we propose to enrich clustering results by defining numerical coefficients that measure the cluster representativity, or equivalently their exceptionality, to indicate the extent to which they are characteristic of the whole dataset. Such coefficients complete the information about the data subgroups and can for instance help analysts to provide linguistic labels for the clusters, e.g. to choose the appropriate modifying adverbs.

We thus define an *exceptionality coefficient*, denoted $cExc$, which takes the reference value 1 for characteristic subgroups and a high value for clusters with low representativity that correspond to minor behaviors. It is based on a specific clustering algorithm, the Outlier Preserving Clustering Algorithm (OPCA) [9], which simultaneously detects the major and minor trends present in a dataset; more precisely, $cExc$ is deduced from the iterative process of OPCA and does not require expensive additional computations to provide additional information.

The article is organized as follows. Section 2 recalls the principle of the Outlier Preserving Clustering Algorithm on which the exceptionality coefficients are based. Section 3 defines the exceptionality coefficients and compares them with other numerical coefficients which also characterize a dataset, namely the *local outlying factors* proposed by Breunig et al. [2] and the typicality degrees proposed by Rifqi [10], we underline their differences and their respective properties. Lastly section 4 illustrates and interprets the results obtained on artificial and real datasets.

2   Outlier Preserving Clustering Algorithm

In this section, we briefly recall the principle of the Outlier Preserving Clustering Algorithm, OPCA [9], which simultaneously identifies subgroups corresponding to major and marginal trends: it is able to build classic clusters, as provided by classic clustering algorithms, but also one-point clusters, corresponding to outliers, as provided by outlier detection methods, and lastly intermediate clusters, corresponding to small sets of similar outliers, which may be overlooked by both clustering and outlier detection techniques.

2.1   Justification

Usually, outliers are considered as noisy points which are to be excluded from the learning dataset, so that they do not disturb the learning process. For instance, robust clustering algorithms [4, 5] decrease the weight associated to such datapoints, so as to reduce their influence on the final result. Yet, in our characterization aim, they are to be considered differently: outliers should not be rejected, but considered as minor but significant groups that should be present as any other cluster.

One approach could be to decompose clustering into two cases, distinguishing the outlier handling from the other points: one could perform a first step of outlier detection method [1, 8, 2] as a preliminary to clustering; one can also model the outliers in a specific cluster [3] or define a specific distribution to handle them [11].

Using such an approach, it could be possible to perform a second clustering step on this specific cluster to identify relevant subgroups among outliers. OPCA takes a different approach which does not distinguish between the two types of points and handles them the same way: as different clustering algorithms are sensitive to different types of clusters, it appears that combining them makes it possible to exploit their different properties, and thus to optimize simultaneously, compactness and separability (see [9] for more details).

2.2   Principle

OPCA is based on the combination, in an iterative process, of the single linkage agglomerative hierarchical algorithm and the fuzzy c-means, denoted AHC_{min} and fcm respectively. The coupling makes it possible to exploit the different properties of each method, namely the ability of AHC_{min} to take into account the group separability and the ability of fcm to provide compact subgroups; the iterative process makes it possible to adapt the outlier definition to local contexts, in particular to take into account variable significant distance scales, depending on the local data density.

More precisely, the algorithm considers a group G and first determines the most appropriate dividing method: if G contains well-separated subgroups, it is decomposed by AHC_{min}; if G has a low separability but has still a low compactness, it is split by fcm. This process is then iterated on each obtained subgroup. The criteria selecting the applied algorithm respectively evaluate the presence of gaps in G data distribution and estimate G compactness as a function of its diameter and its variance, compared to the average variance of its possible subgroups (see [9] for more details).

2.3   Results and Limitations

Figure 1 illustrates the results obtained with artificial one-dimension datasets where datapoints are represented as stars, possibly repeated and vertically shifted in case of multi-occurrences, and clusters are represented by their membership functions defined as Gaussians of order 4 [9]. Dataset 1 (fig. 1a) corresponds to an outlier detection task in a simple case, the algorithm manages to identify the three intuitive subgroups. Dataset 2 (fig. 1b) shows a more complex case with variable densities and a definition of outliers that must depend on the locally significant distances; the obtained fuzzy subsets correspond to a natural description of the data which represents both major and marginal trends. Lastly, Dataset 3 (fig. 1c) shows a dataset which leads to a fuzzy profile identical to the first one; yet the importance of the leftmost cluster is higher than on graph (a) and it should be interpreted differently: a linguistic characterization could be "high", "low" and "abnormally low" in the first case and "high", "intermediate" and "low" in the second one, the absence of adverb showing that the three groups are equivalent. Such instances show that fuzzy profiles are not sufficient to characterize a dataset; we propose to enrich it through exceptionality coefficients to measure the extent to which a cluster is representative of the whole dataset.

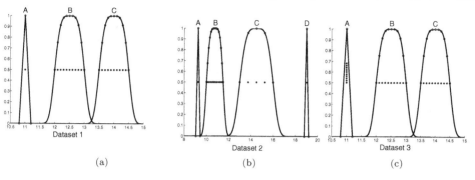

Fig. 1. Profiles of artificial one-dimension databases obtained with the outlier preserving clustering method. The fuzzy membership functions are defined as Gaussian functions of order 4 (see [9]).

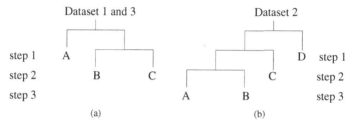

Fig. 2. Chronological account of the groups constitution. (a) for Datasets 1 and 3; (b) for Dataset 2. Letters correspond to clusters as indicated on figure 1.

3 Representativity Measure

The previous clustering algorithm highlights the structure of a dataset through the identification of all relevant subgroups. In fact, it provides a much richer information about the extracted subgroups owing to its iterative process: beside the data assignment, it offers a chronological account of the group constitution; figure 2 shows a tree representation of the group identification history for the three previous datasets. This can be exploited to measure the cluster representativity and it is the basis of the definition of exceptionality coefficients.

In what follows, we will use the notion of *isolation date* or *identification date* for a cluster, associated with the use of OPCA: it corresponds to the iteration step from which a group is not further divided but considered as a group that must appear as such in the final data decomposition; for instance it equals 2 for cluster C of Dataset 2.

3.1 Exceptionality Coefficient Definition

To justify our definition of exceptionality coefficients, we first consider the extreme case of single-point clusters, i.e. outliers. Such points are considered as non-characteristic of the whole dataset with an intensity that depends on their distance to the nearest point: a local outlier, as point B of Dataset 2, better represents the whole dataset than a global outlier, as point D, and thus must have a lower $cEcx$. Now this information is contained in the chronological account of the group constitution through the isolation date: the significant distance scale decreases when the number of iterations of OPCA increases, which means that a datapoint isolated at the end of the process is only a local outlier. Therefore representativity increases when the isolation date increases.

In case of larger groups, this principle still holds, but it must be balanced by the group size: isolation is associated with separability, insofar as an isolated cluster is well-separated from its neighbors; thus it is not directly equivalent to exceptionality. For instance a large and well-separated cluster may represent the whole dataset better than smaller groups identified later which may be justified only at a more refined distance scale.

We propose to measure cluster representativity by the following exceptionality coefficient, where G denotes the group under consideration, $|G|$ its size, and $h(G)$ its isolation date, i.e. the iteration number at which it is not further divided, lastly $\bar{s}_t$ is the average size of groups handled at step t. We then define the *exceptionality coefficient* characterizing cluster G as

$$cExc(G) = \frac{1}{Z} \frac{\max_\Gamma h(\Gamma)}{h(G)} \frac{\bar{s}_{h(G)}}{|G|} \tag{1}$$

where Z is a normalization factor defined to set a reference value: a cluster is fully representative of the whole dataset if it gets a $cExc$ value of 1, its exceptionality increases when $cExc$ increases. The isolation date $h(G)$ is compared to the total number of iterations (this constant factor could be included in Z but helps the lisibility). The group size $|G|$ is considered with respect to the size of equivalent groups $\bar{s}_{h(G)}$, i.e. the size of clusters built at the same step; it makes it possible to take into account the local context and measures a local lack of balance in terms of size.

According to this definition, exceptionality is maximal for early identified clusters of small size, which are indeed the least representative groups, thus it corresponds to the desired properties.

3.2   Comparison with Other Approaches

In this section, we compare the proposed exceptionality coefficients with existing numerical coefficients which also characterize the data, namely *local outlying factors* [2] and typicality degrees [10]. We underline their respective properties which provide different insights on the dataset.

Local Outlying Factors. Breunig et al. [2] propose to extend the classic binary definition of outliers to a graded notion that quantifies the "outlierness" of each point, and define the *local outlying factor*, denoted *lof*, which measures a local isolation degree: for any point x, $lof(x)$ is defined as a quotient between the density around x and the density around x neighbors, where the density around a point y is a function of the average distance between y and its nearest neighbors.

The first difference between $cExc$ and lof concerns the characterized elements: lof is computed for each individual datapoint whereas $cExc$ applies to data subgroups. This difference is linked to the objectives of the two quantities: lof belongs to an outlier detection framework which considers points individually and does neither take into account nor provide any information about natural grouping, whereas $cExc$ aims at enriching clustering results.

lof and $cExc$ can be compared directly in the special case of single-point clusters, which are simultaneously datapoints and subgroups. Then both can be interpreted as local isolation degrees, they only differ in the way they define it: through the density quotient, lof compares average distances to nearest neighbors, whereas $cExc$ compares isolation dates. The latter is equivalent to comparing isolation distances as the iterative property of the clustering algorithm implies that the significative distance scale decreases at each step.

For larger groups, more differences appear: lof values vary and are minimal for points "deep inside the cluster" [2], which are less isolated and thus less outlying than data near the cluster limits. On the contrary, by definition, $cExc$ has the same value for all points in the same cluster. One could characterize the whole group with lof for instance computing the average lof value for points belonging to a same cluster, this could give results similar to $cExc$ (provided the hyperparameters for lof definition are well chosen). Yet in this case, it seems preferable to exploit thoroughly the information offered by OPCA and compute $cExc$ instead of carrying out additional independant computations to evaluate lof.

Typicality Degrees. Exceptionality coefficients can also be seen as evaluating the cluster typicality and are to be compared to the typicality degrees defined by Rifqi [10] in the context of fuzzy prototype construction. These degrees are computed in a supervised learning framework on fuzzy data where each point is associated with a class label and described as a membership function on a numerical domain; they indicate for a datapoint x the extent to which it is typical of the class it belongs to, i.e. the extent to which it is similar to other points of its class and/or distinct from members of the other class. For each point, the typicality degree is computed as the aggregation of its average within-class similarity and inter-class dissimilarity.

Typicality degrees are first different from exceptionality coefficients because, as lof, they characterize each datapoint individually and not data subgroups. But the major distinction is to be made about the considered reference: typicality degrees indicate the extent to which a point is characteristic of the class it belongs to, whereas $cExc$ and lof take the whole dataset as reference.

This reference difference is particularly sensitive on single-point clusters: in the typicality case, outliers appear as having an obviously high within-class similarity as they are the only member of their class, and their isolation leads to a high inter-class dissimilarity. Thus they are viewed as especially typical points whereas for lof and $cExc$ they correspond to exceptional behaviors. This is due to the fact that typicality degrees give a more local information related to a specific class and not to the whole dataset.

Thus the representativity measure defined by $cExc$ is quite different from lof and typicality degrees, which themselves are distinct: as a summary, typicality degrees characterize each point in a supervised framework indicating the extent to which it is typical of the class it belongs to, lof characterize each datapoint in an unsupervised framework, indicating the extent to which it is typical of the whole dataset, $cExc$ characterize each identified subgroup indicating the extent to which it is typical of the whole dataset. Thus, like typicality degrees, $cExc$ takes into account information on cluster decomposition, but it is closer to lof insofar as the it takes as reference all datapoints; it differs from lof on the "granularity" point of view and thus provides a different insight on the data.

4   Experimental Results

In this section, we illustrate the previous differences between the representativity measure, the local outlying factor and the typicality degrees and we highlight the clustering enrichment provided by $cExc$. We use artificial and real datasets, in one or two dimensions so that graphical representations of the results are possible.

4.1   Computations of lof and Typicality Degrees

Local Outlying Factor. *Lof* values depend on the number k of nearest neighbors taken into account to compute the density; for a datapoint x, $lof(x)$ is defined as the maximal value obtained when k varies in a pre-defined interval [$minptsLB$, $minptsUB$] [2]. $minptsLB$ corresponds to the minimal number of points a group has to contain so that other objects can be local outliers with respect to that cluster, $minptsUB$ is the maximal cardinality of a subgroup for which all points can be potentially outliers. In absence of *a priori* knowledge, we set these values to 4 and 20 for our small one-dimension artificial databases, and 10 and 40 for the larger two-dimension dataset (which in this case respectively correspond to the twentieth and the fifth part of the total number of instances).

Typicality Degrees. Rifqi [10] defined typicality degrees in a supervised framework for fuzzy data; applying it to unsupervised learning with numerical data requires to adapt the initial definitions. To define data labels, we apply OPCA and use the obtained clusters as labels, although it induces a strong bias in the typicality degrees: clustering aims at extracting compact and well-separated subgroups, i.e. it optimizes a kind of typicality. Therefore, we expect all typicality degrees to be high: the aim of these experiments is to compare the data characterization with that provided by $cExc$ and lof, rather than exploiting the computed values as such.

As regards the quantities involved in the degree computation, we made the following choices, denoting x and y datapoints, and C_x the class label associated with x:

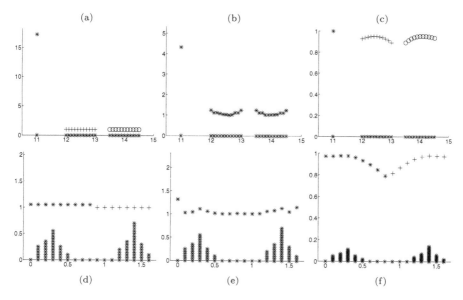

Fig. 3. Values of exceptionality coefficients, *lof*, and typicality degrees for two one-dimensional artificial datasets. The data are represented with ordinates 0, repeated and vertically shifted in case of multiple occurrences, for *cExc* and typicality degrees, the symbols indicate the cluster information. Note that the scale changes from one graph to another.

similarity measure : $s(x, y) = \dfrac{1}{1 + \|x - y\|^2}$

dissimilarity measure : $d(x, y) = \dfrac{1}{\max_{u,v} \|u - v\|} \|x - y\|$

internal aggregator : mean

thus within-class similarity : $R(x) = \text{mean}\{s(x, y), y \in C_x\}$

and inter-class dissimilarity : $D(x) = \text{mean}\{d(x, y), y \notin C_x\}$

external aggregator : probabilistic *t*-conorm

thus final typicality degree : $T(x) = R(x) + D(x) - R(x) * D(x)$

4.2   Artificial Datasets

One-Dimension Data. Figure 3 and 4 illustrate the obtained values of *cExc*, *lof* and typicality degrees for one-dimension artificial data. The datapoints are represented with stars at ordinate 0, possibly repeated and vertically shifted in case of multi-occurrences; note that the scale changes from one graph to another.

General Properties. Fig. 3(a, b, c) corresponds to Dataset 1 (defined on fig. 1a) and illustrates the general properties of the three data characterizations pre-

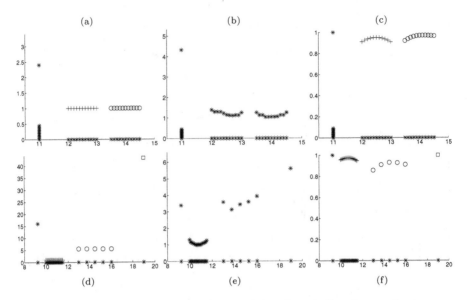

Fig. 4. Values of exceptionality coefficients, *lof*, and typicality degrees for two one-dimensional artificial datasets. Note that the scale changes from one graph to another.

sented in the previous section, in terms of outlier handling: *cExc* and *lof* provide similar results and highlight the fact that the leftmost point is not representative, i.e. is an outlier with respect to the whole dataset; indeed its associated values are 18 for *cExc* and 4.5 for *lof*, both are significantly higher than the reference value 1. On the contrary, in terms of typicality degrees, this datapoint appears as maximally typical of its own class. The graphs also show that *lof* values vary for data within natural groups, and take lower values deep inside the cluster; averaging these values give an equivalent to exceptionality coefficients. These comments are valid for all other datasets, we will not repeat them.

Fig. 3(d, e, f) illustrate another effect of the theoretical differences between *cExc*, *lof* and typicality degrees, in terms of chaining effect: the dataset consists in two natural groups linked through a chain of data close one to another. In this case, OPCA resorts to fuzzy *c*-means to handle the data and identify the two groups; exceptionality coefficients and *lof* values then indicate that the two groups are equivalent (the difference between the two values comes from a slight cardinality difference, and it is not significant). For typicality degrees, it appears that the central data have a low typicality because they are too similar to data belonging to the other class. This difference again is due to the fact that typicality degrees take as reference the cluster itself and not the whole dataset. Note that *lof* values, which only consider local density values, show a slight difference for the extreme data.

Clustering Enrichment. The results obtained with Dataset 3, which was presented on fig. 1c, shown on fig. 4(a, b, c), highlight the information provided by representativity measure and how it complements the clustering results: Dataset 3 only differs from Dataset 1 in the number of occurrences of the leftmost datapoint which constitutes an outlier. For Dataset 3, this point gets $cExc = 2.5$ against 18 for Dataset 1 (see fig. 3a), which is far less significant when compared to the reference value 1; thus $cExc$ makes it possible to distinguish between the two cases and shows that in the second one, the associated cluster is less to be considered as an outlier. On the contrary, *local outlying factors* and typicality degrees hardly make a difference between Datasets 1 and 3: for *lof*, the leftmost points of the two clusters appear slightly more outlying because their neighborhood contains a denser region; likewise, the typicality degrees are slightly higher because the inter-class dissimilarity increases with the additional points. Both for *lof* and typicality degrees, the differences between Datasets 1 and 3 are not significant: they provide information at another granularity level and do not aim at characterizing the dataset as a whole.

Fig. 4(d, e, f) correspond to Dataset 2 defined on fig. 1b and illustrate a more complex case. Exceptionality coefficients distinguish between the local and the global outliers (resp. leftmost and rightmost datapoints) and show that the local one is more representative of the whole dataset; moreover they indicate that the low density group is less typical of the whole dataset than the denser one but more characteristic than the outliers. Thus they enrich the clustering result and complete the subgroups decomposition.

The characterization provided by *lof* values lead to a less intuitive ranking: the most outlying point is also the rightmost point, but there is no real difference between the local outlier and the average *lof* of the low density group. This is due to the fact that the local density is equivalent in the two cases (with the neighborhood definition implied by the hyperparameter choice, the result is different for other hyperparameter values); $cExc$ distinguishes between them because its definition is based on the isolation date, which provides more aggregated information than individual isolation distances. Lastly, this dataset also shows that typicality degrees are sensitive to local density: the low density group has a lower typicality, which is due to the fact that the within-class similarity is lower in this case than for denser groups.

These artificial one-dimension datasets illustrate the possible interpretation of exceptionality coefficients and the differences existing between $cExc$, *local outlying factors* and typicality degrees.

Two-Dimension Artificial dataset. Figure 5 illustrates the results obtained by exceptionality coefficients and *local outlying factors* on an artificial database made of two Gaussians with different variances and two outliers with coordinates $(-1, -0.5)$ and $(-1.5, 3.5)$. The 3D plots (graphs (a) and (b)) respectively show the $cExc$ and *lof* values for each point, the 2D plots (graphs (c) and (d)) underline the identified outliers, here defined as points for which the coefficient value differs from the average by more than one standard deviation. With this definition, it appears that $cExc$ combined to OPCA identifies the two major clusters, which get a maximal representativity coefficients, and the outliers, which get higher exceptionality coefficients, and some other points which indeed are

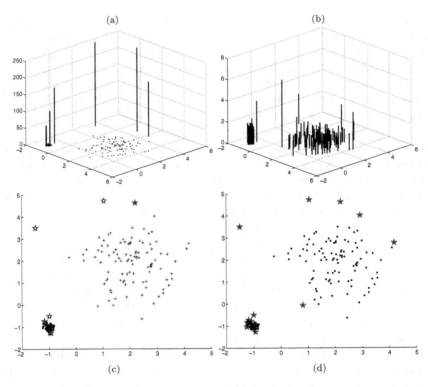

Fig. 5. Two-dimension artificial data handling. (a) exceptionality coefficients; (b) *local outlying factors*; (c) and (d) are the corresponding 2D projections, where stars represent datapoints for which the coefficient values (*cExc* or *lof*, resp.) differ from the average by more than one standard deviation.

locally isolated. It is to be noted that two points get the same maximal *cExc* value, *cExc* = 249.9, corresponding to the outlier $(-1.5, 3.5)$ and an isolated point $(1.05, 4.73)$, this result appears as relevant and intuitive when looking at the data distribution (see fig. 5c).

Local outlying factors give naturally less information as they tell nothing about natural grouping of similar points but they only indicate the most outlying ones; it appears that the contrast between the maximal and minimal values is much lower than for *cExc*. According to our criterion, *lof* identifies 13 outliers (7 are isolated by *cExc*), which only partially overlap with *cExc* results and have a different ranking: the most outlying point for *lof* is none of the predefined outliers, but a locally isolated point situated between the two major groups: its neighborhood contains points from both clusters, which lead to a density contrast and a high *lof* value. Globally, the obtained results seem difficult to justify, as compared to *cExc*: in the latter case, the information is aggregated at a cluster level, and thus it is already summarized and easier to interpret.

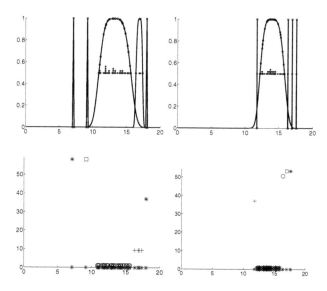

Fig. 6. Real data: evaluation of two students years. First row, profiles obtained with OPCA with Gaussian of order 4 membership functions; second row, exceptionality coefficients.

4.3   Real Dataset

Figure 6 illustrates the information gain provided by the exceptionality coefficients: it shows the results obtained for two student classes, described by their marks for a specific test. The fuzzy profile may lead to think that the two classes are quite similar, they have the same main structure made of a large middle group, with some smaller groups. The left class appears less homogeneous as it contains two students having difficulty but has a more important best student groups.

The exceptionality coefficients modify this impression and stress the difference between the two classes which do not have the same level: the left one can be globally characterized as having better results. Indeed, in the right case, the best students appear as outliers and the data is mostly described by the middle cluster, whereas on the left case, the exceptions correspond to the lower results and the high ones are more characteristic of the whole data.

5   Conclusion

We propose a technique to enrich a clustering result in order to better characterize a dataset: applying a clustering algorithm which detects simultaneously major trends and marginal behaviors, we define a numerical coefficient that quantifies the extent to which the groups are representative of the whole dataset and this representativity measure gives an interesting insight on the data.

The obtained results show that these coefficients provide a useful information and complete the subgroups decomposition. They can be particularly helpful in natural concept modelling, whose aim is to establish a link between numerical values and semantic knowledge expressed by linguistic terms: usually analysts are asked to label many examples and supervised learning methods are applied to determine the associated characterization. The enriched clustering technique makes it possible to extract automatically the relevant subgroups, represent them with fuzzy subsets and provides additional information necessary for labelling and choosing the most appropriate modifying adverb. Thus an expert is not asked to label all data, but only a reduced number of fuzzy characterizations.

References

1. V. Barnett and T. Lewis. *Outliers in statistical data*. Wiley and Sons, 1994.
2. M. Breunig, H. Kriegel, R. Ng, and J. Sander. LOF: Identifying density-based local outliers. In *Proc. of ACM SIGMOD*, volume 29, pages 93–104. ACM, 2000.
3. R. Davé. Characterization and detection of noise in clustering. *Pattern Recognition Letters*, 12:657–664, 1991.
4. R. Davé and R. Khrishnapuram. Robust clustering methods: a unified view. *IEEE Transactions on fuzzy systems*, 5(2):270–293, 1997.
5. H. Frigui and R. Krishnapuram. A robust competitive clustering algorithm with applications in computer vision. *IEEE Transactions on Pattern Analysis and Machine Intelligence*, 21(5):450–465, 1999.
6. F. Höppner, F. Klawonn, R. Kruse, and T. Runkler. *Fuzzy Cluster Analysis, Methods for classification, data analysis and image recognition*. Wiley, 2000.
7. A. Jain, M. Murty, and P. Flynn. Data clustering: a review. *ACM Computing survey*, 31(3):264–323, 1999.
8. E. Knorr, R. Ng, and V. Tucakov. Distance based outliers : algorithms and applications. *Very Large Data Bases Journal*, 8(3–4):237–253, 2000.
9. M.J. Lesot and B. Bouchon-Meunier. Extraction de concepts descriptifs avec exceptions par classification non supervisée hybride. In *Rencontres Francophones sur la Logique Floue et ses Applications, LFA'03*, Tours, France, 2003.
10. M. Rifqi. *Mesure de comparaison, typicalité et classification d'objets flous : théorie et pratique*. PhD thesis, Université de Paris VI, 1996.
11. C. Saint-Jean and C. Frélicot. An hybrid parametric model for semi-supervised robust clustering. In *Int. Conf. on Recent Developments in Mixture Modelling (MIXTURES)*, Hambourg, Germany, 2001.

Consequence Finding in Default Theories

Katsumi Inoue[1], Koji Iwanuma[2], and Hidetomo Nabeshima[2]

[1] National Institute of Informatics
2-1-2 Hitotsubashi, Chiyoda-ku, Tokyo 101-8430, Japan
ki@nii.ac.jp
[2] Department of Computer and Media Engineering, Yamanashi University
4-3-11 Takeda, Kofu 400-8511, Japan
{iwanuma,nabesima}@iw.media.yamanashi.ac.jp

Abstract. Consequence finding has been recognized as an important technique in many intelligent systems involving inference. In previous work, propositional or first-order clausal theories have been considered for consequence finding. In this paper, we consider consequence finding within a default theory, which consists of a first-order clausal theory and a set of normal defaults. In each extension of a default theory, consequence finding can be performed with the "generating defaults" for the extension. Alternatively, we consider all extensions in one theory with the "conditional consequence" format, which explicitly represents how a conclusion depends on which defaults. We also propose a procedure to compute consequences from a default theory based on a first-order consequence-finding procedure SOL. The SOL calculus is then further refined using skip-preference and complement checking, which have a great ability of preventing irrational derivations. The proposed system can be well applied to a multi-agent system with speculative computation in an incomplete communication environment.

1   Introduction

Given an axiom set, the task of *consequence finding* [15] is to discover hidden theorems of a given axiom set. These theorems to be found are not given in an explicit way, but are only characterized by some desired properties. Thus, consequence finding is clearly distinguished from *proof finding* or *theorem proving*. In practice, however, the set of theorems of an axiom set is generally infinite, and hence the complete deductive closure is neither obtainable nor desirable. A more practical way for automated consequence finding is to produce only "interesting" clauses derivable from an axiom set Σ. Criteria of such interesting clauses can be specified by a *production field*, which is a sub-vocabulary of the language of Σ, and each interesting clause that is minimal with respect to subsumption is called a *characteristic clause* of Σ [8].

The use of characteristic clauses enables us to characterize various reasoning problems of interest to AI, such as *query answering* [3, 12], *knowledge compilation* [2], *nonmonotonic reasoning* and *abduction* [8, 10], *inductive logic programming* [9], and *distributed knowledge bases* [19]. In the propositional case, each characteristic clause of Σ is a *prime implicate* of Σ. An extensive survey of consequence finding in propositional logic is given in [18].

H. Christiansen et al. (Eds.): FQAS 2004, LNAI 3055, pp. 459–472, 2004.

In these applications of consequence finding, we need to generate consequences of a given axiom set having some appropriate properties. In particular, we often need to generate clauses containing instances of some given literal L representing a question or an observation. The negation of the other literals in such a generated clause is an abductive hypothesis allowing to derive L [5]. In query answering, both *conditional answering* [3] and *reasoning about validity and completeness* [4] involve consequence finding. For such applications, it is necessary to produce the hypotheses we have to add to a given axiom set in order to prove the given formula. In conditional answering, this functionality enables us query answering under incomplete information. Conditional answers are also useful for various computational issues such as *lazy evaluation* and *resource limited computation* [7], and are applicable to deriving and checking *integrity constraints* as well as *intensional query answering* [5, 1].

In previous work, consequence finding has been considered mainly in *monotonic* propositional or first-order clausal theories. As is recognized in AI, however, nonmonotonic reasoning is a crucial method for reasoning under incomplete knowledge and dynamically changing worlds. In particular, recent technologies for agent systems have to deal with various kinds of incomplete information, and it is important to develop techniques for problem solving under incomplete communication environments. When an agent collects new information from other agents, it should make default assumptions when information about other agents is not available. In multi-agent systems, this kind of default reasoning is also called *speculative computation* [26]. Then, acceptance of new data sometimes happens accidentally, and an agent should update its beliefs according to situation changes. Thus, a desired feature of intelligent agents is to derive new consequences according to new incoming information. By this reason, we need a mechanism of *consequence finding from nonmonotonic theories*[1].

In this paper, we consider *consequence finding in default theories*. Here, a knowledge base consists of a first-order clausal theory together with a set of prerequisite-free normal *defaults* [21]. In each *extension* of a default theory, by computing the "generating defaults" [23] for the extension, consequence finding can be performed in a first-order clausal theory as usual. Since a conclusion from a default theory is tentative, we then consider all extensions in a single theory with the *conditional consequence* format [3]. Here, the literals in each condition are those literals that can be assumed by defaults. The conditional consequence format has also a great advantage of explicitly representing how a conclusion depends on which generating defaults.

We also propose a procedure to compute consequences from a default theory based on a first-order consequence-finding procedure SOL (Skipping Ordered

---

[1] Note that consequence finding is an important technique in implementing nonmonotonic reasoning such as abduction and circumscription [10, 18]. However, previous work on implementing nonmonotonic reasoning is only related to theorem proving in nonmonotonic frameworks. As far as the authors know, implementation of consequence finding from nonmonotonic theories has never been considered in the literature.

Linear resolution) [8, 13, 20]. The use of SOL calculus enables us to produce interesting consequences only to a limited extent rather than to compute all the consequences. The SOL calculus is then further refined using *skip-preference* and *complement checking*, which have a great ability of preventing irrational derivations. The proposed system can be well applied to a multi-agent system with speculative computation in an incomplete communication environment [11][2].

In the rest of this paper, Section 2 defines our default reasoning system and consequence finding from it. Section 3 reviews the consequence-finding procedure SOL [8] and SOL tableaux [13]. Section 4 defines a framework for problem solving with SOL tableaux and the conditional consequence format, and Section 5 gives a refined SOL tableau with skip-preference and complement checking. Section 6 discusses related work, and summarizes contributions and future work of this paper. Due to the space limitation, we omit the proofs of theorems in this paper, and will address them in the full paper.

2   Framework for Default Reasoning

In this section, we define our default reasoning system, and characterize it through consequence finding. We here use Poole's framework for default reasoning [21] (without constraints), which is a subset of Reiter's *default logic* [23] for clausal theories. Poole's framework is very simple yet powerful and practically useful as it can also give the logical account of *abduction* for which many resolution-based procedures exist [22, 10].

According to [16], a *clause* is defined as a multiset of literals, written as a disjunction $L_1 \vee \cdots \vee L_n$, where each L_i $(i = 1, \ldots, n)$ is a literal. The *empty clause* is a clause with $n = 0$, and is denoted as $\square$. For a literal L, $\overline{L}$ denotes the *complement* of L, i.e., when A is an atom, $\overline{A} = \neg A$ and $\overline{\neg A} = A$. For a set Γ of literals, $\overline{\Gamma}$ denotes the set $\{\overline{L} \mid L \in \Gamma\}$. For a set Σ of clauses, $Th(\Sigma)$ represents the set of logical consequences of Σ.

Definition 2.1 A *default theory* is defined as a pair $\Delta = (D, P)$ where

1. D is a set of ground literals called *defaults*[3].
2. P is a set of clauses such that a clause in P contains a literal whose predicate appears in D only if the literal is ground.

The meaning of a default theory in Definition 2.1 is given by *default logic* [23]. For each default theory (D, P), Reiter's *prerequisite-free normal default theory*

$$\left(\left\{ \frac{:L}{L} \,\middle|\, L \in D \right\}, P \right) \tag{1}$$

---

[2] The paper [11] assumes that a given default theory has a unique extension, and deals with updates of such default theories. On the other hand, the present paper generalizes the idea of [11] in that default theories may have multiple extensions.

[3] A default in the form of any first-order ground formula can be converted to a ground literal by the naming method [21].

is associated [21]. This default theory has always its *extensions* [23], which are characterized by the following proposition originally stated in [24].

Proposition 1. [24] *Suppose* (D, P) *is a default theory in Definition 2.1. Then, E is an extension of* (D, P) *iff* $E = Th(P \cup \widehat{D})$, *where* $\widehat{D}$ *is a maximal subset of D such that* $P \cup \widehat{D}$ *is consistent.*

Example 2.1 As a motivating example, we consider the following recommendation system for a journal paper based on a simple qualitative decision theory[4].

- Suppose that a paper is to be evaluated by three reviewers, R_1, R_2, and R_3.
- If the paper is accepted by all members, it is ranked as A (accept without a further review).
- If only two members accept the paper, it is ranked as B (accept with revisions).
- If neither R_1 nor R_2 accepts the paper, it is ranked as C (reject), because they are key persons for the review.
- R_2 and R_3 are positive reviewers and usually accept papers, but R_1 has no such a tendency.

Suppose that the editor gets a review from R_2 who accepts the paper but receives no answers from R_1 and R_3, although it is urgent that a rank should be anyhow determined for the paper. Then, the editor can rationally estimate that by default R_3 may accept the paper, but cannot guess R_1's evaluation at this stage. Then the editor might infer as follows. If R_1 is positive, the paper would be ranked as A. Otherwise, if R_1 is negative, it could be predicted as B. Consequently, the editor should predict that it is either A or B.

By abbreviating *accepts* as a and *rank* as r, this problem can be represented by the following set of clauses P:

$$\neg a(1) \vee \neg a(2) \vee \neg a(3) \vee r(A, [1, 2, 3]),$$
$$\neg a(1) \vee \neg a(2) \vee a(3) \vee r(B, [1, 2]),$$
$$\neg a(1) \vee a(2) \vee \neg a(3) \vee r(B, [1, 3]),$$
$$a(1) \vee \neg a(2) \vee \neg a(3) \vee r(B, [2, 3]),$$
$$a(1) \vee a(2) \vee r(C, []).$$

On the other hand, there are two ways to represent each member's default. The first one is to put the defaults as

$$D_1 = \{a(2), a(3)\}$$

so that we do not have any default for R_1. Another one is to prepare each case for R_1 as a possible *assumption* or an *abducible* in abduction:

$$D_2 = \{a(1), \neg a(1), a(2), a(3)\}.$$

---

[4] This example has in essence the same structure as the meeting-room reservation problem in a multi-agent system, which was introduced in [26].

The difference between the two is that there is the unique extension for (D_1, P), while there are two extensions for (D_2, P), one containing $r(A, [1, 2, 3])$ and the other containing $r(B, [2, 3])$. In the former case, the unique extension includes $r(A, [1, 2, 3]) \vee r(B, [2, 3])$, which also holds in both extensions for the latter case. Hence, $r(A, [1, 2, 3]) \vee r(B, [2, 3])$ is a consequence of both (D_1, P) and (D_2, P).

The main objective of this paper is to find consequences in extensions of a default theory like $r(A, [1, 2, 3]) \vee r(B, [2, 3])$ in Example 2.1. According to Proposition 1, this can be realized by (i) computing each maximal subset $\widehat{D}$ of D such that $P \cup \widehat{D}$ is consistent, and then (ii) utilizing a *consequence-finding* procedure [8, 2, 18, 20] to compute logical consequences of $P \cup \widehat{D}$. Note that this $\widehat{D}$ is called the *generating defaults* for an extension.

3   SOL Tableaux for Consequence Finding

As discussed in Section 1, we are interested in a practical way for automated consequence-finding. To find out "interesting" consequences, production fields and characteristic clauses are defined as follows.

We write $\subseteq_{ms}$ to denote the inclusion relation over multisets. When C and D are clauses, C *subsumes* D if there is a substitution θ such that $C\theta \subseteq_{ms} D$. We say C *properly subsumes* D if C subsumes D but D does not subsume C. For a set Σ of clauses, $\mu\Sigma$ denotes the set of clauses in Σ not properly subsumed by any clause in Σ. We assume that any two clauses subsuming each other are identified in $\mu\Sigma$. Note that $\mu(\mu\Sigma) = \mu\Sigma$ always holds. We say that Σ is *reduced* if $\Sigma = \mu\Sigma$ holds. In the following, we also assume that the given input axiom set Σ of clauses is reduced[5].

Definition 3.1 [8] A *production field* $\mathcal{P}$ is a pair $\langle \mathbf{L}, Cond \rangle$, where $\mathbf{L}$ is a set of literals closed under instantiation, and $Cond$ is a certain condition to be satisfied. When $Cond$ is not specified, $\mathcal{P}$ is just denoted as $\langle \mathbf{L} \rangle$. A clause C *belongs to* $\mathcal{P} = \langle \mathbf{L}, Cond \rangle$ if every literal in C belongs to $\mathbf{L}$ and C satisfies $Cond$. When Σ is a set of clauses, the set of logical consequences of Σ belonging to $\mathcal{P}$ is denoted as $Th_{\mathcal{P}}(\Sigma)$. A production field $\mathcal{P}$ is *stable* if, for any two clauses C and D such that C subsumes D, the clause D belongs to $\mathcal{P}$ only if C belongs to $\mathcal{P}$.

Example 3.1 (1) $\mathcal{P}_1 = \langle \{Ans\}^+ \rangle$ is stable, where $\{Ans\}^+$ is the positive literals whose predicates are Ans. $Th_{\mathcal{P}_1}(\Sigma)$ is the set of all positive clauses derivable from Σ such that the predicate of every literal is Ans.

(2) $\mathcal{P}_2 = \langle \mathbf{L}, length\ is\ fewer\ than\ k \rangle$ is stable. $Th_{\mathcal{P}_2}(\Sigma)$ is the set of clauses implied by Σ consisting of fewer than k literals in $\mathbf{L}$.

(3) $\mathcal{P}_3 = \langle \{\neg P, Q, R\}, length\ is\ more\ than\ 2 \rangle$ is not stable. For example, $D = \neg P \vee Q \vee R$ belongs to $\mathcal{P}_3$. However, $C = \neg P \vee Q$ does not belong to $\mathcal{P}_3$ although C properly subsumes D.

---

[5] This assumption is only necessary for the completeness of SOL tableaux (Theorem 3.1 (2)) with the TCS-freeness to hold [11]. If the SOL tableaux does not incorporate the TCS-freeness, the completeness also holds for non-reduced axiom sets.

The stability of a production field is important in practice [8], and we assume in this paper that production fields are stable.

Definition 3.2 [8] The *characteristic clauses* of Σ with respect to $\mathcal{P}$ are

$$Carc(\Sigma, \mathcal{P}) = \mu Th_{\mathcal{P}}(\Sigma).$$

Let C be a clause. The *new characteristic clauses* of C with respect to Σ and $\mathcal{P}$ are

$$Newcarc(\Sigma, C, \mathcal{P}) = \mu\left[Th_{\mathcal{P}}(\Sigma \cup \{C\}) \setminus Th(\Sigma)\right].$$

Note that Σ is unsatisfiable iff $Carc(\Sigma, \mathcal{P}) = \{\Box\}$ for any stable production field $\mathcal{P}$. This means that proof finding is a special case of consequence finding. On the other hand, if $\Sigma \not\models L$ and $\Sigma \not\models \overline{L}$ for literals L and $\overline{L}$ belonging to $\mathcal{P}$, $Carc(\Sigma, \mathcal{P})$ contains a tautology $L \vee \overline{L}$ as long as $L \vee \overline{L}$ satisfies *Cond*. The definition of the new characteristic clauses is equivalent to the following [8]:

$$Newcarc(\Sigma, C, \mathcal{P}) = Carc(\Sigma \cup \{C\}, \mathcal{P}) \setminus Carc(\Sigma, \mathcal{P}).$$

New characteristic clauses represent *ramifications* of a theory, i.e., "new" consequences derived when the new clause C is input to Σ.

The characteristic clauses $Carc(\Sigma, \mathcal{P})$ can be expressed by incrementally using $Newcarc$ operations [8]. Let $Taut(\mathbf{L})$ be the set of tautologies of the form $L \vee \overline{L}$ such that both L and $\overline{L}$ belong to $\mathbf{L}$. Then, for a set Σ of clauses, a clause C and a stable production field $\mathcal{P} = \langle \mathbf{L}, Cond \rangle$, it holds that

$$Carc(\emptyset, \mathcal{P}) = \mu\{T \mid T \in Taut(\mathbf{L}) \text{ and } T \text{ satisfies } Cond\},$$
$$Carc(\Sigma \cup \{C\}, \mathcal{P}) = \mu\left[Carc(\Sigma, \mathcal{P}) \cup Newcarc(\Sigma, C, \mathcal{P})\right].$$

To compute new characteristic clauses, Inoue [8] defined *SOL resolution* by extending the *Model Elimination* (ME) calculus with the additional *Skip rule*. In computing $Newcarc(\Sigma, C, \mathcal{P})$ for a clause C, SOL resolution focuses on producing only those theorems belonging to $\mathcal{P}$, and treats a newly added clause C as the *start clause*. These features are desirable for consequence finding since the procedure can directly derive the theorems relevant to the added information.

Now, we review the tableaux variant of SOL resolution [13]. There is a sophisticated first-order implementation of SOL tableaux written in Java [20].

Definition 3.3 A *clausal tableau* T is a labeled ordered tree, where every non-root node of T is labeled with a literal. We identify a node with its label, i.e., a literal if no confusion arises. If the immediate successors of a node are literals $L_1, \ldots, L_n$, then the clause $L_1 \vee \cdots \vee L_n$ is called the *tableau clause*. The tableau clause below the root is called the *start clause*. T is a *clausal tableau for* a set Σ of clauses if every tableau clause C in T is an instance of a clause D in Σ. In this case, D is called an *origin clause* of C in Σ.

A *connection tableau* is a clausal tableau such that, for every non-leaf node L except the root, there is an immediate successor labeled with $\overline{L}$. A *marked tableau* T is a clausal tableau such that some leaves are marked with labels `closed` or `skipped`. The unmarked leaves are called *subgoals*. T is *solved* if all leaves are marked. $skip(T)$ denotes the set of literals of nodes marked with `skipped`.

Notice that $skip(T)$ is a *set*, not a multiset. $skip(T)$ is also identified with a clause. In the following, we abbreviate a marked connection tableau as a tableau.

Definition 3.4 A tableau T is *regular* if no two nodes on a branch in T are labeled with the same literal. T is *tautology-free* if no tableau clause in T is tautology. T is *complement-free* if no two non-leaf nodes on a branch in T are labeled with complementary literals.

A tableau T is *skip-regular* if there is no node L in T such that $\overline{L} \in skip(T)$. T is *TCS-free (Tableau Clause Subsumption free)* [16] for a clause set Σ if any tableau clause C in T is not subsumed by any clause in Σ other than origin clauses of C.

Notice that the skip-regularity applies to all over a tableau, so it is effective not only for subgoals but also for non-leaf and solved nodes. The skip-regularity can prevent lots of useless derivations produced from contrapositive clauses. Moreover, the TCS-freeness is important for restricting derivations to generating only *rational* conclusions (see Examples 4.1 and 5.1).

Definition 3.5 (SOL Tableau Calculus)   Let Σ be a set of clauses, C a clause, and $\mathcal{P}$ a production field. Then, an *SOL-deduction deriving a clause S from $\Sigma + C$ and $\mathcal{P}$* consists of a sequence of tableaux $T_0, T_1, \ldots, T_n$ satisfying that:

1. T_0 consists of the start clause C only. All leaf nodes of T_0 are unmarked.
2. T_n is a solved tableau, and $skip(T_n) = S$.
3. For each T_i $(i = 0, \ldots, n)$, T_i is regular, tautology-free, complement-free, skip-regular, and TCS-free for $\Sigma \cup \{C\}$.
4. For each T_i $(i = 0, \ldots, n)$, the clause $skip(T_i)$ belongs to $\mathcal{P}$.
5. T_{i+1} is constructed from T_i as follows. Select a subgoal K, then apply one of the following rules to T_i to obtain T_{i+1}:
   (a) **Skip:** If $skip(T_i) \cup \{K\}$ belongs to $\mathcal{P}$, then mark K with label skipped.
   (b) **Skip-factoring:** If $skip(T_i)$ contains a literal L, and K and L are unifiable with mgu θ, then mark K with skipped, and apply θ to T_i.
   (c) **Resolution:** Select a clause B from $\Sigma \cup \{C\}$ and obtain a variant $B' = L_1 \vee \cdots \vee L_m$ by renaming. If there is a literal L_j such that $\overline{K}$ and L_j are unifiable with mgu θ, then attach new nodes $L_1, \ldots, L_m$ to K as the immediate successors. Next, mark the node L_j with closed and apply θ to the extended tableau.
   (d) **Reduction:** If K has an ancestor node L on the branch from the root to K, and $\overline{K}$ and L are unifiable with mgu θ, then mark K with closed, and apply θ to T_i.

Theorem 3.1. [8, 13, 11]

(1) Soundness: *If a clause S is derived by an SOL-deduction from $\Sigma + C$ and $\mathcal{P}$, then S belongs to $Th_{\mathcal{P}}(\Sigma \cup \{C\})$.*
(2) Completeness: *If a clause F does not belong to $Th_{\mathcal{P}}(\Sigma)$ but belongs to $Th_{\mathcal{P}}(\Sigma \cup \{C\})$, then there is an SOL-deduction deriving a clause S from $\Sigma + C$ and $\mathcal{P}$ such that S subsumes F.*

4   Conditional Consequences

Once we have a consequence-finding procedure, we can compute extensions of a default theory based on Proposition 1. For problem solving in default theories, SOL can be combined with the *answer literal* method [6, 14]. Given a query $\neg Q(X)$ of the clausal form, where X stands for the tuple of free variables in the query, the SOL-deductions with the start clause $\neg Q(X) \vee Ans(X)$ provide all consequences consisting of literals with the predicate Ans only (called *answer literals* [6]). For Example 2.1, the start clause of each SOL-deduction is given as $\neg r(x, y) \vee Ans(x, y)$. In this case, the production field can be specified as $\langle \{Ans\}^+, Cond \rangle$, where $\{Ans\}^+$ denotes the positive literals with the predicate Ans and $Cond$ can contain the maximum length of clauses or the maximum depth of terms in literals. An answer in a more general form can be represented as a *conditional answer* [3].

Definition 4.1 Let $Q(X)$ be a conjunction of literals $L_1 \wedge \cdots \wedge L_k$, where X is the tuple of free variables appearing in $L_1, \ldots, L_k$. Then, the clause $\neg Q(X) = \overline{L_1} \vee \cdots \vee \overline{L_k}$ is called a *query*. Let Σ be a set of clauses, and $A_1 \vee \cdots \vee A_m$ a clause belonging to some production field $\mathcal{P}$, and $\theta_1, \ldots, \theta_n$ substitutions for the variables X. Then, a clause S:

$$A_1 \vee \cdots \vee A_m \vee Q(X)\theta_1 \vee \cdots \vee Q(X)\theta_n \qquad (2)$$

is a *conditional answer (to the query $\neg Q(X)$ relative to Σ and $\mathcal{P}$)* if $\Sigma \models S$ and $\Sigma \not\models A_1 \vee \cdots \vee A_m$. In particular, $S = Q(X)\theta_1 \vee \cdots \vee Q(X)\theta_n$ is a *correct answer (to the query $\neg Q(X)$ relative to Σ)* if $\Sigma \models S$.

A conditional answer of the form (2) represents an implicational formula:

$$\overline{A_1} \wedge \cdots \wedge \overline{A_m} \to Q(X)\theta_1 \vee \cdots \vee Q(X)\theta_n,$$

where the consequent represents a (disjunctive) answer to the query and the antecedent specifies a sufficient condition for the answer to hold.

Definition 4.2 Let Ans be a predicate symbol appearing nowhere in Σ. A *conditional Ans-clause (a CA-clause for short) (relative to Σ and $\mathcal{P}$)* is a clause of the form:

$$A_1 \vee \cdots \vee A_m \vee Ans(X)\theta_1 \vee \cdots \vee Ans(X)\theta_n, \qquad (3)$$

where $A_1 \vee \cdots \vee A_m$, $\mathcal{P}$, and $\theta_1, \ldots, \theta_n$ are the same as in Definition 4.1.

Conditional answers and CA-clauses are also called *conditional consequences*[6]. It can be proved, in a similar way to [14, Theorem 1], that a conditional answer of the form (2) belongs to $Th(\Sigma)$ iff a CA-clause of the form (3) belongs to $Th(\Sigma \cup \{\neg Q(X) \vee Ans(X)\})$. It is also known that SOL resolution is the only known procedure in the ME family which is complete for minimal (conditional) answer computation [12]. Then, by Proposition 1 and Theorem 3.1 (2), the next theorem holds for consequence finding of default theories.

---

[6] We can derive any clausal form of consequences from a default theory. Due to space limitation, we here deal with C-consequences related to some queries.

Theorem 4.1. *Let (D, P) be a default theory, $\neg Q(X)$ a query, and $\widehat{D}$ a maximal subset of D such that $P \cup \widehat{D}$ is consistent. If a clause $Q(X)\theta_1 \vee \cdots \vee Q(X)\theta_n$ is a correct answer to $\neg Q(X)$ relative to $P \cup \widehat{D}$, then there is an SOL-deduction $\mathcal{D}$ from $(P \cup \widehat{D}) + (\neg Q(X) \vee Ans(X))$ and $\langle \{Ans\}^+ \rangle$ deriving a clause:*

$$Ans(X)\sigma_1 \vee \cdots \vee Ans(X)\sigma_u$$

such that $Ans(X)\sigma_1 \vee \cdots \vee Ans(X)\sigma_u$ subsumes $Ans(X)\theta_1 \vee \cdots \vee Ans(X)\theta_n$.

Theorem 4.1 guarantees the completeness of SOL calculus for computing consequences in default extensions. However, it is only meaningful for some *fixed* $\widehat{D}$ as the generating defaults. This $\widehat{D}$ must be maximally consistent with P by definition. In other words, we have to compute $\widehat{D}$ in advance.

Now, we propose an alternative way to compute consequences in default extensions *without computing the generating defaults in advance*. In the proposed method, consequence finding is performed in all extensions at the same time. For this purpose, we utilize the conditional consequence format to associate each conclusion with its depending defaults. This method has additional advantages for *updates* of a default theory. Since all defaults are considered to be *tentative*, the real truth value for a default literal may not agree with the default value. Moreover, the real truth value itself may also be changed frequently. For Example 2.1, the reviewer R_1 may often change his/her decision after communicating with other reviewers. To cope with such a situation change at a later time, it is useful to record the dependency on defaults used to derive a conclusion.

Theorem 4.2. *Let (D, P), $\neg Q(X)$, and $\widehat{D}$ be the same as in Theorem 4.1. If a clause $Q(X)\theta_1 \vee \cdots \vee Q(X)\theta_n$ is a correct answer to $\neg Q(X)$ relative to $P \cup \widehat{D}$, then there is an SOL-deduction $\mathcal{D}$ from $P + (\neg Q(X) \vee Ans(X))$ and $\langle \overline{D} \cup \{Ans\}^+ \rangle$ deriving a CA-clause:*

$$B_1 \vee \cdots \vee B_s \vee Ans(X)\sigma_1 \vee \cdots \vee Ans(X)\sigma_u \tag{4}$$

such that

1. $B_i \in \overline{\widehat{D}}$ *for each $i = 1, \ldots, s$, and*
2. $Ans(X)\sigma_1 \vee \cdots \vee Ans(X)\sigma_u$ *subsumes $Ans(X)\theta_1 \vee \cdots \vee Ans(X)\theta_n$.*

In Theorem 4.2, SOL-deductions are constructed not with the input set $P \cup \widehat{D} \cup \{\neg Q(X) \vee Ans(X)\}$, but with $P \cup \{\neg Q(X) \vee Ans(X)\}$. Hence, we do not need to prepare a maximal $\widehat{D}$ in advance. Moreover, because the production field $\mathcal{P}$ is defined as $\langle \overline{D} \cup \{Ans\}^+ \rangle$, we do not need to know what $\widehat{D}$ is. Here, **Resolution** *operations with unit clauses in D are simulated by* **Skip** *operations to literals belonging to $\langle \overline{D} \rangle$*. Thus, the conditional consequent format enables explicit representation of dependencies on defaults which are used to derive tentative conclusions. This reflects our intuition that defaults are tentative.

Theorem 4.2 characterizes the completeness of SOL calculus for consequence finding in multiple extensions of default theories. That is, we can set the production field as $\mathcal{P} = \langle \overline{D} \cup \{Ans\}^+ \rangle$. For the soundness in this setting, Theorem 3.1 (1) implies that a clause S of the form (4) derived by an SOL-deduction belongs to $Th_P(P \cup \{\neg Q(X) \vee Ans(X)\})$. The problem here is that a clause S is not always a CA-clause, and S never provides a correct answer unless S is a CA-clause. Note that S is a CA-clause iff $P \not\models B_1 \vee \cdots \vee B_s$. The SOL calculus can be used for this consistency checking as follows.

Theorem 4.3. *Let (D, P) be a default theory, and $\neg Q(X)$ a query. If there is an SOL-deduction $\mathcal{D}$ from $P + (\neg Q(X) \vee Ans(X))$ and $\langle \overline{D} \cup \{Ans\}^+ \rangle$ deriving a CA-clause S of the form (4) such that S is not subsumed by any clause in $Carc(P, \langle \overline{D} \rangle)$, then there is an extension E of (D, P) such that*

1. *$\overline{B_i} \in \widehat{D}$ for each $i = 1, \ldots, s$, where $\widehat{D}$ is the generating defaults of E, and*
2. *E contains the correct answer $Q(X)\sigma_1 \vee \cdots \vee Q(X)\sigma_u$.*

In Theorem 4.3, $Carc(P, \langle \overline{D} \rangle)$ represents the set of minimally incompatible constraints on D. That is, if $\overline{L_1} \vee \cdots \vee \overline{L_n} \in Carc(P, \langle \overline{D} \rangle)$, then $L_1, \ldots, L_n$ cannot be assumed to be true simultaneously in any extension. As shown in Section 3, $Carc(P, \langle \overline{D} \rangle)$ can also be computed by SOL.

SOL tableaux in Theorems 4.2 and 4.3 can exclude many irrational derivations, mainly due to the skip-regularity. However, the SOL calculus in this setting still might generate several inappropriate conclusions in a dynamic world. This is because the lack of unit clauses from the generating defaults $\widehat{D}$ in the axiom set often fails to satisfy the TCS-freeness.

Example 4.1 Consider the default theory (D_2, P) in Example 2.1. Recall that $a(2)$ and $a(3)$ are assumed to be true by default. In this case, according to the default set D_2, the production field $\mathcal{P}$ is $\langle \{a(1), \neg a(1), \neg a(2), \neg a(3)\} \cup \{Ans\}^+ \rangle$. In this situation, several irrational tableaux are still derived within SOL. Two examples are depicted in Figure 1, both of which satisfy the skip-regularity but generate the following irrational/redundant conclusions, respectively:

$$\neg a(1) \wedge a(3) \rightarrow Ans(B, [2, 3]) \vee Ans(C, []), \tag{5}$$

$$a(1) \wedge a(3) \rightarrow Ans(B, [1, 3]) \vee Ans(A, [1, 2, 3]). \tag{6}$$

In the consequence (5), the disjunct $Ans(C, [])$ corresponds to the case that the reviewer R_2 does not accept the paper ($\neg a(2)$). However, $a(2)$ holds by default in any extension, which implies that $Ans(C, [])$ is a redundant conclusion. In fact, the tableau clause $a(1) \vee a(2) \vee r(C, [])$ in Figure 1(a) would be subsumed if $a(2)$ could be added as an additional unit clause from the generating defaults $\widehat{D_2}$ to P. Hence, the tableau (a) violates the TCS-freeness for the axiom set $P \cup \widehat{D_2}$. Similarly, $Ans(B, [1, 3])$ in the consequence (6) is redundant.

5   Skip Preference and Complement Checking

Now, we shall further refine SOL tableaux, which is intended to be more appropriate for default reasoning in a dynamic world. We introduce an extension of *skip-preference* [8] to SOL tableaux. The resulting calculus, denoted as *SOL-S(Γ) tableaux*, first performs *complement checking* which is aimed to simulate

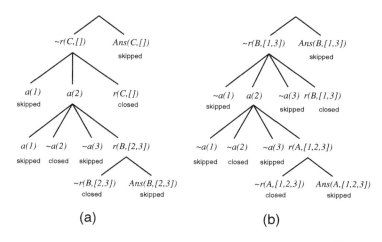

Fig. 1. SOL tableaux violating the TCS-freeness for $P \cup \widehat{D_2}$.

TCS-freeness checking with respect to some set of defaults, and next applies **Skip** operations to literals for the default set as much as possible by ignoring the possibility of **Resolution** operations.

Definition 5.1 (SOL-S(Γ) Tableau Calculus) Let Γ be a set of ground literals. The *SOL tableau calculus with skip-preferring* Γ, denoted as SOL-S(Γ), is obtained from SOL tableaux of Definition 3.5 by inserting the following additional procedure just before (5-a) of Definition 3.5:

(5-0) Check $\overline{\Gamma}$ & Cut, Skip for Γ & Cut:
  5-0-1. Check whether the complement $\overline{K}$ belongs to Γ or not. If so, then do nothing, and prune all alternative rules (5-a)–(5-d) for the subgoal K.
  5-0-2. Otherwise, if K belongs to Γ, then mark K with label `skipped`. Prune all alternative rules (5-a)–(5-d) for the subgoal K.
  5-0-3. Otherwise, go to Step (5-a).

Although the above complement checking of Γ partially achieves the TCS-freeness of $\overline{\Gamma}$ in general, it has a sufficient pruning power for default reasoning. Moreover, complement checking is much easier for implementation. Since the SOL-S(Γ) calculus only restricts the number of SOL deductions, the soundness is immediate by Theorem 4.3. The completeness of SOL-S(Γ) calculus still holds for consequence finding in extensions if Γ is appropriately chosen as follows.

Theorem 5.1. *Let (D, P), $\neg Q(X)$, and $\widehat{D}$ be the same as in Theorem 4.1. Let*

$$\Gamma = \{\, \overline{L} \mid L \in D,\ \overline{L} \text{ does not appear in any clause in } Carc(P, \langle \overline{D} \rangle)\,\}.$$

If $Q(X)\theta_1 \vee \cdots \vee Q(X)\theta_n$ is a correct answer relative to $P \cup \widehat{D}$, then there is an SOL-S(Γ) deduction from $P + (\neg Q(X) \vee Ans(X))$ and $\langle \overline{D} \cup \{Ans\}^+ \rangle$ deriving a CA-clause of the form (4) satisfying the same conditions as in Theorem 4.2.

Example 5.1 Reconsider the situation in Example 4.1. Let Γ be

$$\Gamma = \overline{D_1} = \{\neg a(2), \neg a(3)\} \subseteq \overline{D_2} = \{a(1), \neg a(1), \neg a(2), \neg a(3)\}.$$

Here, $a(1) \vee \neg a(1) \in Carc(P, \langle \overline{D_2} \rangle)$ holds, so that both $a(1)$ and $\neg a(1)$ are excluded from Γ. Although there are a number of tableaux derivable within SOL for this situation, only four tableaux depicted in Figure 2 are derivable within SOL-S(Γ). For example, the two tableaux in Figure 1 are pruned by complement checking of $\neg a(2) \in \Gamma$ in Step 5-0-1. In the tableau of Figure 2(a),

$$a(1) \wedge a(2) \wedge a(3) \rightarrow Ans(A, [1, 2, 3]),$$

is derived, in which $\neg a(1)$ is skipped. On the other hand, in the tableau of Figure 2(b), the complement $a(1)$ is skipped. Notice that such a truth value assignment caused by **Skip** operation is guaranteed to be consistent in an SOL tableau thanks to the skip-regularity in the tableau. The two tableaux (c) and (d) in Figure 2 derive the same conclusion:

$$a(2) \wedge a(3) \rightarrow Ans(A, [1, 2, 3]) \vee Ans(B, [2, 3]),$$

which describes a more general conclusion not depending on the truth value of the literal $a(1)$ (see Example 2.1).

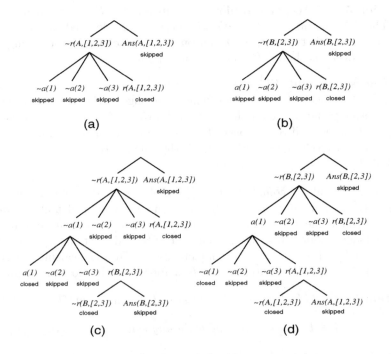

Fig. 2. SOL-S(Γ) tableaux.

6   Related Work and Conclusion

We have considered consequence finding in prerequisite-free normal default theories, and its computation has shown to be done with or without computing the generating defaults. This is implemented using a consequence-finding procedure SOL, which is extended to incorporate the TCS-freeness constraint, the conditional consequence format, skip-preference, and complement checking. The conditional consequence format has a great advantage of explicitly representing how a conclusion depends on defaults in a dynamic world. Skip-preference and complement checking prune lots of irrational/redundant derivations. These new techniques could also be applied to *SFK resolution* [2] with minor changes.

As stated in Section 1, although there are a number of previous works on theorem proving in default theories, there is very little work on consequence finding from nonmonotonic theories. In particular, no previous work supports consequence finding in first-order clausal theories.

Keeping CA-clauses to avoid duplicate computation is similar to labeling propositions with hypotheses in *ATMS* [25]. Since ATMS computes all prime implicates of a propositional theory, it is not easy to lift it to the first-order case. SOL, on the other hand, can be regarded as a first-order version of ATMS, yet can focus search on clauses relevant to a production field.

An important future work is to develop a method of consequence finding within more general default theories. For general defaults, Linke and Schaub [17] generalize Proposition 1 to characterize extensions with generating defaults and additional notions of groundedness, protectedness, and non-conflict. Their methods do not explicitly perform consequence finding, but can be combined with our consequence finding procedure once we get such generating defaults.

References

1. de Giacomo, G. Intensional query answering by partial evaluation. *Journal of Intelligent Information Systems*, 7(3):205–233, 1996.
2. del Val, A. A new method for consequence finding and compilation in restricted languages. In: *Proceedings of AAAI-99*, pages 259–264, 1999.
3. Demolombe, R. A strategy for the computation of conditional answers. In: *Proceedings of ECAI'92*, LNAI 810, pages 134–138, Springer, 1992.
4. Demolombe, R. Answers about validity and completeness of data: formal definitions, usefulness and computation technique. In: *Proceedings of FQAS'98*, LNAI 1495, pages 138–147, Springer, 1998.
5. Demolombe, R. and L. Fariñas del Cerro. An inference rule for hypothesis generation. In: *Proceedings of IJCAI-91*, pages 152–157, Morgan Kaufmann, 1991.
6. Green, C. Theorem-proving by resolution as a basis for question-answering systems. In: B. Meltzer and D. Michie, editors, *Machine Intelligence*, Volume 4, pages 183–205, Edinburgh University Press, 1969.
7. Imielinski, T. Intelligent query answering in rule based systems. *Journal of Logic Programming*, 4:229–257, 1987.
8. Inoue, K. Linear resolution for consequence finding. *Artificial Intelligence*, 56:301–353, 1992.

9. Inoue, K. Induction, abduction, and consequence-finding. In: *Proceedings of the 11th International Conference on Inductive Logic Programming*, LNAI 2157, pages 65–79, Springer, 2001. An extended version is to appear in *Machine Learning*, 55:109–135, 2004, under the title: Induction as consequence finding.
10. Inoue, K. Automated abduction. In: A. C. Kakas and F. Sadri, editors, *Computational Logic: Logic Programming and Beyond—Essays in Honour of Robert A. Kowalski, Part II*, LNAI 2408, pages 311–341, Springer, 2002.
11. Inoue, K. and K. Iwanuma. Speculative computation through consequence-finding in multi-agent environments. *Annals of Mathematics and Artificial Intelligence*, to appear, 2004.
12. Iwanuma, K. and K. Inoue. Minimal answer computation and SOL. In: *Proceedings of JELIA'02*, LNAI 2424, pages 245–257, Springer, 2002.
13. Iwanuma, K., K. Inoue, and K. Satoh. Completeness of pruning methods for consequence finding procedure SOL. In: *Proceedings of the 3rd International Workshop on First-Order Theorem Proving*, pages 89–100, 2000.
14. Kunen, K. The semantics of answer literals. *Journal of Automated Reasoning*, 17:83–95, 1996.
15. Lee, C. T. A completeness theorem and computer program for finding theorems derivable from given axioms. Ph.D. thesis, Department of Electrical Engineering and Computer Science, University of California, Berkeley, CA, 1967.
16. Letz, R. Clausal tableaux. In: W. Bibel, P. H. Schmitt, editors, *Automated Deduction: A Basis for Applications*, Volume 1, pages 39–68, Kluwer, 1998.
17. Linke, T. and T. Schaub. Alternative foundations for Reiter's default logic. *Artificial Intelligence*, 124:31–86, 2000.
18. Marquis, P. Consequence finding algorithms. In: D. M. Gabbay and P. Smets, editors, *Handbook for Defeasible Reasoning and Uncertain Management Systems*, Volume 5, pages 41–145, Kluwer, 2000.
19. McIlaith, S. and E. Amir. Theorem proving with structured theories. In: *Proceedings of IJCAI-2001*, pages 624–631, Morgan Kaufmann, 2001.
20. Nabeshima, H., K. Iwanuma, and K. Inoue. SOLAR: a consequence finding system for advanced reasoning. In: *Proceedings of TABLEAUX 2003*, LNAI 2796, pages 257–263, 2003.
21. Poole, D. A logical framework for default reasoning. *Artificial Intelligence*, 36:27–47, 1988.
22. Poole, D., R. Goebel, and R. Aleliunas. Theorist: a logical reasoning system for defaults and diagnosis. In: N. Cercone and G. McCalla, editors, *The Knowledge Frontier: Essays in the Representation of Knowledge*,
23. Reiter, R. A logic for default reasoning. *Artificial Intelligence*, 13:81–132, 1980.
24. Reiter, R. A theory of diagnosis from first principles. *Artificial Intelligence*, 32:571–95, 1987.
25. Reiter, R. and J. de Kleer. Foundations of assumption-based truth maintenance systems: preliminary report. In: *Proceedings of AAAI-87*, pages 183–187, Morgan Kaufmann, 1987.
26. Satoh, K., K. Inoue, K. Iwanuma, and C. Sakama. Speculative computation by abduction under incomplete communication environments. In: *Proceedings of the Fourth International Conference on MultiAgent Systems*, pages 263–270, 2000.

Personalized Movie Recommender System through Hybrid 2-Way Filtering with Extracted Information

Kyung-Yong Jung[1], Dong-Hyun Park[2], and Jung-Hyun Lee[3]

[1] HCI Laboratory, School of Computer Engineering, Inha University, Korea
Kyjung@gcgc.ac.kr
[2] Department of Industrial Engineering, Inha University, Korea
dhpark@inha.ac.kr
[3] School of Computer Engineering, Inha University, Korea
jhlee@inha.ac.kr

Abstract. Personalized recommender systems improve access to relevant items and information by making personalized suggestions based on previous items of an individual user's likes and dislikes. Most recommender systems use collaborative filtering or content-based filtering to predict new items of interest for a user. This approach has the advantage of being able to recommend previously un-rated items to users with unique interests and to provide explanations for personalized recommendations. We describe a personalized movie recommender system that utilizes WebBot, hybrid 2-way filtering, and a machine-learning algorithm for web page and movie poster's extraction. And we validate our personalized movie recommender system through hybrid 2-way filtering with extracted information in on-line experiments.

1 Introduction

Most recommender system would comprehend user requirements transparently, search the web autonomously for appropriate information, and deliver the answers before user interests diminish. It commonly involves repeated interactions with users having long-term interests such as finding information on autonomous agents. This is in contrast to information retrieval systems such as Infoseek, Lycos, Excite, which focus primarily on users having short-term needs represented in queries that can be fulfilled in few interactions [1]. Personalized recommender systems support decisions of users who purchase some goods in a shopping mall on the web site. They use automated information filtering technology to recommend appropriate items that an active user prefers. The accuracy of prediction and high quality of recommendation lists are important in recommender system. Personalized recommender systems have been studied in data mining, machine learning, pattern recognition, knowledge discovery, and information filtering [6]. Most of recommender systems have used information filtering technology. Information filtering techniques fall in two independent filtering categories: collaborative filtering and content-based filtering [7]. However, most existing

H. Christiansen et al. (Eds.): FQAS 2004, LNAI 3055, pp. 473–486, 2004.

recommender systems are explicit and implicit ratings-based systems e.g. Letizia [11], Ringo [17], SiteSeer [18], Fab [2]. People describe explicitly their interests to the system by rating some data. For instance, when a user moves from one web page to another, the user rates how interesting the pages are. The effort of rating pages could interrupt the normal browsing process, so the fewer ratings required is better. But system performance is totally based on user's ratings [1]. In this study, we present the framework for the personalized movie recommender system through hybrid 2-way filtering with extracted information. The hybrid 2-way filtering consists of collaborative filtering and content-based filtering. We have also developed WebBot: web robot agent that utilizes semi-structured content information about movies gathered from the web page using simple information extraction technique. We apply this framework in the domain of movie recommendation and show that our approach performs significantly better than both pure collaborative filtering and pure content-based filtering.

2 Personalized Item Recommender Filtering Systems

There are various ways to perform personalized information filtering. Different machine learning algorithm can be used to learn a mapping from the features of an item to a number indicating the utility of the item to the user based on previous ratings that the user has made on other items. For example, the words in an article can form its features that can be used to predict whether an article could be interesting for the user. An alternative method is to use ratings of "similar" users to predict the rating on items that the user has not rated. This is called "collaborative filtering". The basic premise is that people with similar taste tend to like similar types of items and the rating of someone similar is a good predictor for the personalized rating of the item. Collaborative filtering can improve in taking advantage of the information.

Collaborative filtering intensifies the personalization from a search point of view, improves the accuracy of searches and decreases time that the user need to use for e.g. following up changed on a particular web site. The basic mechanism behind collaborative filtering systems is the following: a large group of user preferences are registered using a similarity metric. Soon a neighborhood of user is selected, whose preferences are similar to the user preferences that seek advice [6]. Then an average of the preferences for that neighborhood is calculated and the resulting preference function is used to recommend options on which the advice-seeker has not yet expressed any personal opinion [8].

2.1 Collaborative Filtering

Collaborative filtering systems recommend objects for a target user based on the opinions of other users by considering how much the target user and the other users have agreed on other objects in the past. This allows this technique to be used on any type of objects and thus build a large variety of service, since collaborative filtering systems consider only human judgments on the value of objects. These judgments are usually expressed as numerical ratings, revealing the user preference for objects [6,7]. Most collaborative filtering systems collect the user opinions as ratings on a numerical scale, leading to a sparse matrix rating (*user*, *item*) in short $r_{u,i}$. Collaborative filtering technique then uses this rating matrix to predict rating. Several algorithms have been proposed on how to use the rating matrix [6,7,8,13]. In this paper, we apply a commonly used algorithm, which is based on vector correlation using the Pearson correlation coefficient.

Collaborative filtering technique predicts the rating of a particular user u for an item i. And it compares the predicted rating with the rating of all other users who have rated the item i. Then a weighted average of the other users rating is used as a prediction. If I_u is set of items that a user u has rated then we can define the mean rating of user u by Equation (1).

$$w(u,a) = \frac{\sum_{i \in I_u \cap I_a}(r_{u,i} - \overline{r_u})(r_{a,i} - \overline{r_a})}{\sqrt{\sum_{i \in I_u \cap I_a}(r_{u,i} - \overline{r_u})^2 \bullet \sum_{i \in I_u \cap I_a}(r_{a,i} - \overline{r_a})^2}} \qquad \overline{r_u} = \frac{1}{|I_u|}\sum_{i \in I_u} r_{u,i} \qquad (1)$$

Collaborative filtering algorithms predict the rating based on the rating of similar users. When Pearson correlation coefficient is used, similarity is determined from the correlation of the rating vectors of user u and the other users a. It can be noted that $w \in [-1, +1]$. The value of w measures the similarity between the two users' rating vectors. A high value close to $+1$ signifies high similarity and a low value close to 0 signifies low correlation (not much can be deduced) and a value close to -1 signifies that users are often of opposite opinion. The general prediction formula is based on the assumption that the prediction is a weighted average of the other users' rating. The weights refer to the amount of similarity between the user u and the other users by Equation (2). U_i represents the users who rated item i. The factor k normalizes the weights.

$$p^{collab}(u,i) = \overline{r_u} + \frac{1}{\sum_{a \in U_i} w(u,a)}\sum_{a \in U_i} w(u,a)(r_{a,i} - \overline{r_a}) \qquad (2)$$

It is common for the active user to have highly correlated neighbors that are based on very few co-rated item (overlapping; $I_u \cap I_a$). These neighbors based on a small number of overlapping item tend to be bad predictor. To devalue the correlation based on few co-rated items, we multiple the correlation by default voting.

2.2 Content-Based Filtering

Content-based filtering process consists of translating web pages to their vector space representation, finding web pages that are similar to the profile, and selecting the top-scoring pages for presentation to the user. The vector representation is obtained by a text analysis of HTML pages. This is done by extracting keywords from page titles, all level of headings, and anchor hypertexts. This narrow analysis leads to retrieval of fewer pages, but most of retrieved materials are likely to be helpful to the user; as it is reasonable to assume that the author of a web page used these words to give the main aspect of the page. Stop word are filtered out and word stemming is then performed to improved Information Retrieval performance. To provide content-based filtering, we treat the prediction task as a text categorization problem. We view movie content information as web page, and user ratings 0-5 as one six class label. We implemented a bag-of-words naïve Bayesian classifier to learn profiles from a set of rated movies i.e. labeled pages [13]. We use a multinomial text model, in which a page is modeled as an ordered sequence of ordered sequence of word events drawn from the vocabulary. The naïve Bayes assumption states that the probability of each keyword event is dependent on the page class but independent of the word's context and position. For each class c_j, and word, $w_k \in V$, the probability, $P(c_j)$ and $P(w_k|c_j)$ must be estimated from training data. Then the posterior probability of each class given a web page P, is computed using Bayes rule by Equation (3).

$$p(c_j \mid P) = \frac{P(c_j)}{P(P)} \prod_{i=1}^{|P|} P(a_i \mid c_j) \tag{3}$$

Where a_i is the ith word in the page, and $|P|$ is the length of the page in words. Since for any given page, the prior $P(P)$ is a constant, this factor can be ignored if all that is desired is a rating rather than a probability estimate. A ranking is produced by sorting pages by their odds ratio, $P(c_1|P)/P(c_0|P)$, where c_1 represents the positive class and c_0 represents the negative class. An example is classified as positive if the odds are greater than 1, and negative otherwise. In our case, since movies are represented as a vector of "pages", p_m, one for each slot (where s_m denotes the mth slot), the probability of each word given the category and the slot $P(w_k|c_j, s_m)$, must be estimated and the posterior category probability for a movie film, F, computed using Equation (4).

$$p(c_j \mid F) = \frac{P(c_j)}{P(F)} \prod_{m=1}^{|S|} \prod_{i=1}^{|p_m|} P(a_{m,i} \mid c_j, s_m) \tag{4}$$

Where S is the number of slots and $a_{m,i}$ is the ith word in the mth slot. The class with the highest posterior probability determines the predicted rating. The *Laplace* smoothing is used to avoid zero probability estimates [13,14].

3   Recommender System through Hybrid 2-Way Filtering

Hybrid 2-way filtering was modeled as an autonomous agent that provided personalized content for the web site using it. The proposed hybrid 2-way filtering transparently creates and maintains user preferences. It assists users by providing both collaborative filtering and content-based filtering, which are updated in real time whenever the user changes his/her current page using any navigation technique. The WebBot uses the URLs provided in the EachMovie dataset to download movie content from IMDb [12]. Hybrid 2-way filtering keeps track of each individual user and provides that a user online assistance. The assistance includes two lists of recommendations based on two different filtering paradigms: collaborative filtering and content-based filtering. Hybrid 2-way filtering updates the list each time the user changes his/her current page. Content-based filtering is based on the correlation between the content of the pages and the user preferences. The collaborative filtering is based on a comparison between the user path of navigation and the access patterns of past users. Hybrid 2-way filtering may eliminate the shortcomings in each approach. By making collaborative filtering, we can deal with any kind of content and explore new domains to find something interesting to the user. By making content-based filtering, we can deal with pages un-seen by others. Figure 1 depicts the architecture of personalized movie recommender system through hybrid 2-way filtering with extracted information.

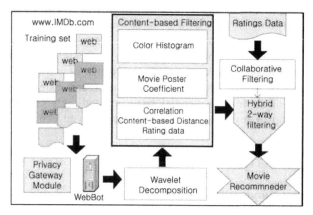

Fig. 1. The Architecture of Hybrid 2-Way Filtering with Extracted Information

The architecture of personalized movie recommender system can be broken down into four modules, which encapsulate fairly distinct functions. Personalized movie recommender system consists of extracting information from WebBot, hybrid 2-way filtering module, privacy and gateway module, and the graphical user interface module. Hybrid 2-way filtering consists of collaborative filtering and content-based filtering on movie poster.

3.1   Extracting Information from WebBot and Building a Database

We have been exploring content-based movie recommending by applying automated text-categorization methods to semi-structured text extracted from the web. Our current prototype system, WebBot: Web Robot Agent, uses a database of movie content information extracted from web pages at Internet Movie Database[1]. Therefore, the system's current content information about titles consists of textual meta-data rather than the actual text of the movies themselves.

An IMDb subject search is performed to obtain a list of movie-description URLs of broadly relevant titles [12]. WebBot then downloads each of these pages and uses a simple pattern-based information-extraction system to extract data about each title. Information extraction is the task of locating specific pieces of information from a

---

[1]   The Internet Movie Database is a good example for a created movie recommender system (http://www.imdb.com).

page, thereby obtaining useful structured data from unstructured text. A WebBot follows the IMDb link provided for every movie in the EachMovie dataset and collects information from the various links off the main URL. We represent the content information of every movie as a set of slots (feature). Each slot is represented simply as a bag of words. The slot we use for the EachMovie dataset are: title, director, cast, genre, plot keywords, user comments, external reviews, plot summary, newsgroup reviews, and awards. IMDb produces the information about related directors and movie titles using collaborative filtering: however, WebBot treats them as additional content information about the movie. The text in each slot is then processed into an unordered bag of words and the examples represented as a vector of bags of words (one bag for each slot). A movie's title and directors are also added to its own related-title and related-director slots, since a movie is obviously "related" to itself, and this allows overlap in these slots with movies listed as related to it. Some minor additions include the removal of a small list of stop-words, the preprocessing of director names into unique tokens of the form first-initial_last-name and the grouping of the words associated with synopses, reviews, and customer comments all into one bag [13].

3.2 Privacy Issues and Gateway Module

To get highest benefit from collaborative filtering, the system should tell where people go on the web, where they click, how long their session lasts, how they rate thing, what kind of persons they are etc. this is what the system developers want more personalized suggestions too, but want their privacy at the same time. Certain questions about privacy and collaborative filtering have already been solved by the development of more general web standards. One solution is Open Profiling Standard (OPS). It was brought to the WWW Consortium (W3C) as a way to give the control of data back to the user. Collaborative filtering requires a large amount of data to facilitate the correlation of a consumer's purchasing pattern, and recommendation cannot be changed or weighted more heavily by an expert's option. Thus, collaborative filtering is appropriate when decisions are not of significance importance, and is used primarily for items that are influenced [8].

The gateway module is a central component where HTTP traffic between a user and the web site is accomplished by this module. It servers to monitor user requests, maintain user session information, and add recommendations in the HTML responses of the Web site. For experimenting purposes, the gateway was implemented as a proxy server to enable us test to the performance of hybrid 2-way filtering on any web site. To overcome the problem of stateless connection in HTTP, WebBot follows users through tracking their IP address. To track user presence, a timeout mechanism is used to delete user's session information after a predetermined amount of idle time. The connection after the specified period having the same IP is identified as a new user. This method is fairly easy to implement. Consequently, the IP of a proxy server may represent two or more people who are accessing the same web site simultaneously in their browsing sessions, causing an obvious conflict. However, the reality is that many large sites use this method and have not any clashes.

3.3   Content-Based Filtering on Movie Poster

Our project goal is to assign in the original movie poster to a relatively small number of groups, where each group represents a set of pixels that are coherent in their color and local movie poster properties; the motivation is to reduce the amount of raw data represented by the movie poster while preserving the information needed for the movie poster understanding task. It is reasonable to expect that movie posters with similar content information will be almost equally interesting to users. The problem is that defining movie poster content information and movie poster similarity is still an open problem [9]. Ongoing research is focusing on two directions. First, each movie poster is described by a textual caption, and captions are compared using techniques derived from page retrieval. Second, analysis and recognition technique are applied to the movie poster pixels to extract automatically features that are compared using some distance measure in the feature space. In this study, we solve the first approach as pure content-based filtering. And we focus on the latter approach, because it can be entirely automated. In our prototype, we have currently implemented two feature extraction components; color histograms and movie poster coefficients.

3.3.1 Color Histograms for Extracted Information

Color is important cue in extracting information from movie poster. Color histograms are commonly used content-based filtering and have proven to be useful. However, the global characterization is poor, because it tasks information about how color is distributed spatially. It is important to group color in localized region and to fuse color with movie poster properties. The original movie posters are available in RGB format, where each pixel is defined by the value (0-255) of the three components red, blue, and green. We treat the hue-saturation-value color space as a cone: for a given point (h, s, v) that models more accurately the human perception of colors. The HSV coefficients are quantized to yield 166 different colors. h and sv are the angular and radial coordinates of the point on a disk of radius v at height v; all coordinates range from 0 to 1. Points with small v are black, regardless of their h and s values. The cone representation maps all such points to the apex of the cone, so they are close to one another. This encoding allows us to operationalize the fact that hue differences are meaningless for very small saturations. However, it ignores the fact that for large value and saturations, hue differences are perceptually more relevant than saturation and value differences. For movie posters, the histogram of these 166 colors is computed. This encoding allows us to operationalize the fact that hue differences are meaningless for small saturation. However, it ignores the fact that for large values and saturations, hue differences and perceptually more relevant than saturation and value differences [9]. To compare two movie posters, we compute the Euclidean distance between their color histograms.

These movie posters are quantized to binary values, so that each pixel of the original movie poster is associated with binary vector of length 9. The histogram of these vectors (length $512 = 2^9$) is the feature vector associated to analysis of the movie poster [9]. As shown in Figure 2, to determine the similarity between movie posters, all movie posters in the content information database are decomposed according to wavelet decomposition using the 2-dimensional Haar transform. From the decomposition a feature histogram is derived, which can then be compared by the use a vector metric. We use a linear estimated for the content-based filtering on movie poster, which is illustrated in the following Equation (5). $P^{poster}(u,i)$ represents the content-based filtering for movie poster i for user u.

$$p^{poster}(u,i) = \sum_j (\sum_{a \in C_j(i)} r_{u,a} / |C_j(i)|) \tag{5}$$

If a prediction is to be made for a user u and a target movie poster i, all the movie posters previously rated by user u are grouped into distance classes $C_j(i)$ according to distance to target movie poster i. The distance are then sorted and grouped.

Fig. 2. Original movie poster / Wavelet decomposition (Haar 2 Wavelet: elapsed 0.060 sec)

3.4 Prediction of User Preference through Hybrid 2-Way Filtering

For the following considerations, we assume an existing collaborative filtering technique, as personalized movie recommender system. The hybrid with content-based filtering on movie poster is therefore rather an extension of collaborative filtering. As research leads to additional content-analysis tools, the extension approach should not limit the number of content-based filtering extensions. Therefore, we use hybrid 2-way filtering predictor $p^{hybrid}(u,i)$ using the following Equation (6).

$$p^{hybrid}(u,i) = \lambda^{collab} p^{collab}(u,i) + \lambda^{content} p^{content}(u,i) + \lambda^{poster} p^{poster}(u,i) \tag{6}$$

In the above equation $p^{content}(u,i)$ corresponds to the pure content-based filtering for the active user and movie i. $p^{collab}(u,i)$, $p^{poster}(u,i)$ are as shown in Equation (2), (5). The weights (λ^{collab}, $\lambda^{content}$, λ^{poster}) are estimated by the use of linear regression with a set-aside subset of the rating, so that the weights are adapted to the relevance feedback of a predictor. The estimation of the weights should be repeated as the content information database. Hybrid 2-way filtering approaches use parameters to control the collaborative filtering, content-based filtering. The parameters determine the weight automatically in the sum of each filtering. We found through our experiment the following value for these parameters: λ^{collab} =0.58, $\lambda^{content}$ =0.39, λ^{poster} =0.03. After reviewing the recommendations, the user may assign their own rating to movies they believe to be incorrectly ranked and retrain the system to produce improved recommendations. As with relevance feedback in information retrieval, this cycle can be repeated several times to produce the good results. Also, as new movies are provided, the personalized recommender system can track any change in a user preferences and alter its recommendations.

4 Performance Evaluation

We use the user-movie ratings provided by the EachMovie dataset [12] and the movie details from the Internet Movie Database (IMDb). The EachMovie dataset was obtained by the DEC Systems Research Center by running a movie recommendation service for 18 months. The data set contains 72,916 users who entered a total of 2,811,983 numeric ratings for 1,628 different movies. Each rating comes from the set {0.0, 0.2, 0.4, 0.6, 0.8, and 1.0} where 0.0 is the lowest score and 1.0 is the highest. The movies are categorized into 10 categories: action, animation, art foreign, classic, comedy, drama, family, horror, romance, and thriller, where a movie may belong to more than one category. In this paper, we represent the content information of every movie as a set of slots. Each slot is represented simply as a bag of words. The slots we use for the EachMovie dataset are: movie title, director, cast, genre, plot, summary, plot keywords, user comments, external reviews, newsgroup reviews, and award. To have a quick turn-around time for our experiments, we only used a subset of the EachMovie dataset. This dataset contains 7,893 randomly selected users and 1,461 movies for which content was available from IMDb. The reduced dataset has 299,997 ratings for 1,289 movies. The dataset provides optional demographic data such as age, gender, and zip code supplied by each person. For each movie, information such as the name, genre, release data and IMDb URL are provided. Finally the dataset provides the actual rating data provided by each user for various movies. User ratings range from one-to-six stars. One stars(★) indicate extreme dislike for a movie and six stars(★★★★★★) indicate high praise. This dataset contained 0.5562 negative user ratings (i.e. ≤3). The distribution over the 1-6 ratings is given in Table 1.

Table 1. Distribution of User Ratings

User rating	★	★★	★★★	★★★★	★★★★★	★★★★★★
No. of movies	291	237	189	198	179	195

The textual data obtained from IMDb has many real-world aspects. The users reported that while rating the movies, some pages retrieved directly from IMDb.com contained synopses that were clearly intended for other movie. There were also spelling errors that a simple approach such as ours would treat as separate instances. In addition, the amount and quality of description of the movies tended to vary across a wide range.

We describe the metrics and experimental methodology. we use to compare different prediction algorithm; and present the result of our experiments. To evaluate
various approaches of filtering, we divided the rating dataset in test-set and training-
set. The rating database is used a subset of the ratings data from the Eachmovie dataset. The qualities of the various prediction algorithms were measured by comparing
the predicted rating values for the withheld ratings to the actual ratings. The metrics
for evaluating the accuracy of a prediction algorithm are used mean absolute error
(MAE) and rank scoring measure (RSM) [3,10]. [2,3,5,10,11,17] used the same
metrics to compare their algorithm. MAE is used to evaluate recommendation system
about the single movie. RSM is used to evaluate the performance for recommender
systems that recommend movies from ranked lists. The statistical significance of
differences in performance between two predictors was evaluated using two-tailed
paired t-tests [14].

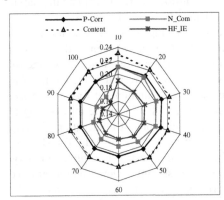 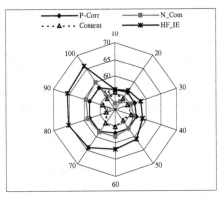

Fig. 3. MAE, RSM at varying the number of users

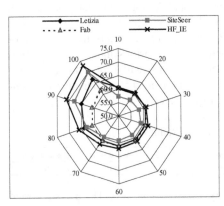 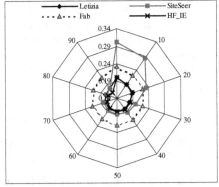

Fig. 4. MAE, RSM at varying nth rating

For evaluation, this paper uses the following methods: The proposed the hybrid 2-way
filtering with extracted information (HF_EI), a collaborative filtering using Pearson
correlation coefficient (P_Corr), the recommendation method using the content based

filtering (Content), and a naïve combined approach (N_Com). The naïve combined approach takes the average of the ratings generated by the collaborative filtering and content-based filtering. The various methods were used to compare performance by changing the number of clustering users. Also, the proposed approach was compared with SiteSeer, Letizia, Fab methods in 5 Related works that use collaborative filtering and content-based filtering by changing the number of user evaluations.

Figure 3 shows the MAE and RSM of the number of users. Figure 3, as the number of users increases, the performance of the HF_IE, and the P_Corr also increases, whereas the method using content based filtering shows no notable change in performance. In terms of accuracy of prediction, it is evident that method HF_IE, which uses hybrid collaborative filtering and content-based filtering, is more superior to method N_Com. Figure 4 is used to show the MAE and RSM when the number of user's evaluations is increased. In Figure 5, the SiteSeer method shows low performance when there are few evaluations; the other methods outperform the SiteSeer method. Although the Letizia method along with the HF_IE shows high rates of accuracy, the HF_IE shows the highest accuracy of all methods.

5 Related Works

There have been a few other attempts to combine content information with collaborative [1,5,16]. One simple approach is to allow both collaborative filtering and content-based filtering to produce separate ranked lists of recommendations, and then merge their results to produce a final list [7]. There can be several schemes to merging the ranked lists, such as interleaving content and collaborative recommendations or averaging the rank or ranking predicted by the two approaches. This is essentially what our hybrid 2-way filtering approach does. This section compares personalized movie recommender system through hybrid 2-way filtering with extracted information (HF_IE) with other recommender systems. Among these systems, three are selected for comparison: SiteSeer [18], Letizia [11], and Fab [2]. The systems were selected because they cover the best feature of the other recommender systems.

SiteSeer [18] is web page recommendation system using collaborative filtering. User profiles are extracted from their bookmark files, taking into account the content of the referenced documents, and the structure of bookmark file. The folders in the bookmark are used to identify the user's categories of interest. Even through there is no technical information on how the representation is done, it is said that the system does not derive any semantic value from the content of the stored URLs. The profiles thus seem to consist of a list of URLs together with their structure. Recommendations occur when the profiles of two users match in term of the URLs contained therein and thus measuring the overlap, by giving additional weight to URLs that do not occur frequently, an approach similar to the *tf idf* approach for content information determination of documents. The user profiles are most likely stored on a central server in order to allow for matching users [16].

Letizia [11] is an agent that assists a user browsing the web. Letizia uses the idle time spent by the user reading the current document to explore the neighborhood looking for web pages that are related to the user interest. Letizia relies in implicit feed-back: Links followed from the currently visited page are assumed to reveal interest in the document containing the link. Bookmaking a page also means this page is interest-ing. Furthermore, as user tent to read from the top left corner to the right bottom cor-ner, links that are omitted during the reading process might express disinterest in the referenced document. There is no ordinal scale for the importance of suggested links but rather a preference ordering. It is reasonable to assume the filtering mechanism involves cosine similarities in the vector space model since the documents to matched are stored as weighted keyword vectors [16]. This agent similar to HF_IE, the purpose of Letizia agent is to provide assistance to the user without the intervention while the user is browsing. However, Letizia learns the areas that are of interest to a user by recording the user's browsing behavior. Letizia uses content-based filtering, while our personalized movie recommender system uses hybrid 2-way filtering with extracted information. Furthermore, Letizia requires considerable bandwidth shortages. On the other side, HF_IE inhabits a web site and operates locally in assisting users. Finally, Letizia requires a Netscape browser to operate, which severely limits its extent. In contrast, HF_IE is a platform independent. HF_IE shows good performance on several web sites in the domain of real estates, and it is expected to be adaptable to different domains with easy modification of the XML-based domain knowledge.

Fab [2] is a system that helps users to discover new and interesting sites. Fab use an alternative approach to combine collaborative filtering and content-based filtering. This system maintains user profiles based on content analysis, and directly compares these profiles to determine similar users for collaborative filtering system. User pro-files are stored in form of weighted keyword vectors and updated on the basis of ex-plicit relevance feedback. Pages and user profiles are matched according to the cosine similarity in the vector space model. A central repository of recommended by a user who exhibits interest in the document whose interest profile matches the page [16]. The system delivers a number of pages that it thinks would interest the users. Users evaluate the web pages and provide explicit feedback to the system. Fab uses the web for collecting pages for recommendation. This is an advantage over HF_IE's ap-proach, since it is restricted to the web site's pages. However, Fab uses considerable bandwidth for collecting these web pages. Moreover, the system does not operate concurrently with users during users browsing session. Users get the recommendations by explicitly accessing their account in Fab's database through the web.

6   Conclusions

We have presented personalized movie recommender system through hybrid 2-way filtering with extracted information (HF_IE). This proposed method represents the domain knowledge and automatically generates WebBot: Web Robot Agent from semi-structured content information about movies gathered from the web pages. We have shown how hybrid 2-way filtering system performs significantly better than col-laborative filtering, content-based filtering, and a naïve combined filtering. The proto-type personalized movie recommender system shows good performance on several web sites in the domain of real estates, and it is expected to be adaptable to different domains with easy modification. More testing on about many web sites in the same domain is in progress to evaluate the personalized recommender system's power more practically. We are aiming at creating a personalized recommender system that can be applied to multi-domain environments.

Acknowledgements

The author would like to thank the anonymous reviewers whose comments helped improve the paper. This research was supported by Inha University that allowed Dong-Hyun Park to have the sabbatical year from September 2002 to August 2003. Sincere thanks go to Jung-Hyun Lee who provided the idea for this thesis.

References

1. M. Ahmad Wasfi, "Collecting User Access Pattern for Building User Profiles and Collaborative Filtering," In Proc. of the International Conference on Intelligent User Interfaces, pp. 57-64, 1999.
2. M. Balabanovic, Y. Shoham, "Fab: Content-based, Collaborative Recommendation," Communication of the Association of Computing Machinery, Vol. 40, No. 3, pp. 66-72, 1997.
3. D. Billsus, M. J. Pazzani, "Learning Collaborative Information Filters," In proc. of the International Conference on Machine Learning, 1998.
4. J. S. Breese, C. Kadie, "Empirical Analysis of Predictive Algorithms for Collaborative Filtering," In Proc. of the Conference on Uncertainty in Artificial Intelligence, Madison, WI, 1998.
5. N. Good, et al., "Combining Collaborative Filtering with Personal Agents for Better Recommendations," In Proc. of National Conference on Artificial Intelligence, pp. 439-446, 1999.
6. K. Y. Jung, J. H. Lee, "Prediction of User Preference in Recommendation System using Association User Clustering and Bayesian Estimated Value," In Proc. of 15th Australian Joint Conference on Artificial Intelligence, LNAI 2557, pp. 284-296, 2002.
7. K. Y. Jung, et al., "Development of Design Recommender System using Collaborative Filtering," In Proc. of 6th International Conference of Asian Digital Libraries, LNCS 2911, pp. 100-110, 2003.
8. S. Kangas, "Collaborative Filtering and Recommendation Systems," Technical Report TTE4-2001-35, VTT Information Technology, 2001.
9. A. Kohrs, et al. "Improving Collaborative Filtering with Multimedia Indexing Techniques to Create User-Adapting Web Sites," In Proc. of the 7th ACM International Conf. on Multimedia, pp. 27-36, 1999.
10. W. S. Lee, "Collaborative Learning for Recommender Systems," In Proc. of the 18th International Conf. on Machine Learning, pp. 314-321, 1997.
11. H. Lieberman, "Letizia: An Agent that Assists Web Browsing," In Proc. of the 14th International Joint Conference on Artificial Intelligence, 1997.

12. P. McJones, EachMovie dataset, URL: http://www.research.digital.com/SRC/eachmovie
13. P. Melville, et al., "Content-Boosted Collaborative Filtering for Improved Recommenda-tions," In Proc. of the National Conference on Artificial Intelligence, pp. 187-192, 2002.
14. T. Mitchell, Machine Learning, McGraw-hill, New York, pp. 154-200, 1997.
15. M. J. Pazzani, "A Framework for Collaborative, Content-based and Demographic Filter-ing," Artificial Intelligence Review, 13(5-6), pp. 393-408, 1999.
16. A. Pretschner, S. Gauch, "Personalization on the Web," Technical Report ITTC-FY2000-TR-13591-01, Information and Telecommunication Technology Center, Dept. of Electrical Engineering and Computer Science, The University of Kansas, 1999.
17. U. Shardanand, P. Maes, "Social Information Filtering: Algorithm: Algorithms for Auto-mating "Word of Mouth"," In Proc. of the Human Factors in Computing System Confer-ence, Denver, 1995.
18. J. Rucker, M. J. Polanco, "SiteSeer: Personalized Navigation for the Web," Communica-tions of the Association of Computing Machinery, Vol. 40, No. 3, pp. 73-75, 1997.

LUCI: A Personalization Documentary System Based on the Analysis of the History of the User's Actions

Rachid Arezki[1], Abdenour Mokrane[1], Gérard Dray[1],
Pascal Poncelet[1], and David W. Pearson[2]

[1] Centre LGI2P EMA, Site EERIE Parc Scientifique Georges Besse
30035 Nimes Cedex 1, France
{rachid.arezki,abdenour.mokrane,gerard.dray,pascal.poncelet}@ema.fr
[2] IUT de Roanne, 20 Avenue de Paris 42334 Roanne, France
david.pearson@univ-st-etienne.fr

Abstract. With the development of Internet and storage devices, online document servers abound with enormous quantities of documents from various themes. The online search of pertinent documents is a fastidious task and "search engine" may overcome this difficulty. However, in such engines, each new document need must be formulated by a new request. Recently, new approaches were proposed to solve this problem by taking into account the user profile. However, these approaches don't consider the evolution in time of the document classes consulted by the user. In this paper, we propose a new approach for learning the user long-term profile for textual document filtering. In this framework, the documents consulted by the user are classified in a dynamic way, then we analyze the distribution in the time of the document classes. The approach aim is to determine, as well as possible, the document classes which interest the user. We also propose a system called *LUCI*, which allows an online document's personalization by using this approach. An empirical study confirms the relevance of our approach.

Keywords: User Modeling, Information Filtering, Long-Term Adaptation and Filtering

1 Introduction

With the development of Internet and storage devices, online document servers abound with enormous quantities of documents from various themes. The online search of pertinent documents is a fastidious task and "search engines" may overcome this difficulty. However, in such engines, each new document need must be formulated by a new request. Recently, considerable efforts have been deployed to overcome this weakness by developing systems able to propose adapted documents to a user without requests formulation. These systems take into account the user profile to propose personalized documents. In this paper, we propose a new approach for user long-term profile learning for textual documents filtering.

H. Christiansen et al. (Eds.): FQAS 2004, LNAI 3055, pp. 487–498, 2004.

It is based on the analysis of the evolution in time of the document classes consulted by the user. Indeed, the documents consulted by the user are classified in a dynamic way, then we analyze the distribution in the time of the documents classes. The approach aim is to determine, as well as possible, the document classes which interest the user. It is achieved by giving more importance to the regularly consulted document classes than those concentrated over short periods. Our approach does not require that the user provides explicitly information to the system.

We have developed a system, called *LUCI*, allowing an online document personalization by using our approach. *LUCI* learns the user profile via the consulted documents and proposes documents dynamically, i.e each time the user modifies its profile (new consulted document), the system proposes to him documents adapted to its new profile.

The article is organized as follows: Section 2 presents the problem of modeling the user long-term interests for a personalized filtering of textual documents. Section 3 describes the functional architecture of the system *LUCI*. Then, Section 4 details our approach for document filtering, based on the distribution in time of the document classes consulted by the user. Section 5 presents the process of documentary filtering. The experimental results, on a documentary corpus of reference, are presented in Section 6, we show that our approach allows to detect and to propose documents of regular interest. Section 7 presents briefly the related work on the user modeling. Finally, Section 8 provides some concluding remarks and directions of future research.

2   Problematic

The objective of our proposal is the learning of users long-term profiles for an effective textual document personalization. To achieve this goal, we classify the consulted documents and we analyze the evolution in time of the classes of these documents. The general idea considers that the document classes regularly consulted have more long-term interest than those concentrated over a short period. For example, a user having shares consults everyday one or two documents on finance. However, this same user gave a talk on dinosaurs, and has consulted more than 100 documents in one day on the dinosaurs. In the long-term (one month for example), the finance theme has more interest, to the user, than the dinosaur one, whereas the number of documents consulted on the dinosaurs is much more significant than the number of documents consulted on finances. In fact, the first thematic represents a regular interest whereas the second one is just a momentary need, i.e. concentrated in a short period. In the long-term (one month in this example) we must be able to propose documents of the thematic finances, because it is a regular interest, and not to propose documents of the thematic dinosaur because it is a spontaneous interest.

In our context, the user is connected to an online documentary base which contains a collection of documents on various themes. The documentary corpus is indexed and each document is associated to a vector. The user is modeled by a set of documents (vectors) consulted through time. The problem of long-term document personalization is to find a model able to take into account the evolution in time of the document classes consulted by the user, and as well as possible to detect the classes of regular interests for a better personalization of documents.

3   LUCI Architecture

The goal of the *LUCI* system is to learn dynamically the user profile and to propose documents adapted to his long-term profile. *LUCI* models the user through the consulted documents, and accordingly it proposes to him new ones. As shown in figure 1, *LUCI* is composed of two sub-systems and a structure defining the user model:

1. *User modeling sub-system:* models the user under his actions. Indeed, it supervises the user's actions by updating the model when a document is consulted.
2. *Filtering documentary sub-system:* proposes documents according to the user model, and when this last one is updated (i.e document is consulted), a new document collection is proposed.
3. *The user model:* is a complex structure which models the user long-term interests.

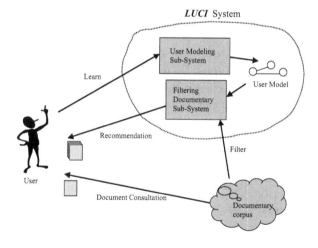

Fig. 1. Functional Architecture

There are many vector space models to represent documents [Cha90,DDL⁺90]. In our context, we consider that the documents are represented by the traditional vector space model [Sal71,SG83]. The extraction of terms (key words) is done by:

- *identification of terms (lexical segmentation),*
- *elimination of the stop words, that is, terms that are not interesting (by using a preset list),*
- *stemming, that is, reduction of the terms to their root[1],*
- *the choice of the most frequent terms (10% of the Existing key words).*

To reduce the advantage of the long documents on the short documents, the used keyword vectors are normalized [SSMB95,Sin97]. Let D be a text document, then $\{(t_1, w_1), ..(t_n, w_n)\}$ is the feature vector of D where t_i is a term (word) that occurs in D and w_i is the weight of term t_i, such as:

$$w_i = \frac{f_i}{\sum\limits_{j=1}^{n} f_j}$$

f_i is the frequency of the term t_i.

We use, to measure the similarity, the *cosine* formula [SG83]: let D_i, D_j be two documents, the similarity of the *cosine* between these two documents is formulated by:

$$SIM(D_i, D_j) = \frac{D_i \bullet D_j}{\mid D_i \mid \times \mid D_j \mid}$$

4   Modeling Long-Term Interests

In this section, we describe our approach to model the long-term interest. Our motivation behind this modeling is to capture, as well as possible, the general user interest. Hence, we consider that a class regularly consulted (permanent interest) has more interest than a class concentrated in a short period (spontaneous "or momentary" interest).
The approach is based on:

1. dynamic classification of the documents consulted by the user,
2. associating a vector with each class, which corresponds to the sum of its document vectors,
3. associating a number with each class, which is its document distribution in the time,
4. using the vectors of classes and their distributions, a vector named *LTV* (Long-Term Vector), which determines the user long-term interest is calculated,
5. proposing documents to the user is done by the calculation of similarity between documents of the corpus and the vector *LTV*.

In the following of this section, we will start by describing in detail the structure of the long-term model. Then, we will describe the method of the

---

[1] We use Porter's stemming algorithm.

dynamic classification of the documents, followed by the calculation method of the document distribution of a class. Finally, we present the calculation of the *LTV* vector.

4.1 Structure of the Long-Term Model

A user is defined by a tuple $X =< id, S >$ where id stands for an unique identifier and S is the set of document classes consulted by the user id, i.e $S = \{C_1, ...C_n\}$, where n stands for number of classes.

A class C_i, i=1 to n, is defined by a tuple $C_i = \{V, Dist_{C_i}, V_{C_i}\}$, such that:

1. V: is a set of tuples which contain the consulted documents of the class C_i (vectors) and their positions (in time).

$$\{(V_1^{C_i}, Pos_1)..(V_{\|C_i\|}^{C_i}, Pos_{\|C_i\|})\}$$

$\|C_i\|$: is the number of documents of the class C_i
$V_j^{C_i}$: is the jth document of the class C_i,
The document position Pos_i stands for its appearance in the time order, over all the consulted documents.
2. $Dist_{C_i}$: is the distribution in time of the documents of the class C_i (see section 4.3),
3. V_{C_i}: the vector of the class C_i, with:

$$V_{C_i} = \sum_{j=1}^{\|C_i\|} V_j^{C_i}$$

Now we will examine how the classes are determined and how the documents are associated to these classes.

4.2 Classification of the Consulted Documents by the User

The algorithm below describes the process of classification of the consulted documents. The creation of the classes is done in a dynamic way. Initially, the number of classes is set to zero ($S = \emptyset$). With the first consulted document, the algorithm creates the class C_1. Then for each consulted document, the algorithm calculates the similarity between the document and the whole of the existing classes. If the document is close to one of the existing classes then the document is added to this class. Otherwise, the algorithm creates a new class and associates this document to it.

The algorithm receives in entry a new document, represented by a vector V_D and the user model $X =< id, S >$. At output, it associates the document V_D and its position to a class.
$\|S\|$: represents the number of classes contained in the user model,
SIM: similarity function between two vectors,
α: represents the threshold of similarity.

Algorithm 1: Algorithm of dynamic classification
Input: Document V_D
Pos_{V_D}: position of the document V_D
the user model $X = < id, S >$
Output: association of V_D to a class of documents
begin
   if $\|S\| = 0$ then
      create a class C_1
      Add (V_D, Pos_{V_D}) to the class C_1
   else
      $k \leftarrow 1$
      for $j = 1$ to $j = \|S\|$ do
         if $SIM(V_{C_j}, V_D) > SIM(V_{C_k}, V_D)$ then
            $k \leftarrow j$
      if $SIM(V_{C_k}, V_D) > \alpha$ then
         Add (V_D, Pos_{V_D}) to the class C_k
      else
         create a new class $C_{\|S\|+1}$
         Add (V_D, Pos_{V_D}) to the class $C_{\|S\|+1}$
end

4.3 Calculation of the Document Distribution Classes

To calculate the distribution in time of the consulted document classes, to each class, we associate a group of dots represented in a two dimensional space. Each point represents a document of the class. A document is represented by two coordinates:

1. its position on all the documents, i.e. its consultation order in time,
2. its position of the document compared to the documents of its class, i.e. its insertion order in its class.

$$Dist_{C_i} = \frac{Pos_{\|C_i\|} - Pos_1 + 1}{N} \times \frac{1}{1 + \sum_{j=1}^{j=\|C_i\|} Distance(D_j, \Delta)}$$

$Dist_{C_i}$: distribution of the class C_i,
$Pos_{\|C_i\|}$: the position of the last consulted document of the class C_i, compared to all the consulted documents,
Pos_1: the position of the first consulted document of the class C_i, compared to the all the consulted documents,
Δ: the regression line of least squares of the group of dots of the class,
D_j: coordinates of the jth document of the class C_i,
N: the number of consulted documents,
$Distance(D_j, \Delta)$: distance between the point D_j and the line Δ.

4.4   Calculation of the Long-Term Vector LTV

From the user's long-term model, a vector defining his long-term interest (LTV), is calculated:

$$LTV = \sum_{i=1}^{\|S\|} Dist_{Ci} \times V_{Ci}$$

$\|S\|$ is the number of classes.

The proposal of documents to the user relating to his long-term interest is done by the calculation of similarities between the documents of the corpus and the vector LTV. If the similarity is greater than given threshold, it recommends the document to the user.

4.5   Example

Suppose that a user have consulted a succession of documents: $D_1, D_2, .., D_9$. At the 9th consulted document, the dynamic algorithm of classification will form 3 classes:
$C_1 = \{D_1, D_5, D_9\}$
$C_2 = \{D_2, D_3, D_4\}$
$C_3 = \{D_6, D_7, D_8\}$
The user model is defined by $X =< id, S >$, such as:
$S = \{C_1, C_2, C_3\}$ where:

1. $C_1 = \{V, Dist_{C_1}, V_{C_1}\}$
   $V = \{(D_1, 1), (D_5, 5), (D_9, 9)\}$
   $Dist_{C_1} = \frac{9-1+1}{9} \times \frac{1}{1+0} = 1$
   $V_{C_1} = D_1 + D_5 + D_9$
2. $C_2 = \{V, Dist_{C_2}, V_{C_2}\}$
   $V = \{(D_2, 2), (D_3, 3), (D_4, 4)\}$
   $Dist_{C_2} = \frac{4-2+1}{9} \times \frac{1}{1+0} = \frac{3}{9}$
   $V_{C_2} = D_2 + D_3 + D_4$
3. $C_3 = \{V, Dist_{C_3}, V_{C_3}\}$
   $V = \{(D_6, 6), (D_7, 7), (D_8, 8)\}$
   $Dist_{C_3} = \frac{8-6+1}{9} \times \frac{1}{1+0} = \frac{3}{9}$
   $V_{C_3} = D_6 + D_7 + D_8$

$$LTV = (1 \times V_{C_1}) + (\frac{3}{9} \times V_{C_2}) + (\frac{3}{9} \times V_{C_3})$$

It is noticed that the number of documents of the classes C_1, C_2, C_3 is identical. However at the calculation of vector LTV the C_1 class is favoured, because it is a regular interest, contrary to the classes C_2 and C_3 which are spontaneous interest.

5   Textual Documents Filtering

The proposal of documents to the user is done by the calculation of similarity between the documents of the documentary corpus and the vector LTV. Each time the user consults a document, its profile is modified, thus the system proposes to him new documents. The algorithm below describes the process of the documentary filtering associated with a new consultation of a document by the user.

Algorithm 2: Algorithm of Textual Documents Filtering
Input:
Document V_D
Pos_{V_D}: position of document V_D
user model $X =< id, S >$
α: constant representing the similarity threshold
Output: proposal of documents to the user
begin

 1. Associate the document V_D to a class of documents (see Algorithm1);
 2. Calculate the vector of the class to which V_D belongs;
 3. Calculate the distribution of the whole classes;
 4. Calculate the vector LTV;
 5. Calculate the similarity between vector LTV and the whole documents of the documentary corpus;
 6. Propose to the user the documents whose similarity is higher than the threshold α;

end

6   Experimentation

In order to validate the proposition, experiments were performed. The main objective is to measure the system ability to propose documents of regular interests.

6.1   Method

The documents used for our empirical study are press articles, collected from 5 different online newspapers in different periods. Our documentary corpus contains documents on 6 different thematics from 200 documents each one. The chosen thematics are: *Cinema, Data Processing, Economy, Football, International policy, National Policy.*

Starting with an empty profile. The user consults a succession of documents. For each consulted document, the *LUCI* system proposes twenty documents closed to his interest. We evaluate each proposed document.

To show the *LUCI* system ability to propose documents of regular interests, the user consults a set of documents of thematic *Data Processing* (12 documents), then, a set of documents of *Economy* (30 documents), followed by a set of documents of thematic *Football* (24 documents). Added to that, a regular consultation of documents of the thematic *Cinema* (11 documents), which represents a regular interest for the user.

We have chosen to compare *LUCI* with the algorithm *LUCI-NEG*, which is the implementation of *LUCI* without considering the distribution in time of the document classes.

6.2 Results

Figures 2 and 3 show the percentages of documents by thematic, proposed to the user, respectively by the *LUCI* system and the algorithm *LUCI-NEG*. It is noticed that starting from iteration 29, the *LUCI* system proposes documents of thematic *Cinema* (thematic regularly consulted), whereas *LUCI-NEG* does not propose any. That is due to the capacity of the *LUCI* system to detect the classes of documents of regular interest.

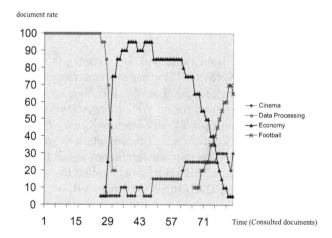

Fig. 2. *LUCI*: Document rate proposed to the user, per thematic

The thematic *Data Processing* is just a momentary need. Indeed, the user is no longer interested by this thematic starting from iteration 14. We notice that *LUCI-NEG* continues to propose significantly the documents of this thematic until iteration 72. Whereas, the number of documents of thematic *Data Processing* proposed by *LUCI*, decreases very quickly and it becomes null at iteration 28. The same observations are made for the thematic *Economy*. That is due to the *LUCI*'s capacity to detect the classes of documents of spontaneous interests and to decrease constantly and quickly the number of documents proposed which belong to these classes.

document rate

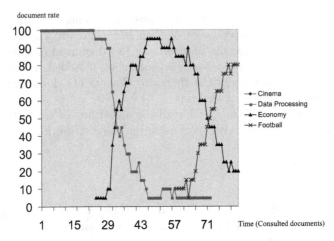

Fig. 3. *LUCI-NEG*: Document rate proposed to the user, per thematic

Other experiments of this type have been realised, they shows that *LUCI* detects better the classes of documents of regular interests than *LUCI-NEG*.

7   Related Work

Recently many systems have been described for documents and information filtering. In *NewsWeeder*, a NetNews Filtering system, *Lang* describe various alternatives to learn static user profiles [Lan95]. *WebMat*, an agent that helps users to effectively browse and search the on Web, it keeps tracks of user interests in different domains through multiple TF-IDF vectors [CS98]. *Fab* is an adaptive system for Web page recommendation which represents user profiles as a single feature vector [Bal97]. *Syskil& Webert* is an intelligent agent that represents a profile as Boolean features using a Naive Bayesian classifier to determine whether a Web page is relevant or not [PB97]. In [WIY01] the authors propose a three-descriptor model to represent a user's interests, and an adaptive algorithm to learn the dynamics of the user's interests through positive and negative relevance feedback. Neural network have been used to learn user profiles for filtering news articles on the Internet [TT98][MS94]. In *NewT* [MZ97] and *GIRAF* [MBVL99] genetic algorithm is employed to learn user interests. In [DN02], the authors use the user profile for an intelligent information retrieval, in which an extended vector space model is presented.

All this research does not take into account the distribution in time of the documents consulted by the user.

8   Conclusion

Having noted that the current systems of document personalization do not take into account the temporal factor when proposing documents to the users. We proposed in this article an approach which takes into account the history of the user's actions and their evolution in time. That by favoring the classes of documents regularly consulted by the user more than those concentrated over a short period. Indeed, we introduced a significant concept into our study, namely the classes of documents of regular interests. The system *LUCI* makes possible to detect these classes and to favor them. The experimental evaluation demonstrated the effectiveness of our approach.

A first prospect for research consists in considering the documents representation and in particular to use approaches like *LSI* [DDL+90] or *TF-IDF* [SG83] for the assignment of the weights. Another prospect for interesting research consists of proposing a variant of our approach taking into account the positive and negative feedback of the user.

References

[Bal97]   M. Balbanovic. An adaptative web page recommendation service. In *Proceeding of the First International Conference on Autonomous Agents*, pages 378–385, 1997.

[Cha90]   J. Chauché. Détermination sémantique en analyse structurelle: une expérience basée sur une definition de distance. *TA Information, vol. 2*, pages 121–167, 1990.

[CS98]   L. Chen and K. Sycara. Webmate: Personal agent for browsing and searching. In *Proceeding of the Second International Conference on Autonomous Agents*, pages 132–139, 1998.

[DDL+90]   S. Deerwester, S. Dumais, T. Landauer, G. Furnas, and R. Harsman. Indexing by latent semantic analysis. *Journal of the Society for Information Science, vol. 41*, pages 391–407, 1990.

[DN02]   C. Danilowicz and H.C. Nguyen. Using user profiles in intelligent information retrieval. In *Proceedings of the 13th International Symposium on Foundations of Intelligent Systems*, pages 223–231. Springer-Verlag, 2002.

[Lan95]   K. Lang. Newsweeder: Learning to filter netnews. In *Proceedings of Machine Learning Conference*, pages 331–339, 1995.

[MBVL99]   M.J. Martin-Bautista, M.A. Vila, and H.L. Larsen. A fuzzy genetic algorithm approach to an adaptive information retrieval agent. *Journal of Americain Society for Information Science.*, 50(9):760–771, 1999.

[MS94]   M. McElligot and H. Sorensen. An evolutionary connectionist approach to personnal information filtering. In *Proceedings of the Fourth Irish Neural Network Conference, Dublin, Ireland*, pages 141–146, 1994.

[MZ97]   A. Moukas and G. Zacharia. Evolving a multiagent information filtering solution in Amalthaea. In *Proceedings of the First International Conference on Autonomous Agents (Agents'97)*, pages 394–403, New York, 5–8, 1997. ACM Press.

[PB97]   M. Pazzani and D. Billisus. Learning and revising user profiles: The identification of interesting web sites. *Machine Learning Journal*, pages 313–331, 1997.

[Sal71]   G. Salton. The smart retrieval system: Experiments in automatic document processing. *Prentice Hall*, 1971.

[SG83]   G. Salton and M.J Mc Gill. Introduction to modern information retrieval. *New York: McGraw-Hill*, 1983.

[Sin97]   A. Singhal. Term weighting revisited. *PhD thesis, Departement of Computer Science, Cornell University*, 1997.

[SSMB95]   A. Singhal, G. Salton, M. Mitra, and C. Buckley. Document length normalization. *Technical Report, Departement of Computer Science, Cornell University*, 1995.

[TT98]   A. Tan and C. Teo. Learning user profiles for personalized information dissemination. In *Proceedings, 1998 IEEE International Joint Conference on Neural Networks, Alaska*, pages 183–188, 1998.

[WIY01]   D.H. Widyantoro, T.R Ioerger, and J. Yen. Learning user interest dynamics with a three-descriptor representation. *Journal of the American Society of Information Science*, 52(3):212–225, 2001.

Author Index